A COMPLETE GUIDE TO

Reptiles

OF AUSTRALIA

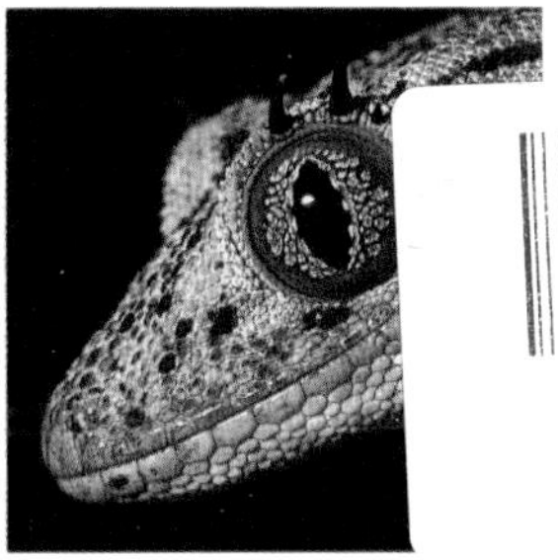

GW00382887

Steve Wilson and **Gerry Swan**

FIFTH EDITION

This fifth edition published in 2017 by
Reed New Holland Publishers

London · Sydney · Auckland
The Chandlery, 50 Westminster Bridge Road, London SE1 7QY, UK
1/66 Gibbes Street, Chatswood, NSW 2067, Australia
5/39 Woodside Avenue, Northcote, Auckland 0627, New Zealand

www.newhollandpublishers.com

First edition published in 2003
Second edition published in 2008
Third edition published in 2010
Fourth edition published in 2013

Copyright © 2017 Reed New Holland Publishers
Copyright © 2017 in text and illustrations: Steve Wilson and Gerry Swan
Copyright © 2017 in images: as credited

All rights reserved. No part of this publication may be reproduced, stored in a retrieval system or transmitted, in any form or by any means, electronic, mechanical, photocopying, recording or otherwise, without the prior written permission of the publishers and copyright holders.

A record of this book is held at the British Library and the National Library of Australia.

ISBN 978 1 92554 602 6

Group Managing Director: Fiona Schultz
Publisher: Simon Papps
Project Editor: Simon Papps
Designers: Simon Rattray, Andrew Davies
Cover design: Andrew Davies, Lorena Susak
Production Directors: James Mills-Hicks

Printer: Toppan Leefung Printing Limited

10 9 8 7 6 5 4 3 2 1

Keep up with New Holland Publishers on Facebookwww.facebook.com/NewHollandPublishers

Picture captions
Front cover: The Superb Dragon (*Diporiphora superba*) is a slender lizard that dwells in foliage along the sandstone gorges of the northern Kimberley region, WA. Surveyor's Pool, Mitchell Plateau, WA. S. Wilson.
Title page: Northern Spiny-tailed Gecko (*Strophurus ciliaris aberrans*) from North West Cape, WA. S. Wilson.

CONTENTS

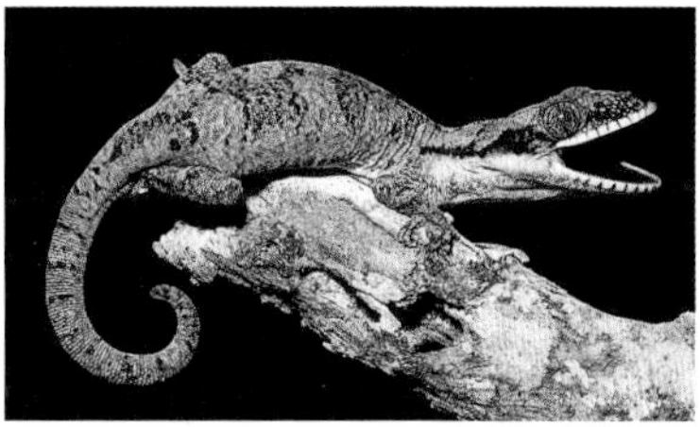

The Ornamental Snake (*Denisonia maculata*) is a vulnerable species that feeds exclusively on frogs. Following rain in Queensland's Northern Brigalow Belt, they emerge from the flood-prone cracking clay soil to hunt. *Denisonia maculata* eating *Litoria alboguttata*. Croyden Stn, Qld. S. Wilson.

A juvenile Smooth-snouted Earless Dragon (*Tympanocryptis intima*) basks in full sun, perched on a black metal chain when the shade temperature was 43°C. It is clearly operating on a fine line, at the very limit of thermal tolerance for any vertebrate. Winton area, Qld. S. Wilson

PREFACE

With taxonomic work continuing unabated and the number of described reptile species steadily climbing, it has been inevitable that Australia's tally would exceed one thousand. That is now the case, and this Fifth Edition of *A Complete Guide to Reptiles of Australia* covers a total of 1011 described species. And there is more to come. We know of species, some quite familiar to naturalists, that remain undescribed, and we are aware of complexes, currently lumped under single names, that await genetic and morphological analysis to describe and name their component members.

The use of scientific names, the binomial system, is structured to provide permanent stability to the nomenclature of animals, plants and other organisms. However there are currently arguments taking place within the herpetological community, some quite heated, regarding the validity of some species descriptions and the names applied to them. It is not the role of a field guide to enter this debate but at the same time we have had to decide which of several contentious names we employ. Our decisions are based on the advice of others with far greater knowledge than us of the complex, labyrinthine rules of zoological nomenclature. Not all readers will agree with our decisions. While debate might continue for some time, and some names may change as a result, the most important thing to us is that the species appear in the book.

When preparing previous editions we decided to include images of preserved material for several of the species for which no live image was available. In this edition we have expanded on that theme, to ensure that all 1011 species are represented by at least one image.

Nearly all species are represented by images of live animals, and only 15 species require photographs of preserved material. A significant proportion of these are blind snakes (family Typhlopidae). It is testament to the secretive nature of these poorly known snakes that 7 of the 45 species, over 15 per cent, have never been photographed as live animals, and a significant proportion of the species are known from fewer than five specimens.

Thanks to the efforts of many hard-working herpetological photographers, Australia's reptile fauna is very comprehensively documented. We are acutely aware of the numerous instances where an image, buried amongst hundreds of others within the pages of this book, is the result of immense endeavours and personal costs. We understand the countless kilometres driven over outback roads in adverse conditions, sometimes fruitlessly over repeated occasions, and the hours spent raking leaf litter, peering into hollows, delving into prickly spinifex or spotlighting for hours, to finally locate and photograph an elusive species. To all contributing photographers, we offer a sincere thank you for your generosity in allowing us to use your images in this book.

The principal role of this field guide is to aid identification. It also aims to encourage conservation and promote an interest in reptile ecology and behaviour.

Steve Wilson and Gerry Swan
December 2016

The Oakview Leaf-tailed Gecko (*Phyllurus kabikabi*) was named in 2008. Just one small population is known to occur in a 120 metre wide band of vine thicket on rock scree inland from Gympie, Qld. More field work will probably expand this range, but there is no doubt this is a highly restricted species. Oakview Forest Reserve. S. Wilson.

ACKNOWLEDGEMENTS

We owe a great debt of gratitude to our dedicated friends and colleagues who have assisted us.

Many thousands of images were submitted for consideration and it has been a great privilege to view such a vast and comprehensive collection. For allowing us access to their photographs we would like to thank: Kieran Aland, Michael Anthony, Jessica Bolton, Rob Browne-Cooper, Clayton Bryce, Brian Bush, John Cann, Sharee Carton, Nick Clemman, Hal Cogger, Henry Cook, John Cornish, Mark Cowan, Lauren Dibben, Michael Dinsdale, Col Dollery, Steve Donnellan, Paul Doughty, Scott Eipper, Adam Elliott, Ryan Ellis, Angus Emmott, Jules Farquhar, Stewart Ford, Greg Fyfe, Glen Gaikhorst, Nic Gambold, Mike Gillam, Graeme Gow, Roger Grace, Allen Greer, Phil Griffin, Greg Harold, Ryan Hart, Paul Horner, Conrad Hoskin, Grant Husband, Mark Hutchinson, Ray Ireland, Ron Johnstone, Cameron de Jong, Jordan de Jong, Angus Kennedy, Dave Knowles, Alex Kutt, Col Limpus, J. Lindley McKay, Ray Lloyd, Michael Lyons, Stewart Macdonald, Roy Mackay, Stephen Mahony, Brad Maryan, Peter McDonald, Rune Midtgaard, Brian Miller, Peter Mirtschin, Andrew Morton/AWC, Paul Oliver, Tom Parkin, T. Peters, Thomas Rasmussen, Eric Rittmeyer, Lewis Roberts, Peter Robertson, Dave Robinson, Brendan Schembri, Matthew Shaw, Glenn Shea, Dean Shipman, Andrew Smith, Dave Stanton, Gary Stephenson, Rob Steubing, Geoff Swan, Mike Swan, Steve Swanson, Dane Trembath, Kanishka Ukuwela, Rob Valentic, Eric Vanderduys, Gary Vas, Jordan Vos, John Weigel, David Williams, John Wombey, Anders Zimny and Stephen Zozaya.

Patrick Couper of the Queensland Museum granted permission to use some of his original illustrations, and the Herpetology Departments of the Australian and Queensland Museums provided access to specimens and data on distribution. Commonwealth Fisheries Research and Development Corporation and Queensland DPI permitted access to sea snake images.

For their companionship and the sharing of a common fascination with all things reptilian, we would like to acknowledge Kieran Aland, Bob Ashdown, Rob Browne-Cooper, Jeanette Covacevich, Greg Czechura, Harald Ehmann, Allen Greer, Peter Harlow, Greg Harold, Tim Helder, Tony and Kate Hiller, Rod Hobson, Dave Knowles, Brad Maryan, Mats Olsson, Ross Sadlier, Glenn Shea, Mike Swan and Eric Vanderduys.

Brad Maryan has moved mountains on our behalf, seeking elusive images, liaising with photographers and acting as our West Australian ambassador. For this, we are extremely grateful.

Underwater World at Mooloolaba generously permitted access to sea turtles in their care. Richard Jackson of Australia Zoo made goannas available for photographing. John Cann was kind enough to read our freshwater turtle text and offer some constructive comments.

Steve Wilson's parents, Joy and Ken Wilson, urged him from an early age to follow his passion. The value of such support cannot be measured. His wife Marilyn has been a source of endless encouragement, provider of technical assistance when computers behave strangely, and willing sharer of our abode with all reptiles except death adders.

Gerry Swan's family have shown considerable patience and tolerance in a house sometimes overrun with reptiles. In particular his wife Marlene has been very supportive, putting up with dust, flies, goanna bites and the ultimate boredom of reading through an earlier draft of this book and diligently noting all the bits whose meaning was obscure.

Eastern Water Skink (*Eulamprus quoyii*) foraging in a shallow pool. Girraween NP, Qld. S. Wilson

HOW TO USE THIS BOOK

The aim of this book is to aid the identification of Australian reptiles by presenting all the species with descriptions generally accepted to 31st December 2016 in compact handbook form. It features descriptions and distribution maps for the 1011 named species from continental Australia, including Norfolk and Lord Howe islands and their satellites. Species restricted to the oceanic territories of Christmas and the Cocos (Keeling) islands are excluded, as are the many species which remain unnamed. Formal descriptions of some of these are pending.

To maintain portable, comprehensive coverage the individual accounts are, by necessity, brief. The book should be used in conjunction with existing larger format books, scientific publications and regional guides.

Classification

Like all organisms, reptiles are classified by arranging them into groups based on similar characteristics and shared evolutionary histories. The levels of classification relevant to this book are: family, genus and species.

The families make up most of the chapters of this book. The family names for all animals end with the letters 'idae'. Each is introduced with an account of the physical and behavioural characteristics of its members.

Within each family there are one or more genera (singular = genus), arranged alphabetically. The genus is the 'pigeonhole' containing related species that share common ancestry and exhibit distinctive features. On occasions a genus contains only one unique species with no close living relatives. Other genera are much more complex, containing up to 90 or more species.

Within each genus are the species. These are the different kinds of reptiles, and at this level of classification lie the individual descriptions, maps and photographs.

Scientific Names

Scientific names are italicised and normally consist of two parts, the capitalised genus and lower-case species (for example, the gecko *Strophurus spinigerus*).

Many species include regionally distinct populations isolated by some aspect of geography. They may differ slightly in size, scale character or colour. Some of these are classified as subspecies, in which case a third name is added (for example, *Strophurus spinigerus inornatus*).

Name Changes

Reptile classification is under constant review and there is no universally accepted list of names. Species are sometimes moved between genera to more accurately reflect their evolutionary history. The gecko *Strophurus spinigerus* appears as *Diplodactylus spinigerus* in older literature but is now acknowledged as part of a separate, distinct group of species. This presents a clearer picture for herpetologists but confuses the reader who attempts to cross-reference information between sources employing different names. It is an annoying problem, but bear in mind that the species name usually remains constant, and the reptile can be accessed directly under that name in the index (for example, *spinigerus, Strophurus*).

Common Names

Many reptiles are widely known by common names. Tiger Snake, Saltwater Crocodile and Loggerhead Turtle are familiar terms. There are also examples of multiple names. For example, Shingleback, Sleepy Lizard, Boggi, Stumpy-tail and Bob-tail apply in different parts of the country to just one species, *Tiliqua rugosa.* Following an increasing trend to include common names where possible, names have been sourced from a variety of books and authoritative websites and employed here.

Identification

Identification is often difficult in the field. While some species are large and distinctive, most are small and require close attention to fine detail; sometimes the presence, absence or condition of merely a single scale must be determined to reach an accurate identification. With experience, many similar species become readily recognisable by subtle nuances in pattern, build or behaviour. These minute cues rarely transpose effectively into print but with time and application the identification process does become easier.

Species Accounts

When studying species accounts, readers should always refer to the genus account as well, because features common to all members of a genus are not repeated for each individual species. When a genus contains only one species, the genus and species accounts are combined.

Each account features a description, notes on distribution and preferred habitat and often a few aspects of behaviour. Descriptions are as simple and brief as accuracy permits, but reference to minute features requiring examination with a magnifying glass or microscope is sometimes unavoidable. Specialised terminology is explained in the glossary.

Diagnostic features of particular relevance are highlighted in **bold type**. When a similar species or genus has an overlapping distribution and is likely to cause confusion, this is mentioned for easy cross-referencing under 'See Also'. Some element in bold type will normally provide the all-important identification clue.

Measurements

Measurements are in millimetres for species under 1 metre long (for example, 325mm), and in metres for species over 1 metre long (for example, 1.2m). Because many lizards lose and re-grow their tails, they are measured by snout–vent length (SVL), which equates to head and body length. Goannas, snakes and crocodiles rarely lose their tails, so their sizes are given as total length (TL). Turtles are measured by carapace length (CL). Measurements usually refer to average adult lengths rather than rare freakish maximums, though record sizes are sometimes added.

Maps

The maps illustrate broad distributional parameters, but few species occur continuously in all habitats throughout the shaded area. Maps are prepared with reference to existing books, museum databases, scientific literature and unpublished observations. They have been drawn as accurately as possible, but because of their small size should be considered as a rough guide only. Also, reptiles are notorious for not reading the right books, and frequently have the audacity to turn up outside the areas we have prescribed for them.

Photographs

Photographs featuring the described species, subspecies and many colour variants accompany the text. For the most part the photographs illustrate typical live animals on their natural backgrounds. However several species are known only from preserved, and sometimes single, specimens. In the absence of a live image, pictures of preserved specimens are included.

Conservation Status

Some reptile populations have severely declined, but fortunately we have not witnessed the catastrophic extinction rate suffered by native mammals. All are protected in Australia. They face a variety of threats, based largely on inappropriate land-use practices, feral predators, unsustainable harvesting (of turtles) and even excessive collecting. The spectre of climate change adds a new and urgent level of uncertainty to the conservation of reptiles and other organisms in Australia and worldwide. Many species not currently considered at risk may seriously decline or even face extinction in the near future. Species listed at federal and/or state levels as being of conservation concern (endangered, threatened, vulnerable, etc.) are indicated accordingly. We have also included the international status of species in the 2004 International Union for Conservation of Nature and Natural Resources (IUCN) Red List of Threatened Species.

Abbreviations Used in Text

approx. approximately; **Aust.** Australia; **brdg, non-brdg** breeding, non-breeding; **Ck/s** Creek/s; **CL** carapace length; **DSF** dry sclerophyll forest; **e.** east; **estn** eastern; ♀ female; **fig.** figure; **Gt** Great; **Gt Aust. Bight** Great Australian Bight; **Gt. Div. Ra.** Great Dividing Range; **incl.** including; **Is.** Island/s; **juv.** juvenile; ♂ male; **Mtns** Mountains; **Nat. Res.** Nature Reserve; **NP** National Park; **NG** New Guinea; **NZ** New Zealand; **n.** north; **ne.** north-east etc.; **nthn** northern; **Pen.** Peninsula; **pop./pops** population/s; **RF** rainforests; **Ra.** Range; **R.** River; **s.** south; **sthn** southern; **sp./spp.** species sing/pl.; **SF** State Forest; **Stn** Station; **ssp.** subspecies; **SVL** snout–vent length; **TL** total length; **vegtn** vegetation; **w.** west; **wstn** western; **WSF** wet sclerophyll forest

GLOSSARY AND ILLUSTRATIONS

These definitions apply to the context in which the words have been used in this book. In other contexts they may have different or additional meanings.

Ablepharine Lacking a moveable eyelid; replacing the lower lid with a fixed, transparent spectacle. See illustration 5c.
Adpress Pressing the hindlimb forward and the forelimb back against the body to gauge relative limb length.
Aestivate To go into an inactive state during periods of drought or high temperatures.
Anterior At or towards the front of the body.
Auricular Relating to the ear.
Autotomy Tail-loss, spontaneously or by reflex.
Basal At or near the base.
Callose/Callus A raised hard or tough condition. Usually applies to lower surfaces of digits.
Carapace The upper shell of a turtle.
Carination Keel or ridge on a scale.
Casque A helmet of thickened skin or bone over the head.
Caudal Relating to the tail.
Chenopod Shrub in the family Chenopodiaceae. Many have small succulent leaves and grow in dry or saline conditions.
Chevron An inverted V-shaped marking.
Cloaca The common chamber into which reproductive and excretory ducts open.
Costal scute See illustration 1.
Crepuscular Active at dawn, dusk or in deeply shaded conditions.
Crest A longitudinal row of elevated, often spiny, scales along the neck, back or tail.
Cryptic Inconspicuous or secretive by way of colour, pattern and/or behaviour.
Dermal Of the skin.
Dewlap A loose flap of skin under the throat.
Distal Furthest from the body, away from the point of attachment.
Diurnal Active by day.
Dorsal Relating to the back or upper surfaces.
Dorsally depressed Flattened from the top.
Dorsolateral Relating to the junction of the upper (dorsal) and side (lateral) surfaces.
Elliptic Usually relates to vertical pupils.
Femoral pore One or more pores beneath the thigh.
Frontal scale See illustrations 3, 7 and 10.
Gular Relating to the throat, or in turtles, a pair of plates on the leading edge of the plastron. See illustrations pp. 36, 40, 44 and 48.
Heterogeneous Refers to that condition where the scales differ in size and/or shape.
Homogeneous Refers to that condition where the scales are similar.
Intergular shield A plate on the midline of the plastron on some turtles. See illustrations pp. 36, 40, 44 and 48.
Internasal scales See illustration 10.
Keel A narrow raised ridge on individual scales, or a low crest or other longitudinal flange.
Labial Of the lips, usually referring to scales bordering the lips.
Lamellae Scales along the underside of the digits.
Laterally compressed Flattened from side to side.
Lateritic soil A reddish, gravelly soil rich in iron or aluminium ore.
Laterodorsal The outer part of the back, usually a dark stripe along the inner edge of a pale dorsolateral stripe.
Loreal scale Scale between nasal and preocular scales. See illustration on p. 512.
Macrocephaly A condition where some aged turtles develop greatly enlarged heads.

Marginal scute See illustration 1.
Mental scale See illustration 2.
Midbody scales The scales counted along an oblique line around the middle of the body. See illustration 11.
Mucronate Ending in a sharp point or spine. Usually refers to the subdigital lamellae of some lizards.
Nasal scale See illustrations 2, 3, 7, 8, 9 and 10.
Nuchal Relating to the nape, or the scute on the leading edge of a turtle carapace. See illustrations 1 and 3.
Ocelli Eye-like, ring-shaped spots.
Osteoderm A bony plate underlying each scale in some reptiles.
Palpebral disc The transparent window in the lower eyelid of some lizards. See illustration 5b
Paravertebral scales A longitudinal row of scales lying on each side of the mid-dorsal line.
Parietal scale See illustrations 3, 7, 9 and 10.
Parthenogenetic Able to reproduce without fertilisation by a male, particularly some geckos that produce female clones.
Pectoral Part of the chest, or part of the plastron of a turtle.
Pelagic Inhabiting the open seas.
Plantar scales Scales of the sole of the foot.
Plastron Lower part of a turtle shell.
Pore Opening to a scale on some lizards, best developed in males, usually filled with a wax-like substance.
Postauricular Behind the ear.
Posterior At or towards the rear.
Postocular Behind the eye.
Preanal pore One or more pores located in front of the vent.
Prefrontal scale See illustrations 3, 7 and 10.
Preocular scale See illustrations 2, 7, 9 and 10.
Primary temporal scales Large scales behind the eye between the parietal and upper labial scales.
Proximal Nearest to the body, close to the point of attachment.
Reticulated Forming a net-like pattern or reticulum.
Rosette A circular arrangement of scales, usually surrounding a tubercle.
Rostral scale See illustrations 2, 3, 7, 8, 9 and 10.
Scapular The dorsal part of the shoulder.
Sclerophyll forest A forest mostly comprising eucalypt (gum) trees which have hard, stiff leaves.
Scutes Enlarged scales on a reptile; horny plates of a turtle shell.
Setae Microscopic hairs or bristles.
Spinifex Spiny-leafed grasses of the genera *Triodia* and *Plectrachne*, which form prickly hummocks. Often called porcupine grass.
Spinose Having spines.
Striation Groove on the surface of a scale.
Subcaudal Beneath the tail. Often applies to scales. See illustration 12.
Subdigital Beneath the digit (finger or toe).
Subocular scale One of a series of scales below the eye. See illustration on p. 398.
Supraciliary scale See illustrations 2 and 3.
Supraocular scale See illustrations 3, 7, 9 and 10.
Suture The groove between non-overlapping scales.
Temporal scale See illustrations 2 and 10.
Trilobed Having three lobes, as in the snouts of some blind snakes.
Tubercle A rounded or pointed projection.
Tuberculate Having tubercles.
Tympanum Eardrum. Visible externally on many lizards. See illustration 2.
Vent The transverse external opening of the cloaca.
Ventral The lower surfaces, or the scales on the belly.
Ventrolateral Junction of the side (lateral) and lower surface (ventral).
Viscous Sticky.

1. SCUTES OF A TURTLE CARAPACE

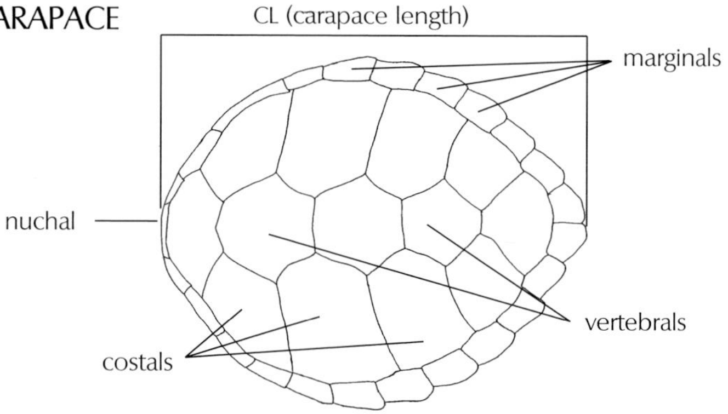

2. SKINK—LATERAL HEAD SHIELDS

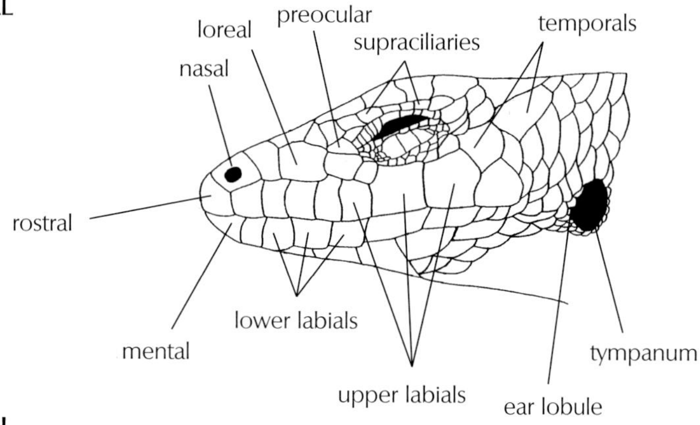

3. SKINK—DORSAL HEAD SHIELDS

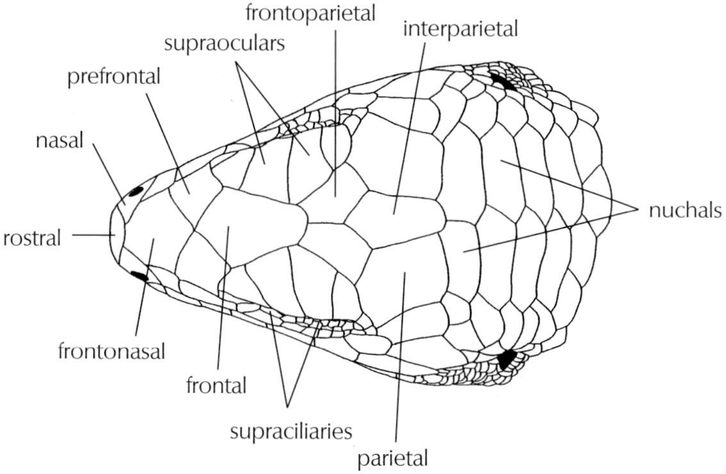

4. LIZARD BODY INDICATING MEASURING POINTS

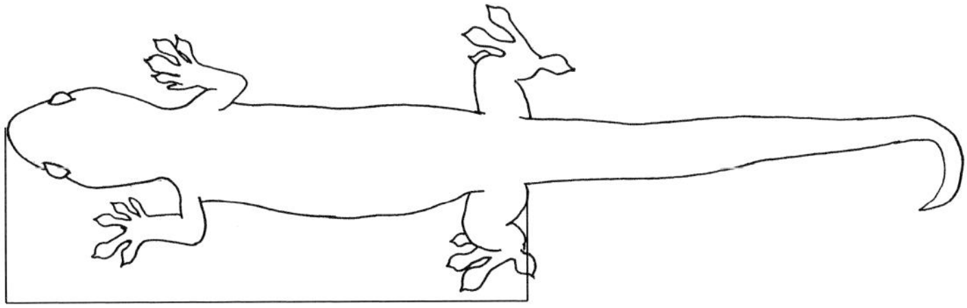

SVL (snout–vent length)

5. CONDITION OF THE LOWER EYELID IN SKINKS

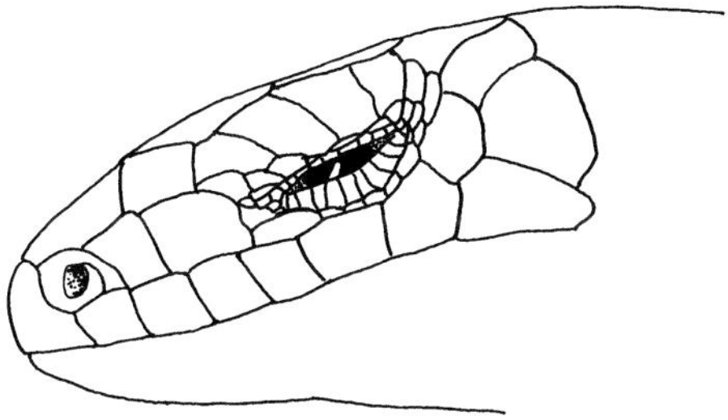

a Moveable and scaly

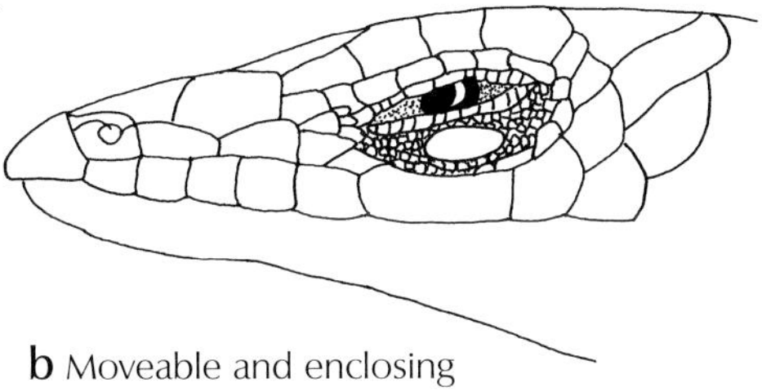

b Moveable and enclosing a transparent palpebral disc

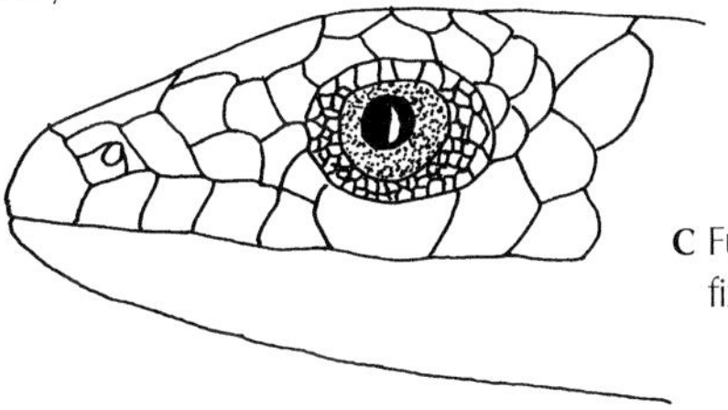

c Fused to form a fixed spectacle

6. BODY STRIPES IN LIZARDS

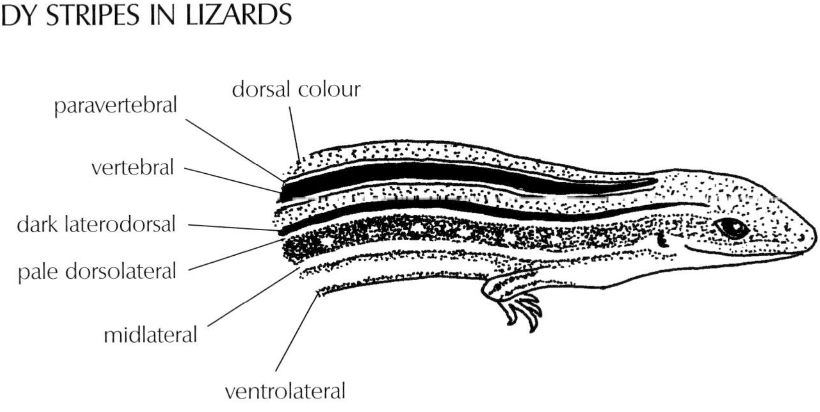

7. BLIND SNAKE—DORSAL HEAD SCALES

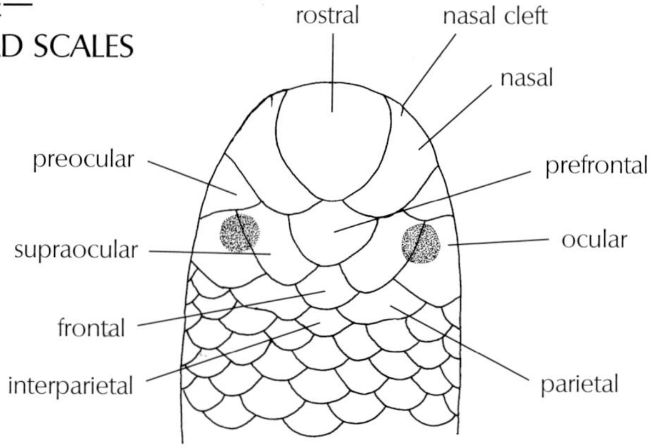

8. BLIND SNAKE—VENTRAL HEAD SCALES

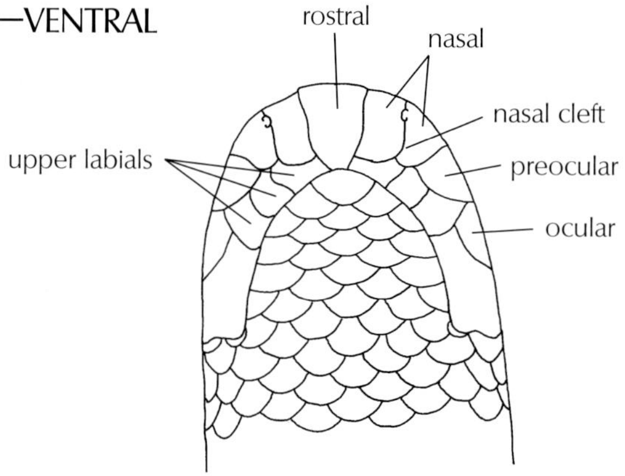

9. BLIND SNAKE—LATERAL HEAD SCALES

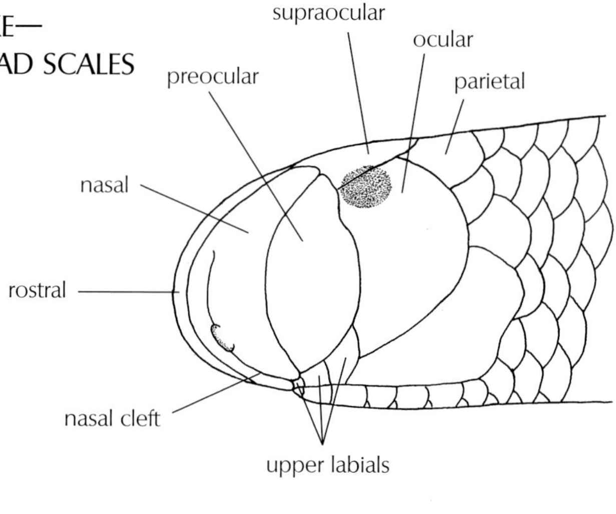

10. ELAPID SNAKE—HEAD SCALES

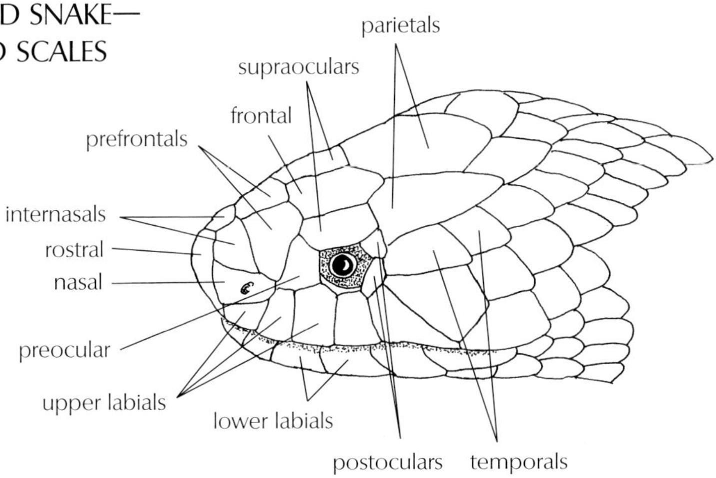

11. SNAKE BODY SCALES SHOWING DIAGONAL COUNTS

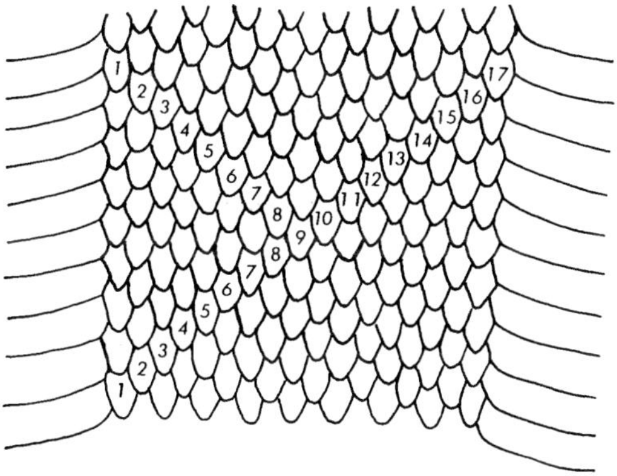

12. SNAKE—DIVIDED OR UNDIVIDED ANAL AND SUBCAUDAL SCALES

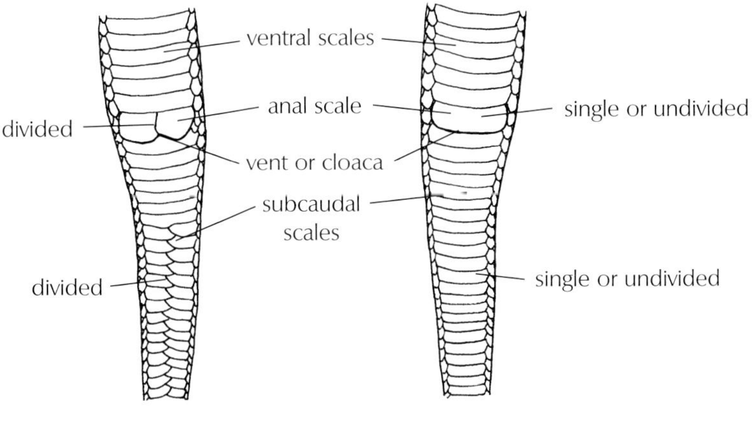

INTRODUCTION

A diverse fauna in an extraordinary land

Australians are the fortunate custodians of a rich and unique reptile fauna. With the current count standing at 1011 described species, and many more still unnamed, it is a fauna as diverse as any in the world and so complex that no single person is ever likely to see all of our species in a lifetime.

We take a certain grim national pride in harbouring some of the world's most lethal snakes, as evidenced by the yarns in any outback pub. We generally tolerate, or even welcome, blue-tongues, geckos and pythons as residents of our homes and gardens, and consider crocodiles and goannas to be an integral part of bush folklore. Reptiles are so abundant in just about every settlement between southern Tasmania and the Torres Strait Islands that we accept them as a normal part of the landscape.

A number of factors have combined to shape this unique Australian herpetological community. Ocean currents, rising and falling sea-levels and shifting continents have injected a strong global influence at the family level, while our geographical isolation has nurtured the evolution of endemic species. With a few notable exceptions, virtually all of the families of reptiles living here are distributed widely in other parts of the world, but they are represented in Australia by a suite of species that occur nowhere else.

Coupled with Australia's isolation is its size; it is a vast expanse of land and coastline encompassing tropical, cool temperate and arid regimes. Another country with comparable mass, United States of America, extends from cold temperate zones to just above the tropics and has extensive hot deserts, yet it only supports just over one-third of the reptile diversity of Australia. It would seem the mosaic of Australian habitats has much to offer.

Australia features warm, shallow, turbid seas fringed with mangroves, clear coral reefs, freshwater wetlands, tropical rainforests and savannahs, arid stony plains and ranges, sand-ridge deserts, alpine areas and cool southern forests and heaths. Each of these is the favoured environment for its own distinctive reptile species. There are also specialists confined to blinding white salt crusts, deeply cracking clays and mist-enshrouded mountain tops.

The arid zones in particular support much of our phenomenal herpetological wealth. One group of grasses, known generally as spinifex or porcupine grasses, covers vast tracts of the interior and west. Spinifex creates such favourable humid shelter sites, within a protective matrix of spiny foliage, that many species of lizards occur only where it grows. A square kilometre of Australian spinifex desert may support more species of reptiles than an area of comparable size anywhere else in the world.

In the species entries in this book, important habitats are frequently discussed as the preferred environment for each species. The ability to recognise particular vegetation associations, forest types or landforms can be invaluable in pinpointing where to begin looking for certain species. Examples of some of these broad habitat types are pictured.

Spinifex *Triodia* sand-plain. G. Swan

Desert dune. S. Wilson

Mallee/spinifex association. G. Swan

Gibber desert. S. Wilson

Arid shrubland. S. Wilson

Stony hills. S. Wilson

Tropical woodland. S. Wilson

Dry sclerophyll forest. S. Wilson

Tropical rainforest. S. Wilson

Vine thicket. S. Wilson

Mangroves. S. Wilson

Tropical wetland. S. Wilson

Alpine heath. S. Wilson

Temperate heath. S. Wilson

CROCODILES
Family Crocodylidae

The family Crocodylidae is one of three extant families within the order Crocodilia, with an evolutionary history spanning more than 200 million years.

Crocodilians include the largest living reptiles. They have several distinctive characteristics: a four-chambered heart and a diaphragm, a long snout with nostrils set at the tip to allow breathing while the body is submerged, jaws lined with sharp conical teeth, a streamlined body heavily armoured with bony plates, a long laterally compressed tail and short limbs with clawed webbed feet.

Crocodilians are efficient predators. Snout shape and diet are closely associated. Those adapted to catch fish or other swift prey have slender snouts, allowing them to sideswipe rapidly under water, while generalists and species that capture powerful prey have broader snouts. They hunt mainly at night, and can often be seen by day basking on river banks.

All lay eggs, exhibiting the most advanced maternal care in reptiles. Females of some species lay in a nest-mound of vegetation which they guard. When the young hatch their mother transports them to water. It seems incongruous that jaws capable of snapping a buffalo's thigh can carry delicate offspring, and sometimes even assist them from the shell.

The family Crocodylidae is represented here by one genus.

Genus *Crocodylus*

Thirteen spp. (2 in Aust.) with a **notch on each side of the upper jaw, accommodating the 4th tooth of the lower jaw** when the mouth is closed. This tooth is always visible, giving crocodiles a somewhat 'toothy grin'. In contrast, Alligators and Caimans (Alligatoridae) have broad flat snouts with all lower teeth accommodated within pits in the upper jaw, and not visible when the mouth is closed. The Gharial (Gavialidae) has an extremely slender snout, sharply demarcated from a bulbous head.

Freshwater Crocodile; Johnstone's Crocodile *Crocodylus johnstoni* TL 2–3m

Snout slender, with **1 row of enlarged nuchal shields set just behind smooth-skinned parietal region**. Grey to brown with darker bands. ■ **NOTES** Freshwater rivers and billabongs. Eats fish, crustaceans, insects, reptiles, amphibians and birds. Not normally dangerous but swimmers have been injured, perhaps when feet were mistaken for a fish. ■ **STATUS** Specially protected (WA); lower risk – least concern (IUCN Red List).

Estuarine Crocodile; Saltwater Crocodile *Crocodylus porosus* TL 3–5m (max. 7m)

Snout broad, with **2 rows of enlarged nuchal shields set well back from smooth-skinned parietal region**. Grey to almost black with darker mottling. ■ **NOTES** Coastal rivers and swamps from wstn Pacific to India. Extends inland along the major drainage systems; occasionally seen in open sea. World's largest living crocodilian. Juv. eat insects, crustaceans, fish and reptiles; adults take mammals, birds and fish, including, on rare occasions, people. Signs along many tropical river banks warn people not to swim. DANGEROUS. ■ **STATUS** Vulnerable (Qld); specially protected (WA); lower risk – least concern (IUCN Red List).

Crocodylus johnstoni. Kununurra, WA. S. Wilson

Crocodylus porosus. Kakadu NP, NT. M. Dinsdale

HARD-SHELLED SEA TURTLES
Family Cheloniidae

Sea turtles are found throughout the world's tropical to warm temperate seas. Six of the seven species belong to the family Cheloniidae, five of which occur in Australia. Cheloniid turtles are characterised by having feet modified to form flippers, but retaining at least **one claw on the forelimbs**. The shell is heavily armoured with **strong horny scutes**, though on the adult Flatback Turtle (*Natator depressus*), these are covered by a thin veneer of soft skin.

Each species tends to have a different diet. The Green Turtle (*Chelonia mydas*) is carnivorous for the first year but adults are largely vegetarian, grazing on marine grasses and algae. The Loggerhead Turtle (*Caretta caretta*) is almost entirely carnivorous, with a heavy skull and jaws to crush crustaceans and molluscs. The Hawksbill Turtle (*Eretmochelys imbricata*) eats sponges and soft corals.

Though wholly aquatic in their feeding and mating, sea turtles remain obligated to land because they are egglayers. Males need never leave the sea, but females must periodically haul themselves ashore to lay. They return to the beach of their birth, normally many hundreds of kilometres from their feeding grounds, demonstrating extraordinary navigational skills.

A female may lay more than one clutch per season but the taxing process of developing a sizeable egg-mass (often more than 100 eggs), let alone the lengthy journeys involved to lay them, means that several years elapse between clutches.

Nesting always occurs on tropical to subtropical beaches. In some cases a lone female will come ashore but some sites are subject to massive aggregations, with hundreds or even thousands of turtles laying each night. Their combined efforts create an extensive layer beneath the beach consisting of millions of eggs.

Turtle reproductive strategy involves producing a glut of hatchlings with the expectation that only a few survive. They suffer an appalling mortality rate. Nests are excavated by pigs and monitor lizards, and as the hatchlings cross the sand they are devoured by crabs and birds. When they reach the sea there are plenty of hungry fish waiting.

The odds seem impossible, yet the result has been relatively stable turtle populations, since the lucky few that grow up have been adequate to replenish adult stock. For thousands of years turtle numbers have tolerated harvesting of eggs and adults by indigenous people, and today they remain an integral part of the diet and culture in many northern Australian communities. In recent years, however, numbers have declined alarmingly, due in part to events occurring beyond our borders.

Only the Flatback Turtle is endemic to Australian waters. Populations of all other species travel widely. Those that breed here may feed elsewhere, and turtles that forage in our seas often nest on distant beaches. They swim a gauntlet of unsustainable capture rates, while rookeries may be afforded no protection at all. Many also end up as trawling by-catch.

Even within Australia turtles face the problems of boat strikes, attempting to swallow ocean junk such as plastic bags, or drowning entangled in fishing lines and submerged nets.

All sea turtles in Australia are listed as having some degree of conservation concern.

Loggerhead Turtle (*Caretta caretta*). South-eastern Qld. S. Wilson

Genus *Caretta*

Loggerhead Turtle *Caretta caretta* CL 1.25m

Head disproportionately massive, particularly on aged individuals. Scutes on carapace not overlapping, with **5 (rarely 6) pairs of costal shields**. Reddish brown to brown, sometimes with darker speckling. ■ **NOTES** Tropical and warm temperate waters worldwide, including those off Aust. coast, particularly Great Barrier Reef. Occasional strays venture south to cooler waters. Mainly carnivorous, eating mostly molluscs, crustaceans, sea urchins and jellyfish. ■ **STATUS** Vulnerable (IUCN Red List; NT); endangered (C'wealth; Qld; NSW; SA; Tas; WA).

Genus *Chelonia*

Green Turtle *Chelonia mydas* CL 1.5m

Scutes on carapace not overlapping, with **4 pairs of costal shields**. Snout not beak-like, with **1 pair of large prefrontal scales (fig.)**. Olive green with black and darker brown markings. ■ **NOTES** Tropical and warm temperate waters worldwide. Occasional strays venture south to cooler waters. Juv. carnivorous but adults graze on seagrasses and seaweeds. This is the sp. most frequently sought for meat and eggs. ■ **STATUS** Endangered (IUCN Red List); vulnerable (C'wealth; Qld; NSW; SA; Tas; WA); near threatened (NT).

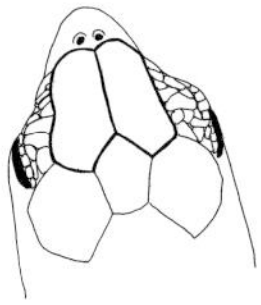

Genus *Eretmochelys*

Hawksbill Turtle *Eretmochelys imbricata* CL 1m

Scutes on carapace overlapping, with **4 pairs of costal shields**. Upper jaw juts forward to form distinctive **beak-like snout**, with **2 pairs of prefrontal scales (fig.)**. Olive green to brown with rich reddish brown to black variegations. ■ **NOTES** Tropical and warm temperate waters worldwide. Represented in Indian and Pacific Oceans by the ssp. *E. i. bissa*, though significant genetic difference is reported between pops from ne. and nw. Aust. Favours rocky areas and coral reefs. Feeds mainly on sponges, but also on soft corals, seagrasses and molluscs. Heavily exploited by the tortoiseshell industry for its overlapping scutes. ■ **STATUS** Critically endangered (IUCN Red List); endangered (Qld); vulnerable (C'wealth; Tas; WA; NT).

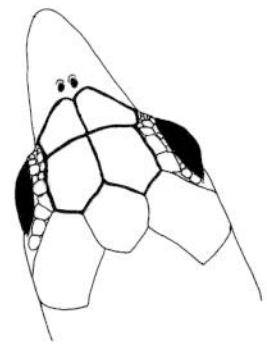

Caretta caretta.
Juvenile. Mon Repos, Qld. S. Wilson

Caretta caretta.
Nesting adult. Mon Repos, Qld. S. Wilson

Chelonia mydas. Raine Is., Qld. M. Shaw

Eretmochelys imbricata. Juvenile.
Mt Adolphus Is., Qld. S. Wilson

Eretmochelys imbricata.
Heron Is., Qld. H. Cogger

Genus *Lepidochelys*

Pacific Ridley Turtle *Lepidochelys olivacea* CL 600–750mm

Nearly round shell. Scutes on carapace not overlapping, with **6 or more pairs of costal shields**. Snout not beak-like, with 2 pairs of prefrontal scales. Olive grey to brown. ■ **NOTES** Tropical areas of Indian, Pacific and parts of Atlantic Oceans, but largely restricted in Aust. to nthn coast of NT and Cape York Pen., Qld. Only low-level nesting occurs in Aust. but enormous rookeries are heavily exploited by man in Central America and Mexico. Feeds on small crabs and shellfish. ■ **STATUS** Vulnerable (IUCN Red List; NT); endangered (C'wealth; Qld; WA).

Genus *Natator*

Flatback Turtle *Natator depressus* CL 800mm–1m

Carapace very depressed with upturned edges, covered on adults by thin fleshy skin. Scutes on carapace not overlapping with **4 pairs of costal shields**. Snout not beak-like, with 1 pair of large prefrontal scales. Olive grey to pale green without pattern. ■ **NOTES** The only sea turtle restricted to Aust. waters, between the Pilbara, WA and e. coast of Qld. Carnivorous, feeding mainly on soft-bodied prey such as sea cucumbers, soft corals and jellyfish. ■ **STATUS** Vulnerable (C'wealth; Qld; WA).

Lepidochelys olivacea. Raragala Is., NT. P. Horner

Natator depressus. Mon Repos, Qld. C. Limpus

LEATHERY SEA TURTLE
Family Dermochelyidae

The family Dermochelyidae contains only the one genus, with a single species, an enormous and quite unique sea turtle commonly known as the Leathery Turtle. It shares with the Cheloniid sea turtles a wholly aquatic lifestyle in which the female comes ashore only to lay eggs, and the male never leaves the water, but it differs markedly in appearance, behaviour and physiology.

This pelagic species is the world's most widespread reptile, foraging in open oceans and coastlines across a vast area from north of the Arctic Circle to south of New Zealand. Sightings occur around most of coastal Australia, though it tends to avoid coral reefs.

Despite a wide range and frequent occurrence in cold seas, the Leathery Turtle nests only in the tropics. There is very limited breeding in mid-eastern Qld, and the nearest significant breeding sites are in eastern Malaysia. There are also large rookeries in Central America. Clutch sizes average about 80 eggs.

Leathery Turtles are dietary specialists, eating only jellyfish and other gelatinous, free-swimming invertebrates. It seems incongruous that their huge mass, sometimes more than 900 kilograms, can be sustained on such insubstantial but obviously nutritious fare. Much of their movement appears to be dictated by the occurrence of jellyfish blooms.

Leathery Turtles are unique among living reptiles in maintaining a body temperature higher than ambient. Specimens found in waters of only 7°C have recorded a body temperature as high as 25°C. They employ a process of heat production and temperature regulation coined 'giganto-thermy', maintaining high body temperatures by a mix of large body size, low metabolic rates and insulating peripheral tissues. This unusual physiology enables Leathery Turtles to roam the world's oceans, and to dive to extraordinary depths exceeding 1100 metres.

Because they wander over vast distances, Leathery Turtles probably face even more threats than the Cheloniid turtles. No individual is confined within the territorial waters of any one nation, so cooperative international legislation is required to effectively protect them. Their most crucial rookeries are heavily exploited, and they share the oceans with an increasing number of plastic bags. The similarity of these to jellyfish is obvious, and their accidental ingestion is one of the biggest killers of Leathery Turtles.

Genus *Dermochelys*

Leathery Turtle; Luth *Dermochelys coriacea* CL 1.8–2.8m

A huge sea turtle with long, **streamlined, leathery or hard rubbery carapace,** strongly pointed at rear, with 7 prominent longitudinal ridges. Instead of horny scutes the leathery cover is embedded with a mosaic of numerous tiny polygonal bones called osteoderms. **Front flippers are enormous and lack claws.** Very dark grey to black, often with paler mottling. Juv. beaded with white along ridge-lines. ■ **STATUS** Vulnerable (IUCN Red List; SA; Tas; WA); critically endangered (Vic; NT); endangered (C'wealth; Qld; NSW).

Dermochelys coriacea. **Adult.** Wreck Rock Beach, Qld. C. Limpus

Dermochelys coriacea. **Juvenile.** Bundaberg, Qld. H. Cogger

SIDE-NECKED FRESHWATER TURTLES
Family Chelidae

Excluding only the unique Pig-nosed Turtle (Family Carettochelydidae) and the introduced Red-eared Slider (Family Emydidae), Australian freshwater turtles are all members of the family Chelidae, restricted to Australia, New Guinea and South America. These 'side-necked' turtles or Pleurodira, have clawed webbed feet and relatively flattened shells covered by tough horny scutes. The head and neck fold horizontally under the front edge of the carapace rather than retracting directly backwards. Many species have unusual fleshy growths called barbels on the chin, believed to have a sensory, tactile function.

Once known in Australia as tortoises, the term 'freshwater turtles' is now widely used, distinguishing these from both their marine allies and the dome-shelled, wholly terrestrial true tortoises of other continents. In Australia juveniles of any species are referred to as 'penny turtles'. Australia is home to 22 described species but many more, some well known to herpetologists, remain undescribed. It is increasingly obvious that some widespread 'species' occur as a suite of populations genetically isolated in different drainage systems. A complicating factor in identification is the shell shape, which changes with age. Many short-necked turtle juveniles have shells with a high central crest and serrated rear margins, becoming flatter and smoother to varying degrees with age.

Feeding, courting and mating take place underwater, though many species commonly bask on protruding logs and rocks, and some frequently undertake lengthy overland journeys between bodies of water. One species, the Fitzroy River Turtle (*Rheodytes leukops)* rarely surfaces. Thanks to extensive vascular linings within its cloaca, it can extract oxygen directly from the water and remain submerged for days.

Freshwater turtles occur in most permanent water on mainland Australia. They also thrive in some temporary waterways by burying themselves as the water recedes and aestivating until rains come.

Long-necked turtles (*Chelodina*) are almost exclusively carnivorous and able to exploit relatively swift prey such as fish and shrimps, thanks to a combination of ambush and a long fast strike. The Western Swamp Turtle (*Pseudemydura umbrina*) is also carnivorous, eating mainly insect larvae, shrimps and tadpoles. Short-necked turtles of the genus *Emydura* are opportunistic omnivores, consuming water plants, fallen fruits and molluscs, plus any small animals slow enough to capture. Omnivorous species, including those with a strong herbivorous bias, such as the Northern Snapping Turtle (*Elseya dentata*), tend to be mainly carnivorous as juveniles.

Mature females of some short-necked turtles exhibit a distinctive condition called macrocephaly or 'big-headedness'. Enlargement of the skull and jaw musculature, sometimes to a grotesque degree, may be associated with crushing mussel shells. In extreme cases the turtle is no longer capable of drawing its head into the shell.

Freshwater turtles lay their eggs on land in sand or soil near water. The Northern Long-necked Turtle (*Chelodina oblonga*) is a unique exception, with some individuals laying in burrows under shallow water. Yet even in this situation, the eggs are placed in sites that will be exposed when the water level drops so development can proceed above water.

Snake-necked Turtle (*Chelodina longicollis*). Nepean River, NSW. J. Cann

Long-necked Turtles Genus *Chelodina*

Seven spp. **with extremely long necks**, usually as long as or longer than carapace. **Forefeet each have 4 claws. Gular shields in contact** in front of intergular shield (fig.). ■ SUBGENERA *C. (Chelodina)* has head and neck equal to or slightly less than carapace length and broad plastron. Under duress they secrete highly pungent fluid. *C. (Macrochelodina)* has head and neck longer than carapace, narrow plastron and less pungent fluid. *C. (Macrodiremys)* has head and neck longer than carapace, and narrow carapace and plastron. ■ NOTES Widespread in waterways of Aust, excluding central arid zones. Also present in NG. These carnivores feed on anything small enough to seize and swallow, such as fish, tadpoles, crustaceans, insects and carrion. They hunt by ambush, using the long neck to strike in a snake-like manner while gaping the mouth to suck in prey.

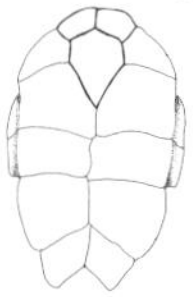

Sandstone Long-necked Turtle *Chelodina burrungandjii* CL 266mm

Long, thick neck and **short, very broad, strongly depressed head.** Carapace oblong, flared posteriorly in the region of 7th–9th marginal scutes, with **slightly upturned sides.** Dark brown to black above with **dark speckling on head and neck.** Cream to pale brown below. ■ NOTES Known from Arnhem Land Plateau and e. Kimberley, occupying permanent pools in sandstone gorges and in rivers and billabongs. Feeds mainly on fish and shrimps, but unlike other long-necked turtles, also eats plant material. Reported to dig nests in river banks, unlike the submerged nests of the allied *C. oblonga.* ■ SEE ALSO *C. oblonga.*

Cann's Long-necked Turtle *Chelodina canni* CL 240mm

Slender neck and wide, robust head. Carapace broad and round. **Plastron expanded anteriorly but not extending beyond inner edge of marginal scutes on carapace.** Brown to black above, often with darker mottling. Cream to yellowish brown below, with some sutures of plastron narrowly marked with black; attractively blotched with red on juv. Head, neck and limbs flushed with pink. ■ NOTES From about Rockhampton, Qld to ne. NT. Also found in NG. Favours lagoons and swamps. Releases pungent fluid when handled. ■ SEE ALSO *C. longicollis.* ■ STATUS Lower risk – near threatened (IUCN Red List—as *C. novaeguineae*).

South-western Long-necked Turtle *Chelodina colliei* CL 310mm

Long, thick neck and broad, strongly depressed head. **Carapace extremely narrow and oval.** Dark brown to black above and paler below. ■ NOTES Waterways from Hill R. se. to Fitzgerald R. Common in lakes of suburban Perth. Usually occurs in permanent water, but capable of aestivating under mud or migrating to nearby water during dry periods.

Chelodina burrungandjii.
Koolpin Gorge, Arnhem Land, NT. J. Cann

Chelodina burrungandjii.
Amalia Gorge, El Questro Stn, WA. S. Wilson.

Chelodina canni.
Ross River area, Qld. S. Wilson

Chelodina colliei.
Swan River drainage, WA. J. Cann

Broad-shelled Long-necked Turtle *Chelodina expansa* CL 480mm

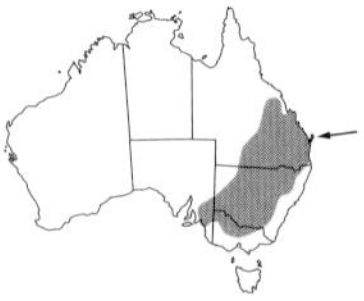

Very long, thick neck and **broad, strongly depressed head. Carapace very broad, oval and flattened** with expanded rear edges. Brown to blackish brown, often with dark flecks or reticulations, and whitish below. ■ **NOTES** Murray/Darling R. systems in SA, Vic, NSW and Qld, reaching coast in se. Qld, extending to Fraser Is. and n. to Rockhampton. Lies concealed in debris on the bottom or among root mats in silty rivers, streams and waterholes. ■ **STATUS** Endangered (Vic); vulnerable (SA).

Snake-necked Turtle *Chelodina longicollis* CL 254mm

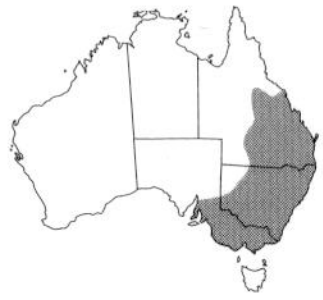

Slender neck and small, moderately depressed head. **Plastron greatly expanded anteriorly, extending beyond inner edges of marginal scutes on carapace.** Rich brown or dark brown to black above, with dark sutures on pale animals. White to cream below with broad black sutures on plastron. Plastron of juv. often attractively marked with black and orange to red. ■ **NOTES** Widespread through estn drainage systems from Adelaide, SA to just s. of Townsville, Qld. Coastal and inland waterways, typically inhabiting swamps, lagoons and slow-moving rivers and creeks, but often seen wandering overland far from any apparent water. Releases pungent fluid when handled. ■ **SEE ALSO** *C. canni.* ■ **STATUS** Data deficient (Vic).

Northern Long-necked Turtle *Chelodina oblonga* CL 360mm

Long, thick neck and **broad, strongly depressed head. Carapace oval** and expanded posteriorly, but **not upturned along edges.** Dark brown to black above and pale below. ■ **NOTES** Nthn Aust. from Ord and Victoria drainages e. to Cape York, Qld. Favours seasonal wetlands subject to extensive wet season flooding but often drying completely during dry season. Also occurs in large slow-moving rivers. Unusual in laying under water, with eggs lying dormant within a submerged burrow until water level drops and development proceeds. ■ **SEE ALSO** *C. burrungandjii.* ■ **STATUS** Lower risk – near threatened (IUCN Red List).

Steindachner's Turtle; Plate-shelled Turtle *Chelodina steindachneri* CL 200mm

Slender neck, small, moderately depressed head and **flat round shell.** Uniform brown above and paler below. ■ **NOTES** Isolated drainages from Irwin R. n. to De Grey R., incl. the most arid regions inhabited by Aust. turtles. In many areas all or most waterways dry up annually, requiring extended aestivation or lengthy overland migration. This sp. can be abundant and obvious in some clear shallow pools.

Chelodina expansa laying eggs.
Moura area, Qld. D. Shipman

Chelodina longicollis.
Glenmorgan, Qld. S. Wilson

Chelodina longicollis.
Sydney region, NSW. J. Cann

Chelodina oblonga.
Darwin, NT. P. Horner

Chelodina steindachneri.
Wooramel River, WA. S. Wilson

Snapping Turtles Genus *Elseya*

Four large spp. with extended **head and neck shorter than carapace**, a thin **horny shield on top of head not extending down toward tympanum, low rounded tubercles over temples**, moderate to spinose tubercles on neck and 5 claws on each forefoot. **Intergular shield much narrower than each gular shield** (A). **Sutures at rear of 2nd and 3rd costal scutes contact 7th and 9th marginal scutes** (B). Juv. and young adults have a high central keel on carapace with weak serrations on rear edges, normally becoming flatter with smoother edges on adults. ■ **NOTES** Waterways of nthn and ne. Aust. Diets primarily herbivorous to broadly omnivorous. ■ **SEE ALSO** *Wollumbinia; Emydura; Rheodytes.*

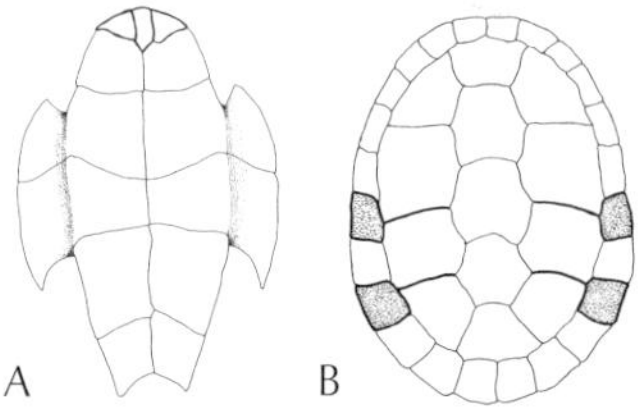

Southern Snapping Turtle *Elseya albagula* CL 420mm

Carapace broadly oval posteriorly, with deeply serrated to spiny rear edge on juv. and young adults. Dark brown to black (adults) to tan (juv.). Head large and robust; dark brown above, and cream, yellow to white (females) or grey to cream (males) below – the colours meeting along a sharp, irregular junction. One of Aust.'s largest chelid turtles. ■ **NOTES** Flowing waters in Mary, Burnett, Fitzroy–Dawson and associated drainage systems, se. Qld. Adults largely herbivorous. ■ **STATUS** Critically endangered (C'wealth); endangered (Qld).

Northern Snapping Turtle *Elseya dentata* CL 340mm

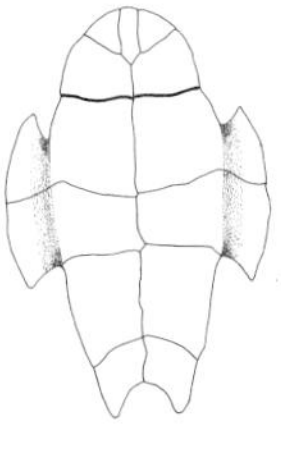

Shell broadly oval and expanded posteriorly. **Suture between humeral and pectoral shields on plastron forms a straight line (fig.).** Head and neck large with conspicuous but rounded tubercles on neck. Brown to dark brown, sometimes with scattered darker flecks but no pale streak on neck. ■ **NOTES** Large rivers and lagoons, particularly deeper sections, in Kimberley and nw. NT, incl. King Edward, Ord, Victoria and Daly Rivers. Mainly herbivorous, eating aquatic plants and fallen leaves, flowers and fruits. Carrion and various small prey also taken. ■ **SEE ALSO** *E. lavarackorum.*

Yellow-headed Snapping Turtle *Elseya irwini* CL 380mm

Shell oblong and fairly straight-sided. **Pale-headed.** Low, rounded and larger spinose tubercles present on neck. Light brown with darker patches above and yellow below, blotched with black in larger animals. Head appears white but is very pale yellow, incl. horny head casque, often piebald, with rose pink flush from snout, under eye to jaw. ■ **NOTES** Burdekin R. drainage n. to South and North Johnstone and Barron Rivers, Qld. Poorly known but probably omnivorous; plant material and snails recorded as food items.

Elseya albagula.
Raglan River, Qld.
J. Cann

Elseya dentata.
Daly River, NT.
J. Cann

Elseya irwini.
Burdekin River, Qld. J. Cann

Elseya irwini.
Johnstone River, Qld. D. Trembath

Gulf Snapping Turtle *Elseya lavarackorum* CL 320mm

Very poorly known. Superficially similar to *E. dentata*, but having an **undulating suture between humeral and pectoral shields in plastron (fig.)** rather than a straight suture. ■ **NOTES** Nicholson R. drainage of Qld, to wstn Gulf of Carpentaria, NT. Originally described from Pleistocene fossil material from Riversleigh, Qld, then subsequently rediscovered as a living sp. ■ **SEE ALSO** *E. dentata*. ■ **STATUS** Endangered (C'wealth); vulnerable (Qld).

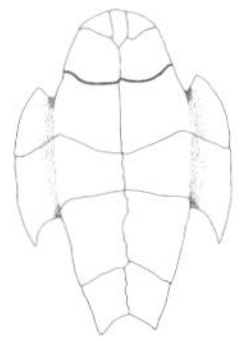

Genus *Elusor*

Mary River Turtle *Elusor macrurus* CL 400mm

Sole member of genus. **Extended head and neck much shorter than carapace, extremely long thick tail** (at least 50% of carapace length on both sexes and up to 70% on large ♂), and 5 claws on each forefoot. Carapace oval to slightly wider posteriorly. Juv. and young adults have a weak central keel on carapace and small serrations on rear edges, becoming flat with completely smooth edges on adults. Gular shields entirely separated by intergular. Many moderately sharp tubercles on neck. Light brown to blackish brown above and grey below, without significant pattern. ■ **NOTES** Mary R. drainage, se. Qld. Omnivorous, eating aquatic algae and bivalves. Commonly emerges to bask on protruding logs. ■ **STATUS** Endangered (C'wealth; Qld; IUCN Red List).

Elseya lavarackorum.
Gregory River, Qld.
J. Cann

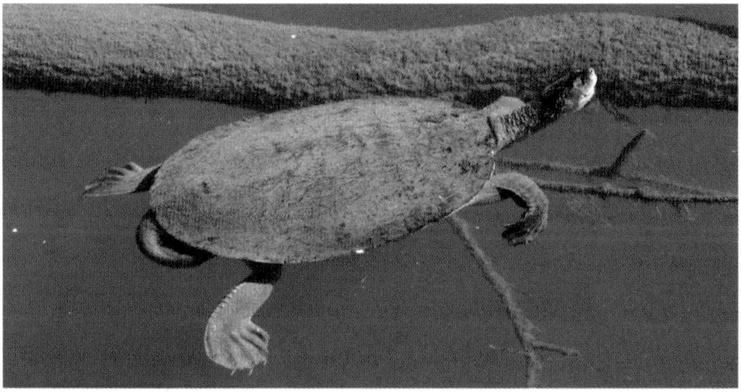

Elusor macrurus.
Mary River,
Kenilworth, Qld.
S. Wilson.

Elusor macrurus.
Mary River
catchment, Qld.
J. Cann

Genus *Emydura*

Four moderate to large spp. with **extended head and neck much shorter than carapace, no horny shield over back of head, smooth temples, smooth necks** (sometimes with low rounded tubercles but not spines), and 5 claws on each forefoot. Nuchal shield usually present but variable in some spp. **Gular shields entirely separated by intergular (fig.)**. Juv. and young adults have a strong to weak central keel on carapace and serrations on rear edges, becoming flatter with smoother edges on adults. Pattern usually includes a **pale streak on face**. Macrocephaly is common in nth. ■ **NOTES** Widespread in nthn and estn Aust., extending into temporary waterways of estn interior. Omnivorous, feeding on water-plants, invertebrates, small vertebrates and carrion. Favours still waters, often seen basking on protruding rocks or logs. ■ **SEE ALSO** *Elseya; Wollumbinia.*

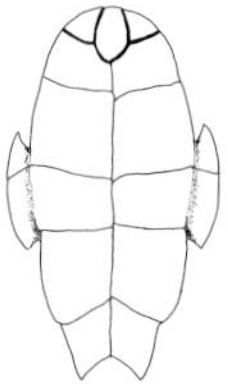

Macquarie Turtle *Emydura macquarii* CL 185–368mm

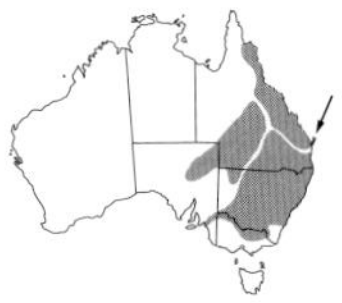

Pale brown to dark brown above, with pale yellow streak extending back from corner of jaw along neck. Pale streak behind eye absent to weak and narrow, or broad and prominent. Extremely variable, particularly in relation to size, carapace shape and iris colour. Pops from different drainage systems represent 4 described though ill-defined ssp. ■ **SSP.** *E. m. macquarii* (Macquarie Turtle) is variable (CL 184–340mm depending on river system). Little or no pale streak behind eye. *E. m. krefftii* (Krefft's Turtle) is large (CL 290mm) with prominent pale streak behind eye. *E. m. emmotti* (Cooper Creek Turtle) is largest (CL 368mm), very deep-bodied with little or no facial pattern on adults. *E. m. nigra* (Fraser Island Turtle) is medium-sized (CL 250mm) with very dark skin and carapace and no dark streak behind eye. ■ **NOTES** Rivers, creeks and lagoons of estn Aust. from se. SA to ne. Qld. *E. m. macquarii* is the most widespread form, associated with the extensive Murray/Darling drainage system of NSW, Qld, Vic and SA, and from Sydney Basin through easterly-flowing rivers of ne. NSW to se. Qld. *E. m. krefftii* extends through estn Qld, from just n. of Brisbane to Princess Charlotte Bay. *E. m. emmotti* extends from Alice, Barcoo and Thompson drainages of central Qld, through Cooper Ck and floodplains to vicinity of Lake Eyre, SA. *E. m. nigra* is confined to lakes on Fraser Is. Most (probably all) races are omnivorous. *E. m. macquarii* and *E. m. krefftii* are conspicuous where they occur, commonly seen basking on protruding logs and rocks. ■ **STATUS** *E. m. macquarii* is vulnerable (Vic; SA).

Emydura macquarii macquarii.
Lake Numalla,
Currawinya NP, Qld.
S. Wilson

Emydura macquarii macquarii
Wynnum, Qld. S. Wilson

Emydura macquarii emmotti.
Cooper Creek, Qld. J. Cann

Emydura macquarii krefftii.
Burnett River, Qld. S. Wilson

Emydura macquarii nigra.
Fraser Island, Qld. J. Cann

Jardine River Turtle; Worrell's Turtle *Emydura subglobosa* CL 250mm

Dull brown above, very brightly marked with prominent stripes on face and neck. ■ **SSP.** *E. s. subglobosa* has a bright yellow stripe running from tip of snout above eye to top of ear, a yellow patch on upper jaw and a broken bright red stripe extending from upper edge of lower jaw along neck. Limbs, plastron and lower edges of carapace variably spotted or splashed with pink to red. Colours are most conspicuous in juv., fading on older animals. *E. s. worrelli* has dark-edged pink to yellow facial and neck stripes, and lacks the red suffusions on limbs, plastron and margins of carapace. ■ **NOTES** *E. s. subglobosa* is restricted in Aust. to Jardine R. drainage on nthn Cape York Pen., Qld but is widely distributed in NG. *E. s. worrelli* extends between Skardon R. drainage, Cape York Pen., Qld and Drysdale and Ord R. drainages, ne. Kimberley, WA. Omnivorous, taking molluscs, snails, pandanus fruits and other vegetable matter. ■ **STATUS** *E. s. subglobosa* is lower risk – least concern (IUCN Red List); vulnerable (Qld). *E. s. worrelli* is near threatened (Qld).

Northern Yellow-faced Turtle *Emydura tanybaraga* CL 285mm

Carapace of adults broadly oval and expanded posteriorly; **hatchlings have carapaces broader anteriorly than posteriorly**. Fawn to dark brownish grey with scattered dark spots above. **Prominent pale yellow facial stripes** from eye to just above ear, and from upper jaw below ear onto side of neck. Iris yellow, enclosing **dark horizontal streak through eye, level with pupil**. Colours fade on large adults but distinctive iris pattern always remains. ■ **NOTES** Known from isolated localities across nthn Aust. between Fitzroy and Isdell R. drainages, WA and Wenlock and Lynd systems, Cape York Pen., Qld.

Northern Red-faced Turtle *Emydura victoriae* CL 250mm

Light brown to blackish brown above, usually with obscure dark flecks, and whitish below flushed with pink. **Prominent red stripe** extends from eye to above and behind ear and another extends from angle of mouth along side of neck. Large adults may lack pattern, and macrocephaly is common. ■ **NOTES** Rivers, billabongs and waterholes of n. Aust., from Victoria R. and Daly R. drainages, NT to rivers of Kimberley region, WA.

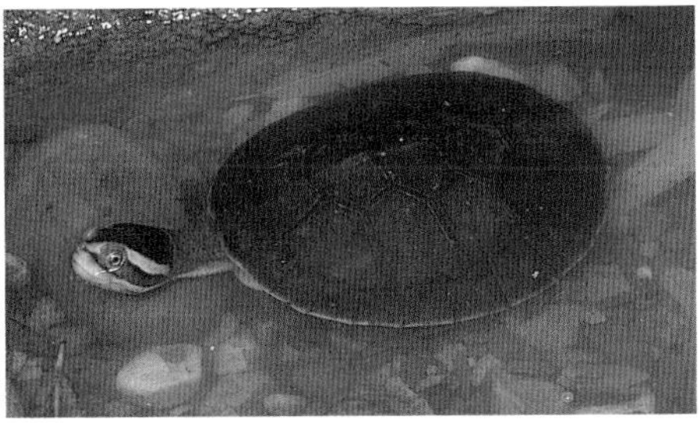

Emydura subglobosa worrelli.
Louie Creek, Qld. S. Wilson

Emydura subglobosa subglobosa.
Jardine River, Qld. J. Cann

Emydura tanybaraga.
Wenlock River,
Qld. R. Lloyd.

Emydura victoriae. El Questro Stn, WA. S. Wilson

Emydura victoriae exhibiting macrocephaly.
Daly River, NT. J. Cann

Genus *Pseudemydura*

Western Swamp Turtle *Pseudemydura umbrina* CL 150mm

Sole member of genus. Smallest Aust. turtle, with **depressed squarish carapace, broad flat head with a horny casque**, and **short neck adorned with large conical tubercles**. Gular shields entirely separated by intergular. Shades of brown above and pale brown to cream below. ■ **NOTES** Restricted to small clay-based temporary swamps at Bullsbrook, near Perth, WA. One of the world's rarest reptiles, with fewer than 500 individuals in the wild, completely enclosed by electrified, vermin-proof fencing. Active in winter when shallow swamps are full, aestivating under dense low vegtn when they dry. Carnivorous, eating insects and crustaceans. ■ **STATUS** Critically endangered (IUCN Red List; C'wealth; WA).

Genus *Rheodytes*

Fitzroy River Turtle *Rheodytes leukops* CL 250mm

Sole member of genus. Extended head and neck much shorter than carapace, and neck adorned with scattered large pointed conical tubercles. Carapace broadly oval (roughly circular with strong posterior serrations on juv.). **Sutures at rear of 2nd and 3rd costal scutes contact 6th and 8th marginal scutes (fig.)**. Forelimbs each with 5 claws. Pupil grey with **white ring around iris**. Medium to dark brown above and pale yellowish brown below, without significant pattern.

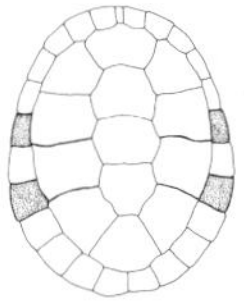

Sides of neck and throat of large ♂ prominently blotched with orange. ■ **NOTES** Fitzroy R. and tributaries. Prefers fast-flowing clear water, sheltering among roots and submerged timber. Does not seem to bask and rarely surfaces to breathe, extracting oxygen from water via unique cloacal pouches. Carnivorous. ■ **SEE ALSO** *Elseya; Wollumbinia.* ■ **STATUS** Vulnerable (C'wealth; Qld; IUCN Red List).

Helmeted Turtles Genus *Wollumbinia*

Four moderate to large spp. with **extended head and neck shorter than carapace**, a thin **horny shield on top of head extending well down almost to tympanum, small pointed tubercles on neck** and 5 claws on each forefoot. Nuchal shield narrow or absent, **intergular shield as wide as or wider than each gular shield (A). Sutures at rear of 2nd and 3rd costal scutes contact 7th and 9th marginal scutes (B).** Juv. and young adults have a high central keel on carapace, becoming flatter on adults, and serrations on rear edges becoming smoother with age but sometimes retained. ■ **NOTES** Waterways of e. and ne. Aust. Omnivorous to mainly carnivorous. ■ **SEE ALSO** *Elseya; Emydura; Rheodytes.*

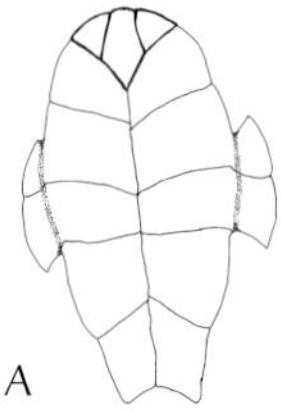

A

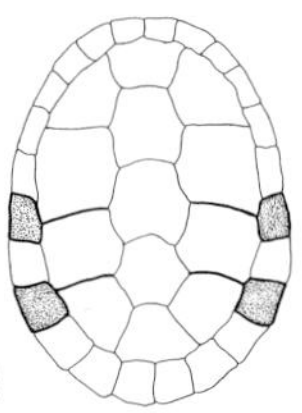

B

Pseudemydura umbrina.
Twin Swamps, WA. J. Cann

Rheodytes leukops. Male (left) and female (right). Fitzroy River, Qld. J. Cann

Bell's Turtle *Wollumbinia bellii* CL 290mm

Many spinose tubercles present on neck. Brown to dark brown above with dark grey mottling, and **yellow streak or stripe along neck** from angle of mouth, through tympanum to forelimb. **Mature turtles have black plastrons.** ■ **NOTES** Narrow watercourses along upper reaches of the MacDonald, Namoi, Severn and Gwydir R. systems of ne. NSW, and an outlying pop. at Bald Rock Ck in se. Qld. ■ **STATUS** Endangered (IUCN Red List); vulnerable (C'wealth; Qld; NSW).

Georges' Turtle *Wollumbinia georgesi* CL 220mm

Pale stripe on neck. Low rounded tubercles present on neck. Pale brown with darker patches or uniform dark olive brown above, and plastron marbled with light bluish green tinge. Continuous yellow stripe extends from angle of jaw along lower side of neck. ■ **NOTES** Bellinger R. and tributaries, favouring deeper pools with clear water in upper reaches. ■ **STATUS** Critically endangered (NSW); data deficient (IUCN Red List).

Saw-shelled Turtle *Wollumbinia latisternum* CL 287mm

Juv. and young adults have a high central keel on **carapace with prominent serrations on rear edges.** With age, carapace becomes flatter and serrations reduced, varying geographically from moderately prominent to almost non-existent. Many spinose tubercles present on neck. Horny head casque extends down each side of head to tympanum. Brown to blackish brown above and cream to yellow below, usually meeting on a sharp junction along sides of face and throat. Iris colour varies, but leading and trailing dark spot on either side of pupil often present. ■ **NOTES** From Richmond R. area, NSW, to Cape York Pen., Qld. Isolated pops in Gregory and Nicholson catchment in Gulf of Carpentaria, and in Liverpool, Mann, South and East Alligator Rivers of NT, w. to upper Mary River Drainage. Tends to favour lagoons, creeks and upper reaches of larger rivers. Broadly omnivorous, and apparently a successful predator of cane toads.

Purvis' Turtle *Wollumbinia purvisi* CL 230mm

Boldly patterned, with **dark stripes on throat and under tail.** Low rounded tubercles present on neck. Medium to dark brown above. A prominent yellow streak, dark-edged above, extends from snout under eye and along neck. Ventral surfaces yellow with darker patches. Throat and underside of tail yellow, divided medially by a grey to black bar which sometimes occupies most of throat. ■ **NOTES** Manning R. drainage, NSW.

Wollumbinia bellii.
MacDonald River, NSW. J. Cann

Wollumbinia bellii.
Girraween NP, Qld. S. Wilson

Wollumbinia georgesi.
Bellinger River, NSW. J. Cann

Wollumbinia latisternum.
Lake Eacham, Qld. S. Wilson

Wollumbinia purvisi.
Manning River, NSW. J. Cann

Wollumbinia purvisi.
Manning River, NSW. J. Cann

PIG-NOSED TURTLE
Family Carettochelydidae

The family Carettochelydidae contains a single distinctive species, commonly known as the Pig-nosed Turtle, restricted to freshwater rivers of northern Australia and New Guinea. It is unrelated to other Australian freshwater turtles, but has a number of distinctive features that place it closer to the soft-shelled turtles (Trionychidae) of Asia, Africa and North America.

In Australia the Pig-nosed Turtle is confined to the Daly, Victoria, Alligator and possibly Roper River systems of the Northern Territory. This turtle favours large, still bodies of water, preferring sandy areas of riverbed with overhanging banks and submerged fallen trees. It is also present in southern New Guinea, where it extends into brackish estuarine waters.

The unusual distribution, with Australian and New Guinea populations separated by the Arafura Sea, is a probably an artefact of previous lower sea-levels when the two regions were a landmass featuring now-submerged river systems.

Pig-nosed Turtles are omnivorous with a preference for vegetable matter. They feed on water-plants such as ribbonweed, and fallen figs, pandanus and eucalypt flowers, and also eat crustaceans, insects, molluscs and carrion.

During the dry season, between July and early November, the females aggregate prior to nesting. They deposit their clutches of 7–19 eggs on sandy banks well above the low waterline. Fully developed young remain within the eggs until rising water-levels or torrential downpours inundate the nests, triggering them to emerge explosively from their shells.

The family contains only one genus and a single unique species.

Genus *Carettochelys*

Pig-nosed Turtle *Carettochelys insculpta* CL 600–700mm

Very large freshwater turtle with **limbs modified to form broad flippers, each with 2 claws. Shell covered by soft pitted skin with no hard dermal scutes**. The common name is derived from the placement of the nostrils at the end of a **prominent, fleshy, trunk-like snout**. The neck is withdrawn straight back into the shell, unlike those of all other Aust. freshwater turtles which retract their necks sideways. Grey to greyish brown with pale patch behind eye and pale ventral surfaces. Large specimens can weigh more than 20kg. ■ **STATUS** Vulnerable (IUCN Red List); near threatened (NT).

Carettochelys insculpta. Daly River, NT. P. Horner

Carettochelys insculpta. Daly River, NT. J. Cann

RED-EARED SLIDER
Family Emydidae

A widespread family occurring naturally in North America, Europe, Northern Africa and parts of South America. One highly invasive species, North America's Red-eared Slider (*Trachemys scripta*) now extends into South East Asia and parts of Australia.

Emydid turtles have moderately domed shells and clawed webbed feet. The neck withdraws along a vertical axis, meaning the head is pulled directly back into the shell.

Emydidae contains more than forty species, mostly aquatic inhabitants of freshwater swamps, rivers, ponds and lakes. A few are adapted to brackish estuarine waters and some are primarily terrestrial. Most are omnivorous, with juveniles consuming significant amounts of animal material. Sliders are probably named for their habit of slipping back into the water from basking perches when disturbed.

The Red-eared Slider, the world's most frequently kept 'pet turtle', is hardy, breeds well in captivity and is attractive. The strikingly patterned young are particularly appealing. Millions are farmed and sold worldwide. Males develop long slender claws on the forefeet, reminiscent of the curved fingernails of a Chinese mandarin. During courtship they face the females and vibrate their claws. Sliders produce numerous large clutches (up to 23 eggs).

It is of concern that the species appears to have become established in Australia via the pet-shop trade. They have been recorded to seriously deplete native turtles wherever they are introduced, and the vista of a dozen or more sliders stacked along a partly submerged log is not something we wish to see in Australia.

Genus *Trachemys*

Red-eared Slider *Trachemys scripta elegans* CL 280mm

Carapace domed, **head withdrawn directly back into shell,** and **bold pattern on face, carapace and plastron.** Yellow bars and narrow lines on carapace, a black blotch on each plastron scute, very narrow pale stripes on head and neck and a bold red stripe behind eye. Pattern bold on juv., weak on adults. ■ **NOTES** Creeks and ponds in Pine Rivers Shire just n. of Brisbane, possibly waterways in the Gold Coast vicinity and near Sydney, NSW. Individuals have been recorded from the ACT, Vic. and WA but whether these are waifs or breeding populations is not known. ■ **STATUS** Class 1 Pest (Qld).

Trachemys scripta elegans. Singapore Botanic Gardens. S. Wilson

Trachemys scripta elegans. Singapore Botanic Gardens. S. Wilson

CHAMELEON, THICK-TAILED, LEAF-TAILED AND KNOB-TAILED GECKOS
Family Carphodactylidae

This distinctive group of geckos is the only lizard family endemic to Australia. All others extend at least to New Zealand or New Guinea and beyond. They share important characteristics with the flap-footed lizards (Pygopodidae) and the two other Australian gecko families, Gekkonidae and Diplodactylidae. They lack eyelids, using their broad flat tongues to wipe the clear spectacles covering their eyes. They also have a voice in the form of a squeak or rasping bark, uttered during social encounters or when provoked. And they share a clutch size of just two eggs. These are soft and parchment-like, and must be deposited in a sheltered humid environment to avoid desiccation.

There are 30 described species of Carphodactylid geckos. They are widespread in Australia with a suite of species occurring in temperate zones, deserts, tropical woodlands and outcrops, and subtropical to tropical rainforests. Most of the rainforest species are leaf-tailed geckos (*Orraya, Phyllurus and Saltuarius*) with extremely restricted distributions that reflect historical expansions and contractions of rainforest habitats.

Carphodactylid geckos are easily characterised by their striking appearance. Most are large species, including some of Australia's largest and heaviest geckos. Some have smooth scales while others feature prominent scattered tubercles, or even large spines surrounded by rosettes of smaller spines. They have flattened or box-shaped heads, long slender limbs, clawed digits lacking any expanded pads and usually highly modified, sometimes extraordinary tails.

The tails are easily discarded, so regenerated tails are common in adults, but they lack the multiple, pre-weakened cleavage points common to many other lizards. The only cleavage is at the base so when the tail is lost it is forfeited in its entirety. However, the tails are by far their most noteworthy feature, and many species and generic names are derived from the bizarre caudal appendages.

The three genera of leaf-tailed geckos have extremely broad, flat tails liberally covered and fringed (when original) with spinose scales. A few species of *Phyllurus* have secondarily evolved narrower, cylindrical tails. Knob-tailed geckos (*Nephrurus*) are named for the unique spherical knob on the tail-tip, the purposes of which remain unclear. Some have fleshy tails but three species (*N. asper* and its allies) have tails reduced to a comical degree. Thick-tailed geckos (*Underwoodisaurus* and *Uvidicolus*) have bulbous tails with tapered tips while the Chameleon Gecko (*Carphodactylus laevis*) has a long, laterally compressed, carrot-shaped tail.

When provoked, Carphodactylids perform impressive threat displays. Thick-tailed and knob-tailed geckos raise and sway their plump bodies high on slender limbs, sinuously wave their tails and launch at their aggressor with mouth agape uttering a loud rasping bark. This behaviour has earned them the alternative name of 'barking geckos'. Leaf-tailed geckos are also highly vocal under stress, but the emphasis is more on waving the tail than raising the body.

Rough-throated Leaf-tailed Gecko (*Saltuarius salebrosus*) on a sandstone rock face decorated with Aboriginal hand stencils. Blackdown Tableland, Qld. S. Wilson

Genus *Carphodactylus*

Chameleon Gecko *Carphodactylus laevis* SVL 130mm

Sole member of genus. This spectacular gecko is **strongly laterally compressed with an acute vertebral ridge**, long slender limbs, a **carrot-shaped tail** and slender, clawed, padless digits. Brown with a fine cream vertebral line and a striking black and white ringed original tail; regenerated tails dark, sombrely streaked and mottled. ■ **NOTES** RF in the Wet Tropics, sheltering under leaf litter, and probably in hollow limbs, tree buttresses and large epiphytes. Forages on the forest floor, often ascending saplings to perch head downwards, presumably to ambush invertebrate prey. The tail is readily discarded, and when a regenerated tail is lost it produces a loud and distinctive squeaking noise as it wriggles around. It is not known whether severed originals behave in the same way, but no other gecko (or reptile) is known to employ this diversionary tactic.

Knob-tailed Geckos Genus *Nephrurus*

Nine **plump-bodied** spp. **with large deep heads** and slender limbs. Digits short, clawed and padless with **small spinose subdigital lamellae. Original tails terminate in a unique spherical knob**. Scales small and granular mixed with low tubercles, or with spines arranged in rosettes comprising large conical tubercles surrounded by smaller tubercles. ■ **NOTES** Dry tropics to arid zones. Terrestrial, dwelling by day in burrows (their own or those of other animals) and foraging at night in open spaces between low vegtn. Diets include arthropods (often incl. scorpions) and smaller geckos. When threatened they raise their bodies and lunge at their aggressor uttering a loud wheezing bark. ■ **SEE ALSO** *Underwoodisaurus*.

Centralian Knob-tailed Gecko *Nephrurus amyae* SVL 135mm

Tail extremely short. Body and limbs adorned with rosettes; largest and **most spinose on rump and hindlimbs**. Rich reddish brown with fine dark transverse lines alternating with rows of paler spots, each centred on a tubercle. Head marked with a fine dark reticulum. Most massive Aust. gecko. ■ **NOTES** Rocky ranges and outcrops of central Aust.

Prickly Knob-tailed Gecko *Nephrurus asper* SVL 115mm

Tail extremely short. Body and limbs adorned with rosettes. Shades of brown to reddish brown with many fine dark transverse lines alternating with rows of paler spots, each centred on a tubercle. Head marked with a fine dark reticulum. **Digits unbanded**. Specimens from Cape York have cream and rich reddish brown bands of approx. equal width. ■ **NOTES** Rocky hills and outcrops in arid to dry tropical parts of Qld, inland to Windorah district. Cape York pop. often occurs on sandy heaths. ■ **SEE ALSO** *N. sheai*.

Carphodactylus laevis.
Lake Barrine, Qld.
S. Wilson

Nephrurus amyae.
King's Creek Stn, NT.
S. Wilson

Nephrurus asper. Heathlands, Qld. S. Wilson

Nephrurus asper. Suttor Creek, Qld. S. Wilson

Pernatty Knob-tailed Gecko *Nephrurus deleani* SVL 100mm

Tail slender, with enlarged white tubercles. Many low conical tubercles on body and limbs. Pale brown mottled with purplish brown. Pattern variable to virtually absent; usually **3 pale V-shaped bars** across base of head, neck and from neck back to mid-dorsal line. **Narrow white vertebral line** often present on juv. ■ **NOTES** Restricted to arid sand-ridges n. and w. of Pernatty Lagoon, SA. ■ **STATUS** Endangered (IUCN Red List); rare (SA).

Pale Knob-tailed Gecko *Nephrurus laevissimus* SVL 93mm

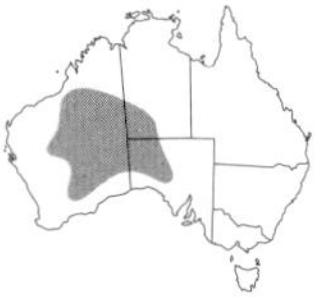

Tail relatively slender, with enlarged white tubercles. **Flanks smooth**; only a few scattered tubercles on vertebral region. Pink to pinkish brown, with or without many small whitish spots, marked with 3 dark brown lines on head and forebody: behind eyes and across base of head, across neck, and curving back from each shoulder. Short dark longitudinal stripes also present on either side of body above hips. ■ **NOTES** Desert sand-ridges vegetated with spinifex.

Smooth Knob-tailed Gecko *Nephrurus levis* SVL 102mm

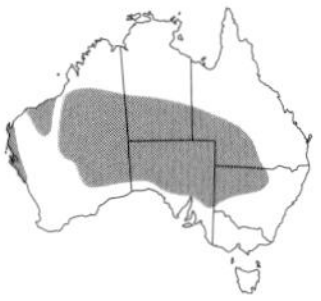

Tail moderately slender to plump and heart-shaped, with enlarged white tubercles. Body and limbs bear small tubercles. Pale pinkish brown to dark purplish brown with 3 pale bands: across base of head, across neck, and back from about level of shoulder to midline. ■ **SSP.** *N. l. levis* has rostral scale about as broad as mental scale. *N. l. occidentalis* has rostral scale usually narrower than mental scale; broader, longer, more depressed tail and usually paler colouration. *N. l. pilbarensis* has large granules scattered among smaller granules on throat and stronger pattern, incl. dark blotches and lines on back, and pale bands intensified by prominent dark edges. ■ **NOTES** Arid, usually sandy regions of all mainland states except Vic. *N. l. occidentalis* occurs on mid-w. coast and hinterland from about Karratha s. to Geraldton, WA; *N. l. pilbarensis* is restricted to arid Pilbara and Gt Sandy Desert; *N. l. levis* occupies remainder of range.

Northern Knob-tailed Gecko *Nephrurus sheai* SVL 120mm

Tail extremely short. Body and limbs adorned with rosettes. Brown with fine dark transverse lines alternating with rows of paler spots, each centred on a tubercle. **Digits strongly banded.** Head marked with a fine dark reticulum. ■ **NOTES** Rocky ranges from the Kimberley region of WA to the Arnhem Escarpment, NT. ■ **SEE ALSO** *N. asper.*

Starred Knob-tailed Gecko *Nephrurus stellatus* SVL 90mm

Small, relatively slender tail, with enlarged pale tubercles. Body covered in low conical tubercles and rosettes. Pale yellowish brown to rich reddish brown marked with 3 narrow white transverse lines between head and forelimb and **many prominent pale spots, each centred on a tubercle or rosette**. In estn parts of range, head is darker and transverse lines are dark purplish brown and broader. ■ **NOTES** Arid and semi-arid sthn WA and Eyre Pen., SA. Occurs on yellow to pinkish sand-plains and sand-ridges vegetated with heath or with mallee and spinifex.

Nephrurus deleani. Pernatty Lagoon, SA. R. Valentic

Nephrurus laevissimus. Yulara, NT. G. Gaikhorst

Nephrurus levis levis.
Currawinya NP, Qld. S. Wilson

Nephrurus levis occidentalis.
North West Cape, WA. S. Wilson

Nephrurus levis pilbarensis.
De Grey River, WA. S. Wilson

Nephrurus sheai.
Oscar Ranges, WA. G. Gaikhorst

Nephrurus stellatus. Eastern population.
Lake Gillies region, SA. S. Wilson

Nephrurus stellatus. Western population.
Mt Holland region, WA. S. Wilson

Mid-line Knob-tailed Gecko *Nephrurus vertebralis* SVL 93mm

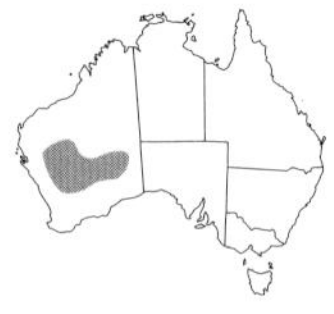

Moderately slender tail, with enlarged white tubercles. Body and limbs bear small conical tubercles. Reddish brown with a prominent **narrow white vertebral stripe from base of head to tail-tip**, and many pale spots each centred on a tubercle. ■ **NOTES** Arid sthn interior of WA, on heavy to stony soils dominated by acacia woodlands and shrublands.

Banded Knob-tailed Gecko *Nephrurus wheeleri* SVL 100mm

Broad depressed tail. **Body and limbs covered with rosettes.** Pink to rich reddish brown, with prominent **broad dark brown bands on body and tail.** ■ **SSP.** *N. w. wheeleri* has 4 bands: across neck and shoulders, rump, tail-base and tail-tip. *N. w. cinctus* has 5 bands, the 1st being split into 2. ■ **NOTES** Arid mid-wstn interior. *N. w. wheeleri* occupies acacia woodlands and shrublands on hard, usually stony soils in the Murchison and nthn Goldfields areas. *N. w. cinctus* occurs on rocky ranges and outcrops vegetated with spinifex in the Pilbara region.

Genus *Orraya*

McIlwraith Leaf-tailed Gecko *Orraya occulta* SVL 108mm

Sole member of genus. **Extremely long-necked,** with flat body and angular, clawed, padless digits. Scales small and granular mixed with large conical tubercles. **Original tail flat and teardrop-shaped, edged by clusters of sharply pointed spines. Regenerated tail round, smooth and flat with spinose tubercles around margins.** Grey with darker mottling. ■ **NOTES** Known only from granite boulders in RF along Peach Ck in McIlwraith Ra., Cape York Pen. Hides by day in crevices and cavities between piled boulders, emerging at night to rest motionless on exposed boulder surfaces. ■ **SEE ALSO** *Phyllurus; Saltuarius.* ■ **STATUS** Vulnerable (Qld).

Leaf-tailed Geckos Genus *Phyllurus*

Nine large spp. with flat bodies and angular, clawed, padless digits. Original tails very distinctive; **cylindrical to extremely flat with a simple flared outer edge and a cylindrical slender tip.** Regenerated tails usually have more **complex flares and short tips**. Scales small and granular mixed with large conical to spinose tubercles (all smooth on regenerated tails). **Rostral scale not contacting nostril.** Superbly camouflaged with **lichen-like flecks**. Most spp. can be identified by distribution; others by examination of rostral scale. ■ **NOTES** RF and rock outcrops between Sydney and Townsville; each sp. occupies a small range. They rest by day on cave walls, in narrow crevices, and inside tree hollows. At night they emerge to rest motionless, usually head-downwards, to ambush passing prey. ■ **SEE ALSO** *Orraya; Saltuarius.*

Mt Elliot Leaf-tailed Gecko *Phyllurus amnicola* SVL 113mm

Flat, strongly flared tail and **small tubercles**. Body and tail pale greyish brown, with darker blotches on body and pale bands on original tail, the **1st pale band broken on midline.** ■ **NOTES** Known only from 400–1000m on Mt Elliot near Townsville. Associated with granite boulders in RF along a creek-line.

Nephrurus vertebralis.
Yuinmery Stn, WA. B. Maryan

Nephrurus wheeleri cinctus.
Pannawonica, WA. S. Wilson

Nephrurus wheeleri wheeleri.
Ned's Creek Stn, WA. S. Wilson

Orraya occulta.
McIlwraith Range, Qld. S. Wilson

Phyllurus amnicola.
Mt Elliot, Qld. S. Wilson

Ringed Thin-tailed Gecko *Phyllurus caudiannulatus* SVL 103mm

Tail narrow and cylindrical. Rostral scale completely divided by midline groove. Large tubercles on body and tail, incl. pronounced raised tubercles mixed with granules under hindlimb. Dark grey to brown with fine dark mottling or blotches and scattered to transversely aligned pale spots. Original tail has 5–6 prominent cream bands; regenerated tail is mottled with blackish brown. ■ **NOTES** Restricted to RF in vicinity of Bulburin SF in mid-estn Qld. Shelters in tree hollows and large numbers may co-habit; 13 recorded on one fig tree. ■ **STATUS** Vulnerable (Qld).

Champion's Leaf-tailed Gecko *Phyllurus championae* SVL 80mm

Tail flat and flared to carrot-shaped. Rostral scale completely divided (fig.). Brown with irregular black blotches; tail heavily mottled with black, and marked with 5 white bands. ■ **NOTES** Known only from two adjacent localities in mid-estn Qld: Cameron Ck and Blue Mtn. RF; associated with boulders and scree.

Gulbaru Leaf-tailed Gecko *Phyllurus gulbaru* SVL 93mm

Tail narrow and cylindrical. Rostral scale partly divided by midline groove. Small tubercles on body with larger tubercles on base and along sides of original tail. Grey with irregular dark blotches, a pair of large dark and pale blotches on hips and 8 pale bands on original tail. ■ **NOTES** Sthn end of Paluma Ra., in steep gullies with boulders, RF and hoop pines. ■ **STATUS** Critically endangered (IUCN Red List; C'wealth); endangered (Qld).

Mt Blackwood Broad-tailed Gecko *Phyllurus isis* SVL 76mm

Smoothest sp. Tail flat and strongly flared with long slender tip. **Rostral scale partly divided by one groove (fig.).** Body greyish brown with darker blotches. Original tail marked on anterior flared portion with **2 pale bands broken on midline by a dark stripe**, and 3 bands on slender tip. Regenerated tails greyish brown with irregular pale blotches. ■ **NOTES** Restricted to RF on Mt Blackwood and Mt Jukes near Mackay. Known only from small outcrops of mossy rocks under a low, dense canopy. ■ **STATUS** Vulnerable (Qld).

Oakview Leaf-tailed Gecko *Phyllurus kabikabi* SVL 81mm

Tail narrow and cylindrical. Rostral scale completely divided by midline groove. Moderate tubercles on body and tail and uniform granules under hindlimb. Brown heavily marked with irregular dark blotches. Original tail darker with 5–6 cream bands; regenerated tail heavily pigmented. ■ **NOTES** Known only from narrow band of vine forest on rock scree in Oakview Forest Reserve, Qld. ■ **STATUS** Endangered (Qld).

Phyllurus caudiannulatus.
Bulburin SF, Qld. S. Wilson

Phyllurus championae.
Cameron Creek, Qld. S. Wilson

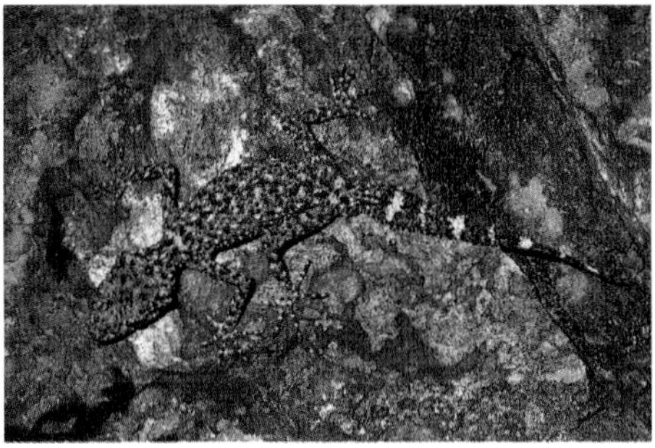

Phyllurus gulbaru. Patterson's Gorge, Paluma Range, Qld. S. Wilson

Phyllurus isis. Mt Blackwood, Qld. S. Wilson

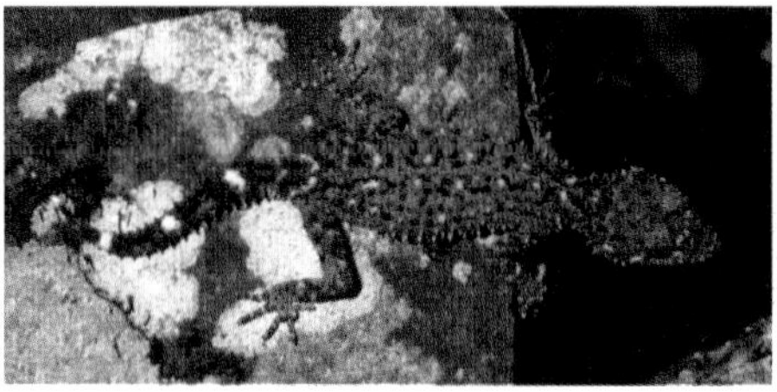

Phyllurus kabikabi.
Oakview Forest Reserve, Qld. S. Wilson

Eungella Broad-tailed Gecko *Phyllurus nepthys* SVL 103mm

Very spinose. Tail flat and flared to carrot-shaped. **Rostral scale partly divided by one groove (fig.).** Greyish brown with irregular dark brown blotches and usually irregular transverse bands of pale grey blotches. **Ventral surfaces distinctively peppered.** Original tail has 4–5 prominent cream bands. Regenerated tail mottled with cream and dark brown, lacking transverse bands.

■ **NOTES** Restricted to RF in the Clarke Ra., w. of Mackay.

Mount Ossa Leaf-tailed Gecko *Phyllurus ossa* SVL 89mm

Moderately spinose. Tail flat and flared with slender tip terminating in minute knob. **Top of rostral scale usually notched by 3 deep grooves (A),** occasionally by **2 grooves,** or rarely an **inverted Y-shaped groove (B).** Grey to brown with prominent dark grey to black blotches; black on slender tail-tip.

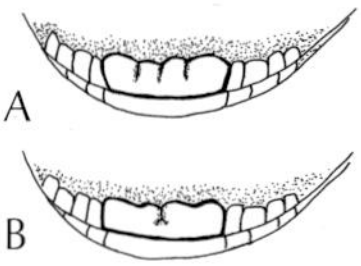

A

B

Original tail banded with cream. Regenerated tail pale grey with dark blotches or black with pale blotches. **SSP.** P. o. *tamoya* has scattered enlarged tubercles on throat (smooth on other ssp.). *P. o. ossa* has uniformly large spinose tubercles on forearm. *P. o. hobsoni* has tubercles on forearm decreasing in size and spinosity towards wrist. ■ **NOTES** Rocks associated with RF in mid-estn Qld. P. o. *tamoya* is known only from Whitsunday Is. *P. o. ossa* occurs in the Mt. Ossa/Mt. Charleton/Mirani area near Mackay. *P. o. hobsoni* lives in the Conway Range/Mt. Dryander area near Proserpine.

Broad-tailed Gecko *Phyllurus platurus* SVL 95mm

Tail flat and flared. Pale brown to dark grey with darker mottling, spots or flecks. No distinctive pale bands on tail, though original tail may bear irregular bands towards tip. ■ **NOTES** Restricted to sandstones from Denman area s. to Kiama and inland to Jenolan Caves. Shelters in crevices and wind-blown sandstone caves, and in human dwellings adjacent to outcrops. Large numbers may share a suitable shelter site; up to 16 individuals recorded in one crevice. In such sites, spider webs are often festooned with their sloughed skins.

Leaf-tailed Geckos Genus *Saltuarius*

Seven very large, spectacular spp. with flat bodies and angular clawed padless digits. **Tails very broad and flat with an elaborate outer flange.** Original tails are spiny with a cylindrical slender tip but regenerated tails are smooth and blunt-tipped. Scales small and granular mixed with large conical to spinose tubercles (all smooth on regenerated tails). Rostral scale contacts nostril (A), or is separated (B). Pattern prominent; **complex lichen-like marbling** renders them nearly invisible against the variegated tree buttresses and boulder faces they inhabit. The genus includes some of our largest and most impressive geckos. ■ **NOTES** RF and rock massifs of granite and sandstone between ne. NSW and Wet Tropics of ne. Qld. ■ **SEE ALSO** *Orraya; Phyllurus.*

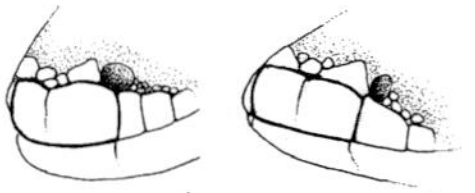

A B

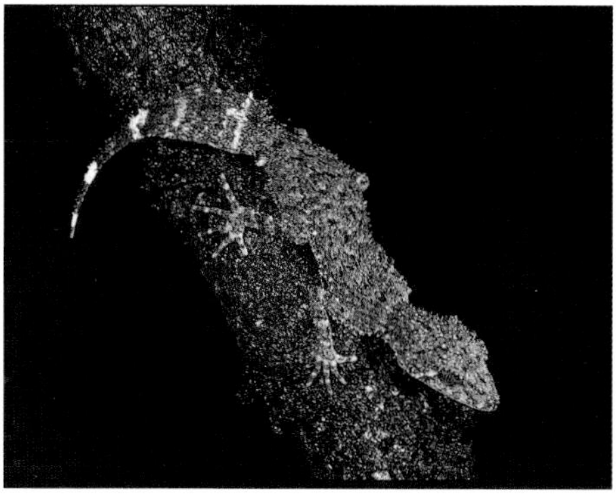

Phyllurus nepthys. Eungella NP, Qld. S. Wilson

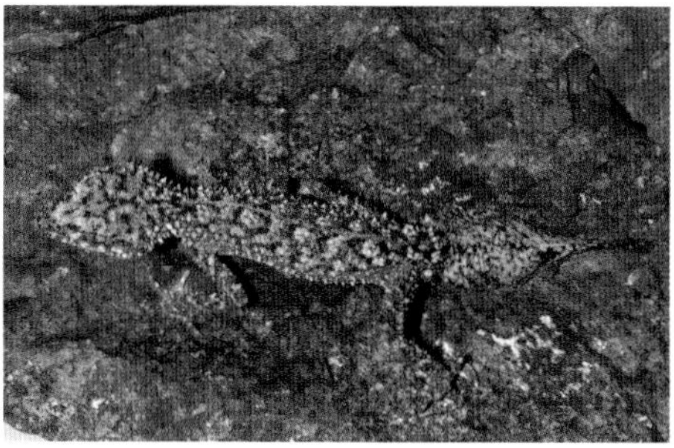

Phyllurus ossa tamoya. Whitsunday Island, Qld. S. Wilson

Phyllurus ossa ossa. Mt Ossa, Qld. S. Wilson

Phyllurus ossa hobsoni. Mt Dryander, Qld. S. Wilson

Phyllurus platurus. Lane Cove NP, NSW. S. Wilson

Northern Leaf-tailed Gecko *Saltuarius cornutus* SVL 144mm

Distinctive **long hooked tubercles on flanks**. Shades of grey, brown to olive with prominent disruptive lichen-like mottling, blotches and variegations. Original tail usually marked with broad irregular pale bands. One of Aust.'s largest geckos. ■ **NOTES** Restricted to RF in the Wet Tropics from Cooktown s. to Mt Spec.

Cape Melville Leaf-tailed Gecko *Saltuarius eximius* SVL 120mm

Long and extremely slender body, short head with **extremely large unpatterned eyes** and long thin limbs. **Original tail has elaborately undulating frilled margin** and fine slender tip less than one third total tail length. Regenerated tail broadly flared and paddle-shaped with rounded posterior margin. Blackish brown to black with sharply contrasting irregular pale bands. ■ **NOTES** Restricted to isolated RF atop the granite boulder-fields of Melville Ra. in Cape Melville NP, Cape York Pen.

Kate's Leaf-tailed Gecko *Saltuarius kateae* SVL 105mm

Rostral scale separated from nostril, scales on side of snout grade evenly down from small to large and **upper surface of digits lacking large spinose tubercles**. Brown with reduced pattern of grey and mid to dark brown blotches, a narrow brown vertebral stripe broken by 6-7 weak paler bands and a weak V-shape between eyes. Regenerated tail greyish with heavy dark mottling. Original tail with irregular, diffuse, **continuous pale bands** and **slender tip free of tubercles**. ■ **NOTES** Sandstone escarpments in open eucalypt forests at Wyan's Creek and Mt Marsh, ne. NSW. ■ **SEE ALSO** *S. moritzi; S. swaini.*

Moritz's Leaf-tailed Gecko *Saltuarius moritzi* SVL 109mm

Rostral scale contacts nostril, scales on side of snout grade evenly down from small to large, and **upper surface of digits usually with large spinose tubercles**. Extremely variable; typically finely marbled with grey and light to dark brown blotches, a narrow dark-edged brown vertebral stripe broken by 3-6 paler bands and usually a prominent deep V-shape back between eyes. Original tail with irregular **continuous pale bands** and **slender tip free of tubercles.** ■ **NOTES** Widespread in WSF, RF and rock outcrops and gorges in ne NSW s of Clarence River. ■ **SEE ALSO** *S. kateae; S. swaini; S. wyberba.*

Rough-throated Leaf-tailed Gecko *Saltuarius salebrosus* SVL 140mm

Prominent tubercles on throat. Shades of grey, usually with some indication of brownish dark-edged vertebral stripe broken by 3 (usually dark-edged) pale dorsal blotches located at about shoulders, midbody and hips. ■ **NOTES** Granite outcrops and sandstone cliffs, caves and overhangs. Pops from Bulburin SF and Bania SF occur in RF. Shelters in rock crevices, on ceilings and walls of wind-blown sandstone caves and in cavities in RF tree trunks.

Saltuarius cornutus.
Woonooroonan NP, Qld. S. Wilson

Saltuarius eximius. Cape Melville, Qld. C. Hoskin

Saltuarius kateae.
Wyan's Creek, NSW. S. Wilson

Saltuarius moritzi.
Coffs Harbour, NSW. G. Swan

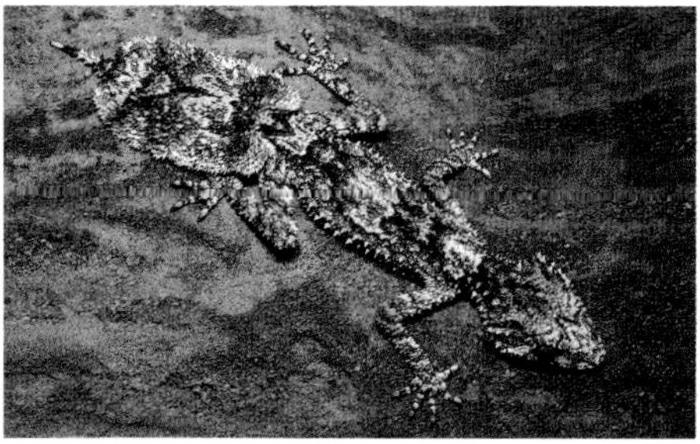

Saltuarius salebrosus.
Cracow, Qld. S. Wilson

Southern Leaf-tailed Gecko *Saltuarius swaini* SVL 134mm

Rostral scale usually contacts nostril, scales on side of snout a mix of small and large granules, and **upper surface of digits usually with large spinose tubercles.** Mottled grey to brown with dark-edged tan vertebral stripe broken by 3-5 paler bands and deep V-shape back between eyes. Original tail with lichen-like blotches, diffuse pale bands and **relatively thick tip with large tubercles**. Regenerated tail with darker marbling. ■ **NOTES** RF on coastal ranges between Mt Glorious, Qld and Richmond Range, NSW. ■ **SEE ALSO** *S. kateae; S. moritzi; S. wyberba.*

Granite Belt Leaf-tailed Gecko *Saltuarius wyberba* SVL 108mm

Rostral scale usually contacts nostril, scales on side of snout grade evenly down from small to large, and **upper surface of digits usually with large spinose tubercles.** Tan to grey with dark blotches, a narrow vertebral stripe broken by 4 paler blotches and wide open V-shape back between eyes. Original tail with 2 narrow **pale irregular bands, discontinuous at midline,** across flared portion, often centred on enlarged tubercles and **fine tip with minute tubercles.** ■ **NOTES** Granite outcrops in open forest between Queen Mary Falls, Qld and Gibraltar Ra., NSW. ■ **SEE ALSO** *S. swaini; S. moritzi.*

Thick-tailed or Barking Geckos
Genus *Underwoodisaurus*

Two **plump-bodied** spp. **with large deep heads** and slender limbs. Original tails plump, carrot-shaped, **tapering gradually to a tip with no terminal knob. Subdigital lamellae transverse.** Scales small and granular mixed with low tubercles. ■ **NOTES** Dry habitats across sthn Aust. with one sp. isolated in arid Pilbara region, WA. Terrestrial, sheltering by day under rocks, logs or in burrows (their own or those of other animals) and foraging at night in open spaces between low vgtn. Diets incl. arthropods and smaller geckos. When threatened, they raise their bodies and lunge at their aggressor, uttering a loud wheezing bark. ■ **SEE ALSO** *Nephrurus; Uvidicolus.*

Common Thick-tailed Gecko *Underwoodisaurus milii* SVL 100mm

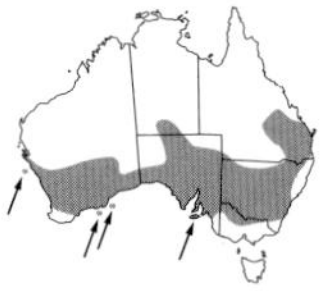

Pink to dark purplish brown with many prominent, **large, cream to yellow spots**, each centred on a tubercle and **tending to form well-defined bands** across back. **Head usually well marked** with lighter patches, incl. lips, snout and across base. Original tail spinose, black with 5–6 prominent white bands. Regenerated tail smooth, blunt and mottled. ■ **NOTES** Widespread across sthn Aust. from Rockhampton area, Qld to just n. of Shark Bay, WA. Common in dry or well-drained habitats incl. DSF, shrublands and rock outcrops, extending into temperate forests in some areas. Can be locally abundant; up to 13 recorded beneath a granite slab in nthn Vic.

Saltuarius swaini.
Border Ranges, NSW. S. Wilson

Saltuarius wyberba.
Girraween NP, Qld. S. Wilson

Underwoodisaurus milii.
Helidon region, Qld. S. Wilson

Pilbara Barking Gecko *Underwoodisaurus seorsus* SVL 100 mm

Pale to medium reddish-brown with numerous **small pale spots** scattered over body and limbs, corresponding with numerous small, low, spinose, scattered dorsal tubercles, **tending to form irregular bands** across back. **Top and sides of head have no pattern**. Limbs and digits long and slender. Original tail spinose, dark reddish-brown with 5 prominent white bands. Regenerated tail smooth, blunt and mottled. ■ **NOTES** Hamersley Ra. in Pilbara region, WA, from n. of Tom Price, se. to near Newman. Rocky areas with spinifex and low tree cover.

Genus *Uvidicolus*

Granite Belt Thick-tailed Gecko *Uvidicolus sphyrurus* SVL 70mm

Sole member of genus. Large deep head and slender limbs. Original tail plump, squarish, **tapering sharply to a tip** with no terminal knob. Subdigital lamellae transverse. Scales small and granular mixed with low tubercles. Brownish grey with darker variegations and small, transversely aligned pale spots, each centred on a tubercle. Original tail spinose, blackish with approx. 4 cream bands. Regenerated tail smooth, blunt and mottled. ■ **NOTES** Restricted to cool highland Granite Belt of New England, NSW, and adjacent Stanthorpe district, Qld, sheltering under rocks and in burrows. ■ **SEE ALSO** *Underwoodisaurus.* ■ **STATUS** Vulnerable (C'wealth; NSW); lower risk – near threatened (IUCN Red List).

Underwoodisaurus seorsus.
Packsaddle Range, WA. R. Lloyd.

Uvidicolus sphyrurus.
Girraween NP, Qld. S. Wilson

DIPLODACTYLID GECKOS
Family Diplodactylidae

Diplodactylid geckos are endemic to Australia and the western Pacific, extending to New Zealand and New Caledonia. Along with the flap-footed lizards (Pygopodidae) and two other Australian gecko families (Gekkonidae and Carphodactylidae) they belong to a clade of lizards called the Gekkota.

The group shares many distinctive features. These include employing the tongue to wipe the clear spectacles covering their lidless eyes, and a voice in the form of a squeak, uttered when stressed or during social encounters. They also share a clutch of no more than two eggs, with an egg descending from each oviduct. Like most lizard eggs, the shells are soft and parchment-like (brittle and hard in Gekkonid geckos). As an adaptation to colder climates, the New Zealand Diplodactylids are livebearers, producing twins. One New Caledonian species is also a livebearer.

Diplodactylidae is represented here by 93 described species. Most have padded digits with enlarged subdigital lamellae, normally including a large terminal pair. In some terrestrial species, however, particularly those inhabiting dry sandy substrates, lamellae have become greatly reduced, sometimes barely enlarged. In the Beaded Gecko (*Lucasium damaeum*) they are all minute and spinose.

Like other geckos, Diplodactylids have a soft, velvety skin texture. Most species lack enlarged tubercles. The spiny-tailed geckos (*Strophurus ciliaris* and its allies) are peculiar exceptions, featuring rows of large tubercles on the back, and tubercles or spines along the dorsal surface of the tail and sometimes above the eyes.

Diversity is highest in arid habitats dominated by spinifex, and in tropical woodlands and outcrops. Several species, including the Eastern Stone Gecko (*Diplodactylus vittatus)* and the Spotted Velvet Gecko (*Oedura tryoni*), penetrate well into areas subject to cold winters and occasional snow.

Diplodactylids are an extremely diverse group, both morphologically and behaviourally. The family includes arboreal, rock-inhabiting, tussock-inhabiting and terrestrial species. Included are Australia's smallest geckos, the clawless geckos (*Crenadactylus* spp.); giant cave geckos (*Pseudothecadactylus* spp.) that feature very broad padded digits plus additional adhesive lamellae under their tail-tips; and striped geckos (*Strophurus* spp.) with simple patterns of bold longitudinal stripes to conceal them among tussocks and grass hummocks. In dry, open areas, many terrestrial Diplodactylids shelter largely or solely in the vertical shafts of insect and spider holes.

While most members of the family are dietary generalists, consuming a range of arthropods and (in the case of larger species), smaller geckos, a number of species are specialists. The beaked geckos (*Rhynchoedura* spp.) the fat-tailed geckos *(Diplodactylus conspicillatus* complex) and the Pretty Gecko *(D. pulcher*) appear to subsist almost entirely on termites.

All geckos are typically nocturnal, but some spiny-tailed geckos regularly bask in dappled sunlight among foliage, occasionally even exposing themselves to full sun at formidable temperatures.

The Soft Spiny-tailed Gecko (*Strophurus spinigerus*) lives in south-western heaths and woodlands, where it can sometimes be found basking among foliage in dappled sunlight.
Perth, WA. S. Wilson

Slender Velvet Geckos
Genus *Amalosia*

Four small slender spp. Dorsally depressed, with **dorsal scales minute**, smooth and granular, **much smaller than ventrals**; more than one cloacal spur; **long slender tail, more or less round in cross-section**; and **subdigital lamellae enlarged at base, divided distally and terminating in a pair of enlarged plates** (fig). Dorsal pattern often fragmented, comprising broad, **pale zigzagging vertebral stripe or series of angular blotches**. ■ **NOTES** Estn and nthn Aust. Arboreal and rock-inhabiting, sheltering behind loose bark and under rock slabs. ■ **SEE ALSO** *Nebulifera; Oedura*

Clouded Gecko *Amalosia jacovae* SVL 61mm

Long, slightly bulbous tail and **pronounced basal webbing between 3rd and 4th toes**. Greyish brown with broad, wavy, dark-edged **pale grey vertebral zone, generally broken or partly broken by narrow irregular bands**. Usually a small dark blotch on neck, and some indication of a dark midlateral stripe extending forward above ear and through eye to snout. Snout, flanks and limbs unspotted, or with a few small pale lateral spots. ■ **NOTES** Dry open eucalypt forests, heaths and outcrops in se. Qld between Kroombit Tops and Warwick and incl. Brisbane area. ■ **SEE ALSO** *A. lesueurii; A. rhombifer.*

Lesueur's Velvet Gecko *Amalosia lesueurii* SVL 80mm

Blotched, with long, moderately depressed tail, **and little basal webbing between 3rd and 4th toes.** Grey to greyish brown with a broad, ragged-edged, paler vertebral region broken into irregular dark-edged blotches from nape to tail-tip. Regenerated tails are variegated with blackish brown. **Snout, flanks and limbs with small pale spots and blotches.** ■ **NOTES** Rocky ranges and outcrops, particularly sandstones and granites, in DSF and woodlands. Shelters in crevices and under rock slabs. ■ **SEE ALSO** *A. jacovae.*

Slim Velvet Gecko *Amalosia obscura* SVL 62mm

Banded, with tail long, slender and round in cross-section. Pale yellowish brown to pinkish brown with **dark brown bands** and broader pale interspaces from nape onto tail, and **small white spots scattered over body**, limbs and tail. Regenerated tails are marked with dark streaks. ■ **NOTES** Nw. Kimberley, e. to Cockburn Ra. Shelters in crevices and under slabs on sandstone plateaux and in gorges.

Zigzag Velvet Gecko *Amalosia rhombifer* SVL 70mm

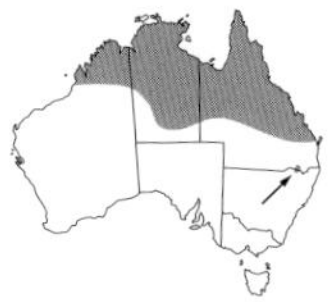

Long, nearly round tail and **no basal webbing between 3rd and 4th toes**. Pale to dark grey or brown with **broad, unbroken, pale zigzagging vertebral stripe** from nape to tail-tip, forking forward at nape and extending through each eye. ■ **NOTES** Widespread in woodlands, sheltering under bark, in hollows and often in buildings. ■ **SEE ALSO** *A. jacovae.* ■ **STATUS** Endangered (NSW).

Amalosia jacovae. Southbrook, Qld. S. Wilson

Amalosia lesueurii. Girraween NP, Qld. S. Wilson

Amalosia obscura.
Mitchell Plateau, WA. S. Wilson

Amalosia rhombifer.
Townsville area, Qld. S. Wilson

Clawless Geckos Genus *Crenadactylus*

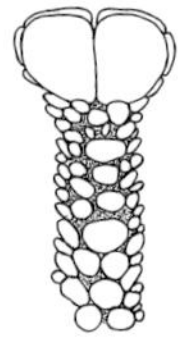

Seven extremely small spp. (Aust's smallest geckos) with maximum SVL of 35mm. Unique in **lacking claws**. Digital pads very wide and **subdigital lamellae enlarged, with two very large terminal plates (fig)**. Pattern incl. pale ocelli (1 sp.) or simple stripes. ■ **NOTES** Widespread in dry habitats from sw. WA to nthn and central Aust. Spp. range from spinifex-inhabiting to terrestrial, sheltering under low vegetation, leaf litter, rocks and surface debris. Very secretive and rarely found far from cover.

Central Uplands Clawless Gecko *Crenadactylus horni* SVL 35mm

Rostral scale fully contacts nostril. **Internasal scale enlarged**. Dorsal scales homogeneous and no enlarged tubercles on original tail. Tan to dark brown with simple striped pattern. Narrow silvery grey vertebral stripe usually present, bordered by dark-edged brown paravertebral stripes, pale dorsolateral stripes from snout onto tail, dark upper lateral stripe from side of snout onto tail and ill-defined dark lateral stripe. ■ **NOTES** Apparently isolated pops in central Aust., each restricted to rocky habitats with spinifex and separated by unsuitable habitat between Ngarutjara and Pukatja homelands, SA, through Finke Gorge, West MacDonnell Ras and Alice Springs n. to Wilora, NT. *Crenadactylus* recorded from sandridges at Ethabuka, sw. Qld, tentatively assigned.

Northern Clawless Gecko *Crenadactylus naso* SVL 31mm

Rostral scale usually narrowly contacts nostril but sometimes separated (esp. in e. Kimberley). Dorsal scales homogeneous with **enlarged tubercles on original tail**. Simple striped pattern, with scattered pale scales within dark stripes.Yellowish grey with pale vertebral stripe often forked at back of head, brown paravertebral stripes, dark-edged pale dorsolateral stripes extend from snout onto tail, weakly developed dark lateral stripes and pale enlarged tubercles on tail. ■ **NOTES** Considered a species complex extending across nthn Aust. from w. Kimberley to nw. Qld. Inhabits spinifex on rocky areas incl. sandstone outcrops, gorges and scree slopes, and in diverse habitats such as vine thickets and woodlands. ■ **SEE ALSO** *C. rostralis*

Western Clawless Gecko *Crenadactylus occidentalis* SVL 33mm

Rostral scale fully contacts nostril. **Dorsal scales homogeneous** and no enlarged tubercles on original tail. Simple striped pattern with **no ocelli**. Tan to pale yellowish brown with narrow silvery grey vertebral stripe, dark brown paravertebral stripes that converge at hips, broad pale dorsolateral stripes extend from snout onto tail, sometimes peppered with orange spots on body, and dark brown upper lateral stripe from side of snout onto tail. ■ **NOTES** Mid-west coast from inland of Geraldton n. to sthn part of North West Cape and extending inland no more than 100km. Recorded from spinifex, coastal dune vegtn and limestone rocks.
■ **SEE ALSO** *C. ocellatus*; *C. tuberculatus*.

Crenadactylus horni.
King's Creek Stn, NT.
S. Wilson

Crenadactylus naso
Kununurra area, WA.
S. Wilson

Crenadactylus naso.
McArthur River, NT.
J. Wombey

Crenadactylus occidentalis.
Hamelin Pool area, WA.
R. Browne-Cooper

South-western Clawless Gecko *Crenadactylus ocellatus* SVL 35mm

Rostral scale fully contacts nostril. Dorsal scales homogeneous and no enlarged tubercles on original tail. Tan to dark brown with **pattern incl. ocelli.** Ill-defined silvery grey vertebral stripe sometimes present. Pale brown dorsolateral zones extend from snout to tail, incl. 7–12 widely spaced pale spots or ocelli comprising clusters of pale scales, sometimes with dark borders, between eye and tail. ■ **NOTES** Dry areas of sw. WA, e. to Israelite Bay and Balladonia and sw. to Waroona. Occupies open wooded areas on sandy, stony and hard substrates and shelters under logs, leaf litter, rocks and other surface debris. ■ **SEE ALSO** *C. occidentalis.*

Pilbara Clawless Gecko *Crenadactylus pilbarensis* SVL 28mm

Rostral scale fully contacts nostril. **Single, greatly enlarged postmental scale.** Dorsal scales homogeneous and no enlarged tubercles on original tail. Striped, with scattered clusters of pale scales. Pale to dark brown with narrow pale vertebral stripe, dark brown paravertebral stripes that converge at hips, broad pale dorsolateral stripes extend from snout onto tail, dark brown upper lateral stripe from side of snout onto tail, and narrow dark lateral stripes, incl. wavy midlateral and broken indistinct lower lateral. ■ **NOTES** Pilbara region, WA, from Shay Gap and Meentheena Cons. Res. s. to Barlee Ra. and Kumarina. Occupies spinifex on rocky hills and gullies on mainland, and sandy surfaces on Dolphin Is.

South-west Kimberley Clawless Gecko *Crenadactylus rostralis* SVL 33mm

Rostral scale separated from nostril. Dorsal scales homogeneous and **no enlarged tubercles on original tail.** Simple striped pattern, usually with some pale mottling within dark stripes. Pale greyish brown with narrow pale vertebral stripe, dark brown paravertebral stripes, broad pale dorsolateral zone extending from snout onto tail, dark brown upper lateral stripe from side of snout onto tail and pale grey ventrolateral stripe sometimes with ill-defined narrow dark edge. ■ **NOTES** Limestone ranges of sw. Kimberley from Napier Ra. sw. to Gogo Stn, and provisionally incl. pop. from Mt. Anderson near Derby. Inhabits spinifex, and recorded in large clumps around limestone areas. ■ **SEE ALSO** *C. naso.*

Cape Range Clawless Gecko *Crenadactylus tuberculatus* SVL 28mm

Rostral scale fully contacts nostril. **Dorsal scales heterogeneous; small with enlarged scattered tubercles** on body, and no enlarged tuberculate scales on original tail. Pale brownish grey with stripes mixed with dark and pale scales and some orange on enlarged tubercles. Narrow pale vertebral stripe on body, dark brown paravertebral stripes that converge at hips, pale dorsolateral stripe from snout onto tail, and dark brown upper lateral stripe from side of snout onto tail. ■ **NOTES** Cape Range on North West Cape, s. to Yardie Ck. Mainly associated with spinifex on limestone, but also coastal dunes. Smallest Aust. gecko. ■ **SEE ALSO** *C. occidentalis.*

Crenadactylus ocellatus.
Ravensthorpe, WA. S. Wilson

Crenadactylus pilbarensis.
Juna Downs Stn, WA. B. Maryan

Crenadactylus rostralis.
Geikie Gorge, WA. P. Oliver

Crenadactylus tuberculatus.
Yardie Creek, WA. S. Zozaya

Genus *Diplodactylus*

Twenty-seven small to moderate-sized robust terrestrial spp. with **broad digits about 4 times as long as wide**, enlarged terminal plates present, subdigital lamellae range from a broad undivided series (A), to greatly reduced (B), **clusters of generally more than 5 spines on each side of cloaca**, relatively short limbs and usually **swollen tails. Caudal glands are absent; unable to produce viscous fluids from back and tail.** Pattern often a pale zigzagging to straight vertebral stripe or series of blotches (small scattered flecks some spp.). Generally sedentary, sheltering under rocks, surface debris and in burrows. Spp. are identified by pattern and whether nostril contacts rostral scale (C) or is separated (D). ■ SEE ALSO *Lucasium; Rhynchoedura; Strophurus.*

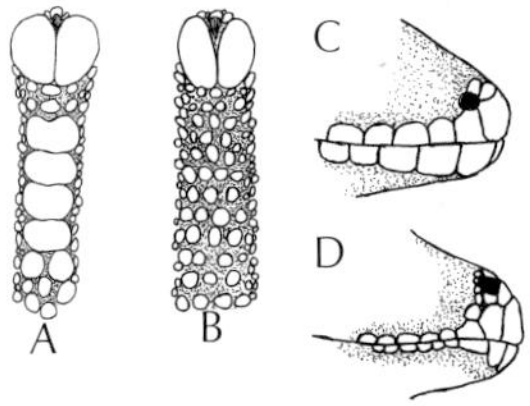

Eastern Deserts Fat-tailed Gecko *Diplodactylus ameyi* SVL 60mm

Robust. **All upper labial scales small and granular (1st not enlarged). Snout broad and blunt when viewed from above and convex along dorsal surface. Original tail short, thick, spade-like and blunt-tipped**, with dorsal scales in transverse rows; usually uniform in size but sometimes incl. alternating rows of large and small scales. Scales on nape small and granular, just slightly larger than granules on side of neck, and mid-dorsal scales on body plate-like, noticeably larger than adj. dorsolateral scales. Subdigital lamellae minute, with a pair of small terminal plates. Shades of brown with **little or no pale streak from eye to snout**, fine dark reticulum and pale spotting; spots tend to be larger and denser on flanks. Dark pigment generally reduced on vertebral zone, and marked with 5–6 irregular pale blotches. ■ NOTES Open arid habitats on sand, clay and stony substrates along estn edge of Eromanga Basin, from nw. NSW n. to Winton area, Qld. ■ SEE ALSO *D. conspicillatus; D. barraganae; D. laevis; D. platyurus.* ■ STATUS Endangered (NSW – as *D. conspicillatus*).

Gulf Fat-tailed Gecko *Diplodactylus barraganae* SVL 49mm

Robust. Only **1st upper labial scale greatly enlarged**; remainder small, granular and the same as adj. scales. **Original tail short, thick, spade-like, blunt-tipped**, with **scales on dorsal surface in transverse rows**, typically incl. alternating rows of large and small scales. **Scales on nape granular, just slightly larger than granules on side of neck, mid-dorsal scales small, only slightly larger than adj. dorsolateral scales**. Subdigital lamellae minute, with a pair of small terminal plates. Brown to reddish brown with prominent **broad pale stripe from eye to snout**. Body with diffuse spotting and obscure reticulations, and often a paler, broken to continuous vertebral zone. ■ NOTES Broad band of open tropical woodland along sthn edge of Gulf of Carpentaria between Roper R. area, NT, and Mt Isa area, Qld. ■ SEE ALSO *D. ameyi; D. conspicillatus; D. hillii; D. platyurus.*

Diplodactylus ameyi. Myendetta Stn, Charleville area, Qld. S. Wilson

Diplodactylus barraganae. Doomadgee, Qld. J. de Jong

Western Fat-tailed Gecko *Diplodactylus bilybara* SVL 63mm

Robust. Only 1st upper labial scale greatly enlarged; remainder small, granular and the same as adj. scales. **Original tail short, thick, spade-like, with an extension at tip**, with scales on dorsal surface in transverse rows, often incl. a large row alternating with two rows of much smaller scales. **Scales on nape granular, just slightly larger than granules on side of neck, but mid-dorsal scales plate-like, noticeably larger than adj. dorsolateral scales.** Subdigital lamellae minute, with a pair of small terminal plates. Reddish brown with prominent broad pale stripe from eye to snout. Body with dark irregular wavy bands and scattered to transverse spots. ■ **NOTES** Central wstn WA, in Carnarvon, w. Pilbara and Gascoyne regions, favouring Mulga woodlands on sandy loams and *Triodia* sandplains. ■ **SEE ALSO** *D. conspicillatus*; *D. laevis*.

South Coast Gecko *Diplodactylus calcicolus* SVL 49mm

Robust, with moderately short thick tail. Rostral scale contacts nostril. **Labial scales enlarged, approximately square.** Subdigital lamellae in a large series with relatively large terminal plates. Pale to dark brown or grey with pale grey dorsal **stripe usually broken into a series of irregular blotches**, occasionally a continuous stripe with scalloped margins. Upper flanks with **circular spots and intermixed irregular darker and lighter scales.** ■ **NOTES** Cool dry habitats, usually on limestone or calcareous coastal sands from near Perth, WA to mouth of Murray R., SA. ■ **SEE ALSO** *D. furcosus, D. g. granariensis, D. lateroides, D. vittatus, D. wiru.*

Cape Range Gecko *Diplodactylus capensis* SVL 64mm

Robust with short thick tail. Rostral scale contacts nostril. Subdigital lamellae large and circular in single series with large terminal plates. Reddish brown with irregular **pale vertebral stripe and 5-8 short transverse bars** along each side of midline. ■ **NOTES** Restricted to rocky nthn end of North West Cape, WA.

Variable Fat-tailed Gecko *Dipodactylus conspicillatus* SVL 62mm

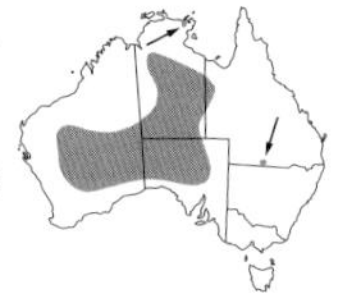

Robust. Only **1st upper labial scale greatly enlarged**; remainder small, granular and the same as adj. scales. **Original tail short, thick, spade-like, blunt-tipped,** with **scales on dorsal surface in transverse rows**, typically incl. alternating rows of large and small scales. **Scales on nape granular, just slightly larger than granules on side of neck, but mid-dorsal scales plate-like, noticeably larger than adj. dorsolateral scales.** Subdigital lamellae minute, with a pair of small terminal plates. Brown to reddish brown with prominent **broad pale stripe from eye to snout**. Body chequered or peppered with dark pigment. Pale spots usually present, particularly on flanks. ■ **NOTES** Very widespread across arid zone from wstn interior to wstn Qld. Open habitats favouring hard soils such as clay, gibber and compacted sands and loams. Shelters in vertical spider holes, blocking the shaft with tail. Appears to be a termite specialist. ■ **SEE ALSO** *D. ameyi*; *D. barraganae*; *D. bilybara*; *D. hillii*; *D. laevis*.

Diplodactylus bilybara.
Hamersley Range, WA.
J. de Jong

Diplodactylus calcicolus.
Eucla, WA. S. Wilson

Diplodactylus capensis.
Shothole Canyon, Cape Range NP, WA. B. Maryan

Diplodactylus conspicillatus.
Emily Gap area, NT.
S. Wilson

Kimberley Fat-tailed Gecko *Diplodactylus custos* SVL 61mm

Robust. Only 1st upper labial scale greatly enlarged; remainder small, granular and the same as adj. scales. **Original tail short, thick, spade-like, with short, acute attenuated tip** and with large **scales on dorsal surface in transverse rows**, typically of uniform size, but sometimes alternating with single rows of smaller scales. **Scales on nape granular, just slightly larger than granules on side of neck, but mid-dorsal scales plate-like, noticeably larger than adj. dorsolateral scales.** Subdigital lamellae minute, with a pair of small terminal plates. Reddish brown with weak pattern; diffuse darker mottling, prominent broad pale stripe from eye to snout and sometimes pale spots. ■ **NOTES** Widespread across Kimberley region, WA, from Kununurra to Derby and Yampi Pen. Recorded from eucalypt woodlands and grasslands, often on stony soils. Probably shelters in vertical spider holes, blocking the shaft with tail. Appears to be a termite specialist. ■ **SEE ALSO** *D. laevis; D. hillii.*

Lake Disappointment Ground Gecko *Diplodactylus fulleri* SVL 51mm

Long-limbed, with tail covered with rings of large rectangular scales. **Rostral scale contacts nostril. Subdigital lamellae small and granular with small terminal plates.** Fawn to pale reddish brown with irregular darker spots and markings. ■ **NOTES** Only known from low samphire shrubs fringing Lake Disappointment, WA, foraging on bare salt crust between shrubs.

Ranges Stone Gecko *Diplodactylus furcosus* SVL 51mm

Robust with short thick tail. Rostral scale contacts nostril. Subdigital lamellae in a large series with relatively large terminal plates. Brown to tan with **narrowly dark-edged** strongly scalloped or zigzagging pale vertebral stripe, or series of blotches, **forking forward at nape to above eyes. Upper flanks usually with circular spots, sometimes dark-edged.** ■ **NOTES** Sthn interior of SA to far wstn NSW, usually associated with rocky areas or stony soils. ■ **SEE ALSO** *D. calcicolus; D. vittatus; D. wiru.*

Northern Pilbara Beak-faced Gecko *Diplodactylus galaxias* SVL 46mm

Moderately short, thick cylindrical tail, **beak-like snout with rostral scale not contacting nostril**, and moderately enlarged **paired subdigital lamellae.** Reddish brown with **fine scattered yellow dorsal spots. A gradual junction between dark flanks and pale ventral surfaces.** ■ **NOTES** Stony hills with spinifex in Pilbara region, from mouth of Fortescue River and Burrup Peninsula, inland along Chichester Ra., WA. Possibly a termite specialist.
■ **SEE ALSO** *D. savagei.*

Diplodactylus custos.
Wyndham area, WA.
S. Wilson

Diplodactylus fulleri.
Lake Disappointment,
WA. B. Maryan

Diplodactylus furcosus.
Cowell, SA. B. Maryan

Diplodactylus galaxias.
Burrup Peninsula, WA.
R. Browne-Cooper

Mesa Gecko *Diplodactylus galeatus* SVL 55mm

Robust, with short thick tail, and **rostral scale contacting nostril. Subdigital lamellae in 2 rows with moderately enlarged terminal plates**. Pale brown to reddish brown with 6–9 large, dark-edged, pale dorsal blotches on body and tail. Top of head pale, bordered posteriorly by a curved dark line from eye to eye. ■ **NOTES** Rock outcrops and ranges of central Aust. Shelters under small stones in mild weather, and in deep crevices, insect or spider holes during hot periods.

Western Stone Gecko *Diplodactylus granariensis* SVL 66–72mm

Rostral scale contacts nostril. Subdigital lamellae in a large series with relatively large terminal plates. ■ **SSP.** *D. g. granariensis* is greyish brown to reddish brown with a broad, pale **straight-edged to weakly scalloped vertebral stripe, forking forward on nape to above eyes. Upper flanks largely patternless.** *D. g. rex* is larger (72 mm) with more massive head and simple pattern of straight-edged pale vertebral stripe and dark mid lateral stripe. ■ **NOTES** *D. g. granariensis* occurs in dry sw. interior of WA, e. to Zanthus. *D. g. rex* occurs further inland on the arid wstn plateau. ■ **SEE ALSO** *D. calcicolus; D. wiru.*

Northern Fat-tailed Gecko *Dipodactylus hillii* SVL 52mm

Robust. 1st upper labial scale greatly enlarged; remainder small, granular and the same as adj. scales. **Original tail short, thick, spade-like, blunt-tipped, with scales on dorsal surface uniformly large, arranged as mosaic, not in transverse rows.** Scales on nape and dorsal body granular, just slightly larger than adj. granules. Subdigital lamellae minute, with a pair of small terminal plates. Shades of brown with dark reticulum, broad pale stripe from eye to snout, and sometimes pale spots on body. ■ **NOTES** Nthn NT s. to Elsey NP, presumably in open woodland on compacted, possibly stony soils. Probably shelters in vertical spider holes, blocking the shaft with tail, and a likely termite specialist. ■ **SEE ALSO** *D. barraganae*; *D. conspicillatus*; *D. custos.*

Kenneally's Gecko *Diplodactylus kenneallyi* SVL 47mm

Robust, with short swollen **tail with regular rings of large scales. Rostral scale not contacting nostril. Subdigital lamellae moderately enlarged granules and terminal plates.** Brown, paler on vertebral region with chocolate brown flanks and many white lateral dots. ■ **NOTES** Known only from the vicinity of Lake Buchanan in the Gibson Desert, WA.

Diplodactylus galeatus.
George Gill Ranges, NT. S. Wilson

Diplodactylus granariensis rex.
Millbillillie Stn, WA. S. Wilson

Diplodactylus granariensis granariensis.
Charles Darwin Nat Res., WA. S. Wilson

Diplodactylus hillii.
Katherine, NT. P. Horner

Diplodactylus kenneallyi.
Lake Buchanan area, WA. R. Miller

Kluge's Gecko *Diplodactylus klugei* SVL 58mm

Slender and short-faced, with **rostral scale contacting nostril. Subdigital lamellae granular, with enlarged terminal plates**. Pale brown to reddish brown with a series of large, dark-edged pale dorsal blotches (occasionally a broad pale vertebral stripe) and scattered pale lateral spots. Top of head pale with dark brown posterior edge. ■ **NOTES** Arid shrublands in Carnarvon Basin and mid-w. coast, from s. of Shark Bay n. to Giralia. ■ **SEE ALSO** *D. pulcher.*

Desert Fat-tailed Gecko *Diplodactylus laevis* SVL 65mm

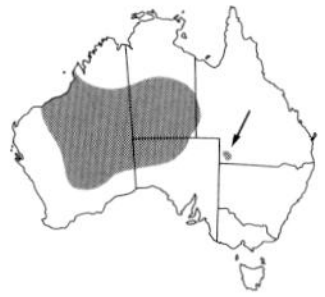

Robust. Only **1st upper labial scale greatly enlarged**; remainder small, granular and the same as adj. scales. **Original tail short, thick, spade-like with long acute attenuated tip; scales on dorsal surface of tail in transverse rows**, incl. alternating rows of large and small scales. **Scales on nape and top of head plate-like, considerably larger than granules on side of neck**, and **mid-dorsal scales on body plate-like, noticeably larger than adj. dorsolateral scales**. Subdigital lamellae minute, with a pair of small terminal plates. Shades of brown with prominent **broad pale stripe from eye to snout**, dark reticulum and usually fine pale spots, particularly on flanks. ■ **NOTES** Widespread across arid interior from Dampier Pen. through Pilbara and Gt. Victoria Desert to sthn NT. Apparently isolated pop. in sw. Qld. Occupies various open habitats favouring compacted sandy loams, hard clays and possibly stony soils. ■ **SEE ALSO** *D. ameyi*; *D. bilybara*; *D. custos*; *D. conspicillatus*; *D. platyurus.*

Speckled Stone Gecko *Diplodactylus lateroides* SVL 51mm

Short, thick, cylindrical tail. Rostral scale contacts nostril. **Labial scales low, wider than high**. Subdigital lamellae circular and paired at base, single and circular to transversely oblong distally, with pair of moderately enlarged terminal plates. **Rusty brown to brownish black** with irregularly sized and shaped paler blotches tending to join, forming ill-defined vertebral stripe or broken series of blotches. ■ **NOTES** Hard, stony areas of laterite or granite with woodlands of jarrah, marri or wandoo along Darling Ra. s. of Perth. Sthn. pop. occurs in Stirling Ra. ■ **SEE ALSO** *D. polyopthalmus*; *D. calcicolus.*

Pilbara Stone Gecko *Diplodactylus mitchelli* SVL 64mm

Robust, with very **large dorsal scales**, short thick tail, and **rostral scale contacting nostril. Subdigital lamellae large and broad, with large terminal plates**. Brown to reddish brown with dark-edged pale vertebral stripe with irregular lateral extensions on either side, and sometimes dark reticulations and flecks on body. ■ **NOTES** Heavy to stony and cracking clay soils with grasses and sparse shrubs in Pilbara region from Dampier to Cockeraga R.

Diplodactylus klugei.
Woodleigh Stn district, WA.
B. Maryan

Diplodactylus laevis.
Nappa Merrie Stn, Qld. S. Wilson

Diplodactylus lateroides.
Mt Dale, WA. S. Wilson

Diplodactylus mitchelli.
Dampier district, WA. S. Wilson

Cloudy Stone Gecko *Diplodactylus nebulosus* SVL 56mm

Short, thick, cylindrical tail. Rostral scale contacts nostril. **Labial scales as high as wide.** Subdigital lamellae circular and rarely transversely oblong, with pair of moderately enlarged terminal plates. Pale to dark brown with large, irregular paler dorsal blotches, sometimes joined to form a continuous, irregular and wavy stripe, and each often containing a short transverse row of fine pale spots.
■ **NOTES** Eucalypt woodlands on hard surfaces such as sandstone outcrops and laterite break-aways, occasionally on softer sands, along sthn w. coast. Sthn pop. occurs in vicinity of Lesueur NP, and up to 30km inland from Green Head and Jurien. Nthn pop. is in vicinity of Geraldton, incl. Yetna, Moresby Ra. and Howawatha Nat. Res. n. to Lower Hutt R.
■ **SEE ALSO** *D. polyophthalmus.*

Ornate Gecko *Diplodactylus ornatus* SVL 58mm

Relatively slender and long-tailed, with **rostral scale contacting nostril. Subdigital lamellae large and transverse, with enlarged terminal plates.** Grey to brown above with a broad pale vertebral stripe forking forward from nape and extending back to tail-tip, and a series of pale lateral blotches.
■ **NOTES** Dry to arid coastal dunes and sand-plains on w. coast, from Exmouth Gulf s. to Jurien and adjacent hinterland.

Eastern Fat-tailed Gecko *Diplodactylus platyurus* SVL 55mm

Robust. **All upper labial scales small and granular (1st not enlarged). Snout finely tapered when viewed from above and steeply sloping along dorsal surface. Original tail short, thick, spade-like and blunt-tipped,** with scales on dorsal surface in transverse rows; usually uniform in size but sometimes incl. alternating rows of large and small scales. Scales on nape small and granular, just slightly larger than granules on side of neck, and mid-dorsal scales on body plate-like, noticeably larger than adj. dorsolateral scales. Shades of brown with **little or no pale streak from eye to snout,** a fine dark reticulum or extensive dark pigment, generally reduced on vertebral zone, and variable pale spotting. ■ **NOTES** Widespread from ne. coast and ne. interior extending from Edward R. on Cape York Pen. s. to Blackdown Tableland area. Dry open woodlands and shrublands, on clays and compacted sands. ■ **SEE ALSO** *D. ameyi; D. barraganae.*

Diplodactylus nebulosus.
Moresby Range, WA. B. Maryan

Diplodactylus ornatus.
Marchagee Reserve, WA.
S. Wilson

Diplodactylus platyurus.
Moranbah area, Qld. S. Wilson

Spotted Sandplain Gecko *Diplodactylus polyophthalmus* SVL 54mm

Short, thick, cylindrical tail. Rostral scale contacts nostril. **Labial scales low, wider than high**. Subdigital lamellae circular and paired at base, single and circular to transversely oblong distally, with pair of moderately enlarged terminal plates. **Brownish grey** with obscure paler spots, often joined to form larger dorsal blotches and sometimes an ill-defined vertebral stripe. ■ **NOTES** Sandy substrates with Banksia and eucalypt woodlands on coastal and adj. sandplains n. of Swan R. Sthn pop. occurs from nthn Perth suburbs to Yanchep NP while nthn pop. extends from Cataby area n. to Eaneabba. ■ **SEE ALSO** *D. lateroides*; *D. nebulosus*.

Pretty Gecko *Diplodactylus pulcher* SVL 62mm

Slender and short-faced with **rostral scale not contacting nostril. Subdigital lamellae granular, with enlarged terminal plates**. Pale brown to reddish brown with a series of large, dark-edged, pale dorsal blotches or broad pale vertebral stripe, and scattered pale lateral spots. Top of head pale yellowish brown edged posteriorly with dark brown. ■ **NOTES** Arid to semi-arid zones from mid-wstn WA and Darling Ra. near Perth to nw. SA. Favours shrublands on heavy soils. ■ **SEE ALSO** *D. klugei*. ■ **STATUS** Rare (SA).

Southern Pilbara Beak-faced Gecko *Diplodactylus savagei* SVL 50mm

Very short, thick cylindrical tail, **beak-like snout with rostral scale not contacting nostril**, and **moderately enlarged paired subdigital lamellae**. Rich reddish brown with **large yellow dorsal spots aligned or joined to form 8-12 transverse rows** between nape and hips. An **abrupt junction between dark flanks and pale ventral surfaces**. ■ **NOTES** Stony hills with spinifex, also occasionally termitaria, cracking clays and loamy plains, in Pilbara and Ashburton regions. Extends from Wodgina to edge of Gt Sandy Desert, incl. Hamersley Ra., and s. to Barlee Ra. and Waldburg Stn. Possibly a termite specialist. ■ **SEE ALSO** *D. galaxias*.

Tessellated Gecko *Diplodactylus tessellatus* SVL 50mm

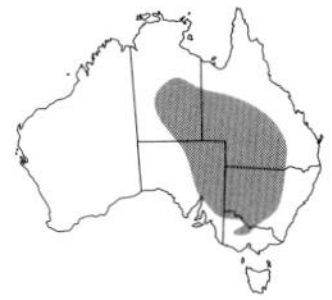

Robust, with **short tail with regular rings of large conical scales and rostral scale contacting nostril**. Subdigital lamellae slightly enlarged, with large terminal plates. Grey to reddish brown above with a variable pattern of darker mottling, often incl. a series of pale spots, usually paired, along the mid-dorsal surface and onto tail. **Dark blotches usually present on belly**. ■ **NOTES** Cracking alluvial clays. Shelters in soil cracks, insect and spider holes.

Diplodactylus polyopthalmus. Dianella, WA.
R. Ellis

Diplodactylus pulcher. Blotched form.
Warburton district, WA. S. Wilson

Diplodactylus pulcher. Striped form.
Charles Darwin Nature Reserve, WA. S. Wilson

Diplodactylus savagei.
Marble Bar area, WA. B. Maryan

Diplodactylus tessellatus.
Morney Stn, Qld. S. Wilson

Eastern Stone Gecko *Diplodactylus vittatus* SVL 50mm

Robust, with moderately short, thick tail and **rostral scale contacting nostril.** Subdigital lamellae in a large series with relatively large terminal plates. Brown or grey with a **narrow pale zigzagging vertebral stripe** (occasionally a series of blotches) **extending forward onto head as a pale cap,** and usually **simple pale lateral spots without dark margins.** ■ **NOTES** Open shrublands to well-forested areas. Penetrates into cool damp regions better than any other *Diplodactylus.* ■ **SEE ALSO** *D. calcicolus; D. furcosus.*

Desert Wood Gecko *Diplodactylus wiru* SVL 54mm

Robust with short thick tail. Rostral scale contacts nostril. Subdigital lamellae in a large series with relatively large terminal plates. Medium to dark brownish grey with **broadly dark-edged,** straight to zigzagging pale vertebral stripe, **expanding onto the head as a pale cap.** Upper flanks with **a series of dark edged pale spots.** ■ **NOTES** Sthn Great Victoria Desert, associated with mallee vegetation on sand with extensive ground litter. ■ **SEE ALSO** *D. calcicolus; D. furcosus; D. granariensis.*

Genus *Hesperoedura*

Reticulated Velvet Gecko *Hesperoedura reticulata* SVL 70mm

Sole member of genus. Dorsally depressed, with **dorsal scales minute,** smooth and granular, **much smaller than ventrals;** single cloacal spur; tail long, moderately dorsally depressed; **and subdigital lamellae enlarged at base, divided distally and terminating in a pair of enlarged plates (fig).**

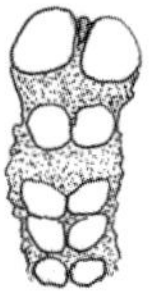

Grey to greyish brown with a broad, dark-edged paler vertebral zone enclosing a broken dark vertebral stripe and irregular dark transverse lines. ■ **NOTES** Woodlands in sthn interior of WA, from Wheatbelt and Goldfields to Darling Range. Favours smooth-barked eucalypts incl. Gimlet, Salmon Gum, Wandoo and Powderbark, sheltering in hollow trunks and limbs.

Genus *Lucasium*

Eleven small to moderate-sized, slender terrestrial spp. with **narrow digits about 7 times as long as wide,** subdigital lamellae usually reduced, ranging from minute and spiny with terminal plates absent (A) to moderately enlarged with a pair of terminal plates (B), **clusters of 2–5 spines on each side of cloaca,** relatively long limbs and generally **long slender tails.**

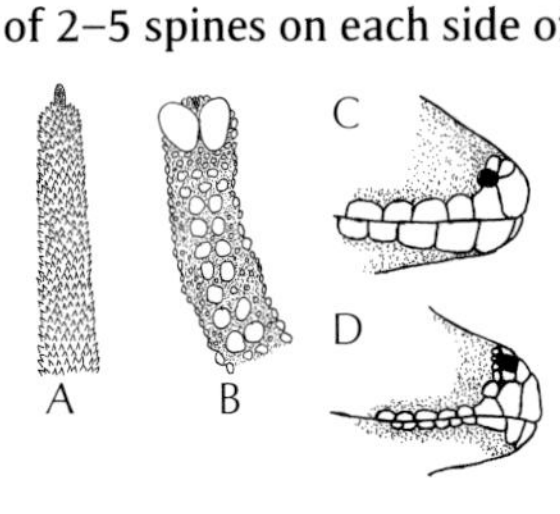

Swift inhabitants of mainly dry open areas, usually sheltering in disused insect and spider holes. Spp. are identified by pattern and whether nostril contacts rostral scale (C) or is separated (D). ■ **SEE ALSO** *Diplodactylus; Rhynchoedura.*

Diplodactylus vittatus.
Sundown NP, Qld. S. Wilson

Diplodactylus vittatus.
Idalia NP, Qld. S. Wilson

Diplodactylus wiru.
Queen Victoria Springs Nature Reserve, WA. B. Maryan

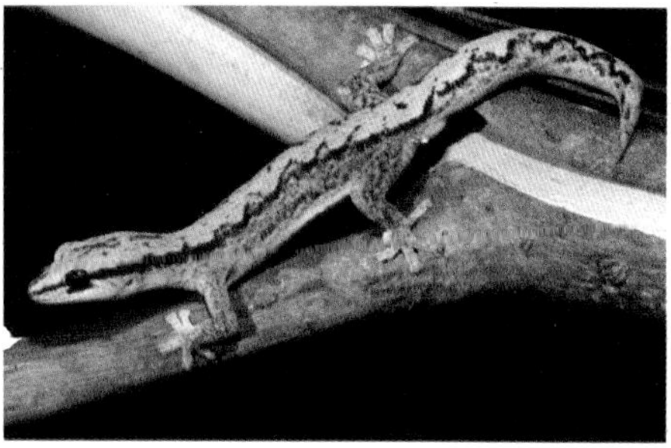

Hesperoedura reticulata.
Bolgart area, WA. S. Wilson.

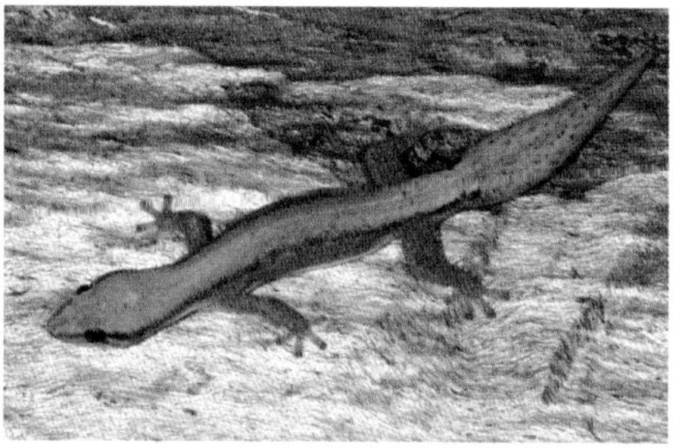

Hesperoedura reticulata.
Charles Darwin Nat. Res., WA. S. Wilson

White-spotted Ground Gecko *Lucasium alboguttatum* SVL 57mm

Rostral scale contacts nostril. Subdigital lamellae granular with moderately large terminal plates. Tan to reddish brown with large, ragged pale dorsal blotches, white lateral spots and a broad dark V-shape on each side of snout. ■ **NOTES** Sand-plains along mid-w. coast from Coral Bay to Perth and adj. inland areas. Shelters in insect and spider holes.

Southern Sandplain Gecko *Lucasium bungabinna* SVL 53mm

Rostral scale contacts nostril. Subdigital lamellae large, mostly single with large terminal plates. Pale to medium tan with prominent, straight to wavy-edged pale vertebral stripe, forking forward on nape and irregular to broken on tail. Flanks spotted. ■ **NOTES** Sandy deserts featuring spinifex or chenopods in Bungalbin and Yellabinna land systems bordering sthn edge of Great Victoria Desert. ■ **SEE ALSO** *L. stenodactylus.*

Gibber Gecko *Lucasium byrnei* SVL 55mm

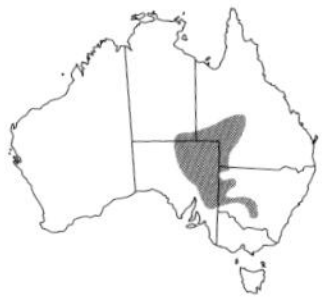

Large-headed, with **rostral scale not contacting nostril**. Subdigital lamellae granular with moderately large terminal plates. Pale yellowish brown to dark reddish brown with 4 irregular pale dorsal blotches and scattered reddish conical tubercles over body. Top of head paler with dark spots. ■ **NOTES** Open shrublands on heavy to stony soils.

Beaded Gecko *Lucasium damaeum* SVL 55mm

All subdigital lamellae minute and spinose. Rostral scale contacts nostril. Pale reddish brown with pale vertebral stripe (straight-edged, deeply notched or broken into a series of blotches), and often a lateral series of large whitish spots. Top of head pale with a narrow dark line from snout to each eye, broadening behind eye and meeting at back of head. ■ **NOTES** Arid to semi-arid sandy areas, usually with spinifex. A swift-moving gecko that forages in open areas and shelters in insect and spider holes.

Pale-striped Ground Gecko *Lucasium immaculatum* SVL 54mm

Rostral scale not contacting nostril. Subdigital lamellae moderately enlarged granules with moderately large terminal plates. Reddish brown with a narrow pale vertebral stripe forking at nape and continuing through eyes to nostrils. A series of narrow pale vertical bars extend from this stripe onto flanks. ■ **NOTES** Shrublands on heavy to stony soils in arid zones.

Main's Ground Gecko *Lucasium maini* SVL 54mm

Large-eyed, with **rostral scale contacting nostril. Subdigital lamellae minute granules, with tiny terminal plates**. Fawn to reddish brown with a series of dark-edged irregular pale dorsal blotches and pale lateral spots. Top of the head pale with scattered dark flecks. ■ **NOTES** Most open, semi-arid habitats from sand-plains to heavy soils. Shelters in spider holes.

Lucasium alboguttatum.
Kalbarri, WA. S. Wilson

Lucasium bungabinna.
Bungalbin Hill area, WA. B. Maryan

Lucasium byrnei.
Betoota district, Qld. S. Wilson

Lucasium damaeum.
Sturt NP, NSW, G. Swan

Lucasium immaculatum.
Morney Stn, Qld. S. Wilson

Lucasium maini.
Charles Darwin Nat. Res. WA. S. Wilson

Yellow-snouted Ground Gecko *Lucasium occultum* SVL 41mm

Rostral scale contacting or separated from nostril. **Subdigital lamellae enlarged, with moderately large terminal plates.** Dark brown above with 4 large, squarish, paler brown dorsal blotches and prominent scattered white spots on flanks and limbs. Top of head paler reddish brown. ■ **NOTES** Woodland with a dense grassy understorey in the Alligator R. region. ■ **STATUS** Endangered (C'wealth); vulnerable (NT).

Mottled Ground Gecko *Lucasium squarrosum* SVL 57mm

Rostral scale not contacting nostril in w. of range, but contacting in e. Subdigital lamellae small and granular, with small terminal plates. Reddish brown with large, dark-edged, irregular pale blotches and spots, occasionally joined to form a wavy-edged vertebral stripe. ■ **NOTES** Acacia shrublands on heavy loams.

Box-patterned Gecko *Lucasium steindachneri* SVL 55mm

Rostral scale not contacting nostril. Subdigital lamellae slightly enlarged with large terminal plates. Pale to dark brown above with pale stripes from above each eye to base of tail, usually connected at about 4 points, forming oval patches of darker ground colour. In n., dorsal pattern often broken into a series of large pale blotches ■ **NOTES** Shrublands and open woodlands on heavy to stony soils in arid and semi-arid areas. ■ **STATUS** Rare (SA).

Sand-plain Gecko *Lucasium stenodactylus* SVL 57mm

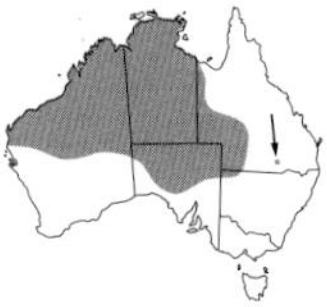

Probably comprises several spp., **with rostral scale usually not contacting nostril. Subdigital lamellae small and granular with small to vestigal terminal plates.** Colour and pattern variable: pinkish to reddish brown with only scattered pale spots, or a broad prominent cream vertebral stripe forking forward on nape and extending back to tail-tip, and prominent pale lateral spots. ■ **NOTES** Widespread through a variety of habitats in arid and semi-arid areas. ■ **SEE ALSO** *L. bungabinna.* ■ **STATUS** Vulnerable (NSW).

Pilbara Ground Gecko *Lucasium wombeyi* SVL 54mm

Rostral scale contacts nostril. Subdigital lamellae a paired series of large granules with large terminal plates. Pale to dark reddish brown with a series of darker reticulations or bands, and usually prominent pale dots over flanks and limbs. ■ **NOTES** Heavy soils of the Pilbara region.

Lucasium occultum.
Kapalga, NT. J. Wombey

Lucasium squarrosum.
Hamelin Pool Stn district, WA. R. Browne-Cooper

Lucasium steindachneri.
White Mountains NP, Qld. S. Wilson

Lucasium stenodactylus. Ethabuka, Qld.
S. Wilson

Lucasium stenodactylus.
North West Cape, WA. S. Wilson

Lucasium stenodactylus.
Kununurra, WA. S. Wilson

Lucasium wombeyi.
Marillana Stn district, WA. S. Wilson

Genus *Nebulifera*

Robust Velvet Gecko *Nebulifera robusta* SVL 80mm

Sole member of genus. Dorsally depressed, with **dorsal scales minute**, smooth and granular, **much smaller than ventrals**; 2-5 cloacal spurs; **broad, depressed tail; subdigital lamellae enlarged at base, divided distally and terminating in a pair of enlarged plates (fig)**; and simple dorsal pattern of angular blotches. Brown to blackish brown with large, squarish, dark-edged pale blotches down back and original tail. Regenerated tail mottled. ■ **NOTES** Coast and interior from ne. NSW to mid-estn Qld. DSF, woodlands and rock outcrops. Shelters under bark, in hollows and rock crevices, and frequently occupies human dwellings. **SEE ALSO** *Amalosia; Oedura*

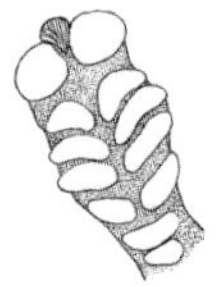

Velvet Geckos Genus *Oedura*

Fourteen moderately large, dorsally depressed spp. **Dorsal scales large**, smooth and granular, **about the same size as ventrals**; one or more cloacal spurs; and **subdigital lamellae enlarged at base, divided distally and terminating in a pair of enlarged plates (fig.).** Dorsal pattern comprises bold to weak **bands, spots or blotches, often strikingly brighter on juv.**, and no indication of vertebral stripe. Colour and pattern usually highly distinctive for each sp. ■ **NOTES** Widespread in woodlands and rock outcrops in estn and nthn Aust. with isolates in arid sthn, central and wstn Aust. Arboreal, rock-inhabiting or both, sheltering under loose bark or rock slabs, in crevices and hollows. ■ **SEE ALSO** *Amalosia; Nebulifera.*

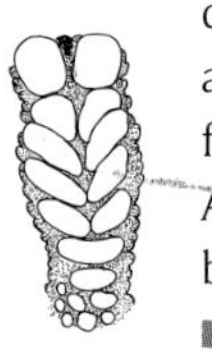

Gulf Marbled Velvet Gecko *Oedura bella* SVL 92mm

Variable, banded to spotted. **Tail relatively short, narrower than head and slightly depressed. All subdigital lamellae narrower than apical pair**. Typically dark purplish brown with about 5 cream to bright yellow bands between nape and hips and 4–7 on original tail. Juv. has broad, prominent sharp-edged bands without spots. With age banded pattern fragments; bands develop ragged edges, dark centres appear within pale bands and pale spots within dark interspaces, until all pattern may be overridden by an irregular mosaic of pale spots and blotches. ■ **NOTES** Rock-inhabiting, on outcrops and gorges on sthn and wstn edges of Gulf of Carpentaria. Extends from Mt Isa area, Qld, to McArthur R. and Borroloola areas, NT. Also Groot Edlandt and an isolated pop. on nthn edge of Barkly Tablelands. ■ **SEE ALSO** *O. cincta; O. marmorata.*

Northern Velvet Gecko *Oedura castelnaui* SVL 90mm

Banded, with plump, moderately long, depressed tail. Yellow-orange to yellowish brown with 5 broad dark-edged **pale bands almost as wide or wider than intervening ground colour** between nape and hips, and about 5 pale bands on original tail; regenerated tails irregularly streaked. Top of head pale, enclosed by broad black stripe sweeping back from each nostril through eye to meet on back of head. ■ **NOTES** DSF, woodlands and rock outcrops. ■ **SEE ALSO** *O. cincta.*

Nebulifera robusta. Kurwongbah, Qld. S. Wilson

Oedura bella. Mt Isa area, Qld. S. Eipper

Oedura castelnaui. White Mountains NP, Qld. S. Wilson

Inland Marbled Velvet Gecko *Oedura cincta* SVL 108mm

Variable, banded to spotted. **Tail moderately long, narrower than head and roughly circular in cross-section. Subdigital lamellae flared, wider than apical pair on 3rd and 4th fingers. Rostral scale fully divided by rostral crease.** Typically dark purplish brown with **dark stripe from behind eye, across nape,** about 5–6 pale bands (grey in estn pop. and more yellow in central pop.) between nape and hips and 5–8 on original tail. Juv. has simple, broad, prominent sharp-edged bands, but pattern fragments with age. Pale bands develop dark centres and ragged edges, and pale spots form within dark interspaces. The original banded pattern is often overridden by irregular mosaic of pale spots and blotches. ■ **NOTES** Estn pop. is primarily arboreal, occasionally rock-inhabiting, in dry woodlands of Cooper and Darling Basins in wstn Qld and interior of NSW. Apparently isolated pops occur in SA; on rocks in Flinders Ra. and on *Allocasuarina* trees in nthn Murray R. area. Central pop., in nthn MacDonnell Ra. area in sthn NT, is rock-inhabiting on outcrops and gorges. STATUS Rare (SA – as *O. marmorata*) ■ **SEE ALSO** *O. castelnaui; O. bella; O. luritja.*

Northern Spotted Velvet Gecko *Oedura coggeri* SVL 70mm

Spotted, with slightly depressed tail. Dull yellowish grey to orange-brown with irregular transverse rows of dark-edged cream spots, tending to join to form transverse bars. Dark margins may be so broad as to obscure the ground colour. A dark-edged pale band extends across nape, its leading edge continuing as a dark stripe through eyes to nostrils. ■ **NOTES** Rocky areas in woodlands on se. Cape York Pen., Qld.

Fringe-toed Velvet Gecko *Oedura filicipoda* SVL 105mm

Banded, with **short broad tail** and distinctive **fringe composed of laterally expanded lamellae around each digit.** Dark brown with prominent yellowish spots on head, body and limbs, widely spaced pale brown bands between nape and hips and **3 pale bands on original tail.** Regenerated tails are mottled with greenish yellow. Juv. has broad prominent sharp-edged bands without spots. ■ **NOTES** Kimberley region, from Mitchell Plateau s. to Mt Daglish. Rock-inhabiting, in sandstone caves and on rock faces. ■ **SEE ALSO** *O. murrumanu.*

Western Marbled Velvet Gecko *Oedura fimbria* SVL 104mm

Variable. Banded to spotted. Tail moderately long, narrower than head and roughly circular in cross-section. Subdigital lamellae flared, wider than apical pair on 3rd and 4th fingers. Typically dark purplish brown with about 5–6 indistinct pale bands, often with darker central regions, between nape and hips and 5–8 on original tail. Juv. has simple, broad, prominent sharp-edged bands, but with age the pattern fragments. Pale bands develop dark centres and ragged edges, and pale spots form within dark interspaces. The original banded pattern is often overridden by an irregular mosaic of pale spots and blotches. ■ **NOTES** Rock-inhabiting, in semi-arid Pilbara, Gascoyne and Murchison regions, WA. Associated with ranges, gorges, caves and break-aways.

Oedura cincta. Eastern population. Morven area, Qld. S. Wilson

Oedura cincta. Central population. Emily Gap, NT. S. Wilson

Oedura coggeri. Chillagoe, Qld. S. Wilson

Oedura filicipoda. Juvenile. Mitchell Plateau, WA. S. Wilson

Oedura filicipoda. Adult. Mitchell Falls, WA. G. Shea

Oedura fimbria. Edah Stn, WA. S. Wilson

Jewelled Velvet Gecko *Oedura gemmata* SVL 103mm

Spotted, with relatively long, broad tail. Pinkish brown to black with many yellow to brown spots over head, body and limbs. Original tails have about 11 narrow white bands. Regenerated tails have transversely aligned pale flecks. ■ **NOTES** Arnhem Escarpment and associated outliers, NT. Shelters in rock crevices and forages on exposed faces.

Gracile Velvet Gecko *Oedura gracilis* SVL 85mm

Slender and **banded,** with **flat head and body** and long, slender, round tail. Pinkish brown with **6–10 dark-edged, pale yellowish brown bands between nape and hips** and a dark stripe from nostril through eye to ear, contrasting with pale lips. ■ **NOTES** Sandstone escarpments and granite outcrops of the Kimberley, s. to King Leopold Ra. and e. to Mt Nyulasy and El Questro.

Quinkan Gecko *Oedura jowalbinna* SVL 69mm

Plain-backed with simple pale bands across neck and base of tail. Pale pinkish grey with faint freckling and 2 dark-edged pale bands. ■ **NOTES** Currently known only from Jowalbinna Station, on heavily dissected escarpments of the Laura Sandstones, Qld. Rock-inhabiting, on sandstone overhangs.

Mereenie Velvet Gecko *Oedura luritja* SVL 99mm

Banded. Tail moderately long and narrow. **Rostral scale less than 50 per cent divided, and usually one cloacal spur.** Purplish brown with 5–6 relatively straight and well-defined yellow bands or transverse series of blotches between nape and hips and 7–8 on original tail. When active at night, dark hues are silvery grey and yellow bands are brighter. **No indication of dark stripe from behind eye across nape.** ■ **NOTES** James Ra., George Gill Ra. and associated sandstone ranges of sthn NT, from Rainbow Valley Conservation Res. w. to Watarrka NP. Restricted to sandstone, and often associated with tight, deep cracks and vertical rock faces. ■ **SEE ALSO** *O. cincta.*

Northern Marbled Velvet Gecko *Oedura marmorata* SVL 97mm

Variable. **Banded to spotted. Tail bulbous, depressed, wider than head and sharply tapered.** Typically dark purplish brown with about 5 cream to bright yellow bands between nape and hips and 4–5 on original tail, sometimes combined with or largely replaced by dark pigment within pale bands and bright pale spots within dark interspaces. Juv. has broad, prominent sharp-edged bands without spots. With age these develop dark centres, ragged edges and may break up with pale spots sometimes overriding pattern. ■ **NOTES** Rock-inhabiting, on gorges and outcrops of nthn NT. ■ **SEE ALSO** *O. bella.*

Oedura gemmata. El Sharana, NT. S. Wilson

Oedura gracilis. El Questro Stn, WA. S. Wilson

Oedura jowalbinna. Jowalbinna Station, Qld. M. Anthony

Oedura luritja. James Range, NT. P. McDonald

Oedura marmorata. Katherine Gorge, NT. S. Wilson

Ocellated Velvet Gecko *Oedura monilis* SVL 85mm

Blotched, with long, slightly depressed tail. Yellowish brown with darker flecks, about 12 dark-edged pale blotches from nape to tail-tip (either arranged as pairs or narrowly joined to form transverse dumbbell shapes) and dark streak through eye to side of neck. Regenerated tails flecked with dark brown. ■ **NOTES** Rock outcrops, open forests and woodlands, particularly ironbarks and cypress pines.

Limestone Range Velvet Gecko *Oedura murrumanu* SVL 103mm

Banded, with relatively flat head and **slightly to moderately swollen tail**. Subdigital lamellae in 6–7 pairs under 4th toe, and **expanded to form lateral fringes on distal portions of each digit**. Purplish brown with narrow pale nuchal band, three broader pale bands across body and **5 pale bands across original tail**. With age, the sharply delineated pattern becomes less discernible with increasing amounts of light and dark mottling. ■ **NOTES** Deeply dissected limestone formations in Oscar Ra., sw. Kimberley region, WA. ■ **SEE ALSO** *O. filicipoda.*

Southern Spotted Velvet Gecko *Oedura tryoni* SVL 87mm

Spotted, with slightly depressed tail. Brown, yellowish brown to reddish brown with many small, prominent, dark-edged pale spots over body, limbs and tail. ■ **NOTES** DSF woodlands and rock outcrops, particularly granite or sandstone, from ne. nw. to mid-estn Qld. Shelters in rock crevices, under slabs and sometimes under bark.

Giant Tree Geckos and Giant Cave Geckos
Genus *Pseudothecadactylus*

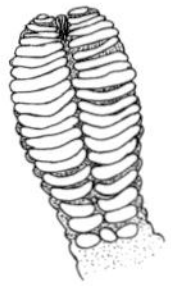

Three very large spp. with cylindrical prehensile **tails tipped below with adhesive lamellae**. Digits broad, flat and, except for innermost, clawed. Subdigital lamellae form broad, divided transverse series along length of digit (fig.). Body scales small and smooth. ■ **NOTES** Nthn Aust. Extremely agile arboreal and rock-inhabiting geckos, can leap between boughs and rocks, and cling with ease using their prehensile tails tipped with specialised lamellae.

Giant Tree Gecko *Pseudothecadactylus australis* SVL 120mm

Deep-headed, with weak pattern; pale brown to olive grey with a series of approx. **6 dark-edged, transversely aligned pale blotches** which often break into pairs, particularly on nape. ■ **NOTES** Nthn Cape York Pen. and islands of Torres Strait. Inhabits woodlands (particularly paperbark), monsoon forests and mangroves. Shelters in hollows, often betraying its presence with a gruff bark when approached by day. In addition to eating invertebrates, has been observed lapping sap.

Oedura monilis. Chesterton Range, Qld.
S. Wilson

Oedura murrumanu. Oscar Range, WA.
S. Mahony

Oedura tryoni. Ipswich region, Qld.
S. Wilson

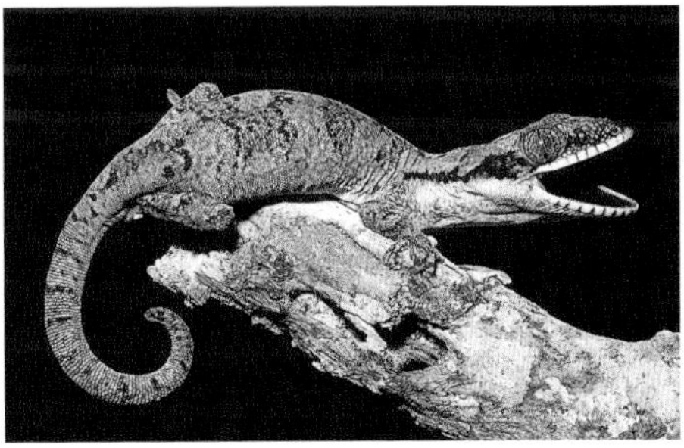

Pseudothecadactylus australis. Prince of Wales Is., Qld. S. Wilson

Pseudothecadactylus australis. Lockerbie Scrub, Qld. S. Wilson

Western Giant Cave Gecko *Pseudothecadactylus cavaticus* SVL 115mm

Cream with 5–7 dark-edged brown bands on body and 9–11 on tail. Head whitish mottled with brown. ■ **NOTES** Restricted to large sandstone outcrops of nw. Kimberley region. Rock-inhabiting, sheltering in rock fissures and caves and foraging on exposed vertical faces.

Northern Giant Cave Gecko *Pseudothecadactylus lindneri* SVL 96mm

Dark purplish brown with irregular cream to pale orange bands, often disrupted on vertebral region. Original tail prominently banded with pale yellow and blackish brown; regenerated tails uniform brown. ■ **NOTES** Sandstone escarpments and caves in the massive formations of wstn Arnhem Land. Shelters in rock crevices, foraging on walls and ceilings of caves and overhangs and often venturing into boughs of adjacent figs. Most active on warm drizzly evenings.

Beaked Geckos
Genus *Rhynchoedura*

Six small, short-limbed spp. with slender, cylindrical body; short, **pointed beak-like snout**; long tail; and no enlarged labial scales. All digits clawed, with small granular subdigital lamellae and a minute pair of terminal plates (fig A.). All spp. similar; shades of reddish brown with darker reticulations, pale spots and pale rim to eye. Identification can be difficult without genetics and locality, with features incl. one or three enlarged mental scales, and number and arrangement of preanal pores; two (fig. B) in contact or separated, or 4-6 in a row (fig. C). ■ **NOTES** Widespread, occurring in open arid and semiarid regions of all mainland states. Terrestrial. Occasionally found under debris, but normally shelter in vertical shafts of spider holes. Some, probably all, feed wholly or largely on termites. ■ **SEE ALSO** *Diplodactylus; Lucasium.*

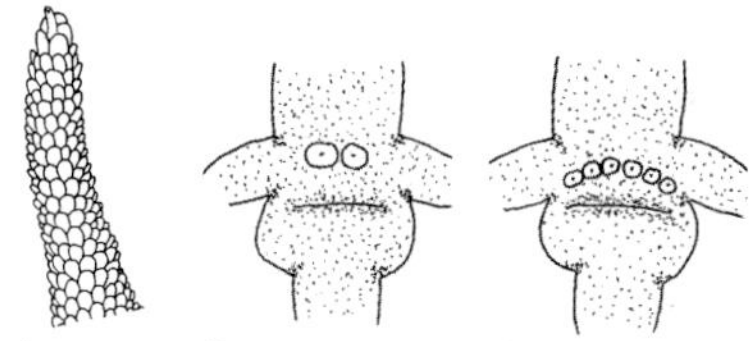

A B C

Border Beaked Gecko *Rhynchoedura angusta* SVL 51 mm

Single enlarged mental scale, **median rostral groove usually strong extending down 30% and up to 55% of scale**, two enlarged preanal pores in contact, relatively flat dorsal scales equal in size to ventrals, and cloacal spurs formed by one enlarged scale. Highly variable; shades of reddish brown with pale vertebral zone with wavy-edges tending to form transverse bars comprising merged spots, overlain on head and body with numerous, **similarly-sized** dark-edged white to pale yellow spots. ■ **NOTES** Mitchell grass and spinifex along narrow band of alluvial flood plains of Bulloo-Bancannia drainage division, from n. of Renmark, SA to Longreach, Qld. ■ **SEE ALSO** *R. eyrensis; R. mentalis; R. ormsbyi.*

Pseudothecadactylus cavaticus. Red Cone Creek, King Leopold Range, WA. S. Wilson

Pseudothecadactylus lindneri. Arnhem escarpment, NT. S. Wilson

Rhynchoedura angusta. Mutawintji NP, NSW. G. Swan

Eyre Basin Beaked Gecko *Rhynchoedura eyrensis* SVL 51 mm

Single enlarged mental scale, **median rostral groove usually strong extending down 30% and up to 70% of scale**, two enlarged preanal pores in contact, relatively flat dorsal scales equal in size to ventrals, and cloacal spurs formed by one enlarged scale. Highly variable; shades of reddish brown with pale vertebral zone with wavy-edges sometimes forming transverse bars comprising merged spots, overlain on head and body with numerous, dark-edged white to pale yellow spots, **tending to be largest on flanks.** ■ **NOTES** Floodplains, sandy and stony terrain in Simpson, Strzelecki and Sturt Stony Deserts and Channel Country across Lake Eyre Basin. ■ **SEE ALSO** *R. angusta; R. mentalis; R. ormsbyi; R. ornata.*

Brigalow Beaked Gecko *Rhynchoedura mentalis* SVL 50 mm

Three enlarged mental scales, no rostral median groove, two enlarged **preanal pores separated by 2-3 scales**, cloacal spurs comprising 2-3 enlarged scales. Dark brown to black with vertebral stripe tan and straight-edged, to pale and comprising interconnected blotches. Fine pale spots on flanks absent from vertebral zone, but sometimes transverse blotches connected to vertebral zone. ■ **NOTES** Mulga on clay soils at just two known sites, Mariala NP and north of Blackall, Qld. ■ **SEE ALSO** *R. angusta; R. eyrensis; R. ormsbyi.*

Eastern Beaked Gecko *Rhynchoedura ormsbyi* SVL 50 mm

Single enlarged mental scale, **median rostral groove usually strong extending down more than 50% and up to 100% of scale**, two enlarged preanal pores in contact, relatively flat dorsal scales equal in size to ventrals, and cloacal spurs formed by one enlarged scale. Highly variable; shades of reddish brown with pale, wavy-edged vertebral zone, overlain with numerous dark-edged white to pale yellow spots, **tending to be largest on flanks.** ■ **NOTES** Eastern arid zone from far nw. Vic to interior of Qld, incl. Murray-Darling Basin, Cobar Peneplain and Mulga Lands bioregion of NSW and Qld. Occupies alluvial flats, sand plains, mulga and eucalypt woodlands. ■ **SEE ALSO** *R. angusta; R. eyrensis; R. mentalis.* ■ **STATUS** Critically endangered (Vic – as *R. ornata).*

Western Beaked Gecko *Rhynchoedura ornata* SVL 57 mm

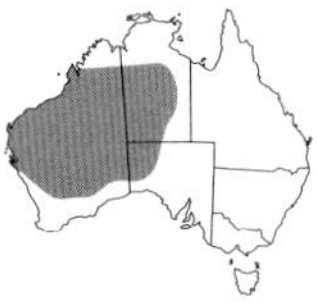

Single enlarged mental scale, **rostral scale usually without median groove,** two enlarged preanal pores in contact, relatively flat dorsal scales equal in size to ventrals, and cloacal spurs formed by one enlarged scale. Highly variable; shades of reddish brown with dark markings tending to form transverse bars, overlaid with numerous cream to yellow spots, their dark edges forming a reticulum. ■ **NOTES** Wstn arid zone, incl. spinifex deserts and mulga, e. to wstn portions of NT and SA. ■ **SEE ALSO** *R. eyrensis; R. sexapora.*

Rhynchoedura eyrensis.
Nappa Merrie Stn, Qld.
S. Wilson

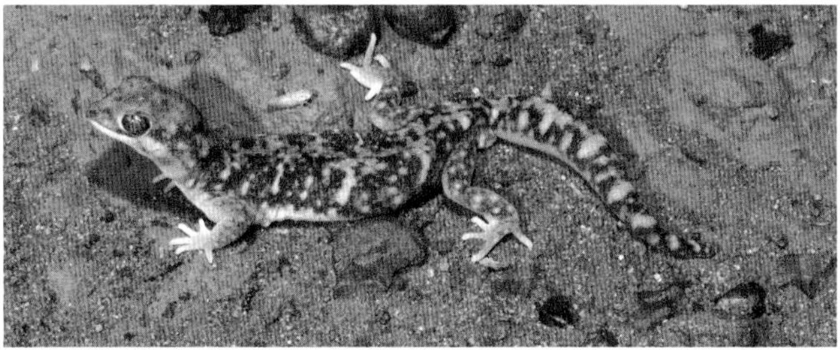

Rhynchoedura mentalis.
Cooladdi area, Qld. S. Wilson

Rhynchoedura ormsbyi.
Morven, Qld. S. Wilson

Rhynchoedura ornata.
King's Creek Stn, NT. S. Wilson

Northern Beaked Gecko *Rhynchoedura sexapora* SVL 48 mm

Single enlarged mental scale, **rostral scale with median groove**, 6 (occasionally 4) **preanal pores arranged in a shallow 'V', dorsal scales slightly gabled, smaller than ventrals**, and cloacal spurs formed by one enlarged scale. Dark brown with paler vertebral zone linked to transverse blotches or bars that extend to flanks, overlain with small pale spots, particularly on flanks. ■ **NOTES** Kimberley region, WA across nthn NT, in tropical woodlands on variety of soil types incl. laterites, sandplains, stony soils and clays. ■ **SEE ALSO** *R. ornata.*

Spiny-tailed, Striped and Jewelled Geckos
Genus *Strophurus*

Nineteen spp. with cylindrical tails and padded feet with **enlarged subdigital lamellae divided at base and single along digit, terminating in a pair of large plates (A)**. Some spp., generally called spiny-tailed geckos, have rows of tubercles along back, **tubercles or spines on tail, and bright coloured iris-rims**. The striped geckos and the Jewelled Gecko have simpler scales but distinctive, **prominent striped or spotted patterns**. Striped geckos are identified by pattern, build and whether the rostral scale contacts the nostril (B) or is separated (C). ■ **NOTES** Widespread wherever dry conditions prevail, from sthn mallee regions through the interior to the tropics. When alarmed, they have the unique ability to **squirt viscous repellent fluid from glands deep within the tail.** This is treacle-like, drying rapidly to cobweb-like filaments. Spiny-tailed geckos are often arboreal, sheltering in hollows, beneath bark or even clinging by day to stems in exposed sunlight. Striped and jewelled geckos live exclusively within spinifex and sedge tussocks. ■ **SEE ALSO** *Diplodactylus.*

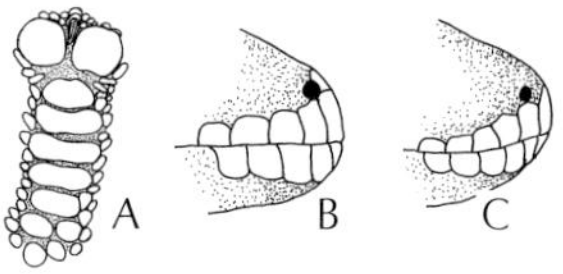

Thorn-tailed Gecko *Strophurus assimilis* SVL 78mm

Spiny-tailed, with **2 wavy or broken lines of large, orange-brown tubercles on back**. Tail spines short and arranged in rings, with largest aligned to form 2 dorsal rows. Grey with a series of dark-edged, paler, chain-like blotches on flanks. Iris pale grey with fine dark venation and black rim. **Mouth-lining dark blue.** ■ **NOTES** Semi-arid to arid shrublands in sthn interior of WA and Eyre Pen., SA. ■ **SEE ALSO** *S. intermedius.*

Northern Spiny-tailed Gecko *Strophurus ciliaris* SVL 89mm

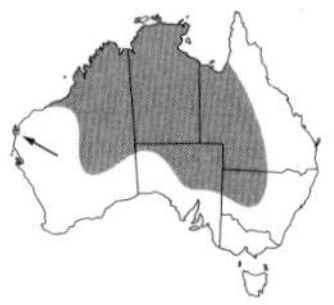

Spiny-tailed, with **long spines above eye, large tubercles scattered over back** and **2 impressive rows of long spines along top of tail. Mouth-lining yellow to orange**. Colouration variable; pale and virtually patternless to brown, sharply dotted with white and blotched with orange. ■ **SSP.** *S. c. ciliaris* has mostly orange spines on tail. Remaining caudal scales flat and granular. N. of range are largest and most spectacular. *S. c. aberrans* has mostly black spines and tubercles; remaining caudal scales are tubercular. ■ **NOTES** Very widespread in arid shrublands, spinifex deserts and tropical woodlands. *S. c. aberrans* occurs from the sw. Kimberley to the nw. coast and interior. Some sthn pops may represent separate undescribed ssp. ■ **SEE ALSO** *S. krisalys*; *S. wellingtonae.*

Rhynchoedura sexapora. Halls Creek area, WA. S. Wilson

Strophurus assimilis. Bungalbin Hills region, WA. B. Maryan

Strophurus ciliaris ciliaris. Katherine, NT. S. Wilson

Strophurus ciliaris aberrans. North West Cape, WA. S. Wilson

Congoo Gecko *Strophurus congoo* SVL 49mm

Slender with relatively short tail. Weakly patterned, with homogeneous body scales and no enlarged tubercles or spines. Iris cream with reddish brown reticulations and mouth-lining pale to dark blue. Cream, pale tan to dark grey with dark peppering, a sharp demarcation between flanks and paler ventral surfaces, and often a faint cream upper lateral stripe on tail. ■ **NOTES** Associated with spinifex (*Triodia bitextura*), in a small area of infertile granitic and rhyolite hilly country in nthn Gt. Div. Ra. near Petford, Qld. Lives only in spinifex.

Jewelled Gecko *Strophurus elderi* SVL 48mm

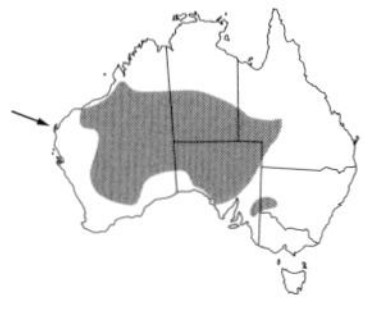

Spotted, with short swollen tail. Brown to dark leaden grey with very distinctive pattern: scattered to transverse rows of **conspicuous, black-edged white spots**, each centred on a small tubercle. There are no other spines or enlarged tubercles. ■ **NOTES** Arid zones, only where spinifex occurs. Dwells exclusively within the prickly hummocks, climbing with ease through a matrix of slender spines. Can exude sticky repellent fluid, but tends to smear rather than squirt it. ■ **STATUS** Vulnerable (NSW).

Arnhem Phasmid Gecko *Strophurus horneri* SVL 36mm

Extremely small, slender and striped with thin limbs, **13–15 upper labial scales** and **rostral scale not contacting nostril**. Yellowish brown with broad darker vertebral and lateral stripes, indistinct thin lower lateral stripes and 3 thin dark ventral stripes. **No thin yellow stripes within pale interspaces** and no spines or enlarged tubercles. ■ **NOTES** Large areas of spinifex among boulders and on sandstone escarpments on Arnhem Plateau, nthn NT. Lives only in spinifex. ■ **SEE ALSO** *S. taeniatus.*

Southern Spiny-tailed Gecko *Strophurus intermedius* SVL 64mm

Spiny-tailed, with **2 continuous parallel lines of large orange-brown tubercles on back**. Tail spines short and arranged in rings, with largest aligned to form **2 dorsal rows**. Grey with a series of dark-edged, paler, chain-like blotches on flanks. Iris pale grey with fine dark lines and orange to maroon rim. **Mouth-lining dark blue.** ■ **NOTES** Semi-arid to arid shrublands and mallee woodlands. Mainly arboreal, but also commonly found in spinifex. ■ **SEE ALSO** *S. assimilis; S. williamsi.*

Southern Phasmid Gecko *Strophurus jeanae* SVL 49mm

Extremely slender and striped, with thin limbs and **rostral scale contacting nostril.** Pale grey, boldly marked above and below with brown or yellow stripes. No spines or enlarged tubercles. ■ **NOTES** Spinifex grasslands. Lives only within spinifex. Recorded to gape its mouth to reveal a bright yellow interior when alarmed. The viscous fluid is bright orange when ejected. ■ **SEE ALSO** *S. mcmillani; S. robinsoni; S. taeniatus.*

Strophurus congoo. Emu Creek via Petford, Qld. E. Vanderduys

Strophurus elderi. Paynes Find, WA. S. Wilson

Strophurus horneri. Kakadu NP, NT. B. Schembri

Strophurus jeanae. Karratha, WA. R. Browne-Cooper

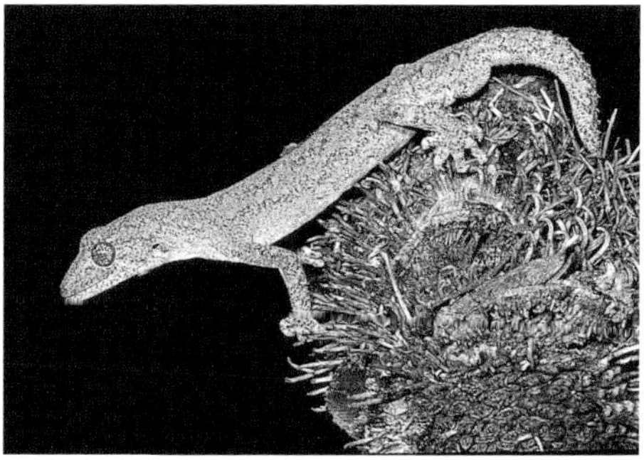

Strophurus intermedius. Big Desert, Vic. R. Valentic

Kristin's Spiny-tailed Gecko *Strophurus krisalys* SVL 70mm

Spiny-tailed, with **spines above eye, 2 rows of large tubercles along each side of midline on body, and 2 widely spaced parallel rows of spines along tail,** separated by 8–13 rows of smaller scales. **Mouth lining deep blue.** Grey with prominent large dark dorsal blotches and hourglass-shaped lateral blotches in n. but tending to be weakly marked to patternless in s. ■ **NOTES** Woodlands, shrublands and spinifex grasslands. ■ **SEE ALSO** *S. ciliaris.*

McMillan's Striped Gecko *Strophurus mcmillani* SVL 53mm

Robust and striped, with **rostral scale widely separated from nostril**. Pale olive grey, patterned above and below with simple, faint, yellowish brown stripes. There are no spines or enlarged tubercles. ■ **NOTES** Nw. Kimberley, dwelling in spinifex growing on sandstone outcrops. ■ **SEE ALSO** *S. jeanae; S. robinsoni; S. taeniatus.*

Robust Striped Gecko *Strophurus michaelseni* SVL 66mm

Robust and striped, with **rostral scale contacting nostril**. Pale olive brown, simply patterned above and below with many pale grey, dark-edged stripes. No spines or enlarged tubercles. ■ **NOTES** Banksia woodlands and heaths, where sedge tussocks or spinifex grow on pale sand-plains. Restricted to mid-to lower w. coast and adjacent interior, between Watheroo NP and Shark Bay. Shelters in sedge or spinifex, emerging at night to climb among adjacent shrubs and low bushes.

Exmouth Spiny-tailed Gecko *Strophurus rankini* SVL 63mm

Technically a spiny-tailed sp., though **spines are absent and tubercles greatly reduced; 2 barely discernible irregular dorsolateral rows on back,** becoming larger (though not spinose), forming 2 parallel rows on tail. Grey with scattered black dots, or a broad, dark, wavy-edged stripe on back and a series of large, pale, chain-like blotches on flanks. Iris pale grey with fine dark lines and a yellow rim. **Mouth-lining blue.** ■ **NOTES** Restricted to a small area on arid mid-w. coast, between North West Cape and Carnarvon, incl. Bernier Is. Hides by day among branches and foliage of coastal shrubs, mainly on pale dunes.

Robinson's Striped Gecko *Strophurus robinsoni* SVL 55mm

Slender and striped, with thin limbs and **rostral scale not contacting nostril**. Brownish grey with 6–8 weak, simple, **wavy, web-like brown lines on each flank**. No spines or enlarged tubercles. ■ **NOTES** Known only from the Upper Keep R. and Middle Ord R. drainages in nw. NT and adj. estn Kimberley region of WA. Lives in spinifex growing on sandstone. ■ **SEE ALSO** *S. jeanae; S. mcmillani; S. taeniatus.*

Strophurus krisalys. Congie Stn, Qld.
S. Wilson

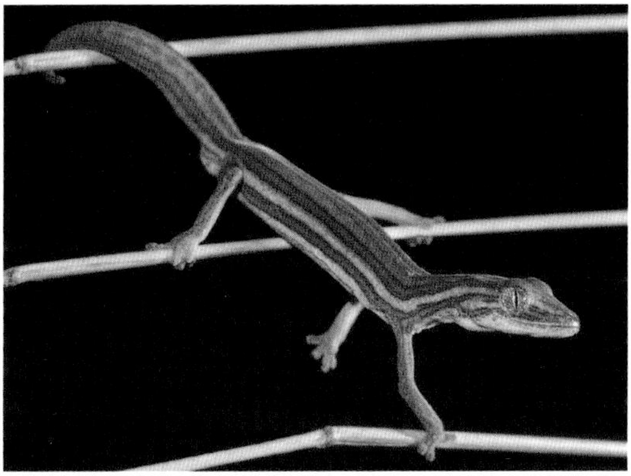

Strophurus mcmillani. Theda Stn, WA.
H. Cook

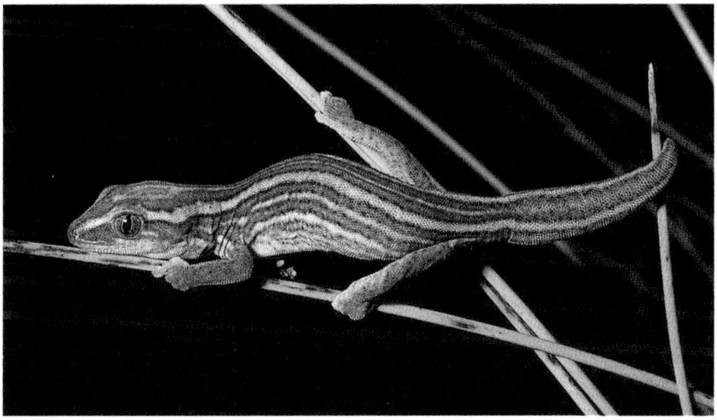

Strophurus michaelseni.
Marchagee Reserve, WA.
S. Wilson

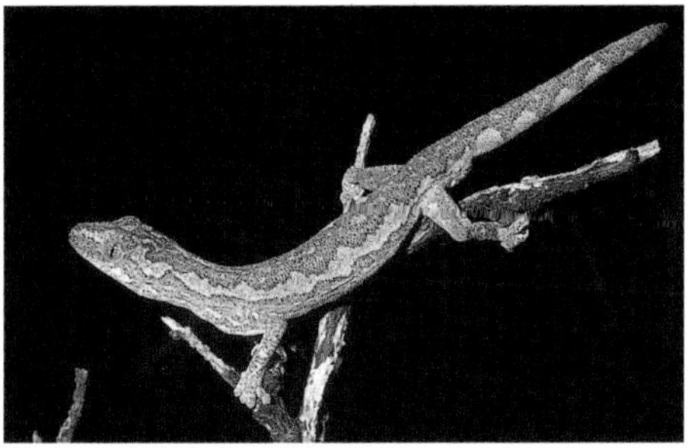

Strophurus rankini.
North West Cape, WA. S. Wilson

Strophurus robinsoni.
Mt Parker, WA. B. Maryan

Soft Spiny-tailed Gecko *Strophurus spinigerus* SVL 74mm

Spiny-tailed, with 2 regular rows of short black spines on back. **Tail spines long, soft and black in 2 rows. Mouth-lining bluish black.** ■ **SSP.** *S. s. spinigerus* is grey with a broad dark grey to black dorsal stripe, peppered with small white spots and with zigzagging edge. Iris maroon to brown, rimmed with yellow in south, and white in coastal areas n. of Kalbarri. *S. s. inornatus* lacks the dark dorsal stripe. Iris rim, if present, is orange-red. ■ **NOTES** Lower w. coast and offshore islands, from Shark Bay to the s. coast. *S. s. inornatus* occupies those areas s. and e. of Darling Ra. Commonly seen clinging to the stems of shrubs in suburban Perth.

Western Spiny-tailed Gecko *Strophurus strophurus* SVL 70mm

Spiny-tailed, with enlarged conical **tubercles randomly scattered over back.** These are larger and arranged in rings on tail, **each tail-ring separated by a distinctive narrow band of pale connective tissue**. Grey with a broad, dark, wavy-edged dorsal stripe. Iris pale grey with fine dark lines and rimmed with yellow, red or white. Mouth-lining bluish grey to bluish black. ■ **NOTES** Semi-arid to arid mid-w. coast and interior, particularly on hard to stony soils supporting low acacia shrublands.

Northern Phasmid Gecko *Strophurus taeniatus* SVL 44mm

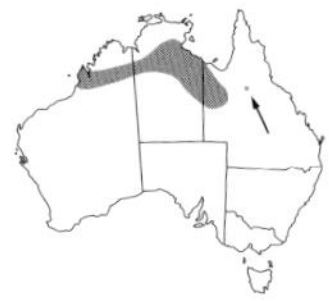

Extremely slender and striped with thin limbs, **10–12 upper labial scales and rostral scale not contacting nostril.** Grey to brown or dull yellow with prominent, broad, sharp-edged dark vertebral, dorsolateral, lateral and mid-ventral stripes and **thinner yellow stripes within pale interspaces.** No spines or enlarged tubercles. ■ **NOTES** Semiarid to arid northern Aust. from Broome, WA, to Mt Isa/Cloncurry area, Qld. A possibly isolated pop. occurs further e. on Gilberton Stn, Qld. Lives only in spinifex, particularly on hard to stony soils. ■ **SEE ALSO** *S. jeanae*; *S. horneri*; *S. mcmillani*; *S. robinsoni.*

Golden-tailed Gecko *Strophurus taenicauda* SVL 73mm

Allied to spiny-tailed geckos though **no spines or enlarged tubercles. Pale grey to cream with a mosaic of black spots and an orange blaze on tail.** ■ **SSP.** *S. t. taenicauda* has bright red iris, large black spots and one golden tail-stripe with undulating edges or transverse extensions. *S. t. albiocularis* has white to cream iris, small black spots, and straight-edged tail-stripe. *S. t. triaureus* has amber iris, small black spots and 3 tail-stripes; broad, straight-edged dorsal and thin undulating laterals separated by narrow black and white vertical lines. ■ **NOTES** DSF and woodlands in Brigalow Belt bioregion, Qld, particularly where cypress pine is present. *S. t. taenicauda* extends nw. to Carnarvon NP and e. to Cecil Plains. *S. t. albiocularis* occurs further n., to sw. of Rockhampton. *S. t. triaureus* occupies narrow band between Mundubbera, Callide and Biloela, Qld. ■ **STATUS** Near threatened (IUCN Red List; Qld).

Strophurus spinigerus spinigerus.
Mosman Park, WA. S. Wilson

Strophurus spinigerus inornatus.
Ellenbrook, WA. B. Maryan

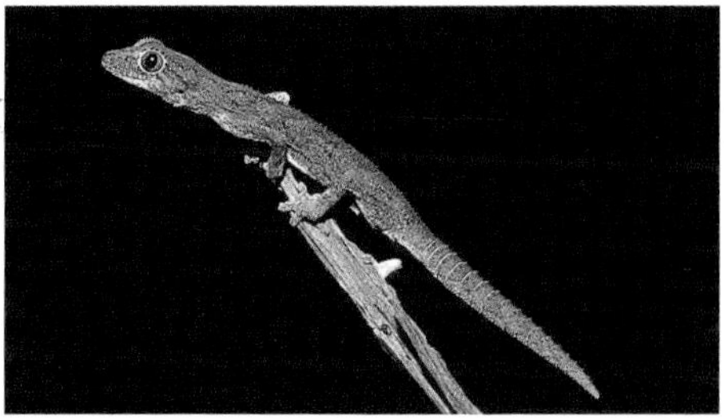

Strophurus strophurus.
Wooleen Stn, WA. S. Wilson

Strophurus taeniatus. Mt Isa area, Qld. S. Wilson

Strophurus taenicauda taenicauda.
Lake Broadwater, Qld. S. Wilson

Strophurus taenicauda albiocularis.
Dingo area, Qld. S. Wilson

Strophurus taenicauda triaureus.
Eidsvold, Qld. S. Wilson

Western-shield Spiny-tailed Gecko *Strophurus wellingtonae* SVL 85mm

Spiny-tailed, with **long spines above eye**, enlarged **tubercles arranged in 2 parallel rows on back**, and **2 rows of long orange or brown spines on tail**. Grey or brownish grey, usually marked with 5–8 pale grey upper lateral blotches between neck and base of tail. Iris greyish white with fine dark lines and maroon rim. **Mouth-lining bluish.** ■ **NOTES** Arid interior from Pilbara region se. to nthn Goldfields. Favours mulga shrublands and woodlands on heavy reddish soils. ■ **SEE ALSO** *S. ciliaris.*

Eastern Spiny-tailed Gecko *Strophurus williamsi* SVL 60mm

Spiny-tailed, with 2–4 nearly parallel rows of large orange-brown tubercles on back and **4 rows of tubercles on tail**. Pale to dark grey, with scattered dark spots, a fine dark reticulum and/or broad, dark, wavy-edged dorsal region. Iris grey with fine dark lines and reddish orange rim. **Mouth-lining bright bluish purple.** ■ **NOTES** Woodlands, particularly where cypress pine and coarse-barked eucalypts (ironbarks) are present. When agitated may open mouth to display bright-coloured interior. ■ **SEE ALSO** *S. intermedius.*

Mount Augustus Striped Gecko *Strophurus wilsoni* SVL 56mm

Stout, **short-tailed**, short-snouted, somewhat intermediate between striped and spiny-tailed geckos, lacking enlarged spines or tubercles. Pale grey to pale reddish brown, **obscurely patterned anteriorly with narrow broken dark lines** which are the margins of faint, broad, pale vertebral and more prominent dorsolateral stripes. Iris bluish grey with fine dark lines, lacking a coloured rim. ■ **NOTES** Shrublands on stony plains and low outcrops in arid interior, from Channar s. to the Robinson Ra., WA. In mild weather it shelters in vertical crevices of small split rocks, or under stones on gibber flats. At night it forages on the ground and ascends low shrubs.

Strophurus wellingtonae.
Waldburg Stn, WA. S. Wilson

Strophurus williamsi.
Charleville, Qld. S. Wilson

Strophurus wilsoni.
Waldburg Stn, WA.
S. Wilson

COSMOPOLITAN GECKOS
Family Gekkonidae

Gekkonids are by far the most widespread of the three Australian gecko families. They extend from the tropics to cool temperate regions that are beyond the range of other geckos. Gekkonid geckos also enjoy a near global distribution, occurring on all continents and colonising many far-flung, isolated islets across the Indian and Pacific Oceans.

Gekkonidae is represented in Australia by 47 described species. Nearly all are endemic, but many are closely related to exotic species. Indeed, five of the seven Australian genera are well represented overseas. Many gekkonid geckos, including the introduced Asian House Gecko (*Hemidactylus frenatus*), adapt easily to human environments.

Gekkonids resemble Diplodactylid and Carphodactylid geckos in having soft, non-glossy scales, with or without tubercles but generally of a velvety texture. Also like other geckos and the pygopodid lizards, gekkonids use the tongue to wipe the clear spectacles covering their lidless eyes. And they share a voice in the form of a squeak or chirrups, uttered when stressed or during social encounters. The egg clutch is normally fixed at two, with an egg descending from each oviduct. However some gekkonids lay just one egg at a time, with subsequent eggs alternating between right and left oviducts.

The distinctive nature of their eggs sets gekkonids apart from all Australian lizards. Typical lizard eggs have soft, pliable shells that are highly permeable. They can lose or gain moisture easily, so they must be deposited in humid sheltered sites. Gekkonid eggs have hard, brittle shells, markedly impervious to moisture-loss. They can be laid in drier environments under bark, in wood cracks or even in the corner of a book case. They travel extremely well, whether in floating debris or the cargo of a modern container ship, and are partly responsible for the family's cosmopolitan distribution and extraordinary dispersal success,

Gekkonid digits range from narrow, clawed and bird-like to flattened, broadly expanded and equipped beneath with transverse plates bristling with microscopic adhesive setae. The family includes terrestrial, arboreal and rock-inhabiting species, but lifestyle is not wholly linked to the presence or absence of toe pads. For example, ring-tailed geckos (*Cyrtodactylus* spp.) have narrow, clawed toes yet they are adept climbers on rough rock surfaces, while some dtellas (*Gehyra* spp.) often shelter beneath terrestrial debris in spite of their well-padded feet.

Like virtually all geckos, gekkonids can readily discard their tails when under duress. Pre-weakened cleavage points are distributed along the tail, so they can economise tail-loss. Depending on circumstances, gekkonids can forfeit the entire tail, a portion or just the tip. In contrast, Carphodactylid and many Diplodactylid geckos have just one cleavage point at the base meaning the tail must be lost in its entirety.

Gekkonids are primarily nocturnal. Their diets are similar to other geckos, comprising mainly arthropods, augmented occasionally by lapping sap or soft fruits.

The family Gekkonidae includes many widely distributed genera containing large numbers of species. *Gehyra* extends from South East Asia to the Pacific Islands. The Dubious Dtella (*Gehyra dubia*) is common in woodlands and human dwellings throughout Queensland.
Chinchilla, Qld. S. Wilson.

Genus *Christinus*

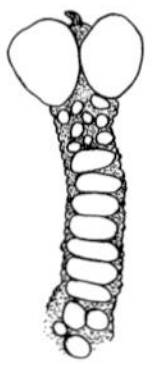

Three spp. with **long fleshy tails**, fine granular scales and digits flattened and expanded to form pads. **Subdigital lamellae in a single series, ending in a large pair of terminal plates (fig.)**. Small claws present and retractable, each set within a groove in the expanded pad. ■ **NOTES** Largely sthn in occurrence, exploiting cool temperate zones and windswept islands more effectively than other geckos. Arboreal and rock-inhabiting, sheltering under loose bark and in crevices. Several undescribed spp. occur.

Nullarbor Marbled Gecko *Christinus alexanderi* SVL 60mm

Subdigital lamellae 9–11. Scales under tail relatively large and overlapping. Grey with a series of narrow, dark, undulating or shallowly zigzagging bands. ■ **NOTES** Nullarbor Plain and hinterland, excluding coastal plains below the escarpment. Its range broadly overlaps with the widespread *C. marmoratus*.

Lord Howe Island Gecko *Christinus guentheri* SVL 80mm

Olive grey to dark brown with a series of W-shaped bands, a pale vertebral stripe and an orange stripe on original tail. ■ **NOTES** Two separate pops, possibly representing separate spp., occur on Lord Howe Is. and its satellites, and on satellites off Norfolk Is. Uncommon on Lord Howe Is. and no longer present on Norfolk Is., due largely to introduced rats, but common to abundant on some offshore islands. Terrestrial and arboreal, sheltering by day under rocks and woody debris. ■ **STATUS** Vulnerable (NSW; C'wealth; IUCN Red List).

Marbled Gecko *Christinus marmoratus* SVL 70mm

Extremely variable, usually with **8–9 subdigital lamellae** (at least within zone of overlap with *C. alexanderi*). **Scales under tail small and non-overlapping**. Pale to dark grey or pinkish brown with dark lines forming irregular marbling, reticulations or zigzagging transverse bands. Irregular pale grey blotches often present, alternating with dark markings and tending to centre on vertebral region. Pattern on tail similar, with a series of reddish brown to bright orange blotches often present, particularly on juv. ■ **NOTES** Most southerly gecko, extending across sthn Aust., incl. many offshore islands, between Warrumbungle Mtns, NSW and Shark Bay, WA. Shelters beneath loose bark and exfoliating rock. WA coastal and island pops are less arboreal, utilising limestones and granites.

Christinus alexanderi. Eucla, WA. S. Swanson

Christinus guentheri.
Blackburn Is. via Lord Howe Island. S. Wilson

Christinus guentheri.
Phillip Is. via Norfolk Island. S. Wilson

Christinus marmoratus.
Deer Park, Vic. S. Wilson

Christinus marmoratus.
Wilson's Inlet, WA. S. Wilson

Bent-toed and Ring-tailed Geckos
Genus *Cyrtodactylus*

Large diverse genus (more than 140 spp.) centred mainly in Asia and Pacific. Six in Aust.; five large banded spp. in ne. Qld and a very small blotched sp. off far nthn WA coast. One other sp. is restricted to the territory of Christmas Is. Small granular dorsal scales mixed with longitudinal rows of larger tubercles, a **ventrolateral skin fold**, clawed, padless, somewhat bird-like digits, and long slender tails. ■ **NOTES** Some are among largest geckos in Aust. Arboreal and rock-inhabiting. Agile climbers on rough surfaces, leaping with ease between boulders. In addition to arthropods, diets of larger spp. incl. frogs and geckos. ■ **SEE ALSO** *Heteronotia*; *Nactus*.

Pascoe River Ring-tailed Gecko *Cyrtodactylus adorus* SVL 123 mm

Small tubercles on forearm and moderately developed dorsal tubercles in 21-24 longitudinal rows at mid-body. Top of head largely without pattern, prominent cream and brown, sharp-edged bands on body and tail incl. usually 3 dark bands on trunk, each with narrow darker posterior edge and often narrow paler anterior edge, **pale interspaces unmarked**, and dark bands on tail-base about twice as wide as pale interspaces. ■ **NOTES** Nthn CYP, on rocky outcrops, mainly granite, in vicinity of lower reaches of Pascoe River, incl. Wattle, Stanley & Kennedy Hills. ■ **SEE ALSO** *C. hoskini.*

Iron Range Ring-tailed Gecko *Cyrtodactylus hoskini* SVL 112 mm

Large, moderately projecting tubercles on forearm and strongly developed dorsal tubercles in 19-24 longitudinal rows at midbody. Coarse dark mottling on top of head and prominent cream and brown bands on body and tail incl. 3 dark bands on trunk, each with narrow darker anterior and posterior edges, and **narrow posterior and anterior vertebral extensions. Pale interspaces usually with dark lateral patch or bar**, and bands on tail-base slightly wider than pale interspaces. ■ **NOTES** Nthn CYP on wstn edge of Iron Range, among granite boulders in open forest interspersed with RF patches and often festooned with ferns, vines and umbrella trees. ■ **SEE ALSO** *C. adorus.*

Kimberley Bent-toed Gecko *Cyrtodactylus kimberleyensis* SVL 45 mm

Very small and slender with small tubercles (absent on base of forearm), in 16-18 longitudinal rows at midbody. Pale brown with broad dark blotches on base of head, dark streak behind eye, small darker blotches and tubercles mottled on back, small pale blotches on lower flanks, neck and face and a pair of dark paravertebral broken stripes on tail-base, breaking into paired dashes at about midpoint. ■ **NOTES** Just one specimen recorded, a gravid female containing one egg, in vine thicket on lateritic slope. Isolated on East Montalivet Is. more than 30 kms off nw. Kimberley coast, WA.

Cyrtodactylus adorus. Kennedy Hills, Qld. K. Aland

Cyrtodactylus hoskini. Tozer Range, Qld. K. Aland

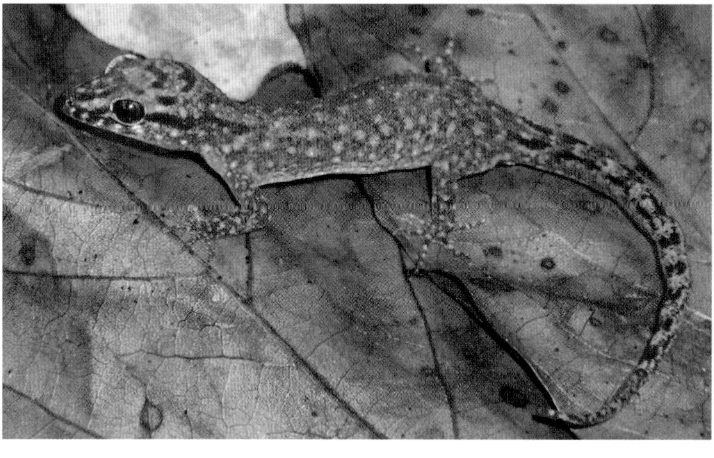

Cyrtodactylus kimberleyensis. East Montalivet Island, WA. R. Browne-Cooper

Southern Ring-tailed Gecko *Cyrtodactylus mcdonaldi* SVL 105 mm

Large, weakly to moderately projecting tubercles on forearm and strongly developed dorsal tubercles in 18-23 longitudinal rows at midbody. **Grey smudges on top of head** and prominent cream and brown bands on body and tail incl. **3 dark bands on trunk, each with narrow darker posterior and just occasionally anterior edges, pale interspaces usually unmarked**, and bands on tail-base just slightly wider than pale interspaces. ■ **NOTES** Nthn Qld from Chillagoe n. to Parrot Ck in Shipton's Flat area. Rocky areas incl. limestone karst at Chillagoe, sandstone at Mt Mulligan and granite at Mareeba. Pop. in Bloomfield area occupies woodland with sparse rocks. ■ **SEE ALSO** *C. tuberculatus.*

McIlwraith Ring-tailed Gecko *Cyrtodactylus pronarus* SVL 132 mm

No tubercles on forearm and moderately developed dorsal tubercles in 20-24 longitudinal rows at midbody. Top of head largely patternless and cream and brown bands on body and tail incl. **3 dark bands on trunk, each with darker posterior edges but diffuse anterior edges merging into paler interspaces.** Pale interspaces usually unmarked, and bands on tail-base more than twice as wide as pale interspaces. ■ **NOTES** Nthn CYP, in small area of McIlwraith Ra at about 500 m altitude. Recorded from granite boulders in well-developed RF at Peach Ck.

Cooktown Ring-tailed Gecko *Cyrtodactylus tuberculatus* SVL 120 mm

Strongly projecting tubercles on forearm and strongly developed dorsal tubercles in 20-24 longitudinal rows at midbody. **Strong dark mottling on top of head**, prominent cream and brown bands on body and tail incl. 3–4 **dark bands on trunk, each with narrow darker anterior and posterior edges**, often a **few dark spots within pale interspaces**, and bands on tail-base just slightly wider than pale interspaces. ■ **NOTES** Sthn CYP from Mt Leswell n. on mainland to Cape Melville, and off-shore n. to Stanley Is. Rocky areas incl. granite boulders and sandstone outcrops, extending onto adjacent aerial root systems of figs and occasionally buildings. ■ **SEE ALSO** *C. mcdonaldi.*

Cyrtodactylus mcdonaldi.
Chillagoe, Qld.
S. Wilson

Cyrtodactylus pronarus.
Peach Creek, Qld.
K. Aland

Cyrtodactylus tuberculatus.
Black Mountain, Qld.
S. Wilson

Dtellas Genus ***Gehyra***

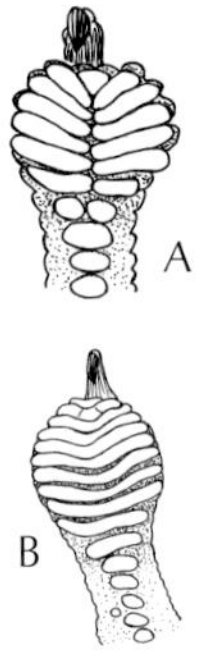

Twenty-six small to moderate spp. with uniform granular scales. **Digits flat with large semi-circular pads, all clawed except the inner digit on each foot, and each claw arising from upper surface of pad.** Subdigital lamellae enlarged; divided (A) or entire (B) in broad transverse series. The spp. are mainly identified by their divided or undivided subdigital lamellae, number of preanal pores on ♂, pattern and build. Identification can be difficult, with sometimes little more than genetic differences, and a likely presence of several undescribed spp. ■ **NOTES** Widespread in dry areas throughout Aust. These swift and agile arboreal and rock-inhabiting geckos shelter beneath loose bark and rock exfoliations. They frequently occur on human dwellings and are often very abundant, sometimes occupying virtually all available shelter sites. Eggs are often deposited communally.

Northern Dtella *Gehyra australis* SVL 81mm

Relatively robust, with **usually 10–11 undivided subdigital lamellae, 21 or fewer preanal pores** and **rostral scale with relatively flat upper edge.** Pale brown to pale pink or almost white, and often completely patternless, particularly when foraging at night. When present, pattern comprises transversely oriented pale blotches with dark leading edges, and sometimes a narrow pale vertebral line. ■ **NOTES** Woodlands and rock outcrops. Arboreal and rock-inhabiting. A common house gecko throughout its range. ■ **SEE ALSO** *G. dubia; G. ipsa; G. koira; G. pamela; G. occidentalis.*

Short-tailed Dtella *Gehyra baliola* SVL 101mm

Robust, with 12–16 **mostly divided subdigital lamellae,** a distinctive **web of skin at rear of hindlimb** and a U-shaped rostral scale enclosing a cluster of smaller scales. Pale yellowish brown to grey with transversely aligned paler spots. ■ **NOTES** Restricted in Aust. to Murray and Darnley Is. of ne. Torres Strait, Qld. Also present in NG. Common in mangroves, woodlands and human dwellings. Arboreal, rock-inhabiting and occupying houses. ■ **SEE ALSO** *G. dubia.*

Borroloola Dtella *Gehyra borroloola* SVL 65mm

Subdigital lamellae divided. Pale pinkish brown to dark brown with transverse rows of dark blotches alternating with rows of cream spots. Pattern usually broken by a narrow pale vertebral line. ■ **NOTES** Rock outcrops and gorges on the Gulf of Carpentaria between Limmen Bight R., NT and Mussellbrook, Qld. Rock-inhabiting.

Gehyra australis. Kununurra, WA. S. Wilson

Gehyra baliola. Murray Is., Qld. H. Cogger

Gehyra borroloola. Limmen Bight River, NT. S. Wilson

Chain-backed Dtella *Gehyra catenata* SVL 55mm

Subdigital lamellae undivided. Pale to dark grey with a wavy dark stripe extending from snout through each eye onto base of tail, joined by dark transverse bars and enclosing **pale dorsal blotches forming a distinctive chain-like pattern.** ■ **NOTES** Woodlands of eucalypts, wattles and she-oaks in the subhumid to semi-arid estn interior. Arboreal. ■ **SEE ALSO** *G. dubia; G. versicolor.*

Dubious Dtella *Gehyra dubia* SVL 65mm

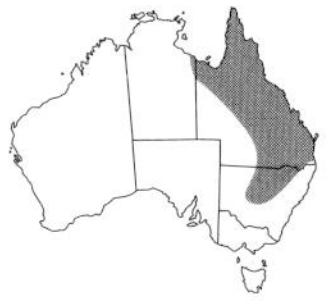

Variable, with **subdigital lamellae undivided** (but sometimes deeply notched) and **steeply sloping upper edges to rostral scale**. Pale grey to pale brown with irregular transverse series of paler grey to white spots, often overlaid with a dark reticulum, or each with a dark leading edge. Y-shaped mark (forked anteriorly) often present on neck and base of head. ■ **NOTES** Woodlands, DSF and rock outcrops from central nthn NSW through central Qld to Cape York Pen. and islands of Torres Strait. Arboreal and rock-inhabiting. Abundant throughout range, frequently occupying human dwellings. ■ **SEE ALSO** *G. australis; G. baliola; G. catenata; G. versicolor.*

Kimberley Karst Gecko *Gehyra girloorloo* SVL 47mm

Subdigital lamellae divided, with 6–7 (usually 6) under expanded portion of 4th toe; 2 pairs of enlarged chin shields, incl. long, narrow postmental scales. Pale purplish brown with very fine darker stippling, irregular dark brown blotches tending to align transversely with intermittent yellow orange edges, alternating with transverse series of pale spots. ■ **NOTES** Rock-inhabiting, in narrow band of limestone outcropping of King Leopold Ra. on Gogo and Mt Piere Stns. ■ **SEE ALSO** *G. nana*; *G. occidentalis.*

Bungle Bungle Dtella *Gehyra ipsa* SVL 96mm

Very large, robust, dorsally depressed with **11–13, usually 12, undivided subdigital lamellae** under 4th toe, **15-20 preanal pores** on ♂ and **42–50 rows of scales (interorbitals) between eyes**. Pale brown with narrow pale dorsal bars, each edged anteriorly with broader dark transverse blotches. ■ **NOTES** Restricted to Purnululu NP (Bungle Bungles) in se. Kimberley region, WA. Rock-inhabiting, foraging at night over exposed rock faces, caves and overhangs. ■ **SEE ALSO** *G. australis*; *G. koira*; *G. occidentalis.*

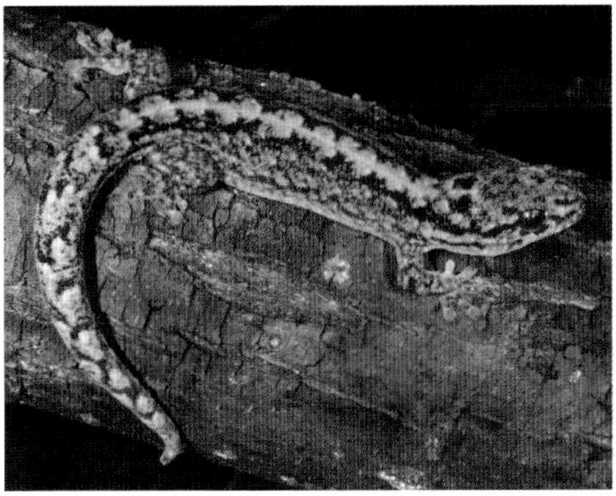

Gehyra catenata. Dingo, Qld. S. Wilson

Gehyra dubia. Girraween NP, Qld. S. Wilson

Gehyra girloorloo.
Galeru Gorge, WA.
T. Parkin

Gehyra ipsa.
Purnululu NP, WA.
S. Wilson

Robust Termitaria Gecko *Gehyra kimberleyi* SVL 61mm

Subdigital lamellae divided, with 6–9 under expanded portion of 4th toe; 2 pairs of enlarged chin shields incl. **long, narrow postmental scales** and smaller outer pair with rounded outer edges; **7–9 upper labial scales**, and 2nd (**A**) or 3rd (**B**) lower labial scale notched by subinfralabial scale (**fig**). Pale tan to dark brown with scattered dark brown blotches, often transversely aligned to form ill-defined bands on body, alternating with rows of smaller pale spots. ■ **NOTES** Widespread from sthn Kimberley to nthn Pilbara. Often associated with termite mounds, but a broad habitat generalist occurring on trees, rocks and ground debris.

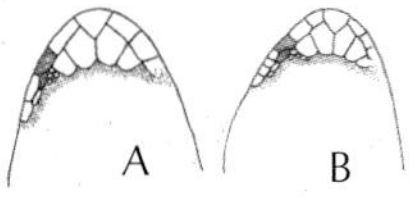

■ **SEE ALSO** *G. montium*; *G. pilbara.*

King's Dtella *Gehyra koira* SVL 86mm

Robust, dorsally depressed with **10–14, usually 12, undivided subdigital lamellae** under 4th toe, **12–18 preanal pores** on ♂ and **35–47 rows of scales (interorbitals) between eyes.** Pale brown with narrow pale dorsal bars, each edged anteriorly with broader dark transverse blotches. ■ **NOTES** Large sandstone massifs in the Ord-Victoria region of nw. NT and adj. ne. WA. Apparently disjunct pop. occurs further s. at Jellabra Rockhole in Gardner Range, nthn Tanami Desert. Rock-inhabiting, foraging at night over exposed rock faces, caves and overhangs.
■ **SEE ALSO** *G. australis*; *G. ipsa*; *G. occidentalis.*

Southern Rock Dtella *Gehyra lazelli* SVL 59mm

Subdigital lamellae divided. Upper edges of rostral scale flat to weakly sloping. Pale or dark grey to brown with numerous irregular dark spots, short wavy lines and streaks mixed with numerous small, scattered, pale spots. **Dark markings and pale spots generally separate, and no continuous dark temporal lines.** ■ **NOTES** Rock-inhabiting, on ranges and outcrops from s. central NSW, through Gawler, Flinders and Mt Lofty Ras to Ceduna and Nuyts Archipelago, SA.
■ **SEE ALSO** *G. versicolor.*

Dwarf Dtella *Gehyra minuta* SVL 45mm

Deep head, short snout, large eyes and **divided subdigital lamellae.** Pale orange-brown with pattern, when present, comprising transverse rows of cream spots alternating with rows of blackish spots which often merge to form dark bands. ■ **NOTES** Isolated rock outcrops in a narrow band of red soil on sw. margin of Barkly Tablelands, semi-arid central NT. Rock-inhabiting. Locally abundant, despite its fragmented occurrence.

Gehyra kimberleyi. Broome Bird Observatory, WA. S. Wilson

Gehyra koira. Keep River, NT. P. Horner

Gehyra minuta. Barry Caves, NT. S. Wilson

Gehyra lazelli. Telowie Gorge, SA. S. Wilson

Central Rock Dtella *Gehyra montium* SVL 51mm

Subdigital lamellae divided, with 7–8 (usually 7) under expanded portion of 4th toe, 2 pairs of enlarged chin shields, **8–11 upper labial scales**, 2nd lower labial scale notched by subinfralabial scale (**fig**). Pinkish brown to reddish brown with **obscure pale spots** and a weak to strong **dark reticulum**. The **pale and dark markings are not normally in contact**. ■ **NOTES** Rock-inhabiting in western arid zone from far ne. SA (e. to Mt Kintore) and sw. NT to Pilbara region, WA. ■ **SEE ALSO** *G.kimberleyi*; *G. moritzi*; *G. pulingka*; *G. variegata*; *G. versicolor.*

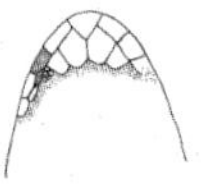

Moritz's Dtella *Gehyra moritzi* SVL 49mm

Subdigital lamellae divided, with 7–8 subdigital lamellae under expanded portion of 4th toe (8 in s. and 7 in n.), usually 2 pairs of enlarged chin shields, 2nd or 3rd lower labial scale notched by subinfralabial scale. Pinkish grey to reddish brown with simple pattern of dark and pale spots. **The pale spots are smallest and regularly circular, while larger dark spots are more irregular in shape**. Nthn pop. is smaller (SVL 40mm) with uniformly small spots. ■ **NOTES** Rock-inhabiting, on ranges and outcrops of Central Aust., s. to James Ra., w. to Kings Canyon and n. to Devils Marbles. ■ **SEE ALSO** *G. montium*; *G. pulingka.*

Multi-pored Gecko *Gehyra multiporosa* SVL 55mm

Dorsally depressed with **subdigital lamellae divided, 6-7 under 4th finger and toe**, and more than 40 precloacal and femoral pores on ♂ with SVL over 50mm. Dark greyish brown, red to salmon with **dark markings tending to form transverse bars**, usually alternating with smaller pale spots or bars. Pattern sometimes interrupted by a thin pale vertebral line or zone. ■ **NOTES** Rock-inhabiting, occupying cliff faces, platforms, boulders, rocky creeks and moist rainforest gullies in rugged sandstones and basalts of nw. Kimberley region, generally within 100 km of coast. Extends from Mitchell Plateau to Walcott Inlet, and many off-shore is. between Cape Voltaire and Doubtful Bay. ■ **SEE ALSO** *G. occidentalis; G. nana.*

Northern Spotted Dtella *Gehyra nana* SVL 54mm

Strongly dorsally depressed, with **divided subdigital lamellae in 5–8 (normally 6–7) pairs under 4th toe**. Pinkish grey to reddish brown with pattern usually prominent; alternating transverse rows of small pinkish white spots and **larger brown spots**. ■ **NOTES** Rock outcrops and ranges in subhumid to arid areas from the Kimberley, WA through nthn NT to nw. Qld. Rock-inhabiting. ■ **SEE ALSO** *G. girloorloo; G. multiporosa; G. occidentalis; G. spheniscus.*

Gehyra montium.
Uluru-Kata Tjuta NP., NT, M. Hutchinson

Gehyra moritzi.
Kings Creek Stn, NT. S. Wilson

Gehyra multiporosa.
Mitchell Plateau, WA.
S. Macdonald

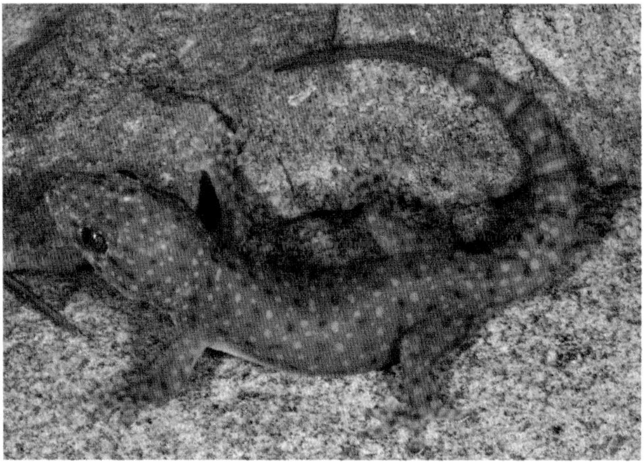

Gehyra nana.
El Questro Stn, WA. S. Wilson.

Kimberley Plateau Dtella *Gehyra occidentalis* SVL 76mm

Dorsally depressed, with **subdigital lamellae divided, 7-10 under 4th toe** and 10-30 precloacal and femoral pores. Chocolate brown with transverse rows of black spots, coalescing to form bands and alternating with bands of paler spots. ■ **NOTES** Rock-inhabiting, occasionally arboreal, in rocky ranges and outcrops of semi-arid sw. (Yampi region) and sthn Kimberley with isolated records on Mt Nyulasy in estn. Kimberley. ■ **SEE ALSO** *G. australis; G. girloorloo; G. ipsa; G. koira; G. nana; G. multiporosa.*

Arnhem Land Dtella *Gehyra pamela* SVL 70mm

Strongly dorsally depressed, with **undivided, deeply grooved or notched subdigital lamellae**, and **19–28 preanal pores**. Reddish grey with prominent to obscure pattern comprising transverse series of large pale spots. ■ **NOTES** Massive rock faces of Arnhem Escarpment, NT. Isolated pops occur as far se. as Roper R. and w. to Bullo R. Rock-inhabiting (the superficially similar *G. australis* tends to be arboreal within zone of overlap). ■ **SEE ALSO** *G. australis.*

Pilbara Dtella *Gehyra pilbara* SVL 55mm

Robust and **deep-headed,** with **divided subdigital lamellae. Postmental scales short and wide**. Pale brown to bright or pale orange with prominent pattern, becoming obscure to absent on large individuals; transversely aligned blackish brown markings, occasionally coalescing to form bands, particularly on tail, and often alternating with transverse rows of circular pale spots. ■ **NOTES** Subhumid to arid regions from mid-estn NT to sthn Kimberley and Pilbara regions, WA. Inhabits large termite mounds, sheltering in them by day and foraging at night on their outer surfaces. Often occurs in high densities, with 15 or more recorded from one mound. ■ **SEE ALSO** *G. kimberleyi; G. punctata; G. variegata.*

Central Spotted Rock Dtella *Gehyra pulingka* SVL 49mm

Subdigital lamellae divided, with 7–8 (usually 8) under expanded portion of 4th toe, usually 3 pairs of enlarged chin shields, 3rd lower labial scale notched by subinfralabial scale (**fig**). Pinkish grey to reddish brown with simple pattern of **prominent pale spots and short, dark wavy lines**. The pale spots are regularly circular, sometimes in transverse rows. ■ **NOTES** Rock-inhabiting, on ranges and outcrops from nw. SA and adj. WA, nw. to Rawlinson Ra., WA, and e. to Kulgera area, sthn NT. ■ **SEE ALSO** *G. montium; G. moritzi.*

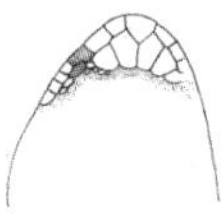

Gehyra occidentalis. Oscar Ranges, WA. G. Gaikhorst

Gehyra occidentalis. Mt Nyulasy, WA. S. Wilson

Gehyra pamela. Kakadu NP, NT. B. Maryan

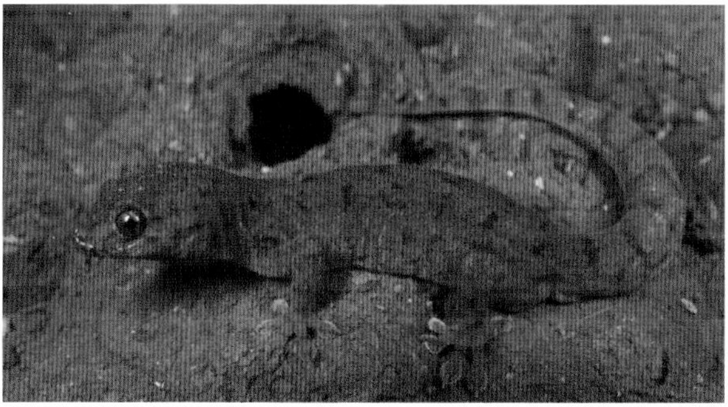

Gehyra pilbara. Brockman Gorge, WA. G. Harold

Gehyra pulingka. Mount Cavenagh area, NT. J. de Jong

Spotted Rock Dtella *Gehyra punctata* SVL 65mm

Moderately robust and dorsally depressed, with **divided subdigital lamellae in 6–10 (normally 8–9) pairs under 4th toe**. Pale yellowish brown or reddish brown to shades of pink with pattern usually prominent; transverse rows of dark brown spots alternating with rows of whitish to yellowish spots. Individuals from s. of range are usually more conspicuously marked, with pale spots yellower and dark spots often pale-edged. ■ **NOTES** Rock-inhabiting, on hills and outcrops from Pilbara region s. to Yalgoo, WA. ■ **SEE ALSO** *G. pilbara.*

Purple Dtella *Gehyra purpurascens* SVL 64mm

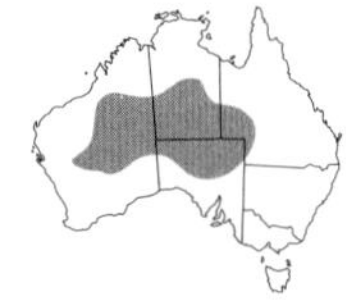

Subdigital lamellae divided. Rostral scale, when viewed from above, almost horizontal. Pale purplish grey with pattern, when present, irregular and **lacking pale spots**; brownish grey to dark grey spots or short streaks forming a reticulum. ■ **NOTES** Arid central interior. Arboreal. ■ **SEE ALSO** *G. montium; G. variegata; G. versicolor.*

Robust Dtella *Gehyra robusta* SVL 75mm

Relatively dorsally depressed, with **subdigital lamellae undivided**. Pinkish brown to orange-brown with transversely aligned dark blotches, often coalescing to form bars, alternating with transverse series of obscure pale spots. Pattern tends to break on vertebral region, leaving narrow pale line. ■ **NOTES** Rocky ranges and outcrops near Lawn Hill, Mt Isa and Winton. Rock-inhabiting.

Small Wedge-toed Gecko *Gehyra spheniscus* SVL 46mm

Dorsally depressed, with **subdigital lamellae divided, 6 under 4th finger and toe, separated at base of digit by wedge of granules**. Brown, red to salmon with alternating transverse rows of pale spots and small dark blotches or broken bars, and often a thin, pale vertebral line. ■ **NOTES** Rock-inhabiting, occupying cliff faces in rugged sandstones of nw. Kimberley region, generally within 100 km of coast. Known from Prince Regent River Nature Reserve, Mitchell Plateau and adj. Katers Is., s. and inland to Galvan's Gorge in Phillips Ra. ■ **SEE ALSO** *G. nana; G. xenopus.*

Gehyra punctata.
Willarrie Pool,
Wooramel River, WA.
D. Knowles

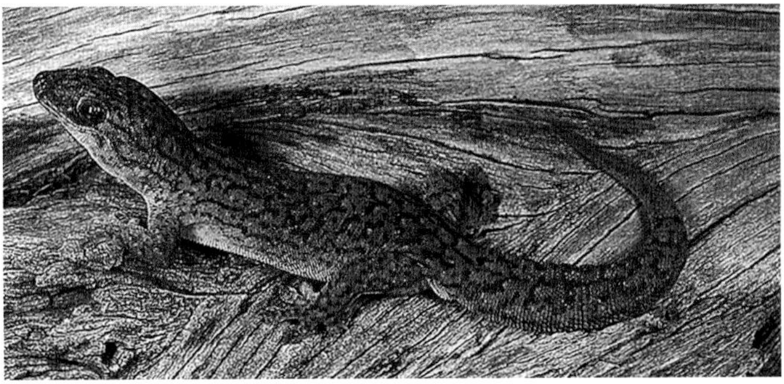

Gehyra purpurascens.
Little Sandy Desert, WA.
B. Maryan

Gehyra robusta.
Mica Creek, Mt Isa area, Qld.
E. Vanderduys

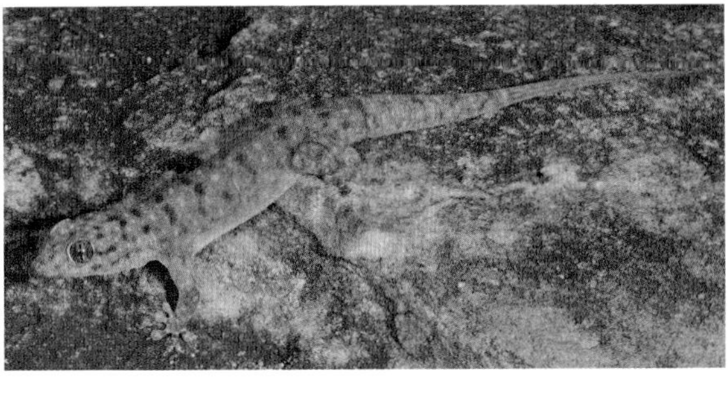

Gehyra spheniscus.
Mitchell Plateau, WA. S. Macdonald

Variegated Dtella *Gehyra variegata* SVL 49mm

Subdigital lamellae divided, with 6–8 (usually 8) under expanded portion of 4th toe, usually 2 pairs of enlarged chin shields, 2nd lower labial scale notched by subinfralabial scale (**fig**). Upper edges of rostral scale weakly to steeply sloping. Extremely variable. Brown to grey with dark lines usually incl. several temporal streaks, often forming irregular, continuous paravertebral and dorsolateral lines, and sometimes transverse lines forming vague ladder-like pattern. **Pale markings present, generally contacting dark markings as posterior highlight or margin**, and often partly enclosed when dark markings are curved. Rock-inhabiting pops tend to have brighter pattern than arboreal pops, with white pigment often expressed as spots. Not diagnosable from *G. versicolor* on morphological features. Within narrow zone of overlap (central wstn SA), separable only using genetics. ■ **NOTES** Vast tracts of dry woodlands, shrublands and rocky areas over sthn half of WA, from sthn Pilbara, se. to wstn interior of SA, almost to Ceduna. Arboreal and rock-inhabiting, but often found beneath ground debris and on buildings. ■ **SEE ALSO** *G. montium; G. purpurascens; G. pilbara; G. versicolor.*

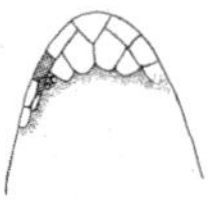

Variable Dtella *Gehyra versicolor* SVL 54mm

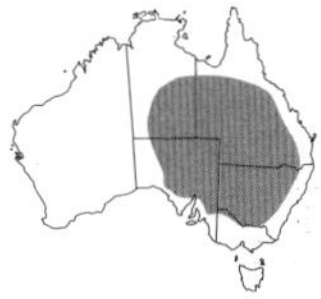

Subdigital lamellae divided, with 7–8 (usually 8) under expanded portion of 4th toe, usually 2 pairs of enlarged chin shields, 2nd lower labial scale notched by subinfralabial scale (**fig**). Upper edges of rostral scale weakly to steeply sloping. Extremely variable. Brown to grey with dark lines, usually incl. several temporal streaks, tending to form irregular, continuous paravertebral and dorsolateral lines, and sometimes transverse lines forming vague ladder-like pattern. **Pale markings present, generally contacting dark markings as posterior highlight or margin**, and often partly enclosed when dark markings are curved. Not diagnosable from *G. variegata* on morphological features. Within narrow zone of overlap (central wstn SA), separable only using genetics. ■ **NOTES** Vast tracts of dry woodlands, shrublands and rocky areas over estn interior, n. to latitude of Hughendon, Qld, s. to Murray Valley of nthn Vic and w. to near Maralinga, SA. Arboreal and rock-inhabiting, but often found beneath ground debris and on buildings. ■ **SEE ALSO** *G. catenata*; *G. dubia*; *G. lazelli*; *G. montium*; *G. purpurascens*; *G. variegata.*

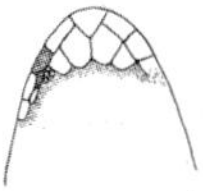

Crocodile-faced Dtella *Gehyra xenopus* SVL 77 mm

Dorsally depressed, with flat head, large eyes and long upturned snout, somewhat crocodile-like in profile. **Subdigital lamellae divided, 8–11 under 4th toe, separated at base of digit by a wedge of granular scales.** Dark brown to greyish brown with irregular transverse rows of large (sometimes dark-edged) circular pale spots. ■ **NOTES** Sandstone outcrops of subhumid nw. Kimberley, incl. offshore islands, from Price Regent R. and Champagny Is. in ne. to Kalumbaru. Rock-inabiting, favouring cliff faces and larger boulders. ■ **SEE ALSO** *G. spheniscus*

Gehyra variegata.
Cockleshell Gully, WA. S. Wilson

Gehyra variegata.
Bolgart area, WA. S. Wilson

Gehyra versicolor.
Julia Creek, Qld.
S. Wilson

Gehyra xenopus.
Little Merten's Falls, Mitchell Plateau, WA. S. Wilson.

Genus *Hemidactylus*

Asian House Gecko *Hemidactylus frenatus* SVL 60mm

Only one sp. in Aust. Somewhat flattened, with granular scales mixed with scattered small tubercles. Digits clawed and expanded to form pads. **Subdigital lamellae broad, with all except the most distal divided by deep cleft (fig.).** Original tails have **transverse rows of enlarged, bluntly spinose tubercles.** White to very dark grey, patternless or with dark and pale flecks; the darker pigment tending to form longitudinal streaks. Gives a **loud recognisable 'chuck...chuck...chuck' call.** ■ **NOTES** This large genus occurs in tropical and temperate regions worldwide. *H. frenatus* is native to South-East Asia, and has been introduced at several locations in cargo; it is established in urban areas from Darwin s. to Ti Tree, NT; along the e. coast from Torres Strait to Lake Macquarie, NSW; and at Kununurra and Argyle Diamond Village in the Kimberley and Sandfire Roadhouse in the Gt Sandy Desert, WA. Virtually restricted to human dwellings and adept at running up windows and across ceilings.

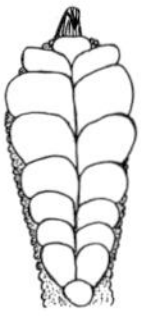

Genus *Heteronotia*

Five described small, long-tailed spp. with small granular scales mixed with many scattered to longitudinally aligned enlarged tubercles, and angular, bird-like, clawed feet—**claws arising from 3 scales, 1 above and 2 below (fig.)**—lacking expanded lamellae. ■ **NOTES** Widespread throughout Aust. Swift and active terrestrial geckos which tend to be extremely abundant, sheltering in soil cracks, under rocks, logs and surface debris. In many dry to arid zones virtually all suitable cover harbours resident geckos. ■ **SEE ALSO** *Nactus*; *Cyrtodactylus*.

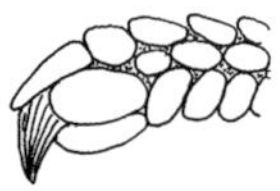

Black Pilbara Gecko *Heteronotia atra* SVL 62mm

Long, slender limbs and tail, greatly enlarged tympanum. Enlarged dorsal tubercles in contact at anterior and posterior edges, and separated on either side by at most, a few small granules. Dark charcoal grey to blackish brown with little pattern; darker temporal stripe and weaker loreal stripe, and sometimes an indication of four pale bands across body, and pale bands across tail. ■ **NOTES** Bare black boulder scree with many crevices and scattered shrubs associated with weathered dolerite mesa near Harding Dam, and at Millstream NP, in nw. Pilbara region,WA.

Bynoe's Gecko *Heteronotia binoei* SVL 54mm

Extremely variable. Dorsal tubercles scattered or arranged in irregular to regular longitudinal rows. Pale greyish brown or reddish brown to almost black with scattered to transversely aligned darker and paler spots, often arranged to form numerous narrow irregular bands. In Central Aust. pale bands may be straight-edged and regular with dark margins. ■ **NOTES** Occurs in dry open habitats over most of Aust., and often the most abundant reptile in many arid areas. Some pops are known to be parthenogenetic while others comprise normal ♂ and ♀ individuals. As currently recognised, a large and problematic complex of species. ■ **SEE ALSO** *H. fasciolatus*

Hemidactylus frenatus. Brisbane, Qld. S. Wilson

Heteronotia atra. Harding River Dam area, WA. B. Maryan

Heteronotia binoei. Currawinya NP, Qld. S. Wilson

Heteronotia binoei. Prince of Wales Is., Qld. S. Wilson

Heteronotia binoei. Pentland, Qld. S. Wilson

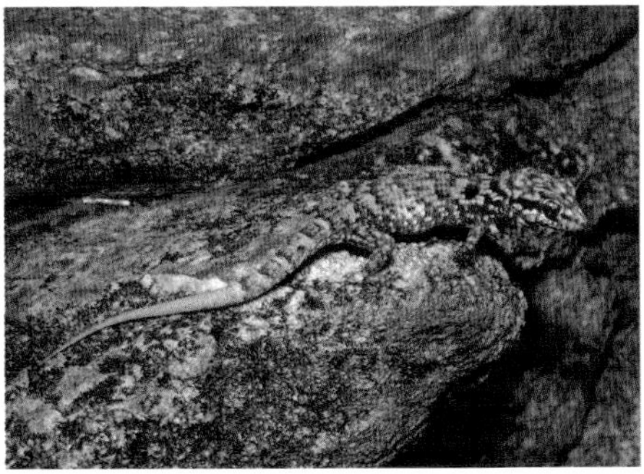

Heteronotia binoei. Drysdale River, WA. S. Wilson

Pale-headed Gecko *Heteronotia fasciolatus* SVL 57mm

Moderately robust. Enlarged dorsal tubercles in longitudinal rows, each tubercle separated by at least one smaller granule at anterior and posterior edges, and by at least two small granules on either side. Dark reddish brown with 5–8 ragged-edged pale bands across body, sometimes breaking or joining other bands. Top of head pale reddish brown with prominent temporal and loreal stripes. Tail marked with 10–13 dark bands, of appr. equal width to pale interspaces. ■ **NOTES** Rocky areas in East and West MacDonnell Ra., n. to Harts Ra., sthn NT. Some local colour variants of *H. binoei* are strikingly similar in appearance. ■ **SEE ALSO** *H. binoei.*

North-west Prickly Gecko *Heteronotia planiceps* SVL 50mm

Slender and long-tailed, with **dorsal tubercles in regular longitudinal rows,** and **prominent sharp-edged bands**. Yellowish brown to reddish brown with 3–4 prominent dark brown bands on body and a **dark temporal stripe joining the first dark brown band across base of head**. Original tails are strongly banded; regenerated tails are brown and patternless. ■ **NOTES** Rock-inhabiting, sheltering in crevices, caves and beneath rocks in ranges and outcrops of the Kimberley, WA through nthn NT to Groote Eylandt. An apparently isolated pop. occurs in the Pilbara, WA.

Desert Cave Gecko *Heteronotia spelea* SVL 55mm

Slender and long-tailed. Enlarged dorsal tubercles in longitudinal rows, each surrounded by at least one smaller tubercle. Yellowish brown to reddish brown with 4–5 strongly contrasting, straight-edged dark brown bands on body and a **dark temporal stripe joining the first dark brown band across neck**. Original tails are strongly banded; regenerated tails are brown and patternless. ■ **NOTES** Rock-inhabiting, sheltering in crevices, caves or beneath rocks in ranges and outcrops of the Pilbara.

Genus *Lepidodactylus*

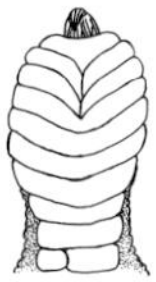

Two small, slender Aust. spp. with depressed bodies, fine granular scales and long tails. Digits flat with **broad transverse subdigital lamellae, undivided at base and divided or undivided distally (fig.)**. ■ **NOTES** This large genus occurs from Asia to NG and Pacific islands. Some spp. have been dispersed among human cargo and many cohabit in human dwellings. Arboreal.

Heteronotia fasciolatus. Emily Gap, NT. S. Wilson

Heteronotia planiceps. Mt Nyulasy, WA. S. Wilson

Heteronotia spelea. Paraburdoo, WA. B. Maryan

Mourning Gecko *Lepidodactylus lugubris* SVL 50mm

Slender, with **tail long and flattened with a lateral fringe of fine spiny scales. Subdigital lamellae divided distally**. Cream, flesh pink to brown with darker flecks and often a series of W-shaped markings from neck onto tail. ■ **NOTES** Associated with trees and buildings on beach and near coastal areas in towns in estn Qld, from islands of Torres Strait to Townsville area. Recently colonised buildings on Heron Is., Sunshine Coast Qld and in Darwin, NT. A parthenogenetic colonist of far-flung Pacific islands and possibly introduced to Aust.

Slender Mourning Gecko *Lepidodactylus pumilis* SVL 48mm

Slender, with long **cylindrical tail** and **undivided subdigital lamellae**. Pale pinkish brown with an obscure pattern comprising a pale vertebral area with narrow, darker, irregular transverse lines. ■ **NOTES** Known only from islands of Torres Strait, occurring in coastal habitats, open and closed tropical forests and human dwellings. ■ **STATUS** Near threatened (Qld).

Genus ***Nactus***

Four small Aust. spp. with slender tails and fine granular scales mixed with rows of large tubercles. Digits slender, padless and clawed, **each claw set between two scales (fig.)**; single dorsal and ventral plates. ■ **NOTES** Restricted in Aust. to Cape York and Torres Strait; other spp. occur between the wstn Indian Ocean and the Pacific, primarily on islands. Very swift and alert, most are terrestrial generalists, sheltering by day beneath logs, stones and leaf litter. One sp. is specialised to dwell on piled boulders. ■ **SEE ALSO** *Heteronotia*; *Cyrtodactylus.*

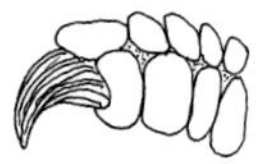

Southern Cape York Nactus *Nactus cheverti* SVL 57mm

Tubercles multi-keeled and conical, in 15–27 (usually 20 or fewer) longitudinal dorsal rows between rear edge of forelimb and front edge of hindlimb. Small pores (1–5, usually 3) sometimes present in front of vent of ♂. About 50% of individuals have smooth thighs, lacking any enlarged tubercles. Scales under tail smooth. Shades of brown with pattern, when present, consisting of pale, transversely aligned blotches with darker leading edges; sharper and tending to form ragged bands on tail. ■ **NOTES** Sthn Cape York Pen., between Cape Melville and Cairns.

Northern Cape York Nactus *Nactus eboracensis* SVL 57mm

Similar in most aspects to *N. cheverti.* Tubercles in 15–37 (usually more than 22) longitudinal dorsal rows between rear edge of forelimb and front edge of hindlimb. Pores in front of vent of ♂ (when present) number 4–11, usually 6. Enlarged tubercles almost always present on thighs. ■ **NOTES** Nthn Cape York Pen., from Princess Charlotte Bay to sthn islands of Torres Strait incl. Thursday, Wednesday, York and Yam.

Lepidodactylus lugubris.
Cooktown, Qld. S. Wilson

Lepidodactylus pumilus.
Morehead area, Papua New Guinea. E. Rittmeyer

Nactus cheverti. Chillagoe, Qld. S. Wilson

Nactus eboracensis.
Tip of Cape York Peninsula, Qld. S. Wilson

Black Mountain Gecko *Nactus galgajuga* SVL 50mm

Very slender and large-eyed, with long limbs and tail. Purplish brown to blackish with broad irregular pale bands or transversely oriented blotches becoming more regular and sharply defined on tail. ■ **NOTES** Restricted to large piled black boulders of Black Mtn, s. of Cooktown. Shelters in crevices and caverns between boulders and forages on exposed rock faces. Extremely swift and agile, able to make well-coordinated leaps between boulders. ■ **STATUS** Vulnerable (Qld).

Pelagic Gecko *Nactus 'pelagicus'* SVL 57mm

Status uncertain. Similar to *N. cheverti* and *N. eboracensis*, but has **keeled scales under the tail**. This is a feature of NG and Pacific *Nactus*, rather than the smooth scales under the tails of Aust. *Nactus*. In other respects, difficult to distinguish. ■ **NOTES** Islands of Torres Strait, from Prince of Wales to outer estn islands and PNG. Other lizards referred to as *N. pelagicus*, incl. parthenogenetic pops, occur on far-flung islands across wstn Pacific.

Nactus galgajuga. Black Mountain, Qld. S. Wilson

Nactus 'pelagicus'. Moa Is., Qld. S. Wilson

FLAP-FOOTED LIZARDS
Family Pygopodidae

Flap-footed lizards are often referred to as 'legless lizards'. They have completely lost their forelimbs and appear quite limbless, but retain vestigial hindlimbs in the form of small scaly flaps. Flap-footed lizards are often killed because of their superficial likeness to snakes. Apart from the hindlimb flaps, they differ from snakes in having a thick fleshy tongue rather than a slender forked tongue. Most species also have obvious ear-openings (never present on snakes); tails much longer than the body (snakes' tails are usually much shorter than the body); and ventral scales that are about the same size as adjacent scales or, if larger, are in a paired series (most snakes have one series of enlarged, transverse ventral scales).

The family is restricted to the Australian region, with 45 described species occurring over most of the country, except south-eastern Victoria, and Tasmania. One species extends north to New Guinea and another is restricted to that island. They tend to favour dry open habitats, particularly the complex heaths of the lower west coast and the spinifex grasslands of the interior.

Pygopodids range from small, worm-like, burrowing insectivores such as *Aprasia* to the large, snake-like Burton's Snake-lizard (*Lialis burtonis*), which preys exclusively on other reptiles. Many species are secretive and nocturnal, seldom seen unless uncovered from beneath stumps or matted, half-buried vegetation. Other species are conspicuous and diurnal, basking among tussocks and heath plants and fleeing with a series of rapid, wriggling leaps when approached. When cornered, some rear their heads and flicker their tongues like small snakes.

The closest relatives of pygopodids are geckos. They share a voice in the form of a harsh squeak, and an ability to lick clean the clear spectacles covering their lidless eyes. The relationship is so close, some scientists have classified them in the one family, essentially regarding the flap-footed lizards as a specialised group of long thin, near-limbless geckos. However, a recent classification based on genetic evidence recognises the Pygopodidae as a distinct family, closely allied to three Australian gecko families. It even appears that some of those gecko families are more closely related to the flap-footed lizards than they are to other geckos. All species of flap-footed lizards are egglayers, producing soft parchment-shelled eggs. As in most geckos, the clutch size is invariably two.

Brigalow Scaly-foot (*Paradelma orientalis*) licking face with its broad fleshy tongue, an ability unique to flap-footed lizards and geckos. Chesterton Range, Qld. S. Wilson

Worm-lizards Genus *Aprasia*

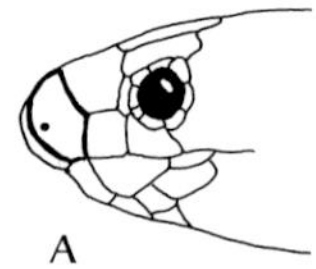

A

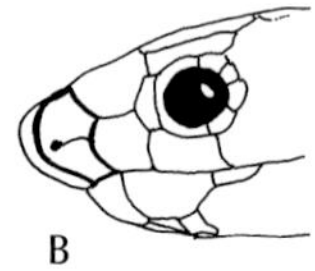

B

Fourteen small, slender, worm-like spp. with **short blunt tails and minute limb flaps. Ear-openings normally absent** (present but greatly reduced on one sp.). Identifying features include whether the 1st upper labial scale is wholly fused (A) or only partly fused (B) with nasal scale. ■ **NOTES** Dry to arid areas of sthn Aust. These burrowing lizards dwell beneath embedded stumps, in insect holes and under rocks and logs. They are often associated with ant nests, probably feeding mainly on the ants' eggs, larvae and pupae. Some have rounded snouts; others are sharply angular and beak-like, reflecting differing burrowing lifestyles and substrates. Many have contrasting tail colours, possibly to distract attention from the head. Mainly nocturnal, though several are active by day.

Eared Worm-lizard *Aprasia aurita* SVL 110mm

Ear-opening present but almost completely covered by notched scale. Snout moderately protrusive, with 1st upper labial scale only partly fused with nasal scale. Body scales in 14 rows. Brown, flushed with pale pink on tail and grey on flanks. Centre of each scale has a dark dash or dot arranged in longitudinal series and tending to coalesce into lines on tail and flanks. ■ **NOTES** Mallee woodlands and spinifex in semi-arid nw. Vic, from Ouyen and Woomelang s. to Wyperfeld NP, and on grey sandy soils at Reedy Creek Range near Millicent, SA. ■ **STATUS** Critically endangered (IUCN Red List); vulnerable (Vic); endangered (SA).

Batavia Coast Worm-lizard *Aprasia clairae* SVL 103mm

Snout long and moderately angular in profile with 1st upper labial scale only partly fused with nasal scale. Midbody scales in 14 rows, ventral scales 152–188 and vertebral scales 138–168. Yellowish to pale brown with obscure dark paravertebral streaks or spots. On tail, these become more continuous and form numerous dark lines. Laterodorsal line more continuous, not clearly delineated from dark brown flanks. Each lateral scale has a pale grey streak. ■ **NOTES** Coastal and near coastal dunes and limestone outcropping from Geraldton s. to Dongara area, and on East Wallabi Is. in Houtman Abrolhos group.

Shark Bay Worm-lizard *Aprasia haroldi* SVL 106mm

Snout protrusive, with 1st upper labial scale only partly fused with nasal scale. Body scales in 14 rows. **Upper labial scales 4** (all other wstn *Aprasia* have 5). Pale yellowish brown fading to white on flanks. Pattern obscure when present; brownish grey streak in centre of each dorsal scale and wavy streak from temple to snout. Tail flushed with pale pink. ■ **NOTES** Pale coastal and near-coastal sands vegetated with low heath and acacia thickets on Edel Land and Dirk Hartog Is., Shark Bay. Shelters beneath leaf litter, limestone slabs, in moist sand under logs and in rotten embedded stumps.

Aprasia aurita.
Wathe Reserve, Vic.
P. Robertson

Aprasia clairae.
Coronation Beach,
WA. B. Maryan

Aprasia haroldi.
Tamala Stn area, WA.
B. Maryan

Red-tailed Worm-lizard; Mallee Worm-lizard *Aprasia inaurita* SVL 136mm

Snout weakly protrusive, with 1st upper labial scale only partly fused with nasal scale. Body scales in 14 rows. Uniform pale yellowish brown to greyish brown on body; **tail bright reddish orange**, boldest towards tip. ■ **NOTES** Semi-arid mallee woodlands on red sands, but occupies pale coastal sands in far w. of range. Shelters in sand beneath stumps or surface debris and in ant nests. Reported to raise brightly coloured tail when threatened. ■ **STATUS** Endangered (NSW).

Gnaraloo Worm-lizard *Aprasia litorea* SVL 98mm

Snout strongly protrusive and angular in profile, with 1st upper labial scale only partly fused with nasal scale. **Midbody scales in 12 rows, ventral scales 162–178 and vertebral scales 158–168.** Yellowish brown above with obscure paravertebral lines of dashes and more continuous **laterodorsal lines not clearly delineated from silvery grey flanks.** Ventral surfaces densely flecked with dark brown. ■ **NOTES** Known only from narrow corridor (1–10km wide) of white sand dunes and white to pink sandplains w. of Lake Macleod, from Gnaraloo Stn s. to Quobba Stn. ■ **SEE ALSO** *A. rostrata.*

Pink-tailed Worm-lizard *Aprasia parapulchella* SVL 140mm

Snout slightly protrusive, with 1st upper labial scale wholly fused to nasal scale. Body scales in 14 rows. Pale grey to greyish brown, merging to pink or pale reddish brown on tail. Dark dot or dash on centre of each scale aligning to form longitudinal series, often coalescing into lines on tail. ■ **NOTES** Sthn ranges around ACT and adjacent NSW; isolated pops near Bendigo, Vic and Gunnedah area, NSW. Favours areas with native grasses and partially buried rocks. Shelters beneath rocks and in ant tunnels. Commonly found with old, sloughed skins, suggesting long-term residence. ■ **STATUS** Endangered (Vic); vulnerable (C'wealth; NSW; ACT).

Black-headed Worm-lizard *Aprasia picturata* SVL 122mm

Snout long and angular, with 1st upper labial scale only partly fused to nasal scale. Body scales in 14 rows. Rich orange-brown with **sharply contrasting black head** and yellowish brown tail. ■ **NOTES** Known only from rocky ridges vegetated with low acacias and eremophilas near Leonora, in arid interior of sthn WA.

Flinders Worm-lizard *Aprasia pseudopulchella* SVL 143mm

Snout slightly protrusive, with 1st upper labial scale wholly fused to nasal scale. Body scales in 14 rows. Greyish brown, darker on head, merging to pink or reddish brown on tail. Dark dot or dash on centre of each scale aligning to form longitudinal series, often coalescing into lines on tail. ■ **NOTES** Stony soils, particularly near creeks and rivers, from Flinders Ra. s. to Adelaide. Shelters in soil beneath stones and rotting stumps. ■ **STATUS** Vulnerable (C'wealth); lower risk – near threatened (IUCN Red List).

Aprasia inaurita.
Port Germein, SA. S. Wilson

Aprasia litorea. Gnaraloo Stn, WA. B. Maryan

Aprasia parapulchella.
Coppin's Crossing, ACT. E. Vanderduys

Aprasia parapulchella.
Bendigo district, Vic. R. Valentic

Aprasia picturata.
Minara Stn, WA. R. Browne-Cooper

Aprasia pseudopulchella.
Burra area, SA. S. Wilson

Granite Worm-lizard *Aprasia pulchella* SVL 120mm

Snout slightly protrusive, with **1st upper labial scale wholly fused to nasal scale** (only sp. with this condition in WA). Body scales in 14 rows. Brown to dark brown, merging to blackish brown on head and tail. Pattern usually obscure; a fine dark dash on centre of each scale, forming narrow lines on tail. ■ **NOTES** Granite and laterite soils on the sthn ranges of sw. WA, n. to the Darling R. Shelters in soil beneath embedded rocks, fallen timber, stumps and surface debris.

Sand-plain Worm-lizard *Aprasia repens* SVL 126mm

Snout long and slightly angular, with 1st upper labial scale only partly fused to nasal scale. Body scales in 12 rows. Pale silvery brown, darker on head and flushed with yellow to pale pink on tail and yellow on throat. Dark dash on the centre of each scale aligning to form longitudinal series, coalescing into lines on tail. ■ **NOTES** Pale coastal sand-plains of sw. WA, n. to Kalbarri and e. to Esperance. Apparently isolated pop. occurs further inland on a sand-plain at Bungalbin. Common near Perth.

Ningaloo Worm-lizard *Aprasia rostrata* SVL 126mm

Snout protrusive, strongly angular and beak-like in profile, with 1st upper labial scale only partly fused with nasal scale. **Midbody scales in 14 rows, ventral scales 172 – 192 and vertebral scales 168-190**. Cream to pale brown with 4 narrow dark lines; weak to prominent paravertebrals and more continuous **laterodorsals sharply delineated from whitish to silvery grey flanks**. Ventral surfaces densely flecked with dark brown. ■ **NOTES** North West Cape s. to Yardie Ck and Learmonth and inland to Bullara Stn. Also Montebello Is. (Hermite and Trimouille) and Barrow Is. off Pilbara Coast. Occupies variety of sandy habitats incl. white coastal dunes and red dunes vegetated with *Triodia*. ■ **SEE ALSO** *A. litorea*. ■ **STATUS** Vulnerable (IUCN Red List; C'wealth; WA)

Black-tipped Worm-lizard *Aprasia smithi* SVL 128mm

Snout sharp-edged and protrusive, with 1st upper labial scale only partly fused to nasal scale. Body scales in 12 rows. Reddish orange to yellowish orange, contrasting sharply with **glossy black head and tail-tip**. Dark brown dashes in centre of each scale forming longitudinal series. ■ **NOTES** Semi-arid mid-w. coast and hinterland from Shark Bay s. to Kalbarri and inland to Towrana. Favours reddish brown sandy loams and yellow sands vegetated with shrublands and low woodlands.

Aprasia pulchella.
Mt Dale, WA. R. Browne-Cooper

Aprasia repens. Hamilton Hill, WA. B. Maryan

Aprasia rostrata. Hermite Is., WA. B. Maryan

Aprasia rostrata, Yardie Creek, WA. B. Maryan

Aprasia smithi. Meadow Stn district, WA. B. Maryan

Lined Worm-lizard *Aprasia striolata* SVL 130mm

Snout slightly protrusive, with 1st upper labial scale only partly fused to nasal scale. Body scales in 12 rows. Pattern extremely variable. Eastern pops are pale brown to grey, **prominently striped with black**, with a pair of broad black lateral stripes, and often 2 narrow dorsal lines or series of dashes. Wstn and Kangaroo Is. pops have little pattern; dashes on each scale may align to form longitudinal series, coalescing into narrow lines on tail. ■ **NOTES** Lower s. coast of WA, sthn SA and sw. Vic. Pops in WA and wstn Eyre Pen. occupy pale coastal sands. In remainder of SA and wstn Vic, found in sand-plains and rock outcrops (including limestone). ■ **STATUS** Near threatened (Vic).

Wicherina Worm-lizard *Aprasia wicherina* SVL 92mm

Snout protrusive, strongly angular and beak-like in profile with 1st upper labial scale only partly fused with nasal scale. Midbody scales in 14 rows, ventral scales 146–162 and vertebral scales 142–156. Yellowish brown with obscure paravertebral rows of smudges and continuous laterodorsal lines of dark streaks, clearly delineated from white to silvery grey flanks. Each lateral scale has dark brown to black streak. Pattern more continuous on tail, forming about 10 narrow lines. ■ **NOTES** Known only from Wicherina Water Res., an elevated sandplain featuring mallee heath over diverse shrub layer and ground cover appr. 40km. e. of Geraldton, WA.

Genus *Delma*

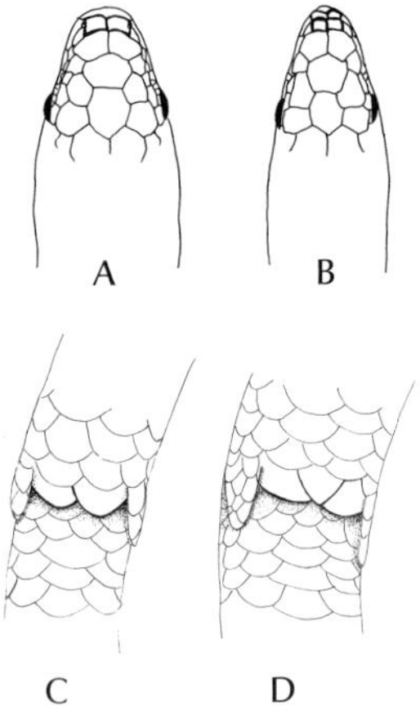

Twenty-two slender spp. with **well-developed hindlimb flaps**, ear-openings, smooth shiny scales, **paired ventral scales usually noticeably larger than adjacent scales**, and tails 2–4 times length of body. Spp. are identified by pattern; whether they have 2 (A) or 4 (B) supranasal scales; position of 3rd or 4th upper labial scales relative to eye; and number of preanal scales, either 2 (C) or 3 (D). ■ **NOTES** Aust.-wide, wherever dry conditions prevail. Some are mainly nocturnal and others diurnal, but most are both according to temperature. They live in dense low vegtn, particularly tussock grasses and spinifex. Within the matrix they move with an easy serpentine gait; on open ground they use a series of wriggling leaps. They eat small invertebrates, mainly insects.

Aprasia striolata.
Lake Bong Bong, Vic.
P. Robertson

Aprasia striolata.
Albany district, WA.
S. Wilson

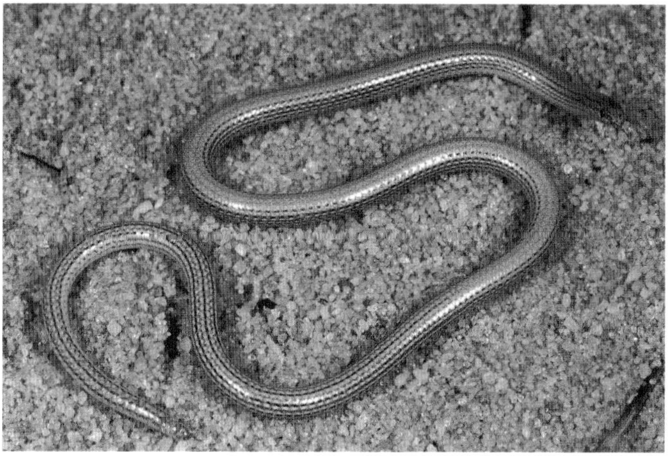

Aprasia wicherina.
Wicherina Water Reserve,
WA. B. Maryan.

Marble-faced Delma *Delma australis* SVL 93mm

Blunt snout with 4th upper labial scale below eye, 2 **supranasal scales** and **3 preanal scales**. Midbody scales usually in 18 rows. **Ventrals not enlarged.** Tail relatively short; less than 2.5 times length of body. Sthn pops are brown to reddish brown with **strong dark variegations or narrow bars on head, nape and forebody extending onto chin and throat**. In n. head markings greatly reduced. ■ **NOTES** Dry to arid sthn Aust., particularly in sandy areas with mallee/spinifex and shrublands. Shelters beneath leaf litter and in spinifex, favouring slightly more humid sites than other *Delma*. In very arid areas it often occurs near creeks. ■ **SEE ALSO** *D. hebesa.* ■ **STATUS** Endangered (NSW).

Northern Delma *Delma borea* SVL 95mm

Fourth upper labial scale below eye, **4 supranasal scales** and **3 preanal scales. Midbody scales in 16 rows.** Tail nearly 3.5 times length of body. Brown to grey with ventrolateral variegations on forebody, pattern usually prominent, but obscure on older individuals. **Head and nape have 3–4 black to dark brown bands**; the narrow pale interspaces tend to be orange above and cream laterally. ■ **NOTES** Dry to arid nthn Aust., favouring heavy to stony soils with grassy ground cover, particularly spinifex. ■ **SEE ALSO** *D. tincta.* ■ **STATUS** Rare (SA).

Spinifex Delma *Delma butleri* SVL 96mm

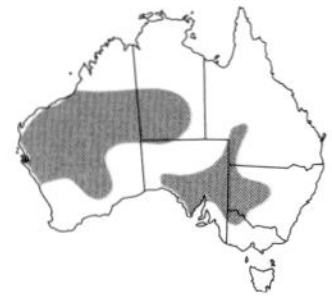

Fourth upper labial scale below eye, **4 supranasal scales** and **3 preanal scales.** Midbody scales in 15–18 (usually 16) rows. Tail nearly 3.5 times length of body. Greyish brown to olive brown with finely dark-edged scales. Pattern usually absent, though narrow, wavy, pale vertical bars often present on sides of head and neck in some pops. Ventral colour-change has been recorded, from white to yellow over a 20-second to 10-minute period. ■ **NOTES** Shelters in spinifex in semi-arid to arid areas. ■ **SEE ALSO** *D. haroldi; D. nasuta.*

Javelin Delma *Delma concinna* SVL 100–112mm

Extremely slender, with long snout, 4th upper labial scale below eye, and large hind limb flaps. Midbody scales usually in 20 rows; **ventrals not noticeably enlarged. Tail about 4 times length of body.** ■ **SSP.** *D. c. concinna* is brownish grey with narrow dark dorsal stripes enclosing a dark grey zone and having a paler outer edge. *D. c. major* is larger with simpler pattern; dark dorsal stripes wider, coalescing to form a broad dark stripe. ■ **NOTES** Heaths on dunes and sand-plains along mid- to lower west coast. *D. c. concinna* occurs between sthn Perth suburbs and Dongara. *D. c. major* occurs at Shark Bay. Diurnal. Dwells in dense matrix of low vegtn and associated leaf litter, fleeing rapidly with a series of wriggling leaps when disturbed.

Delma australis. Coober Pedy area, SA. S. Wilson

Delma australis. Big Desert, Vic. S. Wilson

Delma borea. Koolan Island, WA. B. Maryan

Delma butleri. Peron Peninsula, Shark Bay, WA. B. Maryan

Delma butleri. Nappa Merrie Stn, Qld. S. Wilson

Delma concinna concinna. Cockleshell Gully, WA. S. Wilson

Delma concinna major. Tamala Stn, WA. G. Harold

Desert Delma *Delma desmosa* SVL 90mm

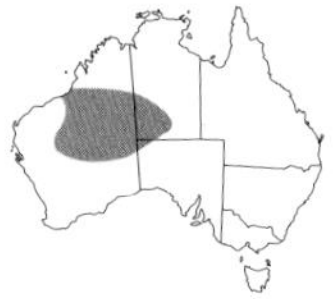

Third (rarely 4th) upper labial scale below eye, 4 supranasal scales and 3 preanal scales. **Midbody scales usually in 16 rows.** Brown with 3–4 dark bands on head and nape; **pattern prominent on juv., fading with age but retained for life.** Interspaces sometimes pale orange-brown dorsally on adults. ■ **NOTES** Spinifex deserts of central and wstn Aust. ■ **SEE ALSO** *D. tincta.* ■ **STATUS** Near threatened (SA).

Pilbara Delma *Delma elegans* SVL 97mm

Fourth upper labial scale below eye, **4 supranasal scales** and **3 preanal scales**. Midbody scales in 18 (rarely 19–20) rows. Tail nearly 4 times length of body. Olive brown to brown; pattern prominent on juv., fading with age. **About 5–6 dark head and neck bands descend obliquely forward**, forking and terminating acutely on sides of head and neck, and broken by yellowish to pale grey interspaces, each broadest and most prominent laterally. Side of forebody bears oblique dark-edged pale bars. ■ **NOTES** Shelters in spinifex in rocky areas in Hamersley Ra. and adjacent lowlands and outcrops of arid Pilbara.

Fraser's Delma *Delma fraseri* SVL 140mm

Fourth upper labial scale below eye, **4 supranasal scales** and **3 preanal scales**. Midbody scales in 16 (occasionally 17; rarely 18–20) rows. Tail nearly 4 times length of body. Pattern prominent on juv., fading with age. Grey to reddish brown (redder on tail) with **3 broad dark head and neck bands** (separated on top by reddish brown interspaces and on the sides by cream vertical bars), extending onto edges of throat as fine dark variegations. ■ **NOTES** Occupies various habitats, from pale coastal sands to woodlands and heaths in dry to semi-arid areas of sw. WA. ■ **SEE ALSO** *D. petersoni.*

Side-barred Delma *Delma grayii* SVL 121mm

Snout long, 4th upper labial scale below eye, **4 supranasal scales** and **3 preanal scales**. Midbody scales in 16 (occasionally 17–18) rows. Tail more than 4 times length of body. Olive brown, copper on upper flanks, with a dark spot on each scale forming longitudinal series, and a row of **vertical cream to yellow bars on sides of head, neck and forebody**. Ventral surfaces yellow. ■ **NOTES** Sandy to lateritic soils with heath and banksia woodlands on lower w. coast and adjacent inland areas between Perth and Shark Bay. Mainly diurnal. Usually seen leaping swiftly through thick low vegtn.

Delma desmosa.
Officer Basin, WA. B. Maryan

Delma elegans.
Mt Brockman, WA. G. Harold

Delma fraseri.
Fitzgerald River NP, WA.
S. Wilson

Delma grayii.
Cervantes, WA. S. Wilson

Neck-barred Delma *Delma haroldi* SVL 75mm

Fourth (occasionally 5th) upper labial scale below eye, **4 supranasal scales** and **3 preanal scales**. Midbody scales in 16 (occasionally 18) rows. Tail more than 3.5 times length of body. Brown, darker on head, with wavy narrow pale bands, broadest laterally, across base of head and nape, and 3–4 additional bands on sides of temples, behind eye and on sides of snout. Anterior dorsal scales each tipped with a dark spot. ■ **NOTES** Spinifex and shrublands on heavy to stony soils. ■ **SEE ALSO** *D. butleri.*

Heath Delma *Delma hebesa* SVL 70mm

Blunt snout with 4th upper labial scale below eye, **2 supranasal scales** and **3 preanal scales**. Midbody scales usually in 18 rows. **Ventrals not enlarged**. Tail relatively short. Pale brown merging into bluish to pale grey on anterior body and pale grey on tail. Top of head bluish to pale grey; patternless or with weak dark variegations. Dark bars or smudges present on lower labial scales and **obscure variegations or bars on sides of neck and forebody but not on chin and throat.** ■ **NOTES** Proteaceous shrublands and mallee heath on s. coastal sandplains from Thomas R. and Cape Arid w. to Canal Rocks and Busselton area. ■ **SEE ALSO** *D. australis.*

Striped Delma *Delma impar* SVL 100mm

First upper labial partly fused with nasal scales, 4th upper labial scale below eye, **2 supranasal scales** and **2 preanal scales**. Midbody scales in 14–16 rows. Tail 2.5–3 times length of body. **Pattern distinctive, prominent and linear**; a broad olive brown vertebral stripe, and narrow dark and pale lateral lines tending to break into oblique bars or rows of spots on tail. ■ **NOTES** Temperate grassy plains from far se. SA to ACT and Hunter Valley region of NSW. Shelters beneath loose rocks and in grass tussocks. Most southerly flap-footed lizard. Much of its habitat on fertile volcanic plains of sthn Vic has been, and is being, dramatically reduced by agricultural and urban development. ■ **STATUS** Endangered (Vic; SA); vulnerable (C'wealth; NSW; ACT; IUCN Red List).

Olive Delma *Delma inornata* SVL 133mm

Snout long, 4th upper labial scale below eye, **4 supranasal scales (usually 2 in SA)** and **3 preanal scales**. Midbody scales in 15–18 (usually 16) rows. Tail up to 4 times length of body. Pattern obscure to virtually absent; olive brown with dark-edged scales. ■ **NOTES** Dry to temperate sthn grasslands and grassy woodlands between se. SA and Darling Downs of se. Qld.

Delma haroldi.
De Grey River region, WA.
D. Robinson

Delma hebesa.
Scaddan, WA. B. Maryan

Delma impar.
Western Melbourne area,
Vic. S. Wilson

Delma inornata.
Bowenville, Qld. S. Wilson

Stripe-tailed Delma *Delma labialis* SVL 115mm

Snout long, 4th upper labial scale below eye, **4 supranasal scales** and **3 preanal scales**. Midbody scales in 16 rows. Tail about 4 times length of body. Reddish brown, yellower on head and greyer on tail. Very distinctive pattern; a lateral row of **cream and pale yellowish brown vertical bars between lips and forebody**, and a **narrow dark dorsolateral stripe** from posterior body well onto tail. ■ **NOTES** From Paluma s. to Keswick Is. and inland to Moranbah. Isolated record from Heathlands in nthn Cape York. WSF and low open forest with a grassy understorey. Diurnal. ■ **STATUS** Vulnerable (IUCN Red List).

Atherton Delma *Delma mitella* SVL 200mm

Snout long, 4th upper labial scale below eye, **4 supranasal scales** and **3 preanal scales**. Midbody scales in 16 rows. Tail very long, about 4 times length of body. Reddish brown, darker copper on head broken by **4 narrow pale bands** (becoming obscure to absent with age), and usually with a distinctive narrow **dark bluish grey stripe along junction between lateral and ventral surfaces**. Ventral surfaces yellow to bright fluorescent lime green. ■ **NOTES** Known only from tall open forests and RF interfaces between Mareeba and Paluma areas. ■ **STATUS** Vulnerable (C'wealth); near threatened (Qld).

Adelaide Delma *Delma molleri* SVL 111mm

Fourth upper labial scale below eye, **2 supranasal scales** and **3 preanal scales**. Midbody scales in 16–18 (usually 18) rows. Tail about 3 times length of body. Pale brown to greyish brown, often with dark smudges on each scale aligning to form indistinct stripes. Pattern prominent on juv., becoming obscure with age; **2 dark bands on head and neck** separated by a pale interspace (2–3 scales wide) from ear to ear. No markings extend onto throat. ■ **NOTES** Adelaide Plains, Yorke Pen. and adjacent ranges in SA, in a variety of habitats including dry to semi-arid grasslands and shrublands, agricultural regions and river flats.

Sharp-snouted Delma *Delma nasuta* SVL 112mm

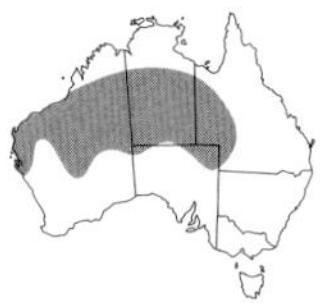

Snout long, 4th upper labial scale below eye, **4 supranasal scales** and **3 preanal scales**. Midbody scales in 16 rows. Tail more than 4 times length of body. Dull olive to brown, each scale with a dark spot or margin forming **reticulated to spotted pattern**, strongest on flanks. ■ **NOTES** Shelters in spinifex on sands, sandy loams or stony soils in semi-arid to arid zones. ■ **SEE ALSO** *D. butleri.*

Delma labialis.
Keswick Is., Qld. S. Wilson

Delma mitella.
Tolga, Qld. S. Wilson

Delma molleri.
Clare Valley, SA. S. Wilson

Delma nasuta.
Docker River, NT. S. Wilson

Peace Delma *Delma pax* SVL 98mm

Third upper labial scale below eye, 4 supranasal scales and **3 preanal scales.** Midbody scales in 16 rows. Tail about 3.5 times length of body. Brown to reddish brown; each scale usually smudged forming indistinct lines. Head and nape pattern of 4 dark bands with reddish brown interspaces; **pattern fades completely with age.** ■ **NOTES** Arid Pilbara region in spinifex grasslands on heavy to stony soils. Also recorded beneath accumulated leaf litter and mats of dead vegetation near dry watercourses.

Painted Delma *Delma petersoni* SVL 128mm

Fourth upper labial scale below eye. **4 supranasal scales** and **3 preanal scales.** Midbody scales in 18 (rarely 17) rows. Tail nearly 4 times length of body. Pattern prominent on juv and fading on adults. Pale brown becoming yellowish brown on tail, with dark head, dark blotch on nape, broad dark bars on face and **dark bands across throat.** ■ **NOTES** Spinifex habitats along sthn edge of Great Victoria Desert between nthn Eyre Pen. and sthn WA. ■ **SEE ALSO** *D. fraseri.*

Leaden Delma *Delma plebeia* SVL 122mm

Fourth upper labial scale below eye, **4 supranasal scales** and **2 preanal scales.** Midbody scales in 14–16 (usually 16) rows. Tail about 3 times length of body. Grey to olive above and sometimes reddish brown on flanks. Top of head very dark on juv., fading with age and contracting to dark smudges on sides of head and neck. ■ **NOTES** DSF and woodlands, usually with a grassy understorey.

North West Cape Delma *Delma tealei* SVL 88mm

Third upper labial scale below eye, 4 supranasal scales and **3 preanal scales. Midbody scales usually in 14 rows.** Greyish brown above with pinkish flush from rear of body onto base of tail, and **greyish lower lateral variegations on anterior body. No dark markings on head and neck of adults.** Juv. colouration not recorded. ■ **NOTES** Stony hills with spinifex on Cape Range Pen., North West Cape. ■ **SEE ALSO** *D. tincta.*

Black-necked Delma *Delma tincta* SVL 92mm

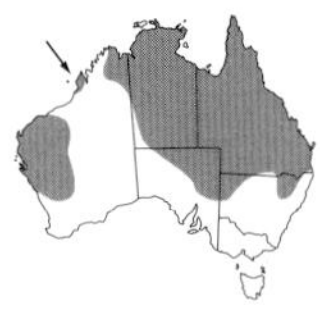

Third upper labial scale below eye, 2 supranasal scales and **3 preanal scales. Midbody scales usually in 14 rows.** Tail nearly 4 times length of body. Greyish brown to reddish brown with ventrolateral variegations on forebody. Head and nape markings prominent on juv., fading to virtual absence with age; 3–4 dark bands with cream to yellow interspaces. ■ **NOTES** Dry to arid regions in a wide variety of habitats, from spinifex deserts to dry forests and rock outcrops. ■ **SEE ALSO** *D. borea; D. desmosa; D. tealei.*

Delma pax.
Burrup Peninsula, WA.
R. Browne-Cooper

Delma petersoni.
Queen Victoria Spring, WA. G. Gaikhorst

Delma plebeia.
Purga Nature Reserve, Qld. S. Wilson

Delma tealei.
Cape Range NP, WA. B. Maryan

Delma tincta.
White Mountains NP, Qld. S. Wilson

Collared Delma *Delma torquata* SVL 63mm

Third upper labial scale below eye, 2 supranasal scales and **2 preanal scales.** Midbody scales in 16 rows. Tail about twice length of body. Reddish brown merging to bluish grey on tail. Head and nape pattern prominent; glossy black, broken by 3–4 narrow, yellow to orange interspaces. **Chin and throat boldly reticulated with grey to black.** ■ **NOTES** Se. Qld, n. to Blackdown Tableland and inland to Bunya Mtns and Millmerran. Recorded from rocky areas associated with dry open forests, and from brigalow associations. Shelters beneath rocks, logs and leaf litter, and possibly in insect and spider holes. ■ **STATUS** Vulnerable (C'wealth; Qld; IUCN Red List).

Genus *Lialis*

Burton's Snake-lizard *Lialis burtonis* SVL 290mm

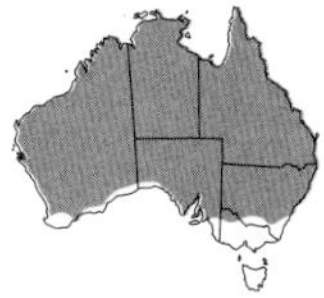

Sole Aust. member of genus; one other (*L. jicari*) is restricted to NG. Very distinctive, with long, **pointed, wedge-shaped snout, fragmented head shields,** vertically elliptic pupils and **very small limb-flaps.** Tail up to 1.7 times length of body. Colour and pattern extremely variable, with many different colour forms present in any given area. Colour ranges from cream and patternless through shades of grey, brown and yellow to brick red with various combinations of stripes, or stripes and lines of spots. Often the only markings are bold white and black stripes through face and forebody. ■ **NOTES** Most widespread Aust. reptile, extending from sthn WA to NG. Absent only from cool high altitudes of Gt Div. Ra., Tas, and parts of sthn mainland. Virtually all habitats from desert sand-ridges and gibber flats to woodlands, DSF and margins of WSF and RF. Nocturnal and diurnal. A lizard specialist, feeding mainly on skinks, but also on geckos, dragons, other pygopodids and small snakes. Usually grips prey at about chest area, holds it fast until suffocated, then swallows it head-first. To facilitate this there is a unique hinge across the head at eye-level, allowing the tips of the snout to meet when the prey is grasped.

Genus *Ophidiocephalus*

Bronzeback *Ophidiocephalus taeniatus* SVL 102mm

Sole member of genus. Moderately slender, with **protrusive snout** and **small limb-flaps.** Scales smooth in 16 rows at midbody; **ventrals not noticeably enlarged.** Tail about 1.5 times length of body. Bronze brown above, paler on head. A **narrow, dark, upper lateral line from head to tail-tip** is sharply delineated from back, and merges below with greyish brown, densely peppered flanks. ■ **NOTES** Near tree-lined watercourses at Charlotte Waters in sthn NT, and Abminga and Coober Pedy areas in nthn and central SA. A sand-swimmer, sheltering in loose upper layers of soil beneath leaf litter overlaying deeply cracking sandy loams. Retreats down deep cracks if disturbed. ■ **STATUS** Vulnerable (C'wealth; IUCN Red List); endangered (NT); rare (SA).

Delma torquata.
Mt Crosby, Qld. S. Wilson

Lialis burtonis.
Three Ways, NT. S. Wilson

Lialis burtonis.
Chesterton Range, Qld. S. Wilson

Lialis burtonis.
Mt Tyson, Qld. S. Wilson

Lialis burtonis.
Sturt NP, NSW. G. Swan

Ophidiocephalus taeniatus.
Coober Pedy area, SA. B. Maryan

Genus *Paradelma*

Brigalow Scaly-foot *Paradelma orientalis* SVL 197mm

Sole member of genus. Robust, with **round snout** and **moderately large limb-flaps.** Scales smooth and glossy in 18 (occasionally 20) rows; ventrals enlarged. Tail about twice length of body. Lead grey to greyish brown with an opaque sheen. **Base of head cream to pale brown, darkening towards snout and contrasting sharply with black bar on nape.** ■ **NOTES** Sandstone ridges, woodlands and vine thickets, including brigalow. Shelters beneath sandstone slabs, logs, dense leaf litter and in grass tussocks. Nocturnal. When alarmed, rears head and forebody and flickers tongue, possibly to mimic venomous snakes. Frequently recorded climbing the rough bark of wattles, possibly to lick exuding sap. ■ **STATUS** Vulnerable (IUCN Red List).

Genus *Pletholax*

Keeled Legless Lizard *Pletholax gracilis* SVL 84–90mm

Sole member of genus. **Extremely slender,** with **pointed snout, small limb-flaps** and **all scales including ventrals strongly keeled,** in 16 rows. Tail nearly 3.5 times length of body. Broad pale grey vertebral stripe, and darker lateral stripe flushed with reddish brown on forebody. Lips, throat and anterior ventral surfaces bright yellow. ■ **SSP.** *P. g. gracilis* has ear-opening. *P. g. edelensis* is larger and lacks ear-opening. ■ **NOTES** *P. g. gracilis* occurs on sand-plains with heaths and banksias between Perth and Kalbarri, while *P. g. edelensis* is restricted to Edel Land Pen. and Dirk Hartog Is., Shark Bay, on dunes with Beach Spinifex (*Spinifex longifolius*) and brown loam supporting *Triodia.* Diurnal. Extremely secretive, basking on dense low vegtn and leaping rapidly for cover when disturbed.

Scaly-foots Genus *Pygopus*

Five very large, robust spp. with round snouts, **prominent ear-openings,** smooth to keeled **scales in 21 or more rows,** enlarged paired ventrals, long tails and **very large, well-developed limb-flaps.** Identification of 3 similar dark-hooded species is determined by presence or extent of dorsal keels and whether nostril contacts 1st upper labial scale (A) or is separated (B). ■ **NOTES** Widespread throughout Aust. When harassed, they rear and flicker their thick fleshy tongues in apparent mimicry of venomous snakes. Hooded spp. have head markings closely resembling those of young brown snakes (*Pseudonaja* spp.). If grasped, scaly-foots struggle violently, utter a long wheezing squeak, rotate within the hand and readily discard their tails. They feed on arthropods, including significant numbers of spiders and scorpions.

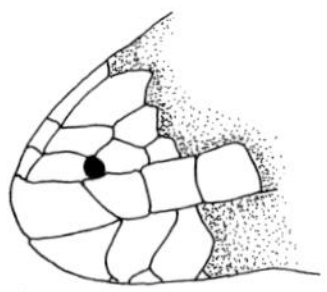

A

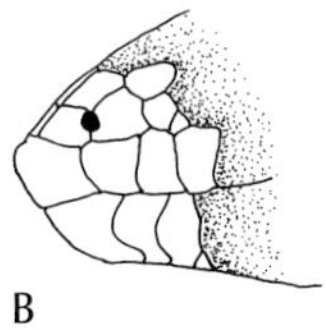

B

Paradelma orientalis.
Chesterton Range, Qld. S. Wilson

Pletholax gracilis edelensis.
False Entrance Well, WA. B. Maryan

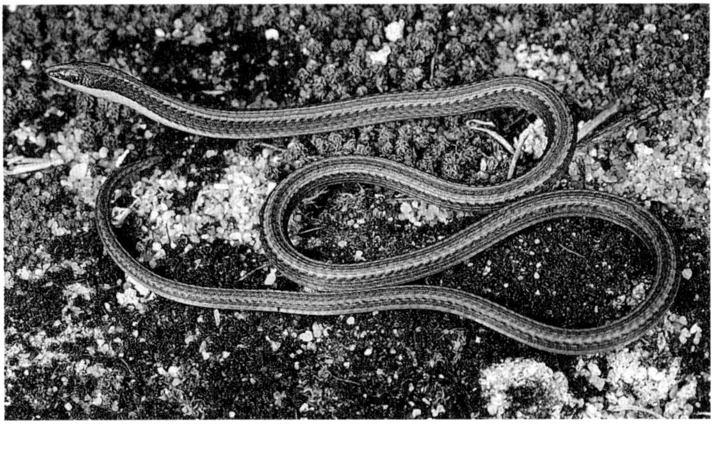

Pletholax gracilis gracilis.
Koondoola, WA. B. Maryan

Common Scaly-foot *Pygopus lepidopodus* SVL 274mm

Strong keels on 10 or more dorsal scale rows, 22 or more midbody scale rows, 2 rows of supraciliary scales and variable colouration; strongly and weakly marked forms occur. Strongly marked lizards are grey with 3 rows of large elongate black blotches with sharp white lateral edges and reddish brown longitudinal interspaces. Weakly marked lizards are either grey, or reddish brown with grey heads and tails. Blotches are largely absent though some trace is normally retained on tail. ■ **NOTES** Open habitats such as heaths and woodlands across sthn Aust, n. to Rockhampton area, Qld. Shelters beneath low vegtn and in dense grasses. Often encountered foraging in open low vegtn on warm sunny mornings, fleeing rapidly when disturbed. Nocturnal in hot weather.

Western Hooded Scaly-foot *Pygopus nigriceps* SVL 227mm

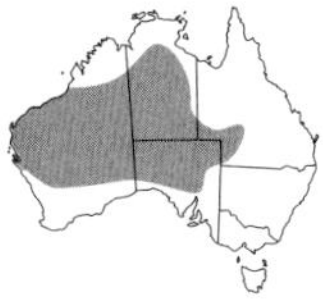

Smooth-scaled, with **dark markings on head and neck, nostril separated from 1st upper labial scale,** and usually **120 or more ventral scales.** Brown to reddish brown with dark brown to black bar across head through eyes onto upper and sometimes lower lips, dark smudge on nostril and broad dark band across neck. Body pattern usually weak; oblique dark lines converging mid-dorsally. ■ **NOTES** Variety of dry habitats, particularly sandy deserts. Shelters in soil cracks and under debris. Nocturnal.

Roberts' Scaly-foot *Pygopus robertsi* SVL 224 mm

Weak keels on 9 dorsal scale rows, **21 mid-body scale rows** and **one row of supraciliary scales**. Pattern reduced; reddish brown to greyish brown with dark bar below eye and sometimes faint grey chin straps. ■ **NOTES** Heath and dry woodland in ne. Qld from Atherton Tableland n. to Shipton's Flat. Pop. in Heathlands area possibly isolated.

Eastern Hooded Scaly-foot *Pygopus schraderi* SVL 198mm

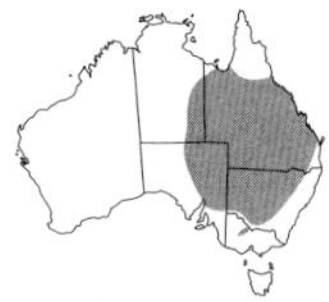

Keeled, with **keels on 10 or more dorsal body-scale rows, dark markings on head and neck, nostril contacting 1st upper labial scale and fewer than 120 ventral scales.** Brown to reddish brown or grey with dark brown to black hood on head, including a prominent to obscure dark band across neck and dark marks under eyes and nostrils. Body pattern prominent to absent; narrow dark and pale broken longitudinal lines, tending to form oblique patterns on tail, and sometimes a continuous vertebral stripe. ■ **NOTES** Dry to arid zones in a variety of open habitats, but typically on stony and heavy soils. Shelters in soil cracks and under debris. Nocturnal. ■ **STATUS** Critically endangered (Vic).

Northern Hooded Scaly-foot *Pygopus steelescotti* SVL 185mm

Weakly keeled, with **keels on less than 10 dorsal body-scale rows, dark markings on head and neck, nostril contacting 1st upper labial scale and fewer than 120 ventral scales.** Pale brown to pale yellowish brown, with **weak pattern**; a dark teardrop under eyes, an indication of dark smudges under nostrils and dark hood on head, including a diffuse dark band across neck. Body pattern weak to absent; narrow dark and pale broken longitudinal lines, tending to form oblique patterns on tail. ■ **NOTES** Tropical woodlands n. of 22°N. Shelters in soil cracks and under debris. Nocturnal.

Pygopus lepidopodus.
Mt Nebo, Qld. S. Wilson

Pygopus lepidopodus.
Big Desert, Vic. S. Wilson

Pygopus lepidopodus.
Fitzgerald River NP, WA. S. Wilson

Pygopus nigriceps.
Kennedy Range, WA. R. Browne-Cooper

Pygopus robertsi.
Mt Sampson, Qld. L. Roberts

Pygopus schraderi.
Moranbah area, Qld. S. Wilson

Pygopus steelescotti.
Wyndham district, WA. G. Harold

SKINKS
Family Scincidae

In terms of abundance, number of species, distribution and diversity of form, skinks are the most successful group of Australian vertebrates. In this volume 437 species are recognised and the number grows as more are described. From wave-washed rocks on Cape York to the chilly heaths of southern Tasmania, skinks are usually the most numerous reptiles. They are also common on all continents except Antarctica, and thrive on some of the most remote oceanic islands.

Skinks are so diverse that few easily discernible features apply to all. Typically they are the smooth, swift lizards we are most familiar with. Most have 4 limbs, 5 fingers and toes, tails that can be discarded and re-grown, shiny, overlapping body scales, and head scales arranged as symmetrical shields. They tend to be sun-loving, basking on the leaf litter and darting for cover when approached. Yet none of these features applies to all skinks.

Based on this simple layout, the skink form is extraordinarily malleable. Many burrowers have elongated bodies with limbs and digits reduced or lost. Progressive loss of limbs and digits has occurred independently several times, reaching its extreme in completely limbless worm-like skinks.

Skinks living on exposed vertical surfaces follow an opposite trend, having flat bodies and longer, more slender limbs and digits. Others are robust and spiny so that they can wedge themselves securely into rock crevices and tree hollows. At another extreme the Shingleback (*Tiliqua rugosa*) is huge and ponderously slow, with a bulbous tail and pinecone-like scales.

The fusing of the eyelid is another modification to have evolved in quite separate skink lineages. Small active skinks in dry climates can lose critical moisture from the surface of the eye; this problem has been solved by capping the eye with a fixed transparent spectacle. Others, including many in temperate and moist habitats, have a moveable lid enclosing a transparent window called a palpebral disc.

Skinks include egglayers and livebearers. Livebearing predominates in cool southern areas where incubation of eggs is hindered by low temperatures. The advantages of warming embryos within the mother's body as she basks outweigh the hindrance to her mobility. In Tasmania virtually all skinks are livebearers while in the tropics most are egglayers.

Most skinks are generalist predators of invertebrates, though some appear to specialise or have distinct preferences. *Coeranoscincus* are large rainforest burrowers with long recurved teeth believed to facilitate predation on earthworms; the Pink-tongued Skink (*Cyclodomorphus gerrardii*) has large rounded teeth at the rear of the mouth to help crack snail shells; several desert striped skinks (*Ctenotus*) feed largely on termites. Medium to large skinks often include smaller skinks in their diets, but with increasing size there is a trend towards omnivory. The largest skinks, blue-tongues (*Tiliqua* spp.) and the Land Mullet (*Bellatorias major*), consume significant amounts of vegetable matter, including fungi.

Not surprisingly, this large and complex family of lizards contains many very similar species. Identification can be extremely difficult, or even impossible, without a microscope. Sometimes merely the presence, absence or modified alignment of a single small scale is all that stands between different species. Where necessary these features are provided here, but in some cases identification problems are unavoidable.

Eastern Blue-tongue (*Tiliqua scincoides*), one of the world's largest skinks. Alton NP, Qld. E. Vanderduys

Genus *Acritoscincus*

Three small spp. with 4 short, well-developed limbs, usually just touching when adpressed on ♂, failing to meet on ♀, each with 5 digits. Lower eyelid moveable, enclosing a transparent disc. No lobules on ear-opening. Parietal scales in contact, **frontoparietals fused into single shield, interparietal reduced, nasals moderately widely separated (fig.)**. Usually marked with

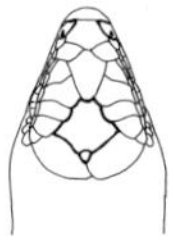

dark longitudinal stripes, including broad straight-edged dark upper lateral stripe; red throat flush on brdg ♂. ■ **NOTES** Cool temp. s. Aust. incl. Tas. Diurnal sun-lovers, basking and foraging for small invertebrates under low rocks and logs, in leaf litter and among grass tussocks. Lays eggs, often communally. ■ **SEE ALSO** *Carinascincus; Lampropholis; Pseudemoia.*

Eastern Three-lined Skink *Acritoscincus duperreyi* SVL 80mm

Silvery grey to greyish brown. Pattern normally prominent; narrow dark vertebral stripe, narrow pale dorsolateral stripes, each with dark inner edge, broad black upper lateral stripe and white midlateral stripe. Orange-red throat flush of varying intensity; boldest on brdg ♂. ■ **NOTES** Se. mainland and Tas, n. to Newnes Plat., NSW and w. to Fleurieu Pen. and Kangaroo Is., SA. Cool temp., forests, woodlands and heaths; favours thick tussock grasses.

Red-throated Skink *Acritoscincus platynotum* SVL 80mm

Pale silvery grey to dark grey or brown above. Broad dark grey to black upper lateral stripe (sometimes with narrow pale upper edge) runs from snout well onto tail. Throat usually tinged with orange-red, most intense on brdg ♂, but present on both sexes at all ages. ■ **NOTES** From Granite Belt of s. Qld, s. to estn Vic. DSF, woodlands and heaths; favours tussock grasses.

Western Three-lined Skink *Acritoscincus trilineatus* SVL 70mm

Olive grey. Pattern, when present, comprises 5 indistinct dark dorsal stripes, narrow greyish white dorsolateral stripe, broad dark grey to black upper lateral stripe and sometimes a narrow pale midlateral stripe. Adults (particularly ♂) display red flush on chin and throat, intensity varying according to locality and season. ■ **NOTES** From Gingin se. to Israelite Bay, WA, and in sthn Eyre Pen., SA. Usually associated with thick vegtn on wetland margins. ■ **STATUS** Rare (SA).

Acritoscincus duperreyi.
Cambridge, Tas.
S. Wilson

Acritoscincus platynotum.
Girraween NP, Qld.
S. Wilson

Acritoscincus trilineatus.
Ellenbrook, WA.
R. Browne-Cooper

Genus *Anepischetosia*

McCoy's Skink *Anepischetosia maccoyi* SVL 50mm

Sole member of genus. Small, long-bodied, with pointed snout, 4 moderately **short, widely spaced limbs, each with 5 digits**, moveable lower eyelid enclosing a small transparent disc, **minute ear-opening**, smooth glossy scales and parietal scales in contact. Rich brown, usually with dark and pale flecks, sometimes a pale vertebral zone or stripe, a **narrow dark dorsolateral line** and cream to orange-yellow ventral surfaces. ■ **NOTES** Woodlands, WSF and RF. Occurs in damp gullies and other moist areas, sheltering in loose soil under rocks, logs and leaf litter. Egglayer. Feeds on small invertebrates. ■ **SEE ALSO** *Hemiergis*. ■ **STATUS** Endangered (SA – as *Nannoscincus maccoyi*).

Genus *Anomalopus*

Seven spp. of **long-bodied skinks** with smooth glossy scales and **limbs absent or greatly reduced**. If present, **digits 3 or fewer, with more fingers than toes**. Lower eyelid moveable, lacking a transparent disc. Ear-opening absent, represented by a depression. ■ **SUBGENERA** *A. (Anomalopus)* are large and limbed; *A. (Vermiseps)* are small and limbless. ■ **NOTES** Forests, heaths and woodlands between Cape York and mid-estn NSW. Burrowers, dwelling in loose soil and humus under rocks, logs and leaf litter. Limbed spp. are unique among Aust. reduced-limbed skinks in having more fingers than toes. Excepting the most sthn sp., *A. swansoni*, all lay eggs. ■ **SEE ALSO** *Coeranoscincus; Coggeria*.

Short-necked Worm-skink *Anomalopus brevicollis* SVL 83mm

Limbless, waxy-tipped snout, eye greatly reduced, **usually 3 supraocular scales**. Pale to dark brown or yellowish brown, head greyish brown, tail greyish brown to black. **Pattern weak**; base of each scale usually darker, tending to align into obscure longitudinal rows of spots on back, lower flanks, chin and throat. ■ **NOTES** From Cracow district n. to Finch Hatton and inland to Clermont area. ■ **SEE ALSO** *A. gowi*.

Speckled Worm-skink *Anomalopus gowi* SVL 108mm

Limbless, waxy-tipped snout, eye greatly reduced, **usually 2 supraocular scales**. Pale to dark brown or yellowish brown with black head and tail-tip. **Pattern prominent**; longitudinal series of dark brown dashes, one per scale above and below. ■ **NOTES** Woodlands and evergreen vine thickets from White Mtns near Torrens Ck, n. to Mt Mulligan. ■ **SEE ALSO** *A. brevicollis*.

Two-clawed Worm-skink *Anomalopus leuckartii* SVL 137mm

Limbed, 2 fingers on forelimb, hindlimb reduced to clawless stump. Brown, greyish brown to purplish brown, paler edges to scales tending to form obscure longitudinal lines. Pale grey to yellowish bar sometimes on nape of juv., often darkening to absence with age. ■ **NOTES** Woodlands and DSF in interior of ne. NSW and se. Qld.

Anepischetosia maccoyi.
Cambewarra Mtn, NSW. S. Wilson

Anepischetosia maccoyi.
Olinda, Vic. S. Wilson

Anomalopus brevicollis.
Cracow, Qld. S. Wilson

Anomalopus gowi.
White Mountains NP, Qld. S. Wilson

Anomalopus leuckartii.
Glenmorgan district, Qld. S. Wilson

Five-clawed Worm-skink *Anomalopus mackayi* SVL 123mm

Limbed, 3 fingers, 2 toes. Greyish brown; sthn pop. often unpatterned, nthn pop. has longitudinal rows of dark spots, 1 per scale, over dorsal and lateral surfaces. Ventral surfaces occasionally have rows of dark spots in n. of range. ■ **NOTES** Small areas of grassy open woodlands in ne. NSW, relict open grasslands of Darling Downs in se. Qld. ■ **STATUS** Vulnerable (C'wealth; IUCN Red List); endangered (NSW; Qld).

Cape York Worm-skink *Anomalopus pluto* SVL 76mm

Limbless, waxy-tipped snout, eye greatly reduced. Pattern virtually absent; brown, darker on tail, paler edges to scales. Ventral surfaces pale brown. ■ **NOTES** Appears restricted to Heathlands area on nthn Cape York Pen., in sandy soils supporting various vegtn types, including monsoon forest, dense heath, open forest and vine thicket.

Swanson's Worm-skink *Anomalopus swansoni* SVL 107mm

Limbless, waxy-tipped snout, eye greatly reduced. Pale to dark brown above, paler below with black tail-tip and obscure pattern; individual scales usually pale-edged. ■ **NOTES** Open forest and heath on well-drained sandy soils from just n. of Sydney to the Hunter R. valley and inland to Sandy Hollow. The only livebearing *Anomalopus,* with litters of 2–3 recorded.

Three-clawed Worm-skink: Verreaux's Skink *Anomalopus verreauxii* SVL 185mm

Limbed, 3 short fingers, hindlimb reduced to stump. Brown to yellowish brown or grey. Juv. has broad prominent yellow bar across base of head, darkening to near-absence (though still usually discernible) with age. ■ **NOTES** DSF, woodlands and WSF margins from about Proserpine, Qld, to Armidale, NSW.

Genus *Bellatorias*

Three large to extremely large, robust spp. with 4 well-developed limbs, each with 5 digits; **4th toe much longer than 3rd.** Lower eyelid moveable, lacking a transparent disc, eyes relatively large, **eyelids with distinctive cream margins,** ear-opening with anterior lobules, **parietal scales separated** (fig.) and body scales smooth to weakly keeled. ■ **NOTES** Restricted to ne. and n., preferring RF or thickly vegetated areas. Terrestrial, sheltering in hollow logs, crevices and burrows. Diurnal but secretive, making a noisy dash for cover when alarmed. Omnivorous livebearers, often living communally in family groups. ■ **SEE ALSO** *Egernia; Tiliqua.*

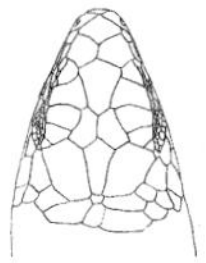

Anomalopus mackayi. Bowenville, Qld. S. Wilson

Anomalopus pluto. Heathlands, Qld. S. Wilson

Anomalopus swansoni. Denman, NSW. S. Wilson

Anomalopus verreauxii. Pittsworth, Qld. S. Wilson

Anomalopus verreauxll. Juveniles. Brisbane, Qld. S. Wilson

Major Skink *Bellatorias frerei* SVL 180mm

Colour and pattern variable; typically shades of brown above, with dark streak on each scale forming fine longitudinal lines, and darker brown to blackish flanks with numerous pale spots. Juv. usually more conspicuously marked. ■ **NOTES** Variety of habitats, from RF and vine thickets to open woodlands and rock outcrops between Coffs Harbour, NSW and sthn NG. Shelters in hollow logs, in burrows and under rocks. ■ **SEE ALSO** *B. major.*

Land Mullet *Bellatorias major* SVL 300mm

Largest *Bellatorias* and among largest Aust. skinks. Adults **uniform glossy black** with conspicuous pale rim to eye. Juv. has prominent pale spots on flanks. Ventral surfaces straw-coloured. ■ **NOTES** Subtropical RF and WSF from Conondale Ra., se. Qld to n. side of Hawkesbury R., NSW. Burrows beneath logs, in lantana and under soil-bound root systems of fallen trees, basking in sunny patches on forest floor. ■ **SEE ALSO** *B. frerei.*

Arnhem Land Gorges Skink *Bellatorias obiri* SVL 208mm

Grey to pale brown with a dark longitudinal streak on each scale. Anterior flanks, from ear to forelimbs, black with occasional white flecking, breaking up to merge with dorsal and lateral colour behind forelimbs. Ventral surfaces, from chin to chest, boldly marked with irregular transverse bars of black flecks. Remainder, back from level of forelimbs, flushed with yellow. ■ **NOTES** Rock crevices in moist, thickly vegetated gorges of sandstone escarpments on wstn edge of Arnhem Land Plateau. ■ **STATUS** Endangered (C'wealth; NT).

Genus *Calyptotis*

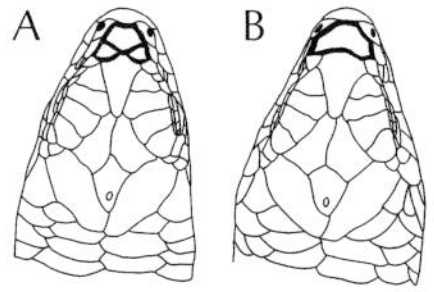

Five small spp. with **short limbs, 5 fingers and toes, moveable lower eyelid lacking a transparent disc**, and distinctive ventral colouration; normally **yellow on chest and belly and pink beneath tail**. The spp. are identified by the presence (A) or absence (B) of prefrontal scales, and whether the ear-opening is exposed or covered by scales. ■ **NOTES** Secretive moisture-lovers, sheltering beneath logs, rocks and leaf litter in RF, eucalypt forests and suburban gardens. Egglayers. Feed on small invertebrates. ■ **SEE ALSO** *Glaphyromorphus; Hemiergis; Saiphos.*

Cone-eared Calyptotis *Calyptotis lepidorostrum* SVL 55mm

Prefrontal scales present. Ear-openings absent, reduced to scaly depressions. Light to dark brown above; 4 narrow dark dorsal lines, strongest and most continuous on nape, and a broad dark dorsolateral stripe. ■ **NOTES** Coast and ranges from Cooloola and the Conondale Ra. n. to Mackay.

Bellatorias frerei. Mt Glorious, Qld. S. Wilson

Bellatorias major. Mt Glorious, Qld. S. Wilson

Bellatorias obiri.
Nourlangie Rock, NT. S. Swanson

Calyptotis lepidorostrum. Cooloola, Qld. S. Wilson

Red-tailed Calyptotis *Calyptotis ruficauda* SVL 55mm

Prefrontal scales and ear-openings present. Light to dark brown above; patternless or with 4 lines of dark dashes. Usually a dark dorsolateral stripe present, often confined to forebody. Tail flushed with reddish brown. ■ **NOTES** Coast and ranges from Buladelah n. to Acacia Plateau.

Garden Calyptotis *Calyptotis scutirostrum* SVL 55mm

No prefrontal scales. Ear-openings absent, reduced to scaly depressions. Light to dark brown above with 4 narrow dark dorsal lines, strongest and most continuous on nape, and a broad dark dorsolateral stripe. ■ **NOTES** Coast and ranges of ne. NSW and se. Qld, from Bostobrick n. to Gympie.

Broad-templed Calyptotis *Calyptotis temporalis* SVL 35mm

Prefrontal scales absent. Ear-openings large. Light to dark brown above; 4 narrow dark dorsal lines, strongest and most continuous on nape, and a broad dark dorsolateral stripe. ■ **NOTES** Coast and ranges between Rockhampton and Proserpine.

Thornton Peak Calyptotis *Calyptotis thorntonensis* SVL 35mm

Somewhat dorsally depressed. **Prefrontal scales present. Ear-openings absent, reduced to scaly depressions.** Light to dark brown above, mottled with black. Dark dorsolateral stripe boldest on forebody. Ventral surfaces cream, **lacking the yellow and pink pigments** that characterise other *Calyptotis.* ■ **NOTES** High altitude RF between Thornton Peak and Upper Roaring Meg in the Wet Tropics. ■ **STATUS** Vulnerable (Qld).

Snow Skinks Genus *Carinascincus*

Eight small, moderately robust to dorsally depressed spp., with well-developed limbs, each with 5 digits, moveable lower eyelid enclosing a transparent disc, ear-opening present, parietal scales in contact, **nasal scales narrowly separated, interparietal moderate in size** and **frontoparietals usually (in all except one species) fused to form a single shield (fig).** ■ **NOTES** Cool-adapted, restricted to sthn temperate areas often subject to regular winter snow. Diurnal and sun-loving, basking in sheltered sites. Livebearing invertebrate feeders. ■ **SEE ALSO** *Acritoscincus; Lampropholis; Pseudemoia.*

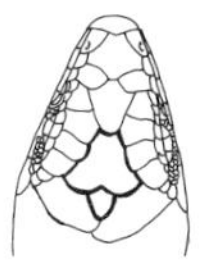

Calyptotis ruficauda.
Bruxner Park, NSW. S. Wilson

Calyptotis scutirostrum.
Mt Glorious, Qld. S. Wilson

Calyptotis temporalis.
Byfield, Qld. S. Eipper

Calyptotis thorntonensis.
Thornton Peak, Qld. S. Wilson

Coventry's Skink *Carinascincus coventryi* SVL 50mm

Paired frontoparietal scales and weak pattern. Metallic brown above, usually with scattered pale flecks and often 3–4 fine dark streaks on each scale, a very narrow pale bronze dorsolateral line, dark grey to black upper flanks (often enclosing scattered pale brown flecks or spots) and grey lower flanks. ■ **NOTES** Highland WSF from Blue Mtns, NSW to the Grampians, Vic. Prefers clearings created by fire, rock outcrops and fallen trees, sheltering in cavities in decaying logs, basking on their surfaces and foraging in adjacent leaf litter.

Northern Snow Skink *Carinascincus greeni* SVL 75mm

Distinctive pattern: black with **many small, pale greenish yellow spots** over head, body, limbs and tail. Ventral surfaces greenish grey. ■ **NOTES** Confined to rocky terrain at altitudes over 1000m in n.-central Tas, from Ben Lomond area w. to Cradle Mtn and s. to Frenchman's Cap. Basks and forages on exposed surfaces, burrowing into waterlogged soil beneath rocks on edges of streams and swamps above the treeline. Will not hesitate to swim or shelter beneath submerged rocks if alarmed, despite low temperatures. Hibernates each winter under a blanket of snow.

Metallic Skink *Carinascincus metallicus* SVL 63mm

Dorsal scales weakly keeled, **paravertebral scales transversely enlarged** and **22–28 midbody scale rows**. Metallic brown above, unmarked or with dark and pale flecks or streaks, and/or a narrow dark vertebral stripe and complete to broken paravertebral stripes. May have narrow, pale copper dorsolateral line and/or obscure pale midlateral stripe. Upper flanks dark grey to black, enclosing many pale flecks. Ventral surfaces often pinkish red, from level of forelimbs to base of tail. Pops from far s. and sw. of Tas have stronger keels, prominent dark dorsal stripes and little or no dark flecking. ■ **NOTES** Widespread over Tas (where it is the most common and most widely distributed lizard), extending to cool areas of se. Vic n. to Mt Baw Baw. Occurs in WSF and DSF, woodlands, heaths, rock outcrops and disturbed areas. ■ **SEE ALSO** *C. microlepidotus; C. pretiosus.*

Southern Snow Skink *Carinascincus microlepidotus* SVL 70mm

Midbody scales in 32–44 rows. Dark brown to olive brown; dark markings create a roughly chequered pattern (sometimes so dense as to exclude all but scattered flecks of ground colour, or coalescing to form a ragged vertebral stripe). Narrow pale dorsolateral stripe, dark brown to black upper flanks (often with pale flecks but **no pale midlateral stripe**) and grey lower flanks with black flecks. ■ **NOTES** Restricted to mountainous areas in central and sthn Tas, n. to Mt Oakleigh and e. to Mt Wellington. Favours rocky herbfields, scree slopes and lake edges, usually above 1000m. Basks, often communally, on exposed rock faces and shelters in crevices or among low vegtn. ■ **SEE ALSO** *C. metallicus; C. orocryptus; C. pretiosus.*

Carinascincus coventryi.
Otway Ranges, Vic. R. Valentic

Carinascincus greeni.
Ben Lomond, Tas. S. Wilson

Carinascincus metallicus.
Griffin Forest Reserve, Tas. S. Wilson

Carinascincus metallicus.
Far south-western form. Melaleuca, Tas. S. Wilson

Carinascincus microlepidotus. Mt Wellington, Tas. E. Vanderduys

Ocellated Skink *Carinascincus ocellatus* SVL 85mm

Distinctively patterned with **small pale blotches**; dark bronze brown to copper brown with many dark-edged cream to silvery grey blotches becoming larger and sparser on flanks. ■ **NOTES** Rocky areas associated with woodlands, heaths and shrublands in lowland Tas and estn islands of Bass Strait. Widespread in the cool temperate zone; scarce in subalpine and alpine regions. Shelters in narrow rock crevices, beneath loose bark and cracks in logs, basking on exposed surfaces.

Tasmanian Mountain Skink *Carinascincus orocryptus* SVL 65mm

Midbody scales in 28–30 (occasionally 32) rows. Brown above, usually with a ragged to broken **black vertebral stripe**; dark flecks or edges to dorsal scales tending to align longitudinally; pale brown dorsolateral stripes; broad black upper lateral stripe; prominent, straight-edged to ragged-edged or broken, **greyish white midlateral stripe** between upper lips and hindlimb; and grey or black flecks on lower flanks. Ventral surfaces pale grey to bright red. ■ **NOTES** Known from only the alpine areas of Mt Eliza, Algonkian Mtn, Mt Hartz and Lake Seal in sthn Tas., and from near sea-level at Strahan. Inhabits dense alpine woodlands with a heath understorey. Apparently arboreal, foraging on bases of trees and in foliage of shrubs. Those on Mt Hartz are rock-inhabiting. In some areas hybridisation occurs with *C. microlepidotus*. ■ **SEE ALSO** *C. microlepidotus.*

Pedra Branca Skink *Carinascincus palfreymani* SVL 95mm

Blackish brown to black with dense pale flecks, narrow dorsolateral lines and black flanks, sometimes with paler flecks or spots. ■ **NOTES** Confined to Pedra Branca Rock, an exposed 1.4ha islet of rugged sandstone approximately 26km s. of Tas. Basks communally to form a dark heat-absorbent mass on exposed surfaces. Feeds on flies, small littoral crustaceans and fish scraps scavenged from the island's seabird colony. Aust.'s most southerly terrestrial vertebrate. Estimated to number about 300 individuals. ■ **STATUS** Vulnerable (C'wealth; IUCN Red List); endangered (Tas).

Tasmanian Tree Skink *Carinascincus pretiosus* SVL 57–70mm

Midbody scale rows 32–36 on mainland Tas; up to 40 on offshore islands. Dark olive brown to brown, with a narrow **black vertebral stripe**, usually a narrow pale dorsolateral stripe, dark brown to black upper flanks (immaculate or enclosing scattered pale flecks), **white midlateral stripe** and grey lower flanks. Ventral surfaces of adults usually flushed with pink. ■ **NOTES** Forests, woodlands and rocky areas throughout most of Tas and offshore islands (excluding estn Bass Strait), n. to King Is. and Albatross Is. Larger on offshore islands and largest on Mewstone Is. ■ **SEE ALSO** *C. metallicus; C. microlepidotus.*

Four-fingered Skinks; Rainbow Skinks Genus *Carlia*

Twenty four small spp. with 4 well-developed limbs, **4 fingers and 5 toes** and a moveable lower eyelid enclosing a transparent disc. Ear-opening present, usually with enlarged lobules. **Dorsal scales usually very weakly to strongly keeled**. Parietal scales in contact, frontoparietals fused

Carinascincus ocellatus.
Launceston, Tas. E. Vanderduys

Carinascincus orocryptus.
Mt Eliza, Tas. M. Hutchinson

Carinascincus palfreymani.
Pedra Branca Rock, Tas. G. Shea

Carinascincus pretiosus.
Melaleuca, Tas. S. Wilson

to form a single shield. ♂ **usually develop distinctive, often spectacular brdg colours** often combining red, green, blue or black. ♀ lack bright colours, but usually have white midlateral stripe. Spp. are identified by ♂ colours; presence, strength and number of dorsal keels; relative size of transparent disc (large, more than half the size of lower eyelid; or small, half the size or less); shape and alignment of ear-opening; and size, shape and arrangement of ear-lobules. ■ **NOTES** Diversity highest in ne. Active, terrestrial sun-lovers, mainly among leaf litter in dry forests, woodlands, river edges and occasionally RF. Many spp. sinuously wave their tails as they forage. All lay clutches of 2 eggs. ■ **SEE ALSO** *Liburnascincus; Lygisaurus.*

Two-spined Rainbow Skink *Carlia amax* SVL 40mm

Robust. **Two strong keels on dorsal scales.** Ear-opening horizontally elongate, usually with small anterior lobule. Olive brown, usually with small pale and/or dark spots, and pale streak under eye, often extending through ear to forelimb. Top of head copper, particularly on brdg ♂. ■ **NOTES** Nw. Qld through nthn NT to Kimberley, WA, inhabiting rock outcrops and scree slopes in dry to semi-arid regions. Forages in leaf litter at bases of trees and rocks. ■ **SEE ALSO** *C. johnstonei.*

Elegant Rainbow Skink *Carlia decora* SVL 49mm

Three keels on hexagonal dorsal scales, large transparent disc occupying more than half lower eyelid and 5 supraciliary scales. Ear-opening vertically elliptical, with **1 large rounded anterior lobule**. Brown with paravertebral rows of black and white dots. Brdg ♂ has orange to copper wash on flanks and orange upper, and sometimes weak lower lateral stripe from forelimb to groin, **blue throat with dark speckling on jaw and sides of neck**, and sometimes fine dark-edges to scales on throat. ♀ **has white mid-lateral stripe with sharp dark edges extending back to groin.** ■ **NOTES** Moist forests, vine thickets and RF margins of e. Qld between about Sarina and Mt Molloy. ■ **SEE ALSO** *C. rubigo.*

Sandy Rainbow Skink *Carlia dogare* SVL 50mm

Moderately robust. **Two strong keels on dorsal scales.** Ear-opening vertically elongate, **broadly edged with black,** with 2 anterior lobules. Sexes differ. Brdg ♂: pale brown, **6 broad pale reddish orange stripes**; paravertebrals, upper laterals and lower laterals; sides of head and neck dark greyish brown, prominently spotted with white. ♀, juv. and non-brdg ♂: brown with obscure pale vertebral and dorsolateral stripes enclosing dark brown back with pale dashes, each with a darker leading edge; greyish brown upper lateral and midlateral stripes; pale curved line under eye to ear. ■ **NOTES** Heaths and low woodlands on white sands from mouth of McIvor R. n. to Bathurst Head and Lizard Is.

Slender Rainbow Skink *Carlia gracilis* SVL 41mm

Three moderately strong keels on dorsal scales. Ear-opening horizontally elongate, with usually 1 small anterior lobule. Brown, coppery brown to grey, darker on head and leading edge of dorsal scales, often with a very narrow pale midlateral stripe from behind ear to hindlimb. Brdg ♂: iridescent greenish blue

Carlia amax.
Katherine, NT. S. Wilson

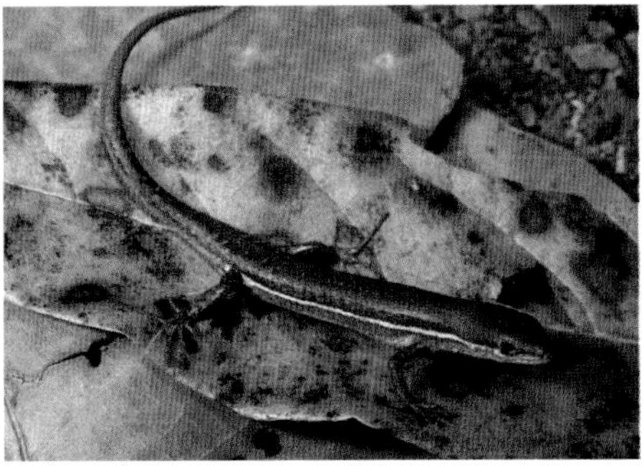

Carlia decora. Female.
Alligator Creek, Mt Elliot, Qld. S. Wilson

Carlia decora. Breeding male.
Whitsunday Island, Qld. R. Midtgaard

Carlia dogare. Breeding male.
Cape Flattery, Qld. S. Wilson

Carlia dogare. Female.
Cape Flattery, Qld. S. Wilson

Carlia gracilis.
Kakadu NP, NT. S. Wilson

head, broad dull red lateral stripe. ■ **NOTES** Far nthn WA and nw. NT. Leaf litter under open forests and along creek and river margins. Common in Darwin gardens.

Whitsunday Rainbow Skink *Carlia inconnexa* SVL 52mm

Mostly two keels on hexagonal dorsal scales (sometimes a mix of 2-and 3-keeled scales), large transparent disc occupying more than half lower eyelid and 5-6 supraciliary scales. Ear-opening usually vertically elliptical with 1-2 round lobules on anterior margin. Grey to brown with heavy black mottling and white markings arranged longitudinally. **Brdg ♂ has black head, and blue throat with intensely black-edged scales.** ■ **NOTES** Known from Hayman, Hook, Whitsunday and Lindeman Islands, usually on stony soils.

Lined Rainbow Skink *Carlia jarnoldae* SVL 49mm

Three keels on dorsal scales. Ear-opening horizontally elongate, with a small pointed anterior lobule and smaller lobules on other edges. Sexes differ. Brdg ♂: brown above, **5–7 narrow dark dorsal lines; upper flanks black with numerous small blue spots, mid to lower flanks and forelimbs bright orange**; top of head coppery brown; lips, side of neck and ventral surfaces pale green. ♀, juv. and non-brdg ♂: brown with black upper flanks, **broad white midlateral stripe from upper lips through ear-opening and along body**. ■ **NOTES** DSF and woodlands, usually on stony soils or rock outcrops, from Collinsville n. to Heathlands.

Rough Brown Rainbow Skink *Carlia johnstonei* SVL 43mm

Two strong keels on dorsal scales. Ear-opening circular or vertically elongate, with **long sharp anterior lobule and many smaller pointed lobules around margin**. Dark reddish brown with scattered pale flecks, each usually with a dark leading edge. Brdg ♂: rich reddish brown flanks; head, neck and foreback black; pale flecks sharp white; chin and throat bluish, with scales broadly edged with black. ■ **NOTES** Nw. Kimberley. Leaf litter, along gorges and well-vegetated rocky creek banks. ■ **SEE ALSO** *C. amax.*

Closed-litter Rainbow Skink *Carlia longipes* SVL 68mm

Robust. **Dorsal scales smooth or with 3 very weak keels**. Ear-opening usually round, occasionally vertical or rarely horizontal, **completely surrounded by sharply pointed lobules**. Sexes differ. Brdg ♂ brown and patternless above with **prominent narrow dorsolateral stripe** from above eye to behind forelimb, dark midlateral zone from head to shoulder **contrasting sharply with pale scales of lower neck and throat**, and merging with rich orange flanks. ♀ and juv. have narrow pale stripe from under eye to above ear, and pale dorsolateral and midlateral stripes enclosing dark upper lateral zone, most prominent anteriorly and fading along body. ■ **NOTES** Coastal ne. Qld between Cape Melville and Gordonvale. ■ **SEE ALSO** *C. rostralis; C. sexdentata.*

Carlia inconnexa. Female.
Whitsunday Island, Qld. S. Wilson

Carlia inconnexa. Male
Whitsunday Island, Qld. S. Macdonald

Carlia jarnoldae. Female.
Townsville district, Qld. S. Wilson

Carlia johnstonei.
Manning Creek, WA. S. Wilson

Carlia jarnoldae. Breeding male.
Petford, Qld. S. Wilson

Carlia longipes. Female.
Cooktown, Qld. S. Wilson

Carlia longipes. Breeding male.
Cooktown, Qld. S. Wilson

Striped Rainbow Skink *Carlia munda* SVL 44mm

Dorsal scales smooth or nearly smooth. Ear-opening horizontally elongate, with a few small lobules on upper edge, occasionally smaller lobules on remaining edges. Brown to greyish brown with dark spots and pale flecks. Narrow, sharp-edged **white midlateral stripe from upper lip to top of ear-opening, continuing back from bottom of ear-opening** for varying distances. Brdg ♂: black lateral flush from head to about forelimb, reddish orange flush from forelimb to hindlimb; scales on side of neck and throat broadly black-edged. ■ **NOTES** Nthn Aust., se. to Ipswich. Isolated pop. on North West Cape and Pilbara, WA. Dry to arid areas supporting DSF, woodlands, shrublands or spinifex, normally on heavy to stony soils. ■ **SEE ALSO** *C. rufilatus.*

Open-litter Rainbow Skink *Carlia pectoralis* SVL 47mm

Three keels on hexagonal dorsal scales, large transparent disc occupying much more than half lower eyelid and 5 supraciliary scales. **Ear-opening usually round**, with rounded anterior lobule and **sharp to blunt lobules around margin**. Brown with paravertebral rows of black and white dots. Brdg ♂ has **orange lateral stripes** (upper and sometimes lower lateral from forelimb to groin), **orange flush on chest, and blue throat with strongly black-edged scales on throat, neck and chin.** ♀ has **pale mid-lateral stripe with diffuse dark edges breaking into flecks at anterior or mid-flanks.** ■ **NOTES** Dry open forests, often with grass tussocks, from Brisbane inland to Great Dividing Range and n. to Carnarvon Ra., Blackdown Tableland and Shoalwater Bay. ■ **SEE ALSO** *C. rubigo; C. schmeltzii.*

Five-carinated Rainbow Skink *Carlia quinquecarinata* SVL 65mm

Robust. **Dorsal scales smooth to weakly carinated.** Ear-opening vertical with sharp **lobules on all margins; small and deeply recessed on posterior margin.** Brown above with large, **longitudinally aligned dark-edged pale dashes.** When present, **pale midlateral line broken into dashes.** ■ **NOTES** Poorly known. Darnley Is., ne. Torres Strait, and probably Murray Is. and NG. Recorded in semi-deciduous notophyll vine forest on basalt. ■ **SEE ALSO** *C. sexdentata.*

Blue-throated Rainbow Skink *Carlia rhomboidalis* SVL 57mm

Interparietal scale fused to frontoparietal scale and smooth scales. Ear-opening circular, with 1–2 large pointed anterior lobules, smaller lobules on remaining margins. Rich brown with black flecks tending to concentrate on paravertebral zone, a narrow gold to pale brown dorsolateral stripe, blackish brown upper flanks and some indication of a pale midlateral stripe. Top of head rich copper. In breeding season, **chin and lips of adults (and often juv.) bright blue, with contrasting red throat.** ■ **NOTES** From Magnetic Is. s. to Clarke Ra. near Mackay. RF, WSF and their margins, basking among leaf litter in sunny patches. ■ **SEE ALSO** *C. rubrigularis.*

Carlia munda. Breeding male.
Shoalwater Bay, Qld. S. Wilson

Carlia munda. Female or non-breeding male.
Chillagoe, Qld. S. Wilson

Carlia pectoralis. Female.
Carnarvon Range, Qld. S. Wilson

Carlia pectoralis. Male.
Woodgate area, Qld. S. Wilson

Carlia quinquecarinata.
Darnley Island, Qld. D. Stanton

Carlia rhomboidalis.
Magnetic Island, Qld. S. Wilson

Crevice Rainbow Skink *Carlia rimula* SVL 39mm

Dorsally depressed with **4–5 weak carinations on dorsal scales, each a series of small points**. Ear-opening vertically elongate, edged by pointed lobules. Copper brown with prominent gold-silver dorsolateral stripe from above eye onto base of tail, its inner edge usually edging a broad ragged-edged black laterodorsal stripe. Upper flanks black. Narrow broken silvery midlateral stripe between forelimbs and hindlimbs; obscure and broken on large ♂. ■ **NOTES** Cape York Pen., between Pascoe R. and Coen. Rocks and leaf litter along creeks edged with vine thickets.

Black-throated Rainbow Skink *Carlia rostralis* SVL 70mm

Robust. **Dorsal scales smooth or with 3 weak keels**. Ear-opening vertically elongate, with large pointed anterior lobules. Sexes differ. Brdg ♂: greyish brown above with a **prominent cream dorsolateral stripe from above eye to behind forelimb**; upper flanks black, fading to brown at mid- or posterior body; **prominent pale midlateral stripe from lips to about forelimb**; lower flanks reddish orange between fore- and hindlimbs, boldest anteriorly; **chin and throat black**. ♀, juv. and non-brdg ♂: prominent pale dorsolateral and midlateral stripes but lack black throat and red pigments. ■ **NOTES** Townsville n. to Kowanyama and Cooktown. Various habitats, incl. DSF, vine thickets and rock outcrops. ■ **SEE ALSO** *C. longipes; C. sexdentata.*

Orange-flanked Rainbow Skink *Carlia rubigo* SVL 44mm

Three keels on hexagonal dorsal scales, large transparent disc occupying much more than half lower eyelid and 5 supraciliary scales. **Ear-opening usually vertically elliptical**, with 1-2 rounded anterior lobules and **smaller rounded lobules on other margins.** Brown with paravertebral rows of black and white dots on posterior half**. Brdg ♂ has orange to copper flush on flanks** sometimes extending onto back and forelimbs, and **blue throat with dark speckling on jaw and sides of neck. ♀ has white mid-lateral stripe from nostril, breaking into dashes at forelimb or mid flanks.** ■ **NOTES** Dry forests and rocky areas along estn interior of Qld n. to w. of Cairns, reaching coast and islands between about Mackay and Townsville. ■ **SEE ALSO** *C. decora; C. pectoralis.*

Red-throated Rainbow Skink *Carlia rubrigularis* SVL 60mm

Interparietal scale fused to frontoparietal scale, smooth scales. Ear-opening circular, with 1–2 large pointed anterior lobules, smaller lobules on remaining edges. Rich brown, with black pigment tending to concentrate on paravertebral zone, a narrow pale dorsolateral stripe, dark upper flanks and indication of a pale midlateral stripe. Top of head copper. **Chin and throat pink**, brightest on brdg ♂. ■ **NOTES** RF from Cooktown s. to Townsville. ■ **SEE ALSO** *C. rhomboidalis.*

Carlia rimula.
Claudie Falls, Qld.
G. Gaikhorst

Carlia rostralis. Breeding male.
Kuranda, Qld. S. Wilson

Carlia rostralis. Female.
Isabella Falls, Qld. S. Wilson

Carlia rubigo. Breeding male.
Magnetic Is, Qld. S. Wilson

Carlia rubigo. Female.
Magnetic Is, Qld. S. Wilson

Carlia rubrigularis.
Josephine Falls, Qld. S. Wilson

Red-sided Rainbow Skink *Carlia rufilatus* SVL 42mm

Three strong keels on dorsal scales. Ear-opening horizontally elongate, usually with 1 small anterior lobule. Dark olive to brown with dark flecks, each with a pale rear edge. **White stripe from upper lip to top of ear-opening, then back from bottom of ear-opening.** Brdg ♂: broad red midlateral stripe; white stripe broadly edged above with black, top of head coppery brown and chin shields dark-edged. ■ **NOTES** Nw. NT and nthn Kimberley, WA. Woodlands and riverine forests. Abundant in well-watered gardens of suburban Darwin. ■ **SEE ALSO** *C. munda.*

Schmeltz's Rainbow Skink *Carlia schmeltzii* SVL 69mm

Robust, with **2–3 strong keels** (varies geographically) on dorsal scales, **small disc occupying about half lower eyelid**, and **7 supraciliary scales. Ear-opening vertically elongate, usually with 2 large squarish anterior lobules.** Brown, with broad pale dorsolateral stripe and grey flanks, the lateral scales broadly dark-edged. Brdg ♂: flanks flushed with bright reddish orange from forelimb to mid- or posterior body; sides of head and neck greyish white with prominent black-edged scales. Pop. on Cape York are smallest and patternless, with 2 keels on dorsal scales; those further s. larger, with 3 keels. Around Townsville both exist. ■ **NOTES** From NSW border n. to Coen and w. to Kowanyama. Various dry habitats, incl. woodlands, rocky ranges and scree slopes. ■ **SEE ALSO** *C. pectoralis.*

Robust Rainbow Skink *Carlia sexdentata* SVL 63mm

Robust. **Dorsal scales smooth or with 3 very weak keels.** Ear-opening usually vertical, occasionally round, **with well developed sharp anterior lobules but moderately to poorly developed lobules on surrounding margins.** Sexes differ. Brdg ♂ brown and patternless above with **ill-defined pale dorsolateral stripe** from above eye to behind forelimb, dark grey upper lateral zone from head to shoulder **not contrasting with pale scales of lower neck and throat**, and merging with rich orange flanks. ♀ and juv. have narrow pale stripe from under eye to above ear, and pale dorsolateral and midlateral stripes enclosing dark upper lateral zone, most prominent anteriorly, usually broken by obscure pale vertical bars in front of forelimb, enclosing irregular pale dashes along its length and fading along body. ■ **NOTES** Torres Strait and Cape York, s. to Princess Charlotte Bay and ne. NT incl. is. off Arnhem Land. ■ **SEE ALSO** *C. longipes; C. rostralis; C. quinquecarinata.*

Storr's Rainbow Skink *Carlia storri* SVL 46mm

Long-tailed, with 2 **strong keels on dorsal scales. Ear-opening circular, edged with pointed lobules.** Pale brown with paler vertebral, dorsolateral and midlateral stripes. Brdg ♂: no pattern; orange flush on limbs and tail. ■ **NOTES** Townsville n. to Torres Strait islands. Also sw. NG. DSF and woodlands over grassy ground cover.

Carlia rufilatus. Breeding male.
Kununurra district, WA. S. Wilson

Carlia rufilatus. Female or non-breeding male.
Darwin, NT. S. Wilson

Carlia schmeltzii. Breeding male.
Shoalwater Bay, Qld. S. Wilson

Carlia sexdentata. Breeding male.
Iron Range, Qld. S. Wilson

Carlia sexdentata. Female.
Moa Is., Qld. S. Wilson

Carlia storri.
Cooktown, Qld. S. Wilson

Southern Rainbow Skink *Carlia tetradactyla* SVL 64mm

Robust. **Dorsal scales smooth or with 3–4 weak striations.** Ear-opening circular, with 1 large blunt anterior lobule. Blackish brown above, longitudinally aligned pale spots or dashes and a broad pale dorsolateral stripe. Brdg ♂: bluish green neck, flanks, throat and ventral surface, and reddish orange upper and lower lateral stripes. ■ **NOTES** Se. Aust., from about Benalla, Vic, along wstn slopes of Gt Div. Ra. to Darling Downs, se. Qld. DSF and woodlands, particularly those with tussock ground cover. Most southerly *Carlia.* Known to lay communally within active nests of a large black ant (*Rhytidoponera* sp.).

Desert Rainbow Skink *Carlia triacantha* SVL 53mm

Robust. **Three strong keels on dorsal scales.** Ear-opening circular, with large pointed anterior lobule, and often edged with many smaller pointed lobules. Greyish brown with faint pale stripe under eye. Brdg ♂: shining coppery green on head and neck and broad red lateral stripe or flush. ■ **NOTES** Woodlands and spinifex grasslands on sandy, stony to loamy soils and sandstone outcrops. Most arid-adapted *Carlia.*

Lively Rainbow Skink *Carlia vivax* SVL 47mm

Slender and long-tailed, with **2 strong keels on dorsal scales. Ear-opening vertically elongate, with 1 large anterior lobule.** Sexes differ. ♀, juv. and non-brdg ♂: greyish brown with 2 dorsal series of dark and pale dashes; pale dorsolateral and midlateral stripes. Brdg ♂: prominent reddish orange lateral flush or broad midlateral stripe; chin and throat pale blue, speckled with dark brown. ■ **NOTES** From about Singleton, NSW, n. to Prince of Wales Is., Qld. DSF, woodlands and heaths on hard, stony or sandy soils.

Cape Melville Rainbow Skink *Carlia wundalthini* SVL 49mm

Interparietal scale fused to frontoparietal scale, and smooth dorsal scales with curved hind edges. Ear-opening circular to horizontally elongate with large sharp anterior lobule and similar lobules around top or sometimes whole margin. Brown, sometimes with paired series of dark dorsal flecks and copper head. Breeding males have colours largely restricted to orange wash on sides of neck and flanks, with little or no indication on throat. Females have broken line of pale dots along flanks. ■ **NOTES** Restricted to upland rainforest isolated on top of the boulder fields of Melville Range, Cape York Pen.

Carlia tetradactyla. Breeding male.
Oakey, Qld. S. Wilson

Carlia triacantha. Breeding male.
El Questro, WA. S. Wilson

Carlia vivax. Female.
Kurwongbah, Qld. S. Wilson

Carlia vivax. Breeding male.
Kurwongbah, Qld. S. Wilson

Carlia wundalthini. Female.
Melville Range, Qld. C. Hoskin

Carlia wundalthini. Breeding male.
Melville Range, Qld. C. Hoskin

Snake-tooth Skinks Genus *Coeranoscincus*

Two large, **long-bodied** spp. with **limbs absent, or greatly reduced with 3 short digits.** Ear-opening represented by a depression. Lower eyelid moveable, lacking transparent disc. Scales smooth and glossy. **Adults sombrely marked, but juv. brightly patterned with stripes or bands.** ■ **NOTES** Restricted to widely separated RF blocks in ne. Qld, and from se. Qld to ne. NSW. Burrowers in moist soil, under leaf litter and in rotten logs. Invertebrate feeders with long, sharp recurved teeth, possibly to grasp earthworms. At least 1 sp. lays eggs. ■ **SEE ALSO** *Anomalopus; Coggeria.*

Limbless Snake-tooth Skink *Coeranoscincus frontalis* SVL 290mm

Completely limbless. Juv. prominently **striped**; dark greyish brown with narrow pale dorsal lines, white upper lateral and black lower lateral stripes, sometimes breaking into vertical bars on tail. Top of head white blotched with brown. Side of head and edges of throat grey, continuous with dark lower lateral stripe. Neck white with dark blotch centred on ear-depression. Adults are brown, sometimes retaining an indication of a pale flush on head and neck, a dark blotch on ear-depression, and a dark lateral stripe. ■ **NOTES** RF on coastal ranges and lowlands from about Thornton Peak south to Mt Spec.

Three-toed Snake-tooth Skink *Coeranoscincus reticulatus* SVL 195mm

Limbs with 3 digits. Juv. prominently **banded**; cream to brown with irregular transverse dark bars, conspicuous anteriorly, often absent posteriorly, dark patches centred on eye and ear-depression. Snout cream. Scales on flanks dark-edged, forming irregular longitudinal streaks. Adults brown to yellowish brown or grey, sometimes retaining vague indications of bands and usually dark eye-patch, ear-marking and pale snout. ■ **NOTES** Subtropical RF and WSF between about Grafton, NSW and Fraser Is., Qld. Most localities are montane on rich dark soils but Fraser Is. and adjacent Cooloola are pale sands in lowlands. Clutches of 2–6 eggs recorded. ■ **STATUS** Vulnerable (C'wealth; NSW); lower risk–near threatened (IUCN Red List).

Genus *Coggeria*

Fraser Island Sand Skink; Satinay Sand Skink *Coggeria naufragus* SVL 127mm

Sole member of genus. Long-bodied, with **4 very short limbs, each with 3 digits**. Ear-opening represented by a depression. Eye small with moveable lower eyelid, lacking transparent disc. **Snout wedge-shaped in profile.** Scales smooth and glossy. Very pale brown above, with weak, broken, dark longitudinal lines and a prominent dorsolateral row of black spots. Flanks and belly grey with black flecks, contrasting sharply with brown back. ■ **NOTES** Fraser Is. Burrower occurring in tall forests and heaths. Invertebrate feeder, probably preying mainly on earthworms. ■ **SEE ALSO** *Anomalopus; Coeranoscincus.*

Coeranoscincus frontalis.
Walter Hill Range, Qld. S. Wilson

Coeranoscincus frontalis. Juvenile.
Mt Bellenden Ker, Qld. S. Wilson

Coeranoscincus reticulatus.
Cunnngham's Gap, Qld. S. Wilson

Coeranoscincus reticulatus. Juvenile.
Maleny district, Qld. S. Wilson

Coggeria naufragus.
Central Station, Fraser Is., Qld.
S. Wilson

Genus *Concinnia*

Seven medium-sized spp. with smooth glossy scales; well-developed limbs which overlap when pressed to side of body, each with 5 digits; lower eyelid moveable lacking a transparent disc; ear-opening without lobules; parietal scales in contact; frontoparietal scale divided; **3rd pair of chin shields separated by 3 longitudinal rows of scales** (A); and **distal subdigital lamellae on 4th toe undivided**. Some are identifiable by pattern, size and locality; others may require examination of scale characters, particularly whether the upper secondary temporal overlaps lower (B), or whether the lower overlaps upper (C). ■ **NOTES** Moist areas from s. coast of NSW n. to about Coen, Cape York Pen. They occupy cavities in tree trunks, logs and rock crevices, incl. rockeries and other garden habitats, and often rest with head and fore-body protruding from cover. Diurnal, sun-loving skinks which feed on arthropods. Livebearers. ■ **SEE ALSO** *Eulamprus*; *Karma*; *Magmellia*.

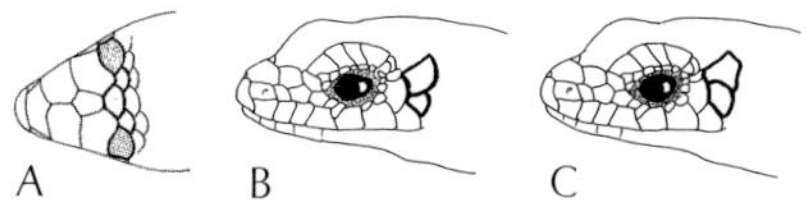

Lemon-barred Forest-skink *Concinnia amplus* SVL 115mm

Dark olive brown with paler scales aligned to form irregular narrow **bands** on body and tail. Prominent dark patch above forelimb. Ventral surfaces lemon yellow. ■ **NOTES** Restricted to RF in vicinity of Mt Blackwood, Conway SF, Eungella NP and Finch Hatton. Associated with boulders beside streams, or among roots and buttresses of large trees, particularly figs under closed forests. Often sleeps at night on exposed rock faces.

Northern Bar-sided Skink *Concinnia brachysoma* SVL 74mm

Midbody scales in 28–32 rows, upper secondary temporal scale overlaps lower and **17–23 lamellae under 4th toe**. Coppery brown above with small black blotches tending to concentrate on paravertebral region, a broad black lateral stripe with deeply zigzagging edges or broken into vertical bars, and many narrow irregular dark bands on tail. ■ **NOTES** Favours rocky habitats, particularly when associated with vine thickets and moist gullies between about Coen and Gayndah. Also present in moist woodlands. Shelters in tree hollows, rock crevices or in burrows under rocks. ■ **SEE ALSO** *C. martini; C. sokosoma; C. tenuis.*

Bartle Frere Bar-sided Skink *Concinnia frerei* SVL 66mm

Lower secondary temporal scale overlaps upper. Dark brown, irregularly marked with transversely elongate black blotches, a black, deeply notched upper lateral zone and irregular narrow dark bands on tail. Ventral surfaces greenish white. ■ **NOTES** Mist-enshrouded RF and boulderscapes on summits of Mt Bartle Frere and Bellenden Ker, and 110km ne. at 1200m. elevation on Mt Lewis in Wet Tropics. Shelters in crevices in timber and rock. ■ **STATUS** Vulnerable (Qld).

Concinnia amplus.
Mt Blackwood, Qld.
S. Wilson

Concinnia brachysoma.
Gayndah district, Qld.
S. Wilson

Concinnia frerei.
Mt Bartle Frere, Qld.
S. Wilson

Martin's Skink *Concinnia martini* SVL 70mm

Lower secondary temporal scale overlaps upper. Coppery brown with many irregular black flecks on back and a broad, deeply notched black upper lateral zone. Lower flanks grey, spotted with white and black. Tail marked with many irregular dark bands. ■ **NOTES** Coast and estn interior from mid-estn Qld s. to about Coffs Harbour, NSW. Shelters in rock crevices and cavities in timber in a variety of habitats including rock outcrops, woodlands, WSF and DSF. Often abundant in and around human dwellings. ■ **SEE ALSO** *C. brachysoma; C. sokosoma; C. tenuis.*

Stout Bar-sided Skink *Concinnia sokosoma* SVL 79mm

Midbody scales in 32–38 rows, upper secondary temporal scale overlaps lower and **19–23 lamellae under 4th toe.** Pale brown with diffuse dark blotches tending to concentrate on paravertebral region, a diffuse, broken, dark upper lateral zone and narrow irregular dark bands on tail. ■ **NOTES** Moist areas within dry rocky habitats on coast and estn interior from Townsville s. to Injune. Shelters in rock crevices. ■ **SEE ALSO** *C. brachysoma; C. martini; C. tenuis.*

Bar-sided Skink *Concinnia tenuis* SVL 85mm

Narrow dark line on nape, upper secondary temporal scale overlaps lower and **22–27 lamellae under 4th toe.** Coppery brown to pale brown, lightly to densely marked with small black blotches; usually a narrow dark longitudinal line on nape; broad, deeply notched black upper lateral stripe (often broken into vertical bars); and many irregular narrow dark bands on tail. ■ **NOTES** Rock outcrops, WSF, DSF, RF and home gardens on coast and estn interior, from ne. Qld s. nearly to Bega, NSW. Shelters in rock crevices and cavities of timber, thriving in garden rockeries and frequently entering houses. ■ **SEE ALSO** *C. brachysoma; C. martini; C. sokosoma.*

Yellow-blotched Forest-skink *Concinnia tigrinus* SVL 85mm

Pale golden brown to dark brown with **narrow black bands across back,** broadening into dark dorsolateral blotches and alternating with a **dorsolateral row of cream to yellow or orange blotches.** Ventral surfaces yellow to pale green. ■ **NOTES** RF and high-altitude heaths from sea-level to about 1600m, between Bloomfield and Kirrama. Basks on fallen logs and tree buttresses, often seen resting with head protruding from hollows.

Concinnia martini.
Helidon, Qld. S. Wilson

Concinnia sokosoma.
Harvey Range, Qld. S. Wilson

Concinnia tenuis.
Southbrook region, Qld.
S. Wilson

Concinnia tigrinus.
Mt Bellenden Ker, Qld. G. Harold

Snake-eyed, Wall or Fence Skinks Genus *Cryptoblepharus*

Twenty-three small, **dorsally depressed** spp. with long limbs, each with 5 slender digits. Eye large and circular, with **lower eyelid fused to form a fixed spectacle, surrounded by granular scales, uppermost much larger**. Scales smooth; **frontoparietals and interparietal fused to form a single shield, and frontal about equal in size to prefrontals (A)**. Identification can be difficult, with features including pattern, build, number of supraciliary scales (5 or 6), whether plantar scales are dark or pale, and smoothly oval (B) to acutely spinose (C). ■ **NOTES** Widespread, excluding se. mainland and Tas. Also Indian and Pacific Oceans, including many isolated islets. Swift, sun-loving skinks that thrive on vertical faces of rocks, trees and buildings, foraging on exposed surfaces and sheltering in narrow crevices. Egglayers. ■ **SEE ALSO** *Morethia.*

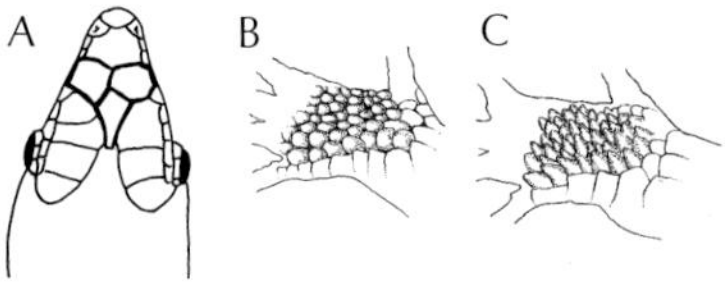

Adams's Snake-eyed Skink *Cryptoblepharus adamsi* SVL 37mm

Striped, with usually **5 supraciliary scales, callused, pale, ovate plantar scales** and relatively short limbs. Narrow dark brown vertebral zone and prominent **broad ragged-edged pale dorsal stripes** with broad, black, ragged inner margins. ■ **NOTES** Arboreal in woodlands, parks and gardens from Mt Molloy s. to Mt Larcom and inland to w. of Mt Surprise, Qld. ■ **SEE ALSO** *C. pulcher; C. virgatus.*

Inland Snake-eyed Skink *Cryptoblepharus australis* SVL 46mm

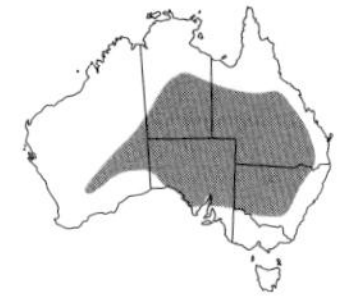

Longitudinally-aligned pattern, with usually **6 supraciliary scales, acute plantar scales, smooth subdigital lamellae** and relatively short limbs. Greyish with variable **complex, ragged pattern** incl. broad dark vertebral zone, dark flecks aligning to form 2 narrow broken paravertebral stripes and broad pale laterodorsal zones. ■ **NOTES** Mainly arboreal, frequently extending onto human structures throughout arid inland. ■ **SEE ALSO** *C. buchananii; C. ochrus; C. pannosus.*

Buchanan's Snake-eyed Skink *Cryptoblepharus buchananii* SVL 49mm

Longitudinally-aligned pattern, with usually **6 supraciliary scales, rounded, usually callused plantar scales** and relatively short limbs. Grey, brown to greyish black with variable **complex, ragged pattern** incl. broad dark vertebral zone, dark flecks aligning to form 2 narrow broken paravertebral stripes and broad pale laterodorsal zones. Colour darkest in s. and pattern weakest in n. ■ **NOTES** Mainly arboreal, frequently extending onto human structures in mid and sthn WA inc. inner suburban Perth. ■ **SEE ALSO** *C. australis; C. plagiocephalus; C. ustulatus.*

Cryptoblepharus adamsi.
Collinsville, Qld.
S. Wilson

Cryptoblepharus australis.
Innamincka, SA.
S. Wilson

Cryptoblepharus buchananii.
Dunsborough, WA.
G. Harold

Swanson's Snake-eyed Skink *Cryptoblepharus cygnatus* SVL 44mm

Longitudinally-aligned pattern, with usually **6 supraciliary scales, rounded, smooth plantar scales, a dark shiny callus on each subdigital lamella** and relatively short limbs. Grey to brown with variable **complex, ragged pattern** incl. broad dark vertebral zone, dark flecks aligning to form 2 narrow broken paravertebral stripes and broad pale laterodorsal zones. ■ **NOTES** Mainly arboreal, frequently extending onto human structures in nthn NT. ■ **SEE ALSO** *C. metallicus; C. gurrmul.*

Dappled Snake-eyed Skink *Cryptoblepharus daedalos* SVL 40mm

Speckled or blotched, with usually **6 supraciliary scales, rounded plantar scales, very long limbs and flat head and body**. Russet to reddish with random, irregular dark flecks and spots. ■ **NOTES** Exclusively rock-inhabiting, in Stokes Range, NT.

Noble Snake-eyed Skink *Cryptoblepharus exochus* SVL 40mm

Longitudinally-aligned pattern, with usually **5 supraciliary scales, acute plantar scales** and relatively short limbs. Olive-brown with fine dark and pale specks and streaks and two widely spaced, **very narrow cream to white laterodorsal stripes.** ■ **NOTES** Exclusively arboreal, inhabiting trunks of Gutta-percha trees on cracking clay soils of Victoria Bonaparte region, NT. ■ **SEE ALSO** *C. metallicus; C. ruber.*

Fuhn's Snake-eyed Skink *Cryptoblepharus fuhni* SVL 47mm

Longitudinally-aligned pattern, with 5 supraciliary scales, round dark plantar scales very flat head and body and **extremely long limbs**. Black to blackish brown with prominent **dorsolateral series of white dots and dashes**. On juv. these tend to join to form lines. Flanks prominently marked with several series of longitudinally oriented pale dashes. ■ **NOTES** Exclusively rock-inhabiting. Restricted to large black boulders of Melville Ra., Cape Melville, on estn Cape York Pen. ■ **STATUS** Vulnerable (Qld).

Arafura Snake-eyed Skink *Cryptoblepharus gurrmul* SVL 44mm

Longitudinally-aligned pattern, with usually **5 supraciliary scales, rounded plantar scales, postnasal scales** and relatively long limbs. Grey-brown to blackish with variable **complex pattern** incl. broad dark vertebral zone, dark flecks aligning to form 2 narrow broken paravertebral stripes and prominent to obscure pale laterodorsal stripes. ■ **NOTES** Littoral zones, inhabiting driftwood and coral rubble, on Oxley, New Year and North Goulburn Islands, off ne. Arnhem Land, NT. ■ **SEE ALSO** *C. cygnatus; C. litoralis.* ■ **STATUS** Endangered (NT).

Cryptoblepharus cygnatus.
Daly River, NT.
S. Wilson

Cryptoblepharus daedalos.
Jasper Gorge, NT.
P. Horner

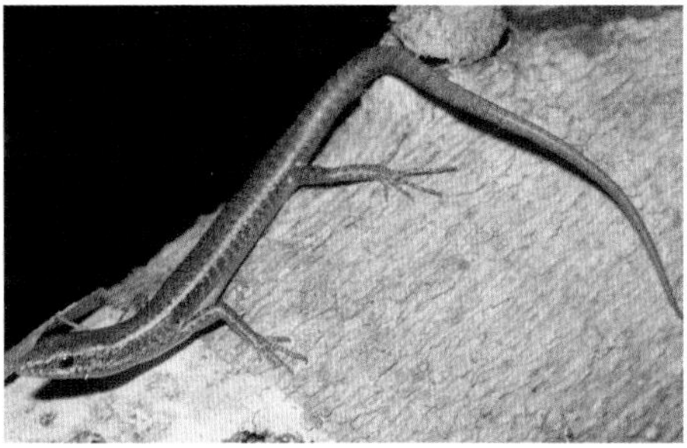

Cryptoblepharus exochus.
Mosquito Flat, NT. P. Horner

Cryptoblepharus fuhni.
Cape Melville, Qld. S. Wilson

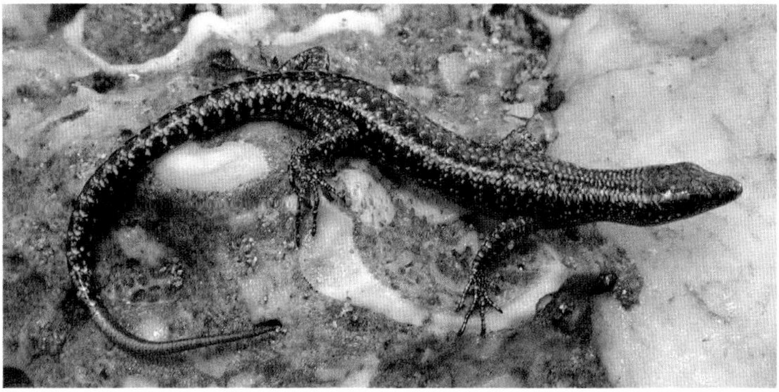

Cryptoblepharus gurrmul.
North Goulburn Island, NT. P. Horner

Juno's Snake-eyed Skink *Cryptoblepharus juno* SVL 43mm

Speckled or blotched, with usually **6 supraciliary scales, rounded plantar scales, very long limbs and flat head and body**. Reddish with random, weak to prominent irregular dark flecks and spots. ■ **NOTES** Exclusively rock-inhabiting, on sandstone escarpments and rocky hills between Bradshaw Stn, NT and Wyndham, WA, s. to Bungle Bungles.

Coastal Snake-eyed Skink *Cryptoblepharus litoralis* SVL 51mm

Very large, with longitudinally-aligned pattern, usually **5 supraciliary scales, rounded, dark plantar scales** and long limbs. Dark brown to greyish black with variable complex, ragged pattern incl. broad dark vertebral zone, dark flecks aligning to form 2 narrow broken paravertebral stripes and pale grey laterodorsal stripes, usually with ragged inner margins. ■ **SSP.** *C. l. litoralis* has 10-14 **(mean 11.8) plantar scales** and 48-62 **(mean 56.6) paravertebral scales.** *C. l horneri* has 9-12 **(mean 10.9) plantar scales** and 50-58 **(mean 54.5) paravertebral scales.** ■ **NOTES** *C. l. litoralis* occurs on coast of Qld, from Gladstone to Torres Strait. *C. l. horneri* occurs on islands off Arnhem Land, NT and on mainland at Murgenella. Forages on exposed coastal rocks, including those in splash zone, and feeds on both terrestrial and small marine invertebrates such as amphipods and polychaete worms. ■ **SEE ALSO** *C. gurrmul; C. metallicus; C. pannosus.*

Blotched Snake-eyed Skink *Cryptoblepharus megastictus* SVL 40mm

Speckled or blotched, with usually **6 supraciliary scales, rounded plantar scales, very long limbs and flat head and body**. Reddish with random, irregular **dark blotches**. ■ **NOTES** Exclusively rock-inhabiting, on sandstone massifs of nthn Kimberley region and rocky off-shore islands, WA.

Merten's Snake-eyed Skink *Cryptoblepharus mertensi* SVL 38mm

Longitudinally-aligned pattern, with usually **5 supraciliary scales, pale acute plantar scales** and relatively short limbs. Brownish grey with variable complex, ragged pattern incl. broad dark vertebral zone about 4 scales wide, dark flecks aligning to form 2 narrow broken paravertebral stripes and pale laterodorsal stripes fading at about midbody. ■ **NOTES** Arboreal, often on *Melaleuca* or *Casuarina* trunks near waterways in Gulf region of NT. ■ **SEE ALSO** *C. metallicus; C. ruber.*

Metallic Snake-eyed Skink *Cryptoblepharus metallicus* SVL 47mm

Longitudinally-aligned pattern, with usually 6 **supraciliary scales, rounded, usually callused plantar scales, smooth subdigital lamellae, 45-56 (modally 48) paravertebral scales** and relatively short limbs. Grey to grey-brown with variable, pale and obscure to dark and prominent, complex ragged pattern incl. broad dark vertebral zone about as wide as paravertebral scales, dark flecks aligning to form 2 narrow broken paravertebral stripes and pale laterodorsal zones. ■ **NOTES** Largely arboreal, but frequently venturing onto human structures and sometimes rocks, across nthn Aust. s. to se. Qld. ■ **SEE ALSO** *C. cygnatus; C. exochus; C. mertensi; C. pannosus; C. ruber; C. tytthos; C. litoralis.*

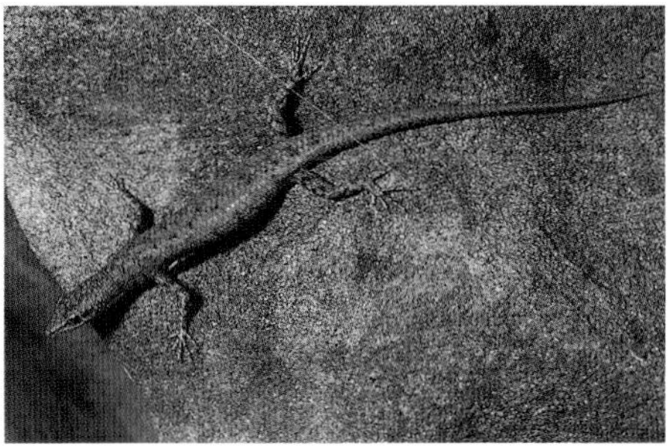

Cryptoblepharus juno.
Kununurra, WA. S. Wilson

Cryptoblepharus litoralis litoralis.
Prince of Wales Is., Qld. S. Wilson

Cryptoblepharus litoralis horneri.
Truant Island, NT. P. Horner

Cryptoblepharus megastictus.
King Leopold Range, WA. B. Maryan.

Cryptoblepharus mertensi.
Roper Bar, NT. P. Horner

Cryptoblepharus metallicus.
Prince of Wales Is., Qld. S. Wilson

Pale Snake-eyed Skink *Cryptoblepharus ochrus* SVL 43mm

Longitudinally-aligned pattern, with usually **5 supraciliary scales, pale, acute plantar scales, weakly-keeled subdigital lamellae, 47-55 (modally 50) paravertebral scales** and relatively short limbs. Pale greyish-brown with variable, obscure to prominent, ragged pattern incl. broad vertebral zone about 4 scales wide, dark flecks aligning to form 2 narrow broken dorsal stripes and smooth-edged **narrow pale laterodorsal stripes** about 1 scale wide. ■ **NOTES** Arboreal, extending onto human structures in ne. SA, s. to Wares Peak. ■ **SEE ALSO** *C. australis; C. pannosus.*

Ragged Snake-eyed Skink *Cryptoblepharus pannosus* SVL 41mm

Longitudinally-aligned pattern, with usually **5 supraciliary scales, pale, acute plantar scales, strongly keeled subdigital lamellae, 43-56 (modally 48) paravertebral scales** and relatively short limbs. Brown, grey to blackish with variable, complex ragged pattern incl. broad dark vertebral zone 3-4 scales wide, dark flecks aligning to form 2 narrow broken dorsal stripes and ragged, **broad** pale grey to cream laterodorsal stripes. ■ **NOTES** Mainly arboreal but extremely versatile, extending onto human structures and rocks, throughout estn Aust. ■ **SEE ALSO** *C. australis; C. metallicus; C. ochrus; C. tytthos, C. litoralis.*

Peron's Snake-eyed Skink *Cryptoblepharus plagiocephalus* SVL 40mm

Longitudinally-aligned pattern, with usually 5 **supraciliary scales, acute, pale plantar scales, moderately keeled subdigital lamellae** and relatively short limbs. Brownish-grey with variable, complex ragged pattern incl. broad dark vertebral zone about 4 scales wide, dark flecks aligning to form 2 narrow broken dorsal stripes and smooth to ragged, broad pale grey to cream latero-dorsal stripes. ■ **NOTES** Typically arboreal, extending onto human structures on coast and interior of WA between Pt Hedland and about Kalgoorlie. Some off-shore island pops wholly terrestrial on limestone and reef debris. ■ **SEE ALSO** *C. buchananii.*

Elegant Snake-eyed Skink *Cryptoblepharus pulcher* SVL 41mm

Striped, with usually **5 supraciliary scales, round, dark plantar scales** and relatively short limbs. Brown to brownish-black with narrow dark vertebral zone about 1 scale wide, black dorsal stripes and prominent, **narrow, smooth-edged pale laterodorsal stripes.** ■ **SSP.** *C. p. clarus* has 24-26 midbody scale rows and generally broader pale laterodorsal stripes. *C. p. pulcher* has 22-26 midbody scale rows and generally narrower pale laterodorsal stripes. ■ **NOTES** Arboreal and rock-inhabiting, often extending onto human structures. *C. p. clarus* extends across sthn Aust. between about Yorke Pen., SA and Ravensthorpe, WA. *C. p. pulcher* is widespread in estn Aust between about Ingham, Qld and Jervis Bay, NSW, incl inner suburban Sydney and Brisbane. ■ **SEE ALSO** *C. adamsi; C. virgatus.*

Cryptoblepharus ochrus.
Coward Springs, SA. S. Wilson

Cryptoblepharus pannosus.
Glenmorgan, Qld. S. Wilson

Cryptoblepharus plagiocephalus.
Kalbarri NP, WA. B. Maryan

Cryptoblepharus pulcher clarus.
Eucla district, WA. R. Browne-Cooper

Cryptoblepharus pulcher pulcher.
Kurwongbah, Qld. S. Wilson

Tawny Snake-eyed Skink *Cryptoblepharus ruber* SVL 47mm

Longitudinally-aligned pattern, with usually **6 supraciliary scales, rounded callose plantar scales, smooth subdigital lamellae, 45-56 (modally 54) paravertebral scales** and relatively short limbs. Brown to grey with variable, complex ragged pattern incl. broad dark vertebral zone 2 scales wide, dark flecks aligning to form 2 narrow broken dorsal stripes and ragged, broad, grey to pale brown laterodorsal stripes. ■ **NOTES** Mainly arboreal, extending onto human structures and rock faces in nw. Aust. ■ **SEE ALSO** *C. metallicus; C. exochus; C.mertensi; C. tytthos.*

Pygmy Snake-eyed Skink *Cryptoblepharus tytthos* SVL 38mm

Small, with reduced, longitudinally-aligned pattern, usually **5 supraciliary scales, pale, acute plantar scales, strongly keeled subdigital lamellae** and relatively short limbs. Brownish grey with variable pattern incl. broad dark vertebral zone 4 scales wide, dark flecks occasionally aligning to form 2 narrow broken dorsal stripes and narrow, often obscure pale grey laterodorsal stripes. ■ **NOTES** Arboreal, extending onto human structures in woodlands and shrublands in nw. Aust and (doubtfully) Mornington Is., Qld. ■ **SEE ALSO** *C. metallicus; C. pannosus, C. ruber.*

Russet Snake-eyed Skink *Cryptoblepharus ustulatus* SVL 41mm

Reduced longitudinally-aligned pattern, with usually **5 supraciliary scales, rounded plantar scales, long limbs and very flat head and body**. Pale russet to brick red with broad vertebral zone about 4 scales wide, sometimes dark flecks aligning to form 2 obscure, broken dorsal stripes, and narrow pale laterodorsal stripes. ■ **NOTES** Exclusively rock-inhabiting in Pilbara region, WA. ■ **SEE ALSO** *C. buchananii.*

Striped Snake-eyed Skink *Cryptoblepharus virgatus* SVL 39mm

Striped, with usually **5 supraciliary scales, round, pale plantar scales** and relatively short limbs. Grey to greyish-brown with broad dark vertebral zone about 2 scales wide, prominent black dorsal stripes and prominent, narrow, **smooth-edged pale laterodorsal stripes**. ■ **NOTES** Arboreal but often inhabiting humans structures in ne. Qld from about Townsville to Torres Strait. ■ **SEE ALSO** *C. adamsi; C. pulcher.*

Spangled Snake-eyed Skink *Cryptoblepharus wulbu* SVL 39mm

Blotched, with usually **6 supraciliary scales, rounded plantar scales, very long limbs and flat head and body**. Reddish-mauve with large, rounded to irregular blackish blotches and scattered pale spots. ■ **NOTES** Exclusively rock-inhabiting, on sandstone faces, boulders and crevices. Restricted to, but locally abundant on, Mt Borradaile, NT.

Cryptoblepharus ruber.
Wave Hill Station, NT. P. Horner

Cryptoblepharus tytthos.
Broome Bird Observatory, WA. S. Wilson

Cryptoblepharus ustulatus.
Mt Bruce, WA. B. Maryan

Cryptoblepharus virgatus.
Cooktown, Qld. S. Wilson

Cryptoblepharus wulbu. Mt Borradaile, NT. P. Horner

Agile Snake-eyed Skink *Cryptoblepharus zoticus* SVL 38mm

Speckled or blotched, with usually **5 supraciliary scales, rounded plantar scales, relatively short limbs and flat head and body**. Reddish with random, weak to prominent irregular **dark flecks and spots**. ■ **NOTES** Exclusively rock-inhabiting, on sandstone escarpments, rocky hills and ridges of sthn gulf region between Limmen Gate NP in NT and Mary Kathleen, Qld.

Striped Skinks Genus *Ctenotus*

One hundred and four small to moderately large, long-tailed spp. with well-developed limbs, each with 5 digits. Scales smooth. **Ear-openings with anterior lobules**. Lower eyelid moveable, lacking transparent disc. **Parietal scales in contact**. Colour and pattern extremely variable; typically **longitudinal stripes** (simple) **or stripes with rows of spots** (complex). Spp. can be difficult to identify. Features employed include size, pattern, number of midbody scales and nature of subdigital lamellae; smooth to broadly callose (A), narrowly callose (B) or finely keeled to mucronate (C and D). Unfortunately, determining these conditions can be subjective. ■ **NOTES** Dry open areas throughout mainland Aust. (not Tas.) and sthn NG, with diversity greatest in spinifex deserts and well-drained tropical areas. Swift and diurnal. Some forage widely across exposed terrain while others skulk along vegtn edges. A few appear to specialise on termites but most are invertebrate generalists. All lay eggs. Largest Aust. reptile genus. ■ **SEE ALSO** *Liopholis.*

A
B
C
D

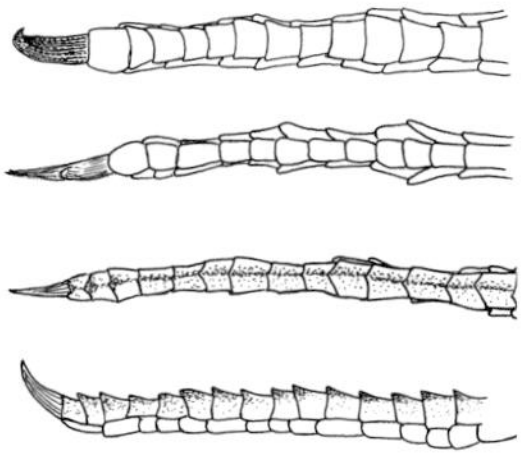

Mitchell Grass Ctenotus *Ctenotus agrestis* SVL 74mm

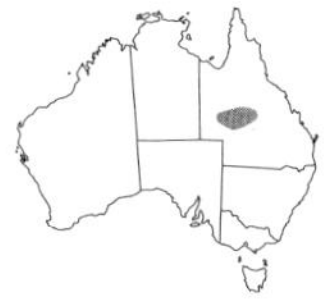

Relatively short-tailed, with simple pattern of **stripes and upper lateral dashes**. Subdigital lamellae broadly callose. Pale greyish brown. Vertebral stripe (broad and black with indistinct pale edge to narrow and obscure) from nape to base of tail; pale dorsolateral stripe from above eye to tail tip; **pale upper lateral stripe broken into dashes from eye to hindlimb**; pale midlateral stripe from nostril to tail; obscure greyish brown lower lateral and ventrolateral stripes. ■ **NOTES** Semi-arid cracking clay plains vegetated with Mitchell grass between Aramac and Boulia incl. Lochern NP, Qld.

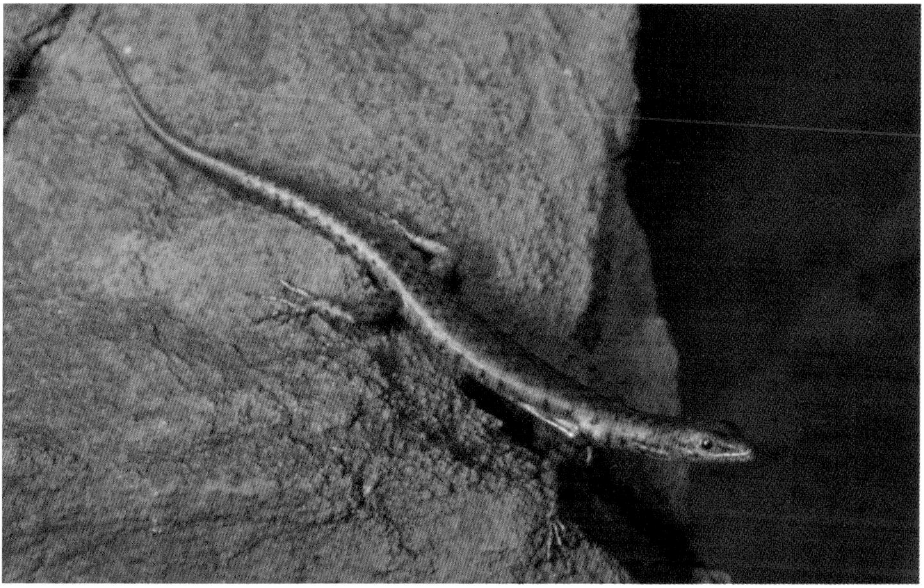

Cryptoblepharus zoticus.
Lawn Hill, Qld. S. Wilson

Ctenotus agrestis.
Aramac, Qld. S. Wilson

Lively Ctenotus *Ctenotus alacer* SVL 62mm

Numerous dorsal stripes and a row of pale upper lateral spots. Subdigital lamellae bluntly keeled to narrowly callose. Black with **6 pale dorsal stripes** (reddish paravertebrals and dorsals, and cream dorsolaterals), **a prominent row of pale upper lateral spots,** and prominent white midlateral stripe (sometimes broken anteriorly) with dark lower edge. Limbs reddish brown with dark stripes. ■ **NOTES** Rocky hills and ranges in wstn Qld, sthn NT and estn WA.

Plain-backed Sandplain Ctenotus *Ctenotus alleni* SVL 93mm

Pattern includes plain back and pale upper lateral spots. Subdigital lamellae narrow to moderately broadly callose. Olive brown with **vertebral stripe absent or reduced to a line on nape.** Black laterodorsal and white dorsolateral stripes; **black upper flanks enclosing 1–2 series of pale dots or short dashes; pale midlateral stripe from forelimb** nearly to end of tail. Limbs brown, streaked with black. ■ **NOTES** Woodland/heaths on yellowish sandy soils on semi-arid coast and hinterland from Nanga s. to Yuna. ■ **SEE ALSO** *C. mimetes.*

Brown-blazed Wedge-snouted Ctenotus *Ctenotus allotropis* SVL 55mm

Prominent pattern includes stripes (**no vertebral stripe**) and a **laterodorsal row of pale spots. Nasal scales in contact. Subdigital lamellae black-keeled; finely mucronate towards tip of digit and blunt at base.** Brown above, with **black laterodorsal stripe enclosing a series of pale spots or dashes,** a narrow white dorsolateral stripe, black upper flanks enclosing 2–3 series of pale, vertically aligned spots, and a prominent white midlateral stripe. Limbs pale brown with dark stripes. ■ **NOTES** Woodlands and shrublands from semi-arid central NSW to se. interior of Qld. ■ **SEE ALSO** *C. schomburgkii; C. strauchii.*

North-west Coastal Ctenotus *Ctenotus angusticeps* SVL 74mm

Pattern weak and fragmented. Subdigital lamellae broadly callose. Dark olive grey with dark and pale mottling and an indication of a dark vertebral stripe. Flanks marked with broken dark-edged ocelli, their pale centres tending to align into broken stripes. ■ **NOTES** Patchily distributed along nw. coast, between Airlie Is. and just n. of Broome. On Airlie Is. it inhabits acacia shrublands, coastal spinifex and particularly tussock grasses at wstn end of island. On mainland lizards have been observed on coastal mudflats vegetated with samphire, sometimes sheltering in crab holes on intertidal zone. ■ **STATUS** Vulnerable (C'wealth; WA))

Ctenotus alacer.
Alice Springs, NT. P. Griffin

Ctenotus alleni.
East Yuna Nature Reserve, WA. B. Maryan

Ctenotus allotropis.
Bollon, Qld. S. Wilson

Ctenotus angusticeps,
Port Hedland, WA.
B. Maryan.

Arcane Ctenotus *Ctenotus arcanus* SVL 87mm

Pattern includes **stripes and upper lateral spots**. Subdigital lamellae narrowly callose. Olive brown to coppery brown above with variable pattern: pale-edged **dark vertebral stripe often reduced to a line on nape of adults** but prominent from nape onto base of tail on juv.; narrow cream dorsolateral and broader black laterodorsal stripes; **black upper flanks enclosing a series of well-spaced sharp white dots**; white midlateral stripe. Limbs reddish brown to olive, striped with black. On Stradbroke Is. and Moreton Is. pattern greatly reduced, pale lateral spots smaller and fragmented into several series, and limbs finely mottled. ■ **NOTES** Se. Qld, from Kroombit Tops, to far ne. NSW, occurring in heaths, woodlands and margins of WSF. On mainland, favours rocky areas. Island pops occur on pale sand, particularly areas edging swamps or freshwater lakes. ■ **SEE ALSO** *C. robustus*.

Ariadna's Ctenotus *Ctenotus ariadnae* SVL 64mm

Simple pattern comprising many narrow stripes. Subdigital lamellae narrowly callose to bluntly keeled. Brown to black with **18–20 narrow pale stripes**. All dorsal stripes well defined, becoming **increasingly ill-defined on flanks, especially anteriorly**. ■ **NOTES** Sandy deserts vegetated with spinifex. ■ **SEE ALSO** C. *dux*.

Jabiluka Ctenotus *Ctenotus arnhemensis* SVL 55mm

Pattern comprises **stripes and upper lateral spots**. Subdigital lamellae moderately broadly callose. Brown above with broad pale-edged black vertebral stripe from nape to base of tail; black laterodorsal and narrow white dorsolateral stripes; blackish brown upper flanks enclosing a row of longitudinally aligned pale blotches; prominent white midlateral stripe (sometimes broken between ear and forelimb); and brown lower flanks. Head brown with **pale stripe under eye**. ■ **NOTES** Open forest and woodlands on pale sandy soils at base of Arnhem Escarpment near Jabiluka. Shelters in shallow burrows beneath rocks and dead vegtn.

Ctenotus arcanus.
Kroombit Tops, Qld. S. Wilson

Ctenotus arcanus.
Pale island colour form.
North Stradbroke Is., Qld. S. Wilson

Ctenotus ariadnae.
Nappa Merrie Stn, Qld. S. Wilson

Ctenotus arnhemensis.
Jabiru, NT. B. Maryan

Ashy Downs Ctenotus *Ctenotus astarte* SVL 82mm

Pattern dominated by pale spots and irregular small dark blotches. Subdigital lamellae bluntly keeled to narrowly callose. Greyish brown to yellowish brown with little indication of a dark vertebral stripe. Dark markings mainly concentrate on mid-dorsal region. Pale spots often align to form irregular broken paravertebral and dorsolateral lines, particularly on juv. Pale dots on upper flanks tend to align vertically. ■ **NOTES** Arid shrublands on stony and cracking soils from Durrie and Caddapan Stns n. to Boulia and Diamantina Lakes area. ■ **STATUS** Rare (SA).

Arnhem Striped Ctenotus *Ctenotus astictus* SVL 51mm

Relatively long-limbed with **simple pattern of stripes**. Subdigital lamellae smooth to broadly callose. Brown above with narrowly pale-edged black vertebral stripe from nape to tail-base; dark laterodorsal and white dorsolateral stripes from above eye onto tail; flanks dark greyish brown with sharp white upper lateral and obscure pale lower lateral stripes. Limbs brown with black stripes. ■ **NOTES** Ne. NT, including near-coastal mainland, and islands in the Wessel and Sir Edward Pellew groups. Open woodlands and shrublands on pale sands near watercourses, and near-coastal areas.

Southern Spinifex Ctenotus *Ctenotus atlas* SVL 69mm

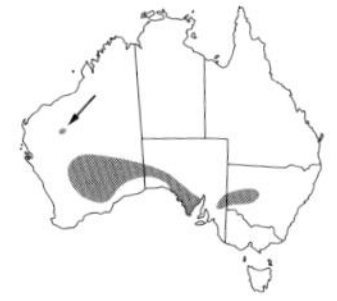

Simple pattern of 8 or 10 pale stripes. Subdigital lamellae narrowly callose. Black with prominent cream to yellowish brown paravertebral, dorsolateral, upper lateral, midlateral and sometimes ventrolateral stripes. Limbs brown, striped with blackish brown. ■ **NOTES** Arid to semi-arid mallee/spinifex associations, between Nymagee, NSW and the Wheat Belt of WA, with an isolated pop. at Turee Creek on upper Ashburton R., WA.

West Coast Long-tailed Ctenotus *Ctenotus australis* SVL 100mm

Pattern prominent; **stripes and upper lateral spots**. Subdigital lamellae broadly callose. Pale brown to coppery brown marked with black vertebral stripe with pale edges (these too may be dark-edged); **black laterodorsal stripe with pale inner margin**; white dorsolateral stripe; black upper flanks enclosing 1–3 series of white dots or dashes; and white midlateral stripe breaking to form **oblique to vertical dark-edged bars from behind forelimb onto sides of neck**. ■ **NOTES** Lower w. coast from Mandurah to Shark Bay. Coastal dunes, sand-plains, and limestones supporting heaths, typically with eucalypt/banksia woodlands.

Ctenotus astarte.
Morney Stn, Qld. S. Wilson

Ctenotus astictus.
Cadell River, NT. P. Horner

Ctenotus atlas.
Lake Gillies region, SA. S. Wilson

Ctenotus australis.
Singleton Beach, WA. S. Wilson

Northern Ctenotus *Ctenotus borealis* SVL 121mm

Weakly patterned with stripes and pale lateral bars. Subdigital lamellae smooth. Pattern obscure on adults but bright on juv.; brown with **indistinct black vertebral stripe** (sometimes absent or reduced to spots and seldom pale-edged); **cream dorsolateral stripe usually absent** or obscure and broken into spots; flanks mottled with greyish brown, tending to form vertical bars; obscure broken pale midlateral stripe; and **dark-edged white stripe under eye**. Hindlimbs speckled with black. ■ **NOTES** Woodlands, rock outcrops and consolidated sand dunes. Genetic evidence indicates very close relationship with *C. robustus*, and the existing taxonomy may require change.

Short-clawed Ctenotus *Ctenotus brachyonyx* SVL 83mm

Weak striped pattern. Subdigital lamellae broadly callose. Brown to olive grey with **broad black vertebral stripe lacking pale edge and ending abruptly at base of tail**; black laterodorsal stripe ending at hips or tail-base; pale dorsolateral stripe extending onto tail; dark brown to dark grey upper flanks sometimes enclosing dark dots or white flecks; and indistinct pale midlateral stripe. Limbs and face patternless. ■ **NOTES** Semi-arid e. in sandy areas with mallee/spinifex associations, occasionally chenopod and mulga shrublands. Genetic evidence indicates very close relationship with *C. inornatus*, and the existing taxonomy may require change.

Short-footed Ctenotus *Ctenotus brevipes* SVL 60mm

Short-limbed with little or no vertebral stripe and **unmarked black upper flanks**. Subdigital lamellae smooth or callose. **Ear-lobules absent**. Brown above with vertebral stripe absent, narrow and confined to nape and anterior body, or reaching hind quarters as a broken dark line. Prominent white dorsolateral stripe and prominent to obscure dark laterodorsal stripes extend back onto tail. Upper flanks black and patternless. Broad white midlateral stripe extends from upper lip to hindlimb. ■ **NOTES** Semi-arid to subhumid woodlands on mid and lower Cape York Pen. Generally skulks close to low vegetation.

Brooks' Wedge-snouted Ctenotus *Ctenotus brooksi* SVL 50mm

Weak pattern of stripes, spots and flecks. Subdigital lamellae usually 24 or more under 4th toe, finely keeled and mucronate, extending onto sole of foot. Orange, pink to rich reddish brown, merging on tail to grey green, with narrow, vaguely pale-edged dark brown vertebral stripe, dark and pale dorsal flecks sometimes forming indistinct lines, dark angular upper lateral blotches extending up to 3rd scale row from vertebral line, and weak white midlateral stripe, often broken anteriorly. ■ **NOTES** Sand-ridges of Victoria and Great Sandy Deserts. ■ **SEE ALSO** *C. taeniatus*.

Ctenotus borealis.
Darwin, NT. R. Browne-Cooper

Ctenotus brachyonyx.
Chesterton Range, Qld. S. Wilson

Ctenotus brevipes.
Undara, Qld.
S. Wilson

Ctenotus brooksi.
King's Creek Stn, NT.
S. Wilson

Plain-backed Kimberley Ctenotus *Ctenotus burbidgei* SVL 58mm

Reduced pattern of stripes and upper lateral spots. Subdigital lamellae narrowly to broadly callose. Yellowish brown to greyish brown usually with **no black vertebral stripe**; black laterodorsal and white dorsolateral stripes; blackish upper lateral zone sometimes enclosing a series of pale circular to squarish spots, and obscure pale grey midlateral stripe. Limbs brown, streaked blackish brown. ■ **NOTES** Sandstone outcrops and escarpments of nw. Kimberley. ■ **SEE ALSO** *C. mastigura.*

Blue-tailed Ctenotus *Ctenotus calurus* SVL 49mm

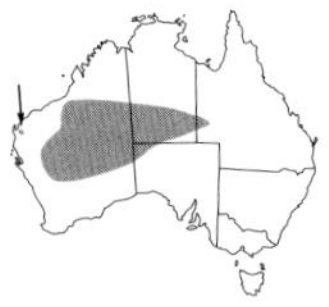

Slender, with **simple striped pattern**. Subdigital lamellae finely keeled and mucronate. Black with 8 sharp white stripes, **blue tail** and reddish orange flush on head. Forelimbs orange with dark brown streaks. Hindlimbs black with white stripes. ■ **NOTES** Sandy deserts with spinifex from central and sthn interior of WA to wstn QLD. Isolated pop. occurs at Exmouth Gulf, WA. Waves its conspicuous blue tail when foraging.

Capricorn Ctenotus *Ctenotus capricorni* SVL 65mm

Robust, with pattern of **stripes and upper lateral spots**. Subdigital lamellae moderately broadly callose. Olive brown with pale-edged black vertebral stripe from nape onto base of tail; sometimes a narrow indistinct pale brown dorsal stripe; obscure narrow black laterodorsal stripe to base of tail; narrow whitish dorsolateral stripe extending well onto tail; pale greyish brown upper flanks enclosing series of obscure white dots or dashes (2 series sometimes present in front of forelimb); and greyish white midlateral stripe. Limbs olive brown, streaked with greyish white. ■ **NOTES** Semi-arid, sandy areas with spinifex, in association with shrub and woodland communities. ■ **STATUS** Near threatened (Qld).

Chain-striped Heath Ctenotus *Ctenotus catenifer* SVL 56mm

Complex pattern including dark dorsal flecks. Subdigital lamellae bluntly keeled to narrowly callose. Brown to olive grey above, flecked with black and sometimes with an irregular black vertebral stripe. Ragged-edged **black laterodorsal stripe, enclosing a series of white dashes, borders a broken white dorsolateral stripe.** Upper flanks black, enclosing white dots. **Limbs brown, peppered with black.** ■ **NOTES** Heaths on pale sand in lower sw. WA, n. to Busselton and e. to Point Dempster incl. humid areas of s. coast. Isolated nthn record at Badgingarra NP. ■ **SEE ALSO** *C. labillardieri.*

Ctenotus burbidgei.
Prince Regent River Reserve, WA.
P Doughty.

Ctenotus calurus.
Hay River, Simpson Desert, NT.
S. Wilson

Ctenotus capricorni.
Jericho, Qld. S. Wilson

Ctenotus catenifer.
Albany district, WA. S. Wilson

Brown-backed Ctenotus *Ctenotus coggeri* SVL 80mm

Robust, with **greatly reduced pattern**. Subdigital lamellae broadly callose. Olive brown above with **no black vertebral stripe**; black laterodorsal and white dorsolateral stripes, blackish brown upper flanks, and prominent **white midlateral stripe extending continuously through hindlimb onto tail.** Limbs brown; hindlimbs marked with prominent lighter stripes. **Ventral surfaces yellow** from throat to base of tail. ■ **NOTES** Wstn Arnhem Escarpment. Restricted to sandstone habitats. ■ **SEE ALSO** *C. inornatus.*

Collett's Ctenotus *Ctenotus colletti* SVL 42mm

Sharp-snouted, with **simple striped pattern**. Subdigital lamellae each with a fine weak keel. Black with **12 pale stripes**; narrow orange-brown paravertebrals and 4 narrow dorsal stripes, white dorsolateral stripes, broad black upper flanks and broad white midlateral and ventrolateral stripes. Limbs pale brown striped with dark brown. ■ **NOTES** Semi-arid acacia scrub in sw. Kimberley.

Ten-lined Ctenotus *Ctenotus decaneurus* SVL 50mm

Simple striped pattern. Subdigital lamellae moderately callose. Black with 8-10 (usually 10) sharp, narrow, pale stripes; **paravertebrals separate throughout their entire length**; dorsals from base of head to tail; dorsolaterals from above eye and midlateral from beneath eye, well onto tail; and lower laterals from below ear to groin. **SSP.** *C. d. decaneurus* has 24-28 (usually 26) midbody scales. *C. d. yampiensis* has 29-32 (usually 30) midbody scales. ■ **NOTES** Woodlands and shrublands on stony hills. *C. d. decaneurus* extends from Kimberley region, WA to nthn NT and wstn Qld. *C. d. yampiensis* occurs in nw. Kimberley in vicinity of Collier Bay. ■ **SEE ALSO** *C. storri; C. vagus.*

Darling Range Heath Ctenotus *Ctenotus delli* SVL 63mm

Back patternless and pale dorsolateral stripe broken. Subdigital lamellae narrowly callose. Uniform dark olive to coppery brown above with narrow black laterodorsal stripe, white dorsolateral stripe broken into a series of dashes, a black upper lateral zone marked with scattered white dots, and a **white midlateral stripe broken into a series of dashes. Limbs brown, finely peppered with black.** ■ **NOTES** Darling Ra. in jarrah and marri woodlands over a shrubby understorey on lateritic, sandy and clay soils. ■ **SEE ALSO** *C. gemmula.*

Ctenotus coggeri.
Nourlangie Rock, Kakadu NP, NT. G. Gaikhorst

Ctenotus colletti.
Roebuck Plains Stn, WA. B. Maryan

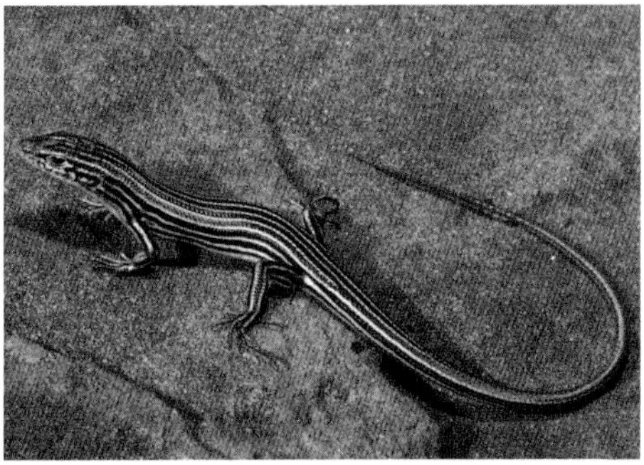

Ctenotus decaneurus decaneurus. 275km west of Wyndham on Gibb River Rd, WA. S. Wilson

Ctenotus decaneurus yampiensis.
Mt Elizabeth Station, WA. G. Harold

Ctenotus delli.
Kalamunda district, WA. S. Wilson

Pilbara Striped Ctenotus *Ctenotus duricola* SVL 60mm

Simple pattern of **stripes and sometimes pale upper lateral spots.** Subdigital lamellae narrowly to broadly callose. **Midbody scales in 26–32 rows.** Black to dark reddish brown with 6–8 white to brownish white stripes; paravertebrals and dorsolaterals; broad dark **upper lateral zone often enclosing an anterior series of small pale spots**; white midlateral stripe; and sometimes a white ventrolateral stripe. Limbs pale reddish brown; forelimbs streaked, and hindlimbs striped, with dark brown. ■ **NOTES** Hard clay or stony soils vegetated with spinifex on nw. coast including Barrow Is. and adjacent interior. ■ **SEE ALSO** *C. piankai.*

Narrow-lined Ctenotus *Ctenotus dux* SVL 65mm

Simple pattern of **18 or more pale stripes.** Subdigital lamellae narrowly callose to bluntly keeled. Coppery brown to metallic olive above with pale-edged black vertebral stripe, black laterodorsal and white dorsolateral stripes. Flanks marked with about 7 pale lines or stripes; **midlateral and ventrolateral stripes broad, white, prominent and extending forward onto neck,** and remainder narrow and wavy, especially between ear and forelimb. Limbs brown, streaked with dark brown. ■ **NOTES** Desert sand dunes dominated by spinifex. ■ **SEE ALSO** *C. ariadnae.*

Brown-tailed Finesnout Ctenotus *Ctenotus ehmanni* SVL 41mm

Numerous **pale dorsal stripes and a row of pale upper lateral spots.** Subdigital lamellae finely keeled to mucronate. Blackish brown above with 10 pale stripes: **brownish white paravertebrals commencing on tip of snout,** dorsals from top of head and dorsolaterals from above eye; black upper flanks enclosing a series of prominent white spots between neck and hindlimb; white midlateral stripe from upper lip, through top of ear-opening onto tail; and black lower lateral and white ventrolateral stripes. Limbs prominently striped. ■ **NOTES** Nw. Kimberley between King Edward R. and Hann R. Recorded from eucalypt woodland with sparse ground cover on sandy soil.

Port Essington Ctenotus *Ctenotus essingtonii* SVL 65mm

Little or no vertebral stripe, upper flanks immaculate or spotted. Subdigital lamellae smooth or callose. Brown to brownish grey above with vertebal stripe absent or obscure and confined to nape and forebody. Prominent white dorsolateral stripe and prominent to obscure dark laterodorsal stripes extend back onto tail. Black upper flanks variable; immaculate, enclosing **a few pale spots between eye and forelimb, or with a series of evenly spaced spots.** Pale midlateral stripe extends from upper lip to hindlimb. Lower flanks mottled pale brown. ■ **NOTES** Nthn and nw. NT, favouring woodlands on sandy soils. Often forages widely across open spaces. ■ **SEE ALSO** *C. quirinus.*

Ctenotus duricola.
North West Cape, WA. D. Knowles

Ctenotus dux.
Ethabuka Stn, Qld. S. Wilson

Ctenotus ehmanni.
King Edward River, WA. A. Zimny

Ctenotus essingtonii.
Darwin, NT. S. Wilson

Bight Wedge-snouted Ctenotus *Ctenotus euclae* SVL 57mm

Pale with **wavy dorsal stripes and black upper lateral stripe. Subdigital lamellae finely keeled and mucronate, extending onto sole of foot.** Silvery white with narrow black vertebral stripe, 4 narrow wavy blackish dorsal stripes, broad black upper lateral stripe commencing along 4th scale row from vertebral line, either immaculate or enclosing white spots, and sharp white midlateral stripe. ■ **NOTES** White sands on Gt Aust. Bight of SA and WA.

Brown-backed Yellow-lined Ctenotus *Ctenotus eurydice* SVL 75mm

Rounded snout, **8 prominent pale stripes and white upper lateral spots.** Subdigital lamellae moderately to broadly callose. Olive brown above with broad pale-edged black vertebral stripe, broad black laterodorsal and narrow whitish dorsolateral stripes. Upper flanks black, with or without a few small white anterior spots, or a row of widely spaced spots. **White midlateral stripe extends from behind nostril to top of ear-opening, continuing back from posterior mid-portion of ear** onto tail. Whitish lower lateral stripe is bordered by a narrow brownish ventrolateral line. Limbs brown striped with black. ■ **NOTES** Rocky areas, mainly in cool uplands, between New England area, NSW and Monto district, se. Qld. ■ **SEE ALSO** *C. taeniolatus.*

Black-backed Yellow-lined Ctenotus *Ctenotus eutaenius* SVL 90mm

Prominent stripes, including pale upper lateral stripe normally broken into dashes anteriorly. Subdigital lamellae broadly callose. Blackish brown with pale-edged black vertebral and olive brown dorsal stripes; black laterodorsal and white dorsolateral stripes; pale yellowish brown upper lateral stripe, usually broken anteriorly and extending forward to temple; white midlateral stripe; and usually some indication of a broad white lower lateral stripe on anterior body. ■ **NOTES** Magnetic Is. w. to the Gt Basalt Wall and n. to Chillagoe. Dry woodlands, often associated with granite and basalt outcrops.

West Coast Ctenotus *Ctenotus fallens* SVL 95mm

Six pale stripes and a row of upper lateral spots. Subdigital lamellae broadly callose. Pale to dark greyish brown, darker on juv., with pale-edged black vertebral stripe (the pale paravertebrals may have dark outer edges), white dorsolateral and black laterodorsal stripe, dark brown upper flanks enclosing a series of pale spots or diffuse blotches, white midlateral stripe, and pale grey lower flanks enclosing diffuse pale spots. Limbs brown striped with darker brown or black. ■ **NOTES** Coastal dunes, sand-plains and offshore islands, from Cape Cuvier south to Pinjarra. Favours low coastal vegtn on pale sandy soils, but extends inland to granites (less commonly laterites) of Darling Ra. Genetic evidence indicates very close relationship with *C. inornatus*, and the existing taxonomy may require change.

Ctenotus euclae.
Eucla district, WA. B. Maryan

Ctenotus eurydice.
Girraween NP, Qld. S. Wilson

Ctenotus eutaenius.
Great Basalt Wall, Qld. S. Wilson

Ctenotus fallens.
Melaleuca Park, WA. S. Wilson

Kakadu Ctenotus *Ctenotus gagudju* SVL 54mm

Frontoparietal scales fused to form a single shield and pattern comprising **stripes and lateral spots.** Subdigital lamellae bluntly to narrowly keeled. Brown above with black vertebral stripe either absent or narrow with no pale edge and terminating at hindlimbs; narrow black laterodorsal and pale yellow dorsolateral stripes; blackish brown upper flanks enclosing a prominent row of white spots; prominent pale midlateral stripe broken anteriorly; and reddish brown lower flanks with scattered pale blotches. Limbs brown with dark stripes. ■ **NOTES** Wstn Arnhem Escarpment in lowland woodlands on reddish lateritic soils near Magela and Nourlangie Cks.

Jewelled Sandplain Ctenotus *Ctenotus gemmula* SVL 58mm

Plain back, broken white dorsolateral stripes and spotted flanks. Subdigital lamellae bluntly keeled. Uniform pale yellowish brown to silvery brown above with black laterodorsal and broken white dorsolateral stripes, black upper flanks usually enclosing series of prominent white spots, and wavy or broken white midlateral stripe. **Limbs yellowish brown, boldly marbled with black and white.** ■ **NOTES** Apparently disjunct pops occur on lower w. coastal plain, and s. coast and adjacent interior. Pale sand-plains supporting heaths in association with banksia or mallee woodlands. ■ **SEE ALSO** *C. ora; C. delli.*

Giant Desert Ctenotus *Ctenotus grandis* SVL 105–122mm

Robust, with **narrow dark dorsal stripes, no pale stripes**, and numerous pale lateral spots. Subdigital lamellae narrowly to broadly callose. **Second loreal scale lacks high angular apex.** Rich reddish brown with 5 narrow dark dorsal stripes, and grey flanks with numerous **whitish lateral flecks tending to align vertically**. Limbs dark brown with pale spots. ■ **SSP.** *C. g. grandis* grows to 300mm total length and has 30–32 midbody scales. *C. g. titan* is longer (371mm), with 32–38 midbody scales and subdigital lamellae more widely callose. ■ **NOTES** Spinifex deserts. *C. g. grandis* extends from interior of WA to central NT. *C. g. titan* occurs on nw. coast and hinterland, including Barrow Is., Pilbara and North West Cape. ■ **SEE ALSO** *C. hanloni.* ■ **STATUS** Rare (SA)

Greer's Ctenotus *Ctenotus greeri* SVL 65mm

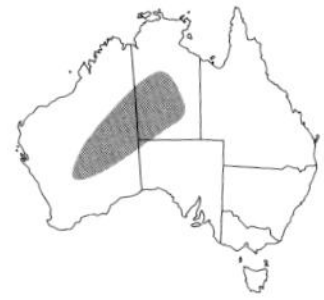

Pattern includes **stripes and pale spots**. Subdigital lamellae narrowly to bluntly callose. Dark brown, paler and redder on forebody, with **broad, pale-edged dark vertebral stripe, a laterodorsal series of white dots or dashes,** white dorsolateral stripe, upper lateral series of white dots, and narrow **white midlateral stripe, well developed posteriorly and wavy or broken into short dashes between forelimb and ear.** Limbs brown with dark stripes. ■ **NOTES** Wstn arid zones on reddish sandy loams supporting mulga, and mallee and spinifex associations. ■ **SEE ALSO** *C. uber.* ■ **STATUS** Rare (SA)

Ctenotus gagudju. Gubara Track, Kakadu NP, NT.
B. Maryan

Ctenotus gemmula.
Melaleuca Park, WA. S. Wilson

Ctenotus grandis titan.
Bullara Stn, WA. S. Wilson

Ctenotus grandis grandis.
Telfer, WA. G. Harold

Ctenotus greeri.
Mt Linden, WA. G. Harold

Chained Ctenotus *Ctenotus halysis* SVL 58mm

Complex pattern of **stripes and upper lateral streaks**. Toes laterally compressed with callose subdigital lamellae. Black to blackish brown with 10-12 pale stripes; creamish white paravertebral, dorsal and dorsolateral stripes enclose dark stripes of equal width, **upper flanks enclose a chain-like series of pale streaks and spots** back to groin, sometimes merging posteriorly to form narrow stripe; prominent pale midlateral stripe extends from ear onto tail; lower flanks marked with 1-2 narrow pale stripes. ■ **NOTES** Low rocky hills with sandy loam and spinifex in central to estn Kimberley region, WA.

Nimble Ctenotus *Ctenotus hanloni* SVL 71mm

Dark dorsal stripes and **many pale lateral spots**. Subdigital lamellae bluntly keeled to narrowly callose. **Second loreal scale usually has a high angular apex**. Rich reddish brown to olive with 5 dark dorsal stripes, including a broad vertebral between cream dorsolateral stripes. **Flanks densely marked with horizontally oriented whitish flecks**. Limbs brown with dark flecks and streaks. ■ **NOTES** Wstn arid zones, from base of North West Cape to wstn NT. Sandy to loamy flats and lower dune slopes vegetated with spinifex. ■ **SEE ALSO** *C. grandis.*

Five-lined Ctenotus *Ctenotus hebetior* SVL 60mm

Five dark dorsal stripes and **spotted flanks**. Subdigital lamellae moderately broadly callose. ■ **SSP.** (ill-defined): *C. h. hebetior* is brown with 5 narrow, indistinct dark dorsal stripes, white dorsolateral stripe, dark reddish brown upper flanks enclosing 2 series of pale spots or dashes, and white midlateral stripe, broken anteriorly. Limbs pale brown, streaked with darker brown. *C. h. schuettleri* has more prominent pattern, including more sharply defined vertebral and midlateral stripes. ■ **NOTES** Central to sw. Qld (*C. h. hebetior*); nw. Qld (*C. h. schuettleri*). Sandy dune slopes and flats with spinifex, and red loams with low woodlands and grasslands. ■ **SEE ALSO** *C. leonhardii.*

Dusky Ctenotus *Ctenotus helenae* SVL 95mm

Little or no pattern. Subdigital lamellae broadly callose. Olive brown to iridescent greenish brown, patternless or with dark vertebral stripe (rarely pale-edged) and faint indications of dark laterodorsal and pale dorsolateral stripes, dark lateral flecks and pale midlateral stripe. ■ **NOTES** Various semi-arid to arid habitats, usually in association with spinifex. Genetic evidence indicates very close relationship with *C. inornatus*, and the existing taxonomy may require change ■ **SEE ALSO** *C. inornatus.*

Ctenotus halysis.
Mornington Wildlife Sanctuary, WA. R. Lloyd.

Ctenotus hanloni.
Bullara Stn, WA. S. Wilson

Ctenotus hebetior hebetior.
Windorah, Qld. S. Wilson

Ctenotus hebetior schuettleri.
Mary Kathleen Dam, Qld. S. Wilson

Ctenotus helenae.
Giralia Stn, WA. S. Wilson

Hill's Ctenotus *Ctenotus hilli* SVL 50mm

Few dorsal stripes and prominent upper lateral spots. Subdigital lamellae narrowly callose to bluntly keeled. Brown with vertebral stripe absent or reduced to narrow line lacking pale edge; broad dark laterodorsal and white dorsolateral stripes; dark purplish brown upper flanks enclosing a prominent series of oblong white spots or dashes; white midlateral stripe broken into dashes anteriorly; and reddish brown lower flanks, uniform or marked with a series of white spots. Limbs pale brown, striped with dark brown. ■ **NOTES** Open forests and woodlands, usually on laterite-based soils.

North West Cape Ctenotus *Ctenotus iapetus* SVL 68mm

Simple pattern of stripes. Subdigital lamellae bluntly keeled to moderately broadly callose. Black with 12 prominent pale stripes: paravertebrals, dorsals, dorsolaterals, upper laterals, midlaterals and ventrolaterals. **All stripes on back extend onto base of head.** Limbs striped with cream and brown. ■ **NOTES** Sand-plains and dunes with dominant ground cover of spinifex on arid nw. coast. ■ **SEE ALSO** *C. maryani.*

South-western Odd-striped Ctenotus *Ctenotus impar* SVL 66mm

Eleven pale stripes, including white vertebral stripe. Subdigital lamellae bluntly keeled. Black with 11 (12 if vertebral splits in two) pale stripes: vertebral, inner and outer dorsals, dorsolaterals, midlaterals and ventrolaterals. Limbs brown streaked with black. ■ **NOTES** Pale sand-plains supporting heaths, often in association with mallee or banksia woodlands on lower w. coast, s. coast and sw. interior of WA.

Ingram's Ctenotus *Ctenotus ingrami* SVL 84mm

Pattern of **simple stripes, including very prominent pale dorsolateral and midlateral stripes.** Subdigital lamellae broadly callose. Olive brown above with a narrow to broad black vertebral stripe edged by narrow pale paravertebrals; black laterodorsals and white dorsolaterals; black upper flanks, very broad white midlateral extends through ear-opening to snout; and white lower laterals. ■ **NOTES** Woodlands, including brigalow and belah, on heavy to stony soils in subhumid areas from Nyngan, in nthn interior of NSW to estn interior of Qld.

Ctenotus hilli.
Darwin, NT. S. Wilson

Ctenotus iapetus.
Bullara Stn, WA. S. Wilson

Ctenotus impar.
Mt Holland, WA. S. Wilson

Ctenotus ingrami.
Glenmorgan, Qld. S. Wilson

Plain Ctenotus *Ctenotus inornatus* SVL 95mm

Pattern normally greatly reduced but pale dorsolateral stripes usually strong. Subdigital lamellae broadly callose and **upper labial scales usually 8. First 3 supraciliary scales much larger than remainder**. Dark brown to olive brown with pattern indistinct on adults but often prominent on juv. Pale-edged black vertebral stripe normally absent or reduced to a line on nape but occasionally prominent to base of tail; **prominent white to cream dorsolateral stripe** with narrow black upper edge; blackish brown upper flanks enclosing pale mottling, flecks or longitudinally aligned blotches; and obscure **pale midlateral stripe passing above hindlimb**, usually most prominent posteriorly. Limbs brown with dark streaks. ■ **NOTES** Subhumid to semi-arid nthn Aust. from Broome, WA to estn Cape York Pen., Qld. Wide variety of habitats, including rock outcrops, river margins and sandy loam flats supporting woodlands, spinifex and spear grass. Genetic evidence indicates very close relationship with *C. brachyonyx, C. fallens, C. helenae, C. saxatilis* and *C. severus*. Existing taxonomy of this complex may require change. ■ **SEE ALSO** *C. coggeri; C. helenae; C. robustus; C. saxatilis; C. superciliaris.*

Blacksoil Ctenotus *Ctenotus joanae* SVL 86mm

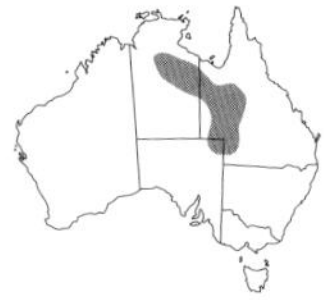

Robust, with simple pattern of stripes, including broad black vertebral stripe and broad areas of olive brown. **Subdigital lamellae bluntly keeled and prefrontal scales separated**. Broad black vertebral and narrow pale paravertebral stripes extend from nape to base of tail; narrow white dorsolateral and broad black laterodorsal stripes from behind eye onto tail. Upper flanks pale to dark olive brown to purplish brown, sometimes with a few anterior pale spots. **Whitish midlateral stripe extends forward to ear or snout**. Lower flanks pale olive brown with faint pale ventrolateral stripe. ■ **NOTES** Cracking clay plains vegetated with Mitchell grasses in semi-arid areas. Shelters in deep soil cracks. ■ **SEE ALSO** *C. rimacola.* ■ **STATUS** Rare (SA).

Alligator Rivers Ctenotus *Ctenotus kurnbudj* SVL 54mm

Slender, with complex pattern of **stripes and spots, including dark upper lateral blotches on tail**. Subdigital lamellae narrowly callose. Brown above with **no black vertebral stripe**; broad black **laterodorsal stripe enclosing cream spots which break into alternating series of black and cream blotches on tail**, and often on body; narrow pale dorsolateral stripe; black upper flanks enclosing several series of longitudinally aligned white flecks; narrow broken white midlateral stripe between forelimb and hindlimb; dark brown to black lower flanks with scattered white spots. Hindlimbs brown with black stripes or elongate blotches. ■ **NOTES** Woodlands, usually on heavy soils, near West Alligator R. and Wildman R.

Ctenotus inornatus.
Boodjamulla NP, Qld.
R. Valentic

Ctenotus joanae.
Brunette Downs Stn,
NT. P. Horner

Ctenotus kurnbudj.
West Alligator River,
NT. B. Maryan

Red-legged Ctenotus *Ctenotus labillardieri* SVL 75m

Continuous pale dorsolateral stripes, reddish brown limbs with bold black marbling, and yellow ventral surfaces. Subdigital lamellae broadly callose. Variable: **plain-backed in n., merging to dark-flecked in s.,** but **almost always with black pigmentation on some dorsal scales.** In n.: rich brown to olive and patternless above with narrow black laterodorsal and prominent sharp-edged white dorsolateral stripes; immaculate black upper flanks (occasionally a few obscure pale spots); sharp white midlateral stripe; black lower flanks; and ragged-edged white lower lateral stripe. In s.: many black dorsal flecks, often concentrating to form an obscure vertebral stripe; broader black laterodorsal and ragged-edged white dorsolateral stripes; and scattered pale lateral spots. ■ **NOTES** High rainfall regions of sw. and s. coast and near-coastal ranges. Heaths, forests and rock outcrops, penetrating WSF and other moist habitats more effectively than other *Ctenotus.* ■ **SEE ALSO** *C. ora; C. catenifer.*

Lancelin Island Ctenotus *Ctenotus lancelini* SVL 80mm

Long-bodied, with broadly callose subdigital lamellae and distinctive pattern; pale brown, merging to grey on tail, with **longitudinally aligned dark dorsal streaks**, ill-defined black laterodorsal stripes enclosing pale spots, unbroken pale dorsolateral stripes, black upper flanks enclosing a row of pale lateral spots, and white midlateral stripe (broken and indistinct anteriorly). **Limbs yellow or orange with dark streaks.** ■ **NOTES** Limestone outcrops on Lancelin Is. (approximately 9 ha in area) off lower w. coast. One record from adjacent mainland at Lancelin. ■ **STATUS** Vulnerable (IUCN Red List; C'wealth; WA).

Gravelly-soil Ctenotus *Ctenotus lateralis* SVL 85mm

Simple pattern of stripes, sharpest on juv. Subdigital lamellae each with broad dark callus. Reddish brown to olive brown with pale-edged black vertebral stripe, narrow black laterodorsal and prominent white to cream dorsolateral stripes, brown flanks enclosing brownish white to grey upper lateral stripe, white midlateral stripe, and usually a narrow pale grey lower lateral stripe. Limbs striped with dark brown and cream. ■ **NOTES** Spinifex/woodland associations on hard, often stony soils.

Centralian Coppertail *Ctenotus leae* SVL 60mm

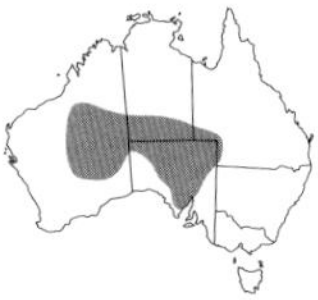

Simple pattern of 8 pale stripes. Subdigital lamellae finely keeled and mucronate. Blackish brown with pale paravertebral, dorsal and dorsolateral stripes, dark upper flanks and broad white midlateral stripes. **All aspects of pattern flushed with red from hips onto tail.** Limbs pinkish brown with obscure darker stripes. ■ **NOTES** Desert sand dunes vegetated with spinifex.

Ctenotus labillardieri.
Mt Dale, WA. S. Wilson

Ctenotus lancelini.
Lancelin Is., WA. B. Maryan

Ctenotus lateralis.
Mary Kathleen Dam, Qld.
S. Wilson

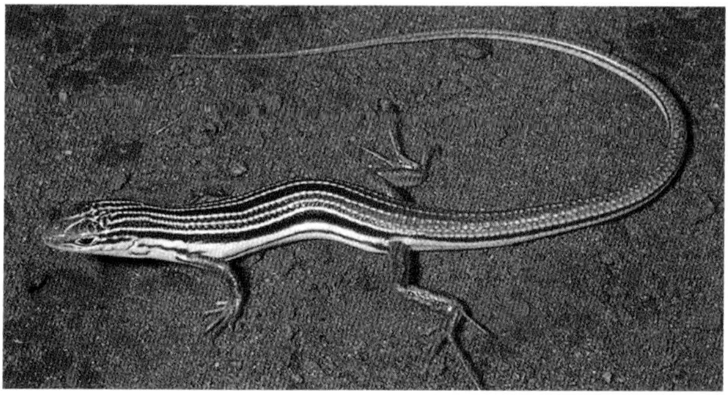

Ctenotus leae.
King's Creek Stn, NT. S. Wilson

Common Desert Ctenotus *Ctenotus leonhardii* SVL 78mm

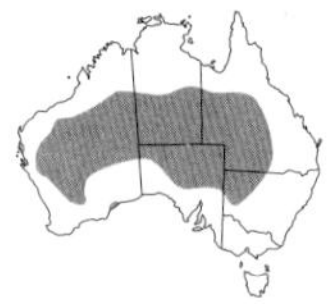

Complex pattern of **stripes and spots**, including **3 dark stripes on back** and **pale midlateral stripe not extending forward beyond forelimb**. Subdigital lamellae narrowly callose. Dark brown to reddish brown with pale-edged dark vertebral stripe; dark laterodorsal and pale dorsolateral stripes; dark brown upper flanks enclosing 1–3 series of whitish dots; well-developed pale midlateral stripe from hindlimb to midbody but breaking into a series of dashes anteriorly; and brown lower flanks marked with obscure pale spots. Limbs brown with dark stripes. ■ **NOTES** Arid stony, sandy to heavy loam soils vegetated mainly with acacia woodlands and shrublands. Forages widely in open spaces between vegtn.
■ **SEE ALSO** *C. hebetior; C. regius.*

Maryan's Ctenotus *Ctenotus maryani* SVL 54mm

Simple pattern of stripes. Subdigital lamellae keeled and weakly mucronate. Dark reddish brown above, paler on flanks, with 12 prominent pale stripes: narrow paravertebral, dorsal, dorsolateral and upper lateral stripes, and broad white midlateral and lower lateral stripes. **Stripes do not extend onto base of head; they terminate at level of nuchal scales**. Limbs striped with cream and brown. ■ **NOTES** Associated with spinifex on dunes, sand-plains and clay soils in arid Carnarvon Basin, from Giralia Stn s. to Carey Downs and inland to Kennedy Ra., WA. ■ **SEE ALSO** *C. iapetus.*

Whiptail Ctenotus *Ctenotus mastigura* SVL 88mm

Long-tailed, with **only 3 supraocular scales** and **simple pattern of stripes**. Subdigital lamellae broadly callose to smooth. Dark iridescent olive brown above with a narrow, pale-edged dark vertebral stripe tending to disappear with age; prominent narrow whitish dorsolateral stripe bordered above and below with black; brownish grey upper flanks; and greyish white midlateral stripe. Limbs and tail reddish brown and virtually patternless. ■ **NOTES** Spinifex on lateritic soils, grassy woodlands and basalt outcrops on Mitchell Plateau in far nw. Kimberley. ■ **SEE ALSO** *C. burbidgei.*

Median-striped Ctenotus *Ctenotus mesotes* SVL 41mm

Complex pattern of broken stripes and spots terminating at rump, finely keeled subdigital lamellae and 6 lower labial scales. Blackish brown to pale grey with pale paravertebral stripes tending to merge, reducing dark vertebral stripe to line on nape, and pale dorsolateral stripes often broken into pale streaks and spots. Flanks with numerous irregular pale spots and streaks, and sometimes a pale midlateral stripe present posteriorly. Pattern usually discontinuous and densely spotted, relieved only by broad pale vertebral zone. ■ **NOTES** Far nthn Kimberley region, WA, from Truscott, Kalumburu and Sir Graham Moore Is. Recorded from woodlands associated with sandstone, sand and laterite. ■ **SEE ALSO** *C. tantillus.*

Ctenotus leonhardii.
Jervois Stn, NT. S. Wilson

Ctenotus maryani.
Nyang Stn area, WA. G. Harold

Ctenotus mastigura.
Mitchell Plateau, WA. P. Griffin

Ctenotus mesotes.
Truscott, WA. P. Doughty

Military Ctenotus *Ctenotus militaris* SVL 65mm

Five dark dorsal stripes and **reddish brown flanks with numerous pale spots.** Subdigital lamellae bluntly keeled. Pale brown above with dark vertebral, dorsal and laterodorsal stripes and pale dorsolateral stripes. Upper flanks reddish brown, darkening posteriorly, enclosing 1–3 series of pale spots. Indication of white midlateral stripe on posterior body, breaking into dots or dashes anteriorly. Lower flanks reddish brown with one or more series of pale spots. Limbs reddish brown with dark stripes. ■ **NOTES** Woodland with grassy understorey, often including spinifex, on sandy soils from semi-arid Kimberley, WA to nw. NT. Also recorded on cracking clay plains.

Checker-sided Ctenotus *Ctenotus mimetes* SVL 82mm

Pattern of **stripes and spots**, including **little or no dark vertebral stripe** and **large, squarish, pale upper lateral spots.** Subdigital lamellae narrowly to moderately broadly callose. Brown above, duller on forebody and brighter and redder on hips and tail, with black laterodorsal and white dorsolateral stripes. Upper flanks black, enclosing 2–3 series of pale spots tending to align vertically, forming narrowly separated rectangular blotches. **White midlateral stripe extends forward to side of head.** Lower flanks similar to upper, but narrower and less regular. Limbs reddish brown, spotted with blackish brown. ■ **NOTES** Semi-arid to arid sw. interior, on sandy to stony red loams supporting woodlands and shrublands. Apparently isolated pop. occurs on nthn edge of Nullarbor Plain. ■ **SEE ALSO** *C. alleni.*

Atherton Ctenotus *Ctenotus monticola* SVL 61mm

Slender, with pattern of **stripes and spots.** Subdigital lamellae narrowly to moderately broadly callose. Pale brown to reddish brown above with narrowly pale-edged, narrow black vertebral stripe from nape onto base of tail; sometimes an indication of a narrow dark dorsal stripe; black laterodorsal; and narrow white dorsolateral stripes. Flanks blackish brown enclosing 1–3 **upper lateral series of brownish white dots tending to align vertically.** Narrow white midlateral stripe from below eye to hindlimb. Lower flanks dark brown, irregularly spotted with brownish white. Limbs brown with darker streaks or stripes. ■ **NOTES** Eucalypt woodlands over a grassy understorey, often in association with granite, in vicinity of Mareeba and Herberton. ■ **STATUS** Vulnerable (Qld).

Long-snouted Ctenotus *Ctenotus nasutus* SVL 46mm

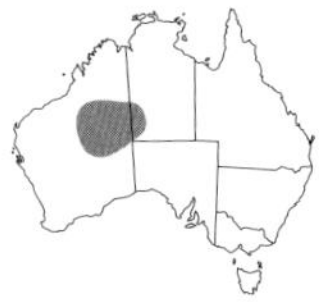

Slender, sharp-snouted. **Simple pattern of 8 pale stripes.** Subdigital lamellae finely keeled and mucronate. Blackish brown above, redder on head, with broad black vertebral stripe (widest of dark dorsal markings) and pale brown paravertebral, dorsal and dorsolateral stripes. Upper flanks black, above a broad white midlateral stripe, edged below with a faint narrow black line. Limbs cream to orange-brown, striped with blackish brown. ■ **NOTES** Sand-ridge deserts vegetated with spinifex from interior of WA to sw. NT.

Ctenotus militaris.
Smoke Creek, WA. G. Harold

Ctenotus mimetes.
Pullagaroo Stn, WA. S. Wilson

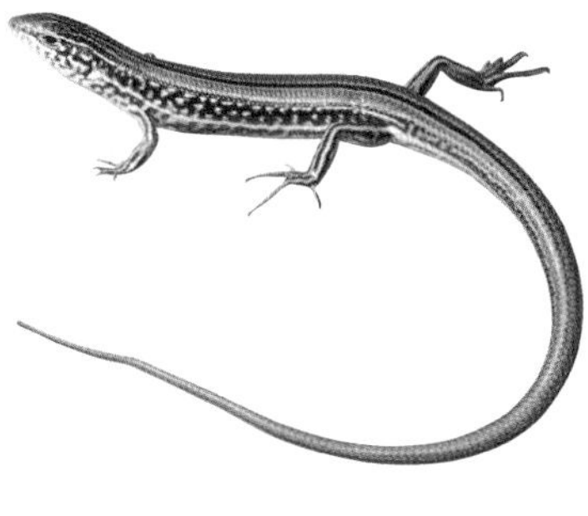

Ctenotus monticola.
Mareeba, Qld. S. Wilson

Ctenotus nasutus.
King's Creek Stn, NT. S. Wilson

Pin-striped Finesnout Ctenotus *Ctenotus nigrilineatus* SVL 49mm

Slender, with **simple pattern of 8 pale stripes**. Subdigital lamellae mostly finely keeled and mucronate. Black with narrow orange-brown paravertebral, dorsal and dorsolateral stripes, and broad white midlateral stripes. Dark interspaces on back are narrow and of equal width. Limbs orange-brown with black stripes. ■ **NOTES** Known from spinifex plains adjacent to granite outcrops and watercourses near Woodstock, Meentheena and Nullagine in hilly interior of Pilbara.

Cooktown Ctenotus *Ctenotus nullum* SVL 79mm

Pattern incl. **weak black vertebral stripe** and **large, squarish, upper lateral blotches**. Subdigital lamellae broadly callose. Olive to reddish brown above, with thin, pale-edged black vertebral stripe on nape or for varying distances along body and tail and black laterodorsal and pale dorsolateral stripes. Upper flanks black enclosing a series of squarish, cream to reddish brown spots normally contacting a pale midlateral stripe. Lower flanks grey with white blotches. Limbs olive to reddish brown with 3 black stripes. ■ **NOTES** Rocky areas, particularly sandstones, near Laura and Cooktown. Also associated with granite at base of Black Mtn, near Cooktown.

Saltbush Ctenotus *Ctenotus olympicus* SVL 69mm

Reduced, ragged pattern of stripes and lateral spots. Subdigital lamellae each with a narrow dark brown callus. Pale to dark brown above with narrow, often obscure, dark vertebral stripe from nape to hips. Pale edge, if present, ill-defined. Black laterodorsal stripes, if present, with irregular inner edges broken by scattered pale-centred scales. Cream dorsolateral stripe, if present, usually breaks between forelimbs and hindlimbs, occasionally reaching hips. Upper flanks black with 3–4 series of small irregular pale spots. Midlateral stripe represented by pale dashes, sometimes coalescing in front of hindlimb. Limbs reddish brown with dark streaks. ■ **NOTES** Heavy, often stony soils supporting shrublands in Lake Eyre and Lake Torrens Basins, SA, extending n. to sthn NT and sw. Qld, and e. into adjacent NSW. ■ **SEE ALSO** *C. orientalis*. ■ **STATUS** Critically endangered (Vic).

Coastal Plains Ctenotus *Ctenotus ora* SVL 60 mm

Back patternless, **with pale dorsolateral stripe unbroken and lacking any white spots above**. Bronze brown above, **immaculate and lacking any black pigment**, with prominent white dorsolateral and midlateral stripes, and weaker, more diffuse pale ventrolateral stripe. Upper flanks brownish black enclosing some fine white flecks. Limbs reddish orange with black patches. ■ **NOTES** Open eucalypt woodland over *Banksia* and low vgtn on sandy coastal plain and coastal dunes s. of Perth, from Pinjarra s. to Yallingup Brook. ■ **SEE ALSO** *C. gemmula*; *C. labillardieri*

Ctenotus nigrilineatus.
Meentheena Cons. Park, WA.
B. Maryan

Ctenotus nullum.
Isabella Falls, Qld. S. Wilson

Ctenotus olympicus.
Dutton Bluff, SA. G. Harold

Ctenotus ora.
Yallingup area, WA. R. Lloyd.

Eastern Spotted Ctenotus *Ctenotus orientalis* SVL 82mm

Pattern of **stripes and spots, including a laterodorsal series of pale spots.** Subdigital lamellae each with a narrow dark callus. Pale greyish brown to pale brown above with **prominent pale-edged black vertebral stripe**, black laterodorsal stripes enclosing a series of pale brown spots or dashes, and prominent pale dorsolateral stripes. Upper flanks black enclosing 2–4 irregular series of pale spots. White midlateral stripe extends forward from hindlimb, breaking well before forelimb. Limbs pale greyish brown to yellowish brown, striped with dark brown. ■ **NOTES** Dry woodlands and shrublands of semi-arid to temperate sthn Aust., from Nullarbor Plain, WA to nthn Vic, sthn NSW and ACT. ■ **SEE ALSO** *C. olympicus; C. uber.*

Pale-backed Ctenotus *Ctenotus pallescens* SVL 45mm

Slender, with **complex pattern of stripes and spots.** Subdigital lamellae finely keeled and mucronate. **Midbody scales usually in 28 rows. Nasal scales separated.** Pale greyish brown above, often with red suffusion. Pattern (fading to virtual absence with age): may have dark vertebral stripe; **dark laterodorsal stripe enclosing a series of transversely elongate pale spots**; and pale dorsolateral stripe. Upper flanks blackish brown enclosing a series of reddish brown to greyish white vertical bars. Prominent white midlateral stripe from snout to hindlimb, above a ventrolateral series of alternating greyish white spots or squarish blotches. Limbs reticulated with dark brown. ■ **NOTES** Sandy, flat areas with low woodlands and tussock grasses in semi-arid to arid central NT and e. Kimberley, WA. ■ **SEE ALSO** *C. schomburgkii; C. tantillus.*

Leopard Ctenotus *Ctenotus pantherinus* SVL 90–114mm

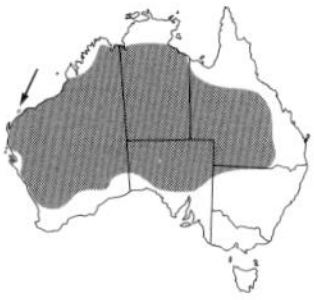

Robust, with **rows of dark-edged pale spots.** Subdigital lamellae finely keeled to mucronate; broadly callose on 1 ssp. Coppery brown to olive with 8–12 rows of black-edged, longitudinally oriented white dashes. ■ **SSP.** *C. p. pantherinus* is smallest, has 30–36 midbody scale rows and sometimes a narrow dark vertebral stripe. *C. p. acripes* (SVL 94mm) has more midbody scale rows (36–40), spinose scales on soles of feet and no dark vertebral stripe. *C. p. ocellifer* (SVL 102mm) has no vertebral stripe. *C. p. calx*, the largest ssp., has flat, callose subdigital lamellae and no vertebral stripe. ■ **NOTES** Arid and semi-arid sandy to stony regions with low ground cover, particularly spinifex. *C. p. pantherinus* occurs in sw. WA; *C. p. acripes* on Barrow Is. off nw. coast of WA, and from estn NT to central Qld; *C. p. ocellifer* occupies spinifex deserts of WA, sthn NT, nthn SA, and far nw. NSW; and *C. p. calx* in e. Kimberley, WA and ne. NT. ■ **STATUS** *C. p. ocellifer* is endangered (NSW).

Ctenotus orientalis.
Big Desert, Vic. S. Wilson

Ctenotus pallescens.
Smoke Creek, WA. G. Harold

Ctenotus pantherinus acripes.
Windorah, Qld. S. Wilson

Ctenotus pantherinus calx.
Halls Creek, WA. S. Wilson

Ctenotus pantherinus ocellifer.
Gibson Desert, WA. S. Wilson

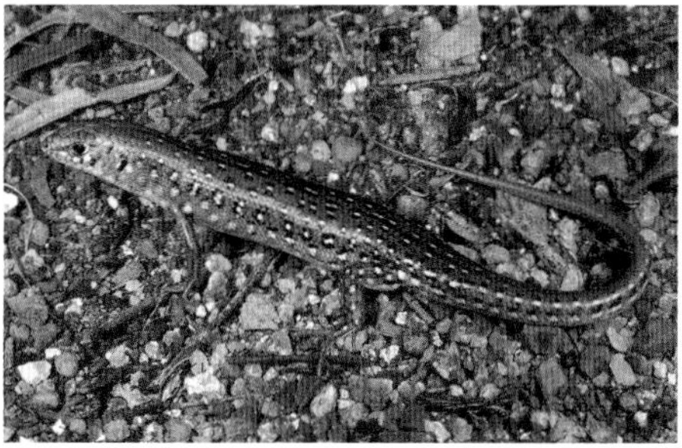

Ctenotus pantherinus pantherinus.
Meckering, WA. B. Maryan

Pianka's Ctenotus *Ctenotus piankai* SVL 60mm

Slender, with **simple pattern of pale stripes**. Subdigital lamellae bluntly keeled to narrowly callose. **Prefrontal scales in contact. Midbody scales in 24–26 rows**. Reddish brown to dark brown with 6 (occasionally 8) cream to pale yellowish brown paravertebral, dorsolateral and midlateral stripes, and occasionally a ventrolateral stripe. Limbs brown with darker stripes. ■ **NOTES** Spinifex deserts, on dunes and sandy flats, occasionally rocky areas, from nw. coast and interior of WA to central and sthn NT and nw. SA. ■ **SEE ALSO** *C. duricola*; *C. vagus*. ■ **STATUS** Rare (SA).

Pretty Ctenotus *Ctenotus pulchellus* SVL 85mm

Robust, with complex pattern of **dark dorsal stripes, dark upper flanks, orange lower flanks,** little or no pale midlateral stripe and numerous pale lateral spots. Subdigital lamellae narrowly to broadly callose. Reddish brown above with 5 dark stripes: broad vertebral, narrow dorsals and broad laterodorsals. White dorsolateral stripe extends from above eye onto tail. Flanks densely dotted with white; upper flanks blackish brown, contrasting with orange-red flush over mid- to lower flanks and sides of head. Limbs reddish brown with dark stripes. ■ **NOTES** Arid nw. Qld and ne. NT. Pop. from Qld occurs on heavy red soils with spinifex; in NT also occurs on cracking clays with Mitchell grass.

Fourteen-lined Ctenotus *Ctenotus quattuordecimlineatus* SVL 70mm

Simple striped pattern. Subdigital lamellae bluntly keeled to narrowly callose. Black, flushed reddish on tail and lower back, with 14 (occasionally 16) pale stripes: paravertebrals, dorsals, dorsolaterals, 2 upper laterals, midlaterals and ventrolaterals (occasionally 2 ventrolaterals). ■ **NOTES** Dunes and sand-plains in spinifex deserts.

Quinkan Ctenotus *Ctenotus quinkan* SVL 80mm

No dorsal pattern. Subdigital lamellae moderately callose. Pale reddish brown with cream dorsolateral stripes, immaculate black upper flanks and pale pinkish red midlateral stripe from ear to hindlimb, bordered below by a black line. Limbs brown, striped with black. ■ **NOTES** Sandstone escarpments in estn Cape York Pen., between Laura and the coast n. of Cooktown.

Arnhem Land Ctenotus *Ctenotus quirinus* SVL 65mm

No vertebral stripe, upper flanks blotched. Subdigital lamellae callose, occasionally smooth. Dark olive brown to pale grey brown above, usually with narrow cream dorsolateral stripes, little or no dark laterodorsal stripes, and broad **dark upper lateral zone enclosing a regular series of large pale spots or squarish blotches**. Prominent pale midlateral stripe extends from upper lip to hindlimb. Lower flanks dark with obscure pale blotches. ■ **NOTES** Nthn and ne. NT, in open forest, open woodlands and shrublands, often on sandy soils. ■ **SEE ALSO** *C. essingtonii*.

Ctenotus piankai.
Rudall River NP, WA. G. Harold

Ctenotus pulchellus.
Mt Isa district, Qld. S. Wilson

Ctenotus quattuordecimlineatus.
Condun Well, WA. S. Wilson

Ctenotus quinkan.
Isabella Falls, Qld. R. Browne-Cooper

Ctenotus quirinus.
Maningrida, NT. P. Horner

Cape Heath Ctenotus *Ctenotus rawlinsoni* SVL 80mm

Simple striped pattern. Subdigital lamellae moderately callose. Black with 6 prominent pale stripes: paravertebrals, dorsolaterals and broad white midlaterals that are wavy or broken from ear to forelimb. Upper lateral zone broad and black. Limbs pale reddish brown to cream, striped with black. ■ **NOTES** Only known from a small area of heath on white coastal sands near Cape Bedford and Cape Flattery, estn Cape York Pen. ■ **STATUS** Vulnerable (Qld).

Royal Ctenotus *Ctenotus regius* SVL 73mm

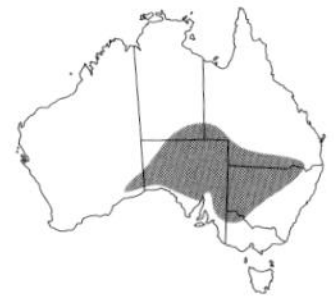

Complex pattern of **stripes and upper lateral spots.** Subdigital lamellae broadly keeled to narrowly callose. Brown above with narrow blackish vertebral stripe, prominent pale paravertebrals, black laterodorsals and pale dorsolateral stripes. Upper flanks dark reddish brown to black, enclosing 1–2 series of scattered pale spots or dashes. **Prominent unbroken white midlateral stripe extends forward well beyond forelimb.** Lower flanks brown, sometimes with scattered pale spots. ■ **NOTES** Semi-arid to arid interior, on heavy to sandy reddish soils supporting open woodlands and shrublands, often in association with spinifex. ■ **SEE ALSO** *C. leonhardii.*

Crack-dwelling Ctenotus *Ctenotus rimacola* SVL 94mm

Pattern of **stripes and diffuse upper lateral blotches,** becoming drab with age. **Subdigital lamellae smooth and prefrontal scales usually in contact.** ■ **SSP.** *C. r. rimacola* is greyish brown above with prominent broad dark vertebral and laterodorsal stripes, narrow diffuse pale paravertebral and prominent narrow white dorsolateral stripes. Upper flanks enclose a series of 9–20 large pale blotches. Pale midlateral stripe most prominent posteriorly and sometimes broken into elongate blotches. Lower flanks grey with obscure pale blotches. Hindlimbs obscurely striped with brown. *C. r. camptris* is olive brown with narrower vertebral stripe, obscure laterodorsal and dorsolateral stripes and mottled hindlimbs. ■ **NOTES** Open plains of deeply cracking clay in Victoria R. district of nw. NT (*C. r. rimacola*), and nthn floodplains of Ord R. and Keep R. near WA/NT border (*C. r. camptris*). ■ **SEE ALSO** *C. joanae.* ■ **STATUS** *C. r. camptris* is vulnerable (NT).

Ctenotus rawlinsoni.
Cape Flattery, Qld.
S. Donnellan

Ctenotus regius.
Currawinya NP, Qld.
S. Wilson

Ctenotus rimacola rimacola.
Kirkimbie, NT. P. Horner

Eastern Striped Ctenotus *Ctenotus robustus* SVL 123mm

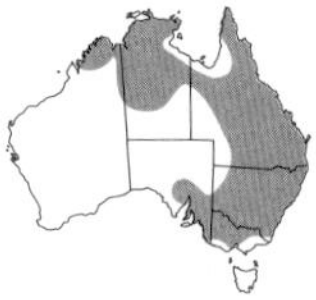

Robust, with complex pattern of **stripes and upper lateral blotches**, smooth to broadly callose subdigital lamellae, and **usually 7 upper labial scales**. Brown to olive brown above with prominent pale-edged black vertebral stripe, black laterodorsal and prominent pale dorsolateral stripes. Upper flanks dark olive brown to dark brown, enclosing 1–2 series of **diffuse pale upper lateral blotches or dashes** (sharper spots on juv.). **Pale midlateral stripe extends forward beyond forelimb** to ear or upper lip; usually **prominent below eye**. Lower flanks variegated with grey and obscurely spotted with white. Limbs brown with darker streaks, stripes or marbling. Some pops from sandy areas of mid-e. coast and adjacent offshore islands lack all pattern. ■ **NOTES** Wide variety of habitats, from tropical and temperate woodlands to heaths and rock outcrops throughout estn and nthn Aust., and extending further se. than any other *Ctenotus*. It seems likely that several species are involved, and there is genetic evidence indicating very close relationship of various pops with *C. borealis* and *C. spaldingi*. The existing taxonomy may require change. ■ **SEE ALSO** *C. arcanus; C. inornatus; C. saxatilis; C. superciliaris.*

Beaded Ctenotus *Ctenotus rosarium* SVL 43mm

Weak dorsal and strong upper lateral pattern and narrowly callose subdigital lamellae. Copper brown above with narrow, finely pale-edged black vertebral stripe from nape to forebody, midbody or base of tail, and narrow, dark laterodorsal and pale dorsolateral stripes extending back to just beyond hips. Upper flanks blackish brown enclosing a row of prominent circular off-white spots on body and continuing as a black stripe along sides of tail. Prominent white midlateral stripe extends forward to between eye and snout. Blackish brown lower lateral stripe encloses diffuse anterior pale blotches. Limbs prominently striped. ■ **NOTES** Spinifex-dominated open woodlands on narrow band of red sandy soils of desert uplands region in ne. interior, from White Mountains NP s. nearly to Aramac.

Ruddy Ctenotus *Ctenotus rubicundus* SVL 101mm

Robust, **without pattern**. Subdigital lamellae narrowly callose. Back, top of head and forelimbs rich reddish brown, paler on flanks. Side of head brown. Hips, hindlimbs and tail greyish brown. Each scale faintly dark-edged, otherwise pattern absent. ■ **NOTES** Rocky hills and escarpments vegetated with spinifex in interior of Pilbara.

Rufous Finesnout Ctenotus *Ctenotus rufescens* SVL 43mm

Slender, sharp-snouted, with **simple pattern of 12 pale stripes**. Subdigital lamellae mostly with a fine weak keel. Blackish brown above with reddish suffusion on foreback and narrow pale paravertebral, inner and outer dorsal and dorsolateral stripes, and broader white midlateral and ventrolateral stripes. **Broad dark upper lateral zone extends forward and splits into 2 on temple.** ■ **NOTES** Arid mid-w. coast near North West Cape, Mardathuna and Boodarrie. Inhabits red sand-dunes and adjacent flats vegetated with spinifex. Rarely forages in open areas, tending to skulk at margins of vegtn.

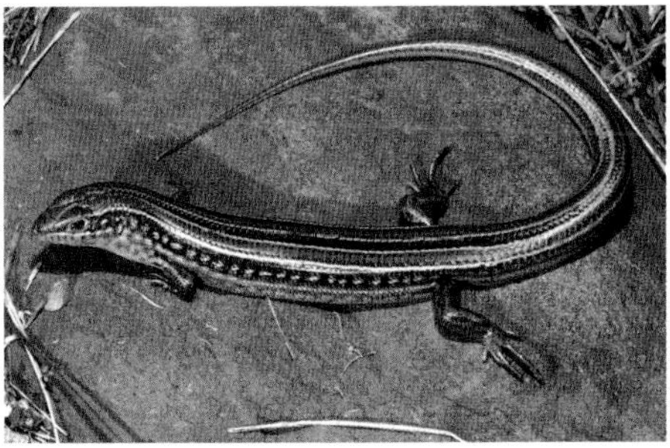

Ctenotus robustus.
Warrill View, Qld. S. Wilson

Ctenotus robustus. Weakly patterned coastal and island form. North Stradbroke Is., Qld. S. Wilson

Ctenotus robustus. Patternless coastal and island form. Moreton Is., Qld. E. Vanderduys

Ctenotus robustus.
El Questro Stn, WA. S. Wilson

Ctenotus rosarium.
Fortuna Stn, Qld. A. Kutt

Ctenotus rubicundus.
Mt Whaleback, WA. B. Maryan

Ctenotus rufescens.
Bullara Stn, WA. S. Wilson

Rusty-shouldered Ctenotus *Ctenotus rutilans* SVL 53mm

Complex pattern, including stripes **and coppery red head and forebody.** Subdigital lamellae bluntly keeled to narrowly callose. Rich reddish brown, sometimes with narrow pale-edged black vertebral stripe. Broad **black laterodorsal stripe enclosing pale spots or short dashes**; narrow pale dorsolateral stripe or series of dashes; blackish brown upper flanks enclosing several series of pale reddish brown dots; prominent pale midlateral stripe restricted to front of hindlimb and base of tail; and clearly delineated reddish brown lower flanks enclosing pale reddish brown dots. ■ **NOTES** Stony soils vegetated with spinifex in arid Hamersley Ra. and Mt Augustus area.

Rock Ctenotus *Ctenotus saxatilis* SVL 100mm

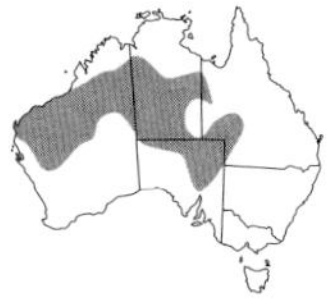

Robust, with complex pattern of **stripes and upper lateral spots**, broadly callose subdigital lamellae, and usually **8 upper labial scales**. Olive brown to reddish brown above with prominent pale-edged dark vertebral stripe, black laterodorsal and white dorsolateral stripes. Upper flanks blackish brown, with a series of large diffuse pale spots. **Pale midlateral stripe extends forward from hindlimb to about forelimb. No pale stripe under eye.** Limbs brown, with darker streaks and stripes. ■ **NOTES** Widespread, mainly in rocky areas, though commonly associated with river floodplains in sthn NT. Possibly comprises several species and there is genetic evidence indicating very close relationship with *C. inornatus*. The existing taxonomy may require change ■ **SEE ALSO** *C. inornatus; C. robustus.*

Spotted Black-soil Ctenotus *Ctenotus schevilli* SVL 85mm

Pattern dominated by pale spots. Subdigital lamellae smooth to bluntly keeled. Olive brown, flanks often flushed with pale reddish brown, with many small pale spots, scattered on back and tending to align vertically on flanks. Blackish dorsal blotches may form an irregular vertebral stripe from midbody onto base of tail. Forelimbs usually patternless, and hindlimbs with obscure darker streaks. ■ **NOTES** Open plains of deeply cracking clay with Mitchell grass from Richmond s. to Muttaburra and Aramac. ■ **STATUS** Near threatened (Qld).

Ctenotus rutilans.
Hamersley Range, WA. R. Lloyd

Ctenotus saxatilis.
Burrup Peninsula, WA. R. Browne-Cooper

Ctenotus saxatilis.
Windorah district, Qld. S. Wilson

Ctenotus schevilli.
Hughendon area, Qld.
E. Vanderduys

Barred Wedge-snouted Ctenotus *Ctenotus schomburgkii* SVL 52mm

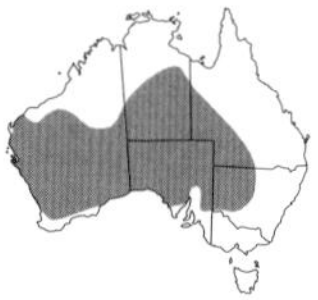

Extremely variable, with **complex pattern of stripes and spots, nasal scales usually separated, midbody scales usually in 26 rows** and **subdigital lamellae finely keeled and mucronate**. Three colour forms occur, all with limbs reddish brown marbled with black. Wstn form: olive to orange-brown with black vertebral stripe, black variegations over back, black (often broken or obscure) laterodorsal and white dorsolateral stripes, black upper flanks with reddish vertical bars and white midlateral stripe. Sw. form: back olive brown and patternless (occasionally a narrow black vertebral stripe often restricted to nape), black laterodorsal and white dorsolateral stripes, black upper flanks enclosing whitish to reddish spots or blotches and white midlateral stripe. Estn form: reddish brown to olive with 5 dark dorsal stripes, cream dorsolateral stripe, black upper flanks enclosing reddish brown blotches, and white midlateral stripe. ■ **NOTES** Dry to arid areas, from sand-plains with heath or spinifex to rocky ridges. Wstn form occurs in wstn interior, sw. form in sw. interior and estn form extends e. from about 120°E, a line roughly drawn through Newman, Wiluna and Kalgoorlie, WA. ■ **SEE ALSO** *C. allotropis; C. pallescens; C. strauchii.*

Gibber Ctenotus *Ctenotus septenarius* SVL 72mm

Long-limbed, with complex pattern including **5–7 dark dorsal stripes and lateral spots**. Subdigital lamellae narrowly callose. Rich reddish brown above, brighter on hips and base of tail, with narrow, pale-edged black vertebral stripe, 2–4 dark dorsal stripes, dark laterodorsal and pale dorsolateral stripes. Dark stripes tend to fade and fragment posteriorly, with sometimes only the vertebral stripe extending back to posterior body or base of tail. Upper flanks black, enclosing numerous prominent white spots. Pale midlateral stripe extends from side of head to hindlimb, often broken anteriorly. Lower flanks dark brown with white spots. Limbs reddish brown with black stripes. ■ **NOTES** Sparsely vegetated stony hills and gullies. Formerly referred to in Qld as *C. aphrodite.*

Gravel-downs Ctenotus *Ctenotus serotinus* SVL 50mm

Robust, with **pattern dominated by pale spots**. Subdigital lamellae smooth to bluntly keeled. Olive brown with sparse pale spots, ragged-edged black vertebral stripe with diffuse pale edges and diffuse pale dorsolateral stripe. Upper flanks dark olive brown, enclosing several series of small white spots, tending to align vertically. Diffuse pale grey midlateral stripe (broken anteriorly) from behind eye onto tail. Limbs obscurely striped with dark and pale brown. Juv. more strongly marked, with vertebral and paravertebral stripes sharp-edged, dorsolateral stripe prominent with dark inner edge and midlateral stripe bolder. ■ **NOTES** Known only on dunes and adjacent stony soils in Diamantina Lakes area. ■ **STATUS** Vulnerable (Qld).

Ctenotus schomburgkii. Plain south-western form. Lake Cronin, WA. S. Wilson

Ctenotus schomburgkii. Eastern form. Currawinya NP, Qld. S. Wilson

Ctenotus schomburgkii. Western form. Charles Darwin Nat. Res. WA. S. Wilson

Ctenotus septenarius. Morney Stn area, Qld. S. Wilson

Ctenotus serotinus. Diamantina Lakes area, Qld. D. Knowles

North-western Sandy-loam Ctenotus *Ctenotus serventyi* SVL 57mm

Complex pattern of stripes, including **5 dark dorsal stripes, well-developed pale midlateral stripe, and upper lateral spots**. Subdigital lamellae bluntly keeled to narrowly callose. Pale brown above with narrow pale-edged black vertebral stripe; narrow dark dorsal stripes (fading to brown with age); and narrow dark laterodorsal and pale dorsolateral stripes. Upper flanks dark brown, enclosing 1–2 series of brownish white dots and/or short dashes. Prominent white midlateral stripe extends forward to upper lips. Limbs pale brown striped with darker brown. ■ **NOTES** Shrublands and woodlands on sandy loams, in arid to semi-arid sthn Kimberley, nw. coast and Pilbara.

Stern Rock Ctenotus *Ctenotus severus* SVL 91mm

Complex pattern of **stripes and upper lateral spots**, including **narrow brown strip between dark upper flanks and pale dorsolateral stripe**. Subdigital lamellae broadly callose. Brown to reddish brown above with dark vertebral stripe absent, reduced to a line on nape, or narrow, lacking pale edge and ending at hips, and broad dark laterodorsal and prominent pale dorsolateral stripes. Upper flanks blackish brown, enclosing diffuse pale spots and edged above with narrow strip of brown dorsal colour. Pale midlateral stripe diffuse and indistinct. Limbs brown with darker streaks. ■ **NOTES** Granite outcrops and heavy to stony soils dominated by acacia woodlands and shrublands in arid mid-w. and interior of WA. Genetic evidence indicates very close relationship with *C. inornatus*, and the existing taxonomy may require change

Spalding's Ctenotus *Ctenotus spaldingi* SVL 100mm

Variable, with complex pattern of **stripes and upper lateral spots**, and **only 3 supraocular scales**. Shades of brown, olive or reddish brown above, with dark vetebral stripe absent to prominent and pale-edged and narrow black laterodorsal and white dorsolateral stripes from above eye onto tail. Upper flanks dark brown to black, enclosing a series of pale squarish blotches. White midlateral stripe from forebody or below eye to base of tail. Limbs pale brown, with indistinct dark stripes or streaks. ■ **NOTES** Woodlands, rock outcrops and grassy coastal dunes from nthn NT to nthn interior of Qld, Cape York Pen. and Torres Strait islands. Extends n. to sthn NG. Genetic evidence indicates very close relationship with nthn pop. of *C. robustus*.

Storr's Ctenotus *Ctenotus storri* SVL 40mm

Slender, with **simple pattern of 8 pale stripes, including paravertebrals fused for part of their length**. Subdigital lamellae narrowly callose. Brown with paravertebral, dorsal, dorsolateral and midlateral stripes; the paravertebral stripes commence as one on nape and rejoin at about level of hindlimb, or remain fused to form a broad pale vertebral line. Limbs yellowish brown, striped with black. ■ **NOTES** Woodland/grassland associations on sandy flats of coastal nw. NT. ■ **SEE ALSO** *C. decaneurus.*

Ctenotus serventyi.
Burrup Peninsula, WA.
R. Browne-Cooper

Ctenotus severus.
Paynes Find, WA. S. Wilson

Ctenotus spaldingi.
Moa Is., Qld. S. Wilson

Ctenotus storri.
Mandorah, NT. S. Wilson

Eastern Barred Wedge-snouted Ctenotus *Ctenotus strauchii* SVL 55mm

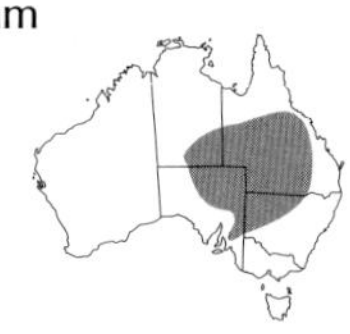

Variable, with **complex pattern of stripes and spots, nasal scales usually in contact**, and **finely keeled and mucronate subdigital lamellae**. ■ **SSP.** *C. s. strauchii* is brown, sometimes with pale-edged black vertebral stripe from nape to base of tail. **Black laterodorsal stripe encloses pale spots or short dashes**, edged by white dorsolateral stripe. Upper flanks black with 1–3 series of pale, usually vertically aligned, dots. White midlateral stripe extends forward to upper lip. Lower flanks greyish brown to black, sometimes enclosing small irregular white spots. Limbs pale brown, streaked or mottled with black. *C. s. varius* is paler with more diffuse pattern; olive grey to pale reddish brown with vertebral stripe narrow and faint, pale dorsolateral stripe present but dark laterodorsal stripe ragged and discontinuous or broken into variegations, dots and flecks; and upper flanks black with numerous scattered pale spots or broken into vertical bars or rectangular blotches. ■ **NOTES** Hard stony soils with sparse low ground cover of woodlands and shrublands in dry to semi-arid regions of estn interior. *C. s. strauchii* extends from ne. Qld through nw. NSW to se. SA. *C. s. varius* extends through sw. Qld and nw. NSW to sthn NT and nthn SA. ■ **SEE ALSO** *C. allotropis; C. schomburgkii.*

Stripe-headed Ctenotus *Ctenotus striaticeps* SVL 50mm

Simple pattern of **stripes including paravertebrals converging on top of snout**. Subdigital lamellae finely keeled and mucronate. Black with 6–8 prominent pale stripes, suffused anteriorly with orange: paravertebrals, dorsolaterals, midlaterals and (if present) ventrolaterals. Limbs black, boldly striped with pale orange. ■ **NOTES** Semi-arid to arid nw. Qld and adjacent NT, on hard stony soils vegetated with spinifex.

Stuart's Ctenotus *Ctenotus stuarti* SVL 54mm

Complex pattern of **stripes and upper lateral spots**. Olive brown above with broad, pale-edged, black vertebral stripe. **Dark laterodorsal and pale dorsolateral stripes present but normally broken into series of flecks and streaks**. Upper flanks brown with 2 irregular series of pale blotches. Pale midlateral stripe from forelimb to hindlimb, often indistinct and broken anteriorly. Lower flanks mottled greyish white with diffuse pale spots and blotches. Limbs brown, streaked with black. ■ **NOTES** Known only from Swim Creek and Kapalga, in open woodlands on sandy substrates, including areas subject to seasonal flooding.

Ctenotus strauchii strauchii.
Currawinya NP, Qld. S. Wilson

Ctenotus strauchii varius.
Plenty Hwy on Qld/NT border. S. Wilson

Ctenotus striaticeps.
Mt Isa district, Qld. S. Wilson

Ctenotus stuarti.
Opium Creek Stn, NT. P. Horner

Sharp-browed Ctenotus *Ctenotus superciliaris* SVL 81mm

Vertebral stripe prominent to absent, pale dorsolateral stripe usually present and lateral pattern broken into variegations. **Little or no pale subocular stripe**. Subdigital lamellae broadly callose. **Only 1st and 2nd supraciliary scales enlarged**; remainder very small and largely to completely obscured by angular brow. Extremely variable but typically shades of brown with pale-edged dark vertebral stripe present in s. and on juv., but often weak to absent on nthn adults. Pale dorsolateral stripe usually prominent, and lateral variegations and blotches bordered below by ill-defined pale lower lateral stripe extending forward from groin to midbody. ■ **NOTES** Dry tropical zones through Pilbara and Kimberly regions, WA, to nthn NT, s. to nthn margin of arid zone. ■ **SEE ALSO** *C. inornatus; C. robustus.*

Eyrean Ctenotus *Ctenotus taeniatus* SVL 56mm

Extremely variable but usually including a vaguely pale-edged dark vertebral stripe. **Subdigital lamellae usually 23 or fewer under 4th toe, finely keeled and mucronate, extending onto sole of foot.** Pink, orange to brown according to substrate. Pattern ranges from little more than a narrow dark vertebral line with a series of weak, dark upper lateral botches, to a chequered pattern of dark-centred dorsal scales and black lateral flecks, or to 5 sharp, straight, black dorsal stripes, pale dorsolateral stripes, black upper flanks extending up to 3rd scale row from vertebral line and enclosing whitish spots, and white midlateral stripe. ■ **NOTES** Sand-ridges from Simpson Desert to central SA. Isolated, boldly patterned pop. on pale sands of wstn Vic and adjacent SA. ■ **SEE ALSO** *C. brooksi.* ■ **STATUS** Vulnerable (NSW – as *C. brooksi*).

Copper-tailed Skink *Ctenotus taeniolatus* SVL 80mm

Simple pattern of stripes. Subdigital lamellae bluntly keeled. Rich brown above (the dorsal colour often contracted to form a narrow stripe) with sharply pale-edged, prominent black vertebral stripe, black laterodorsal and white to yellowish dorsolateral stripes. Upper flanks black, unpatterned except for a white spot or short pale streak on side of head. White midlateral stripe extends from above upper lip, curving sharply over ear to tail, above black lower lateral and ventrolateral stripes. Limbs reddish, striped or streaked with black. Tail often rich copper in s. and pale olive or brown in n. ■ **NOTES** Coast and ranges of estn Aust, in various woodlands and heaths. Particularly favours rock outcrops such as sandstone or granite. Common in bushland peripheral to Sydney and Brisbane. ■ **SEE ALSO** *C. eurydice.*

Tanami Ctenotus *Ctenotus tanamiensis* SVL 91mm

Robust, with **pattern dominated by longitudinal series of white dots and dashes**. Subdigital lamellae bluntly keeled to narrowly callose. Reddish brown with broad, pale-edged, dark vertebral stripe and dorsal and dorsolateral series of pale dashes. Flanks reddish brown with numerous small, vertically aligned dots, and sometimes a pale midlateral row of flecks. Limbs pale reddish brown with darker stripes. ■ **NOTES** Recorded from reddish sand-plains with spinifex in Tanami Desert.

Ctenotus superciliaris.
Prince Regent area, WA. S. Zozaya

Ctenotus superciliaris.
Broome Bird Observatory, WA. S. Wilson

Ctenotus taeniatus. Weakly patterned.
Durrie Stn, Qld. S. Wilson

Ctenotus taeniatus. Strongly patterned.
Big Desert, Vic. S. Wilson

Ctenotus taeniolatus.
Girraween NP, Qld. S. Wilson

Ctenotus tanamiensis.
Tanami Desert, NT. M. Gillam

Kimberley Wedge-snouted Ctenotus *Ctenotus tantillus* SVL 45mm

Complex pattern of **stripes and upper lateral spots**. Subdigital lamellae finely keeled. **7 lower labial scales and nasal scales in contact**. Olive brown above, with or without 3–5 narrow dark stripes; a finely pale-edged dark vertebral stripe, narrow dark dorsal (often absent) and laterodorsal stripes, and pale dorsolateral stripe (sometimes broken into a series of dashes). Upper flanks black, enclosing an irregular series of small white spots. Whitish midlateral stripe well developed, broken or absent. Lower flanks brown with obscure white spots or blotches. Limbs pale brown, striped with dark brown. ■ **NOTES** Sandy flats adjacent to sandstone outcrops, from Kimberley, WA to adj. NT. ■ **SEE ALSO** *C. pallescens; C. mesotes.*

Hinchinbrook Ctenotus *Ctenotus terrareginae* SVL 90mm

Long-tailed, with pattern of **simple stripes, including plain back**. Subdigital lamellae broadly callose. Dark brown above with weak vertebral stripe restricted to nape and foreback; black laterodorsal and white dorsolateral stripes extending from front of eye onto tail; black upper flanks, white midlateral stripe from snout onto hindlimbs and tail; and black lower flanks with white blotching on neck and anterior body, coalescing to form a dark lower lateral stripe from midbody onto tail. Limbs reddish brown with black and white stripes. ■ **NOTES** Rocky areas between Paluma and Hinchinbrook Is.

Western Spotted Ctenotus *Ctenotus uber* SVL 70mm

Long-tailed, with pattern of **stripes and spots, including a laterodorsal series of pale spots**. Subdigital lamellae bluntly keeled to narrowly callose. ■ **SSP.** *C. u. uber* has nasal scales rarely in contact. Reddish brown to orange-brown with **dark vertebral stripe narrow to absent.** Broad dark laterodorsal stripe encloses a series of pale spots. Narrow pale dorsolateral stripe sometimes broken into a series of spots or short dashes. Upper flanks dark brown, enclosing 2–4 series of small dots, sharply delineated from reddish brown lower flanks. **Pale midlateral stripe barely discernible to absent**. Limbs brown with dark stripes or streaks. *C. u. johnstonei* has a well-developed vertebral stripe and nasal scales in contact. ■ **NOTES** *C. u. uber* occurs mainly on hard reddish soils of semi-arid to arid central, sthn and wstn interior. *C. u. johnstonei* is known from an area of chenopod shrubland at the base of a sandstone hill near Balgo, ne. interior of WA, and possibly extends further w. ■ **SEE ALSO** *C. greeri; C. orientalis.*

Uneven-striped Ctenotus *Ctenotus vagus* SVL 44mm

Simple striped pattern. Subdigital lamellae moderately callose. **Prefrontal scales separated.** Dark brown with 10-12 narrow pale stripes; prominent paravertebrals and dorsolaterals from base of head onto tail; **darker brownish cream dorsals and (if present) laterodorsals narrow and indistinct** to hips, sometimes broken, ragged-edged and merging with ground colour; whitish midlateral stripe onto tail; and indistinct lower lateral stripe to groin. ■ **NOTES** Drysdale River and Purnululu NP in nthn and se. Kimberley region, WA. Recorded on red sand with spinifex. No known live image. ■ **SEE ALSO** *C. decaneurus; C. piankai.*

Ctenotus tantillus.
Kununurra, WA.
S. Wilson

Ctenotus terrareginae.
Hinchinbrook Is., Qld.
S. Wilson

Ctenotus uber johnstonei (?).
235 km SSW Port Hedland, WA. R. Browne-Cooper

Ctenotus uber uber.
Waldburg Stn, WA. S. Wilson

Ctenotus vagus. Preserved holotype.
Purnululu NP, WA. R. Ellis

Scant-striped Ctenotus *Ctenotus vertebralis* SVL 55mm

Very slender, with **simple reduced pattern of stripes**, ranging from prominent to virtually absent. Subdigital lamellae broadly callose. Pale coppery brown to olive brown above with black vertebral stripe ranging from broad and pale-edged to a narrow dark line or completely absent, and a narrow pale dorsolateral stripe, continuous or broken, with or without a black anterior inner margin. Upper flanks black and patternless, above a pale midlateral stripe and grey lower flanks. Limbs greyish brown and normally patternless. ■ **NOTES** Woodlands over grasses and leaf litter on sandy soils adjacent to rock outcrops in subhumid ne. NT. Tends to skulk close to low vegetation rather than forage in open areas.

Wide-striped Sandplain Ctenotus *Ctenotus xenopleura* SVL 49mm

Pattern consists of **pale stripes and upper lateral spots**. Subdigital lamellae with weak blunt keels. Black with 10 pale stripes: narrow paravertebral, dorsal and dorsolateral stripes, black upper flanks enclosing 1–2 series of elongate white spots, and broad white midlateral and lower lateral stripes. Limbs yellowish brown, striped with black. ■ **NOTES** Isolated patches of spinifex and heath on yellow sandy soils near Boorabbin, Bungalbin, McDermid Rock and Toomey Hills, in semi-arid sthn interior of WA.

Shark Bay Sand Ctenotus *Ctenotus youngsoni* SVL 84mm

Robust, thick-tailed, with complex pattern of **stripes and pale dorsal blotches**. Subdigital lamellae broadly callose. Olive grey to pale greyish brown, extending as a broad vertebral zone to base of tail and edged by very **broad black laterodorsal stripes, each enclosing or partially enclosing a series of large blotches of ground colour**. Whitish dorsolateral stripe from above ear to base of tail. Flanks olive, flecked with black. Pale midlateral stripe indistinct to absent. Limbs olive, speckled with black. Tip of snout yellow. ■ **NOTES** Restricted to wstn pen. of Shark Bay, s. to Tamala and including Dirk Hartog Is. Pale coastal dunes vegetated with heath.

Hamelin Pool Ctenotus *Ctenotus zastictus* SVL 60mm

Slender, long-tailed, with complex pattern of **8 pale stripes and pale latero-dorsal and upper lateral spots**. Subdigital lamellae narrowly to moderately broadly callose. Blackish with narrow white paravertebral stripes, latero-dorsal series of white to yellowish dashes, narrow white dorsolateral stripes, prominent upper lateral series of white dots and dashes, narrow white midlateral stripe and white ventrolateral stripe. Limbs blackish brown, striped with white. ■ **NOTES** Restricted to an isolated stand of spinifex on red sands at Hamelin and Coburn Stns, immediately s. of Shark Bay. ■ **STATUS** Vulnerable (IUCN Red List; C'wealth; WA).

Ctenotus vertebralis.
Kakadu NP, NT. B. Maryan

Ctenotus xenopleura.
Bungalbin Hill area, WA. B. Maryan

Ctenotus youngsoni.
Tamala Stn area, WA. S. Wilson

Ctenotus zastictus.
Hamelin Pool Stn area, WA. B. Maryan

Little Zebra Ctenotus *Ctenotus zebrilla* SVL 40mm

Simple pattern of 8 pale stripes. Subdigital lamellae finely dark-keeled and mucronate. Black to blackish brown with narrow pale brown paravertebral and dorsal stripes (aspects of dorsal pattern sometimes reduced to absent), broader white dorsolateral and midlateral stripes and wavy dark lower lateral stripes. Limbs striped pale brown and black. ■ **NOTES** Rocky hills with dry woodlands and low grasses in subhumid sthn interior of Cape York Pen.

Slender Blue-tongued, She-oak and Pink-tongued Skinks
Genus *Cyclodomorphus*

Nine moderate to large, smooth-scaled spp. with long bodies and relatively short limbs, each with 5 digits, the 4th toe not markedly longer than 3rd toe. Lower eyelid moveable, lacking a transparent disc. **Parietal scales widely separated (A). No row of subocular scales; granular scales below eye contact upper labial scales (B).** Ear-opening present, usually with small anterior lobules. ■ **NOTES** Related to the blue-tongued skinks (*Tiliqua*). Mainly crepuscular to nocturnal inhabitants of dense low vegtn, but often seen basking in sheltered sites. She-oak and pink-tongued skinks occur in moist estn areas; slender blue-tongues prefer dry interior and w. When threatened, many gape their mouths and flicker their fleshy tongues; some even rear in apparent mimicry of snakes. Omnivorous, feeding on invertebrates (particularly snails), flowers and fruits. Livebearers. ■ **SEE ALSO** *Tiliqua.*

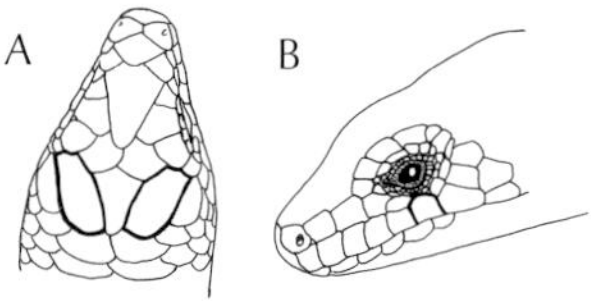

Gilled Slender Blue-tongue *Cyclodomorphus branchialis* SVL 88mm

Black patches on sides of neck and anterior flanks. Yellowish brown to greyish brown with short, broad dark spots on many scales tending to align transversely, particularly on tail, and 3 prominent, vertically elongate black bars on sides of neck and anterior flanks. ■ **NOTES** Semi-arid shrublands on heavy red soils from Irwin R. n. to Murchison R. and inland to Mt Magnet. ■ **SEE ALSO** *C. celatus.* ■ **STATUS** Vulnerable (WA).

Tasmanian She-oak Skink *Cyclodomorphus casuarinae* SVL 174mm

Moderately long tail (**68–84 subcaudal scales** when original) and variable colouration. Shades of grey to reddish brown or black, occasionally patternless but normally with dark sides to each scale forming broken stripes, often mixed with pale streaks and dark markings forming irregular narrow bands, and dark bar under eye. Juv. have a broad dark band on nape. ■ **NOTES** Restricted to various open habitats in Tas, from heath and tussock grassland to edges and clearings in closed forests.

Ctenotus zebrilla.
Porcupine Gorge, Qld. S. Wilson

Ctenotus zebrilla.
Abingdon Downs Stn, Qld.
E. Vanderduys

Cyclodomorphus branchialis.
Ajana, WA. D. Knowles

Cyclodomorphus casuarinae.
Melaleuca, Tas. S. Wilson

Western Slender Blue-tongue *Cyclodomorphus celatus* SVL 121mm

Midbody scales usually 20–22. Grey to white with dark streaks on most dorsal scales, **each streak extending full length of scale**, becoming weaker on nape and sometimes forming 3 or more vertical bars on side of neck (**never solid black bars**). Juv. darker, with dark head and pale spots. ■ **NOTES** Mid- and lower w. coast, from Gnaraloo s. to Swan R., on various sandy and limestone-based soils supporting shrublands, heaths and hummock grasses. Common in coastal dunes behind Perth's suburban beaches. ■ **SEE ALSO** *C. branchialis; C. melanops.*

Pink-tongued Skink *Cyclodomorphus gerrardii* SVL 200mm

Large head distinct from neck, long prehensile tail and pink tongue on most adults but blue on juv. Pale brown, pinkish brown to grey; pattern prominent to virtually absent, comprising broad dark bands on body and tail. Bands may become progressively reduced to margins, forming pairs of narrow bands, or be lost entirely. Patternless individuals usually retain dark tip on snout. Juv. prominently marked with sharp-edged dark and pale bands. ■ **NOTES** Humid e. coast and ranges between Springwood, NSW and Cairns, Qld, in various habitats, favouring moist conditions. Partially arboreal. Diurnal and nocturnal. Most active after rain on warm nights, foraging for slugs and snails which constitute bulk of diet.

Giant Slender Blue-tongue *Cyclodomorphus maximus* SVL 232mm

Simple pale spots. Yellowish brown to reddish brown with pale yellow to cream hind-edges to scales forming transverse bands of spots on posterior two-thirds of body and tail, fading on flanks. Juv. more prominently marked, including 2 broad dark bands across nape, separated by pale yellowish brown interspaces. ■ **NOTES** Escarpments or boulder-strewn habitats with various vegtn, from spinifex to dense vine thickets, in nw. Kimberley.

Spinifex Slender Blue-tongue *Cyclodomorphus melanops* SVL 132mm

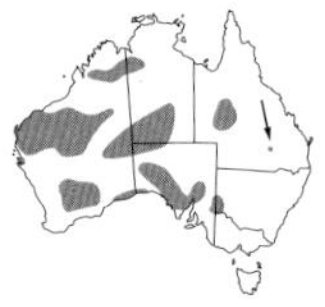

Midbody scales usually 24–29. Shades of brown to olive; may have weak pattern, comprising **dark central spot or fleck on most scales**. Juv. usually prominently marked with fine cream spots. **Subcaudal scales 58 or more** on original tail. ■ **SSP.** *C. m. melanops* normally has dark spots extending onto ventral surfaces, most prominent posteriorly. Paravertebral scales 62–80. *C. m. elongatus* is mostly patternless (rarely a few dark ventral flecks) with 61–85 paravertebral scales. *C. m. siticulosus* is mostly patternless (rarely a few dark ventral flecks) with 56–63 paravertebral scales. ■ **NOTES** Widespread through arid and semi-arid regions. *C. m. melanops* occurs in spinifex habitats of sthn Kimberley, nw. and central Aust. *C. m. elongatus* occurs among spinifex, from sthn interior of WA, through SA, wstn NSW and sthn NT to central Qld, with isolated pop. in open woodland/grassland near Amby, in se. interior of Qld. *C. m. siticulosus* occurs among chenopod shrubs and limestone rocks of Nullarbor Plain, SA. ■ **SEE ALSO** *C. celatus; C. venustus.* ■ **STATUS** *C. m. elongatus* is endangered (NSW).

Cyclodomorphus celatus.
City Beach, WA. S. Wilson

Cyclodomorphus gerrardii.
Eungella, Qld. S. Wilson

Cyclodomorphus gerrardii.
Mt Glorious, Qld. S. Wilson

Cyclodomorphus maximus.
Mitchell Plateau, WA. S. Wilson

Cyclodomorphus melanops elongatus.
Lark Quarry district, Qld. S. Wilson

Cyclodomorphus melanops melanops.
Kununurra, WA. S. Wilson

Cyclodomorphus melanops siticulosus.
Mother and young.
Eyre Hwy, near WA/SA border, SA. B. Maryan

Mainland She-oak Skink *Cyclodomorphus michaeli* SVL 174mm

Very long tail (**91 or more subcaudal scales** when original). Olive green to reddish brown with pattern absent or weak; dark edges to scales form broken wavy stripes and occasionally irregular narrow bands, and dark bar under eye. ■ **NOTES** Isolated pockets between estn Gippsland, Vic and New England, NSW. Edges and clearings in WSF to sandy coastal heaths and dense tussocks margining wetlands. ■ **STATUS** Near threatened (Vic).

Alpine She-oak Skink *Cyclodomorphus praealtus* SVL 119mm

Short tail (**57 or fewer subcaudal scales** when original). Olive green, grey to yellowish brown or reddish brown with dark edges to each scale forming wavy broken stripes, and paler scales arranged in irregular broken transverse rows. Belly sometimes flushed with bright red. ■ **NOTES** Aust. Alps above 1500m, from Wellington Plains Vic to Kiandra, NSW. Alpine herbfields, areas of thick tussock grasses and subalpine woodlands. ■ **STATUS** Endangered (C'wealth; NSW); critically endangered (Vic).

Saltbush Slender Blue-tongue *Cyclodomorphus venustus* SVL 101mm

Short tail (**44–54 subcaudal scales** when original), occurring in two distinct pops. Sthn pops: grey to pinkish brown. Some paler scales have heavy dark central streaks, tending to form irregular transverse series. Dark streaks coalesce on sides of neck to form 3–4 vertical bars. Nthn pops: weakly marked, retaining only dark neck bars. ■ **NOTES** Coastal samphire flats near Port Pirie and Port Germein, SA (sthn pop.), and cracking clay and stony plains from ne. SA through nw. NSW to Cunnamulla, Qld (nthn pop.). ■ **SEE ALSO** *C. melanops.* ■ **STATUS** Endangered (NSW).

Genus *Egernia*

Seventeen moderate to very large robust spp. with 4 well-developed limbs, each with 5 digits; **4th toe much longer than 3rd.** Lower eyelid moveable and lacks transparent disc, eyes relatively small, **no distinctive pale margin around eyelids**, ear-opening with anterior lobules, **parietal scales separated** (fig.) and body scales smooth, striated, multi-keeled to spinose. ■ **NOTES** Widespread. Various forms and lifestyles, from very spiny spp. to smooth-scaled spp. most of which wedge themselves firmly into crevices in rock or wood. Omnivorous livebearers, often living communally in family groups. Diurnal. ■ **SEE ALSO** *Bellatorias; Tiliqua.*

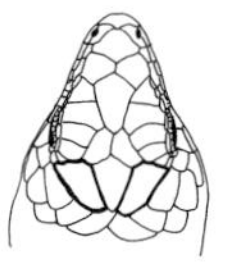

Cunningham's Skink *Egernia cunninghami* SVL 200mm

Spiny, with **tail long and round in cross-section**, and 1 large spine on each dorsal scale, longest and most pronounced on tail. Extremely variable, ranging from very dark brown to almost black with no pattern, or speckles, blotches or narrow bands. ■ **NOTES** Widespread in se. Aust. Isolated pops (mostly distinctly marked) from Fleurieu Pen., SA to Carnarvon Ra., central Qld. Dwells communally in crevices in rock outcrops and basks on exposed rock close to cover. In some areas, also inhabits hollow logs. ■ **STATUS** Endangered (SA).

Cyclodomorphus michaeli.
Chifley, NSW. S. Wilson

Cyclodomorphus praealtus.
Falls Creek, Vic. S. Wilson

Cyclodomorphus venustus. Northern form.
Mt Margaret Stn, Qld. S. Wilson

Cyclodomorphus venustus. Southern form.
Pt Germein, SA. R. Browne-Cooper

Egernia cunninghami.
Main Range NP, Qld. S. Wilson

Egernia cunninghami.
Girraween NP, Qld. S. Wilson

Egernia cunninghami.
Yalwal Plateau, NSW. S. Wilson

Western Pilbara Spiny-tailed Skink *Egernia cygnitos* SVL 117 mm

Spiny with moderately narrow tail bearing relatively short thick spines. On body, each dorsal scale has **short, stout, upward-projecting central spine, just extending beyond scale** and flanked on each side by smaller spine about two thirds the length. **Nasal scale completely divided by groove**. Rich reddish brown with short **dark bars or transverse blotches from about level of arms onto tail**. ■ **NOTES** Pilbara region, WA, excluding most of Chichester subregion but incl. Chichester Ra. Rocky outcrops, sheltering in crevices. ■ **SEE ALSO** *E. depressa*; *E. epsisolus.*

Southern Pygmy Spiny-tailed Skink *Egernia depressa* SVL 107mm

Spiny with short, wide, flat tail bearing long recurved spines. On body, each dorsal scale has **long, thin, flat central spine, projecting well back beyond scale** and flanked on each side by smaller spine about half the length. **Nasal scale completely divided by groove.** Reddish brown on forebody, merging to grey at about midbody, with irregular bands of pale blotches from nape to midbody and dark blotches on posterior body and tail. ■ **NOTES** Woodlands, particularly mulga in arid mid-w. and sthn.interior of WA, s. to Kalgoorlie and Wongan Hills areas, nw. to below North West Cape and ne. to Newman area. Shelters in hollows of standing and fallen trees. ■ **SEE ALSO** *E. cygnitos; E. epsisolus.*

Kimberley Crevice-skink *Egernia douglasi* SVL 215mm

Robust, relatively flat, with striated dorsal scales. Olive brown to reddish brown with 2 broad ragged-edged dark dorsal stripes from snout to anterior body and broad ragged-edged dark upper lateral stripe from in front of eye to behind forelimb. Lips whitish, often with dark brown bars on chin and throat. Ventral surfaces yellow. ■ **NOTES** Nw. Kimberley, WA, in vicinity of Yampi Sound, incl. Leopold Ra. and Artesian Ra. Also Mt Barnett Stn in central Kimberley and apparently isolated pop. near Lissadel Stn in e. Kimberley. Rock-inhabiting.

Central Pygmy Spiny-tailed Skink *Egernia eos* SVL 110 mm

Spiny with short, wide, slightly rounded tail bearing long, weakly recurved lateral spines. On body, each dorsal scale has **short, stout, upward-projecting central spine, just extending beyond scale** and flanked on each side by smaller spine more than two thirds the length. **Nasal scale completely divided by groove**. Yellowish brown with short dark transverse bars on posterior body and tail, and prominent **orange-brown streak from ear to above arm**. ■ **NOTES** Estn interior of WA and adjacent NT in vicinity of Warburton and Peterman Ra., and isolated record at Well 46 on Canning Stock Route, WA. Recorded in granite crevices and mulga wood.

Egernia cygnitos.
Yalleen Stn, WA. H. Cook

Egernia depressa.
Paynes Find, WA. S. Wilson

Egernia douglasi. Artesian Range, WA. Australian Wildlife Conservancy/A. Morton

Egernia eos.
Warburton area, WA. T. Rasmussen.

Eastern Pilbara Spiny-tailed Skink *Egernia epsisolus* SVL 110 mm

Spiny with moderately wide tail bearing relatively short, thick spines. On body, each dorsal scale has **short, stout, upward-projecting central spine, just extending beyond scale** and flanked on each side by smaller spine about half to two thirds the length. **Nasal scale undivided dorsally but grooved below nostril**. Pale yellowish brown to pale reddish brown with short, **white-edged dark bars on posterior body and tail.** ■ NOTES Chichester subregion, excl. Chichester Ra. in eastern Pilbara region, with isolated record s. of Telfer in Little Sandy Desert, WA. Exfoliating granite outcrops, sheltering in crevices. ■ SEE ALSO *E. depressa*; *E. cygnitos.*

Goldfields Crevice-skink *Egernia formosa* SVL 96–107mm

Relatively flat, with smooth scales. Pale brown to olive above with numerous oblong black spots (usually coalescing anteriorly to form broad paravertebral stripes) from top of head to base of tail; broad, **pale patternless laterodorsal zone** from head to midbody; and ragged-edged dark brown to black upper flanks. Nthn pop. larger and redder with weaker pattern. ■ NOTES Semi-arid to arid woodlands in central to sthn interior WA; disjunct pop. in rocky ranges and gorges of Pilbara. Mainly shelters beneath bark or in hollow timber in s., and in rock crevices in n.

Hosmer's Skink *Egernia hosmeri* SVL 180mm

Spiny, with **3–4 sharp keels on each dorsal scale** and **1 long prominent spine on each scale on cylindrical tail**. Pale yellowish brown to reddish brown, darker on head, with dark flecks and pale blotches on anterior body, tending to fade posteriorly. ■ NOTES Subhumid to arid ne. Aust. Rocky ranges and outcrops, with colonies in rock crevices, or occasionally hollows in dead timber.

King's Skink *Egernia kingii* SVL 244mm

Very large, with several weak keels on each dorsal scale. Colour and pattern range from black to dark grey, brown or olive; patternless or with few to numerous small pale spots of varying intensity. ■ NOTES Sw. WA, n. on mainland to Hutt R. and east to Duke of Orleans Bay. Most abundant on offshore islands, n. to Three Bays Is. and e. to Archipelago of the Recherche. Rock outcrops and coastal heaths or shrublands on sand or limestone, sheltering in crevices or burrows, including those of penguins and shearwaters. Frequently feeds on eggs in seabird rookeries.

Eastern Crevice-skink *Egernia mcpheei* SVL 143mm

Relatively flat, with bluntly keeled dorsal scales and **27–32 midbody scale rows**. Brown, with dark streaks forming narrow broken lines, dark upper flanks and pale blotches on lips. Ventral surfaces bright orange to orange-yellow. ■ NOTES Forests and rock outcrops along coast and eastern side of Gt Div. Ra., from Barrington Tops, NSW n. to Main Ra. area, Qld. Shelters in crevices in rocks and timber. ■ SEE ALSO *E. saxatilis; E. striolata.*

Egernia epsisolus.
Abydos Stn, WA. B. Maryan

Egernia formosa.
Pinjin Stn, WA. D. Knowles

Egernia hosmeri.
Dajarra area, Qld. S. Wilson

Egernia kingii.
Yunderup, WA. D. Robinson

Egernia kingii. Juvenile.
Boullanger Is., WA. D. Robinson

Egernia mcpheei.
Guy Fawkes NP, NSW. G. Swan

South-western Crevice-skink *Egernia napoleonis* SVL 133mm

Relatively flat, with **2–4 sharp keels on each dorsal scale**. Olive brown to grey with dark spots tending to align in 3 longitudinal dorsal series, excluding a **broad pale dorsolateral zone**. Many small pale dots often scattered over back and flanks. Ventral surfaces salmon pink to orange-brown. ■ **NOTES** Heaths, woodlands, WSF, DSF and rock outcrops from Green Head se. to Twilight Cove. Arboreal and rock-inhabiting, sheltering under bark, in rock crevices and in hollow stems of grasstrees. ■ **SEE ALSO** *E. richardi.*

Pilbara Crevice-skink *Egernia pilbarensis* SVL 120mm

Robust, with **smooth scales** and virtually no pattern. Reddish brown, darkest on anterior flanks, sometimes with pale lateral dots. ■ **NOTES** Rocky ranges and outcrops of arid Pilbara region, WA, from coast (including Rosemary Is.) to Chichester Ra. Shelters in narrow rock crevices.

Richard's Crevice-skink *Egernia richardi* SVL 105mm

Relatively flat, with weakly keeled dorsal scales and **no pale dorsolateral suffusion**. Olive brown to grey above, sometimes with red flush on foreback, with about 8 series of small dark oblong spots often edged laterally with white. Upper flanks black, with scattered white spots. Lips white. ■ **NOTES** Semi-arid woodlands and outcrops, from sthn interior of WA to nthn Eyre Pen., SA. Shelters in hollow timber, beneath loose bark or in narrow rock crevices. ■ **SEE ALSO** *E. napoleonis; E. striolata.*

Yakka Skink *Egernia rugosa* SVL 240mm

Very large and robust, with thick tail, **parietal scales fragmented into several smaller scales**, and very large, plate-like ear-lobules. Brown with broad darker brown to black mid-dorsal zone, narrow pale brown dorsolateral stripe and brown flanks. ■ **NOTES** Dry open forests, woodlands and rocky areas from St George and Bollon regions to sthn Cape York Pen. Dwells communally in hollow fallen timber, deep rock crevices, in burrows excavated under rocks and logs or disused rabbit burrows. Extremely secretive, its presence often indicated by a communal defecation site. Diurnal to crepuscular. ■ **STATUS** Vulnerable (C'wealth; Qld).

Egernia napoleonis.
Denmark, WA. R. Browne-Cooper

Egernia pilbarensis.
Cleaverville, WA. R. Browne-Cooper

Egernia richardi.
Lake Cronin, WA.
S. Wilson

Egernia rugosa.
Alton NP area, Qld.
S. Wilson

Black Rock Skink *Egernia saxatilis* SVL 135mm

Relatively flat, with **2–5 sharp keels on each dorsal scale,** and **30–42 midbody scale rows.** ■ **SSP.** *E. s. saxatilis* is mid-brown to almost black, with dark dashes on scales aligned into broken lines. Upper flanks black with scattered dark brown scales. Upper lips white. Ventral surfaces, from chest onto tail, dull to bright orange. Throat whitish, variegated with black. *E. s. intermedia* is darker, usually black to very dark grey. ■ **NOTES** *E. s. saxatilis* is restricted to Warrumbungle Mtns, ne. interior of NSW. *E. s. intermedia* extends s. from Newnes Plateau, NSW to the Grampians, wstn Vic. Shelters mainly in narrow rock crevices; occasionally in timber. ■ **SEE ALSO** *E. mcpheei; E. striolata.*

Stokes' Skink; Gidgee Skink *Egernia stokesii* SVL 158–194mm

Spiny; 2 spines on each dorsal scale, becoming large single spines on short flat tail. ■ **SSP.** *E. s. badia* (SVL 194mm) is usually reddish brown with angular pale blotches arranged in irregular bands. A wholly black pop. is also known. *E. s. stokesii* (SVL 158mm) is weakly patterned, or brown to black with clusters of pale scales forming prominent blotches. *E. s. zellingi* (SVL 180mm) is brown with weak pattern; dark and pale scales form small blotches arranged in irregular transverse rows. ■ **NOTES** Widespread though patchy in dry to semi-arid habitats. *E. s. stokesii* occurs under limestone slabs on Houtman Abrolhos Is. off mid-w. coast of WA, and Edel Land Pen. and Baudin Is., Shark Bay. *E. s. badia* occupies rock crevices and hollow timber in sw. interior of WA and on Dirk Hartog Is., Shark Bay. *E. s. zellingi* lives in rock crevices and hollow timber in estn interior of Aust. ■ **SEE ALSO** *E. depressa.* ■ **STATUS** *E. s. stokesii* is lower risk–least concern (IUCN Red List); *E. s. badia* is endangered (C'wealth); vulnerable (WA).

Tree Skink *Egernia striolata* SVL 119mm

Relatively flat, with **2–5 striations or blunt keels on each dorsal scale.** Dark olive to grey, darker along vertebral zone, with a **broad pale dorsolateral suffusion** from nape to midbody or base of tail. Upper lateral zone black, usually boldest anteriorly and fading at midbody or hips. Upper lips white to pale grey. Ventral surfaces pale orange to dull yellow, with dark bars on chin and throat. ■ **NOTES** DSF, woodlands and rock outcrops of estn Aust., from nthn Eyre Pen., SA to ne. Qld. Shelters in hollow timber, beneath loose bark and in narrow rock crevices. ■ **SEE ALSO** *E. mcpheei; E. richardi; E. saxatilis.*

Egernia saxatilis saxatilis.
Warrumbungle NP, NSW. G. Swan

Egernia saxatilis intermedia.
Kanangra Boyd NP, NSW. G. Shea

Egernia stokesii badia.
Morawa, WA. D. Robinson

Egernia stokesii stokesii.
Useless Loop area, WA. B. Maryan

Egernia stokesii zellingi.
Broken Hill area, NSW. S. Wilson

Egernia striolata.
Boondall, Qld. S. Wilson

Genus *Emoia*

Large diverse genus (more than 100 spp.), represented in Aust. by only 2 spp. in nthn Cape York Pen. and Torres Strait; a third sp. is restricted to the oceanic territory of Christmas Is. Smooth-scaled, with 4 well-developed limbs each with 5 digits, moveable lower eyelid enclosing a transparent disc, frontoparietal scales joined to form a single shield, and parietal scales in contact. Aust. spp. are moderately large, with long pointed snouts and long slender tails and digits. ■ **NOTES** Consummate rafters, with pops thriving on islands, including remote oceanic atolls, between South-East Asia and estn Pacific. They are less successful on larger landmasses. Swift, diurnal egglayers, with an almost invariable clutch size of 2 eggs.

Mangrove Skink *Emoia atrocostata* SVL 85mm

Shades of brown to greyish brown above with pale spots and dark flecks, and a broad ragged-edged dark upper lateral zone from behind eye to hips. ■ **NOTES** Restricted to mangroves and rocks of extreme coastal areas, along intertidal zone from tip of Cape York Pen. through Torres Strait islands to NG and the South Pacific, through South-East Asia to Taiwan. Basks and forages on exposed sites, avoiding breaking waves in the splash zone and quickly returning to forage after they subside. Powerful swimmer, readily taking to water if pursued. ■ **STATUS** Near threatened (Qld).

Long-tailed Skink *Emoia longicauda* SVL 98mm

Sharp-snouted, with weak pattern. Coppery brown to pale yellowish brown, with or without scattered pale flecks. **Lips, lower lateral and ventral surfaces yellowish green to bright lemon yellow.** ■ **NOTES** RF clearings and edges, from McIlwraith Ra., Cape York Pen. through islands of Torres Strait to NG and the Solomon Is. Arboreal and highly agile, able to leap with ease between branches.

Genus *Eremiascincus*

Ten Aust. spp. (others in estn Indonesia and Timor) with 4 moderately well-developed limbs, each with 5 digits, moveable lower eyelid lacking a transparent disc, parietal scales in contact, paired frontoparietal scales, smooth glossy body scales (with a series of low ridges on posterior body and tail-base on some spp), obvious ear-openings without lobules and patterns comprising simple bands, a reticulum, or spots and dashes often concentrating to form a dark upper lateral zone. ■ **NOTES** Widespread from sandy deserts to nthn tropical river margins. Mostly nocturnal to crepuscular and mainly egg-layers (1 sp. variously reported as live-bearer and egg-layer). ■ **SEE ALSO** *Glaphyromorphus.*

Emoia atrocostata.
Boigu Is., Qld. S. Wilson

Emoia longicauda.
Moa Is., Qld. S. Wilson

Brown-sided Bar-lipped Skink *Eremiascincus brongersmai* SVL 98mm

Flecked pattern, with usually **6 upper labial scales**. Reddish brown above, sometimes with 4–6 longitudinal series of dashes, an irregular **dark dorsolateral streak on forebody** and **rich brown flanks enclosing many prominent small white dots.** ■ **NOTES** Nw. Kimberley. Shelters in moist sites under leaf litter and logs. ■ **SEE ALSO** *E. isolepis.*

Orange-sided Bar-lipped Skink *Eremiascincus douglasi* SVL 80mm

Flecked and spotted pattern with usually **6 upper labial scales.** Brown to dark brown above with many dark streaks or spots, **broad dark upper lateral streak on forebody** and **rich burnt orange flanks enclosing many prominent small white dots.** ■ **NOTES** Extends widely through woodlands and forests of nthn NT, mainly in moist areas such as logs and suburban compost heaps, but also in dry litter near beaches. Often seen foraging at dusk. ■ **SEE ALSO** *E. isolepis.*

Eastern Narrow-banded Sand-swimmer *Eremiascincus fasciolatus* SVL 123mm

Banded pattern. Low dorsal ridges present on posterior body and tail, one lower labial scale contacts postmental scale, usually 8 upper labial scales, with the last labial scale divided horizontally, and **a row of subinfralabial scales present (fig)**. Pale yellowish brown to reddish brown with 10–16 narrow bands, no more than one scale wide on body, and 25–35 very narrow bands on original tail. ■ **NOTES** Estn interior of Qld, reaching coast at Rockhampton, Port Curtis and Curtis Is., extending n. to Mt Cooper Stn and Blackbraes NP, and inland to Roma and Moonie areas. Occupies open subtropical forests, semiarid woodlands and heathlands, generally on hard substrates. ■ **SEE ALSO** *E. richardsonii.*

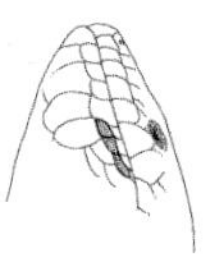

Northern Narrow-banded Skink *Eremiascincus intermedius* SVL 88mm

Strongly banded pattern. Low dorsal ridges present on posterior body and tail, **one lower labial scale broadly contacts postmental scale, 7 upper labial scales**, scales along top of 4th toe have **transverse sutures along at least distal third of digit**, and **subdigital lamellae deeply grooved**, usually along more than half of digit, and divided basally. Brown to reddish brown with 6–16 transverse to oblique narrow bands, less than 2 scales wide, on body and up to 42 perfectly transverse bands on original tail. ■ **NOTES** Sandridge deserts and sandy plains with shrubs and spinifex through most of NT, n. to about Elsey NP and e. to Mt Isa area, Qld. ■ **SEE ALSO** *E. pallidus; E. phantasmus; E. richardsonii.*

Eremiascincus brongersmai.
Mitchell Plateau, WA. P. Griffin

Eremiascincus douglasi.
Humpty Doo area, NT. S. Wilson

Eremiascincus fasciolatus.
Glenmorgan district, Qld. S. Wilson

Eremiascincus intermedius.
Tanami Desert, NT. B. Schembri

Northern Bar-lipped Skink *Eremiascincus isolepis* SVL 72mm

Flecked and spotted pattern with usually **7 upper labial scales** and **no dark dorsolateral streak**. Shades of brown to rich reddish brown with many dark spots, tending to align longitudinally on back, **becoming more concentrated on upper flanks** and sparser on mid- to lower flanks. ■ **NOTES** Widespread across nthn Aust., occupying a variety of habitats from river floodplains and margins of swamps to dry grassy areas. Shelters in moist conditions under rocks, logs and leaf litter. ■ **SEE ALSO** *E. brongersmai; E. douglasi; E. musivus.*

Mosaic Desert Skink *Eremiascincus musivus* SVL 59mm

Spotted pattern, but lacking heavily speckled dark brown flanks. Pale yellowish to orange brown with pale vertebral stripe from base of head to base of tail, pale and dark spots aggregated to form a diffuse reticulum, larger pale dashes on flanks and narrow dark bands on tail. ■ **NOTES** Desert shrublands, buffel- and spinifex grasslands of nw. Aust, between about Dampier and Mandora. ■ **SEE ALSO** *E. isolepis.*

Western Narrow-banded Skink *Eremiascincus pallidus* SVL 77mm

Weakly banded pattern. Low dorsal ridges present on posterior body and tail, usually **1 lower labial scale broadly contacts postmental scale, 7 upper labial scales**, scales along top of 4th toe have transverse sutures along length of digit, and **subdigital lamellae un-grooved**. Reddish, orange to pinkish without dorsal pattern, often a little indication of bands on sides of body, and 32–37 perfectly transverse bands, less than a scale wide, on original tail. ■ **NOTES** Interior of WA reaching coasts of Pilbara and North West Cape, and extending into far nw. SA and w. NT. Inhabits sandy deserts, particularly dunes, often with sparse vegetation, on loose substrates and avoiding stony soils. ■ **SEE ALSO** *E. intermedius; E. phantasmus; E. richardsonii.*

Lowlands Bar-lipped Skink *Eremiascincus pardalis* SVL 70mm

Flecked and spotted pattern with **1 lower labial scale contacting postmental scale**. Brown with short oblique dark bars on sides of head and dark flecks over back, tending to concentrate and form dense black spots on paravertebral area and flanks. ■ **NOTES** Woodlands and monsoon forests of Cape York Pen., s. to Cairns. Shelters in soft soil beneath rocks, logs and leaf litter. ■ **SEE ALSO** *Glaphyromorphus nigricaudis.*

Eremiascincus isolepis.
Broome, WA. S. Wilson

Eremiascincus musivus.
Karratha area, WA. G. Harold

Eremiascincus pallidus.
Bullara Station, WA. S. Wilson

Eremiascincus pardalis.
Cape Melville, Qld. G. Gaikhorst

Ghost Skink *Eremiascincus phantasmus* SVL 92mm

Weakly banded pattern. Low dorsal ridges present on posterior body and tail; 2 **lower labial scales contact postmental scale, usually 8 upper labial scales**, scales along top of 4th toe have transverse sutures along half to almost entire digit and subdigital lamellae in two rows basally. Pale pinkish brown to pale grey with pattern very weak on body and often represented by obscure bands on flanks. Original tail has 29–39 very narrow bands. ■ **NOTES** Primarily low-lying areas of Lake Eyre Basin in ne. SA, extending to wstn NSW, sw. Qld and sthn NT. Inhabits sandy deserts, particularly dunes, often with sparse vegetation, on loose substrates and avoiding stony soils. ■ **STATUS** Data deficient (Vic – as *fasciolatus*). ■ **SEE ALSO** *E. intermedius; E. pallidus; E. richardsonii.*

Broad-banded Sand-swimmer *Eremiascincus richardsonii* SVL 113mm

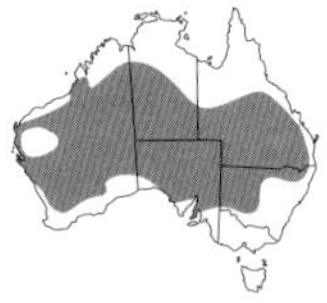

Strongly banded pattern. Low dorsal ridges present on posterior body and tail. Pale brown to dark reddish brown with **broad dark bands, as wide as, or slightly narrower than pale interspaces**; 8–14 bands between nape and hips and 19–32 bands on tail. These may be straight and simple, or oblique and branching. ■ **NOTES** Arid zones of all mainland states except Vic, tending to occur mainly on heavy and stony soils. Shelters under thick leaf-litter, in loose sand under vegetation, in soil cracks and in disused burrows. ■ **SEE ALSO** *E. fasciolatus; E. intermedius; E. pallidus; E. phantasmus.*

Genus *Eroticoscincus*

Elf Skink *Eroticoscincus graciloides* SVL 32mm

One tiny sp. with large eyes, pointed snout, 4 short limbs with 4 fingers and 5 toes, moveable lower eyelid enclosing a transparent disc, parietal scales in contact and minute circular ear-openings. Dark brown to reddish brown (shining iridescent when viewed obliquely) with fine dark streaks on dorsal and upper lateral scales; narrow, ill-defined dark dorsolateral line on body; rusty dorsolateral stripe on tail; and dark markings aligned to form an obscure M-shape on rear of head. ■ **NOTES** Vine thickets, WSF and RF from Fraser Is. s. to Ipswich. Shelters beneath damp leaf litter, logs and stones, foraging in shaded, moist situations.

Genus *Eugongylus*

Brown Sheen-skink *Eugongylus rufescens* SVL 169mm

One Aust. sp. (others in NG region), with long body, short, well-developed limbs, each with 5 digits, moveable scaly lower eyelids, ear-openings with small anterior lobules and parietal scales in contact. Reddish brown to grey (iridescent green/purple when viewed obliquely). Juv. prominently marked with many narrow, widely spaced pale bands. Adults normally patternless, sometimes retaining a vague indication of bands. ■ **NOTES** Monsoon forests from tip of Cape York Pen. through islands of Torres Strait to NG. Secretive, sheltering in cavities in rotting logs, and beneath logs and moist leaf litter. Egglayer.

Eremiascincus phantasmus.
Nappa Merrie Stn, Qld. S. Wilson

Eremiascincus richardsonii.
Currawinya NP, Qld. S. Wilson

Eroticoscincus graciloides.
Buderim, Qld. S. Wilson

Eugongylus rufescens.
Lockerbie Scrub, Qld. S. Wilson

Water Skinks Genus *Eulamprus*

Five spp. of moderate to large skinks with smooth glossy scales; well-developed **limbs which overlap when adpressed to side of body**, each with 5 digits; eyelid moveable, lacking a transparent disc; ear-opening without lobules; parietal scales in contact (separated on 1 sp.); **3rd pair of chin shields separated by 5 longitudinal rows of scales (fig); at least some distal subdigital lamellae divided on 4th toe**. Most are bronze to copper above, often with paler dorsolateral and sometimes dark dorsal stripes, and dark flanks encl. pale flecks or spots. ■ **NOTES** Widespread in estn Aust., in moist or water-side habitats, incl. creek banks, heaths and forests. Diurnal sun-loving skinks which bask on rocks and logs, often beside water. Some frequently enter water to hunt or escape danger. They feed on arthropods, frogs, tadpoles and smaller lizards. Livebearers. ■ **SEE ALSO** *Glaphyromorphus; Concinnia; Karma; Magmellia.*

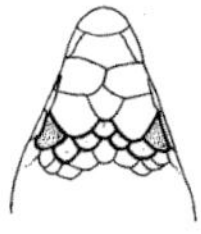

Yellow-bellied Water Skink *Eulamprus heatwolei* SVL 100mm

Black anterior margin to ear-opening. Pale to dark bronze brown with a **pale streak from above eye to neck**, sparse to dense **small black spots over back**, black upper flanks enclosing irregular white spots (each covering a single scale), **patternless yellow belly** and **white throat with black patches**. ■ **NOTES** Creek, river and swamp margins from New England Plateau, NSW to about Goulburn R., Vic. Isolated pop. occurs in Fleurieu Pen., SA. Commonly seen basking on waterside rocks and logs. ■ **SEE ALSO** *E. quoyii; E. tympanum.* ■ **STATUS** Vulnerable (SA).

Alpine Water Skink *Eulamprus kosciuskoi* SVL 85mm

Olive brown with narrow black vertebral and laterodorsal stripes (weak to absent in n.), **yellow dorsolateral stripes**, and black flanks enclosing several series of cream to yellow spots. Lower flanks pale yellow to grey with black spots across belly. ■ **NOTES** Alpine woodlands, heaths and tussock grasslands. Isolated pops occur in Snowy Mtns of NSW and adjacent areas of Vic, New England Plateau and Barrington Tops, ne. NSW and Stanthorpe area, Qld. Basks on rocks and tussocks, often near small streams. ■ **STATUS** Critically endangered (Vic).

Blue Mountains Water Skink *Eulamprus leuraensis* SVL 70mm

Prominent stripes, and **parietal scales separated by interparietal**. Very dark brown to black with very narrow yellow paravertebral and dorsolateral stripes and many yellow lateral spots. Ventral surfaces bright yellow with coarse, dark, longitudinally aligned variegations. ■ **NOTES** Swampy heaths over sandstone at Wentworth Falls, Leura and Newnes Plateau in the Blue Mtns. Basks on dense grass tussocks, sheltering beneath them or in burrows, including those of crustaceans, when disturbed. ■ **STATUS** Endangered (C'wealth; NSW; IUCN Red List).

Eulamprus heatwolei.
Leura, NSW. S. Wilson

Eulamprus kosciuskoi.
Falls Creek area, Vic. S. Wilson.

Eulamprus kosciuskoi.
Polblue Swamp, Barrington Tops NP, NSW. S. Wilson

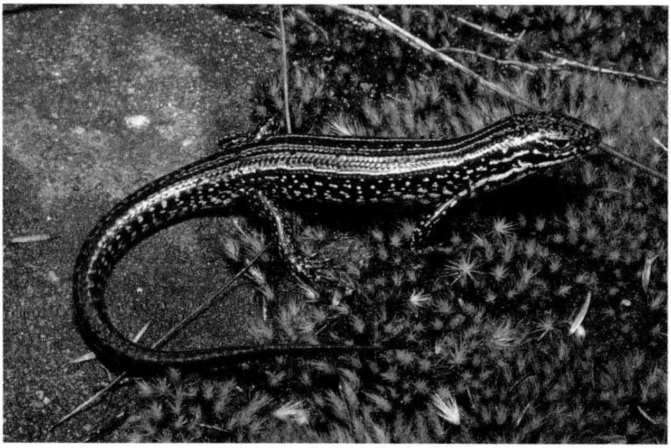

Eulamprus leuraensis.
Leura, NSW. S. Wilson

Eastern Water Skink *Eulamprus quoyii* SVL 115mm

Very large and robust. Coppery brown to golden brown above with irregular black flecks or blotches, a broad to narrow **yellow dorsolateral stripe** from above eye to midbody or hips, black upper flanks enclosing several series of pale spots, and grey lower flanks with black flecks. ■ **NOTES** Variety of waterside habitats from Cairns, Qld s. along coast and ranges to se. NSW and inland to se. SA via Darling/Murray R. drainage system. Basks on rocks or logs, readily taking to water if disturbed. ■ **SEE ALSO** *E. heatwolei; E. tympanum.*

Southern Water Skink; Dreeite Water Skink *Eulamprus tympanum* SVL 93–97mm

Pale anterior margin to ear-opening and **no indication of pale dorsolateral stripe.** ■ **SSP.** *E. t. tympanum* (Southern Water Skink) has 36–44 (usually 42 or fewer) midbody scale rows. Brown above, with or without irregular black flecks; black upper flanks enclosing many small white to yellow spots; and a pale anterior edge to ear-opening continuous with pale streak running back from top of ear. Ventral surfaces cream to yellow, usually flecked with black; light to dark grey on throat. *E. t. marnieae* (Dreeite Water Skink) has 40–48 (usually 43 or more) midbody scale rows. It is larger, with short black transverse dorsal bars and bright yellow ventral surfaces with bold black longitudinal bars. ■ **NOTES** *E. t. marnieae* inhabits basalt outcrops and drystone walls near Lakes Corangamite and Bolac, sw. Vic. *E. t. tympanum* occupies cool temperate habitats, usually beside water, from Blue Mtns, NSW through sthn Vic to se. SA. Basks on waterside rocks and logs, sheltering in cracks in fallen timber, beneath logs and rocks. ■ **SEE ALSO** *E. heatwolei; E. quoyii.* ■ **STATUS** *E. t. marnieae* is endangered (C'wealth); critically endangered (Vic); *E. t. tympanum* is rare (SA).

Genus *Glaphyromorphus*

Eleven small to medium-sized spp. with smooth glossy scales, **short to very short limbs, each with 5 digits, failing to meet when adpressed** (overlapping on one sp.), lower eyelid moveable and lacking a transparent disc, ear-opening without lobules and parietal scales in contact. **Rarely any pink on ventral surfaces.** Identification features include whether 1 (A) or 2 (B) lower labial scales contact postmental scale. ■ **NOTES** Widespread in ne. and nthn Aust. where damp conditions prevail. Nocturnal, crepuscular to diurnal, foraging in shaded environments. Very short-limbed spp. are cryptic, rarely seen in exposed areas. Egg-layers, though one sp. reportedly has livebearing pop. Arthropod feeders. ■ **SEE ALSO** *Calyptotis; Eulamprus; Eremiascincus.*

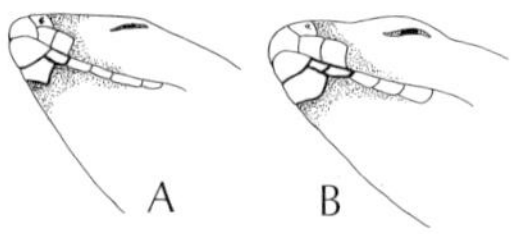

Mount Elliot Mulch-skink *Glaphyromorphus clandestinus* SVL 72mm

Long-bodied with short, widely spaced limbs and long tail. Bronze to brown with light to heavy dark speckling, barred lips and dark flecks on flanks, concentrated on edges of scale rows to form prominent to obscure **dark lateral lines.** ■ **NOTES** Known only from 425m altitude at Mt Elliot, Bowling Green Bay NP. In moist humus under granite slabs at Alligator Ck.

Eulamprus quoyii.
Murray River, Vic. R. Valentic

Eulamprus quoyii.
Sundown NP, Qld. S. Wilson

Eulamprus tympanum marnieae.
Nerrin Nerrin, Vic. R. Valentic

Eulamprus tympanum tympanum.
Otway Ranges, Vic. G. Harold

Glaphyromorphus clandestinus.
Mt Elliot, Qld. C. Hoskin

Slender Mulch-skink *Glaphyromorphus cracens* SVL 58mm

Long-bodied, with short, widely spaced limbs and **2 lower labial scales contacting postmental scale**. Pale to dark brown above (with or without 2–4 longitudinal series of small dark spots), broad black upper lateral stripe, grey lower flanks with small dark spots and cream to pale yellow ventral surfaces.
■ **NOTES** Woodlands, DSF and rock outcrops on and w. of Atherton and Windsor tablelands. Dwells in loose soil under logs, stones and leaf litter.
■ **SEE ALSO** *G. crassicaudus; G. pumilus.*

Northern Mulch-skink *Glaphyromorphus crassicaudus* SVL 55mm

Long-bodied, with short, widely spaced limbs, very long tail, **1 lower labial scale contacting postmental scale, and more than 18 subdigital lamellae under 4th toe.** ■ **SSP.** (ill-defined): *G. c. crassicaudus* is variable; shades of brown to coppery brown with narrow dark paravertebral lines, series of dots or broad vertebral stripe, and **dark brown to black upper lateral stripe with edges prominent and sharp-edged.** *G. c. arnhemicus* lacks vertebral stripe. ■ **NOTES** *G. c. crassicaudus* occurs in monsoon RF, woodlands and disturbed gardens from Cape York Pen. to islands of Torres Strait and NG. *G. c. arnhemicus* is isolated in ne. NT. ■ **SEE ALSO** *G. cracens; G. darwiniensis; G. pumilus.*

Top End Mulch-skink *Glaphyromorphus darwiniensis* SVL 59mm

Long-bodied, with short, widely spaced limbs and **fewer than 18 subdigital lamellae under 4th toe.** Brown above with grey flanks and pattern, when present, comprising a broad darker vertebral stripe. ■ **NOTES** Variety of forests and woodlands in nthn NT and nw. Kimberley. Secretive, dwelling under leaf litter or fallen timber. ■ **SEE ALSO** *G. crassicaudus.*

Brown-tailed Bar-lipped Skink *Glaphyromorphus fuscicaudis* SVL 90mm

Robust, with relatively well-developed limbs. Brown above, darker on tail, with many darker, wavy to broken bands tending to break into spots or flecks on posterior body, and a dark reticulum on side of neck enclosing an irregular **dorsolateral series of cream to pale yellow blotches** from neck to midbody.
■ **NOTES** RF from Carwell Ra. n. nearly to Cooktown. Shelters beneath rotting logs and damp leaf litter. ■ **SEE ALSO** *G. nigricaudis.*

Atherton Tableland Mulch-skink *Glaphyromorphus mjobergi* SVL 90mm

Long-bodied, with short, widely spaced limbs. Rich brown above, often with a black spot on each scale and an anterior **dorsolateral series of cream to pale yellow blotches** alternating with larger dark blotches. ■ **NOTES** Montane RF above 650m, from about Tully Falls n. to Mt Carbine Tableland. Shelters in and beneath rotting logs.

Glaphyromorphus cracens.
Chillagoe, Qld. S. Wilson

Glaphyromorphus crassicaudus crassicaudus.
Moa Is. Qld. S. Wilson

Glaphyromorphus darwiniensis.
Raft Point, NT. S. Wilson

Glaphyromorphus fuscicaudis.
Walter Hill Range, Qld. S. Wilson

Glaphyromorphus mjobergi.
Ravenshoe area, Qld. S. Wilson

Black-tailed Bar-lipped Skink *Glaphyromorphus nigricaudis* SVL 90mm

Robust, with relatively well-developed limbs, **2 lower labial scales contacting postmental scale** and **no pale dorsolateral blotches**. Brown with narrow wavy dark bands from nape, fading at midbody and extending onto flanks. ■ **NOTES** Woodlands and margins of monsoon RF and vine thickets, from nthn and estn Cape York Pen., Qld to sthn NG and in far ne. Arnhem Land, NT. Secretive and nocturnal, sheltering beneath rocks, logs or leaf litter. Mostly egglayers but a livebearing pop. occurs on sthn Cape York Pen. ■ **SEE ALSO** *G. fuscicaudis; Eremiascincus pardalis.*

McIlwraith Bar-lipped Skink *Glaphyromorphus nyanchupinta* SVL 53mm

Robust, with relatively well-developed limbs separated by no more than one forelimb length when adpressed, 2 lower labial scales contact postmental scale and **7 upper labial scales with 5th below eye**. Brown with dark wavy bars across dorsal and lateral surfaces. These are most prominent anteriorly and break up on flanks but extend back to hind limbs. Upper labial scales mainly dark, each with a pale central dot. ■ **NOTES** Restricted to RF on McIlwraith Range, Cape York Pen. Recorded under logs at 530m altitude, but is probably more widespread in uplands.

Cape Melville Bar-lipped Skink *Glaphyromorphus othelarrni* SVL 93mm

Robust, with **well-developed limbs contacting when adpressed**, 2 lower labial scales contact postmental scale and **8 upper labial scales with 6th below eye**. Pale to dark brown above, immaculate or with dark spots or wavy bars on anterior body. Flanks have dark, longitudinally aligned flecks or wavy vertical bars. These are strongest on sides of neck but extend to forebody, and break into flecks that reach groin and base of tail. Upper labial scales mainly pale with dark vertical bars along sutures. ■ **NOTES** Restricted to isolated RF of Melville Range, Cape York Pen., from uplands at 600m altitude to lowlands at 110m altitude. Associated with thick leaf litter among boulders.

Dwarf Mulch-skink *Glaphyromorphus pumilus* SVL 55mm

Long-bodied, with short, widely spaced limbs, **1 lower labial scale contacting postmental scale.** Brown to coppery brown or greyish brown with dark dashes forming broken to continuous paravertebral lines. **Dark, ragged-edged upper lateral zone fragmented by numerous pale spots and flecks.** ■ **NOTES** Woodlands and coastal dunes to vine thickets, margins of RF and rock outcrops of estn Cape York Pen. s. to Cairns area. Shelters beneath leaf litter and in soft soil under rocks and logs. ■ **SEE ALSO** *G. cracens; G. crassicaudus.*

Glaphyromorphus nigricaudis.
Lockerbie Scrub, Qld. S. Wilson

Glaphyromorphus nyanchupinta.
McIlwraith Range, Qld. C. Hoskin

Glaphyromorphus othelarrni.
Melville Range, Qld. C. Hoskin

Glaphyromorphus pumilus.
Lake Wicheura, Qld. S. Wilson

Fine-spotted Mulch-skink *Glaphyromorphus punctulatus* **SVL 70mm**

Long-bodied, with short, widely spaced limbs and **1 lower labial scale contacting postmental scale**. Brownish grey to pale or rich brown with pattern either absent or consisting of simple dark flecks or spots on each dorsal and lateral scale. ■ **NOTES** Woodlands and vine thickets, particularly those on sandy soils, from about Gayndah to between Townsville and Cairns. Shelters beneath leaf litter and in soft soil under logs and rocks.

Genus *Gnypetoscincus*

Prickly Forest Skink *Gnypetoscincus queenslandiae* **SVL 84mm**

Sole member of genus. **All scales strongly keeled**. Limbs well developed, each with 5 digits, parietal scales in contact, eye large with moveable lower eyelid lacking a transparent disc, and ear-opening large without lobules. Dark brown with obscure, broken, pale transverse bands. ■ **NOTES** RF from near Rossville s. to Kirrama. Commonly found in cool damp conditions in and under rotting logs but rarely encountered foraging. Shuns direct sunlight. Slow-moving. Livebearer, feeding on arthropods, slugs, small snails, earthworms and other invertebrates.

Genus *Harrisoniascincus*

Beech Skink *Harrisoniascincus zia* **SVL 55mm**

One small sp. with short, well-developed limbs, each with 5 digits, and a long tail. Lower eyelid moveable, enclosing a transparent disc. Ear-opening present. **Frontoparietal scales paired**, parietals in contact, **interparietal large** and **nasals widely separated (fig.)**. Brown with scattered dark and pale flecks, weak narrow pale dorsolateral line, and dark upper flanks merging with pale-flecked mid- to lower flanks. Tail suffused with reddish brown, brightest towards tip. Belly bright yellow. ■ **NOTES** Cool highland RF and antarctic beech forests of se. Qld and ne. NSW. Secretive, basking among leaf litter on edges of sunny clearings. Egglaying invertebrate feeder. ■ **SEE ALSO** *Lampropholis; Saproscincus.*

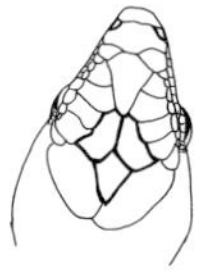

Genus *Hemiergis*

Seven small, long-bodied spp. with very short, widely spaced limbs bearing 5, 4, 3 or 2 digits (fingers and toes equal in number), **moveable lower eyelid enclosing a transparent disc,** (disc absent in 1 species) and **ear-opening usually absent,** represented by a depression (present in 2 spp.). Scales smooth and glossy. Ventral surfaces yellow to reddish orange. ■ **NOTES** Widespread in sthn Aust. Secretive, dwelling in loose damp soil under rocks, logs and leaf litter. Livebearers, feeding on small invertebrates. ■ **SEE ALSO** *Anepischetosia; Calyptotis; Lerista; Saiphos.*

Glaphyromorphus punctulatus.
Keswick Is., Qld. S. Wilson

Gnypetoscincus queenslandiae.
Wooroonooran NP, Qld.
S. Wilson

Harrisoniascincus zia.
Lamington Plateau, Qld.
S. Wilson

Southern Earless Skink *Hemiergis decresiensis* SVL 45–50mm

Three fingers and toes, 24–26 mid-body scale rows. Rich brown above with broad dark dorsolateral stripes, narrower paravertebral lines or series of dashes (occasionally absent), and orange to yellow belly. ■ **SSP.** *H. d. decresiensis* (SVL 45mm) has relatively well-developed limbs, weak or absent paravertebral lines and broad prominent dorsolateral stripes. *H. d. continentis* (SVL 50mm) is more robust, with paravertebral lines often well developed. ■ **NOTES** Woodlands, WSF, DSF and shrublands of se. SA. *H. d. decresiensis* is restricted to Kangaroo Is.; *H. d. continentis* occupies mainland SA.

South-western Mulch-skink *Hemiergis gracilipes* SVL 89mm

Largest *Hemiergis*. Long-tailed with **5 fingers and toes, no transparent disc in moveable lower eyelid and large ear-opening with exposed tympanum.** Brown above with black spots tending to form paravertebral stripes, a black, often ragged-edged dorsolateral line usually enclosing white spots, and grey flanks reticulated with black and spotted with white. Ventral surfaces, from chest to behind vent, yellow. Throat white. ■ **NOTES** Restricted to moist forests, heaths and swamp margins in sw. WA, from Samson Brook se. to Cheyne Beach. Shelters beneath logs and in mats of leaf litter and abandoned stick-ant nests.

Western Earless Skink *Hemiergis initialis* SVL 42–50mm

Short-tailed, with **5 fingers and toes** and a **complete row of subocular scales between eye and upper labial scales.** Brown to reddish brown above with usually 2–4 longitudinal rows of dark spots, narrow dark dorsolateral stripes, grey flanks and bright reddish orange ventral surfaces from chest to base of tail. Throat grey. ■ **SSP.** *H. i. initialis* is largest, with prefrontal and frontonasal scales distinct. *H. i. brookeri* has prefrontals fused to frontonasal scale. ■ **NOTES** Dry forests and woodlands, often on gravelly soils from Darling Ra. to s. coast and sthn interior of WA (*H. i. initialis*) and across Gt Aust. Bight (*H. i. brookeri*). ■ **SEE ALSO** *H. millewae.*

Rusty Earless Skink *Hemiergis millewae* SVL 58mm

Five fingers and toes, ear-depression visible, sometimes exposing a tympanum, and **5th upper labial contacts eye**. Dark olive above, paler on flanks, usually with a burnt orange dorsolateral stripe and prominent black spots on tail. ■ **NOTES** Semi-arid mallee woodlands with spinifex, between nw. Vic and se. interior of WA. Shelters in debris beneath spinifex. ■ **SEE ALSO** *H. initialis.* ■ **STATUS** Critically endangered (Vic).

Hemiergis decresiensis continentis.
Pt Pirie, SA. G. Harold

Hemiergis decresiensis decresiensis.
Duck Lagoon, Kangaroo Is. S. Wilson

Hemiergis gracilipes.
Bunbury, WA. R. Browne-Cooper

Hemiergis initialis brookeri.
Koonalda Stn area, SA. G. Harold

Hemiergis initialis initialis.
Sawyer's Valley, WA. S. Wilson

Hemiergis millewae.
Kimba area, SA. G. Harold

Peron's Earless Skink *Hemiergis peronii* SVL 79mm

Long-tailed, with **3 or 4 fingers and toes.** Brown to olive brown with paravertebral (and occasionally mid-dorsal) lines of dark dashes, sometimes forming a broad dark vertebral stripe, and a narrow broken black dorsolateral line often edged above with a rusty tinge. Ventral surfaces bright yellow. ■ **SSP.** *H. p. peronii* has 4 fingers and toes. *H. p. tridactyla* has 3 fingers and toes. ■ **NOTES** Forests, heaths and shrublands in lower sw. and sthn interior of WA, sthn SA and sw. Vic (*H. p. peronii*), and sw. coast of WA (*H. p. tridactyla*). ■ **STATUS** *H. p. peronii* is near threatened (Vic).

Two-toed Earless Skink *Hemiergis quadrilineatum* SVL 75mm

Long-tailed, with **2 fingers and toes.** Pale to dark reddish brown, yellowish brown or greyish brown with paravertebral lines or series of dashes (sometimes coalescing to form a broad dark vertebral stripe), distinct narrow black dorsolateral stripe and grey to brownish grey flanks. Ventral surfaces, from chest to base of tail, bright yellow. ■ **NOTES** Lower w. coast and offshore islands, on sandy and limestone-based soils. Common in gardens of suburban Perth.

Eastern Earless Skink *Hemiergis talbingoensis* SVL 60 mm

Three fingers and toes, 18-22 midbody scale rows. Brown above with narrow dark dorsolateral and paravertebral lines or series of dashes (occasionally absent) and orange to yellow belly. ■ **SSP.** *H. t. talbingoensis* has 22 midbody scale rows, 7-8 lamellae under fourth toe and dorsal pattern ranges from prominent and continuous to broken and obscure. *H. t. davisi* has 20 (rarely 22 or 18) midbody scale rows, 6 or fewer lamellae under fourth toe and dorsal pattern usually strong. ■ **NOTES** WSF, DSF and woodlands from sthn Vic to nthn NSW; *H. t. talbingoensis* extends from Vic to mid-estn NSW and *H. t. davisi* occurs n. of Abercrombie R., NSW.

Forest Skinks Genus *Karma*

Two medium-sized spp. with smooth, shiny scales; well-developed limbs which overlap when pressed to side of body, each with 5 digits; lower eyelid moveable, lacking a transparent disc; ear-opening without lobules; parietal scales in contact; frontoparietal scale divided; and **3rd pair of chin shields separated by 5 longitudinal rows of scales (fig); Distal subdigital lamellae on 4th toe undivided.** ■ **NOTES** Subtropical RF and temperate Beech forest of se. Qld and ne. NSW. Diurnal skinks which occupy cavities in fallen logs, occasionally rock crevices. Often seen beside walking tracks, resting with head and forebody protruding from shelter site. Livebearing arthropod feeders. ■ **SEE ALSO** *Concinnia*; *Eulamprus.*

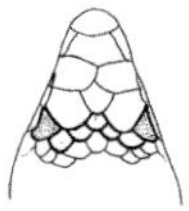

Hemiergis peronii peronii.
Lake Yeagerup, WA. S. Wilson

Hemiergis peronii tridactyla.
Kirup, WA. B. Maryan

Hemiergis quadrilineatum.
Balga, WA. S. Wilson

Hemiergis talbingoensis davisi.
Glen Innes, NSW. R. Valentic

Hemiergis talbingoensis talbingoensis.
Strathbogie Ranges, Vic. S. Wilson

Murray's Skink *Karma murrayi* SVL 108mm

Robust, with a **dusting of fine pale lateral dots**. Golden brown to coppery brown with many scattered to transversely aligned dark dorsal flecks, several large black lateral blotches between ear and forelimbs, and yellow and black mottled flanks with prominent, fine, white to bluish white dots. **Ventral surfaces pale yellow** between forelimbs and hindlimbs. ■ **NOTES** Subtropical RF and WSF from Barrington Tops, NSW to Conondale Ra., Qld. Often observed resting quietly in diffuse sunlight with head protruding from hollows in rotten logs and buttresses. ■ **SEE ALSO** *K. tryoni.*

Tryon's Skink *Karma tryoni* SVL 104mm

Robust, with **scattered light and dark scales on flanks**. Golden brown to coppery brown with dark transverse, often broken, dorsal bands continuous with a series of dark dorsolateral blotches, several large black lateral blotches between ear and forelimbs, and grey flanks marked with scattered black and white scales. **Ventral surfaces rich enamel yellow** between forelimbs and hindlimbs. ■ **NOTES** Restricted to upland subtropical RF of the McPherson Ra. bordering NSW and Qld. Often observed resting quietly in diffuse sunlight with head protruding from hollows in rotten logs and buttresses along walking trails. ■ **SEE ALSO** *K. murrayi.* ■ **STATUS** Vulnerable (Qld).

Genus *Lampropholis*

Eleven small spp. with 4 well-developed limbs, each with 5 digits, moveable lower eyelid enclosing a transparent disc, small ear-opening and fragile tail. Scales smooth; **parietals in contact, frontoparietals fused to form a single shield** and **nasals widely separated (fig.)**. ■ **NOTES** Widespread in moist areas of estn Aust. These skinks range from long-limbed, dorsally depressed

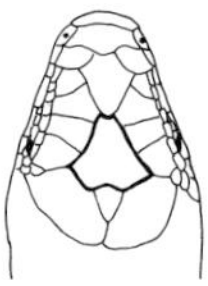

rock-inhabitants to short-limbed, long-bodied ground-dwellers. Included are the small, active, sun-loving brown skinks that frequent parks and suburban gardens of our main estn towns and cities. Egglayers, often depositing their clutches communally. They feed on small invertebrates. ■ **SEE ALSO** *Acritoscincus; Carinascincus; Harrisoniascincus; Pseudemoia; Saproscincus.*

Diamond-shielded Sunskink *Lampropholis adonis* SVL 50mm

Robust, with **interparietal scale fused with frontoparietals to form one shield**. Brown to reddish brown above. Flanks grey, delineated from dorsal colour by a narrow, ill-defined pale dorsolateral line. Brdg ♂ develops a prominent reddish flush on flanks and sides of tail, red reticulations beneath tail and blue on throat. ■ **NOTES** RF clearings and creek edges between Blackall Ra. and Proserpine, with an isolated pop. in shaded gorges of Carnarvon Ra.

Karma murrayi.
Lamington Plateau, Qld.
S. Wilson

Karma tryoni.
Lamington Plateau, Qld.
S. Wilson

Lampropholis adonis.
Yandina, Qld. S. Wilson

Friendly Sunskink *Lampropholis amicula* SVL 35mm

Weak-limbed, with only **5 supraciliary scales**. Copper brown above with dark dashes or peppering, and dark grey to black flanks contrasting with, and delineated from, dorsal colour by a fine pale dorsolateral line. ■ **NOTES** DSF, heaths and margins of vine thickets in ne. NSW and se. Qld, n. to the Burnett R. and inland to the Gt Div. Ra. Secretive, sheltering, basking and foraging among leaf litter and rarely venturing far from cover.

Montane Sunskink *Lampropholis caligula* SVL 54mm

Long-bodied, with **3 supraocular and 6 upper labial scales**. Shiny copper brown above, patternless or with obscure, longitudinally aligned dark dashes and scattered paler flecks. Narrow pale dorsolateral stripe usually present. Flanks dark grey to black, paler on lower flanks and sharply delineated from dorsal colour. ■ **NOTES** Cool highland swamps with a dominant ground cover of tussock grasses, sedges and snow gums at Barrington Tops.
■ **SEE ALSO** *L. delicata*; *L. guichenoti*.

Rainforest Sunskink *Lampropholis coggeri* SVL 45mm

Short-snouted, with drab pattern. Reddish brown above, flecked with cream spots and black dashes. Flanks grey to brown, flecked with paler spots and dark dashes, clearly delineated from brown back by ill-defined, narrow pale dorsolateral stripe, with **dark upper and pale lower lateral colours grading evenly**. Ventral surfaces densely spotted with black on body and sparsely spotted on tail. ■ **NOTES** RF clearings and edges in ne. Qld, from Cooktown area s. to Bluewater Ra. near Townsville.
■ **SEE ALSO** *L. delicata*; *L. robertsi*.

Bunya Mountains Sunskink *Lampropholis colossus* SVL 56mm

Reddish brown to olive brown with pale dorsolateral stripes and broken to entire black laterodorsal stripes. Upper flanks dark brown to black, sharply delineated from pale grey to brown lower flanks. Pale midlateral stripe complete, broken or absent. **Ventral surface bright yellow to cream** with black speckling beneath tail sometimes aligning to form broken lines. ■ **NOTES** Known only from Bunya Pine and RF associations at Bunya Mtns, se. Qld. ■ **SEE ALSO** *L. delicata*.
■ **STATUS** Near threatened (Qld).

Couper's Sunskink *Lampropholis couperi* SVL 49mm

Drably marked, with **extensive black ventral pigment**. Uniform brown above with narrow pale dorsolateral stripe clearly delineating back from grey flanks. Ventral surfaces grey with extensive black flecking, forming spots on chin and throat and reticulations beneath tail. ■ **NOTES** RF between Mt Nebo and Rockhampton. Most abundant along well-vegetated creek banks and RF clearings.

Lampropholis amicula.
Chaelundi SF, NSW. G. Swan

Lampropholis caligula.
Barrington Tops NP, NSW. B. Maryan

Lampropholis coggeri.
Thornton Peak, Qld. S. Wilson

Lampropholis colossus.
Bunya Mtns, Qld, S. Wilson

Lampropholis couperi.
Mt Nebo, Qld. S. Wilson

Garden Skink *Lampropholis delicata* SVL 51mm

Variable, with **7 supraciliary, 4 supraocular and 7 upper labial scales.** Brown, greyish brown to copper above, often with dark and pale flecks, dashes and streaks. May have narrow (often broken) pale dorsolateral line. Upper lateral zone dark brown to black. White midlateral stripe prominent to absent, but **upper and lower flanks normally clearly delineated** (at least in estn Qld). Ventral surfaces cream. ■ **NOTES** Widespread, from Cairns to sthn SA and ne. Tas. Cool temperate to tropical habitats including RF, WSF, DSF, woodlands, heaths and disturbed areas. Common garden lizard in Melbourne, Sydney and Brisbane. ■ **SEE ALSO** *L. caligula; L. coggeri; L. colossus; L. guichenoti; L. elongata.*

Elongate Sunskink *Lampropholis elongata* SVL 53mm

Long-bodied, with **short, widely spaced limbs** and **3 supraocular scales.** Shiny bronze brown above with very narrow dark laterodorsal and pale dorsolateral lines and broad dark brown upper lateral stripe. ■ **NOTES** Eucalypt woodland over tussock grasses on stony, granite and basalt soils at 1180–1455m altitude in vicinity of Grundy Fire Tower and 'The Flags' on Gt Div. Ra. ■ **SEE ALSO** *L. delicata; L. guichenoti.*

Grass Skink *Lampropholis guichenoti* SVL 48mm

Variable, with 5–7 (**usually 6**) **supraciliary scales, 4 supraocular and 7 upper labial scales.** Shades of brown to grey (copper on head) with dark flecks and pale scales, and a weak to prominent, ragged-edged, **dark vertebral stripe** from nape to base of tail. Flanks dark brown to black, edged obscurely above with a pale dorsolateral line, and usually more prominently with a pale midlateral stripe. ■ **NOTES** Forests, woodlands and disturbed areas from Kangaroo Is., SA to Cooloola, Qld. Common in Adelaide, Melbourne and Sydney. ■ **SEE ALSO** *L. caligula; L. delicata; L. elongata.*

Saxicoline Sunskink *Lampropholis mirabilis* SVL 50mm

Long-limbed, dorsally depressed, with prominent, distinctive pattern. Olive grey to copper brown, marked over back, flanks and limbs with dark blotches mixed with scattered white flecks or spots. Narrow pale dorsolateral stripe sometimes present. Top and sides of head and neck copper brown with little or no pattern. ■ **NOTES** Rock-inhabiting, foraging on and around boulders in thickets of hoop pine and pockets of RF. Restricted to Townsville district, including Magnetic Is. ■ **STATUS** Near threatened (Qld).

Lampropholis delicata. Noosa River, Qld. S. Wilson

Lampropholis elongata. Riamukka SF, NSW. G. Swan

Lampropholis guichenoti. Cooloola NP, Qld. S. Wilson

Lampropholis mirabilis. Mt Elliot, Qld. S. Wilson

Roberts' Sunskink *Lampropholis robertsi* SVL 49mm

Reddish brown to golden brown above, sometimes with black dashes, delineated from black to dark brown upper flanks by narrow pale dorsolateral stripe. May have pale brown midlateral stripe, often broken into spots, but **upper and lower flanks clearly delineated**. Ventral surfaces grey with black spots on chin and throat, reticulations under tail and black pigment edging scales. ■ **NOTES** Misty RF and boulderscapes on mtn tops from Thornton Peak s. to Mt Bartle Frere. ■ **SEE ALSO** *L. coggeri.*

Sliders Genus *Lerista*

Ninety-three small to medium elongate spp. with minute ear-openings and smooth scales. Eyelid moveable and enclosing a transparent disc or fused to form a fixed spectacle. Some have 4 well-developed limbs, each with 5 digits, but there is a progressive loss of limbs and digits, reaching its extreme with 2 completely limbless spp. Pattern usually includes stripes or series of dots or dashes. Identification can be difficult; some species are determined by number of limbs and digits, nature of lower eyelid (moveable or fused), colour and pattern, but others require microscopic examination of scale details. ■ **NOTES** Terrestrial burrowers endemic to Aust., thriving in dry conditions, particularly in the ne., centre and w. They range from relatively unspecialised inhabitants of leaf litter to superbly adapted, shovel-snouted sand-swimmers that leave meandering trails across desert dunes. Egglayers. Invertebrate feeders. ■ **SEE ALSO** *Hemiergis.*

Yellow-tailed Slider *Lerista aericeps* SVL 52mm

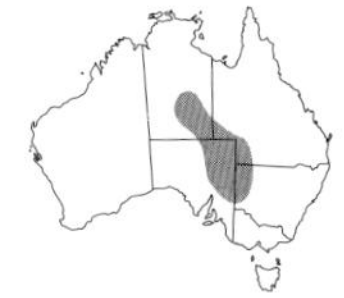

Slender, with **4 well-developed limbs, each with 4 digits. Lower eyelid fused.** Pale to dark reddish brown with 4 dorsal rows of dark spots, a dark streak between nostril and eye continuing as an upper lateral series of dark spots along body, fine dark edges and faint dark flecks on each scale, and a bright yellow to copper flush on tail. ■ **NOTES** Leaf litter under shrubs in sandy spinifex deserts. ■ **STATUS** Vulnerable (NSW – as *L. xanthura*).

Retro Slider *Lerista allanae* SVL 88mm

Moderately robust, with **no forelimb (usually represented by a depression) and 1 digit on hindlimb**. Lower eyelid moveable. Brown to greyish brown with a **dark spot on each dorsal and lateral scale** and dark-edged ventral scales, particularly under tail. ■ **NOTES** Restricted to road verges and other small areas with friable soils, amid pastoral land dominated by heavy soils in vicinity of Capella, Clermont and Logan Downs Stn in central Qld. ■ **SEE ALSO** *L. colliveri.* ■ **STATUS** Endangered (C'wealth; Qld); critically endangered (IUCN Red List).

Cape Range Slider *Lerista allochira* SVL 37mm

Two digits on forelimb and 3 digits on hindlimb. Lower eyelid fused. Dark olive brown with little pattern; a small dark spot on each scale and usually an obscure dark dorsolateral stripe on tail. ■ **NOTES** Dissected limestone gorges and plateaux on North West Cape, WA.

Lampropholis robertsi.
Mt Bartle Frere summit, Qld. S. Wilson

Lerista aericeps.
Milparinka area, NSW. P. Robertson

Lerista allanae.
Cleremont area, Qld. S. Wilson

Lerista allochira.
Vlaming Head, North West Cape, WA. B. Maryan

Limbless Fine-lined Slider *Lerista ameles* SVL 58mm

Slender and **completely limbless.** No trace of forelimbs; hindlimbs represented by depressions. Lower eyelid moveable. Silvery grey to brown with 6 darker longitudinal lines from nape to tail. ■ **NOTES** Recorded in soft soil under granite rocks on low weathered outcrops near Mt Surprise. ■ **STATUS** Vulnerable (Qld).

Fortescue Three-toed Slider *Lerista amicorum* SVL 49mm

Four well-developed limbs, each with 3 digits, 5 supraciliary scales, fused frontoparietal scales and **fused lower eyelid.** Grey above with dark-edged scale rows, narrow pale dorsolateral stripe, dark upper lateral stripe comprising dark pigment confined to scale sutures and **bright yellow tail.** ■ **NOTES** Alluvial flood plains of upper Fortescue River, between Weeli Wolli and Neds Creek Stn, WA. ■ **SEE ALSO** *L. jacksoni; L. muelleri; L. timida; L verhmens.*

Dampierland Limbless Slider *Lerista apoda* SVL 77mm

Very slender and **completely limbless. Minute eye, located under a transparent scale.** Snout flat, sharp and protrusive. Whitish with 4 dorsal lines of faint brown dots. Flanks and ventral surfaces dark brown, spotted with darker brown. ■ **NOTES** Dampier Land in semi-arid wstn Kimberley, from transition zone between coastal dunes and red sands supporting acacia thickets, to rock outcrops. Dwells in soft upper layers of sand beneath leaf litter.

Bight Slider *Lerista arenicola* SVL 66mm

Four well-developed limbs, each with 5 digits, and 4 supraocular scales. Lower eyelid moveable. **Pattern weak**; pale grey above with diffuse, ragged-edged, dark upper lateral stripe, white midlateral stripe and very narrow, diffuse, dark lower lateral stripe. Those in the far estn parts of range have narrow dark paravertebral and dorsal lines. ■ **NOTES** Shelters in leaf litter on pale coastal sands along the Gt Aust. Bight between Twilight Cove, WA, and lower w. coast of Eyre Pen., SA. ■ **SEE ALSO** *L. bougainvillii; L. microtis.* ■ **STATUS** Rare (SA).

Kalbarri Robust Slider *Lerista axillaris* SVL 87mm

Robust, with 2 **digits on forelimb and 3 digits on hindlimb.** Lower eyelid moveable. Pale greyish brown with dark brown flecks on back and tail and **narrow dark upper lateral stripe.** Ventral surfaces yellow. ■ **NOTES** Recorded under acacia litter and limestone rocks on brown sandy loam s. of Kalbarri and near Binnu on the lower mid-w. coast. ■ **SEE ALSO** *L. macropisthopus.*

Lerista ameles.
Mt Surprise, Qld. S. Zozaya

Lerista amicorum.
Roy Hill Station, WA. G. Harold

Lerista apoda.
Coconut Well area, WA. D. Knowles

Lerista arenicola.
Eyre Hwy, near WA/SA border, SA.
B. Maryan

Lerista axillaris.
Kalbarri district, WA. B. Maryan

Bayne's Slider *Lerista baynesi* SVL 91mm

Robust, with **forelimb reduced to a stump or bearing 1 digit, and 1–2 digits on hindlimb**. Lower eyelid moveable. Pale grey to yellowish brown with pattern weak to absent; 4 narrow dark dorsal lines or rows of dashes and a narrow, dark, ragged-edged upper lateral stripe, occasionally split into 2–3 separate lines. ■ **NOTES** Shelters in leaf litter on pale coastal sands along Gt Aust. Bight, from far w. of SA to Twilight Cove, WA, with an isolated pop. further w. on Bilbunya Dunes. ■ **STATUS** Rare (SA).

Western Two-toed Slider *Lerista bipes* SVL 62mm

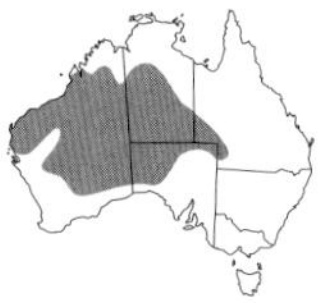

Slender, with flat protrusive snout, **no trace of forelimb; hindlimb with 2 digits**. Lower eyelid moveable. **Upper labial scales 5. Supraciliary scales present, 2 supraocular scales contacting frontal scale (fig.) and midbody scales in 18 rows**. Yellowish brown to reddish brown with 2 lines of dark

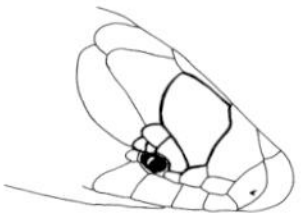

dashes along back and a broad dark brown upper lateral stripe. ■ **NOTES** Arid sandy areas, from nw. coast and offshore islands of WA to sw. Qld. Inhabits loose upper layers of sand under leaf litter. ■ **SEE ALSO** *L. greeri; L. labialis; L. simillima.*

Northern Slider *Lerista borealis* SVL 57mm

Two digits on forelimb and 3 digits on hindlimb. Lower eyelid moveable. **Last of 5 supraciliary scales is large**. Greyish brown to reddish brown with obscure dark brown dots and flecks. ■ **NOTES** Sandy areas, particularly adjacent to rocky hills and outcrops, from Kimberley region of WA to adjacent areas of NT. ■ **SEE ALSO** *L. walkeri.*

Bougainville's Slider *Lerista bougainvillii* SVL 70mm

Four well-developed limbs, each with 5 digits, and 3 supraocular scales. Lower eyelid moveable. **Pattern prominent**. Silvery grey to pale brown, often flushed with yellow or red on tail, usually with 4 lines of dark dashes along back and a broad black lateral stripe. ■ **NOTES** Se. mainland and ne. Tas. Retains strongest limb development and penetrates cool temperate zones more effectively than other *Lerista*. ■ **SEE ALSO** *L. arenicola; L. microtis.*

Bungle Bungle Robust Slider *Lerista bunglebungle* SVL 67mm

Moderately robust, with **2 digits on forelimb and 3 digits on hindlimb**. Lower eyelid moveable. Pale brown with 6 lines of dark brown dots and a dark upper lateral stripe. ■ **NOTES** Known only from Purnululu NP (Bungle Bungles) in semi-arid se. Kimberley region, WA.

Lerista baynesi.
Madura, WA.
R. Browne-Cooper

Lerista bipes.
Bullara Stn, WA. S. Wilson

Lerista borealis.
Bindoola River, WA. S. Wilson

Lerista bougainvillii.
Telowie Gorge, SA. S. Wilson

Lerista bunglebungle
Purnululu NP, WA. R. Lloyd

Carpentarian Slider *Lerista carpentariae* SVL 69mm

Slender, with **forelimb absent, hindlimb reduced to a stump or with 1 digit, midbody scales in 16 rows** and **1 loreal scale**. Lower eyelid moveable. Cream to pale brown with narrow dark paravertebral lines, sometimes an indication of narrow broken dorsal lines, and a broad dark brown lateral stripe. ■ **NOTES** Sandy soils on Groote Eylandt and Sir Edward Pellew Is. in wstn Gulf of Carpentaria, NT. ■ **SEE ALSO** *L. karlschmidti; L. stylis.*

Lyre-patterned Slider *Lerista chordae* SVL 45mm

Four well-developed limbs, each with 4 digits. Lower eyelid moveable. Greyish brown to bronze with 4 lines of dark dorsal dashes, and a dark brown upper lateral stripe from snout to tail-base. Tail bright red on juv.; pale orange-yellow on adults. ■ **NOTES** Woodlands with spinifex and other tussock grasses on sandy soils in vicinity of Torrens Creek in ne. interior.

Bold-striped Four-toed Slider *Lerista christinae* SVL 39mm

Four well-developed limbs, each with 4 digits. Lower eyelid fused. Silvery grey to almost white flushed with pink on tail, with **6 prominent, sharp-edged black stripes**: paravertebrals, upper laterals and lower laterals. ■ **NOTES** Complex heaths and banksia woodlands on pale sand-plains along lower w. coast, between Eneabba and Ellenbrook and including Rottnest Is.

Vine-thicket Fine-lined Slider *Lerista cinerea* SVL 71mm

Very slender. Appears virtually limbless; **no trace of forelimb, 1 digit on minute hind limb; 1 loreal scale**; prefrontal scale present or absent; lower eyelid moveable. Grey to silvery brown with 6 narrow lines of dark dashes but **no dark lateral stripe**. Tail flushed with red on juv. ■ **NOTES** Charters Towers region, on division of Suttor and Lower Burdekin R. drainage sub-basins. Recorded under rocks, logs and soil in vine thickets. ■ **SEE ALSO** *L. hobsoni; L. rochfordensis; L. storri.* ■ **STATUS** Vulnerable (Qld).

Sharp-blazed Three-toed Slider *Lerista clara* SVL 49mm

Four well-developed limbs, each with 3 digits, 5 supraciliary scales, paired frontoparietal scales and **fused lower eyelid.** Pale brown to grey above with pale dorsolateral stripe prominent (brown-backed individuals) to diffuse (grey-backed), prominent **straight-edged dark upper lateral stripe** and **immaculate pearly white lower lateral and ventral surfaces.** ■ **NOTES** Coast and hinterland of nw. WA incl. many Pilbara islands.

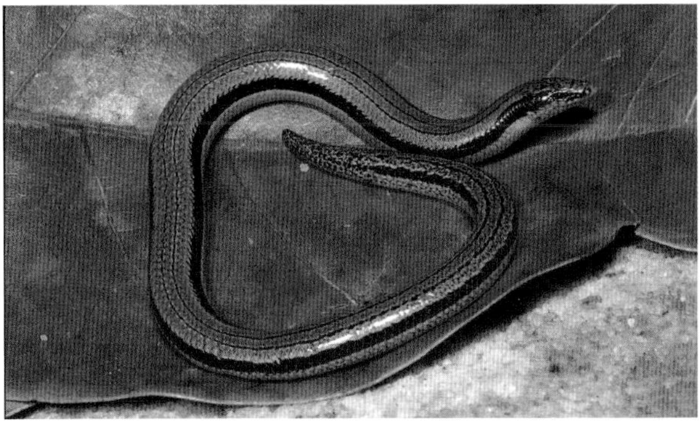

Lerista carpentariae.
Alyangula, Groote Eylandt, NT.
R Valentic

Lerista chordae.
Woura Park Stn, Qld. E. Vanderduys

Lerista christinae.
Ellenbrook, WA. R. Browne-Cooper

Lerista cinerea.
Warrawee Stn, Qld. S. Wilson

Lerista clara.
Gascoyne region, WA. D. Robinson

Colliver's Slider *Lerista colliveri* SVL 84mm

Moderately robust, **with forelimb reduced to a minute stump and 1 digit on hindlimb**. Lower eyelid moveable. Tan, **each scale with a dark streak** forming a series of dorsal and lateral lines, breaking into dark-edged scales on lower flanks. ■ **NOTES** Open woodlands and rock outcrops from just w. of Townsville to Hughenden area. ■ **SEE ALSO** *L. allanae.*

Blinking Broad-striped Slider *Lerista connivens* SVL 85mm

Moderately robust, with **no forelimb (represented by a groove) and 2 digits on hindlimb. Lower eyelid moveable. Midbody scales usually in 22 rows.** Pale greyish brown to almost white with broad vertebral stripe composed of a dark zone and 2 rows of dark spots, a dark upper lateral stripe and bright yellow lower lateral and ventral surfaces. ■ **NOTES** Shrublands on sands and red loams. Shelters in loose upper layers of sand beneath leaf litter. ■ **SEE ALSO** *L. varia.*

Great Desert Slider *Lerista desertorum* SVL 93mm

Robust, with **2 digits on forelimb and 3 digits on hindlimb**. Lower eyelid moveable. Pale reddish brown to yellowish brown with 2 thin dark paravertebral lines or rows of spots, a broad dark upper lateral stripe and yellow ventral surfaces. ■ **NOTES** Shrublands, sheltering in loose sand under thick leaf litter.

South-western Four-toed Slider *Lerista distinguenda* SVL 46mm

Four well-developed limbs, each with 4 digits. Lower eyelid fused. Midbody scales usually in 18 rows. Nasal scales separated. Grey to silvery brown with 2–4 longitudinal lines of dark dorsal dots, a black upper lateral stripe, white midlateral stripe and red flush on tail. ■ **NOTES** Various habitats in sw. WA and Eyre Pen., SA. Shelters under rocks, logs and leaf litter; often found in abandoned stick-ant nests. ■ **SEE ALSO** *L. elegans.* ■ **STATUS** Rare (SA).

Southern Four-toed Slider *Lerista dorsalis* SVL 71mm

Four well-developed limbs, each with 4 digits. Lower eyelid moveable. Pale olive grey with back patternless or with 2-4 narrow black stripes or rows of dashes and a broad, sharp-edged black upper lateral stripe, often edged with white. Distinctive nthn pop. in SA has prominently striped body and vivid red tail. ■ **NOTES** Shrublands and open woodlands under rocks, logs and leaf litter.

Myall Slider *Lerista edwardsae* SVL 95mm

Robust, with **forelimb reduced to a minute stump set in a groove, and hindlimb with 2 digits**. Lower eyelid moveable. Pale brownish grey to silver with narrow dark paravertebral lines from nape to tail-tip, broken dorsal lines usually from hips onto tail, a broad dark upper lateral stripe and yellow lower flanks and ventral surfaces. ■ **NOTES** Semi-arid woodlands, particularly mallee, on sandy soils. Shelters in loose sand under leaf litter.

Lerista colliveri.
Great Basalt Wall, Qld. G. Harold

Lerista connivens.
Carbla Stn, WA. R. Browne-Cooper

Lerista desertorum.
Alice Springs, NT. S. Wilson

Lerista distinguenda.
Kardadup, WA. R. Browne-Cooper

Lerista dorsalis. Southern pop.
Eyre Hwy, near WA/SA border, SA. B. Maryan

Lerista dorsalis. Southern pop.
Laura Bay, SA. R. Valentic

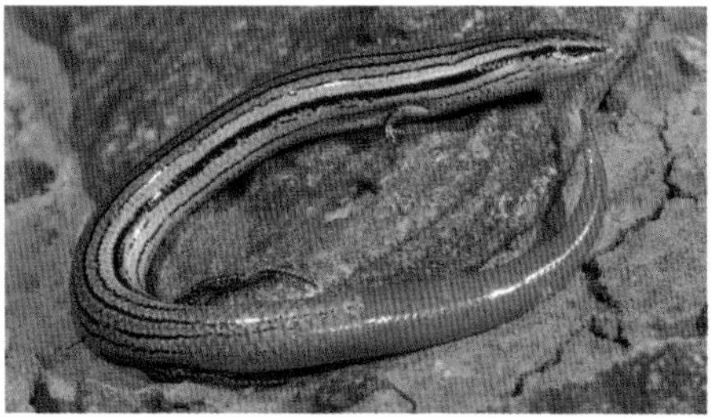

Lerista dorsalis. Northern pop.
Lake Torrens area, SA. B. Schembri

Lerista edwardsae.
Ceduna, SA. S. Wilson

Elegant Slider *Lerista elegans* SVL 43mm

Four well-developed limbs, each with 4 digits. Lower eyelid fused. Midbody scales in 16 rows. Nasal scales in contact. Grey to brown with 2 series of dark dorsal dashes, black upper lateral stripe, white midlateral stripe and often a red flush on tail, particularly on juv. ■ **NOTES** Sandy coastal plains from Monte Bello Is. s. to Augusta. Shelters under rocks, logs and leaf litter. ■ **SEE ALSO** *L. distinguenda.*

Woomera Slider *Lerista elongata* SVL 60mm

Four well-developed limbs, each with 3 digits. Lower eyelid moveable. Pale reddish brown to greyish brown with 4 (occasionally 2) dorsal rows of dark dots and a **broad, sharp-edged dark upper lateral stripe.** ■ **NOTES** Arid interior of SA. Shelters in leaf litter at base of low vegtn. ■ **SEE ALSO** *L. terdigitata.*

Noonbah Robust Slider *Lerista emmotti* SVL 103mm

Four short limbs, each with 2 digits. Lower eyelid moveable. Fawn to brown, each scale with a dark streak aligning to form rows of dark spots. ■ **NOTES** Arid eastern interior, from about Muttaburra in central Qld s. to nw. NSW to adjacent SA. Shelters under leaf litter at bases of trees and shrubs. ■ **SEE ALSO** *L. punctatovittata.*

Meekatharra Slider *Lerista eupoda* SVL 87mm

Two digits on very short forelimb and 3 digits on hindlimb. Lower eyelid moveable. Pale brown with broad, sharp-edged dark vertebral and upper lateral stripes. ■ **NOTES** Open mulga areas on loamy soils in the arid sthn interior of WA, between about Meekatharra and Cue. ■ **SEE ALSO** *L. gerrardii.*

Pilbara Flame-tailed Slider *Lerista flammicauda* SVL 56mm

Four well-developed limbs, each with 4 digits. Lower eyelid moveable. Brown with prominent dark upper lateral stripe. **Tail orange-red,** dotted with dark brown. ■ **NOTES** Hamersley and Barlee Ranges in the arid Pilbara region. Shelters under spinifex and leaf litter near stony watercourses. ■ **SEE ALSO** *L. zietzi.*

Eastern Mulch-slider *Lerista fragilis* SVL 60mm

Four well-developed limbs, each with 3 digits. Lower eyelid moveable. Olive brown to greyish brown with 4 narrow lines of dark dorsal dashes and a narrow dark upper lateral stripe. Tail often flushed with red, particularly on juv. ■ **NOTES** Dry to semi-arid estn interior, usually on sandy soils supporting DSF, woodlands or shrublands. Shelters in soil under rocks, logs and leaf litter.

Lerista elegans.
Balga, WA. S. Wilson

Lerista elongata.
Coober Pedy, SA. C. de Jong

Lerista emmotti.
Noonbah Stn, Qld. S. Wilson

Lerista eupoda.
Cue district, WA. B. Maryan

Lerista flammicauda.
Pannawonica, WA. G. Harold

Lerista fragilis.
Denham Park Stn, Qld. S. Wilson

Centralian Four-toed Slider *Lerista frosti* SVL 60mm

Four well-developed limbs, each with 4 digits. Lower eyelid moveable. Olive grey to olive brown with 2–4 dorsal lines of faint dots or dashes and a narrow dark upper lateral stripe, sharp-edged and sometimes with a pale margin above, and ragged or diffuse below. ■ **NOTES** Sandy flat areas associated with rocky ranges. Shelters in soil under rocks and leaf litter.

Gascoyne Broad-striped Slider *Lerista gascoynensis* SVL 70mm

No forelimb (represented by a groove; sometimes a minute stump) and hindlimb with 2 digits. Lower eyelid fused. Supraciliary scales 3. Brownish white with dark **narrow vertebral stripe** enclosing 2 rows of small dark dots, and a broad dark upper lateral stripe. Lower flanks and ventral surfaces yellow. ■ **NOTES** Gascoyne R. valley n. to Kennedy Ra. Lives under leaf litter in acacia shrublands. ■ **SEE ALSO** *L. nichollsi; L. petersoni.*

Bold-striped Robust Slider *Lerista gerrardii* SVL 87mm

One digit on very short forelimb and 2 digits on hindlimb. Lower eyelid moveable. Pale yellowish brown merging to bluish grey on tail, with straight-edged dark vertebral and upper lateral stripes. ■ **NOTES** Woodlands and shrublands in arid and semi-arid sw. interior, reaching the coast near Geraldton. Shelters under leaf litter. ■ **SEE ALSO** *L. eupoda.*

South-eastern Kimberley Sand-slider *Lerista greeri* SVL 62mm

Slender, with flat protrusive snout, **no trace of forelimb and 2 digits on hindlimb. Lower eyelid moveable. Preocular scale present. Upper labial scales 6. Supraciliary scales present, 2 supraocular scales contacting frontal scale, and midbody scales in 20 rows.** Pale brown to reddish brown with 2 paravertebral rows of dark dots or narrow lines, and broad dark upper lateral stripe. ■ **NOTES** Semi-arid s. and e. Kimberley, WA and presumably adjacent NT. ■ **SEE ALSO** *L. bipes; L. labialis; L. griffini; L. simillima.*

Stout Sand-slider *Lerista griffini* SVL 67mm

Moderately robust, with **flat protrusive snout, no trace of forelimb and 2 digits on hindlimb. Lower eyelid moveable. No preocular scale.** Brown to reddish brown with 2 paravertebral rows of small dark dashes, sometimes an indication of broken dark dorsal lines, and broad dark upper lateral stripe. ■ **NOTES** Sandy areas in Dampier Land in w. Kimberley, e. Kimberley and adjacent NT, and mid-nthn Barkly Tableland. ■ **SEE ALSO** *L. greeri.*

Gnaraloo Three-toed Slider *Lerista haroldi* SVL 40mm

Four well-developed limbs, each with 3 digits, 4 supraciliary scales, paired frontoparietal scales and **fused lower eyelid**. Yellowish brown with **little pattern**; dark brown speckling and dark streak from nostril to eye. ■ **NOTES** Arid upper w. coast, between Cape Cuvier and Gnaraloo.

Lerista frosti.
Alice Springs, NT. G. Harold

Lerista gascoynensis.
Dairy Creek, Gascoyne region, WA.
R. Browne-Cooper

Lerista gerrardii.
Ninghan Stn, WA. S. Wilson

Lerista greeri.
Derby, WA. G. Harold

Lerista griffini.
Kununurra, WA. S. Wilson

Lerista haroldi.
Gnaraloo Stn, WA. G. Harold

Hobson's Fine-lined Slider *Lerista hobsoni* SVL 68mm

Very slender. Appears virtually limbless; **no trace of forelimb, 1 digit on minute hind limb; 2 loreal scales**; prefrontal scale present; lower eyelid moveable. Silvery-grey with 6 narrow lines of dark dashes but **no dark lateral stripe.** ■ **NOTES** Recorded under surface debris and leaf litter in open forests of Upper Burdekin R. Drainage Basin. ■ **SEE ALSO** *L. cinerea; L. storri.*

Humphries Worm-slider *Lerista humphriesi* SVL 64mm

Slender, with flat protrusive snout, **no trace of forelimb, hindlimb reduced to minute stump, moveable lower eyelid, 2 loreal scales** and **1 supraciliary scale**. Pale brownish grey with paravertebral lines of dark dashes, fainter and more broken laterodorsal lines and a broad dark brown upper lateral stripe. Head flushed with orange and tail with greyish white. ■ **NOTES** Acacia shrub-lands on sand-plains of semi-arid mid-w. coast, between Shark Bay and Murchison R. Shelters under embedded stumps and in loose sand under leaf litter. ■ **SEE ALSO** *L. praepedita.*

McIvor River Slider *Lerista ingrami* SVL 36mm

Four well-developed limbs, each with 4 digits. Lower eyelid fused. Pale greyish brown with 4 dorsal rows of fine black dots, a prominent dark brown upper lateral stripe with sharp upper and lower edges, and a pale to bright orange tail. ■ **NOTES** White coastal sands, including first coastal dunes, on se. Cape York Pen. near the mouth of the McIvor R. Shelters in loose soft sand under debris. ■ **STATUS** Vulnerable (Qld).

Robust Worm-slider *Lerista ips* SVL 72mm

Robust, with **flat protrusive snout, no trace of forelimb and 2 digits on hindlimb. Lower eyelid moveable**. Pinkish brown and virtually patternless; faint dark flecks. ■ **NOTES** Red sand-ridges with spinifex of the Gt Sandy and Gibson Deserts from WA to sw. NT. Shelters in loose sand under spinifex and leaf litter, and forages in exposed areas, leaving meandering tracks on dune crests.

Jackson's Three-toed Slider *Lerista jacksoni* SVL 43mm

Four well-developed limbs, each with 3 digits, 4 supraciliary scales, paired frontoparietal scales and **fused lower eyelid**. Dusky grey with little pattern; sometimes weak lines of dorsal spots and an indistinct upper lateral stripe reduced to a series of spots. ■ **NOTES** Pilbara Plateau and adjacent coast, WA. ■ **SEE ALSO** *L. amicorum; L. muelleri; L. timida; L verhmens.*

Kalumburu Kimberley Slider *Lerista kalumburu* SVL 60mm

One digit on very short forelimb and 3 digits on hindlimb. Lower eyelid moveable. Brown with a darker central spot in each scale, tending to form obscure lines on flanks. ■ **NOTES** Nthn Kimberley, from Napier Broome Bay s. to Carson Escarpment. Shelters in loose soil under rocks, logs and leaf litter.

Lerista hobsoni.
Myola Stn, Qld. S. Wilson

Lerista humphriesi.
Zuytdorp Cliffs, WA. B. Maryan

Lerista ingrami.
Cape Flattery, Qld. S. Wilson

Lerista ips.
Little Sandy Desert, WA. B. Maryan

Lerista jacksoni.
Pt Hedland area, WA. G. Harold

Lerista kalumburu.
Theda Stn, WA. H. Cook

Karl Schmidt's Slider *Lerista karlschmidti* SVL 70mm

Slender, with **no forelimbs, hindlimb reduced to small stump, 16 midbody scale rows** and **2 loreal scales**. Lower eyelid moveable. Olive brown to greyish brown with narrow dashes through each scale forming a series of thin dark lines along body and tail. ■ **NOTES** Open flat sandy areas in ne. NT. Also recorded near Townsville in ne. Qld. Shelters in loose sand under logs and leaf litter. ■ **SEE ALSO** *L. carpentariae; L. stylis.*

Shark Bay Broad-striped Slider *Lerista kendricki* SVL 67mm

Slender, with **no forelimb (represented by a groove or pit and sometimes a minute stump)** and **2 digits on hindlimb. Lower eyelid fused**. Pale grey, fawn or brown with a **broad dark vertebral stripe continuous with dark head** and enclosing 4 series of dark dots on back, and a **narrow dark upper lateral stripe**. ■ **NOTES** Semi-arid mid-w. coast, from base of Peron Pen. to s. of the mouth of Murchison R. Shelters under leaf litter at bases of shrubs on white to reddish sands. ■ **SEE ALSO** *L. yuna.*

Kennedy Range Broad-striped Slider *Lerista kennedyensis* SVL 58mm

Slender, with **prominent ventrolateral keel on anterior body, forelimb represented by a small stump arising from a groove, and 2 digits on hindlimb**. Lower eyelid fused. Pale orange-brown with paravertebral series of dark dots and a narrow, diffuse, dark upper lateral stripe. ■ **NOTES** Red sand-ridges vegetated with acacia, banksia and spinifex atop the Kennedy Ra.

King's Three-toed Slider *Lerista kingi* SVL 46mm

Four well-developed limbs, each with 3 digits, 5 supraciliary scales, paired frontoparietal scales and **fused lower eyelid**. Usually brown above, sometimes olive to grey, with paravertebral and dorsal rows of dark spots or streaks, sometimes coalesced to form narrow lines, weakly to moderately strong pale dorsolateral stripe, and narrow dark upper lateral stripe with continuous upper edge and deeply scalloped lower edge as dark pigment becomes restricted to scale sutures. ■ **NOTES** Heath and woodland communities in sw. interior. ■ **SEE ALSO** *L. timida.*

Eastern Two-toed Slider *Lerista labialis* SVL 60mm

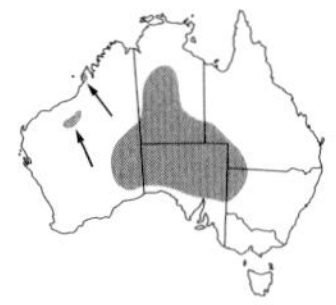

Slender, with flat protrusive snout, **no trace of forelimb; hindlimb with 2 digits**. Lower eyelid moveable. **Upper labial scales usually 6. No supraciliary scales. Only 1 supraocular scale contacts frontal scale (fig.). Midbody scales in 18–20 rows**. Pale brown to reddish brown with a paravertebral series of small dark dots and a dark upper lateral stripe. ■ **NOTES** Shelters in loose upper layers of sand under leaf litter across vast tracts of sandy deserts. ■ **SEE ALSO** *L. bipes; L. greeri; L. simillima.*

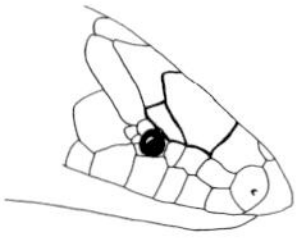

Lerista karlschmidti. Opium Creek Stn, NT. B. Maryan

Lerista kendricki. Shark Bay, WA. S. Wilson

Lerista kennedyensis. Kennedy Range, WA. D. Knowles

Lerista labialis. Yulara, NT. S. Wilson

Lerista kingi. Karara Nature Reserve, WA. S. Wilson

Perth Lined Slider *Lerista lineata* SVL 55mm

Slender, with **2 digits on forelimb and 3 digits on hindlimb**. Lower eyelid fused. Pale brownish grey with prominent black paravertebral lines, a broad black upper lateral stripe and narrow pale midlateral stripe. ■ **NOTES** Sandy coastal heath and shrubland on lower w. coast between Perth and Leschenault Peninsula and incl. Rottnest Is., with an isolated pop. on the mid-w. coast at Woodleigh Stn and another apparent isolate at Busselton in the sw.

Line-spotted Robust Slider *Lerista lineopunctulata* SVL 103mm

Variable, with **moveable lower eyelid** and **5 supraciliary scales**. Subject to geographic variation. Sthn form: **forelimb represented by a stump**, and **2 digits on hindlimb**; pale greyish brown to grey, with 6 or more series of dots or dashes forming narrow broken lines. Nthn form: **forelimb absent, represented by a groove**, and **1 digit on hindlimb**; pale yellowish brown with little pattern; obscure dark margins to scales, dark bars on upper lip and dark flush on head. The 2 forms merge at about Shark Bay. ■ **NOTES** Coastal dunes and sand-plains on w. coast, from Leschenault Peninsula to North West Cape, dwelling in soft upper layers of loose sand beneath leaf litter at bases of coastal shrubs. ■ **SEE ALSO** *L. varia.*

Unpatterned Robust Slider *Lerista macropisthopus* SVL 96mm

Variable, with usually **2 digits on forelimb and 3 on hindlimb, moveable lower eyelid** and weak pattern. ■ **SSP.** *L. m. macropisthopus* is greyish brown to pink without pattern. *L. m. fusciceps* has dark flush on head. *L. m. galea* has **1 digit (occasionally 2) on forelimb and 2 on hindlimb**, and often a narrow, diffuse dark lateral stripe. *L. m. remota* is pale brown with heavy dark stippling on head and rows of dark dots on back and flanks. ■ **NOTES** Acacia shrublands and woodlands in semi-arid to arid sthn WA; in sw. interior (*L. m. macropisthopus*); mid-w. coast and interior (*L. m. fusciceps*); lower Murchison region (*L. m. galea*); and central interior (*L. m. remota*). All forms shelter in loose soil under leaf litter at bases of shrubs. ■ **SEE ALSO** *L. axillaris.*

Micro Three-toed Slider *Lerista micra* SVL 46mm

Four well-developed limbs, each with 3 digits, 4 supraciliary scales, paired frontoparietal scales and **fused lower eyelid**. Usually brown above, sometimes olive to grey, with prominent to obscure paravertebral and sometimes dorsal series of dark spots, little or no pale dorsolateral stripe, and narrow ragged upper lateral stripe composed of dark pigment centred around scale sutures. ■ **NOTES** Upper w. coast and hinterland of WA, from Murchison R. n. to Gnaraloo. ■ **SEE ALSO** *L. rolfei; L. occulta.*

Lerista lineata.
Jandakot, WA. S. Wilson

Lerista lineopunctulata. Northern form.
Tamala Stn, WA. S. Wilson

Lerista lineopunctulata. Southern form.
Port Denison, WA. B. Maryan

Lerista macropisthopus fusciceps.
North West Cape, WA. S. Wilson

Lerista macropisthopus galea.
Galena, WA. S. Wilson

Lerista macropisthopus macropisthopus.
Kellerberrin, WA. B. Maryan

Lerista macropisthopus remota.
Little Sandy Desert, WA. B. Maryan

Lerista micra.
Carbla Station area, WA. B. Maryan

South Coast Five-toed Slider *Lerista microtis* SVL 52–60mm

Four well-developed limbs, each with 5 digits, and 4 supraocular scales. Lower eyelid moveable. **Pattern prominent, at least on flanks.** ■ **SSP.** *L. m. microtis* is dark olive grey to brown above, with or without dark flecks; narrow black laterodorsal stripe; pale dorsolateral stripe; broad prominent sharp-edged black upper lateral stripe; white midlateral stripe; black lower lateral stripe; and greyish white ventrolateral stripe. *L. m. intermedia* (SVL 57mm) is paler, with dark dorsal spots tending to align into 3 stripes, and narrower dark upper lateral stripe. *L. m. schwaneri* (SVL 60mm) resembles *L. m. intermedia* but with more midbody scale rows (22–24 vs usually 20). ■ **NOTES** Coastal heaths and WSF margins along lower w. coast and sw. of WA e. to Bremer Bay (*L. m. microtis*); s. coast of WA between East Mt Barren and Israelite Bay (*L. m. intermedia*); and w. coast of SA (*L. m. schwaneri*). All forms shelter in soil under logs, rocks and leaf litter. In WA disused stick-ant nests are often used. ■ **SEE ALSO** *L. arenicola; L. bougainvillii.* ■ **STATUS** *L. m. schwaneri* is rare (SA).

Mueller's Three-toed Slider *Lerista muelleri* SVL 50mm

Four well-developed limbs, each with 3 digits, 3 supraciliary scales (2nd fused with 1st supraocular scale), paired frontoparietal scales and **fused lower eyelid.** Brown to olive above with little pattern; usually no paravertebral and dorsal lines of spots, no pale dorsolateral stripe, and a broad, diffuse dark lateral stripe composed of dark blotches on anterior portions of each scale. ■ **NOTES** Pilbara Plateau and nearby rocky outliers, n. to Pt Hedland area, WA. ■ **SEE ALSO** *L. amicorum; L. jacksoni; L. timida; L. verhmens.*

Pilbara Robust Slider *Lerista neander* SVL 88mm

Four short limbs, each with 2 digits. Lower eyelid moveable. Greyish brown with 8–10 rows of dark brown spots. ■ **NOTES** Arid wstn interior of WA, in e. Hamersley and Ophthalmia Ranges. Shelters in loose soil under leaf litter and spinifex.

Nevin's Three-toed Slider *Lerista nevinae* SVL 41mm

Four well-developed limbs, each with 3 digits, 4 supraciliary scales, paired frontoparietal scales and **fused lower eyelid.** Very pale brown to almost white above with prominent black paravertebral and upper lateral stripes. ■ **NOTES** Coastal dunes vegetated with *Acacia* and low shrubs between Point Sampson and Cape Lambert, nw. WA. ■ **STATUS** Vulnerable (WA).

Lerista microtis intermedia.
Quagi Beach, WA. R. Browne-Cooper

Lerista microtis microtis.
Albany district, WA. S. Wilson

Lerista microtis schwaneri.
Wedge Island, SA. T. Peters

Lerista muelleri.
Cherrata Station, WA. G. Harold

Lerista neander.
Savory Creek, WA. B. Maryan

Lerista nevinae.
Wickham area, WA. G. Harold

Inland Broad-striped Slider *Lerista nichollsi* SVL 68mm

No forelimb (represented by a groove or pit and sometimes a minute stump); hindlimb with 2 digits. Lower eyelid fused. Supraciliary scales 4. Pale grey to almost white with prominent pale to dark brown vertebral stripe enclosing 2 rows of dark dots, and a broad black upper lateral stripe. Lower flanks and ventral surfaces yellow. ■ **NOTES** Acacia shrublands in arid lower mid-wstn interior. Shelters in loose soil under leaf litter at bases of shrubs. ■ **SEE ALSO** *L. gascoynensis.*

Hidden Three-toed Slider *Lerista occulta* SVL 39mm

Four well-developed limbs, each with 3 digits, 5 supraciliary scales, paired frontoparietal scales and **fused lower eyelid**. Dark purplish brown with prominent to obscure paravertebral and dorsal lines of dark spots, little or no pale dorsolateral stripe, dark upper lateral stripe with upper edge solid or comprising a series of blotches and lower edge fragmented with pigment centred around scale edges, and freckled lower flanks and ventral surfaces. ■ **NOTES** Wstn interior of WA in vicinity of Gascoyne Junction and flats along wstn face of Kennedy Range. ■ **SEE ALSO** *L. micra; L. rolfei.*

Onslow Broad-striped Slider *Lerista onsloviana* SVL 70mm

No forelimb (represented by a groove), 2 digits on hindlimb. Lower eyelid fused. Supraciliary scales 2. Brownish white with a narrow, sharp-edged dark vertebral stripe composed of paravertebral series of dark dashes enclosing a brown zone, and a dark upper lateral stripe with straight upper and ragged lower edges. ■ **NOTES** Red sands, loams and white coastal dunes on nw. coastal plains from Onslow to Giralia and Barradale. Shelters under leaf litter at bases of shrubs.

North-eastern Slider *Lerista orientalis* SVL 49mm

Four well-developed limbs, each with 4 digits. Lower eyelid fused. Brownish grey to copper brown with 4 longitudinal rows of dots (1 per scale) from nape to tail and a broad **dark upper lateral stripe with sharp upper and diffuse lower edges**. Tail often flushed with red. ■ **NOTES** Shrublands and woodlands on heavy stony soils. Often associated with leaf litter near water-courses. ■ **SEE ALSO** *L. zonulata.*

Pale Broad-striped Slider *Lerista petersoni* SVL 70mm

No forelimb (represented by a groove or pit and sometimes a minute stump); hindlimb with 2 digits. Lower eyelid fused. Supraciliary scales 4. Pale grey to almost white with **broad diffuse dark vertebral stripe** composed of 2–4 series of spots, and a **broad dark upper lateral stripe**. Lower lateral and sometimes ventral surfaces yellow. ■ **NOTES** Arid mid-w. and adjacent interior of WA. Normally associated with leaf litter under acacias on heavy loams and stony soils, though sometimes occurring on slopes of red dunes. ■ **SEE ALSO** *L. gascoynensis.*

Lerista nichollsi.
Yalgoo district, WA. B. Maryan

Lerista occulta.
Kennedy Range, WA. G. Harold

Lerista onsloviana.
Onslow district, WA. B. Maryan

Lerista orientalis.
Gordon Downs, WA. D. Robinson

Lerista petersoni.
Bullara Stn, WA. S. Wilson

Southern Robust Slider *Lerista picturata* SVL 92mm

Forelimb bearing 1–2 digits or reduced to stump and hindlimb with 1–2 digits. Lower eyelid moveable. Pale grey to yellowish brown with 4 narrow dark dorsal lines, a broad dark brown upper lateral stripe, and pale yellow lower flanks and ventral surfaces. ■ **NOTES** Woodlands such as mallee communities on sandy loams in semi-arid sthn interior of WA. Shelters in soft sand under leaf litter at bases of shrubs.

Keeled Slider *Lerista planiventralis* SVL 72mm

Flat, wedge-shaped snout, **2 digits on forelimb, 3 digits on hindlimb, moveable lower eyelid** and distinctive **ventrolateral keel along body.** ■ **SSP.** *L. p. planiventralis* has 22–24 midbody scale rows. Pale grey to coppery brown (varying according to substrate colour) with 4 narrow dark dorsal lines and a dark upper lateral stripe. *L. p. decora* has 20 midbody scale rows and broader, more prominent upper lateral stripe. *L. p. maryani* has only 17–18 midbody scale rows and a narrow diffuse upper lateral stripe. ■ **NOTES** Sandy areas on w. coast; mid-w. coast from North West Cape s. to Shark Bay (*L. p. planiventralis*); lower w. coast from Peron Pen. s. to Badgingarra (*L. p. decora*); and nw. coast between Onslow and Barradale (*L. p. maryani*). All forms forage by day in exposed sandy areas, leaving many meandering tracks.

Yampi Sand-slider *Lerista praefrontalis* SVL 67mm

Slender, with flat protrusive snout, **no trace of forelimb, hindlimb with 2 digits** and **2 prefrontal scales on each side**. Lower eyelid moveable. Pale reddish brown with 2 rows of dark brown dashes and a broad dark lateral stripe. ■ **NOTES** Status uncertain. Known from a single specimen uncovered in litter among sand at base of a cliff on King Hall Is. in Yampi Sound, nw. Kimberley. No live image available. ■ **STATUS** Vulnerable (WA).

West Coast Worm-slider *Lerista praepedita* SVL 65mm

Slender, with flat protrusive snout, **no trace of forelimb, hindlimb reduced to minute stump, moveable lower eyelid, 1 loreal scale** and **no supraciliary scales.** Very pale brownish grey with narrow broken paravertebral lines of dark dashes and a dark upper lateral stripe. Tail flushed with grey. ■ **NOTES** Mid- to lower w. coast from North West Cape s. to Mandurah. Dwells in loose sand under leaf litter, rocks and embedded stumps. ■ **SEE ALSO** *L. humphriesi.*

Eastern Robust Slider *Lerista punctatovittata* SVL 100mm

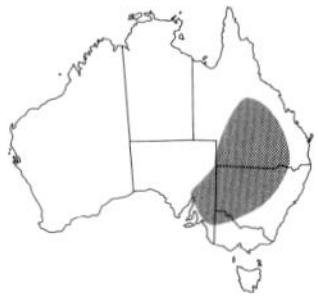

Robust, with **1 digit on very short forelimb and 2 digits on hindlimb. Lower eyelid moveable.** Shades of brown with dark sutures on head shields, dark bars on lips and usually dark marks on each scale aligning to form longitudinal rows of spots. ■ **NOTES** Wide variety of habitats in semi-arid open sandy areas. ■ **SEE ALSO** *L. emmotti.*

Lerista picturata.
Zanthus, WA. D. Knowles

Lerista planiventralis decora.
Kalbarri NP, WA. S. Wilson

Lerista planiventralis maryani.
Barradale area, WA. B. Maryan

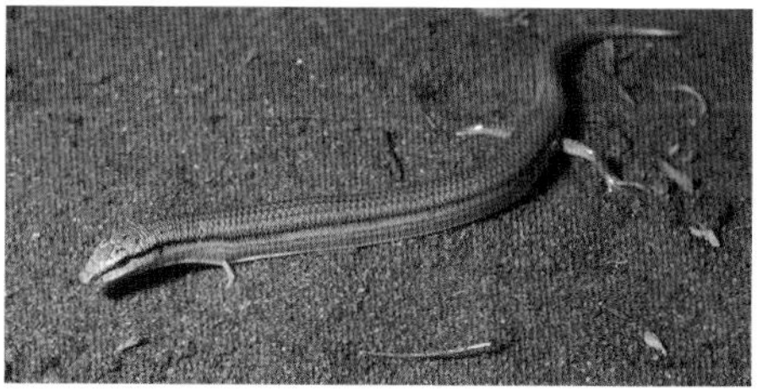

Lerista planiventralis planiventralis.
Bullara Stn, WA. S. Wilson

Lerista praefrontalis. Preserved holotype.
King Hall Island, WA. R. Ellis

Lerista praepedita.
Melaleuca Park, WA. S. Wilson

Lerista punctatovittata.
Glenmorgan, Qld. S. Wilson

Great Victoria Desert Slider *Lerista puncticauda* SVL 86mm

Two digits on forelimb and 3 digits on hindlimb. Lower eyelid moveable. Pale brown to yellowish brown with or without an upper lateral series of narrowly to widely separated dark brown spots. Tail flushed with pink and heavily dotted with brown. Ventral surfaces pale yellow. ■ **NOTES** Arid shrublands in vicinity of Queen Victoria Spring on sw. edge of Gt Victoria Desert.

Dark-streaked Slider *Lerista quadrivincula* SVL 52mm

Four well-developed limbs, each with 4 digits. Lower eyelid moveable. Olive brown with 4 dorsal lines of dark dashes and a weak dark upper lateral stripe. ■ **NOTES** Only one specimen known from a single locality at Maitland R. on the arid coastal plain near Karratha. No live image available.

Dusky Slider *Lerista robusta* SVL 64mm

Robust, with flat protrusive snout, **no trace forelimb and hindlimb with 2 digits. Lower eyelid moveable.** Pale reddish brown with little pattern; 4 indistinct dorsal series of dots or short dashes and a diffuse dark upper lateral stripe. ■ **NOTES** Arid grasslands s. of St George Ra., sthn interior of Kimberley.

Rochford Slider *Lerista rochfordensis* SVL 82mm

Slender with **no trace of forelimb and 1 digit on minute hindlimb.** Lower eyelid moveable. **Midbody scales in 16 rows.** Pale beige to grey with 8-10 prominent narrow dark lines, each along a scale row. Ventral surface immaculate. ■ **NOTES** Known only from vine thickets at 2 localities no more than 20 kms apart and each comprising only a few hundred square metres; Rochford Scrub and Boori Stn, se. of Charters Towers, Qld. ■ **SEE ALSO** *L. cinerea.*

Rolfe's Three-toed Slider *Lerista rolfei* SVL 48mm

Four well-developed limbs, each with 3 digits, 5 supraciliary scales, paired frontoparietal scales and **fused lower eyelid.** Pale brown to grey above with paravertebral and dorsal lines of dark spots usually obscure, weak to moderately prominent pale dorsolateral stripe, dark upper lateral stripe with ragged lower edge sometimes fragmented into vertically aligned blotches, **a line of un-pigmented scales below upper lateral stripe**, and irregular dark spots on lower lateral and ventral surfaces. ■ **NOTES** Arid shrublands of Gascoyne region in wstn interior of WA, n. to Ashburton River Valley. ■ **SEE ALSO** *L. micra; L. occulta; L. timida.*

Dampierland Slider *Lerista separanda* SVL 32mm

Four well-developed limbs, each with 4 digits. Lower eyelid fused. Pale pinkish brown with each scale finely edged with brown, a prominent dark upper lateral stripe and reddish pink flush on tail and hindlimbs. ■ **NOTES** Sandy areas of sw. Kimberley coast, between Kimbolton and Nita Downs.

Lerista puncticauda.
Queen Victoria Springs, WA. D. Knowles

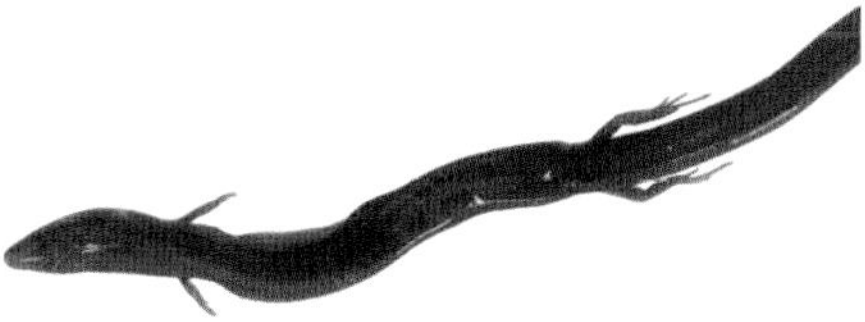

Lerista quadrivincula. Preserved holotype.
Maitland River, Karratha area, WA. R. Ellis

Lerista robusta.
Nookanbar Stn, WA.
D. Robinson

Lerista rochfordensis.
Amity Stn, Qld. S. Wilson

Lerista rolfei.
Mt Phillips Station, WA. B. Maryan

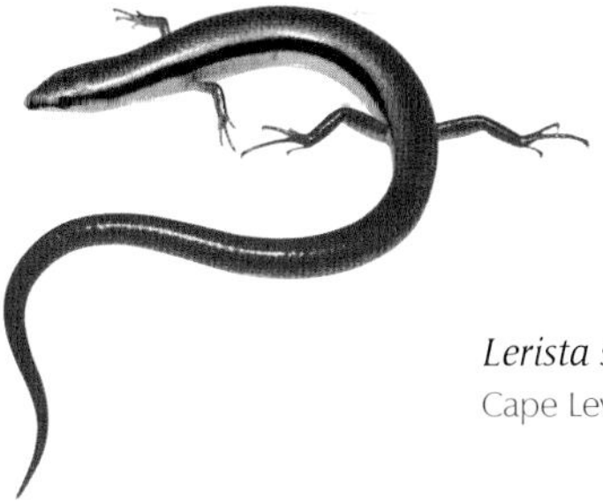

Lerista separanda.
Cape Leveque, WA. A. Greer

Fitzroy Sand-slider *Lerista simillima* SVL 54mm

Slender, with flat protrusive snout, **no trace of forelimb, hindlimb with 2 digits.** Lower eyelid moveable. **Upper labial scales 6, supraciliary scales absent, 2 supraoculars contacting frontal (fig.) and midbody scales in 20 rows.** Pale

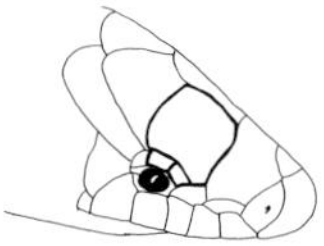

brown with 2 lines of dark brown dots from nape onto tail and a broad dark upper lateral stripe. ■ **NOTES** Acacia thickets and woodlands on red sandy loams, between Liveringa Stn and Fitzroy Crossing in semi-arid sw. Kimberley. ■ **SEE ALSO** *L. bipes; L. greeri; L. labialis.*

Musgrave Slider *Lerista speciosa* SVL 51mm

Four well-developed limbs, each with 3 digits. Lower eyelid moveable. Dark brown with back patternless or with 4 narrow black dorsal stripes breaking into spots on tail, a broad sharp-edged black lateral stripe and a white midlateral stripe. ■ **NOTES** Known only from between Mt Morris and Sentinel Hill areas in w. and ne. Musgrave Ra. in arid nw. SA. ■ **STATUS** Vulnerable (SA).

Spotted Broad-striped Slider *Lerista stictopleura* SVL 58mm

Blunt-snouted, with **1 digit on forelimb and 2 digits on hindlimb.** Lower eyelid fused. Orange-brown above with 4 rows of dark dashes from nape onto tail, a pale orange-yellow laterodorsal stripe margining a narrow black lateral stripe, and **orange-brown flanks with 3–5 series of angular black spots.** ■ **NOTES** Acacia shrublands around Mt Augustus in arid mid-w. interior. Shelters in leaf litter and in soil beneath logs and stumps.

Chillagoe Fine-lined Slider *Lerista storri* SVL 70mm

Slender, appearing virtually limbless; **no trace of forelimb, hindlimb minute and stylar (no digits); 1 loreal scale.** Lower eyelid moveable. **Prefrontal scales absent.** Brown to silvery grey with fine dark broken lines along body and tail but **no dark lateral stripe.** ■ **NOTES** Woodlands on sandy soils and outcrops between Chillagoe and Mt Surprise, s. to Charters Towers area. ■ **SEE ALSO** *L. cinerea; L. hobsoni.* ■ **STATUS** Vulnerable (Qld).

Single-toed Slider *Lerista stylis* SVL 60mm

Slender, appearing virtually limbless; **no trace of forelimb, hindlimb reduced to a minute stump, midbody scales in 18 rows** and **1 loreal scale.** Lower eyelid moveable. Pale yellowish brown to pale greyish brown with paravertebral lines of dark dashes, an indication of dorsal lines, and a black upper lateral stripe. ■ **NOTES** Woodlands in sandy areas. ■ **SEE ALSO** *L. carpentariae; L. karlschmidti.*

Lerista simillima.
Fitzroy Crossing, WA. D. Robinson

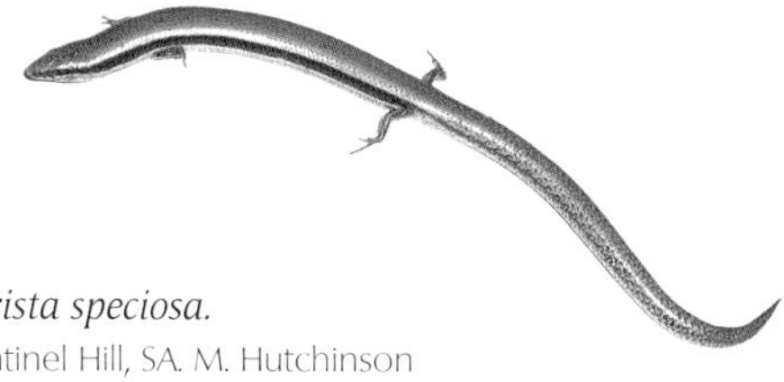

Lerista speciosa.
Sentinel Hill, SA. M. Hutchinson

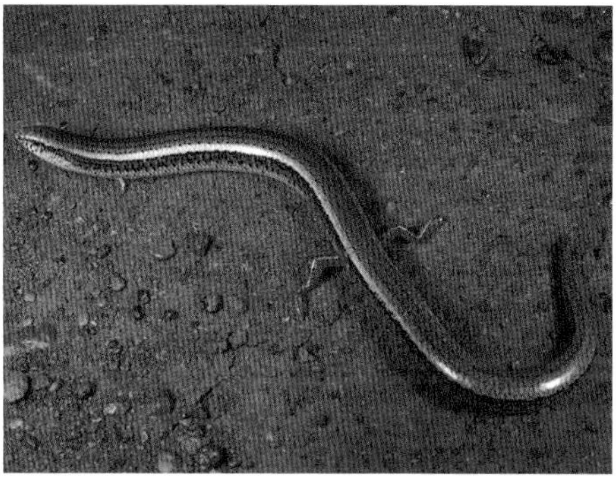

Lerista stictopleura.
Mt Augustus, WA. B. Maryan

Lerista storri.
Van Lees Stn, Qld. S. Wilson

Lerista stylis.
Gove, NT. S. Wilson

Ribbon Slider *Lerista taeniata* SVL 44mm

Slender, with **4 well-developed limbs, each with 4 digits. Lower eyelid fused.** Reddish brown, flushed with coppery red on head and neck, dorsal pattern reduced to fine dark edges on scales or 4 fine dark longitudinal lines. Broad blackish upper lateral stripe from snout to tail. ■ **NOTES** Sand-plain deserts with spinifex from estn Kimberley, WA through Tanami Desert, NT to central SA.

Southern Three-toed Slider *Lerista terdigitata* SVL 70mm

Four well-developed limbs, each with 3 digits. Lower eyelid moveable. Olive grey to olive brown with 4–6 dorsal rows of dots and a **narrow, ragged-edged dark upper lateral stripe.** ■ **NOTES** Variety of open habitats including mallee woodlands and chenopod shrublands, sheltering in soil beneath leaf litter, rocks and logs. ■ **SEE ALSO** *L. elongata.*

Dwarf Three-toed Slider *Lerista timida* SVL 49mm

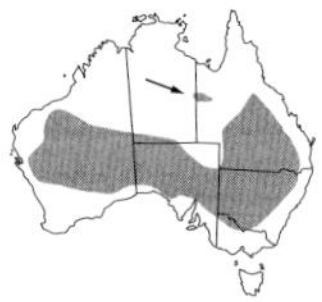

Four well-developed limbs, each with 3 digits, 5 supraciliary scales, fused frontoparietal scales and **fused lower eyelid**. Usually brown above, sometimes olive to grey, with paravertebral and dorsal series of dark spots or streaks, often coalesced to form narrow lines, weak to moderately strong pale dorsolateral stripe, and dark upper lateral stripe with continuous upper edge and deeply scalloped lower edge as dark pigment becomes restricted to scale sutures. ■ **NOTES** Dry to arid areas of all mainland states, dwelling under rocks, logs and leaf litter in various forest, woodland and shrubland communities. ■ **SEE ALSO** *L. amicorum; L. jacksoni; L. kingi; L. muelleri; L. rolfei; L verhmens.* ■ **STATUS** Endangered (Vic).

Dark-backed Mulch-slider *Lerista tridactyla* SVL 56mm

Four well-developed limbs, each with 3 digits. Lower eyelid moveable. Olive grey to olive brown with 4 dorsal rows of dots and a **broad, sharp-edged dark upper lateral stripe.** ■ **NOTES** Shelters in soil beneath leaf litter and logs in semi-arid woodlands.

Slender Broad-striped Slider *Lerista uniduo* SVL 61mm

Slender, with **no forelimb (represented by a groove),** and **2 digits on hindlimb. Lower eyelid fused.** Brownish white with narrow to moderately broad, pale to dark brown vertebral stripe enclosing 2–4 series of dark dots, and a broad dark upper lateral stripe. Lower flanks and ventral surfaces yellow. ■ **NOTES** Arid mid-w. coast and hinterland. Shelters in loose soil under leaf litter at bases of shrubs growing on sand, loose clay and loams.

Lerista taeniata.
Tanami Desert, NT. R.J. Johnstone

Lerista terdigitata.
Fowler's Bay, SA. R. Browne-Cooper

Lerista timida.
Girraween NP, Qld. S. Wilson

Lerista tridactyla.
Balladonia area, WA. B. Maryan

Lerista uniduo.
Tamala Stn, WA. S. Wilson

Leaden-bellied Fine-lined Slider *Lerista vanderduysi* SVL 67mm

Very slender, appearing virtually limbless; **no trace of forelimb; hindlimb minute with 1 digit; 1 loreal scale**. Lower eyelid moveable. Prefrontal scales absent. Rich glossy brown with 4 series of streaks forming narrow broken paravertebral and laterodorsal lines, and a broad, **prominent dark lateral stripe** from behind eye onto tail. **Ventral surface dark**, suffused with brown to grey. ■ **NOTES** Known only from vine thickets within Western Cape and Gulf Drainage, in vicinity of Blackbraes NP and Gilberton Stn.

Variable-striped Robust Slider *Lerista varia* SVL 84mm

No forelimb (represented by a groove or pit), 2 digits on hindlimb, usually 20 midbody scale rows and **4 supraciliary scales. Lower eyelid moveable.** Pale brown to brown with **weak pattern**: an obscure dark vertebral stripe enclosing faint dark dots and usually an ill-defined narrow upper lateral stripe. ■ **NOTES** Shrublands on sand and shell-grit between Cape Cuvier and Shark Bay. ■ **SEE ALSO** *L. connivens; L. lineopunctulata.*

Powerful Three-toed Slider *Lerista verhmens* SVL 50mm

Four well-developed limbs, each with 3 digits, 5 supraciliary scales, paired frontoparietal scales and **fused lower eyelid**. Grey with paravertebral and dorsal lines of spots and streaks, weak to moderately strong dorsolateral stripe, and dark upper lateral stripe varying from narrow and largely solid to broad with dark pigment confined to scale sutures. ■ **NOTES** Stony hills of wstn Pilbara region, WA. ■ **SEE ALSO** *L. amicorum; L. jacksoni.*

Slender Worm-slider *Lerista vermicularis* SVL 42mm

Slender, with flat protrusive snout, **no trace of forelimb, 2 digits on hindlimb** and an **angular junction between lateral and ventral surfaces. Lower eyelid fused.** Pale yellowish brown to pale reddish brown with little pattern: sometimes 2–4 series of small dark dorsal dots and a narrow dark brown upper lateral stripe, most prominent on tail. ■ **NOTES** Crests of red sand-ridges in Gt Sandy Desert. Forages just beneath surface of exposed sand, leaving meandering trails.

Ravensthorpe Range Slider *Lerista viduata* SVL 45mm

Four well-developed limbs, each with 5 digits. Lower eyelid moveable. Olive grey with 4 dorsal series of dark spots and dashes and a dark upper lateral stripe with sharp upper and diffuse lower edges. ■ **NOTES** Known only from Ravensthorpe Ra. Shelters among leaf litter at bases of trees and shrubs in eucalypt woodlands on loam or loamy clay soils.

Lerista vanderduysi.
Blackbraes NP, Qld. S. Wilson

Lerista varia.
Dirk Hartog Is., WA. R. Browne-Cooper

Lerista verhmens.
Cape Lambert, WA. G. Harold

Lerista vermicularis.
Telfer, WA. B. Maryan

Lerista viduata.
Ravensthorpe, WA. G. Harold

Side-striped Fine-lined Slider *Lerista vittata* SVL 63mm

Slender, appearing virtually limbless; **no trace of forelimb, hindlimb minute with 1 digit. Lower eyelid moveable. Prefrontal scales absent.** Silvery grey to silvery brown with 4 narrow dark dorsal lines and dark brown lateral stripe. Tails of juv. and subadults flushed with orange. ■ **NOTES** Known only from vine thickets on sandy soil from Mt Cooper Stn near Charters Towers, w. to Kidston and Blackbraes NP. ■ **STATUS** Vulnerable (C'wealth; Qld); endangered (IUCN Red List).

Walker's Slider *Lerista walkeri* SVL 63mm

Four short limbs, each with 2 digits. Last of 5 supraciliary scales is small. Lower eyelid moveable. Dark greyish brown with small dark spots on each scale, aligned longitudinally. ■ **NOTES** Coast and islands of nw. Kimberley region. ■ **SEE ALSO** *L. borealis.*

Wilkin's Slider *Lerista wilkinsi* SVL 75mm

Slender, with **no trace of forelimb, hindlimb very small with 2 digits. Lower eyelid moveable.** Silvery grey to silvery brown with dark brown markings on scales forming narrow longitudinal lines and red flush on tail, particularly on juv. ■ **NOTES** Rocky ranges near Warrigal Ra. and White Mtns. Shelters in soft sand and leaf litter accumulated at bases of trees and in rocky depressions.

Yellow-tailed Plain Slider *Lerista xanthura* SVL 40mm

Four well-developed limbs, each with 4 digits. Lower eyelid fused. Pale grey to coppery brown with each scale dark-edged, and **head and tail flushed with bright yellow.** ■ **NOTES** Arid sand-plains with spinifex in Gibson Desert. Shelters under leaf litter and spinifex. Relationship between this sp. and *L. aericeps* from further e. remains uncertain.

Yuna Broad-striped Slider *Lerista yuna* SVL 66mm

Slender, with **no forelimb (represented by a groove or pit and occasionally a minute stump)** and **2 digits on hindlimb. Lower eyelid fused.** Pale grey to almost white with very broad, greyish brown vertebral stripe enclosing 4 series of dark spots, and a **broad dark upper lateral stripe.** ■ **NOTES** Pale sand plains in vicinity of Yuna, in semi-arid lower wstn interior. Shelters in soft soil under leaf litter at bases of shrubs. ■ **SEE ALSO** *L. kendricki.*

Pilbara Blue-tailed Slider *Lerista zietzi* SVL 54mm

Four well-developed limbs, each with 4 digits. Lower eyelid moveable. Coppery brown; narrow dark upper lateral stripe with straight sharp upper edge and diffuse ragged lower edge; **steely blue tail.** ■ **NOTES** Shelters among rocks and leaf litter along watercourses and gorge floors in the Pilbara, from Wittenoom to Newman, including Hamersley Ra. ■ **SEE ALSO** *L. flammicauda.*

Lerista vittata.
Mt Cooper Stn, Qld. S. Wilson

Lerista walkeri.
Surveyors Pool, Mitchell Plateau, WA. S. Wilson

Lerista wilkinsi.
White Mountains NP, Qld. S. Wilson

Lerista xanthura.
Great Sandy Desert, WA. B. Maryan

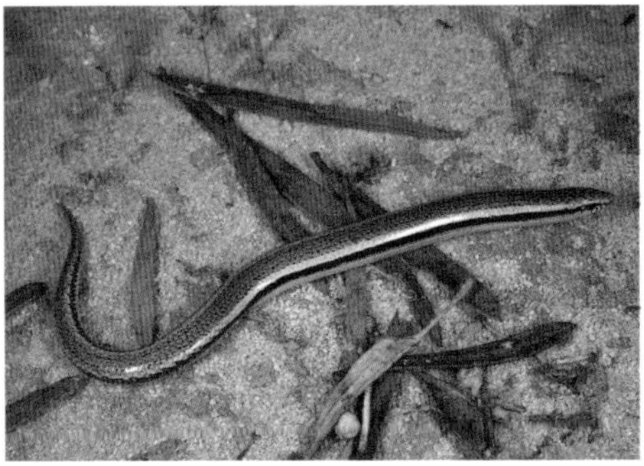

Lerista yuna.
Yuna district, WA. B. Maryan

Lerista zietzi.
Hamersley Ranges, WA. S. Wilson

Wide-striped Four-toed Slider *Lerista zonulata* SVL 50mm

Four well-developed limbs, each with 4 digits. Lower eyelid fused. Pale to dark olive brown, redder on tail, with 4–6 dorsal rows of small dark dots and a broad, blackish brown **upper lateral stripe with sharp upper and lower edges.** ■ **NOTES** Dry stony hilly areas from Windsor Tableland s. to Charters Towers. ■ **SEE ALSO** *L. orientalis.*

Four-fingered Rock Skinks Genus ***Liburnascincus***

Four moderate-sized spp with **long limbs and digits, 4 fingers and 5 toes** and a moveable lower eyelid enclosing a transparent disc. Ear-opening present with enlarged lobules. Dorsal scales keeled, sometimes with rows of small points. Parietal scales in contact, frontoparietals fused to form a single shield. ♂ **does not develop distinctive, brdg colours.** ■ **NOTES** Restricted to e. Qld. Swift, agile, sun-loving rock-inhabitants that sinuously wave tails as they forage and execute well-co-ordinated leaps between boulders. ■ **SEE ALSO** *Carlia; Lygisaurus.*

Bamboo Range Rock Skink *Liburnascincus artemis* SVL 58mm

Robust and long-limbed with predominantly 2 weak to strong keels on dorsal scales (some 3-keeled scales usually present). Ear-opening round, edged with conspicuous pointed lobules, largest anteriorly. **Midbody scales 34–36 (mean 35). Inner row of plantar scales large and block-like, about twice the size of remaining densely packed plantar scales.** Head and anterior body copper merging back to grey, with paired paravertebral series of dark and pale spots on back. Vertebral region patternless. Whitish lines extend back from eye, breaking to form dorsolateral series of pale dashes or spots and small black spots. ■ **NOTES** Known only from Bamboo Ra. in Cape York Pen. but probably more widespread on continuous low rocky hills comprising Gt Div. Ra. in the region. ■ **SEE ALSO** *L. mundivensis.*

Coen Rainbow Skink *Liburnascincus coensis* SVL 68mm

Dorsally depressed with **3–5 longitudinal rows of small tubercles on each dorsal scale.** Ear-opening vertically elongate, edged by small rounded lobules. Blackish brown with broad, **golden or silver, wavy-edged or broken stripes;** vertebral from nape to tail-base, dorsolateral from head to hips continuing as a ragged line to tail-tip, and midlateral blotches from ear to hindlimb. ■ **NOTES** McIlwraith and Table Ra., from Coen n. to Pascoe R. Forages on rock faces and boulders, particularly in vine thickets along creeks.

Lerista zonulata.
Chillagoe, Qld.
S. Wilson

Liburnascincus artemis.
Musgrave Roadhouse area, Qld. S. Macdonald

Liburnascincus coensis.
Coen, Qld. S. Wilson

Outcrop Rock Skink *Liburnascincus mundivensis* SVL 56mm

Robust, with **2–3 moderately strong keels** on dorsal scales. Ear-opening round, edged with pointed lobules. **Midbody scales 34–42 (mean 38). Plantar scales grade evenly from large inner row to smaller outer scales.** Olive brown with numerous large blackish blotches, often aligned to exclude vertebral zone. Scattered pale flecks often coalesce to form obscure vertebral, dorsolateral and midlateral stripes, prominent on juv. Top of head copper. ■ **NOTES** Forages on exposed rock faces and occasionally on tree roots associated with outcrops and boulder scree from between Cooktown and Laura s. to inland from Gladstone, Qld. ■ **SEE ALSO** *L artemis.*

Black Mountain Skink *Liburnascincus scirtetis* SVL 64mm

Dorsally depressed, with protrusive eyes and upturned snout. Dorsal scales with weak carinations, each a series of small points. Ear-opening vertically elongate, edged with long pointed lobules. Blackish brown and patternless, or with obscure pale greenish flecks; most prominent on juveniles, and tending to form indistinct vertebral and dorsolateral stripes. ■ **NOTES** Restricted to piled black granite boulders of Black Mtn, s. of Cooktown. Alert, inquisitive, but difficult to approach. Dwells on bare boulder surfaces. ■ **STATUS** Vulnerable (Qld).

Genus ***Liopholis***

Eleven small to moderate sized spp. with 4 well-developed limbs, each with 5 digits; **4th toe much longer than 3rd.** Lower eyelid moveable, lacking transparent disc, eyes relatively large, **eyelids with distinctive cream margins**, ear opening with anterior lobules, **parietal scales separated (fig.)** and body scales smooth (weakly keeled in one species).

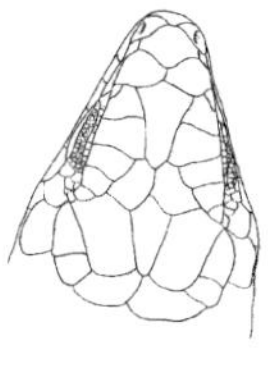

■ **NOTES** Widespread, from southern heaths and alpine outcrops to central deserts. Most utilise burrows that range from simple to complex systems, sometimes with multiple entrances. Others dig simple tunnels under rocks. Omnivorous livebearers, often living communally in family groups. Mainly diurnal with several spp. crepuscular to nocturnal. ■ **SEE ALSO** *Ctenotus.*

Guthega Skink *Liopholis guthega* SVL 111mm

Smooth-scaled, with **17–20 subdigital lamellae under 4th toe, prominent stripes and spots, dark upper flanks** but **no dark vertical bar above forelimb.** Blackish brown on back and upper flanks with pale grey to greyish brown vertebral and dorsolateral stripes and numerous longitudinal rows of sharp pale spots. Juv. very dark with weak stripes and prominent white to pink spots; large adults have weaker, more ragged pattern. ■ **NOTES** Rocky areas in woodlands, tussock grasslands and heaths above 1600m at Mt Kosciuszko NP, NSW and Bogong High Plains, Vic. Large colonies share burrow networks under boulders and shrubs. ■ **SEE ALSO** *L. montana, L. whitii.* ■ **STATUS** Endangered (C'wealth); critically endangered (Vic).

Liburnascincus mundivensis.
Chillagoe, Qld.
S. Wilson

Liburnascincus scirtetis.
Black Mountain, Qld.
S. Wilson

Liopholis guthega.
Mt Kosciuszko NP, NSW. M. Swan.

Desert Skink *Liopholis inornata* SVL 84mm

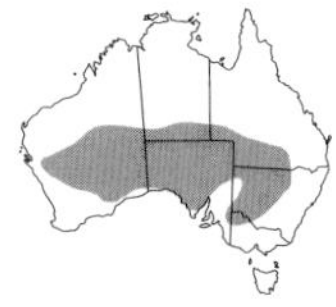

Smooth-scaled, with **deep blunt head. Yellowish brown to rich coppery red**, varying according to substrate, usually with longitudinal rows of black spots on back and vertically aligned black spots on flanks, represented on sides of tail as dark bars. ■ **NOTES** Arid to semi-arid sthn Aust. between Shark Bay, WA and Thrushton NP, Qld. Sand-ridges or sand-plains with spinifex or shrubs, excavating multi-entranced burrows with concealed escape exits. Crepuscular to nocturnal. ■ **SEE ALSO** *L. slateri.*

Great Desert Skink; Tjakura *Liopholis kintorei* SVL 187mm

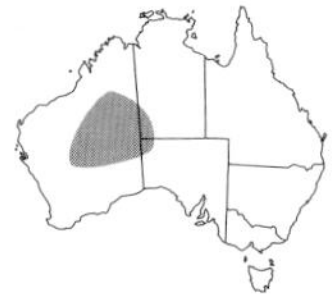

Largest *Liopholis*. Smooth-scaled, with deep blunt head. Rich reddish brown above with dark brown edges to scales forming narrow longitudinal lines. Flanks grey to bluish grey with dark pigment tending to form diffuse vertical bars. ■ **NOTES** Arid sand-flats and clay-based or loamy soils vegetated with spinifex. Excavates large complex multi-entranced communal burrow systems and uses shared defecation sites. Crepuscular to nocturnal. ■ **STATUS** Vulnerable (IUCN Red List; C'wealth; WA; NT); endangered (SA).

Masked Rock Skink *Liopholis margaretae* SVL 116mm

Smooth-scaled, with pattern prominent to virtually absent. ■ **SSP.** (ill-defined): *L. m. margaretae* reddish brown with faint dark edges to scales, forming narrow lines, or with prominent longitudinally aligned dark streaks and lines of pale spots. *L. m. personata* is said to be paler with longer limbs, pale dorsolateral stripe and weak dark laterodorsal stripe. Not all specimens exhibit these characters. ■ **NOTES** Arid central Aust. highlands, from sthn NT to nw. SA (*L. m. margaretae*); Flinders Ra., SA (*L. m. personata*). Shelters under slabs, in crevices and burrows in rocky habitats.

Eastern Ranges Rock Skink *Liopholis modesta* SVL 112mm

Smooth-scaled, with weak pattern. Brown to greyish brown with narrow dark lines, a few large pale spots between upper lips and anterior flanks and conspicuous pale ear-lobules and rim around eye. **No pale streak on upper lip.** ■ **NOTES** DSF, woodlands and rock outcrops between Hunter Valley, NSW and se. Qld, with an isolated pop. in Yathong Nat. Res., central NSW. Shelters in burrows and depressions beneath rocks or logs. ■ **SEE ALSO** *L. whitii.*

Mountain Skink *Liopholis montana* SVL 111mm

Smooth-scaled, with **19–25 subdigital lamellae under 4th toe, weak pattern, dark upper flanks** but **no dark vertical bar above forelimb**. Reddish brown above with greyish brown vertebral zone. Dorsal pattern absent or reduced to 2 rows of dark brown marbling. Upper flanks black, enclosing one or more rows of pale spots. Juv. have prominent white spots alternating with dark stripes but pattern fades as they grow. ■ **NOTES** Areas of granite associated with tall open forest and heath in Southern Highlands of ACT and NSW, s. along Gt. Div. Ra. to upper Yarra River valley, Vic. Colonies occupy burrow networks under rocks. ■ **SEE ALSO** *L. guthega; L. whitii.* ■ **STATUS** Data deficient (Vic).

Liopholis inornata.
Ethabuka, Qld. S. Wilson

Liopholis kintorei.
Yulara area, NT. S. Wilson

Liopholis margaretae personata.
Flinders Ranges, SA. J. Cornish

Liopholis margaretae margaretae.
King's Creek Stn, NT. S. Wilson

Liopholis modesta.
Lake Broadwater, Qld. S. Wilson

Liopholis montana.
King's Spur, Vic. N. Clemman

Bull Skink *Liopholis multiscutata* SVL 96mm

Smooth-scaled, with interparietal scale of adults slightly narrower to slightly wider than frontal scale. Grey to greyish brown with black dorsal stripe enclosing 1–2 series of pale spots or dashes and a pale dorsolateral stripe. ■ **NOTES** Sandy soils with heaths and open woodlands between Bernier Is., off Shark Bay, WA, and Big Desert in nw. Vic. Excavates multi-entranced burrows at bases of low shrubs in open areas. ■ **SEE ALSO** *L. pulchra; L. whitii.* ■ **STATUS** Critically endangered (Vic).

South-western Rock Skink *Liopholis pulchra* SVL 110mm

Weakly keeled dorsal scales. ■ **SSP.** *L. p. pulchra* is pale brown to reddish brown, sometimes with dorsal pattern. Broad vertebral stripe bordered by broad dark dorsal stripe enclosing a series of pale spots, a pale dorsolateral stripe and grey flanks flecked with black. Weakly marked lizards have plain backs and flecked flanks. *L. p. longicauda* has a much longer tail (proportionally longer than all other *Liopholis*) and an orange ventral flush. ■ **NOTES** Forests, woodlands and heaths on rocky ranges and sthn coast, n. along Darling Ra. to just n. of Perth, and e. to Stirling Ra. and Cheyne Beach (*L. p. pulchra*); and islands of Jurien Bay on lower w. coast (*L. p. longicauda*). Shelters in burrows beneath rocks and in crevices. *L. p. longicauda* also uses petrel burrows. ■ **SEE ALSO** *L. multiscutata.* ■ **STATUS** *L. p. longicauda* is vulnerable (C'wealth; WA).

Slater's Desert Skink *Liopholis slateri* SVL 85mm

Smooth-scaled, with **deep blunt head** and **grey to greyish brown** colouration. ■ **SSP.** *L. s. slateri* has black dorsal spots or flecks aligned in longitudinal rows or narrow lines. Flanks similar, including pale flecks. *L. s. virgata* has a black vertebral stripe. ■ **NOTES** Heavy loamy soils on alluvial plains in central Aust. (*L. s. slateri*), and far nthn SA, between Oodnadatta and the Everard Ra. (*L. s. virgata*). Excavates multi-entranced burrows beneath low vegtn. Crepuscular to nocturnal. ■ **SEE ALSO** *L. inornata.* ■ **STATUS** *L. s. slateri* is endangered (C'wealth); vulnerable (NT); *L. s. virgata* is endangered (SA).

Night Skink *Liopholis striata* SVL 112mm

Smooth-scaled, with **deep blunt head** and **vertically elliptic pupils**. Brown to brick red with dark lateral edges to scales forming longitudinal lines. ■ **NOTES** Sand-plains and interdunes vegetated with spinifex, from arid central interior of WA to sthn NT and nw. SA. Excavates deep multi-entranced burrow systems. Predominantly nocturnal and crepuscular.

Liopholis multiscutata.
Lancelin Is., WA. S. Wilson

Liopholis pulchra longicauda.
Boullanger Is., WA. D. Robinson

Liopholis pulchra pulchra.
Stirling Range NP, WA. S. Wilson

Liopholis slateri slateri.
Palm Valley, NT. G. Fyfe

Liopholis striata.
Ti Tree, NT. R. Valentic

White's Skink *Liopholis whitii* SVL 113mm

Smooth-scaled, with **pale streak on upper lip** and **interparietal scale much narrower than frontal scale**. Striped and plain-backed forms occur. Striped forms have a broad rusty brown vertebral stripe, broad dark brown to black dorsal stripes enclosing a series of pale spots, and pale dorsolateral stripes. Flanks usually paler and greyer with large dark-edged pale spots, and a **dark vertical bar above forelimb enclosing 1–3 pale spots**. Plain-backed forms lack dorsal pattern but usually retain lateral pattern. Both forms occur in all pops except Tas, where only striped forms are recorded. ■ **NOTES** DSF, woodlands and heaths, particularly where rock outcrops are present, in cool temperate se. Aust. Extends from Kangaroo Is. and islands off sthn Eyre Pen., SA through Tas and Vic to Granite Belt, sthn Qld. Isolated pop. at Mutawintji NP, wstn NSW. Excavates burrows or shallow depressions and tunnels beneath rocks or logs. ■ **SEE ALSO** *L. guthega; L. modesta; L. montana; L. multiscutata.* ■ **STATUS** Endangered (wstn NSW pop.).

Genus *Lissolepis*

Two medium sized, robust spp. with 4 well developed limbs, each with 5 digits; **4th toe much longer than 3rd.** Lower eyelid moveable, lacking a transparent disc, relatively small eyes, **no distinctive pale margin around eyelids**, ear-opening with anterior lobules, **parietal scales separated** (fig.) and body scales smooth and glossy. ■ **NOTES** Restricted to widely-separated cool moist conditions in se. and sw. Nocturnal to diurnal. Secretive, basking in sheltered sites and using burrows in dense vegetation around wetlands. Omnivorous livebearers.

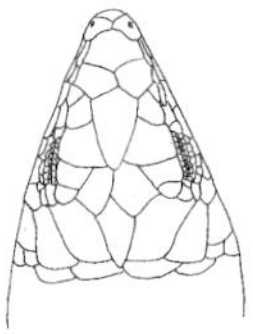

Swamp Skink *Lissolepis coventryi* SVL 100mm

Black above with coppery bronze markings aligning to form broad ragged-edged stripes: paravertebrals (sometimes joined to form a wide vertebral) and dorsolaterals. Upper flanks black, merging to grey on lower flanks, spotted with white. ■ **NOTES** Cool temperate, low-lying wetlands incl. swamp margins, tea-tree thickets and even tidal salt-marshes. Secretive, often dwelling in dense low vegtn. Nocturnal to diurnal. Shelters in burrows, incl. those of crustaceans. ■ **STATUS** Endangered (SA); vulnerable (Vic).

Mourning Skink *Lissolepis luctuosa* SVL 129mm

Yellowish brown to dark brown above with about 6 longitudinal rows of oblong to square black spots, a ragged-edged black upper lateral stripe and lemon yellow to yellowish brown flecks on mid- to lower flanks. Ventral surfaces flushed with yellow and often spotted with black. ■ **NOTES** Dense vegtn surrounding swamps, lakes, creeks and rivers on humid coast and hinterland, from Perth se. to Cheyne Beach. Nocturnal to diurnal.

Liopholis whitii. Plain-backed form.
Girraween NP, Qld. S. Wilson

Liopholis whitii. Plain form.
Mutawintji NP, NSW. G. Swan

Liopholis whitii. Striped form.
New England NP, NSW. S. Wilson

Lissolepis coventryi.
Tooradin, Vic. S. Wilson

Lissolepis luctuosa.
Lake Herdsman, WA.
S. Wilson

Litter-skinks Genus ***Lygisaurus***

Eleven small spp. with 4 well-developed limbs, **4 fingers and 5 toes** and a usually moveable lower eyelid enclosing a transparent disc (fused to form a fixed spectacle on 1 sp.). **Ear-opening conspicuous**, usually with enlarged lobules. Dorsal scales smooth (rows of small points on 1 sp.). Parietal scales in contact, frontoparietals fused to form a single shield. Pattern usually weak but **brdg ♂ usually develop distinctive red flush on head and/or tail**. Spp. are identified by size of disc in lower eyelid, shape of ear-opening, nature and arrangement of ear-lobules and number of upper labial scales. ■ **NOTES** Largely confined to ne. Alert but secretive, sun-loving leaf litter inhabitants that seldom venture far from surface cover. ■ **SEE ALSO** *Carlia; Liburnascincus; Menetia; Pygmaeascincus.*

Secretive Litter-skink *Lygisaurus abscondita* SVL 30mm

Large disc in lower eyelid, ear-opening round to slightly horizontal with sharp lobules around margin, 7 upper labial scales. Dark olive brown, paler on hindlimbs and tail. Lips heavily barred with black. ■ **NOTES** Only known from Donkey Springs and Bulleringa NP near Mt Surprise, in woodlands and sandstone outcrops.

Large-disced Litter-skink *Lygisaurus aeratus* SVL 30mm

Large disc in lower eyelid, ear-opening horizontally elongate, numerous sharp lobules around margin, usually **6 upper labial scales.** Olive brown, top of head copper, dark bars on lips, dark flanks often speckled with white. **Tail brown without orange flush,** sometimes paler than body, and generally with **bold dark speckling below.** ■ **NOTES** Woodlands, grasslands and rock outcrops from just n. of Townsville to Rokeby Stn area. ■ **SEE ALSO** *L. malleolus.*

Tree-base Litter-skink *Lygisaurus foliorum* SVL 39mm

Lower eyelid fused to form a spectacle. Ear-opening horizontally elongate, with 1 or more sharp to flat lobules. Brown to greyish brown, with fine white peppering on flanks and dark flecks or bars on lips. Brdg ♂: pinkish orange throat, hindlimbs and tail. ■ **NOTES** DSF and woodlands from Townsville, Qld to Sydney, NSW.

Rainforest Edge Litter-skink *Lygisaurus laevis* SVL 37mm

Small disc in lower eyelid. Ear-opening horizontally elongate, with many sharp lobules of approx. equal size around edge and 7 upper labial scales. Reddish brown above (iridescent green and purple from some angles), sometimes with fine black dashes on each scale forming narrow lines. Flanks greyish brown to black, usually with pale flecks. Brdg ♂: red throat and tail. ■ **NOTES** RF and margins from Cooktown s. to Bramston Beach. ■ **SEE ALSO** *L. sesbrauna.*

Lygisaurus abscondita.
Bulleringa NP, Qld. C. Dollery

Lygisaurus aeratus.
Shipton's Flat, Qld. E. Vanderduys

Lygisaurus foliorum.
Kurwongbah, Qld.
S. Wilson

Lygisaurus laevis.
Kuranda, Qld.
S. Wilson

Translucent Litter-skink *Lygisaurus macfarlani* SVL 37mm

Small disc in lower eyelid. Round ear-opening with large blunt anterior lobule and several small flat lobules around margin, usually 6 upper labial scales. Pale or rich brown to olive grey; dark head, barred lips, pale brown dorsolateral stripe, dark brown upper flanks and sometimes a narrow obscure pale brown to cream midlateral line. Brdg ♂: red limbs, tail, chin and throat, pattern reduced to absent. ■ **NOTES** Woodlands, vine thickets and coastal vegtn from Princess Charlotte Bay on Cape York Pen. to Torres Strait islands, Qld, with disjunct populations in ne. Arnhem Land and Melville Is., NT. Also in sthn NG. ■ **SEE ALSO** *L. tanneri.*

Red-tailed Litter-skink *Lygisaurus malleolus* SVL 32mm

Large disc in lower eyelid, ear-opening round to slightly horizontally elongate with sharp lobules around margin, 7 upper labial scales. Brown with **orange flush on hindlimbs and tail. Tail virtually patternless below.** Lips heavily barred with black. ■ **NOTES** Eucalypt woodlands from just s. of Cairns to just n. of Cooktown. ■ **SEE ALSO** *L. aeratus; L. tanneri.*

Fire-tailed Litter-skink *Lygisaurus parrhasius* SVL 33mm

Dorsal scales with weak carinations, each a series of small points. Ear-opening round, surrounded by long pointed lobules. Pattern distinctive; **black with sharply contrasting white vertebral, dorsolateral and midlateral stripes and a bright red tail.** Head coppery brown. Becomes more bronze with age, stripes darker and tail browner, diffusing the pattern. ■ **NOTES** Glennie Tableland, a sandstone plateau 60km nw. of Lockhart R. community on ne. Cape York Pen. Recorded on large sandstone fragments at bases of cliffs and the scree slope below them. Probably forages mainly on exposed rock faces, sheltering in crevices and accumulated litter.

Chillagoe Litter-skink *Lygisaurus rococo* SVL 39mm

Long-limbed and dorsally depressed with **large disc in lower eyelid. Round ear-opening with flat blunt lobules around edge.** Coppery brown (iridescent metallic green from some angles) with no pattern. ■ **NOTES** Limestone outcrops and granite boulders around Chillagoe. Forages on exposed rock surfaces and adjacent leaf litter. ■ **STATUS** Near threatened (Qld).

Eastern Cape Litter-skink *Lygisaurus sesbrauna* SVL 34mm

Small disc in lower eyelid, round ear-opening with large, sharp anterior lobules and smaller sharp lobules around margin, and usually 7 upper labial scales. Reddish brown to yellowish brown with narrow dark-edged pale dorsolateral stripes, and often a dark vertebral stripe and 2–3 fine dark paravertebral lines. Brdg ♂: brown with red tail, hindlimbs and possibly throat. ■ **NOTES** Monsoon forests and moist areas in open forests, woodlands and heaths on Cape York Pen., from Silver Plains n. to tip. ■ **SEE ALSO** *L. laevis.*

Lygisaurus macfarlani. Breeding male.
Badu Is., Qld. S. Wilson

Lygisaurus malleolus.
Mt Molloy, Qld. G. Harold

Lygisaurus parrhasius.
Glennie Tableland, Qld. S. Wilson

Lygisaurus rococo.
Chillagoe, Qld. S. Wilson

Lygisaurus sesbrauna.
Lockerbie Scrub, Qld. S. Wilson

Tanner's Litter-skink *Lygisaurus tanneri* SVL 37mm

Small disc in lower eyelid, round ear-opening may have low, flat ear-lobules, and **usually 7 upper labial scales.** Pale to dark brown with obscure pale flecks, sometimes with vague pale dorsolateral stripes, particularly on juv. Brdg ♂: red throat and tail. ■ **NOTES** Riverine RF and monsoon forests from Endeavour R. n. to Starcke Wilderness. ■ **SEE ALSO** *L. macfarlani; L. malleolus.* ■ **STATUS** Vulnerable (Qld).

Sun-loving Litter-skink *Lygisaurus zuma* SVL 34mm

Large disc in lower eyelid. Round to nearly horizontal ear-opening with low flat lobules around edges and **7 upper labial scales.** Iridescent greyish brown above, coppery on head, longitudinal rows of dark flecks concentrating on flanks to form a dark upper lateral zone. Brdg ♂: red throat and tail. ■ **NOTES** Mackay district, n. to Kirrama area, Qld, inhabiting various eucalypt-dominated open forests and riverine gallery forests.

Genus *Magmellia*

Orange-speckled Forest Skink *Magmellia luteilateralis* SVL 92mm

Sole member of genus. Medium-sized sp. with smooth, shiny scales; well-developed limbs which overlap when pressed to side of body, each with 5 digits; lower eyelid moveable, lacking a transparent disc; ear-opening without lobules; parietal scales in contact; frontoparietal scale divided; and **3rd pair of chin shields separated by 5 longitudinal rows of scales (fig); distal subdigital lamellae on 4th toe undivided.** Rich brown to bronze brown above with scattered darker scales or flecks, a large dark patch above forelimb, sometimes smaller dark patches on side of neck and above ear, and burnt **orange flanks** enclosing many prominent fine white spots. ■ **NOTES** Known only from RF above 900m in Eungella NP. Normally seen resting quietly on large rotting logs, retreating within them when approached. ■ **SEE ALSO** *Concinnia; Eulamprus.* ■ **STATUS** Vulnerable (Qld).

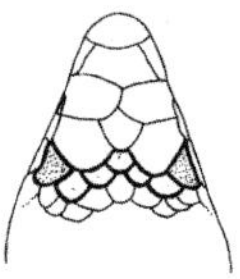

Lygisaurus tanneri.
Cooktown area, Qld.
S. Wilson

Lygisaurus zuma.
Mt Charleton, Qld.
S Wilson

Magmellia luteilateralis.
Eungella NP, Qld.
S. Wilson

Dwarf Skinks Genus *Menetia*

Five tiny spp. (incl. some of Aust's smallest reptiles) with well-developed limbs, 4 fingers and 5 toes, **ear-opening minute to absent without lobules, lower eyelid fused to form a fixed spectacle** and 11 or more scales along top of 4th toe. Scales smooth, parietals in contact, frontoparietals fused to form a single shield and **interparietal scale distinct**. Identification can be difficult, requiring microscopic examination to determine whether only 2nd (A), or 1st and 2nd (B) supraciliary scales contact 1st supraocular scale, and whether there are 3 (C) or 4 (D) scales in a line between eye and nostril. ■ **NOTES** Secretive diurnal skinks that bask, shelter and forage among leaf litter, rarely venturing into exposed areas. Egglaying. Invertebrate feeders. ■ **SEE ALSO** *Lygisaurus; Pygmaeascincus.*

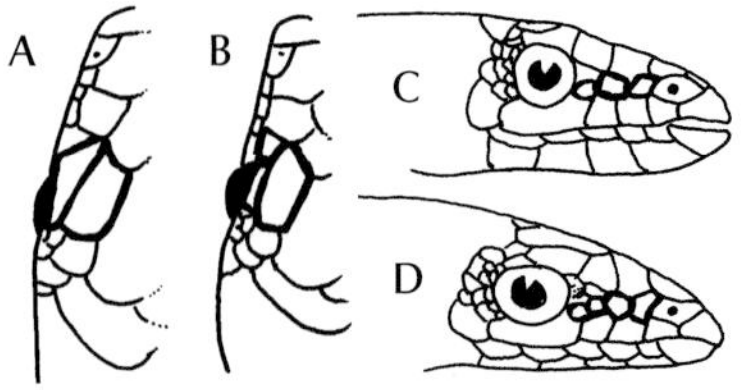

Top-end Dwarf Skink *Menetia alanae* SVL 25mm

Drably marked, with 2 **supraciliary scales (1st much smaller, and only 2nd contacting supraocular scale)**, 22–24 midbody scales, **4 scales in a line between eye and nostril** and weak pattern with **no pale midlateral stripe**. Pale brown with paravertebral series of fine dark flecks and dark brown upper flanks merging to paler grey on lower flanks. ■ **NOTES** Subhumid to humid nw. NT, usually on sandy coastal and alluvial soils in woodlands or forests.

Jabiluka Dwarf Skink *Menetia concinna* SVL 31mm

Two supraciliary scales (1st much smaller, and only 2nd contacting supraocular scale), 20 midbody scales, 4 scales in a line between eye and nostril and a **pale midlateral stripe**. Pale brownish grey with fine darker spotting, a broad dark upper lateral stripe and a prominent white midlateral stripe from below eye to midbody or tail. ■ **NOTES** Sandy soils with woodlands and dense leaf litter, in East Alligator R. drainage on wstn Arnhem Land escarpment near Jabiluka. ■ **SEE ALSO** *M. greyii.*

Common Dwarf Skink *Menetia greyii* SVL 38mm

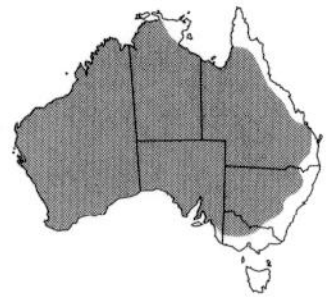

Two supraciliary scales (1st much smaller, and only 2nd contacting supraocular scale), 3 scales in a line between eye and nostril and a **pale midlateral stripe**. Brownish grey to grey with dark dorsal dashes sometimes forming broken lines and broad dark upper lateral and white midlateral stripes. Shark Bay pop. (formerly referred to as *M. amaura*) lacks visible ear aperture, has 1–2 supraciliary scales, pale midlateral stripe reduced to line from below eye to position of ear and simple pattern of pale flecks. Mature ♂ has yellow flush on belly and pink flush on throat. ■ **NOTES** Widespread in dry areas on a variety of soils and open vegtn types. ■ **SEE ALSO** *M. concinna.*

Menetia alanae.
Litchfield NP, NT.
B. Maryan

Menetia concinna.
West Alligator River,
NT. B. Maryan

Menetia greyii.
Mutawintji NP, NSW.
G. Swan

Menetia greyii.
Tamala Stn, WA.
S. Wilson

Main's Dwarf Skink *Menetia maini* SVL 25mm

Drably marked, with 2 **supraciliary scales (2nd not much larger than 1st and both contacting supraocular scale), 3 scales in a line between eye and nostril** and pale midlateral stripe absent, weak or prominent. Pale or dark coppery brown to greyish brown with dark flecks on each scale, sometimes a vague pale anterior dorsolateral line and dark brown to black flanks. ■ **NOTES** Variety of dry open habitats from nthn WA to interior of Qld.

Western Dwarf Skink *Menetia surda* SVL 32mm

Variable, with **3–4 supraciliary scales (3 contacting supraocular scale)** and **4 scales in a line between eye and nostril.** ■ **SSP.** *M. s. surda* is pale to dark olive brown with a dark upper lateral stripe. *M. s. cresswelli* lacks the dark upper lateral stripe. ■ **NOTES** *M. s. surda* occurs in the Pilbara, while *M. s. cresswelli* occupies the Shark Bay area. Undetermined ssp. occur on North West Cape and Kennedy Ra.

Genus *Morethia*

Eight small spp. with 4 well-developed limbs, each with 5 digits, and **lower eyelid fused to form a fixed spectacle**. Scales smooth; parietals in contact, **frontoparietals fused with interparietal to form a single shield**, and **frontal much larger than each prefrontal (fig.)**. Spp. are identified by pattern, and nature of suture-line between supraciliary and supraocular scales. Throats of brdg ♂ become bright orange-red in most spp. ■ **NOTES** Widespread in dry or well-drained open habitats. Diurnal. Swift terrestrial sun-lovers which forage among leaf litter around bases of low vegtn and rock outcrops. Egglaying invertebrate feeders. ■ **SEE ALSO** *Cryptoblepharus; Notoscincus.*

Saltbush Morethia *Morethia adelaidensis* SVL 53mm

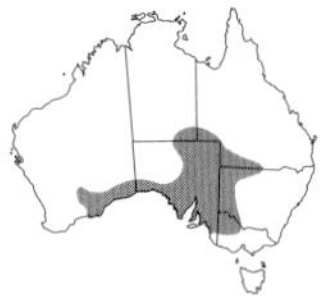

Usually 5 supraciliaries, the last 3 largest and penetrating deeply between supraoculars (fig.). Grey, olive grey to brown, sometimes tinged with reddish brown, with dark dashes forming 2 broken lines, often an obscure pale dorsolateral stripe, broad dark brown upper lateral stripe enclosing scattered pale flecks, and a pale wavy-edged midlateral stripe. ■ **NOTES** Favours chenopod-dominated shrublands, often associated with woodlands, in dry to arid sthn Aust. ■ **STATUS** Endangered (Vic).

Boulenger's Morethia *Morethia boulengeri* SVL 50mm

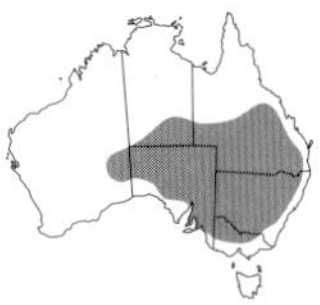

Usually 6 supraciliaries, 1st and 3rd largest, and remainder decreasing in size (fig.) to form a roughly straight-edged junction behind 1st supraocular. Coppery brown to greyish brown above with dark longitudinally aligned dashes, and broad black upper lateral and broad white midlateral stripes. Tail flushed with red on juv. ■ **NOTES** Woodlands, shrublands and DSF, mainly on heavy soils. ■ **SEE ALSO** *M. butleri.*

Menetia maini.
El Questio Stn, WA. S. Wilson

Menetia maini.
Bullita, NT. P. Horner

Menetia surda cresswelli.
Wandina Stn, WA. B. Maryan

Menetia surda surda.
Burrup Peninsula, WA. B. Maryan

Morethia adelaidensis.
Currawinya NP, Qld. S. Wilson

Morethia boulengeri.
Currawinya NP, Qld. S. Wilson

Woodland Dark-flecked Morethia *Morethia butleri* SVL 56mm

Six supraciliaries; 1st largest, forming a straight line along junction with supraoculars (fig.). Coppery brown to greyish brown and usually patternless

above, with a broad black upper lateral stripe and strong to weak white midlateral stripe. Tail flushed with red on juv. ■ **NOTES** Woodlands and chenopod shrublands in semi-arid to arid zones, from Shark Bay through sthn interior of WA to nw. Eyre Pen., SA. ■ **SEE ALSO** *M. boulengeri.*

West Coast Pale-flecked Morethia *Morethia lineoocellata* SVL 49mm

Usually 6 supraciliaries; 3rd, 4th and 5th largest and penetrating deeply between supraoculars (fig.). Olive grey to olive brown, copper on head,

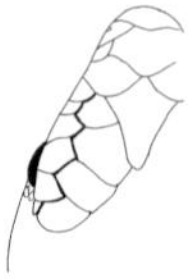

with prominent white-edged black spots, strong to weak pale dorsolateral stripe and usually prominent pale midlateral stripe. ■ **NOTES** Variety of habitats, mainly on sandy soils, including coastal dunes, samphire flats and woodlands, from Montebello Is. and North West Cape s. to Cape Leeuwin.

Shrubland Pale-flecked Morethia *Morethia obscura* SVL 56mm

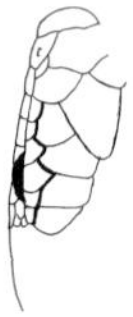

Usually 6 supraciliaries; 4th largest, and last 3 forming a roughly straight line along junction with supraoculars (fig.). Olive brown to olive grey, with or without an obscure pattern of dark-edged white spots or flecks, and sometimes a weak pale midlateral stripe. ■ **NOTES** Woodlands, heaths and shrublands in dry to semi-arid sthn Aust.

Fire-tailed Skink *Morethia ruficauda* SVL 46mm

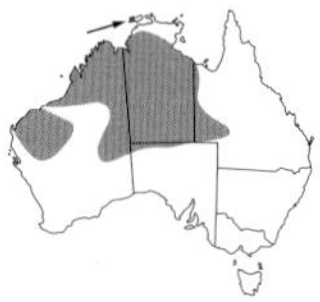

Boldly striped, with **4 supraciliaries; penetrating deeply between supraoculars to form ragged junction (fig.).** ■ **SSP.** *M. r. ruficauda* is **glossy black**

with sharp **white dorsolateral stripes converging on snout,** white midlateral stripes extending to lips, red flush on hips and hindlimbs and fiery red on tail. *M. r. exquisita* has a prominent white vertebral stripe. ■ **NOTES** Dry to arid rocky areas. *M. r. ruficauda* extends from nw. Qld to nw. WA. *M. r. exquisita* occurs in the Pilbara, Gascoyne and North West Cape regions, WA. ■ **SEE ALSO** *M. storri*

Northern Fire-tailed Skink *Morethia storri* SVL 38mm

Striped, with 4 supraciliaries penetrating deeply between supraoculars to form ragged junction (fig.). Pale brown to olive brown with narrow pale dorsolateral stripes **extending forward to above eye,** broad dark

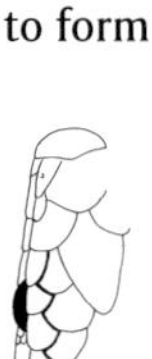

upper lateral stripes, white midlateral stripes extending forward to lips and red flush on lower back and hindlimbs, intensifying on tail. ■ **NOTES** Woodlands and shrublands, mainly in dry rocky areas, in nthn NT, with an apparently isolated pop. on Dampier Land in wstn Kimberley, WA. ■ **SEE ALSO** *M. ruficauda*

Morethia butleri.
Hamelin Stn, WA.
D. Robinson

Morethia lineoocellata.
Rottnest Is, WA. S. Wilson

Morethia obscura.
Mt Dale, WA. R. Browne-Cooper

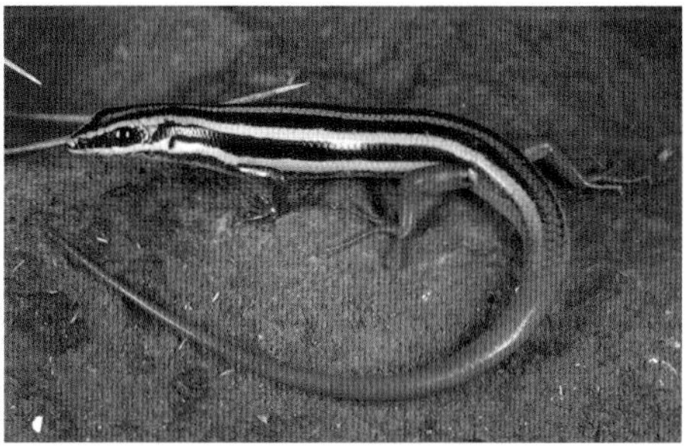

Morethia ruficauda exquisita.
Burrup Peninsula, WA. R. Browne-Cooper

Morethia ruficauda ruficauda.
Broome, WA. S. Wilson

Morethia storri.
Berrimah, NT.
B. Maryan

Eastern Fire-tailed Skink *Morethia taeniopleura* SVL 42mm

Striped, with 5 supraciliaries; 3rd and 4th penetrating deeply between supraoculars (fig.). Brown to greyish brown with prominent pale dorsolateral stripe extending forward to about nostril, broad black upper lateral and broad white lower lateral stripes and reddish flush on hips, hindlimbs and base of tail, becoming more intense on tail. ■ **NOTES** Woodlands, DSF and rock outcrops from Cape York s. to Ipswich.

Genus *Nangura*

Nangur Spiny Skink *Nangura spinosa* SVL 95mm

Sole member of genus. Robust, with **spinose to strongly keeled scales**, most pronounced on tail, and weakly keeled ventral scales. Parietal scales widely separated. Ear-opening large without lobules. Lower eyelid moveable, lacking a transparent disc. Brown with weak pattern; irregular dark dorsal bands and yellowish lateral bars. ■ **NOTES** Known only from vine thickets near Murgon and Kilkivan. Rests with head and forebody protruding from burrow excavated under tree buttresses, surface roots or rocks on sloping terrain. Ambushes passing invertebrates, rarely forages. Livebearing, with young cohabiting mother's burrow for at least 9 months. ■ **STATUS** Critically endangered (C'Wealth); endangered (Qld).

Genus *Notoscincus*

Two small spp. with large eyes, 4 well-developed limbs, each with 5 digits, and **lower eyelid fused to form a fixed spectacle completely surrounded by granules**. Scales smooth; parietals in contact, **frontoparietals fused to form a single shield, interparietal free, upper labials 6**, and **subdigital lamellae divided**. ■ **NOTES** Nthn Aust., from tropical river margins to arid regions. Secretive sun-lovers which bask and forage among leaf litter and close to low vegtn. Egglaying invertebrate feeders. ■ **SEE ALSO** *Morethia; Proablepharus.*

Western Striped Snake-eyed Skink *Notoscincus butleri* SVL 42mm

Pale coppery brown with bold black vertebral and dorsal stripes, broader black upper lateral stripe, white midlateral stripe and narrow dark ventrolateral stripe. ■ **NOTES** Arid, rocky, near-coastal Pilbara. Associated with spinifex-dominated areas near creek and river margins.

Ornate Snake-eyed Skink *Notoscincus ornatus* SVL 39mm

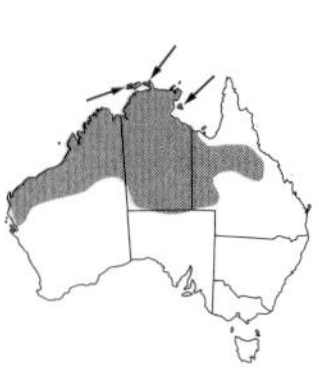

Coppery brown to bronze with plain to spotted dorsal pattern.
■ **SSP.** *N. o. ornatus* has back patternless or with 1 or 3 dorsal rows of black dots and/or dashes, black upper lateral series of dark squarish bars and a white midlateral stripe. *N. o. wotjulum* has more solid pattern, including a broad unbroken black upper lateral stripe. ■ **NOTES** *N. o. wotjulum* occurs in far nthn NT and the Kimberley, WA, but those from Lake Argyle, WA are difficult to determine; both races occur on Groote Eylandt, NT. Sandy flats and dunes to woodlands and river margins. ■ **STATUS** *N. o. ornatus* is rare (SA).

Morethia taeniopleura.
Wivenhoe Dam, Qld.
S. Wilson

Nangura spinosa.
Nangur SF, Qld.
S. Wilson

Notoscincus butleri.
Millstream NP, WA. R. Browne-Cooper

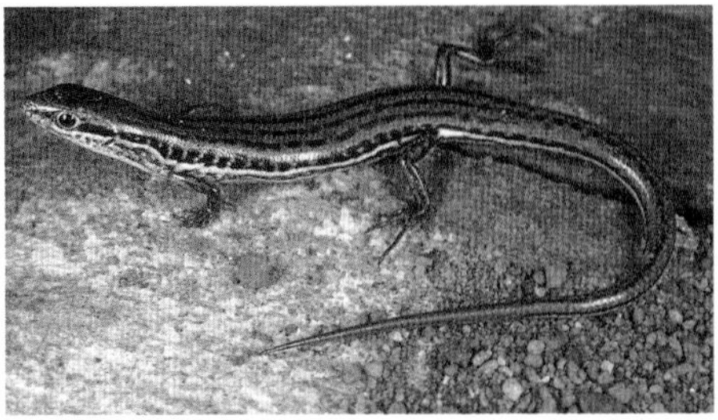

Notoscincus ornatus ornatus.
Burrup Peninsula, WA. R. Browne-Cooper

Notoscincus ornatus ornatus.
Mt Cooper Stn, Qld. S. Wilson

Notoscincus ornatus wotjulum.
Kununurra district, WA. S. Wilson

Genus *Oligosoma*

Lord Howe Island Skink *Oligosoma lichenigera* SVL 80mm

Sole Aust. sp. placed tentatively in a NZ genus. Four well-developed limbs each with 5 digits. Lower eyelid moveable, enclosing a small transparent spectacle; ear-opening present. Scales smooth and small (36 or more midbody rows), parietals separated and frontoparietals paired. Metallic brown to olive above, usually with longitudinally aligned dark flecks or streaks, a pale dorsolateral stripe, and dark upper flanks enclosing pale spots and darker flecks, merging with pale lower flanks and cream to yellow ventral surfaces. ■ **NOTES** Restricted to Lord Howe Is. and its outliers, including Ball's Pyramid and Blackburn (Rabbit) Is., and on Philip Is. off Norfolk Is. Uncommon on main islands but common under stones on offshore islands. Diurnal in winter and nocturnal in summer, feeding on invertebrates (including amphipods) and birds' eggs. Egglaying. The two separate pops probably represent separate spp. Egglaying. ■ **STATUS** Vulnerable (C'wealth; NSW; IUCN Red List).

Snake-skinks Genus *Ophioscincus*

Three worm-like spp. with **limbs completely absent** or **reduced to minute stumps**. Eye very small with **moveable lower eyelid. Ear-opening absent**, represented by a scaly depression. **Snout blunt, tipped with a waxy cuticle.** ■ **NOTES** Confined to moist parts of mid-estn Aust., living in loose soil under stones, logs and leaf litter, and in tunnels of insects and spiders. Egglayers, feeding on invertebrates, including earthworms.

Cooloola Snake-skink *Ophioscincus cooloolensis* SVL 69mm

Completely limbless, with **no prefrontal scales** and **18–19 midbody scale rows.** Silvery grey with 2–4 lines of black spots, 1 per scale, a broad, sharp-edged black lateral stripe and yellow to orange ventral surfaces, black beneath tail. ■ **NOTES** White sands supporting heaths, woodlands and RF at Cooloola and adjacent Fraser Is. Apparently isolated pop. occurs to the n. at Kroombit Tops.

Yolk-bellied Snake-skink *Ophioscincus ophioscincus* SVL 97mm

Completely limbless, with **prefrontal scales** and **20–24 midbody scale rows.** Silvery white to pale brownish grey with 4–6 lines of dashes, reducing to 2–4 on tail, a broad, sharp-edged black lateral stripe and yellow to orange ventral surfaces, black beneath tail. ■ **NOTES** WSF, RF and moist pockets in DSF from Brisbane n. to Bulburin SF.

Short-limbed Snake-skink *Ophioscincus truncatus* SVL 79mm

Four limbs reduced to minute stumps. Brown, pinkish brown, greyish brown to grey, darkening on tail, with narrow lines or rows of dashes often joined on flanks to form a broader stripe. Ventral surfaces cream to bright yellow, black beneath tail. ■ **NOTES** Mainland pops inhabit RF and WSF of coastal ranges between Conondale Ra., se. Qld and about Macksville, ne. NSW. Island pops occur in a quite different habitat: woodlands and heaths on pale sandy soils in Moreton Bay, Qld.

Oligosoma lichenigera.
Blackburn Island via Lord Howe Island, NSW. S. Wilson

Oligosoma lichenigera.
Phillip Island via Norfolk Island. S. Wilson

Ophioscincus cooloolensis.
Cooloola NP, Qld. S. Wilson

Ophioscincus ophioscincus.
Mt Glorious, Qld. S. Wilson

Ophioscincus truncatus. Island population.
North Stradbroke Is., Qld. S. Wilson

Ophioscincus truncatus. Mainland population.
Mary Cairncross Park, Qld. S. Wilson

Genus ***Proablepharus***

Five small, very slender spp. with slender limbs, each with 5 digits. Eye large with **lower eyelid fused to form a fixed spectacle.** Ear-opening present. Frontoparietal scales divided or fused to form a single shield, interparietal free or fused with frontoparietals, parietals in contact, **upper labials 7–8** and **subdigital lamellae entire.** ■ **NOTES** Widespread through arid to dry tropical zones. Extremely cryptic, diurnal skinks which bask, shelter and forage in and near leaf litter and thick low vegtn. Egglaying invertebrate feeders. ■ **SEE ALSO** *Notoscincus.*

Lyon's Snake-eyed Skink *Proablepharus barrylyoni* SVL 51mm

Striped, with **fused frontoparietal and interparietal scales** and **4 supraocular scales.** Based on preserved material, dark brown with 10-14 narrow pale stripes; dorsals, dorsolaterals and midlaterals are prominent from behind head to proximal third of tail, while additional lateral stripes are ill-defined and variable. Brdg ♂ has orange-red flush on outer edge of throat and jaw line. Straw-coloured tails suggest an orange flush in life. ■ **NOTES** Known only from grassland with scattered trees on seasonally inundated cracking clay soils at one locality on Springfield Stn, Qld. No live image available. ■ **SEE ALSO** *P. kinghorni.*

Kinghorn's Snake-eyed Skink *Proablepharus kinghorni* SVL 45mm

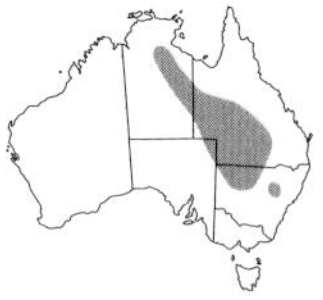

Striped, usually with **fused frontparietal scales, free interparietal scale** and **4 supraocular scales.** Brownish white to pale grey, with dark edges to scales usually coalescing to form stripes. On obscurely marked individuals these are most prominent on forebody. Tip of snout pinkish. **Tail dull to bright red.** ■ **NOTES** Deeply cracking clay plains and heavy red loams with tussock grasses. Shelters in deep soil cracks and beneath leaf litter and surface debris. ■ **SEE ALSO** *P. naranjicaudus, P. barrylyoni.* ■ **STATUS** Rare (SA).

Orange-tailed Snake-eyed Skink *Proablepharus naranjicaudus* SVL 46mm

Striped, with **fused frontoparietal and interparietal scales** and **4 supraocular scales.** Dark brown to black (juv.) to brown (adults) with cream to pale yellow stripes from rear of head to base of tail. Hindlimbs and tail bright orange. Pattern boldest on juv; weak to virtually absent on adults. ■ **NOTES** Grasslands on cracking clay soils in Ord–Keep–Victoria region, nw. NT. ■ **SEE ALSO** *P. kinghorni.*

Spinifex Snake-eyed Skink *Proablepharus reginae* SVL 41mm

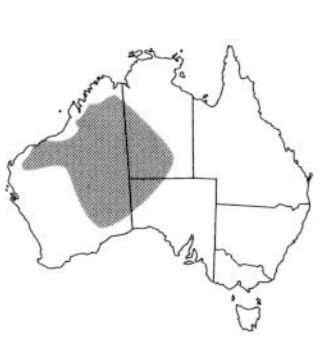

Long-tailed, with large eye, **divided frontoparietal scales** and **4 supraocular scales.** Brown to olive brown with dark edges to scales forming an obscure reticulum, or with a dark anterior spot on each scale. Brdg ♂ develop red flush on sides of head and neck. ■ **NOTES** Infrequently encountered; known from widely scattered localities from nw. and interior of WA to wstn NT. Associated with spinifex in sandy to stony areas.

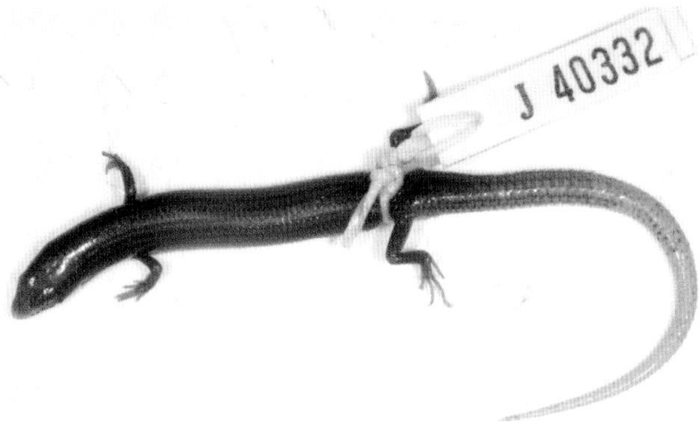

Proablepharus barrylyoni. Preserved specimen.
Springfield Stn, Qld. S. Wilson

Proablepharus kinghorni.
Durham Downs Stn, Qld. S. Wilson

Proablepharus naranjicaudus.
Pigeon Hole Station, NT. J. L. McKay

Proablepharus reginae. Breeding male.
Queen Victoria Springs area, WA. B. Maryan

Slender Snake-eyed Skink *Proablepharus tenuis* SVL 32mm

Frontoparietal scales usually partly or completely fused, in WA and NT, and divided in Qld; 3 supraocular scales. Copper brown to olive grey with a fine dark spot on most scales. Mature ♂ develop red flush on sides of head and neck. ■ **NOTES** Open forests and woodlands across nthn Aust., often with spinifex or speargrass.

Genus *Pseudemoia*

Six small spp. with 4 well-developed limbs, each with 5 digits. **Lower eyelid moveable, enclosing a large circular transparent disc**, ear-opening without lobules, parietal scales in contact and **frontoparietals paired (fig). Breeding ♂ develop red pigment on throat and/or flanks** in most spp. ■ **NOTES** Restricted to cool temperate se. and sthn Aust., including alpine regions, particularly where tussock grasses are present. Active sun-loving skinks which bask and forage among tussocks and low vegtn. Livebearing invertebrate feeders. ■ **SEE ALSO** *Acritoscincus; Carinascincus; Lampropholis.*

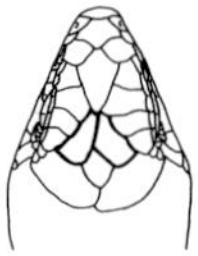

Bight Coast Skink *Pseudemoia baudini* SVL 53mm

Supraciliary scales 6–8 (rarely 5). Grey to greyish brown with striped pattern boldest in w.; usually a narrow black vertebral, pale dorsolateral and sometimes black laterodorsal stripes, and light and dark dorsal speckling, mainly on posterior body and tail of estn pop. Flanks dark grey with a **prominent, straight-edged white midlateral stripe**. Ventral surfaces flushed with pink to orange on brdg ♂. ■ **NOTES** Coastal dunes and calcareous soils supporting shrublands, extending disjunctly along semi-arid coast and islands of Gt Aust. Bight, from Point Culver and Roe Plain, WA e. to sthn Eyre Pen., SA. ■ **SEE ALSO** *P. entrecasteauxii* (wstn pops). ■ **STATUS** Rare (SA).

Alpine Bog Skink *Pseudemoia cryodroma* SVL 55–60mm

Stripes few and continuous, and **no pale dorsal flecks**. Metallic greenish brown with a narrow black vertebral stripe (sometimes very thin but rarely absent) and pale dorsolateral stripe but **no other dark dorsal stripes**, broad dark upper lateral zone and a white midlateral stripe (rose pink to scarlet on brdg ♂ but **no red ventral colour**). ♀ largest. ■ **NOTES** Mt Baw Baw, Bennison, Dargo and Bogong High Plains. Grasslands and heaths, woodlands and boggy creeks on mountain plateaux above 1000m. Active in cool sunny weather, retiring to cover during warm periods. ■ **SEE ALSO** *P. entrecasteauxii; P. pagenstecheri.* ■ **STATUS** Endangered (Vic).

Proablepharus tenuis.
Kununurra district, WA. S. Wilson

Pseudemoia baudini.
Eyre Hwy, near WA/ SA border, SA. B. Maryan

Pseudemoia cryodroma.
Falls Creek, Vic. S. Wilson

Southern Grass Skink *Pseudemoia entrecasteauxii* SVL 58–64mm

Extremely variable, usually with **5 supraciliary scales** and usually **disrupted stripes**. Olive brown, greyish brown to very dark metallic brown with or without **pale and/or dark speckling**; a black vertebral stripe (sometimes obscure or ragged-edged); black, usually broken laterodorsal stripes sometimes present; **pale dorsolateral stripe centred on 4th scale row from midline** usually present, at least anteriorly; and dark upper flanks with or without light brown mottling and small white dots. Pale midlateral stripe variable: distinct, broken posteriorly by darker speckling, or completely obscured by speckling. ♂ brdg colours variable; red flushes on midlateral stripe, beneath tail, limbs, belly and chest, throat, chin and lips. ♀ largest. ■ **NOTES** Cool and cold temperate zones from Mt Canobolas, NSW to Tas, and w. to sthn Eyre Pen., SA. Occupies a variety of forests, woodlands, heaths, grasslands and alpine herbfields. ■ **SEE ALSO** *P. baudini; P. cryodroma; P. pagenstecheri; P. rawlinsoni.*

Tussock Skink *Pseudemoia pagenstecheri* SVL 59–62mm

Extremely variable, with **5 supraciliary scales**, usually **continuous stripes** and **little or no pale speckling**. Brown to olive with straight-edged black vertebral stripe (often edged by small white longitudinally aligned flecks in south); **black laterodorsal stripes; pale dorsolateral stripe centred on 4th scale row from midline**; tan to black upper flanks; and white to pale grey midlateral stripe. Brdg ♂ develop orange to red midlateral stripe but **no red ventral colours.** ♀ largest. ■ **NOTES** Disjunct through highlands of NSW and ne. Vic to low-altitude basalt plains of sthn Vic, s. to Tas and e. to estn SA. Tussock grasslands with few or no trees. ■ **SEE ALSO** *P. cryodroma; P. entrecasteauxii; P. rawlinsoni.* ■ **STATUS** Vulnerable (Vic; Tas); rare (SA).

Glossy Grass Skink *Pseudemoia rawlinsoni* SVL 62mm

Supraciliary scales 6. Olive grey with **continuous stripes and no pale flecks;** black vertebral stripe (sometimes reduced or absent), black laterodorsal stripe, prominent **cream dorsolateral stripe centred on 3rd scale row from midline**, dark brown upper lateral flanks and prominent white midlateral stripe (weak orange anteriorly on brdg ♂). ■ **NOTES** Disjunct from se. SA and sw. Vic to highlands of ne. Vic and se. NSW, Cape Barren Is. in Bass Strait and ne. Tas. Inhabits swamp and lake edges, salt-marshes and boggy creeks with dense vegtn. ■ **SEE ALSO** *P. entrecasteauxii; P. pagenstecheri.* ■ **STATUS** Vulnerable (Vic; SA); rare (Tas).

Spencer's Skink *Pseudemoia spenceri* SVL 65mm

Long-limbed and dorsally depressed. Olive brown to coppery brown with broad black ragged-edged laterodorsal stripe (sometimes very broad and obscuring all but a narrow vertebral line of ground colour) usually enclosing 1–2 series of pale dots and dashes, prominent cream dorsolateral stripe, broad black upper lateral stripe and narrow pale midlateral stripe. ■ **NOTES** WSF, subalpine woodlands and rock outcrops in humid mountain areas, extending disjunctly from Blue Mtns, NSW to Otway Ra. and the Grampians, Vic. Arboreal and rock-inhabiting, foraging and basking on exposed surfaces of trees and rocks and sheltering in narrow cavities.

Pseudemoia entrecasteauxii. Breeding male.
Kosciuszko NP, NSW. R. Valentic

Pseudemoia entrecasteauxii. Spotted form.
Lake Corangamite, Vic. R. Valentic

Pseudemoia pagenstecheri.
Falls Creek, Vic.
S. Wilson

Pseudemoia rawlinsoni.
Tooradin, Vic. P. Robertson

Pseudemoia spenceri.
Cooma, NSW. S. Swanson

Pygmy Skinks Genus *Pygmaeascincus*

Three tiny spp. (incl. some of Aust's smallest reptiles) with widely spaced well-developed limbs, 4 fingers and 5 toes, **ear-opening minute without lobules, lower eyelid partially fused** (an immoveable spectacle with a suture along upper edge), 5 supraciliary scales with 3 contacting 1st supraocular scale and **10 or fewer scales along top of 4th toe**. Parietal scales in contact, **frontoparietal and interparietal scales fused to form one shield**. Brdg ♂ has orange flush on tail. Identification features incl. whether upper palpebral scales are small (A) or large (B), and number of pretemporal scales: 2 (C) or 1 (D). ■ **NOTES** Estn Qld, in dry forests and other well-drained habitats. Swift, secretive skinks that forage over and through leaf-litter at bases of trees and shrubs, seldom venturing into exposed areas. Egglayers. ■ **SEE ALSO** *Lygisaurus*; *Menetia*.

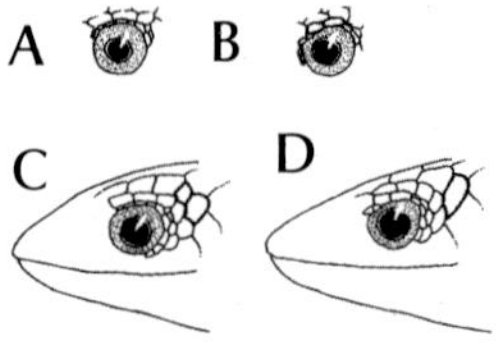

Koshland's Dwarf Skink *Pygmaeascincus koshlandae* SVL 28mm

Upper palpebral scales small. Uniform medium brown above with darker sides. Lips whitish, flecked with brown. ■ **NOTES** Ne. Qld, from Almaden and Mt Mulligan to Palmer R. and Shipton's Flat. Recorded from a limestone outcrop adjacent to a woodland with high grass cover.
■ **SEE ALSO** *P. timlowi*.

Magnetic Island Dwarf Skink *Pygmaeascincus sadlieri* SVL 27mm

Upper palpebral scales large, 2 pretemporal scales. Pale brown with a narrow paler dorsolateral stripe and dark brown flanks. ■ **NOTES** Only known from Magnetic Is. ■ **SEE ALSO** *P. timlowi*. ■ **STATUS** Vulnerable (Qld).

Low's Dwarf Skink *Pygmaeascincus timlowi* SVL 29mm

Upper palpebral scales large, 1 pretemporal scale. Dark brown to grey, darker on flanks, with obscure dark and pale streaks and fine dark spotting on flanks and sides of tail. ■ **NOTES** Variety of wooded habitats from Meandarra e. to Helidon and n. to se. Cape York Pen. ■ **SEE ALSO** *P. koshlandae*; *P. sadlieri*.

Pygmaeascincus koshlandae.
Almaden area, Qld.
E. Vanderduys

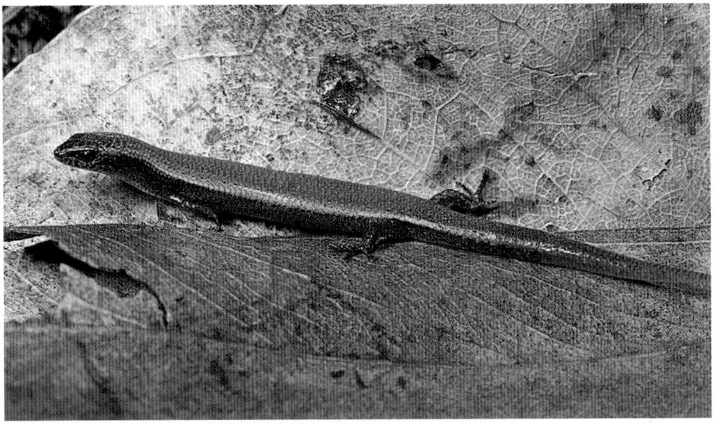

Pygmaeascincus sadlieri.
Magnetic Island, Qld.
S. Wilson

Pygmaeascincus timlowi.
Chinchilla, Qld.
S. Wilson

Genus *Saiphos*

Three-toed Skink *Saiphos equalis* SVL 75mm

Sole member of genus. Long-bodied, with **4 short, widely spaced limbs, each with 3 digits. Lower eyelid moveable, lacking a transparent disc. Ear-opening absent, represented by a depression.** Glossy brown to coppery brown, usually with several dorsal series of narrow dark lines or rows of dashes and sharply contrasting darker flanks. Ventral surfaces yellow to bright orange from chest to base of tail and black beneath tail. ■ **NOTES** WSF, DSF, woodlands and occasionally RF from Jamberoo, NSW n. to Kroombit Tops, Qld. Shelters in soft damp soil under rocks, logs and leaf litter. Livebearing invertebrate feeders. ■ **SEE ALSO** *Calyptotis; Hemiergis.*

Shadeskinks Genus *Saproscincus*

Twelve small spp. with well-developed limbs, each with 5 digits (4 fingers on 1 sp.) and moveable lower eyelid enclosing a transparent disc. Ear-opening present. Scales weakly glossed to matt-

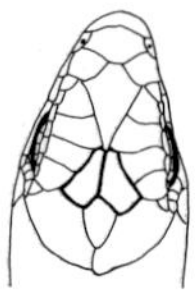

textured, parietals in contact and **frontoparietals paired (fig.)**. Pattern includes a **pale spot on rear base of hindlimb** and usually a **rusty dorsolateral stripe on tail.** ■ **NOTES** Moist areas of estn Aust. Diurnal to crepuscular. Active in shade or dappled sunlight in sheltered humid habitats. Egglayers with a clutch of 2, often laid communally. Invertebrate feeders. ■ **SEE ALSO** *Harrisoniascincus; Lampropholis.*

Southern Wet Tropics Shadeskink *Saproscincus basiliscus* SVL 49mm

Midbody scales in 22–29 rows and **paravertebral scales in 50–59 rows.** Pale brown to reddish brown, usually with dark and pale flecking, often a dark-edged pale dorsolateral stripe (at least anteriorly) and usually a dark, ragged-edged upper lateral zone extending back for varying distances along body. ■ **NOTES** RF in the sthn portion of the Wet Tropics from Mt Elliot n. to Roaring Meg. Ventures into exposed areas more readily than most other *Saproscincus.* ■ **SEE ALSO** *S. lewisi.*

Challenger Shadeskink *Saproscincus challengeri* SVL 57mm

Long-tailed, with usually **6 supraciliary scales** and **several large pale blotches on anterior dorsal surface of tail.** Colour variable. ♂ and most ♀ are brown, sometimes with scattered pale brown scales, and ragged-edged anterior dorsolateral stripe of dark flecks, sometimes reaching posterior body, where it may have a reddish brown upper margin, or onto tail. Ventral surfaces with irregular brown spots, and a narrow dark ventrolateral stripe on tail, sharply delineating dark lateral and pale ventral surfaces. Some ♀ are uniform brown with a prominent pale-edged dark dorsolateral stripe. Others are plain brown above with contrasting dark upper flanks and broad prominent white lateral stripe. ■ **NOTES** Restricted to McPherson Ra. and hinterland, from sea-level to 500m. Active and conspicuous in closed forests. ■ **SEE ALSO** *S. rosei; S. spectabilis.*

Saiphos equalis.
Girraween NP, Qld.
S. Wilson

Saproscincus basiliscus.
Curtain Fig NP, Qld. S. Wilson

Saproscincus challengeri.
Lamington NP, Qld. S. Wilson

Czechura's Shadeskink *Saproscincus czechurai* **SVL 34mm**

Short-tailed, with pointed snout. Brown to dark reddish brown, paler brown to grey on flanks, with small dark and pale flecks (sometimes coalescing to form wavy lines) and a narrow, dark-edged, rusty dorsolateral stripe, often weak or broken on body but normally prominent on hips and tail. Brdg ♂ develop black flush, prominently spotted with white, over sides of head and neck, and orange on hindlimbs and tail. ■ **NOTES** Highland RF from Cardwell Ra. n. to Shipton's Flat. Secretive, normally remaining close to shaded sheltered sites and dwelling among stones, logs and leaf litter adjacent to creeks and streams.

Eungella Shadeskink *Saproscincus eungellensis* **SVL 67mm**

Long-tailed, with 26–34 subdigital lamellae under 4th toe and usually 6 supraciliary scales. Colour variable. ♂ brown above with scattered paler scales and a near continuous dorsolateral row of dark markings. Ventral surfaces either marked uniformly with dark flecks forming broken lines, or with lines only on outer surfaces, and scattered flecks centrally. ♀ either similar but darker, or plain brown above, with dark brown dorsolateral stripe, its upper margin pale-edged, and paler brown to grey flanks. ■ **NOTES** RF above 700m, normally near streams, in Clarke Ra. ■ **STATUS** Vulnerable (Qld).

Hannah's Shadeskink *Saproscincus hannahae* **SVL 38mm**

Relatively short-tailed. Brown to reddish brown above with dark spots on some scales forming broken longitudinal lines. Flanks paler with longitudinal rows of dark flecks, clearly delineated from back by a brown to reddish brown, often broken dorsolateral stripe. Lips barred. Dark V-shape on base of head. ■ **NOTES** RF between Proserpine and Sarina. Secretive, seldom venturing far from the cover of leaf litter, logs and rocks, particularly along creek edges.

Northern Wet Tropics Shadeskink *Saproscincus lewisi* **SVL 42mm**

Midbody scales in 22–24 rows and **paravertebral scales in 46–50 rows.** Brown to bronze with scattered dark flecks and sometimes a narrow pale dorsolateral stripe with dark lower edge sharply delineating flanks from back. Flanks brown; uniform or with dark or pale flecks. ■ **NOTES** RF in the nthn portion of the Wet Tropics from Cape Tribulation n. to Mt Webb. ■ **SEE ALSO** *S. basiliscus.*

Weasel Skink *Saproscincus mustelinus* **SVL 55mm**

Long-tailed, with **distinctive pale mark behind eye**. Brown, orange-brown, rich red to grey, paler on flanks, with pale and dark flecks and an obscure pale dorsolateral stripe with irregular dark edges between eye and hips, becoming prominent and orange-brown from hips onto tail. ■ **NOTES** WSF, temperate RF and moist areas in woodlands and heaths, from Otway Ra., sthn Vic to New England Plateau, ne. NSW. Seldom ventures far from cover.

Saproscincus czechurai.
Lamb Range, Qld. S. Wilson

Saproscincus eungellensis.
Eungella NP, Qld. S. Wilson

Saproscincus hannahae.
Mt Blackwood, Qld. S. Wilson

Saproscincus lewisi.
Shipton's Flat, Qld. S. Wilson

Saproscincus mustelinus.
Hunters Hill, NSW. S. Wilson

Coastal Shadeskink *Saproscincus oriarus* SVL 43mm

Long-tailed, with usually **6 supraciliary scales.** Pale to dark brown with a narrow dark continuous or broken dorsolateral stripe, brown to nearly black upper flanks and a narrow, dark-edged white midlateral stripe (broken posteriorly) running from snout, under eye, through ear to base of hindlimb. Ventral surfaces patternless or with dark edges to scales forming regular longitudinal rows. Tail with a narrow dark ventrolateral stripe, sharply delineating dark lateral and pale ventral surfaces. ■ **NOTES** Well-vegetated coastal paperbark thickets and littoral RF between Smiths Lakes, NSW and North Stradbroke Is., Qld. ■ **SEE ALSO** *S. rosei; S. spectabilis.*

Rose's Shadeskink *Saproscincus rosei* SVL 64mm

Long-tailed, with usually **7 supraciliary scales** and **17–24 subdigital lamellae under 4th toe**. Extremely variable geographically, within pops and sexually. Typically brown above with narrow, ragged-edged dark dorsolateral stripes on body, reddish brown dorsolateral stripes on hips and tail and narrow dark ventrolateral stripes on tail. Backs of sthn pops are uniform or with scattered paler scales, while those of nthn pops often feature a mosaic of lighter and darker scales. The reddish brown hip stripe, most typical of ♀, is ill-defined in s. but very prominent and sharp-edged in n. Rarely, ♀ are uniform brown above with sharply contrasting dark flanks and a prominent white midlateral stripe. Ventral surfaces cream, with scattered brown spots in s., becoming regularly aligned in longitudinal rows northwards. Mature ♂ develop a pale yellow ventral wash. ■ **NOTES** RF on coastal ranges and estn edge of Gt Div. Ra., from just s. of Gympie, Qld to Barrington Tops, NSW. Shelters, basks and forages among fallen logs, leaf litter and rocks. ■ **SEE ALSO** *S. challengeri; S. oriarus; S. spectabilis.*

Cape Melville Shadeskink *Saproscincus saltus* SVL 42mm

Very slender with extremely long limbs and digits, flat head and 6–7 supraciliary scales. Golden brown with scattered dark flecks above. Flanks brown to dark brown, usually darkest on upper flanks, regularly spotted with gold to yellow. ■ **NOTES** Restricted to boulders associated with RF, isolated by boulder fields on Cape Melville, Cape York Pen. Agile, long-limbed skinks, able to leap between boulders and move rapidly across rocks when pursued.

Gully Skink *Saproscincus spectabilis* SVL 59mm

Long-tailed, with usually **7 supraciliary scales** and **22–28 subdigital lamellae under 4th toe**. Brown above, uniform or with scattered paler and darker scales, a dark ragged dorsolateral stripe present at least anteriorly, flanks ill-defined to conspicuously darker and sometimes a pale midlateral stripe. Ventral surfaces white to bold lemon yellow with dark flecks. On boldly marked lizards these form dark edges to scales, creating roughly longitudinal streaks. ■ **NOTES** RF and moist gullies. Widespread though disjunct between Mt Tamborine, Qld and Sydney, NSW. ■ **SEE ALSO** *S. challengeri; S. oriarus; S. rosei.*

Saproscincus oriarus.
Broken Head, NSW. S. Wilson

Saproscincus rosei. Female.
Lamington NP, Qld. S. Wilson

Saproscincus rosei.
Lamington NP, Qld. S. Wilson

Saproscincus saltus.
Cape Melville, Qld. C. Hoskin

Saproscincus spectabilis.
Neutral Bay, NSW. S. Wilson

Four-fingered Shadeskink *Saproscincus tetradactylus* SVL 33mm

Short-tailed, with **only 4 fingers**. Brown to dark reddish brown, paler on flanks, with black longitudinal dashes, a narrow reddish brown dorsolateral stripe with broken dark edges, often an obscure dark W-shaped mark on rear of head between eyes, and barred lips. Ventral surfaces pale lemon yellow. ■ **NOTES** Lowland and highland RF from Kuranda s. to Paluma. Secretive, sheltering beneath stones, logs and leaf litter in shaded moist areas.

Genus *Techmarscincus*

Bartle Frere Skink *Techmarscincus jigurru* SVL 70mm

Sole member of genus. Dorsally depressed, with long limbs each with 5 long slender digits, **moveable lower eyelid enclosing a large transparent disc** and ear-opening present. Parietal scales in contact and **frontoparietals paired**. Coppery brown with prominent black dots, each with a conspicuous posterior cream dash, a ragged-edged broken pale dorsolateral stripe, black flanks, often with obscure paler flecks, and a broken white midlateral stripe. Top of head rich copper. ■ **NOTES** Cool, mist-enshrouded granite outcrops surrounded by dense RF on Mt Bartle Frere at altitudes of 1440–1620m. Diurnal; basks and forages on exposed rock surfaces and shelters in crevices and beneath exfoliations. Egglaying invertebrate feeders. ■ **STATUS** Vulnerable (Qld).

Blue-tongued Skinks; Shinglebacks Genus *Tiliqua*

Six moderate to extremely large, very robust spp. with 4 short limbs, each with **5 short digits of approximately equal length**. Lower eyelid moveable, lacking a transparent disc. Ear-opening present, usually with lobules. Scales smooth to rugose; **parietals separated** and frontoparietals paired. **A row of subocular scales between eye and upper labial scales (fig.)**. ■ **NOTES** Aust.-wide. One other in NG. These slow-moving terrestrial skinks are among our most familiar reptiles. In spite of their large size they continue to thrive in urban areas, penetrating the suburbs of all capital cities. When harassed they inflate their bodies, hiss, gape the mouth and protrude the flat blue tongue. Diurnal, sheltering under logs, in thick low vegtn and in burrows. Omnivorous, feeding on flowers, fruits and foliage, arthropods, snails, eggs and small vertebrates. Livebearers. ■ **SEE ALSO** *Cyclodomorphus; Egernia.*

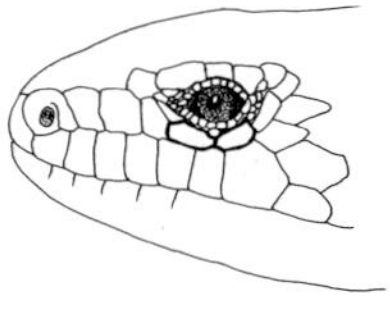

Saproscincus tetradactylus.
Curtain Fig NP, Qld. S. Wilson

Techmarscincus jigurru.
Mt Bartle Frere summit, Qld. S. Wilson

Pygmy Blue-tongue *Tiliqua adelaidensis* SVL 90mm

Large head, short slender tail and smooth scales. Pale yellowish brown to pale bluish grey; patternless or with irregular blackish streaks and small blotches sometimes coalescing into a ragged vertebral stripe. ■ **NOTES** Apparently restricted to highly modified treeless grasslands in a small area of grazing country in the vicinity of Burra, SA, though historically extending s. to Adelaide. Believed extinct until its rediscovery in 1992 after an absence of 33 years. Shelters in the vertical shafts of spider holes, emerging infrequently to ambush passing insect prey. ■ **STATUS** Endangered (C'wealth; SA; IUCN Red List).

Centralian Blue-tongue *Tiliqua multifasciata* SVL 289mm

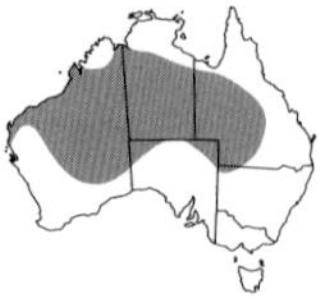

Robust, with very short body, short slender tail, smooth scales and **many narrow bands**. Pale grey to greyish brown with 9–14 orange to yellowish brown bands on body and 8–10 on tail, and a prominent broad black stripe from eye to above ear. ■ **NOTES** Semi-arid to arid red sand-plains, sand-dunes or stony hills vegetated with spinifex. ■ **STATUS** Vulnerable (NSW).

Southern Blue-tongue; Blotched Blue-tongue *Tiliqua nigrolutea* SVL 300mm

Relatively long, thick tail, smooth scales and **pattern of pale blotches**. Brown to black with large whitish, yellow, pale brown to salmon pink blotches arranged irregularly or aligned in transverse or longitudinal series on body and forming bands on tail. Pops from nthn upland areas are darkest, with reddest markings. ■ **NOTES** Cool temperate forests, woodlands and heaths from nthn Tas to Blue Mtns, NSW. Widespread in sthn lowlands, becoming increasingly altitude-dependent northwards.

Western Blue-tongue *Tiliqua occipitalis* SVL 320mm

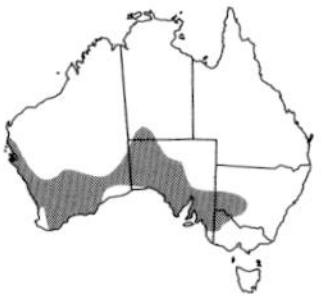

Slender, with long body, long slender tail and smooth scales. Yellowish brown to pale greyish brown with about 4–6 **broad dark brown bands** on body, 3–4 forming complete rings on tail, and a broad dark stripe from eye to above ear. ■ **NOTES** Dry to arid open sandy areas supporting shrublands, heaths and mallee woodlands with spinifex. ■ **STATUS** Vulnerable (NSW); near threatened (Vic).

Tiliqua adelaidensis.
Burra area, SA. S. Wilson

Tiliqua multifasciata.
Newman, WA. S. Wilson

Tiliqua nigrolutea.
Port Albert, Vic. S. Wilson

Tiliqua nigrolutea. Northern upland form.
Lithgow, NSW. S. Wilson

Tiliqua occipitalis.
Melaleuca Park, WA. S. Wilson

Shingleback; Bobtail; Stumpy-tail; Sleepy Lizard; Pinecone Lizard; Boggi

Tiliqua rugosa SVL 260–310mm

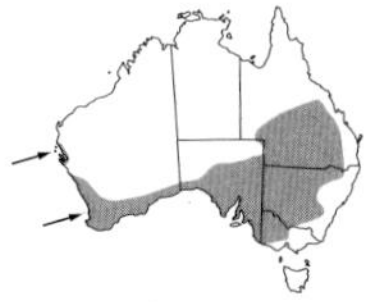

Very robust, with **broad triangular head, short blunt tail** and **extremely large rugose scales.** ■ **SSP.** *T. r. rugosa* is variable in colour: brown, olive brown to black, usually with irregular pale bands on body and tail. Head usually paler and often boldly flushed with orange. Ventral surfaces cream to white with dark streaks, stripes or bars. *T. r. konowi* is smaller, with narrower head and darker, less variable colour: dark grey with pale peppering above and below. *T. r. aspera* is more robust, with broader head, shorter thicker tail and larger, more rugose body scales. Colour and pattern variable but no orange flush on head. *T. r. palarra* has relatively narrow dark head, pale streaks and spots and a large brown mid-ventral patch. ■ **NOTES** Dry to arid sthn Aust. in most open habitats, from DSF to mallee woodlands, shrublands and coastal dunes. *T. r. rugosa* occurs in sw.; *T. r. konowi* on Rottnest Is., WA; *T. r. aspera* from Nullarbor Plain, WA to estn Qld; and *T. r. palarra* on mid-w. coast, from Shark Bay to Carnarvon, WA. The many regional common names indicate our familiarity with this distinctive lizard. Pairs appear to mate for life, meeting each spring. ■ **STATUS** *T. r. konowi* is is vulnerable (WA).

Common Blue-tongue; Eastern Blue-tongue; Northern Blue-tongue

Tiliqua scincoides SVL 300–320mm

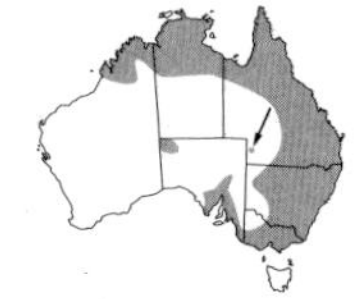

Long body, long thick tail, smooth scales and **greatly enlarged, long temporal scales.** ■ **SSP.** *T. s. scincoides* is highly variable, but typically incl. about 6–9 pale bands between nape and hips and 7–10 on tail, and often a broad prominent dark stripe from eye to above ear. *T. s. intermedia* is larger. Bands often broken into variegations or invaded by heavy mottling on back but distinct, flushed with yellow to orange and alternating with black bars on flanks; dark stripe behind eye obscure to absent. ■ **NOTES** Virtually all habitats throughout estn and nthn Aust., excluding alps and closed RF. *T. s. scincoides* occupies estn portion of range while *T. s. intermedia* extends across n.

Tiliqua rugosa aspera.
Quilpie area, Qld. S. Wilson

Tiliqua rugosa palarra.
Carnarvon, WA. B. Bush

Tiliqua rugosa konowi.
Rottnest Island, WA. S. Wilson

Tiliqua rugosa rugosa.
Kelmscott, WA. S. Wilson

Tiliqua scincoides intermedia.
South Alligator River, NT. B. Maryan

Tiliqua scincoides scincoides.
Brisbane, Qld. S. Wilson

DRAGONS
Family Agamidae

This large family of lizards extends from the western Pacific through Australia and Asia to Africa and Europe. There are 89 species currently recognised in Australia, with diversity greatest in the arid to dry tropical areas. Alpine regions, wet sclerophyll forests and rainforests support few species, and only one reaches Tasmania.

Dragons are diurnal lizards characterised by their upright posture and small, rough, non-glossy body scales. Many are adorned with spines, sometimes forming elaborate crests. Others have developed impressive dewlaps, folded erectable capes or spinose 'beards'. Limbs are well developed, the hindlimbs usually significantly longer, each with 5 strongly clawed digits. The tongue is broad, thick and fleshy. Tail autotomy (loss of the tail along specialised cleavage points) does not occur, although some species have limited powers of regeneration if part of the tail is damaged or lost. Femoral and/or preanal pores are present in most species, and their number and arrangement are important aids to species identification (fig.).

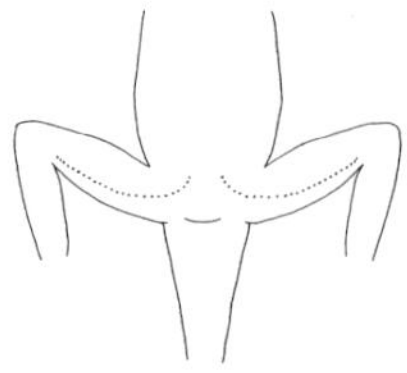

All Australian dragons are oviparous, excavating burrows in which to deposit their clutches of 2–30 parchment-shelled eggs. They feed on insects and other small arthropods, though some larger species include reptiles, nestling birds and small mammals in their diets. There is also a trend for larger species to be omnivorous, consuming significant amounts of flowers, fruit and other plant material.

Dragons are mainly terrestrial, but several are arboreal and many seek elevated sites such as rocks, shrubs, stumps and fallen timber. From these perches they survey their surroundings with a keen eye. Thanks to their acute vision, behaviour patterns are strongly visually cued. Colour intensity is enhanced by mood and temperature, and mature males often display the brightest hues and patterns. Many species engage in complex courtship, territorial and other social communication involving ritualised display sequences such as head-bobbing, arm-waving, push-ups and occasionally fighting.

Most dragons rely on speed to escape predators, and some reach mind-boggling velocity across open terrain. Many even raise their bodies to sprint on their hindlimbs. Some of these are colloquially referred to as 'bicycle lizards'. At the other end of the spectrum, the Thorny Devil (*Moloch horridus*) achieves no more than a slow jerky gait, like a clockwork toy.

Other dragons are masters of camouflage. Some Earless Dragons (*Tympanocryptis* spp.) bear a striking resemblance to the pebbles strewn across the bleak arid plains they inhabit, while rainforest dragons (*Lophosaurus* spp.) cling cryptically to saplings and buttresses, sliding discreetly from view if approached.

Dragons also have some spectacular defensive responses. The most famous examples are bearded dragons (*Pogona* spp.) and the Frilled Lizard (*Chlamydosaurus kingii*), which create a sudden flash of colour and an apparent increase in size by gaping the mouth to reveal a bright-coloured interior while erecting a large spinose pouch under the throat or frill around the neck.

Blue-lined Dragon (*Diporiphora winneckei*) basking on a spinifex hummock. Windorah, Qld. S. Wilson

Genus *Amphibolurus*

Four moderate-sized spp. with long limbs and tails and **3–5 crests of slightly enlarged to spinose scales** (an erectable nuchal and vertebral crest, and 1–2 dorsal crests on each side) and exposed tympanum. Pattern usually includes **2 broad pale dorsal stripes or series of blotches.** ■ **NOTES** Largely associated with woodlands in temperate to semi-arid sthn areas, and riverine vegtn in the interior. Partly arboreal, often perching on trunks and limbs. These swift, alert dragons run on hindlimbs when alarmed. ■ **SEE ALSO** *Diporiphora; Gowidon; Lophognathus.*

Burns' Dragon *Amphibolurus burnsi* SVL 135mm

Well-developed **spinose nuchal and vertebral crest and 1 or more additional dorsal crests on each side. Thighs covered with large scattered spinose scales** mixed with small keeled scales and a **large row along rear of thighs**. Shades of grey to almost black with 2 prominent pale dorsolateral stripes from ear to hips, discontinuous with broad pale stripe along lower jaw from chin to side of neck. Narrower pale midlateral stripe may be discernible. Pattern brightest and crests largest on mature ♂. ■ **NOTES** Occurs in dry woodlands of ironbark, cypress pine and brigalow, and among large eucalypts along inland watercourses.

Centralian Tree Dragon *Amphibolurus centralis* SVL 122mm

Prominent nuchal crest, a vertebral crest and 1-2 dorsal crests on each side, 2-3 longitudinal series of enlarged spinose scales on each side at rear of head, and **dorsal scales with both converging and parallel keels.** Keels on innermost dorsal scales parallel to midline, keels on outer crests parallel to or converging on midline and keels on remaining small dorsal scales converging back towards midline. Brownish with broad pale dorsolateral stripe enclosing dark bars or spots and with wavy upper edge, extending forward to side of neck, discontinuous with broad pale stripe from lower jaw back to postauricular fold. Crests largest and pattern brightest (contrasting white against black) on mature ♂ ■. **NOTES** Known from interior of NT n. to Larrimah and s. to James Ra. Also Mt Isa, Winton and Longreach areas, Qld, and probably occurring through intervening region. Poorly known but recorded from riverine vegtn and sami-arid timbered areas

---

Jacky Lizard *Amphibolurus muricatus* SVL 120mm

Moderately robust, with **5 crests**, including well-developed nuchal and vertebral crest. **Thighs covered with large scattered spinose scales** mixed with small keeled scales. **Mouth-lining bright yellow**. Grey with a series of pale dorsal blotches, sometimes coalescing to form broad, wavy to straight-edged stripes. **No dark stripe between nostril and eye.** ■ **NOTES** DSF and woodlands. Though present in estn highlands, it does not occur in alpine areas. Usually encountered perched on fallen or standing timber. ■ **SEE ALSO** *A. norrisi; Diporiphora nobbi; Rankinia diemensis.* ■ **STATUS** Rare (SA).

Amphibolurus burnsi.
Alton NP, Qld. S. Wilson

Amphibolurus centralis.
Conner's Well, NT. H. Cogger

Amphibolurus muricatus.
Girraween NP, Qld. S. Wilson

Mallee Tree Dragon *Amphibolurus norrisi* SVL 115mm

Five crests, including well-developed nuchal and vertebral crest. **Thighs covered with large scattered spinose scales** mixed with small keeled scales. **Mouth-lining bright yellow**. Pale grey with obscure pale dorsal stripes broken into lozenge-shapes or with their inner edges notched. **Dark streak from snout through eye to ear**. ■ **NOTES** Mallee woodlands in association with heath or spinifex across semi-arid sthn Aust., extending disjunctly from nw. Vic to se. WA. Usually encountered on ground or perched on fallen timber. ■ **SEE ALSO** *A. muricatus; Diporiphora nobbi.*

Genus *Chelosania*

Chameleon Dragon *Chelosania brunnea* SVL 118mm

Sole member of genus. Short-limbed, with blunt-tipped tail, **strongly laterally compressed head and body, granular eyelids with small apertures and a distinctive dewlap on throat**. No femoral or preanal pores. Reddish brown to grey with dark variegations and streaks, including marks radiating from eye and broad dark bands on tail. ■ **NOTES** Tropical woodlands, from the Kimberley, WA through nthn NT (s. to Daly Waters) to far nw. Qld. Arboreal, perching on trunks and limbs of standing trees. Secretive and infrequently seen; usually encountered crossing roads. Common name refers to laterally compressed form, slow deliberate gait and small eye aperture surrounded by scaly lids. If harassed, presents broadest lateral aspect, raises nuchal crest and distends deep gular pouch. ■ **STATUS** Near threatened (NT).

Genus *Chlamydosaurus*

Frilled Lizard; Frillneck *Chlamydosaurus kingii* SVL 258mm

Sole member of genus. Very distinctive, with **a loose frill of scaly skin attached to the neck**. At rest it folds like a cape over the neck and shoulders; erect, it stands at 90 degrees to encircle the head and neck. Frill colour variable: WA and NT lizards have red or orange in the frill while those from Qld are grey. ■ **NOTES** Tropical woodlands of nthn and estn Aust., s. to Brisbane. Arboreal. Seldom encountered during dry season, presumably remaining in the canopy. Frequently seen during wet season, perching 1–2m from ground on trunks of standing rough-barked trees and often descending to ground after rain. Runs erect on hindlimbs, dashing to the nearest tree when disturbed. If confronted, the frill is suddenly erected (up to 30cm across) and the mouth gaped, presenting a startling change in colour and form. The frill is also erected during social displays. Like most cryptic arboreal dragons, frilled lizards slide slowly from view when approached.

Amphibolurus norrisi.
Big Desert, Vic. S. Wilson

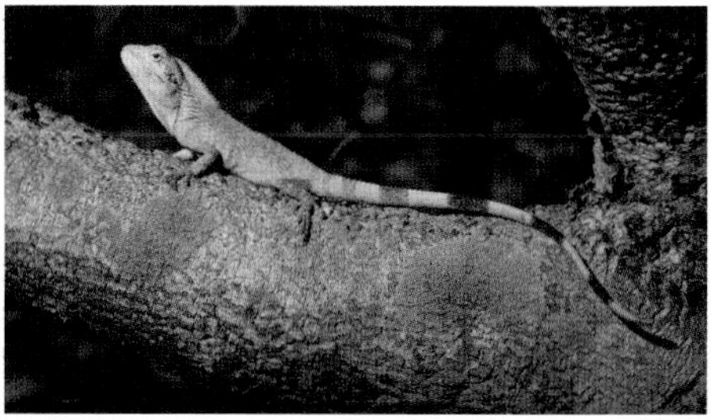

Chelosania brunnea.
Umbrawarra Gorge, Pine Creek area, NT.
N. Gambold

Chelosania brunnea. Gravid female.
Cape Leveque area, WA. S. Wilson

Chlamydosaurus kingii. Defensive display.
Kakadu NP, NT. S. Wilson

Chlamydosaurus kingii. Resting posture.
Kununurra, WA. S. Wilson

Genus *Cryptagama*

Hidden Dragon *Cryptagama aurita* SVL 46mm

Sole member of genus. Very squat, with short limbs. **Tail shorter than body** and blunt-tipped. **Tympanum exposed.** Dorsal scales small, mixed with enlarged tubercles. Pale reddish brown to brick red, suffused with pale brownish grey on head and back. ■ **NOTES** Arid ne. interior of WA and adjacent NT, on stony soils with spinifex. Superbly evolved to mimic gibber stones. ■ **SEE ALSO** *Tympanocryptis.*

Genus *Ctenophorus*

Thirty-two small to moderate-sized spp. with a **row of enlarged scales curving under each eye (fig.)**. Tympanum exposed (except on *butleri, maculosus* and *parviceps*). Dorsal spines range from absent or confined to nuchal crest and sides of neck, to scattered over back. Femoral and preanal pores present. Mature ♂ have varying amounts of black ventral colouration. ■ **NOTES** Widespread over dry to arid areas. Most are extremely swift dragons exhibiting a variety of different forms and lifestyles: small heath dragons scamper among low shrubs and tussocks; dorsally depressed rock dragons forage on exposed rock, perch on protruding stones and shelter in crevices; small striped 'military dragons' forage mainly in open sandy spaces between shrubs and spinifex and dive into low vegtn when pursued; round-headed, relatively short-limbed netted and painted dragons perch on low elevated sites and shelter in burrows at bases of shrubs; and long-limbed crested and lozenge-marked dragons perch on fallen timber in semi-arid southern woodlands.

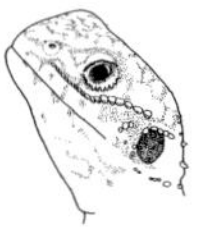

Western Heath Dragon *Ctenophorus adelaidensis* SVL 52mm

Very small with **short limbs and tail**, small **dorsal scales mixed with scattered enlarged spinose scales** and a **row of enlarged spines along each side of tail-base**. Grey with a broad unmarked vertebral stripe edged by black triangular blotches, 2 narrow dark dorsolateral lines and a row of ill-defined upper lateral blotches. Ventral surfaces with black (♂) or grey (♀) chevron on throat and a patch on chest continuous with **3 dark ventral stripes** converging in front of vent. ■ **NOTES** Sandplains with heath or banksia along lower w. coast and hinterland, from Kalbarri s. to Perth. Relatively slow compared to most *Ctenophorus*, tending to scuttle rather than sprint. ■ **SEE ALSO** *C. chapmani.*

Shark Bay Heath Dragon *Ctenophorus butleri* SVL 43mm

Tympanum hidden. Very small **with short limbs and tail**, small **dorsal scales mixed with scattered enlarged scales** and **14-20 femoral and preanal pores.** Shades of grey with unmarked vertebral stripe, 8-10 dark hourglass-shaped transverse bars, dark upper flanks with black blotches and **bright yellow patch on chin and lips.** ■ **NOTES** Pale dunes and sandplains on mid-west coast between Shark Bay and Kalbarri. Relatively slow compared to most *Ctenophorus*, tending to scuttle rather than sprint. ■ **SEE ALSO** *C. parviceps.*

Cryptagama aurita.
Wave Hill, NT.
P. Horner

Ctenophorus adelaidensis.
Jandakot, WA.
S. Wilson

Ctenophorus butleri.
Tamala Stn, WA.
S. Wilson

Western Ring-tailed Dragon *Ctenophorus caudicinctus* SVL 89mm

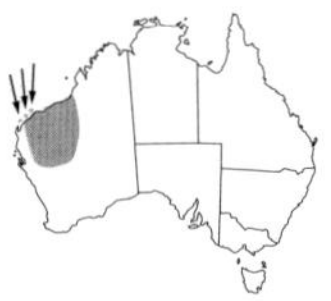

Robust rock dragon. Sexes differ in n. (Pilbara) but less so in s. (Gascoyne and Murchison districts). ♀, juv. and sthn ♂ tend to be reddish brown with 2–4 longitudinal rows of large dark spots alternating with thin pale bands or transverse rows of smaller spots. Mature Pilbara ♂ is pale reddish brown to dull blood red, with pigment on flanks tending to concentrate into about 3 wavy longitudinal reddish streaks. Tail yellowish brown with prominent narrow dark rings. ■ **NOTES** Rocky ranges, outcrops and stony flats of WA from nw. coast and offshore islands, through Pilbara to Murchison district. ■ **SEE ALSO** *C. infans*; *C. slateri*; *C. graafi*.

Southern Heath Dragon *Ctenophorus chapmani* SVL 52mm

Very small with **short limbs and tail**, small **dorsal scales mixed with scattered enlarged spinose scales** and a **row of enlarged spiny scales along each side of tail-base**. Shades of grey with a broad unmarked vertebral stripe edged by black triangular blotches, 2 narrow dark dorsolateral lines and a row of ill-defined upper lateral blotches. **Ventral surfaces with irregular dark marbling**. ■ **NOTES** Sandplains with heath or mallee across sthn Aust. from Stirling Ra., WA to Yorke Pen., SA. Relatively slow compared to most *Ctenophorus*, tending to scuttle rather than sprint. ■ **SEE ALSO** *C. adelaidensis*.

Black-collared Dragon *Ctenophorus clayi* SVL 58mm

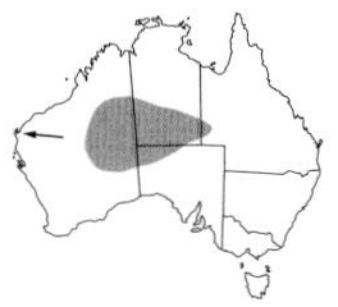

Stout, with round head, blunt snout, short limbs and tail. Fawn to reddish brown with dark reticulum, narrow pale vertebral stripe and a series of large dark blotches. Prominent **black patch on side of neck**, sometimes extending around throat to form a collar. Mature ♂ has prominent yellow patch on either side of gular fold. ■ **NOTES** Red sand-ridges with spinifex in central and wstn deserts, with an isolated pop. on North West Cape, WA. Shelters in burrows beneath spinifex hummocks.

Crested Dragon; Bicycle Lizard *Ctenophorus cristatus* SVL 110mm

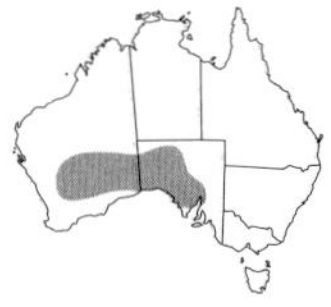

Long-limbed and long-tailed, with **prominent nuchal and dorsolateral crests of spines**. Pattern brightest on ♂, duller on ♀, and invariably drab on juv. Head, forelimbs and anterior body cream, yellow to fiery red, boldly mottled with black. Ragged black dorsolateral stripe runs to hips. Posterior body, hindlimbs and base of tail grey. Last three-quarters of tail strikingly ringed with black and cream to orange. ■ **NOTES** Semi-arid woodlands in sthn Aust., e. to Spencer Gulf in SA. Terrestrial, perching on elevated sites such as fallen timber. Extremely swift, running on hindlimbs.

Ctenophorus caudicinctus. Male.
Maitland River, WA. R. Browne-Cooper

Ctenophorus caudicinctus. Female.
Woolgerong Rock, WA. B. Maryan

Ctenophorus chapmani.
Nullarbor Plain, SA. S. Wilson

Ctenophorus clayi.
Uluru district, NT. J. Cornish

Ctenophorus cristatus. Mature male.
Bungalbin Hill, WA.
B. Maryan

Tawny Dragon *Ctenophorus decresii* SVL 82mm

Flat-bodied, with smooth to keeled scales on snout, **small pale tubercles scattered on flanks** of sthn pop., and no keels on vertebral line. ♀ and juv. are brown to grey, darker on flanks, with scattered dark dots. ♂ are grey to brown with darker upper lateral stripe margined above and usually below (at least anteriorly) with white, yellow, orange to red. ♂ throat colour varies geographically. Sthn ♂ (Kangaroo Is. and sthn Mt Lofty Ras) have dark lateral stripe constricted into blotches, and prominent blue throat with yellow to orange along gular fold. Nthn ♂ (nthn Mt Lofty and Flinders Ra.) are variable, with orange, yellow, orange and yellow, or grey throats. ■ **NOTES** Rocky ranges and outcrops of estn SA, from Kangaroo Is. and Mt Lofty Ra., to Flinders Ra. and Olary Spur. Adults restricted to rocks, but juv. often encountered foraging on surrounding soils. Rock-inhabiting, sheltering in narrow crevices and perching on prominent rocks. ♂ are territorial, regularly displaying by head-bobbing and tail-coiling. ■ **SEE ALSO** *C. mirrityana; C. fionni; C. vadnappa.*

Long-tailed Sand Dragon *Ctenophorus femoralis* SVL 57mm

Small and slender, with total of 18–32 **preanal pores confined to inner halves of thighs and curving slightly forward towards midline**. Pattern weak: brick red to dull orange with small pale spots, smaller dark flecks and usually a pair of obscure pale broken dorsolateral stripes. Pale midlateral stripe more prominent. ♂ has black patch on breast. ■ **NOTES** Arid mid-w. coast and hinterland between North West Cape and Kennedy Ra. Inhabits sand-ridges and sand-plains vegetated with spinifex, foraging on open red sand between low vegtn. Entirely terrestrial, rarely or never perching on elevated sites. ■ **SEE ALSO** *C. isolepis; C. rubens.*

Peninsula Dragon *Ctenophorus fionni* SVL 96mm

Flat-bodied rock dragon with **smooth to keeled scales on snout** and **lacking pale flank tubercles and keels on vertebral scales.** ♀ is brown to brick red with sparse to dense dark speckling and mottling. ♂ is subject to extreme geographic variation, with each isolated pop. having its own distinctive and often striking colouration and, to a lesser extent, size. Various races tend to have grey backs, brown heads and many transversely aligned white, cream, yellow to orange dorsal spots. ■ **NOTES** Rocky ranges and outcrops of Eyre Pen., adjacent interior of SA and offshore islands. Rock-inhabiting, sheltering in narrow crevices and perching on protruding rocks. ♂ readily display with impressive push-ups, tail-coiling and head-bobbing. ■ **SEE ALSO** *C. decresii; C. vadnappa.*

Ctenophorus decresii. Mature male.
Wilpena Pound, SA. S. Wilson

Ctenophorus decresii. Female.
Telowie Gorge, SA. S. Wilson

Ctenophorus femoralis.
Bullara Stn, WA. S. Wilson

Ctenophorus fionni. Mature male.
Arcoona, SA. J. Read

Ctenophorus fionni. Mature male.
Gawler Range, SA. S. Swanson

Ctenophorus fionni. Female.
Gawler Range, SA. S. Swanson

Ctenophorus fionii. Mature male.
Tumby Bay area, SA. S. Wilson

Mallee Military Dragon *Ctenophorus fordi* SVL 58mm

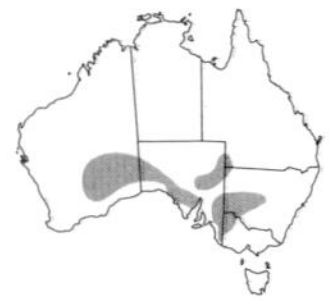

Total of 22–43 **femoral and preanal pores in a straight line extending about three-quarters of the way along thighs.** Brown to reddish brown with prominent pale dorsolateral and lateral stripes, the dorsolaterals edged above and below with black blotches. Throat of ♂ marked with black spots or bars, often coalescing to form V-shape. ■ **NOTES** Semi-arid to arid sandy areas vegetated with spinifex, usually in association with mallee. In some areas of SA it occurs on dunes supporting canegrass. Forages in open sandy areas, dashing for cover of grasses when pursued. ■ **SEE ALSO** *C. isolepis; C. maculatus.*

Gibber Dragon *Ctenophorus gibba* SVL 82mm

Stout, with round head, blunt snout, short limbs and tail. Yellowish brown, reddish brown to grey with a fine dark reticulum or flecking, 6–8 pairs of dark spots between nape and hips and often a similar series on flanks. **Sides of tail marked with 20–30 dark squarish blotches.** Elongate black blotch present on chin, followed by a larger round blotch on throat and a large patch on chest. Pale yellow suffusion may be present on anterior chest and shoulders. ■ **NOTES** Sparsely vegetated gibber plains in arid ne. interior of SA. Basks on low protruding rocks and shelters in burrows in soft soil between stones.

Graaf's Ring-tailed Dragon; Tantalka *Ctenophorus graafi* SVL 79mm

Robust rock dragon. Sexes differ. ♀ is reddish brown with dark flecks and paravertebral series of dark spots, not widely separated and not well aligned transversely. Little or no indication of the transverse pale spots present on other ring-tailed dragons. Mature ♂ is dull yellowish brown (duller than ♀) with little indication of paravertebral spots. Base of tail un-banded and distal three quarters with obscure dark bars. ■ **NOTES** Rocky ranges and granite outcrops along nthn edge of Gt Victoria Desert in estn interior of WA, from Warburton R. e. to Barrow Ra. ■ **SEE ALSO** *C. caudicinctus; C. infans; C. slateri.*

Goldfields Ring-tailed Dragon *Ctenophorus infans* SVL 67mm

Robust rock dragon with little difference between adult and juv. colouration. Brick red to orange brown with paravertebral series of dark brown dots merging to form bands on tail, and alternating on body with narrow transverse rows of pale dots or lines. ■ **NOTES** Rocky ranges and outcrops in WA Goldfields region from Leinster and Laverton sw. to Kookynie. ■ **SEE ALSO** *C. caudicinctus; C. graafi; C. slateri.*

Ctenophorus fordi. Female.
Menzies, WA. S. Wilson

Ctenophorus fordi. Mature male.
Menzies, WA. S. Wilson

Ctenophorus gibba.
Maree, SA. S. Wilson

Ctenophorus graafi.
Warburton area, WA. T. Rasmussen

Ctenophorus infans.
Leinster, WA. B. Maryan

Central Military Dragon *Ctenophorus isolepis* SVL 70mm

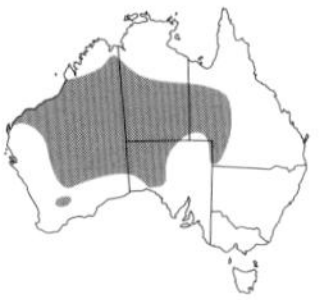

Total of 42–68 **femoral and preanal pores in a line along full length of thighs and curving sharply forwards at midline.** Reddish brown with dark-edged whitish spots and pale dorsolateral and midlateral stripes. ♂ bears broad black stripe from chin to middle of abdomen, constricting on throat and extending on anterior edges of forelimbs. ■ **SSP.** *C. i. isolepis* has unbroken dorsolateral stripes. *C. i. gularis* has broken dorsolateral stripes and more extensive ventral black colouration. *C. i. citrinus* is dull to bright yellow above with broken dorsolateral stripes. ■ **NOTES** Arid wstn two-thirds of Aust., in sand-ridge deserts and loamy flats. *C. i. isolepis* extends from North West Cape through sthn Kimberley to nthn interior of NT and wstn Qld. *C. i. gularis* occurs from interior of WA to far wstn Qld. *C. i. citrinus* occupies yellow sand-plains with heath and spinifex in sthn interior of WA. Entirely terrestrial, rarely perching on elevated sites and foraging on bare ground between low open vegtn. ■ **SEE ALSO** *C. femoralis; C. fordi; C. maculatus; C. rubens.*

Spotted Military Dragon *Ctenophorus maculatus* SVL 54–67mm

Total of 38–58 **femoral and preanal pores along full length of thighs and curving slightly forwards at midline.** ■ **SSP.** *C. m. maculatus* is brown with cream dorsolateral and pale grey midlateral stripes. ♂ bears small black patch on chin, spots on lower lips, chevron on throat and kite shape on chest. *C. m. griseus*, largest race, is grey with dorsolateral stripe usually broken and flushed anteriorly with red. *C. m. badius*, smallest race, is reddish with yellow dorsolateral stripe. *C. m. dualis* ♂ resembles *C. m. griseus* while ♀ is drab reddish brown with more obscure pattern. ■ **NOTES** Semi-arid to arid shrublands and hummock grasslands. *C. m. maculatus* occurs on w. coast n. to Shark Bay; *C. m. badius* occurs further n. on mid-w. coast and adjacent interior; *C. m. griseus* inhabits the sthn interior and s. coast of WA; *C. m. dualis* occurs along a narrow band of mallee on sthn edge of Nullarbor Plain. Entirely terrestrial, foraging in open areas around margins of low ground cover. ■ **SEE ALSO** *C. fordi; C. isolepis.* ■ **STATUS** Rare (SA).

Lake Eyre Dragon *Ctenophorus maculosus* SVL 69mm

Stout, with round head, blunt snout, short limbs and tail. **Tympanum hidden.** White to very pale brown with fine dark reticulum or flecking and 2 prominent rows of large, circular black blotches between nape and hips. A black streak runs from chin to gular fold. Both sexes develop varying red ventral flushes during the breeding season. ■ **NOTES** Restricted to featureless salt lakes in arid interior of SA, dwelling near margins of salt lakes and burrowing beneath the buckled salt crust. Elevated rims of ant nests provide meagre shade and perching sites, and during periodic flooding lizards burrow into sandy shorelines.

Ctenophorus isolepis citrinus.
Bungalbin, WA. R. Browne-Cooper

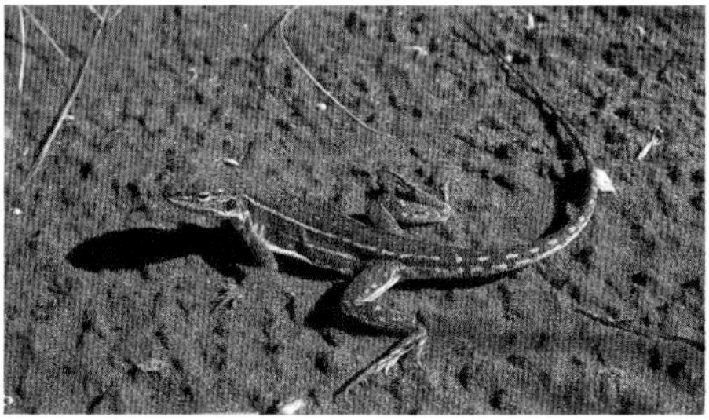

Ctenophorus isolepis isolepis. Female.
Bullara Stn, WA. S. Wilson

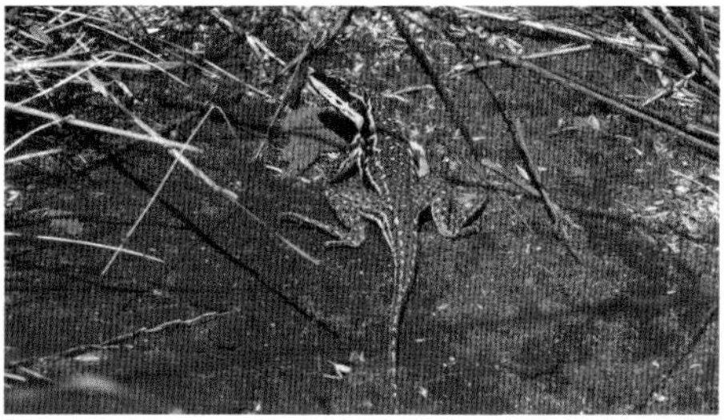

Ctenophorus isolepis gularis. Male.
Windorah, Qld. S. Wilson

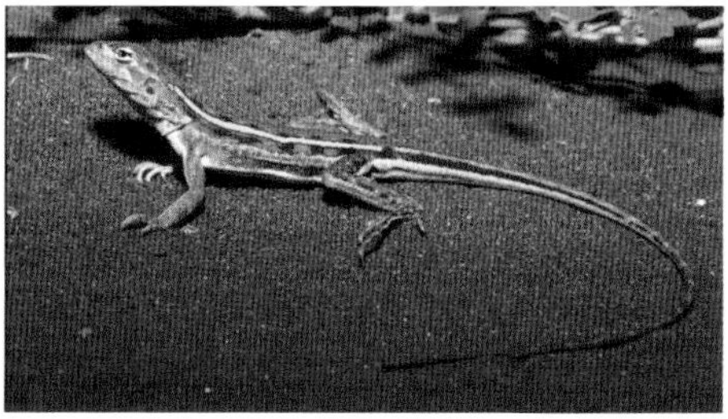

Ctenophorus maculatus badius.
Mt Narryer Stn, WA. D. Knowles

Ctenophorus maculatus dualis. Male (upper) and female (lower). Eucla district, WA. G. Harold

Ctenophorus maculatus griseus.
Forrestania area, WA. S. Wilson

Ctenophorus maculatus maculatus.
Tamala Stn, WA. S. Wilson

Ctenophorus maculosus.
Lake Eyre South, SA. P. Robertson

McKenzie's Dragon *Ctenophorus mckenziei* SVL 77mm

Long-limbed and long-tailed, with **low spiny nuchal crest**. Blackish brown with narrow greyish white vertebral stripe, broad wavy-edged orange-brown dorsolateral stripe or series of blotches, and **irregular greyish white transverse lines.** ♂ bears broad dark stripe on throat and kite-shaped patch on chest. ■ **NOTES** Semi-arid sthn woodlands of mallee growing over acacia and chenopod shrubs. Known from two widely spaced localities: near Ponier Rock and Noondoonia Stn in se. interior of WA, and Colona Stn area, sw. SA. Forages in open spaces between shrubs, sheltering in burrows at their bases. ■ **SEE ALSO** *C. scutulatus.* ■ **STATUS** Rare (SA).

Barrier Range Dragon *Ctenophorus mirrityana* SVL 91mm

Flat-bodied, with smooth to lightly wrinkled scales on snout, and no enlarged tubercles on flanks. ♀and juv. are brown with thin pale vertebral line, dark lateral stripe and brown, grey and terracotta speckling. Adult ♂ is blue grey to pale blue with broad black upper lateral stripe from behind eye to groin, enclosing a thinner, broken orange stripe. Orange wash over eyes, snout and upper jaw. Throat cream with orange flush that may cover entire throat, parallel grey stripes and a **broad black midline stripe from snout to gular fold.** ■ **NOTES** Rock inhabiting on ranges and outcrops of wstn NSW incl. Barrier Ra. nth of Broken Hill, Mutawintji NP and Koonenberry Mtn, nth of Mutawintji. ■ **STATUS** Endangered (NSW). ■ **SEE ALSO** *C. decresii.*

Lake Disappointment Dragon *Ctenophorus nguyarna* SVL 78mm

Robust with short, deep head and **numerous enlarged dorsal scales tending to form transverse bars on sides.** ♂ is orange with black variegations, numerous small dark-edged pale spots and a broad silvery grey vertebral stripe from nape onto tail, enclosing sharp-edged black bars (sometimes off-set at midline) on body. **Tail pale with black vertical bars along sides.** Ventral surfaces white with black triangle on throat and kite-shaped patch on chest. ♀ is duller greyish orange, with vertebral stripe weaker and narrower, and no dark ventral pigment. ■ **NOTES** Known only from low samphire shrubs fringing a remote salt lake, Lake Disappointment. Forages on bare salt crust, digs shallow burrows at bases of shrubs and ♂ basks and displays (head-bobbing, back-arching and tail-waving) on top of shrubs. ■ **SEE ALSO** *C. salinarum.*

Central Netted Dragon *Ctenophorus nuchalis* SVL 115mm

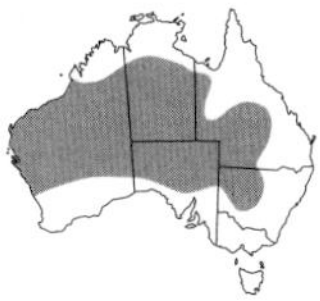

Robust, with round head, **very blunt snout**, short limbs and tail, small spiny nuchal crest and total of 12–34 **femoral and preanal pores arranged in a curve, sweeping forward to anterior thigh**. Pale yellowish brown with dark reticulum and narrow pale vertebral stripe. Breeding ♂ develops bright orange-red flush over head and throat. ■ **NOTES** Widespread through semi-arid to arid areas. Abundant and conspicuous throughout the interior, basking on low elevated sites and sheltering in burrows at bases of shrubs and stumps. During winter inactivity entrances to burrows are plugged with soil. ■ **SEE ALSO** *C. reticulatus.*

Ctenophorus mckenziei.
Noondoonia Stn, WA. R. Browne-Cooper

Ctenophorus mirrityana. Female.
Mutawintji NP, NSW. S. Wilson

Ctenophorus mirrityana. Male.
Mutawintji NP, NSW. S. Wilson

Ctenophorus nguyarna. Male.
Lake Disappointment, WA. B. Maryan

Ctenophorus nguyarna. Female.
Lake Disappointment, WA. B. Maryan

Ctenophorus nuchalis.
Mutawintji NP, NSW. G. Swan

Ornate Dragon *Ctenophorus ornatus* SVL 93mm

Extremely dorsally depressed rock dragon. Adult ♂ subject to geographic variation in colour and pattern. ♀ and juv. are shades of brown to grey with coarse dark marbling, usually a vertebral series of large pale blotches or ocelli, transverse series of small pale dots, and obscure bands on tail. Adult ♂ has brighter colour, with patterns including various pale mid-dorsal blotches or a straight-edged stripe, and strikingly ringed tails. Sw. forms are darker and inland pops redder to match their substrates. ■ **NOTES** Dry to semi-arid sw. WA. Restricted to granite, favouring bare expanses strewn with exfoliations and boulders. Shelters in narrow rock crevices, basks on elevated rocks and sprints across open rock sheets.

North-western Heath Dragon *Ctenophorus parviceps* SVL 46mm

Tympanum hidden. Very small with **short limbs and tail**, small **dorsal scales mixed with scattered enlarged scales** and **26-34 femoral and preanal pores**. Pale brown with weak pattern: broad pale bluish grey to yellowish brown vertebral stripe edged by broad, slightly darker dorsal zone encl. pale, longitudinally elongate hourglass-shaped blotches. ■ **NOTES** Pale coastal sands and shell grit with open heaths and beach spinifex (*Spinifex longifolius*) between North West Cape and Carnarvon, and also Bernier Is., WA. Relatively slow compared to most *Ctenophorus*, tending to scuttle rather than sprint. ■ **SEE ALSO** *C. butleri*.

Painted Dragon *Ctenophorus pictus* SVL 65mm

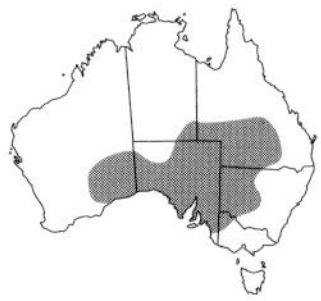

Moderately stout, with short deep head and **uniform body scales**. Extremely variable. Adult ♂ is brown, yellowish brown to orange with dark-edged pale bars, blotches or spots overlaying a dark vertebral stripe. Brdg ♂ has blue flush over lower lips, throat and limbs and bright yellow to orange over anterior chest and shoulders. ♀ and juv. are duller, lacking blue and bright yellow pigment. ■ **NOTES** Semi-arid to arid regions, favouring shrublands and hummock grasslands on sandy and saline soils. Forages in open areas, rests on low perches, and digs short burrows at bases of shrubs. ■ **SEE ALSO** *C. salinarum*.

Western Netted Dragon *Ctenophorus reticulatus* SVL 108mm

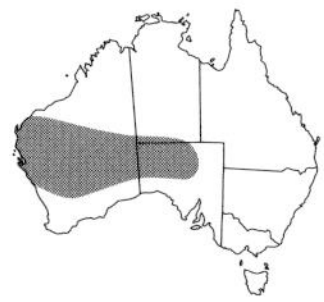

Robust, with round head, **very blunt snout**, short limbs and tail, small nuchal crest and a total of 30–56 **femoral and preanal pores arranged in a straight line along rear edge of thigh**. Juv. is olive grey with dark paravertebral spots alternating with bands of small whitish spots. ♀ loses pale spots and develops a series of elongate dark grey blotches. Adult ♂ is red with black reticulum; deep red when brdg, with reddish flush on chin and throat. ■ **NOTES** Arid to semi-arid regions, particularly on heavy (often stony) soils with open acacia-dominated woodlands and shrublands. Basks on low stones and stumps, sheltering in shallow burrows under rocks or logs, and at bases of shrubs. ■ **SEE ALSO** *C. nuchalis*.

Ctenophorus ornatus. South-western male.
Darling Range, WA. S. Wilson

Ctenophorus ornatus. Inland male.
Paynes Find district, WA. D. Knowles

Ctenophorus ornatus. Female.
Ravensthorpe district, WA. S. Wilson

Ctenophorus parviceps.
North West Cape, WA. S. Wilson

Ctenophorus pictus. Female.
Currawinya NP, Qld. S. Wilson

Ctenophorus pictus. Male.
Ballera district, Qld. S. Wilson

Ctenophorus reticulatus.
Pittosporum Creek, WA. B. Maryan

Rufus Sand Dragon *Ctenophorus rubens* SVL 83mm

Total of 50–72 **femoral and preanal pores in a line along full length of thighs and curving sharply forward at midline**. Sexes vary. ♀ is dark reddish brown with pale dorsolateral and midlateral stripes, sparse brown dots and dark-edged white spots or bars. ♂ is pinkish brown, flushed with brown on head and reddish brown on tail, with pattern obscure to virtually absent; pale dorsolateral stripes barely discernible. ♂ has extensive black over throat, chest, limbs, abdomen and sometimes vent. ■ **NOTES** Sandy areas with shrublands and spinifex in arid Exmouth Gulf and adjacent interior of WA, with isolated pop. on sand-plain s. of Hamelin Pool. Entirely terrestrial, foraging in open sandy areas around margins of low ground cover. ■ **SEE ALSO** *C. femoralis; C. isolepis.*

Rusty Dragon *Ctenophorus rufescens* SVL 90mm

Strongly dorsally depressed, with very long limbs and tail. ♀ and juv. are reddish brown with irregular black blotches along either side of midline and on upper flanks. ♂ is pink to brown and virtually patternless, with brighter orange on flanks and tail. ■ **NOTES** Granite outcrops featuring open expanses strewn with exfoliated rock, in arid nw. SA, sw. NT and adjacent WA. Perches on protruding rocks and shelters in crevices and under slabs.

Claypan Dragon *Ctenophorus salinarum* SVL 70mm

Moderately stout, with short deep head and **enlarged smooth scales scattered over flanks**. Grey to reddish brown with dark-edged pale spots coalescing into bars on vertebral region and centred on enlarged flat scales on flanks. Brdg ♂ brightest, with pale orange flush on side of head and a dark patch on chest. Similar to *C. pictus*, but lacks blue or bright yellow. ■ **NOTES** Arid to semi-arid chenopod shrublands around salt lakes and claypans and in adjacent sandy heaths. Shelters in burrows at bases of shrubs. ■ **SEE ALSO** *C. nguyarna; C. pictus.* ■ **STATUS** Rare (SA).

Lozenge-marked Dragon *Ctenophorus scutulatus* SVL 115mm

Long-limbed and long-tailed, with well-developed spinose nuchal crest. Pale reddish brown to greyish brown with pattern brightest anteriorly; short dark transverse bars across nape and forebody, and a broad pale orange to grey dorsolateral stripe constricted to form dark-centred lozenge-shaped blotches between nape and base of tail. Brdg ♂ has a broad black stripe on throat and a black patch on chest. ■ **NOTES** Semi-arid to arid zones on hard to stony soils supporting acacia woodlands and chenopod shrublands. Extremely swift, foraging in open areas and occasionally ascending fallen timber to bask. ■ **SEE ALSO** *C. mckenziei.*

Ctenophorus rubens. Mature male.
Hamelin Stn, WA. A. Elliott

Ctenophorus rufescens.
Mimilli, Everard Ranges, SA. B. Miller

Ctenophorus salinarum.
Mt Celia Stn district, WA. B. Maryan

Ctenophorus scutulatus.
Wooleen Stn, WA.
S. Wilson

Slater's Ring-tailed Dragon *Ctenophorus slateri* SVL 100mm

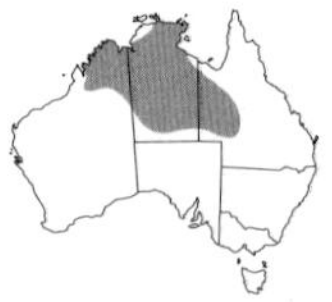

Robust rock dragon. Sexes differ. ♀ is dull reddish brown with widely separated paravertebral series of small dark dots. Pale dorsolateral dots sometimes present, occasionally forming transverse rows. Mature ♂ is dull fawn to reddish brown with weak pattern; dark paravertebral spots sometimes present. Tail obscurely marked with brown bands. ■ **NOTES** Rocky ranges and outcrops from central Aust., nw. to Kimberley region and e. to interior of Qld. ■ **SEE ALSO** *C. caudicinctus; C. infans; C. graafi.*

Ochre Dragon *Ctenophorus tjantjalka* SVL 73mm

Moderate-bodied rock dragon with **wrinkled scales on snout** and **keeled vertebral scales** on ♂. ♀ and juv. are pale greyish brown to brick red with dark flecks and bands of pale spots. Mature ♂ is blue-grey and without pattern, or brown with dark upper flanks and **irregular cream vertical bars darkening to salmon pink laterally**. Vertebral region brown to grey. Tail obscurely banded. ■ **NOTES** Arid SA, from Painted Hill nw. to base of Everard Ra. on low, weathered, crumbling outcrops and stony hills. ■ **SEE ALSO** *C. vadnappa.*

Red-barred Dragon *Ctenophorus vadnappa* SVL 85mm

Moderate-bodied rock dragon with **wrinkled scales on snout and keeled vertebral scales**. ♀ and juv. are pale brown with vertical rows of dark flecks on flanks. Mature ♂ has a **bright blue vertebral stripe** and **black flanks with vertical bars of vivid orange-red blotches**. ■ **NOTES** Rocky outcrops and ranges in semi-arid to arid SA, from nthn Flinders Ra. to hills n. of Lake Torrens. Rock-inhabiting. Shelters in crevices and perches on prominent elevated sites. ♂ displays with a series of push-ups with the tail coiled vertically. ■ **SEE ALSO** *C. fionni; C. tjantjalka.*

Yinnietharra Rock Dragon *Ctenophorus yinnietharra* SVL 87mm

Very **dorsally depressed.** Adult ♂ is bluish grey with reddish brown vertebral flush and obscure dark grey marbling. **Distal two-thirds of tail strikingly ringed with black and orange-brown**. ♀ and juv. are dull reddish brown to greyish brown with obscure dark grey blotches and often weak pale vertebral and transverse dorsal lines. ■ **NOTES** Low weathered granite outcrops on Yinnietharra Stn, in arid central-wstn interior. Basks on low rocks and shrubs. ■ **STATUS** Vulnerable (IUCN Red List; C'wealth; WA).

Ctenophorus slateri.
Morney Stn, Qld. S. Wilson

Ctenophorus slateri.
George Gill Range, NT. S. Wilson

Ctenophorus tjantjalka. Male.
Painted Hill, SA. A. Kennedy

Ctenophorus tjantjalka. Male.
Davenport Range, SA. S. Donnellan

Ctenophorus vadnappa. Mature male.
Flinders Ranges, SA. S. Wilson

Ctenophorus vadnappa. Female.
Gammon Ranges, SA. S. Wilson

Ctenophorus yinnietharra. Female.
Yinnietharra Stn, WA. S. Wilson

Ctenophorus yinnietharra. Male.
Yinnietharra Stn, WA. S. Wilson

Genus *Diporiphora*

Twenty-one spp. with **tympanum exposed; dorsal crests absent, or up to 5 rows of enlarged scales**; femoral pores usually absent (0–6 present on each side on 2 spinose estn spp.); preanal pores usually present, up to 6 on each side. **Pattern, if present, typically includes pale vertebral and dorsolateral stripes overlaying dark transverse dorsal bars.** Identification can be difficult, determined in part by presence, strength or absence of postauricular (A), gular (B) and scapular (C) folds. ■ **NOTES** Widespread across dry tropical n., wstn mulga zones, central to sthn arid zones and estn woodlands and moist forests. Predominantly terrestrial (one sp. entirely arboreal), basking on the ground or perching on fallen timber, termite mounds and spinifex. Some current spp. are poorly defined and conflict with genetic evidence. It is highly likely that additional taxa are present and some re-descriptions required. Descriptions and maps should be regarded as provisional in nthn Aust. ■ **SEE ALSO** *Amphibolurus.*

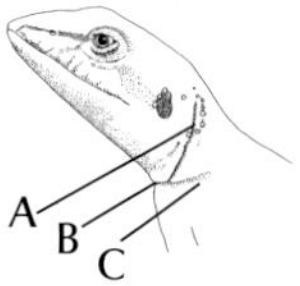

Carnarvon Dragon *Diporiphora adductus* SVL 67mm

Very slender, with long limbs and tail. No gular or postauricular folds, scapular fold weak to absent, no crest, and homogeneous dorsal scales with keels parallel to midline. Pale brown to reddish brown with silver vertebral stripe and narrower prominent dorsolateral stripes, dark dorsal bars absent or reduced to about 4-6 paired blotches, and dark-edged pale lateral stripe. Ventral surfaces white with a pair of narrow dark stripes from chin to vent. ■ **NOTES.** Spinifex and shrubs, mainly on dunes and red sandy loams, in nthn portion of Carnarvon Basin, WA.

White-lipped Two-lined Dragon *Diporiphora albilabris* SVL 55mm

Robust and short-limbed, with moderately strong gular fold, very strong postauricular fold and scapular fold weak to absent. **Dorsal scales heterogeneous**; small vertebral and paravertebral scales and **enlarged, strongly keeled raised series along dorsolateral stripes.** ■ **SSP.** (ill-defined): *D. a. albilabris* is brown to reddish brown with obscure narrow grey vertebral stripe and cream dorsolateral stripes overlaying 5–6 broad dark brown bars between nape and hips. Prominent white stripe extends from lips to side of neck. Ventral surfaces orange. Throat white, with 2–3 grey chevrons. *D. a. sobria* has little or no pattern, though plain and marked individuals may occur together. ■ **NOTES** Grassy woodlands and rocky areas of nw. Aust. *D. a. albilabris* occurs in the Kimberley, WA; *D. a. sobria* occurs in nthn NT.

Diporiphora adductus.
Yardie Creek, WA.
S. Wilson

Diporiphora albilabris albilabris.
Drysdale River, WA.
S. Wilson

Diporiphora albilabris sobria.
Adelaide River area, NT. B. Maryan

Amelia's Spinifex Dragon *Diporiphora ameliae* SVL 67mm

Postauricular fold present bearing a series of low spines, scapular fold present, gular fold absent, and dorsal scales homogeneous with keels parallel to midline. ♂ is brown with grey vertebral zone, prominent yellow dorsolateral stripes overlying a series of 8 dark bars, and when brdg, a prominent red flush on tail base. **Ventral surfaces striped, with 4 grey stripes or longitudinally aligned mottling on body**, and 6 narrow grey stripes on chin and throat forming 3 V-shaped markings converging anteriorly. ♀ has grey dorsolateral stripes, more prominent dorsal bars and prominent dark ventral pattern. ■ **NOTES** Hard pebbly soils with spinifex on dissected ridges of Goneaway Tablelands, Qld. Known from Noonbah and Valetta Stns and Bladensberg NP. ■ **SEE ALSO** *D. winneckei*.

Mulga Dragon *Diporiphora amphiboluroides* SVL 94mm

Short-limbed, **with blunt-tipped tail and 5 low crests** of enlarged spinose scales on back; vertebral largest and continuous, remainder smaller and disrupted. Preanal pores present, 1–3 on each side. Grey to greyish brown with dark upper flanks and a pattern of longitudinal streaks, stripes and dashes, incl. a paravertebral series of 3–5 elongate dark blotches between head and hips. ■ **NOTES** Mulga woodlands and shrublands on heavy (often stony) soils in arid central and wstn interior, reaching coast near Carnarvon. Relatively slow-moving. Mainly terrestrial, blending superbly with fallen timber thanks to its 'woody' colouration and cryptic behaviour. Slowly slides from direct view (rather than fleeing) if approached.

Arnhem Two-lined Dragon *Diporiphora arnhemica* SVL 63mm

Moderately slender, with weak gular and scapular folds, and strong postauricular fold. **One femoral pore on each side**. Brown to grey with narrow grey vertebral and pale grey to cream dorsolateral stripes overlaying and interrupting 8–9 dark reddish brown to brown bands between nape and hips. Pale midlateral stripe may extend between forelimb and hindlimb. Brdg ♂ usually lacks dark dorsal bars and develops red flush on limbs. Throat often longitudinally streaked with grey. ■ **NOTES** Favours woodlands over ground cover of speargrass or spinifex, usually in association with stony soils. Swift, perching on rocks and termite mounds and sprinting rapidly for cover if approached.

Tommy Roundhead *Diporiphora australis* SVL 50mm

Moderately robust, with gular, scapular and spiny postauricular folds and **enlarged dorsolateral scale row**. Colour variable: typically grey to yellowish brown or reddish brown with pale grey vertebral stripe and cream to yellow dorsolateral stripes overlaying and interrupting a series of dark bars between nape and hips. Pale midlateral stripe dark-edged and prominent to weak or absent. ■ **NOTES** Various dry timbered habitats along coast and estn interior, from ne. NSW to sthn Cape York Pen.

Diporiphora ameliae. Gravid female.
Valetta Stn, Qld. S. Wilson

Diporiphora ameliae. Breeding male.
Valetta Stn, Qld. A. Emmott

Diporiphora amphiboluroides.
Mt Clare Stn, WA. S. Wilson

Diporiphora arnhemica.
Halls Creek, WA. S. Wilson

Diporiphora australis.
Warrill View, Qld. S. Wilson.

Diporiphora australis.
Karawatha Forest, Qld. S. Wilson

Robust Two-lined Dragon *Diporiphora bennettii* SVL 80mm

Moderately robust, with weak gular fold, strong spiny postauricular fold, weak to absent scapular fold, large head and short limbs and tail. Brown to reddish brown with darker blotches. Little or no indication of longitudinal stripes. ■ **NOTES** Woodlands, normally associated with rocky areas, particularly sandstones.

Two-lined Dragon *Diporiphora bilineata* SVL 60mm

No gular, scapular or postauricular folds. **Dorsolateral row of scales enlarged.** Shades of grey, yellowish brown to reddish brown with pattern prominent to virtually absent. Narrow pale grey vertebral stripe and narrow white to yellow dorsolateral stripes overlay and interrupt a series of dark bars between nape and hips. Dark blotch often present on shoulder below dorsolateral stripe. Pale midlateral stripe occasionally present. Weakly patterned individuals tend to retain some indication of dorsolateral stripes, though some have only small and sparse dark-edged pale spots. Mature ♂ of some Qld pops develop a black flush on throat. ■ **NOTES** Woodlands and sandy coastlines from nw. NT to Cape York Pen., Qld.

Crystal Creek Dragon *Diporiphora convergens* SVL 34mm

Slender and long-limbed, with strong gular and scapular folds. Postauricular fold absent. Dorsal scales keeled, their keels converging towards midline. Brown with obscure pattern comprising a series of faint narrow dark bars; widely broken at midline. Edges of eyelids white. ■ **NOTES** Known only from one specimen from Crystal Ck on Admiralty Gulf in nw. Kimberley. No known live image.

Lally's Two-lined Dragon *Diporiphora lalliae* SVL 76mm

Slender, with strong gular fold and weak to moderately strong scapular fold. Postauricular fold moderately strong and spinose throughout most of range; weak in the Kimberley, WA. Pale to reddish brown with broad grey vertebral stripe and narrow white to cream dorsolateral stripes overlaying and interrupting a series of short rectangular dark bars. Obscure pale midlateral stripe may be present, most prominent posteriorly. Some are patternless save for a few scattered dark and pale flecks. Brdg ♂ tends to develop a pink flush on sides of tail-base. ■ **NOTES** Dry to arid woodlands with spinifex on heavy to stony soils.

Diporiphora bennettii.
Little Mertens Falls, Mitchell Plateau, WA. S. Wilson

Diporiphora bilineata.
Douglas Daly region, NT. S. Wilson

Diporiphora bilineata. Black-throated male.
Iron Range, Qld. S. Wilson

Diporiphora convergens. Preserved holotype.
Admiralty Gulf, WA. B. Maryan.

Diporiphora lalliae.
Three Ways, NT. S. Wilson

Linga Dragon *Diporiphora linga* SVL 60mm

Well-developed gular and scapular folds. Post auricular fold absent. **Dorsal scales weakly keeled, almost smooth.** Pale yellowish brown to greyish brown with narrow white to yellow dorsolateral stripes. **Vertebral stripe absent.** ♀ has dark pigment, including series of 6–9 blotches along inner edge of pale stripes and flecks over body and limbs. Irregular pale midlateral stripe may be present. Dark-edged ocelli on ventral surfaces. ♂ tends to lack dark markings and, when brdg, develops bright pink over flanks, thighs and tail-base, and bright yellow stripes. ■ **NOTES** Sand-ridges vegetated with spinifex and mallee in arid sthn interior, between Queen Victoria Springs, WA and vicinity of Lake Acraman, SA. Basks on spinifex hummocks, taking shelter in them if disturbed. ■ **SEE ALSO** *D. reginae.*

Yellow-sided Two-lined Dragon *Diporiphora magna* SVL 87mm

Weak to moderately strong scapular fold, spiny postauricular fold (weak to absent in WA) and no gular fold. Yellowish brown to olive green with pattern usually prominent only on juv. and subadults. Pale grey vertebral and narrow white dorsolateral stripes overlay a series of narrow dark bars between nape and hips. Adults have only a dark patch on anterior flanks and sometimes a weak dorsolateral stripe. Ventral surfaces white to bright yellow. ■ **NOTES** Dry areas, favouring grassy woodlands on heavy soils.

Common Nobbi Dragon *Diporiphora nobbi* SVL 84mm

Variable. **Five regular dorsal crests**, including moderately well-developed nuchal and vertebral crest. **Large spinose scales on dorsal surface of thigh grade back evenly into smaller scales. No scattered enlarged spinose dorsolateral scales, and an arc of spines present behind ear.** Mouth-lining pink. Grey to pale brown with a series of dark angular blotches along each side of midline and 2 white to pale yellow dorsolateral stripes. Brdg ♂ develop mauve to red flush on sides of tail-base, and body stripes become bright yellow. ■ **NOTES** Mallee/spinifex associations in se. SA and nw. Vic, through DSF, woodlands and RF along coast and ranges to n. Qld. ■ **SEE ALSO** *D. phaeospinosa; Amphibolurus muricatus; A. norrisi.*

Grey-striped Western Desert Dragon *Diporiphora paraconvergens* SVL 58mm

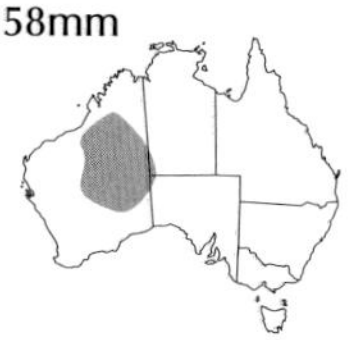

Very slender, with long limbs and tail. Gular and postauricular folds weak, scapular fold present, no crest, and homogeneous dorsal scales with keels converging towards midline. Red to pink with broad, faint pale vertebral stripe, narrower pale dorsolateral stripes, dark dorsal bars absent or reduced to obscure paired blotches, and narrow pale lateral stripe. Mature ♂ have yellow heads. Ventral surfaces white with a pair of dark stripes from chin to vent, converging on neck and before level of hindlimbs. ■ **NOTES** Sand dunes of western deserts.

Diporiphora linga.
Barton, SA.
J. Cornish

Diporiphora magna.
Larrimah, NT. S. Wilson

Diporiphora nobbi.
Yara property, NSW. G. Swan

Diporiphora nobbi.
Girraween NP, Qld. S. Wilson

Diporiphora paraconvergens.
Telfer area, WA. G. Harold

Black-throated Nobbi Dragon *Diporiphora phaeospinosa* SVL 72 mm

Five irregular dorsal crests. No arc of spines present behind ear, **tympanum has a series of enlarged spine rows extending anteriorly, and enlarged spinose scales scattered randomly over dorsolateral area.** Greyish brown with a series of dark angular blotches along each side of midline and 2 white to pale yellow dorsolateral stripes, deep red flush on tail, brightest on base, and black on throat and chest of ♂ ■ **NOTES** Heaths and moist eucalypt forests among sandstone outcrops in mid-estn interior of Qld, in vicinity of Carnarvon/Bigge Ras area and Blackdown Tableland. ■ **SEE ALSO** *D. nobbi*

Pindan Dragon *Diporiphora pindan* SVL 60mm

Slender, with very weak scapular fold, no gular or postauricular folds, no crest and homogeneous dorsal scales with keels parallel to midline. Pattern variable; uniformly pale and without pattern; or dark brown to black with prominent yellow dorsolateral stripes; or brown with moderately broad, silver vertebral stripe and pale yellow dorsolateral stripes overlaying, interrupting and often slightly displacing a series of about 8 irregular dark bars between nape and hips. ■ **NOTES** Grassy woodlands, acacia thickets and spinifex on reddish sandy soils, from Dampier Pen. e. to Tanami Desert.

Red-rumped Two-lined Dragon *Diporiphora reginae* SVL 70mm

Moderately robust, with gular fold, no postauricular fold, and scapular fold weak to absent. **Dorsal scales strongly keeled.** Greyish brown to reddish brown with white to yellow dorsolateral stripes but **no vertebral stripe or dark bands.** Brdg ♂ develops bright orange-red flush on sides of tail-base. ■ **NOTES** Spinifex, heath and mallee associations on sandy soils of sthn interior between Fraser Ra., WA and Moonaree Stn, SA. Favours long unburned spinifex, basking on hummocks and sheltering in them when disturbed. ■ **SEE ALSO** *D. linga.*

Superb Dragon *Diporiphora superba* SVL 90mm

Extremely slender, with very long thin limbs, digits and tail. Gular, scapular and postauricular folds absent. **Pale stripes and dark bands absent.** Pale lime green to greenish yellow with prominent lemon yellow blotch on anterior flanks and sometimes a broad pale reddish brown vertebral zone. Ventral surfaces yellow. ■ **NOTES** Sandstone plateaux of humid to subhumid nw. Kimberley, WA. Completely arboreal, dwelling almost exclusively in foliage of shrubs. Slow-moving.

Diporiphora phaeospinosa.
Blackdown Tableland NP, Qld. S. Wilson

Diporiphora pindan.
Cape Leveque, WA. S. Wilson

Diporiphora reginae.
Queen Victoria Springs area, WA. G. Gaikhorst

Diporiphora superba.
Surveyors Pool, Mitchell Plateau, WA. S. Wilson

Southern Pilbara Tree Dragon *Diporiphora valens* SVL 78mm

Robust, with gular and scapular folds strong, postauricular fold weak or absent, no crest, and homogeneous dorsal scales with keels parallel to midline. Pale to dark brown with pattern reduced to simple pale dorsolateral stripes, or with broad pale silver vertebral and narrower prominent pale yellow dorsolateral stripes overlaying and interrupting a series of **9–11 narrow, dark bars between nape and hips**, and usually a narrow pale lateral stripe. Ventral pattern (when present) incl. **dark longitudinal stripes on gular region; two outer and one medial.** ■ NOTES Acacia and spinifex on stony ground of sthn Pilbara; Hamersley Ra, with outliers in Little Sandy Desert, WA. ■ SEE ALSO *D. vescus.*

Northern Pilbara Tree Dragon *Diporiphora vescus* SVL 62mm

Moderately robust, with moderate gular fold, strong scapular fold and weak postauricular fold, no crest, and homogeneous dorsal scales with keels parallel to midline. Pale brown with pattern reduced to simple pale dorsolateral stripes, or with broad pale silver vertebral and narrower prominent pale dorsolateral stripes overlaying and interrupting a series of **6 narrow, dark bars between nape and hips**. Ventral pattern (when present) incl. **dark longitudinal stripes on gular region; two outer but usually no medial.** ■ NOTES Sand and clay plains and coastal dunes of nthn Pilbara region, incl. Chichester and Roebourne subregions. ■ SEE ALSO *D. valens*

Canegrass Dragon; Blue-lined Dragon *Diporiphora winneckei* SVL 64mm

Very slender, with long limbs and tail. Gular and **postauricular folds weak without spines**, scapular fold strong, no crest, and homogeneous dorsal scales with keels converging towards midline. Pale brown with broad grey vertebral stripe and narrow white to yellow dorsolateral stripes. Dark dorsal bars absent or reduced to 6–8 paired blotches. **Ventral surfaces with 2 stripes converging at chest and pelvis,** silver grey on ♂ and yellow on ♀, incl. broad dark medial marking on throat. ■ NOTES Sand-ridges featuring Cane Grass (*Zyglochloa*) and sometimes spinifex in estn arid zone. ■ SEE ALSO *D. ameliae.*

Genus *Gowidon*

Two Aust. spp., with one extending to sthn NG. Long-limbed dragons with extremely long, slender tails more than 3 times SVL, **one vertebral crest of enlarged scales** continuous with a moderately high nuchal crest, **uniform dorsal scales with keels converging back towards midline**, exposed tympanum and prominent pale dorsolateral stripes. ■ NOTES Nthn and central Aust., mainly associated with watercourses and gorges, perching and displaying (head-bobbing and arm-waving) on elevated sites such as trunks, branches and rock faces. Extremely alert, swift dragons, which sprint on hindlimbs. ■ SEE ALSO *Amphibolurus*; *Lophognathus.*

Diporiphora valens.
Hope Downs, WA. G. Harold

Diporiphora vescus. Gravid female.
Turner River, WA. R. Lloyd.

Diporiphora vescus. Male.
Wodgina area, WA.
J. Vos

Diporiphora winneckei.
Windorah, Qld.
S. Wilson

Long-nosed Dragon *Gowidon longirostris* SVL 114mm

Very long snout. Grey to reddish brown with prominent **pale dorsolateral stripes discontinuous or narrowly continuous with pale stripe along lower jaw**. A black patch behind each ear encloses a white spot. A series of short, dark reddish brown dorsal bars and narrow pale midlateral stripe often present. Adults have 3 prominent orange spots down each side of belly. ■ **NOTES** Arid wstn interior. Usually seen on trunks and branches along gorges and eucalypt-lined permanent and ephemeral watercourses, with some coastal pops inhabiting mangroves. ■ **SEE ALSO** *G. temporalis.*

Swamplands Lashtail *Gowidon temporalis* SVL 109mm

Moderately long snout. Grey to reddish brown with prominent **pale dorsolateral stripes broadly continuous with pale stripe along upper and lower lips**. Irregular darker bands or blotches may be present, particularly on foreback. ■ **NOTES** Nthn coast and islands, between far nthn NT and Torres Strait, Qld. Also present in coastal sthn NG. Tropical woodlands, favouring pandanus- and paperbark-lined watercourses. Usually encountered basking on limbs and trunks of waterside vegtn. ■ **SEE ALSO** *G. longirostris.*

Genus *Intellagama*

Water Dragon *Intellagama lesueurii* SVL 245mm

Sole member of genus. Prominent spinose nuchal and vertebral crests, long powerful limbs and laterally compressed body and tail. Tympanum exposed. Body scales small and uniform with widely spaced transverse rows of larger scales. ■ **SSP.** *I. l. lesueurii* (Eastern Water Dragon) is olive to brown with dark stripe from eye to neck, dark bands on body and red flush on chest. *I. l. howittii* (Gippsland Water Dragon) generally lacks stripe behind eye, dark body bands are reduced, red ventral pigment is replaced by dark olive green and throat of mature ♂ is black blotched with yellow, orange and sometimes blue. ■ **NOTES** Margins of waterways in estn Aust. *I. l. howittii* occurs from Gippsland, Vic to Shoalhaven R., NSW; *I. l. lesueurii* extends n. to about Cooktown, Qld. A powerful swimmer readily taking to water if disturbed. Both ssp. thrive in urban areas such as Canberra, Sydney and Brisbane.

Gowidon longirostris.
Bullara Stn, WA. S. Wilson

Gowidon temporalis. Mature male.
Saibai Is., Qld. S. Wilson

Intellagama lesueurii howittii. Female.
Walhalla, Vic. S. Wilson

Intellagama lesueurii lesueurii. Male.
Brisbane, Qld. S. Wilson

Intellagama lesueurii howittii. Male.
Canberra, ACT. E. Vanderduys

Genus *Lophognathus*

Gilbert's Dragon; Ta-ta Lizard *Lophognathus gilberti* SVL 128mm

Sole described member of genus. Long-limbed with long slender tail, **one vertebral crest of enlarged scales** continuous with a well-developed spinose nuchal crest, **smaller uniform dorsal scales with keels aligned parallel to midline** and exposed tympanum. Shades of grey, reddish brown to black with 2 broad pale dorsolateral stripes from neck to hips, broad white stripe along lower jaw from chin to side of neck, and narrow pale line from eye to above ear. Dark bars sometimes present on back, often indicated by notches along inner edges of pale stripes. Crests largest and pattern brightest (contrasting white against black) on mature ♂. ■ **NOTES** Perches on trunks and branches in woodlands and river margins across nthn Aust. The colloquial name Ta-ta Lizard refers to its frequent arm-waving signals. An extremely alert, swift dragon that sprints on hindlimbs. ■ **SEE ALSO** *Amphibolurus; Gowidon.*

Rainforest Dragons Genus *Lophosaurus*

Two moderately large, laterally compressed Aust. spp. with long limbs; large, impressive, spinose nuchal crests; large vertebral crests; deep dewlaps and angular brows. One other sp. in NG. ■ **NOTES** Restricted to subtropical and tropical RF of estn Aust. Slow-moving and cryptic, usually encountered basking in filtered sunlight after rain. They perch on buttresses and sapling stems, tending to slide discreetly from view rather than dash for cover. Eggs are laid in RF clearings, including road edges and walking tracks.

Boyd's Forest Dragon *Lophosaurus boydii* SVL 150mm

Nuchal and vertebral crests very large, and discontinuous above level of forelimbs. Large tooth-like spines along leading edge of gular pouch and enlarged plate-like scales on lower corner of jaw. Angular brow obvious on adults but not on juv. Colour varies from rich purplish brown to greenish brown or grey. Side of neck flushed with black and bisected by a broad horizontal cream to white bar. ■ **NOTES** RF of ne. Qld, from Mt Spec n. to Shipton's Flat.

Southern Angle-headed Dragon *Lophosaurus spinipes* SVL 110mm

Nuchal crest large and continuous, with moderately large vertebral crest. Angular brow is extremely pronounced on both adults and juv. Colour varies through shades of brown, grey and green, and pattern (when present) comprises irregular mottling, blotches or variegations. ■ **NOTES** Subtropical RF and adjacent margins of WSF from Gosford, NSW n. nearly to Gympie, Qld.

Lophognathus gilberti. Mature male.
Kununurra, WA. S. Wilson

Lophognathus gilberti. Female.
Mt Isa, Qld. S. Wilson

Lophosaurus boydii.
Mossman Gorge, Qld. S. Wilson.

Lophosaurus spinipes.
Lamington NP, Qld. E. Vanderduys

Genus *Moloch*

Thorny Devil *Moloch horridus* SVL 110mm

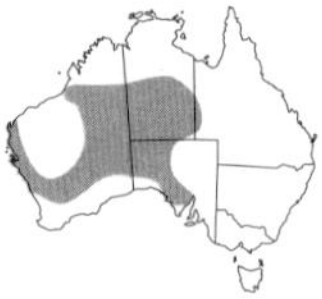

Sole member of genus. Distinctive and spectacular, with **large thorn-like spines over head, body, limbs and tail**, and a unique spinose hump on neck. Very robust, with short limbs and tail. Rich orange-red to yellow, with large prominent darker blotches broken by narrow pale vertebral stripe and usually dorsolateral stripes. ♀ considerably larger than ♂. ■ **NOTES** Arid and semi-arid sandy regions. Walks very slowly with a jerky gait and tail held in an upward curve. Feeds exclusively on small black ants, up to 5000 per meal.

Bearded Dragons Genus *Pogona*

Six moderate to very large spp. with relatively short limbs and weakly to strongly dorsally depressed bodies. Tympanum exposed. Many spines over body, limbs and tail, including **a row across base of head, a row at rear edge of lower jaw, extending across throat to form a 'beard'** in most spp., and **prominent long spines along flanks.** ■ **NOTES** Widespread over most of Aust., including many urban areas. Semi-arboreal, perching on limbs, stumps and fence posts. Omnivorous, consuming invertebrates, small vertebrates, foliage, fruits and flowers. When harassed, flattens body, extends beard and gapes mouth to reveal yellow or pink interior.

Common Bearded Dragon; Eastern Bearded Dragon *Pogona barbata* SVL 250mm

Robust and strongly depressed, with **well-developed squarish 'beard'** including enlarged spines across throat, and **a broad row of many long spines along flanks. Spines across rear of head arranged in backward curving arc. Interior of mouth usually bright yellow**. Shades of grey with 2 rows of pale blotches from nape to hips. ■ **NOTES** Woodlands and DSF from Cairns, Qld, to southern Eyre Pen., SA. One of Aust.'s most familiar reptiles, due to its size, conspicuous perching behaviour and widespread occurrence in populated areas. ■ **SEE ALSO** *P. vitticeps*. ■ **STATUS** Vulnerable (Vic).

Downs Bearded Dragon *Pogona henrylawsoni* SVL 148mm

Robust, with **bulbous head, short limbs and tail. 'Beard' poorly developed with no enlarged spines across throat**, a few enlarged spines at rear of jaw, a cluster on shoulders and 1–4 rows of long spines along flanks. Pale olive brown to yellowish brown with 2 rows of pale blotches between nape and hips. ■ **NOTES** Restricted to treeless cracking clay plains vegetated with Mitchell grass, from about Croydon s. to about Augathella. The featureless nature of its habitat restricts perching sites to any low mound of earth or small rock, however slightly raised above the surrounding terrain. Shelters in soil cracks.

Moloch horridus.
Uluru district, NT.
S. Wilson

Pogona barbata.
Brisbane, Qld.
S. Wilson

Pogona henrylawsoni.
Longreach, Qld.
S. Wilson

Small-scaled Bearded Dragon *Pogona microlepidota* SVL 180mm

Narrow head and poorly developed 'beard', lacking a row of spines across throat, and **3–5 rows of long spines along flanks.** Dull yellowish brown to reddish brown with obscure narrow broken pale bands. Tail dark greyish brown, narrowly banded with dull yellowish brown. Mature ♂ may exhibit a more sharply contrasting pattern, and reddish brown flush on lips and side of head. ■ **NOTES** Woodlands and sandstones of nw. Kimberley, WA.

Dwarf Bearded Dragon *Pogona minor* SVL 115-163mm

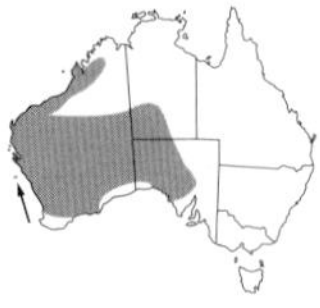

Variable, with poorly developed 'beard' **(spines confined to rear edges of jaw and not extending across throat), a widely spaced row of spines in a straight line across base of head and only 1 row of long spines along flanks.** ■ **SSP.** *P. m. minor* (SVL 149mm) is moderately slender and narrow-headed, with a longitudinal row of spines along each side of nape. Interior of mouth yellow in s. and pinkish white in n. Grey to greyish brown with 2 rows of pale blotches between nape and hips, occasionally coalescing to form wavy broken stripes and sometimes joined by weak narrow transverse lines. *P. m. minima* is similar but smaller (SVL 115mm) and more slender, with longer limbs and tail. *P. m. mitchelli* is larger (SVL 163mm) with broader head and no longitudinal row of spines on nape (replaced by 2 small clusters). Colour brighter; brdg ♂ develops bright reddish flush over head and a black 'beard'. ■ **NOTES** Woodlands and shrublands from wstn half of SA to WA, n. to wstn Kimberley but excluding the Nullarbor and lower sw. *P. m. minima* is restricted to Houtman Abrolhos Is. off lower w. coast and *P. m. mitchelli* occurs n. from nthn Pilbara; *P. m. minor* occupies the remainder. ■ **STATUS** *P. minor minima* is vulnerable (WA).

Nullarbor Bearded Dragon *Pogona nullarbor* SVL 140mm

Robust and strongly depressed, with moderately weak 'beard' of transverse spines across throat and **3–7 rows of long spines along flanks. Spines across rear of head arranged in backward-curving arc. Interior of mouth yellow.** Shades of grey to orange-brown with 6–7 narrow irregular pale bands on back and tail and sometimes 2 series of pale blotches between nape and hips. Throat marked with 3–4 dark chevrons, the smaller inside the larger. ■ **NOTES** Restricted to shrublands of the Nullarbor Plain.

Central Bearded Dragon *Pogona vitticeps* SVL 250mm

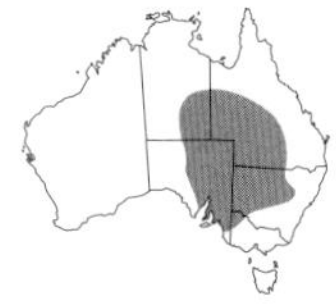

Robust and strongly depressed, with broad head, **well-developed rounded 'beard' including a row of spines across throat**, and only **1–2 rows of long spines along flanks. Spines across rear of head arranged in a straight line. Interior of mouth pink.** Shades of grey to rich reddish orange with 2 rows of pale blotches from nape to hips, sometimes coalescing to form broad wavy stripes and occasionally joined by pale transverse bars. Some individuals have bright orange flush on side of head, particularly around eye. Mature ♂ often has black 'beard'. ■ **NOTES** Semi-arid to arid woodlands in estn interior. ■ **SEE ALSO** *P. barbata.*

Pogona microlepidota.
Theda Stn, WA. H. Cook

Pogona minor minor.
Singleton Beach, WA. S. Wilson

Pogona minor minima.
Houtman Abrolhos Islands, WA. B. Maryan

Pogona minor mitchelli.
Bedford Downs Stn, WA. S. Wilson

Pogona nullarbor.
Rawlinna, WA. G. Harold

Pogona vitticeps.
Blackall district, Qld.
S. Wilson

Genus *Rankinia*

Mountain Heath Dragon *Rankinia diemensis* SVL 82mm

Sole member of genus, with heterogeneous dorsal scales (small mixed with scattered enlarged spinose scales), relatively short limbs and tail, and **row of enlarged spinose scales along each side of tail-base**. Tympanum exposed. Broad grey to reddish brown vertebral stripe from nape to base of tail, edged by broader white to pale grey dorsal stripes, with straight outer edges and deeply serrated inner edges forming prominent zigzagging pattern. Obscure pale bar usually present between eyes. ■ **NOTES** Heaths, woodlands, DSF and margins of WSF of temperate se. Aust., from Tamworth area, NSW s. along Gt Div. Ra. and coastal ranges to nthn and estn Tas (where it is the world's most southerly dragon). Pops living in forests favour clearings. Not swift relative to other dragons, tending to scuttle rather than sprint. Perches on low stones or fallen timber. ■ **STATUS** Grampians pop. is critically endangered (Vic). ■ **SEE ALSO** *Tympanocryptis; Amphibolurus muricatus*

Earless Dragons Genus *Tympanocryptis*

Fifteen small squat spp. with **heterogeneous dorsal scales** (small mixed with enlarged spinose scales) and relatively short limbs and tails. **Tympanum concealed by scaly skin**. Pattern often dominated by pale longitudinal lines and broad dark dorsal bars. ■ **NOTES** Status of some estn pops unresolved, probably incl. undescribed spp. Dry open habitats in arid areas, particularly the bleak gibber plains and cracking clays of the interior, extending into se. temperate grasslands. Some spp. can expose themselves to ferocious summer temperatures with apparent ease. Terrestrial, perching on low elevations such as stones and scuttling over open spaces between shrubs and tussocks. ■ **SEE ALSO** *Cryptagama; Rankinia.*

Centralian Earless Dragon *Tympanocryptis centralis* SVL 55mm

Scales on top of head rough and distinctly keeled, and neck much narrower than base of head. Only 2 (preanal) pores. Greyish brown to reddish brown, redder on flanks, with narrow pale vertebral and dorsolateral lines overlaying 6–7 broad dark dorsal bars between nape and hips, the dorsolateral lines often only visible where they cross these bars. Pale bar between eyes. ■ **NOTES** Stony hills and plains. ■ **SEE ALSO** *T. lineata.*

Coastal Pebble-mimic Dragon *Tympanocryptis cephalus* SVL 64mm

Head rounded with angular snout, low keels on snout and lower keels on top of head. Two preanal pores but no femoral pores. Enlarged scales with raised spines on back, arranged in **transversely aligned clusters of 5–7**. Ventral scales keeled. **Anterior and dorsal edge of thigh has weakly defined row of enlarged scales, not forming a conspicuous ridge**. Shades of brown with 5 irregular darker tan blotches on vertebral zone, and sometimes an indication of broken, pale vertebral and dorsolateral stripes. ■ **NOTES** Pilbara coast, extending about 40km inland, in Karratha and Roebourne area from Mardie Pool, e. to Balla Balla Ck about 50km e. of Roebourne, WA. Presumed to occur on rocky loams and clays. ■ **SEE ALSO** *T. diabolicus; T. fortescuensis.*

Rankinia diemensis. Rocky Cape NP, Tas. S. Wilson

Tympanocryptis centralis. Alice Springs area, NT. G. Gaikhorst

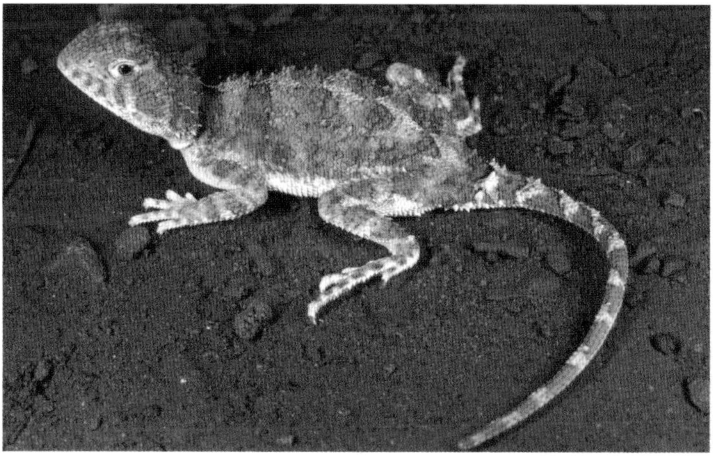

Tympanocryptis cephalus. Roebourne, WA. B. Maryan

Condamine Earless Dragon *Tympanocryptis condaminensis* SVL 63mm

Scales on top of head rough incl. unkeeled, weakly and strongly keeled scales, and neck slightly narrower than head. Two preanal pores but no femoral pores. Brown to grey with narrow pale vertebral stripe, and broader dorsolateral and narrow midlateral stripes overlaying a series of broad dark bands. Pale bar across head between eyes and 3 prominent pale spots on snout. Lower lateral and ventral surfaces have strongly contrasting irregular dark and pale banding and speckling, concentrated mainly on throat and upper chest, and with pale pigment predominating. Some specimens, possibly mature ♂, develop bright orange throats during spring. ■ **NOTES** Restricted to small fragmented areas of estn Darling Downs, Qld, from just w. of Toowoomba to Dalby, n. to Pirrinuan/Jimbour area and s. to Clifton. Original grassland habitat now reduced to roadside verges. Lizards restricted to these and adj. intensely farmed, mixed crops of cotton, maize and sorghum. ■ **STATUS** Endangered (C'wealth; Qld).

Hamersley Pebble-mimic Dragon *Tympanocryptis diabolicus* SVL 60mm

Head rounded with **scales on snout smooth to rugose with weak keels**, and weak, unaligned keels on top of head. Two preanal pores but no femoral pores. Enlarged scales with low spines on back, arranged in **transversely aligned rows of 2–5. Keels of scales on upper surfaces of arms aligned to form lines. Anterior edge of thigh has enlarged scales forming a conspicuous ridge. Ventral scales weakly keeled. Rich reddish brown**, often with greyish black wash, three black-edged white lines on nape and about 3 large dark blotches on back. ■ **NOTES** Probably favours clay-based stony soils. Occurs along nthn edge of Hamersley Ra. in Pilbara region, e. to about Mt Newman, WA. ■ **SEE ALSO** *T. cephalus; T. fortescuensis; T. gigas; T. pseudosephos.*

Fortescue Pebble-mimic Dragon *Tympanocryptis fortescuensis* SVL 65mm

Head rounded with **scales on snout smooth to rugose with low keels**, and moderately strong, unaligned keels on top of head. Two preanal pores but no femoral pores. Enlarged scales with low spines on back, arranged in **transversely aligned rows of 2–5. Keels of scales on upper surfaces of arms aligned to form lines. Anterior edge of thigh has row of enlarged scales forming conspicuous ridge. Ventral scales weakly keeled. Light to medium reddish brown**, mostly patternless but sometimes with ill-defined darker blotches. ■ **NOTES** Cracking clay soils with stones in Pilbara region, WA, centred on Fortescue Marsh area between Balfour Downs in se. Pilbara and Millstream-Chichester NP, n. to Meentheena Nat. Res. ■ **SEE ALSO** *T. diabolicus; T. cephalus; T. pseudosephos.*

Tympanocryptis condaminensis.
Bongeen, Qld. S. Wilson

Tympanocryptis condaminensis.
Bongeen, Qld. S. Wilson

Tympanocryptis diabolicus.
Juna Downs Stn, WA. R. Lloyd

Tympanocryptis fortescuensis.
Redmont, WA. B. Maryan

Gascoyne Pebble-mimic Dragon *Tympanocryptis gigas* SVL 66mm

Head rounded with scales on snout rugose, occasionally with weak, unaligned keels, and weak unaligned keels on top of head. Two preanal pores but no femoral pores. **Enlarged scales with low spines scattered on back (not in transverse clusters).** Keels of scales on upper surfaces of arms not aligned but those on lower arm tend to align to form lines. Scales on upper surface of hind limbs heterogeneous. Anterior edge of thigh has row of enlarged scales. Ventral scales smooth. Very pale brown to cream, with dark nuchal region encl. 3 pale stripes, and 1–2 large dark blotches on back. ■ **NOTES** Gascoyne region, WA, incl. Yinnietharra and Williambury Stns, Wandagee and Nanutarra area, on stony and clay soils incl. quartz. ■ **SEE ALSO** *T. diabolicus; T. pseudosephos.*

Nullarbor Earless Dragon *Tympanocryptis houstoni* SVL 60mm

Scales on top of head rough and distinctly keeled; neck indistinct, as broad as base of head. Only 2 (preanal) pores. Pale brown to yellowish brown with **very broad, pale grey vertebral stripe** and narrow white dorsolateral stripes overlaying about 6 dark dorsal bands. Pale bar between eyes and 3 pale spots on snout. ■ **NOTES** Chenopod shrublands on clay soils of Nullarbor Plain. ■ **SEE ALSO** *T. lineata.*

Smooth-snouted Earless Dragon *Tympanocryptis intima* SVL 61mm

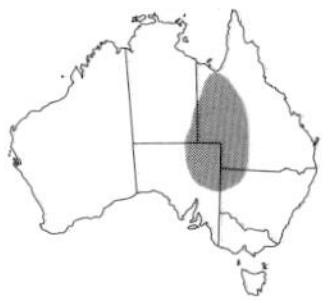

Head rounded, with smooth to very weakly keeled scales. Enlarged dorsal tubercles, mostly single and arranged roughly in longitudinal rows. Pale yellowish brown to brick red, usually with broad, weak dark bands often broken on midline. ■ **NOTES** Arid stony regions including featureless gibber plains.

Lined Earless Dragon *Tympanocryptis lineata* SVL 58mm

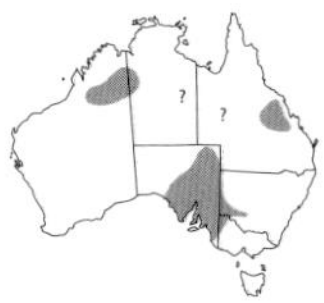

Scales on top of head rough and distinctly keeled. Neck indistinct, as broad as base of head. A total of only 2 (preanal) pores and **no femoral pores. Dorsal tubercles broader than long.** Colouration variable: typically shades of brown or grey to brick red with **light bar between eyes**, oblique bars on sides of head and **narrow pale vertebral** and dorsolateral stripes interrupting about 5 dark bands between nape and hips. Pops from nthn WA are more slender with longer limbs, and could be a separate sp. The name *macra* is available. ■ **NOTES** Status of WA and Qld pops uncertain. Widespread in dry to arid open habitats, incl. gibber plains, stands of mallee and chenopod shrublands. ■ **SEE ALSO** *T. centralis; T. houstoni; T. pinguicolla; T. tetraporophora.* ■ **STATUS** Critically endangered (Vic)..

Tympanocryptis gigas.
Williambury Station, WA. B. Bush

Tympanocryptis houstoni.
Cocklebiddy, WA. B. Maryan

Tympanocryptis intima.
John Hills, Qld.
S. Wilson

Tympanocryptis lineata.
Moomba area, SA. S. Wilson

Tympanocryptis lineata.
Gindie, Emerald area, Qld. S. Wilson

Five-lined Earless Dragon *Tympanocryptis pentalineata* SVL 60mm

Rough, prominently keeled scales on top of head. Two preanal and 2 femoral pores; **5 prominent pale stripes.** Enlarged spinose scales scattered over body. Brownish black with weak, narrow grey vertebral stripe, and narrow white dorsolaterals and laterals separated on flanks by several broad dark vertical bars. The lateral stripes comprise a row of enlarged, sharp pale scales. ■ **NOTES** Flood plains vegetated with grasses and low shrubs sw. of Normanton, in estn Gulf of Carpentaria. ■ **SEE ALSO** *T. tetraporophora.*

Grassland Earless Dragon *Tympanocryptis pinguicolla* SVL 55mm

Scales on top of head rough and distinctly keeled, and neck indistinct, as broad as base of head. Dorsal tubercles longer than broad. Narrow cream vertebral, dorsal and midlateral stripes interrupt broad dark brown bands over a pale brown background. ■ **NOTES** Confined to scattered remnants of treeless native grassland on plains w. of Melbourne, in ACT and adjacent NSW. Shelters in invertebrate holes and soil cracks. Not seen in Vic since the 1960s. ■ **SEE ALSO** *T. lineata.* ■ **STATUS** Endangered (C'wealth; NSW; ACT); vulnerable (IUCN Red List); critically endangered (Vic).

Goldfields Pebble-mimic Dragon *Tympanocryptis pseudosephos* SVL 56mm

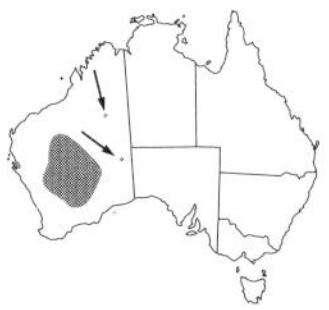

Head rounded with scales on snout rugose, occasionally with weak, unaligned keels, and weak unaligned keels on top of head. Two preanal pores but no femoral pores. **Enlarged scales with low spines on back, arranged in transversely aligned rows of 4–7. Keels of scales on upper surfaces of arms not aligned** but those on lower arm tend to align to form lines. **Anterior edge of thigh has row of enlarged scales forming conspicuous ridge. Ventral scales smooth.** Medium to dark reddish brown, often with dark greyish black suffusion. ■ **NOTES** Widespread over Goldfields region from Norseman area n. nearly to se. edge of Pilbara. Hard, stony soils, often with sparse vegetation incl. mulga and mallee woodlands. ■ **SEE ALSO** *T. diabolicus; T. fortescuensis; T. gigas.*

Tympanocryptis pentalineata. Normanton area, Qld. J. de Jong

Tympanocryptis pinguicolla. Canberra, ACT. S. Wilson

Tympanocryptis pseudosephos. Pebble-mimicking pose. Twin Peaks Stn, WA. S. Wilson

Tympanocryptis pseudosephos. Twin Peaks Stn, WA. S. Wilson

Eyrean Earless Dragon *Tympanocryptis tetraporophora* SVL 74mm

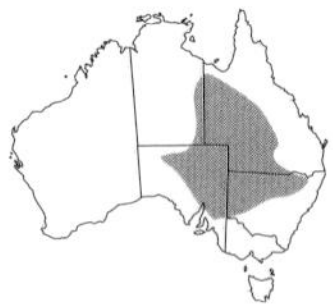

Scales on top of head rough and distinctly keeled, and neck much narrower than head. A total of **4 pores (a preanal and femoral pore on each side)**. Colouration variable, with weak to strong pattern but **no pale bar between eyes**; brown with narrow pale vertebral and dorsolateral stripes interrupting about 5 dark bands on body. Mature ♂ has yellow to orange on throat, edges of belly and scattered on scales over sides of head; ♀ has yellow flush on rear belly and grey on base of head. ■ **NOTES** Vast tracts of arid estn interior, often on sparsely vegetated stony and clay-based soils. Active during high temperatures, perching on small stones or bushes with body angled into sun. Often adopts an upright bipedal pose with hind limbs and tail-base functioning as tripod. ■ **SEE ALSO** *T. lineata; T. pentalineata.*

Even-scaled Earless Dragon *Tympanocryptis uniformis* SVL 50mm

Flat, weakly keeled scales on top of head. Two (preanal) pores. Enlarged dorsal tubercles absent, replaced by simple, very sharply keeled scales barely raised above surrounding scales. Dull grey brown; pattern obscure or absent. Vague broad dark bands may extend across body, darker dorsolateral stripes may be present, and tail has pale and dark grey bands. ■ **NOTES** Known only from Darwin and Victoria River area in nthn NT.

Roma Earless Dragon *Tympanocryptis wilsoni* SVL 53mm

Rough, prominently keeled scales on top of head. Two preanal pores and 2 femoral pores. Enlarged spinose scales scattered over body. Three pale stripes on body and 3 prominent pale spots on snout. Yellowish brown with narrow pale vertebral and dorsolateral stripes overlaying a series of broad dark dorsal bands. Lower lateral and ventral surfaces with heavy brownish black speckling, concentrated ventrally on throat and upper chest, and with dark pigment predominating. ■ **NOTES** Known only from small areas of grassland from just w. of Roma to about Amby, Qld. ■ **STATUS** Vulnerable (Qld).

Tympanocryptis tetraporophora.
Kynuna, Qld. S. Wilson

Tympanocryptis uniformis.
Victoria River area, NT. G. Husband

Tympanocryptis wilsoni.
Roma area, Qld. S. Wilson

MONITORS OR GOANNAS
Family Varanidae

This family of approximately 50 species is distributed from Africa through Asia to Australia and the western Pacific. It includes the world's largest living lizard, the Komodo Dragon (*Varanus komodoensis*), a massive heavyweight exceeding 3 metres in total length. Australia's largest lizard, the Perentie (*V. giganteus*) probably ranks about third, at over 2 metres.

Australia is the stronghold for the family, with 30 described species. The terms 'monitor' and 'goanna' are interchangeable. Monitor is employed worldwide, while goanna is a strictly Australian term derived from 'iguana', a group of large, unrelated lizards from the Americas.

Large foraging monitors walk with a distinctive, unhurried, almost swaggering gait, constantly flicking their slender, deeply forked tongues as they investigate crevices and excavate burrows. All are carnivorous, consuming almost anything that can be caught and eaten. Small species are mainly predators of invertebrates, other reptiles, frogs and bird's eggs, while large monitors are often scavengers of carrion. Their teeth are long, sharp and recurved, suitable for grasping but not cutting. Prey is normally swallowed whole with a jerking motion of the head and neck, though portions can sometimes be ripped from a carcass.

All monitors are egglayers, producing clutches of up to 35 parchment-shelled eggs. Some bury their eggs in burrows but others, including the familiar eastern Australian Lace Monitor (*V. varius*), exclusively utilise termite nests to incubate their eggs. The termites seal the eggs within the nest, creating a natural, climate-controlled humidicrib, and there is now convincing evidence that the mother Lace Monitor actually returns to expose the eggs just prior to hatching.

Newly born young of all species are extremely secretive and seldom seen. Despite the abundance of Lace Monitors in state forests, national parks and picnic grounds, very few herpetologists encounter hatchlings. Most are found accidentally when trees are felled.

The males of many species engage in ritualised combat during the mating season. Bouts are impressive to witness, with both individuals standing upright, grasping each other about the body with the forelimbs and endeavouring to topple their opponent.

The tail, ranging from about the same length as the body to almost twice as long, varies according to its function. For large monitors a robust muscular tail is an effective defensive weapon that can be used as a powerful lash. Several smaller rock-inhabiting monitors have spiny tails which they employ to block the entrance of a burrow or crevice. Some monitors are semi-aquatic, with laterally compressed tails that aid swimming, and the tails of some arboreal, canopy-dwelling monitors are prehensile to assist climbing.

All members of the family are currently placed in one genus.

Lace Monitor (*Varanus varius*). Rival males of many species engage in chest to chest combat.
Woodgate area, Qld. S. Wilson

Genus *Varanus*

Small to extremely large lizards with long heads and necks, narrow snouts, well-developed limbs with 5 strongly clawed digits, deeply forked tongues and thick, loose-fitting skin with tough granular scales. There are no spines on the body, though some spp. have spiny tails.
■ **NOTES** Widespread over most of mainland Aust., but absent from Tas. The majority occur in the nthn and arid regions, with some localities supporting up to 10 different spp. In temperate sthn areas, numbers drop to 1 or 2.

Spiny-tailed Monitor *Varanus acanthurus* TL 63cm

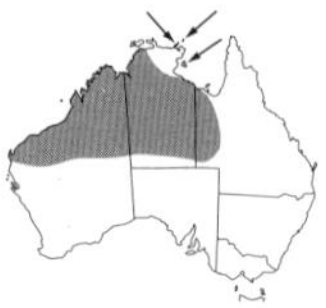

Very spiny tail, round in cross-section, and usually **pale stripes on neck**.
■ **SSP.** *V. a. acanthurus* (SVL 24cm) is red to brown or almost black with numerous **cream or yellow spots, many of them dark-centred, forming ocelli**. The pattern may be obscure in some pops. Tail dark with lighter rings, becoming obscure towards the tip. *V. a. insulanicus* (genetically closer to *V. baritji* and possibly a distinct species) is larger (SVL 25cm) and darker, with more banded pattern. ■ **NOTES** Rocky ranges and heavy to stony soils. *V. a. acanthurus* occurs on mainland Aust. while *V. a. insulanicus* occupies islands off ne. NT, incl. Groote Eylandt and the Wessel group. Terrestrial and rock-inhabiting, sheltering in crevices and in burrows under rocks and old termite mounds. ■ **SEE ALSO** *V. baritji; V. primordius.*

Black-spotted Spiny-tailed Monitor *Varanus baritji* TL 70cm

Very spiny tail, round in cross-section. Reddish brown with numerous small darker and lighter spots, sometimes scattered, aligned more or less transversely, arranged to form a reticulum or circular clusters, but **no dark-centred ocelli or stripes on neck. Throat bright yellow**. Tail dark with lighter rings, becoming obscure towards the tip. ■ **NOTES** Rock outcrops and stony hills, sheltering in crevices and in burrows under rocks and old termite mounds.
■ **SEE ALSO** *V. acanthurus; V. primordius.*

Short-tailed Pygmy Monitor *Varanus brevicauda* TL 23cm

Elongate body, short limbs and **moderately deep head. Tail thick, strongly keeled, shorter than head and body**, and round in cross-section. **Scales at front and leading edge of arms oval, each surrounded by ring of granules**. Reddish brown to yellow brown, obscurely marked with numerous scattered dark and light flecks that **tend to form ocelli**. ■ **NOTES** Sandy spinifex deserts. Extremely secretive, foraging close to edges of spinifex hummocks and sheltering in burrows at their bases. One of world's 2 smallest monitors. ■ **SEE ALSO** *V. sparnus.* ■ **STATUS** Rare (SA).

Varanus acanthurus acanthurus. Kununurra district, WA. S. Wilson

Varanus acanthurus insulanicus. Wessell Islands, NT. N. Gambold

Varanus baritji. Adelaide River area, NT. S. Wilson

Varanus brevicauda. Koordarrie Stn, WA. G. Gaikhorst

Pilbara Pygmy Monitor *Varanus bushi* TL 35cm

Tail round in cross-section, bearing keeled scales. **Dorsal scales markedly elongate.** Pale greyish brown with reddish tinge on back and paler grey tail, with **dark blotches on fore-back, bands across back and base of tail, and narrow dark longitudinal stripes on remainder of tail.** Throat and belly intensely spotted. ■ **NOTES** Mulga and eucalypt woodlands in Pilbara region, sheltering behind loose bark and in hollows, occasionally rock crevices. ■ **SEE ALSO** *V. caudolineatus; V. gilleni.*

Stripe-tailed Monitor *Varanus caudolineatus* TL 32cm

Tail round in cross-section, bearing keeled scales. **Dorsal scales slightly elongate.** Grey, often with a reddish brown tinge on back, marked with **numerous dark spots over body and base of tail**, and **4–5 dark longitudinal stripes on remaining two-thirds of tail.** ■ **NOTES** Arid mid-wstn interior, favouring hard and stony soils with mulga woodlands or shrublands. Arboreal, sheltering under bark and in hollows. Several pops occupy crevices in rocky outcrops. ■ **SEE ALSO** *V. bushi; V. gilleni.*

Blue-tailed Monitor *Varanus doreanus* TL 1.3m

Tail strongly laterally-compressed with scales not in regular rings, **more than 145 midbody scale rows, distinctly pale forks on tongue.** Black with numerous small, sharp, yellow spots on head, body and limbs, dark bands across throat and **blue pigment in pale markings on tail.** ■ **NOTES** RF on far nthn Cape York Pen., with records from Iron Ra. and possibly Lockerbie Scrub. Also NG. Status in Aust. uncertain, and subject to confusion with *V. indicus*. Examination of all Aust. specimens of both spp. is warranted. A related sp., *V. finschi*, also reported on Cape York Pen. but with no confirmed specimens or localities. ■ **SEE ALSO** *V. indicus.*

Pygmy Desert Monitor *Varanus eremius* TL 46cm

Tail round to triangular in cross-section. Brick red to pale reddish brown with **dark and pale spots and 4–5 dark longitudinal stripes along tail.** ■ **NOTES** Sandy deserts with spinifex, from sw. Kimberley, WA through central Aust. to sw. Qld. Terrestrial. Extremely shy, foraging among spinifex hummocks and sheltering in deep burrows. Readily investigates fresh diggings.

Perentie *Varanus giganteus* TL 2.4m

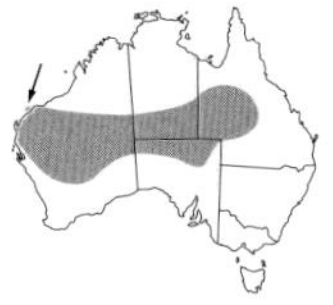

Long-necked with **angular brow**, powerful limbs and long, laterally compressed tail. Cream or white, heavily speckled or completely obscured with dark brown or black, and with large, circular, dark-edged pale spots arranged in rows across body and tail. Sides of **head, neck and throat cream with prominent mesh-like black reticulations.** ■ **NOTES** Arid regions. Usually associated with rocky ranges and outcrops, but also widespread over vast tracts of sandy deserts. Terrestrial. Forages widely and shelters in caves, deep crevices and burrows. Aust.'s largest lizard.

Varanus bushi.
Roebourne area, WA. R. Browne-Cooper

Varanus caudolineatus.
Twin Peaks Stn, WA. S. Wilson

Varanus doreanus.
Iron Range, Qld. J. Bolton

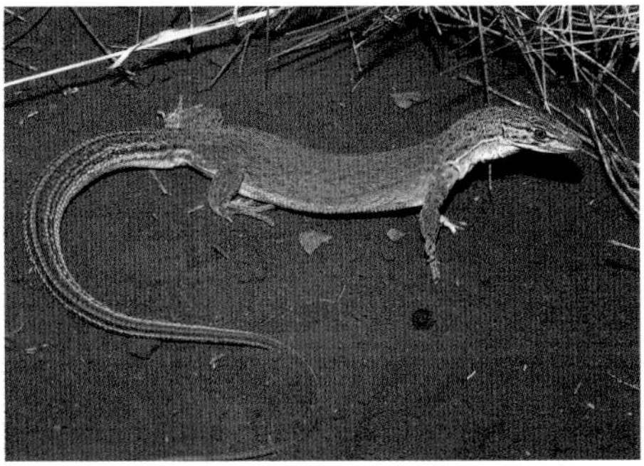

Varanus eremius.
Giralia Stn, WA. S. Wilson

Varanus giganteus.
North West Cape, WA. S. Wilson

Varanus giganteus. Juvenile.
Boulia district, Qld. S. Wilson

Pygmy Mulga Monitor *Varanus gilleni* TL 38cm

Tail round in cross-section, bearing keeled scales. **Dorsal scales almost round.** Grey, often with a reddish brown tinge on back, marked with **narrow dark bands across body** and base of tail, and **narrow dark longitudinal stripes on remainder of tail.** ■ **NOTES** Arid areas, from n. of Spencer Gulf, SA through central Aust. to nw. WA. Arboreal. Usually associated with mulga or desert oak, sheltering under loose bark and in hollows. ■ **SEE ALSO** *V. bushi; V. caudolineatus.*

Kimberley Rock Monitor *Varanus glauerti* TL 80cm

Slender, with flat head and body and very long, thin, slightly laterally compressed tail. Reddish brown to dark brown with transverse rows of large light grey to olive spots. **Tail strikingly patterned with sharply contrasting narrow bands of black and cream.** ■ **NOTES** Gorges and escarpments of the Kimberley, WA and adjacent NT, with a disjunct pop. in wstn Arnhem Land, NT. Rock-inhabiting, sheltering in deep narrow crevices.

Twilight Monitor; Black-palmed Monitor *Varanus glebopalma* TL 1m

Slender, with long neck and limbs and long, slightly laterally compressed tail. Grey to reddish brown with a complex reticulum of blackish brown lines over body, neck and sides of the head. **Basal half of tail black, the remainder a sharply contrasting creamy yellow. Palms and soles of feet black.** ■ **NOTES** Gorges and escarpments from the Kimberley, WA to Mount Isa, Qld. Rock-inhabiting and extremely swift, wary and agile. Mainly diurnal but commonly forages after sunset.

Sand Goanna; Gould's Goanna *Varanus gouldii* TL 1.2–1.6m

Laterally compressed tail. Colouration very variable: light yellow to blackish brown with dense dark speckling and pale spots, many dark-centred and many clustered. A prominent **pale-edged dark stripe runs back from eye**. Basal portion of tail dark with narrow pale bands; **terminal third to quarter of tail cream to yellow and patternless. Throat often streaked with grey. Other dark ventral markings, if present, not arranged on transverse rows.** ■ **SSP.** (ill-defined): *V. g. flavirufus* is paler and generally redder. ■ **NOTES** Most widespread and abundant goanna, found over most of mainland Aust. *V. g. flavirufus* occupies sandy deserts and *V. g. gouldii* occurs over the remainder. Forages widely over most dry open habitats. Terrestrial. Shelters in deep sloping burrows. Often confused with *V. panoptes*, but much less robust. ■ **SEE ALSO** *V. panoptes.*

Varanus gilleni.
Ethabuka, Qld. S. Wilson

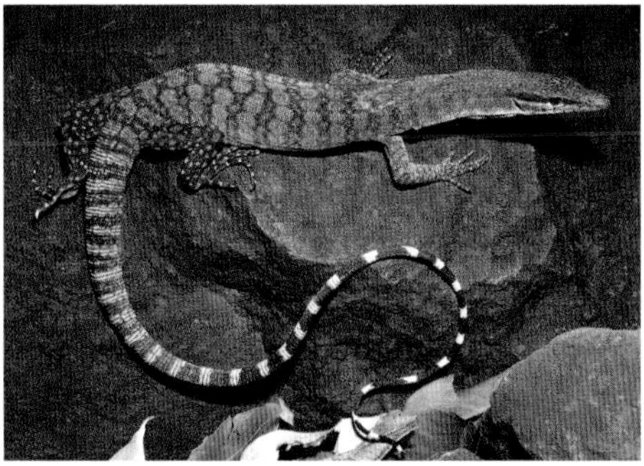

Varanus glauerti.
Mitchell Plateau, WA. S. Wilson

Varanus glauerti.
Nourlangie Rock area, NT. R. Hart

Varanus glebopalma.
El Questro Stn, WA. S. Wilson

Varanus gouldii flavirufus.
Nappa Merrie Stn, Qld. S. Wilson

Varanus gouldii gouldii.
Southern Cross area, WA. S. Wilson

Southern Pilbara Rock Monitor *Varanus hamersleyensis* TL 45cm

Slender with long tail, round in cross-section at mid-point and smooth scales on top of head with supraocular scales gradually merging with larger interocular scales. Dark reddish brown, often paler on head, with numerous dark dorsal spots often coalescing into narrow transverse bars and wavy lines forming a reticulum. Tail brown with darker spots but **no cream and dark caudal rings.** ■ **NOTES** Rock faces, gorges and overhangs in dissected ironstones of Hamersley Ra. in sthn Pilbara e. nearly to Newman, w. to Mt Rica and s. to Rocklea Stn. Extremely swift and agile on exposed vertical rock faces. ■ **SEE ALSO** *V. pilbarensis.*

Mangrove Monitor *Varanus indicus* TL 1.2m

Tail strongly laterally-compressed with scales not in regular rings, **less than 145 midbody scale rows, dark forks on tongue**, Black with prominent yellow, greenish yellow or greenish pale spots over head, body, limbs and tail. ■ **NOTES** RF, coastal mangrove and riverine habitats in nthn Cape York Pen., Torres Strait is., and nthn NT. Also widespread from wstn Pacific to estn Indonesia. Terrestrial, arboreal and semi-aquatic, readily taking to water when disturbed. Status of Cape York Pen. pops uncertain, with *V. doreanus* confirmed to occur there. Examination of all Aust. specimens from both NT and Qld is warranted. ■ **SEE ALSO** *V. doreanus.* ■ **STATUS** Near threatened (NT).

Canopy Goanna *Varanus keithhornei* TL 77cm

Extremely slender, with long limbs and digits, and very **long, thin, prehensile tail.** Blackish with fine cream spots tending to concentrate to form thin paired chevrons on body and rings on tail. Tip of snout is sometimes light bluish green. ■ **NOTES** RF and vine thickets of the McIlwraith and Iron Ranges on Cape York Pen., Qld. Arboreal, inhabiting the RF canopy and employing its light build and prehensile tail to forage among slender branches and outer foliage.

Long-tailed Rock Monitor *Varanus kingorum* TL 33cm

Slender, with **tail long, slender, keeled and round in cross-section.** Greyish brown to reddish brown with small black spots tending to join, forming a reticulated pattern over head, body and limbs, and aligning to form narrow stripes on tail. ■ **NOTES** Estn Kimberley, WA and adjacent areas of nw. NT. Rock-inhabiting. Extremely wary, staying close to the shelter of narrow rock crevices.

Mertens' Water Monitor *Varanus mertensi* TL 1.1m

Strongly laterally compressed tail, topped with 2-keeled crest, and nostrils on the upper part of the snout directed upwards. Dark olive grey to olive brown with numerous **small, dark-edged cream to yellow spots.** ■ **NOTES** Edges of watercourses and lagoons in far northern Aust., from Kimberley region of WA to Cape York, Qld. Semi-aquatic and arboreal, it usually drops from branches into the water when disturbed. It can remain submerged for a considerable time and forages extensively in water. ■ **STATUS** Vulnerable (NT).

Varanus hamersleyensis.
Ophthalmia Range, WA. B. Maryan

Varanus indicus.
Adelaide River, NT. G. Stephenson

Varanus kingorum.
Mt Nyulasy, WA. S. Wilson

Varanus mertensi.
Kununurra, WA. S. Wilson

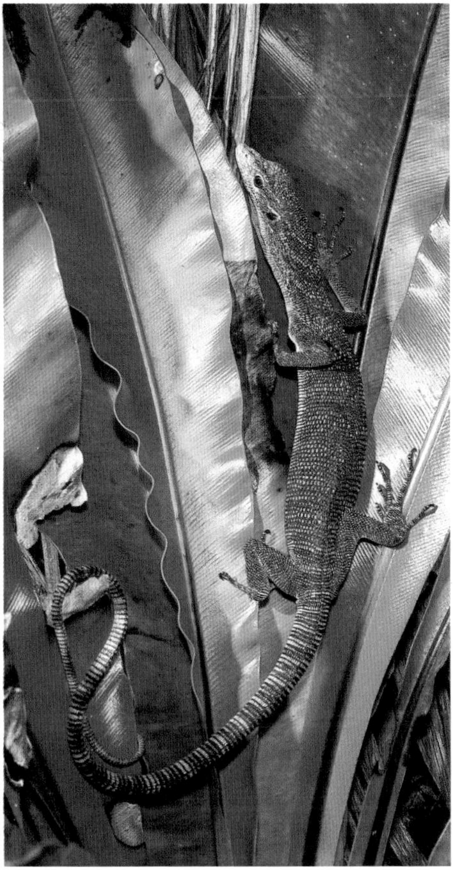

Varanus keithhornei.
Iron Range area, Qld. S. Wilson

Mitchell's Water Monitor *Varanus mitchelli* TL 70cm

Slender, with strongly **laterally compressed tail**. Dark grey to black with many small yellow spots or dark-centred ocelli. **Throat and sides of neck marked with black spots and bars** and often flushed with yellow. ■ **NOTES** Margins of pandanus-lined watercourses, swamps and lagoons, from the Kimberley, WA to nw. Qld. Arboreal and semi-aquatic, sheltering under bark and in hollows of overhanging limbs, and readily taking to the water when disturbed. ■ **STATUS** Vulnerable (NT).

Yellow-spotted Monitor *Varanus panoptes* TL 1.4m

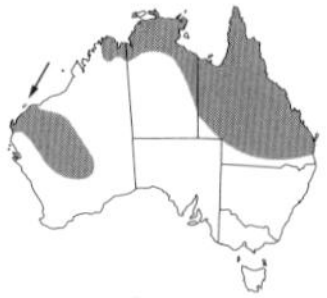

Robust, with laterally compressed tail. Pale-edged dark stripe runs back from eye. Blackish brown to reddish brown with alternate transverse rows of large blackish spots and smaller circular, dark-edged pale spots extending about halfway along tail. **Throat and belly often marked with transverse extensions of the dark dorsal and lateral spots.** ■ **SSP.** *V. p. panoptes* has **distal portion of tail pale with narrow dark bands**. *V. p. rubidus* is redder, with no dark bands on tail-tip. ■ **NOTES** Widespread across nthn Aust. *V. p. panoptes* extends from far nthn WA to Brisbane, Qld; *V. p. rubidus* occurs in the Pilbara, Gascoyne and adjacent regions of WA. Forages widely over a broad range of habitats, from grassland to woodlands and riverine flats. Much heavier and more robust than *V. gouldii*. ■ **SEE ALSO** *V. gouldii*. ■ **STATUS** Vulnerable (NT).

Northern Pilbara Rock Monitor *Varanus pilbarensis* TL 48cm

Slender with long tail, round in cross-section at mid-point and smooth scales on top of head with supraocular scales gradually merging with larger interocular scales. Pale to bright reddish brown with transverse rows of pale greyish brown spots. Distal half of **tail cream with prominent, narrow, dark brown rings**. Sides of head and neck have dark reddish brown mesh-like reticulations extending onto throat. ■ **NOTES** Rock-inhabiting, in ranges, dissected plateaux and boulder piles of nthn Pilbara. Primarily n. of Fortescue Basin, nw. to Burrup Pen. and e. to Ord Ra., Yarrie Mine and Carawine Gorge. Extremely swift and agile on exposed rock faces and boulder piles. ■ **SEE ALSO** *V. hamersleyensis*.

Emerald Monitor; Wyniss *Varanus prasinus* TL 75cm

Extremely slender, with long limbs and digits and very long, thin, prehensile tail. **Bright green** with black pigment forming a fine reticulum, or clustering to form chevrons on back. Palms and soles of feet black. ■ **NOTES** Restricted in Aust. to several islands in Torres Strait, s. to Moa Is., where it is known as Wyniss. Widespread in NG. Arboreal, living in the upper canopy of RF and monsoon forests. Employs its light build and prehensile tail to forage among slender branches and outer foliage. ■ **STATUS** Near threatened (Qld).

Varanus mitchelli.
Waterfall Creek, NT.
S. Swanson

Varanus panoptes panoptes.
Longreach area, Qld. R. Valentic

Varanus panoptes rubidus.
Bullara Stn, WA. S. Wilson

Varanus pilbarensis.
Port Hedland, WA. H. Cook

Varanus prasinus.
Moa Is., Qld. S. Wilson

Northern Ridge-tailed Monitor *Varanus primordius* TL 25cm

Robust, with **spiny tail**, round in cross-section. Grey to reddish brown with numerous dark flecks tending to form fine reticulations. **No pale stripes on neck or yellow ventral pigments.** Pale grey-brown underneath, darkest under throat. ■ **NOTES** Outcrops, rocky ranges and woodlands. Terrestrial and rock inhabiting, excavating shallow burrows and sheltering in crevices and under rocks. ■ **SEE ALSO** *V. acanthurus; V. baritji.* ■ **STATUS** Near threatened (NT).

Heath Monitor *Varanus rosenbergi* TL 1.3m

Laterally compressed tail. Dark grey to black with considerable yellow flecking and **narrow blackish bands**, transverse on body and curving forward on neck. Wider intervening lighter bands may have large yellow spots aligned across body. Pale-edged dark stripe runs back from eye. Tail banded blackish brown and yellow to tip; on some individuals tail-tip may be uniformly dark. ■ **NOTES** Open woodlands and heaths on sandy soil from sw. WA to wstn Vic, with isolated pops in ACT and the mid-coast of NSW. Terrestrial. Clutches of eggs are laid in termite mounds. ■ **STATUS** Vulnerable (NSW; SA); endangered (Vic).

Spotted Tree Monitor *Varanus scalaris* TL 60cm

Tail round in cross-section. **Scales on top of head grade evenly into smaller scales above eyes.** Colour and pattern variable; typically greyish brown to black with prominent ocelli comprising dark-centred pale spots. In some pops these ocelli are fragmented to form a reticulum, sometimes overlaid with broad reddish brown bands. Tail dark with irregular narrow pale rings, at least on base. ■ **NOTES** Currently a complex that includes several undescribed spp. Between them they occupy various timbered habitats, from sparse woodlands to RF, across nthn Aust. Arboreal, sheltering in tree hollows or under loose bark. ■ **SEE ALSO** *V. tristis.*

Varanus primordius.
Northern NT. G. Harold

Varanus scalaris.
Diamantina Lakes area, Qld. S. Wilson

Varanus scalaris.
Kakadu NP, NT. B Maryan

Varanus scalaris.
Beagle Bay, WA. D. Knowles

Varanus rosenbergi.
Fitzgerald River NP, WA. S. Wilson

Varanus scalaris.
Badu Is., Qld. S. Wilson

Varanus scalaris.
El Questro, WA. S. Wilson

Rusty Monitor *Varanus semiremex* TL 60cm

Distal two-thirds of tail laterally compressed. Scales on top of head dark and smoothly polished. Greyish brown with scattered to dense blackish flecks, often forming reticulations. Throat and chest often rusty yellow. Nthn pops from Cape York Pen. tend to be darker, with more prominent pattern comprising dark-centred pale ocelli. ■ **NOTES** Coastal Qld, from Gladstone to Cape York. Inhabits mangroves and margins of swamps and freshwater streams, sheltering in hollow limbs or trunks. Crabs are included in the diet.

Dampier Peninsula Monitor *Varanus sparnus* TL 22cm

Very elongate body, short limbs and **flat head.** Tail thick, strongly keeled, shorter than head and body, and round in cross-section. **Scales at front and leading edge of arms large and squarish, with no small granules at their periphery.** Pale reddish brown freckled with fine black spots that **do not form ocelli.** ■ **NOTES** Probably restricted to Dampier Peninsula, WA. Recorded from pindan shrubland, featuring low *Corymbia* over mixed *Acacia* shrubs and *Triodia* on reddish brown sandy loams. A newly described sp., possibly the world's smallest monitor lizard. ■ **SEE ALSO** *V. brevicauda.*

Spencer's Monitor *Varanus spenceri* TL 1.2m

Very **robust and blunt-headed,** with **short laterally compressed tail,** about as long as head and body. Shades of grey to greyish brown with **simple pattern of pale bands,** transverse on body and tail and V-shaped on nape. These become more obscure on older individuals. ■ **NOTES** Treeless, deeply cracking clay plains vegetated with Mitchell grass. Terrestrial, sheltering in soil cracks.

Storr's Monitor *Varanus storri* TL 40cm

Robust, with **tail thick, spiny and round in cross-section. No stripes present on neck.** ■ **SSP.** *V. s. storri* is pale or dark brown to reddish brown, often paler on vertebral region, with fine dark reticulations, ocelli or flecks on body and limbs. A dark streak, sometimes pale-edged, runs from eye to ear. *V. s. ocreatus* has longer appendages and enlarged scales under distal part of hindlimb. ■ **NOTES** Nthn Aust. *V. s. storri* occurs in ne. interior of Qld. *V. s. ocreatus* occurs in nw. Qld and adjacent NT and from ne. NT to the Kimberley, WA. Terrestrial and rock-inhabiting, favouring low weathered outcrops which may support large communities.

Varanus semiremex. Southern form.
Mid-eastern Qld. S. Wilson

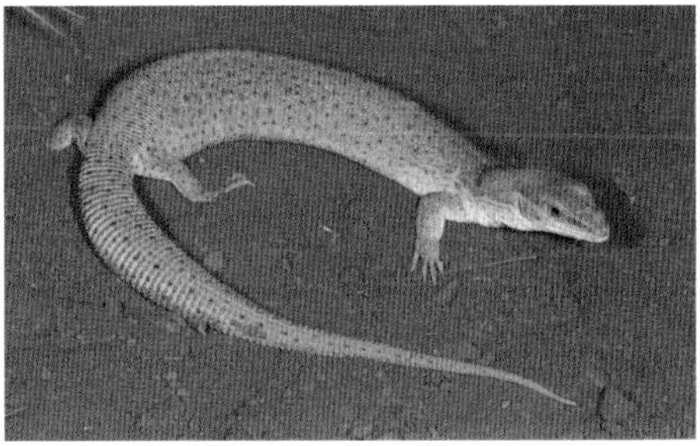

Varanus sparnus.
Mt Jowlaenga area, WA. R. Ellis

Varanus spenceri.
Winton district, Qld.
E. Vanderduys

Varanus storri storri.
Charters Towers, Qld. S. Wilson

Varanus storri ocreatus.
Gibb River Rd near Kalumburu turn-off, WA.
S. Wilson

Black-headed Monitor; Freckled Monitor *Varanus tristis* TL 76cm

Tail long, strongly keeled and round in cross-section. **Scales on top of head sharply delineated from smaller scales above eyes.** ■ **SSP.** (ill-defined): *V. t. tristis* is pale grey, brown to black with numerous pale ocelli aligned transversely. Head and neck black. Tail black with pale spots forming narrow rings on base; remainder patternless. *V. t. orientalis* has head and neck colour similar to body, with pale markings extending well onto neck. ■ **NOTES** Widespread in dry to arid regions. *V. t. tristis* is essentially wstn and *V. t. orientalis* estn, but the 2 merge and coexist in some areas and could be no more than broad geographical pattern trends. They occur in woodlands and rock outcrops, sheltering under bark, in hollow timber, rock crevices and frequently in disused fairy martins' nests. ■ **SEE ALSO** *V. scalaris.*

Lace Monitor *Varanus varius* TL 2.1m

Powerful, with long, slender, laterally compressed tail. Dark grey to dull bluish black with numerous scattered cream spots forming spotted or solid bands. Juv. far more brightly and clearly patterned. Snout strongly marked with **prominent black and yellow bands extending under chin.** Tail narrowly banded with black and cream on basal portion; bands become broad distally. A banded phase ('Bell's form'), occurring in dry parts of Qld and NSW, has simple broad black and yellow bands across body and tail. ■ **NOTES** Occurs in well-timbered areas, from dry woodlands to cool temperate sthn forests. Arboreal, ascending large trees when disturbed. Forages widely, frequently becoming habituated to picnic and camping grounds and regularly raiding farms for poultry and eggs. Clutches of eggs are laid in arboreal or terrestrial termite mounds. ■ **STATUS** Endangered (Vic); rare (SA).

Varanus tristis.
Black-headed form.
Eulo, Qld. S. Wilson

Varanus tristis.
Freckled form.
Wallumbilla, Qld.
S. Wilson

Varanus varius.
Mt Nebo, Qld. S. Wilson

Varanus varius. 'Bell's form'.
Sundown NP, Qld. S. Wilson

BLIND SNAKES
Family Typhlopidae

A group of about 250 species of worm-like snakes living in the warmer parts of the world, from tropical America, Africa and south-eastern Europe to Asia, Australia and the western Pacific. Australia is home to 45 described species, occurring over most of the continent except the lower south-eastern mainland and Tasmania.

The family is represented in Australia by two genera. *Anilios* is regionally endemic to Australia and New Guinea and includes all of the native species. The Asian genus *Indotyphlops* is represented by one introduced species, *I. braminus.*

Blind snakes are secretive burrowers with bodies of uniform thickness and blunt heads and tails. They have poor vision, but appear to be extremely light-sensitive and shun any exposure to sunlight. All are non-venomous and completely harmless, relying on their cryptic habits to escape detection. If handled, many are able to emit a foul-smelling substance from their cloacal glands.

Blind snakes are Australia's only insectivorous snakes. They feed on termites and the eggs, larvae and pupae of ants. Some of the large robust species even appear to specialise on the notorious bulldog ants (*Myrmecia* spp.), famous for aggressively defending their nests with vicious stings. Blind snakes probably dwell mainly in the galleries of their hosts and are also encountered in loose soil beneath rocks and logs, or foraging on the surface at night, particularly after rain. Their glossy, close-fitting scales facilitate easy passage though soil and tunnels, and possibly protect them from retaliatory prey.

Thanks to their cryptic behaviour and generally similar appearance, blind snakes have been largely neglected in biological studies. They remain one of our most poorly known groups of vertebrates, with many more species yet to be named. Even the basic biological functions of courtship and mating have never been recorded, and we only presume all blind snakes are egglayers, based on records of a handful of species. At least one, the introduced Flowerpot Snake (*Indotyphlops braminus*), exists as all-female, parthenogenetic populations.

A consequence of the scant attention that blind snakes have received is the general perception, even among many herpetologists, of uniformity within the family. Yet there are significant differences which no doubt reflect substantial behavioural variation. For example, snouts range from smoothly rounded to acute or beaked, and body diameter from thread-like to plump, almost sausage-like. At least one extraordinarily thin blind snake, *Anilios longissimus*, probably lives only in deep subterranean cavities. It has recently been found that females of several species (and possibly a large number) are significantly longer and thicker than males.

Blind snakes are regarded as a primitive lineage of snakes, partly because of their retention of a vestigial pelvis, linking them to a limbed ancestor shared by snakes and lizards.

Robust Blind Snake (*Anilios ligatus*), a thick-bodied blind snake that appears to prey on the eggs, larvae and pupae of large stinging ants. Theodore area, Qld. S. Wilson

Genus *Anilios*

Sole Aust. genus, representing the family in the Asia/Pacific region. Extremely slender to very robust snakes with highly polished, close-fitting scales of uniform size around body (ventrals not enlarged). Tail short, blunt and terminating abruptly; tipped with a small spur on all but one species. Head scales large, few in number and arranged symmetrically. Eyes greatly reduced and covered by a transparent scale. Mouth minute and set below the head, well back from the snout. ■ **NOTES** Distinguished from other typhlopid genera (and from other snakes) by the unique structure of the hemipenes, which are long, slender and solid. Most snakes have stout, hollow, evertible structures, often ornamented with spines and barbs. Because many spp. of *Anilios* have not had their hemipenes examined, their placement in this genus is based more on geography than morphology. While a small number of spp. can be identified by distinctive build or colouration, most require a midbody scale count and a microscopic examination of head scales, particularly whether the nasal cleft contacts the 1st (A) or 2nd (B) upper labial scale, or the prefrontal scale (C); and whether the snout is round (D) or trilobed (E). Several spp. are known from single specimens and some have never been photographed alive.

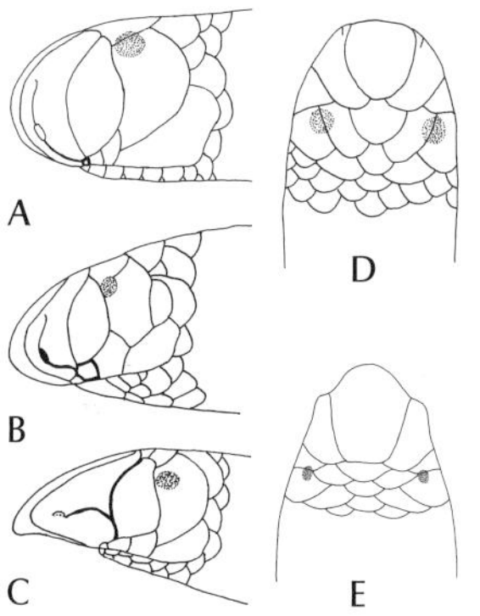

Small-headed Blind Snake *Anilios affinis* TL 220mm

Slender, with snout rounded from above and bluntly angular in profile. Midbody scales in 18 rows. Nasal cleft extends from 2nd upper labial scale to rostral scale, completely dividing nasal scale but not visible from above. Pinkish brown, paler on head and merging with paler ventral surfaces. ■ **NOTES** From central Qld s. to White Rock near Ipswich and inland to the NSW border. Recorded from dry open woodlands and a sandstone outcrop. Also recorded in the Solomon Is.

Pilbara Blind Snake *Anilios ammodytes* TL 252mm

Slender, with snout rounded from above and in profile. Midbody scales in 20 rows. **Nasal cleft clearly visible from above** extending from preocular scale, reaching or nearly reaching rostral scale to divide or nearly divide nasal scale. **Rostral scale relatively long and narrow, constricted anteriorly, creating concave sides.** Pink to pinkish purple, merging gradually with pale ventral surfaces. ■ **NOTES** Arid Pilbara region, from North West Cape to hinterland of Eighty Mile Beach, WA. ■ **SEE ALSO** *R. diversus.*

No-spined Blind Snake *Anilios aspina* TL 278mm

Slender, with snout rounded from above and in profile, and **no spine on tail-tip**. Midbody scales in 18 rows. Nasal cleft extends from 2nd upper labial scale, not dividing nasal scale but visible from above. Pale pinkish tan with faint dark edges to scales. ■ **NOTES** Grasslands on cracking clay plains. Known only from near Barcaldine and Julia Ck, central Qld.

Anilios affinis.
White Rock, Ipswich area, Qld. S. Wilson

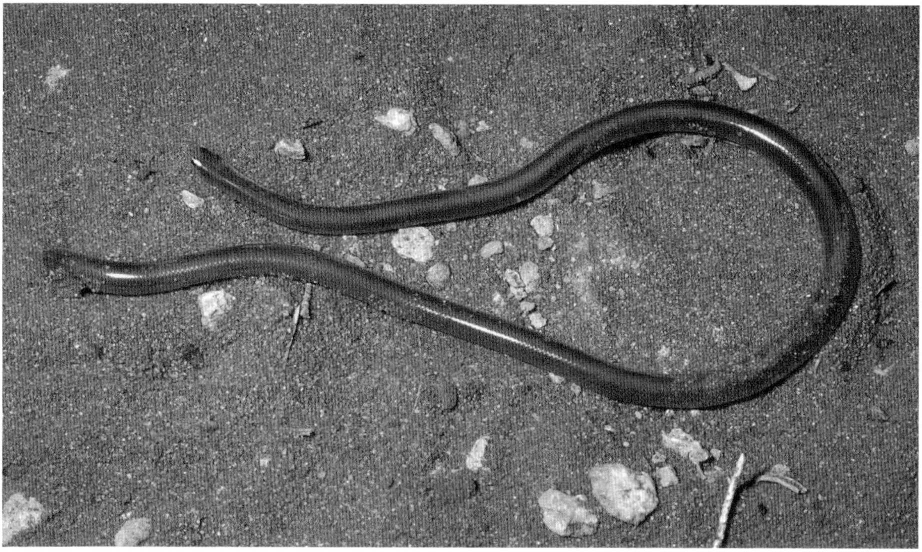

Anilios ammodytes.
Bullara Stn, WA. S. Wilson

Anilios aspina.
Julia Creek, Qld. E. Vanderduys

Southern Blind Snake *Anilios australis* **TL 350mm**

Moderately robust, with **snout rounded from above and in profile.** Midbody scales in 22 rows. Nasal cleft usually extends from 2nd upper labial scale (rarely from junction of 1st and 2nd or from preocular) to between nostril and rostral scale. Not visible from above. Purplish brown (adults) to purplish pink (juv.) with or without prominent junction between dark upper and cream lower surfaces. ■ **NOTES** Midwest to sw. WA, between about Shark Bay and Cape Arid. Occupies a variety of humid to semi-arid habitats, from WSF to mallee/spinifex associations and shrublands. ■ **SEE ALSO** *R. bicolor.*

Wagga Wagga Blind Snake *Anilios batillus* **TL 320mm**

Snout pointed from above and in profile. Midbody scales in 24 rows. Nasal cleft extends from 2nd upper labial scale through nasal scale to rostral scale, completely dividing nasal scale but barely visible from above. Rich brown above and yellowish below. ■ **NOTES** Known from only one specimen, presumed to have been collected at Wagga Wagga, NSW in the late 1800s. While there is no doubt that it represents a distinct and unusual species, it is not certain that the locality is correct, nor that the specimen is from Aust.

Dark-spined Blind Snake *Anilios bicolor* **TL 418mm**

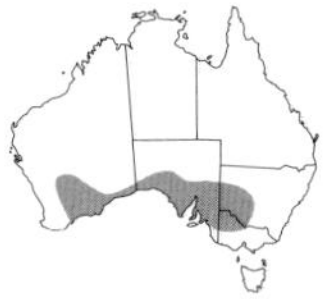

Moderately robust with **snout weakly to moderately trilobed from above and angular in profile.** Midbody scales in 22 rows. Nasal cleft extends from 2nd upper labial scale to between nostril and rostral. Not visible from above. Tail-spine very large and heavily pigmented. Dark brown to greyish brown above and cream to white below, with sharp junction between the colours. ■ **NOTES** Southern third of Aust., from nw. of Kalgoorlie to wstn slopes of Gt Div. Ra. ■ **SEE ALSO** *R. australis.*

Prong-snouted Blind Snake *Anilios bituberculatus* **TL 450mm**

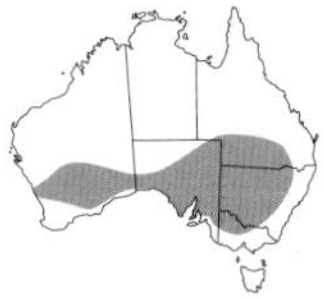

Moderate to slender, with **snout strongly trilobed from above and slightly angular in profile**. Midbody scales in 20 rows. Nasal cleft extends from 2nd upper labial scale to between nostril and rostral scale. Not visible from above. Pink to dark purplish brown or almost black, fading to whitish on lower flanks and ventral surfaces. ■ **NOTES** Subhumid to arid sthn Aust.

Anilios australis.
King's Park, WA.
S. Wilson

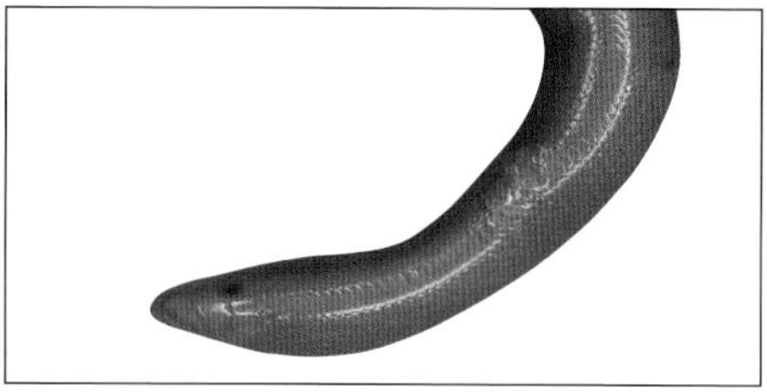

Anilios batillus. Preserved holotype; lateral.
Wagga Wagga, NSW. S. Wilson

Anilios batillus. Preserved holotype; dorsal.
Wagga Wagga, NSW. S. Wilson

Anilios bicolor.
Hattah, Vic. M. Swan

Anilios bituberculatus.
Currawinya NP, Qld. S. Wilson

Faint-striped Blind Snake *Anilios broomi* TL 250mm

Striped, with snout rounded from above and in profile. Midbody scales in 20 rows. Nasal cleft extends from 2nd upper labial scale to rostral, completely dividing nasal scale, and not or scarcely visible from above. Pale brown, merging to dark grey on tail, with dark reddish brown centres to dorsal scales aligning to form narrow longitudinal stripes. Ventral surfaces whitish. ■ **NOTES** Tropical woodlands in the dry belt along the wstn edge of the Wet Tropics, from about Innot Hot Springs ne. to about Cooktown.

Centralian Blind Snake *Anilios centralis* TL 306mm

Moderately slender, with short snout, rounded from above and beak-like in profile. Midbody scales in 20 rows. Nasal cleft extends from 2nd upper labial scale to nostril or a little beyond. Not visible from above. Purplish brown, fading on lower flanks. ■ **NOTES** Known only from Alice Springs area.

Cape York Striped Blind Snake *Anilios chamodracaena* TL 210mm

Striped, with snout rounded from above and in profile. Midbody scales in 18 rows. Nasal cleft extends from 2nd upper labial scale to about halfway between nostril and rostral scale. Not visible from above. Yellowish cream to off-white with black tail, **prominently marked above and below with 18 narrow dark stripes**. Head usually black. ■ **NOTES** Tropical woodlands of wstn Cape York Pen., from Weipa s. to Inkerman Stn and e. to Lockhart R. Settlement, Qld.

Northern Blind Snake *Anilios diversus* TL 352mm

Moderately slender, with rounded snout. Midbody scales in 20 rows. **Nasal cleft just visible from above,** extending from preocular scale, usually reaching rostral to completely divide nasal. **Rostral usually elliptic**, occasionally with slightly concave sides. Pinkish brown to purplish brown, merging with pale ventral surfaces. ■ **NOTES** Subhumid to arid nthn Aust. ■ **SEE ALSO** *R. ammodytes.*

Desert Blind Snake *Anilios endoterus* TL 376mm

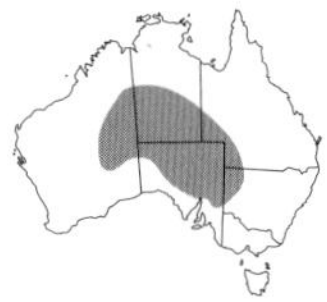

Moderately slender, with snout weakly trilobed from above and angular in profile. Midbody scales in 22 rows. Nasal cleft extends from preocular scale to nostril, a little beyond, or to rostral scale. Not visible from above. Pink to reddish brown, with ragged junction between dark lateral and pale ventral colouration. ■ **NOTES** Arid sandy areas with spinifex or shrublands. ■ **STATUS** Endangered (NSW).

Anilios broomi.
Cooktown, Qld.
S. Wilson

Anilios centralis.
Alice Springs, NT. G. Fyfe

Anilios chamodracaena.
Nassau River mouth, Qld. A. Smith

Anilios diversus.
Kununurra, WA. S. Wilson

Anilios endoterus.
Coward Springs, SA. S. Wilson

Ruby Gap Blind Snake *Anilios fossor* **TL 245mm**

Snout rounded from above, with very slight inflation of nasal region creating very weakly trilobed appearance, and rounded in profile. Midbody scales in 20 rows. Nasal cleft extends from 2nd upper labial but does not reach rostral scale and is not visible from above. Rostral scale large and round. In preservative, pale yellowish brown above and yellow below. ■ **NOTES** Known from one specimen, collected at Ruby Gap Nature Park, NT, on upper reaches of Hale R., presumably in *Eucalyptus camaldulensis* woodland on sandy loam soil. No known live image available.

Gane's Blind Snake *Anilios ganei* **TL 335mm**

Moderately robust, with snout rounded from above and in profile. Midbody scales in 24 rows. Nasal cleft extends vertically from 2nd upper labial scale onto top of head, completely dividing nasal scale and clearly visible from above. Greyish brown above and cream below, with ragged junction between dark lateral and pale ventral colours. ■ **NOTES** Known from widely separated areas between Newman and Pannawonicka, WA. Possibly associated with moist gorges and gullies.

Northern Beaked Blind Snake *Anilios grypus* **TL 415mm**

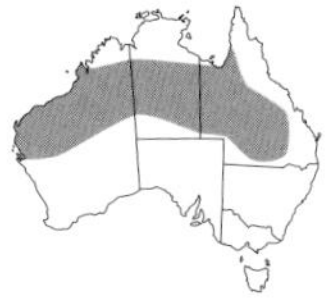

Extremely slender, with snout angular from above and **beak-like in profile**. Midbody scales in 18 rows. Nasal cleft usually extends from 2nd upper labial scale (rarely from 1st labial or preocular) to or towards rostral scale. Not visible from above. Pinkish brown to dark reddish brown, merging with cream ventral surfaces, with cream snout and **black head and tail**. ■ **NOTES** Subhumid to arid nthn interior of Aust.

Black-tailed Blind Snake *Anilios guentheri* **TL 294mm**

Very slender, with snout rounded from above and in profile. Midbody scales in 18 rows. Nasal cleft extends from 2nd upper labial scale to between nostril and rostral scale. Not visible from above. Purplish brown with pale-tipped snout and **black tail**. ■ **NOTES** Subhumid to semi-arid nthn Aust. from nthn NT to sthn and estn Kimberley, WA.

Northern Hook-snouted Blind Snake *Anilios hamatus* **TL 377mm**

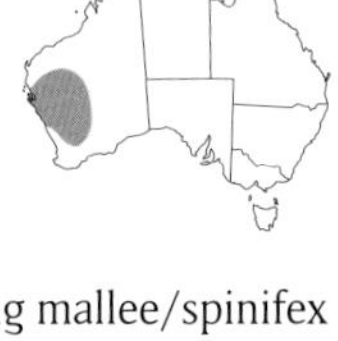

Robust, with snout very weakly trilobed from above and weakly to strongly angular in profile. Midbody scales in 22 rows. Nasal cleft usually extends from 2nd upper labial scale (occasionally from its junction with 1st upper labial) to nostril. Not visible from above. Purplish brown, paler on juv., with prominent and jagged junction between dark lateral and pale ventral colouration. ■ **NOTES** Semi-arid mid-w. coast to arid wstn interior. Various habitats including mallee/spinifex associations, samphire flats and mulga woodlands and shrublands.

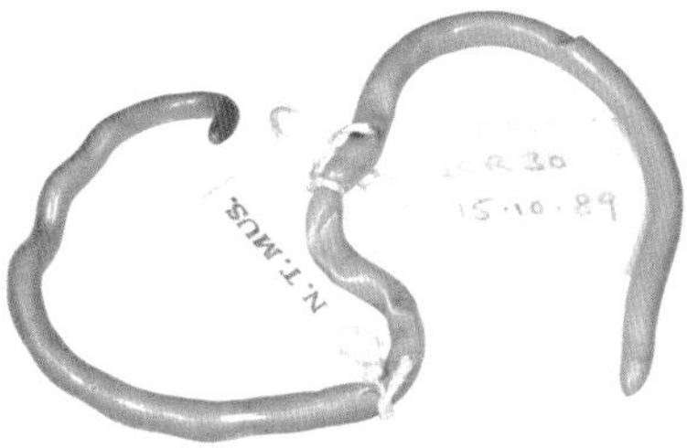

Anilios fossor. Preserved holotype.
Ruby Gap Nature Park, NT. G. Shea

Anilios ganei.
Hamersley Stn., WA. H. Cook

Anilios grypus.
Port Hedland area, WA.
R. Browne-Cooper

Anilios guentheri.
Edith Falls, NT. R. Valentic

Anilios hamatus.
Yuin Stn area, WA. G. Harold

How's Blind Snake *Anilios howi* TL 210mm

Moderately slender, with snout rounded from above and in profile. Midbody scales in 18 rows. Nasal cleft extends from 2nd upper labial scale to rostral scale, completely dividing nasal scale but not visible from above. Dark brown, darker on head, neck and tail, fading to brown on lower lateral and ventral surfaces. ■ **NOTES** Stony clay-based soil in Admiralty Gulf, nw. Kimberley, WA.

Fassifern Blind Snake *Anilios insperatus* TL 96mm

Very small and moderately slender with snout weakly trilobed from above and bluntly angular in profile. Midbody scales in 16 rows. Nasal cleft extends from 2nd upper labial but does not reach rostral scale and is not visible from above. In preservative, uniformly cream above and below with no indication of any pigment. ■ **NOTES** Known from one specimen, collected under a rock on clay soil in cleared pasture adj. to stony slope with open forest of *Eucalyptus crebra, E. moluccana* and *Corymbia citriodora* at Warrill View in Fassifern Valley, Qld. No known live image available. ■ **STATUS** Vulnerable (Qld).

Kimberley Blind Snake *Anilios kimberleyensis* TL 296mm

Slender, with depressed head and snout rounded from above and in profile. Midbody scales in 22 rows. Nasal cleft extends from 2nd upper labial scale to above nostril. Clearly visible from above. Dark brown to silvery grey, fading on lower lateral and ventral surfaces. Snout pale. ■ **NOTES** Nw. Kimberley, WA, to about Litchfield NP, ne. NT.

Murchison Blind Snake *Anilios leptosoma* TL 375mm

Very slender, with snout weakly trilobed from above, and angular in profile. Midbody scales in 16 (rarely 18) rows. Nasal cleft extends from 2nd upper labial scale to rostral, completely dividing nasal scale but not visible from above. Pink to purplish brown, fading on lower lateral and ventral surfaces. Snout paler. ■ **NOTES** Mid-w. coast, between Wooramel R. and Geraldton. Favours sandy soils. Recorded under rocks, and in sand beneath thick acacia leaf litter.

Cape York Blind Snake *Anilios leucoproctus* TL 250mm

Slender, with snout rounded from above and in profile. Midbody scales in 20 rows. Nasal cleft extends from 2nd upper labial scale, failing to reach rostral. Visible from above. **Dark purplish brown above and below.** ■ **NOTES** Ne. Cape York Pen. and estn islands of Torres Strait, Qld to sthn NG.

Anilios howi.
Mitchell Plateau, WA. P. Griffin

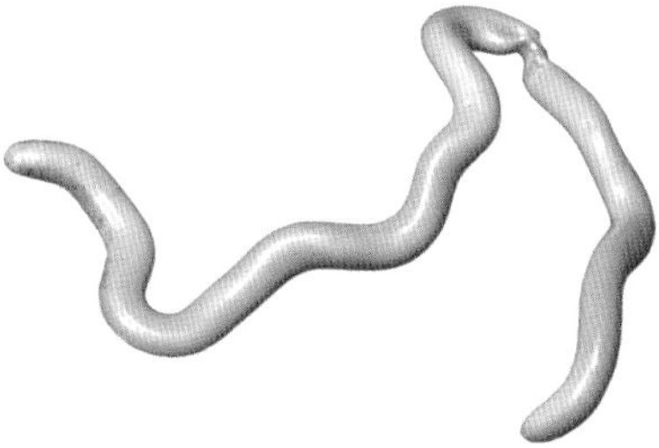

Anilios insperatus. Preserved holotype.
Warrill View, Qld. S. Wilson

Anilios kimberleyensis.
Litchfield NP, NT. P. Horner

Anilios leptosoma.
Kalbarri area, WA. B. Maryan

Anilios leucoproctus.
Prince of Wales Island, Qld. S. Wilson

Robust Blind Snake *Anilios ligatus* TL 500mm

Extremely robust, with snout rounded from above and in profile. Midbody scales in 24 rows. Nasal cleft extends from 1st upper labial scale almost to rostral scale. Visible from above. Dark greyish brown to dark purplish brown above and cream to dull pink below, with the junction between the colours sharp and straight-edged. ■ **NOTES** Central nthn NSW to to Cape York Pen. with apparently disjunct pop. from nw. Qld to sthn Kimberley, WA. Feeds on the eggs, larvae and pupae of stinging ants such as *Myrmecia* spp.

Barrow Island Blind Snake *Anilios longissimus* TL 268mm

Extremely slender (body diameter no more than 2.3mm), with strongly depressed head and snout squarish from above and rounded in profile. Midbody scales in 16 rows. Nasal cleft extends from 2nd upper labial to just beyond nostril; not visible from above. **Translucent and devoid of pigment** except for dark eyes and a 'ghost' of dark scale-edges. ■ **NOTES** Known from a single specimen collected on the outer surface of a bore casing, removed from considerable depth at Bandicoot Bay on Barrow Is., WA. It probably dwells deep in totally dark subterranean cavities, and may be Aust.'s only true reptilian troglodyte. No known live image available.

Buff-snouted Blind Snake *Anilios margaretae* TL 306mm

Very slender, with snout trilobed from above and angular in profile. Midbody scales in 18 rows. Nasal cleft extends from 2nd upper labial scale to between nostril and rostral scale; not visible from above. Pink to purplish grey with pale yellowish brown snout. Ventral surfaces pale grey. ■ **NOTES** Known only from Lake Throssell area in arid se. interior of WA and Maralinga area on sthn edge of Gt. Victoria Desert, SA.

Small-eyed Blind Snake *Anilios micromma* TL 205mm

Slender, with **very small eyes** and snout rounded from above and in profile. Midbody scales in 18 rows. Nasal cleft extends from 2nd upper labial scale to rostral scale, completely dividing nasal scale; visible from above. No data on colour available. ■ **NOTES** Known from only one specimen, collected in 1924 at Leopold Downs Stn in semi-arid sw. interior of the Kimberley, WA. No known live image available.

Groote Eylandt Dwarf Blind Snake *Anilios minimus* TL 218mm

Slender, with snout slightly squared from above and round in profile. Midbody scales in 16 rows. Nasal cleft extends from 2nd upper labial scale to a little beyond nostril; not visible from above. Yellowish brown, darker on head and tail, usually with narrow dark stripes. ■ **NOTES** Apparently occurs on sandy soils in subhumid ne. NT. Known only from Groote Eylandt and from Lake Evella, 170km NNW on the Arnhem Land mainland. No known live image available.

Anilios ligatus.
Currawinya NP, Qld. S. Wilson

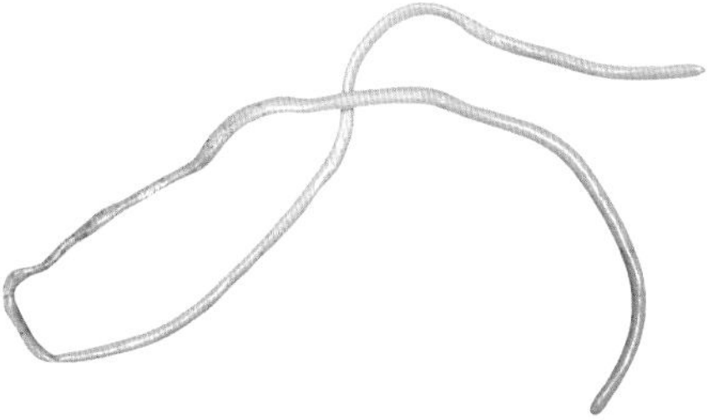

Anilios longissimus. Preserved holotype.
Barrow Is., WA. B. Maryan

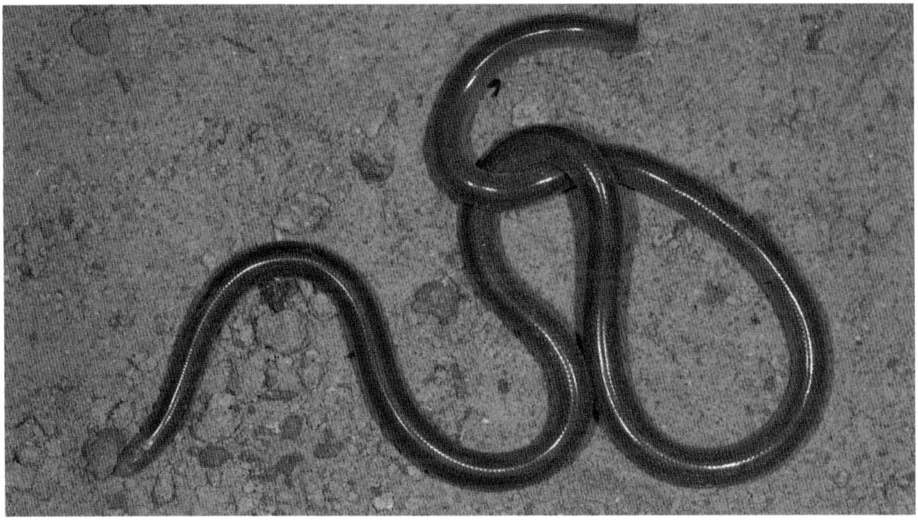

Anilios margaretae.
Appr. 200 km se. of Lake Throssell, WA. S. Ford

Anilios micromma. Preserved holotype.
Leopold Downs Station, WA. R. Ellis

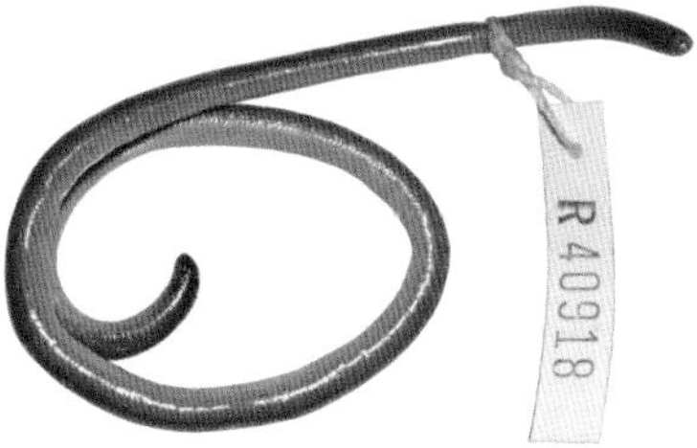

Anilios minimus. Preserved specimen.
Lake Evella, NT. G. Shea

Slender Blind Snake *Anilios nema* TL 270mm

Slender, with snout rounded from above and in profile. Midbody scales in 16 rows. Nasal cleft extends from 2nd upper labial scale to between nostril and rostral scale. Not visible from above. Pinkish brown above and slightly paler below. ■ **NOTES** Known only from Darwin area, NT. Recorded in well-vegetated gardens, under bricks and concrete on dark soils with thick leaf litter.

Blackish Blind Snake *Anilios nigrescens* TL 750mm

Moderately robust, with snout rounded from above and in profile. Midbody scales in 22 rows. Nasal cleft extends from 1st upper labial scale nearly to rostral; visible from above. Pinkish brown (juv.) to dark purplish brown or almost black (adults) with base of each scale usually paler, forming an obscure reticulum. Ventral surfaces pinkish white, with junction between dark upper and pale lower colours weakly delineated but ragged. Often a dark patch present on either side of vent. ■ **NOTES** Humid to subhumid e. coast and ranges. Occurs in a variety of habitats, from RF to woodlands and rock outcrops. Frequently encountered beneath rocks or logs, in cavities under embedded stumps, and even several metres above ground in standing rotten timber.

Pilbara Hook-snouted Blind Snake *Anilios pilbarensis* TL 365mm

Moderately elongate, with snout weakly trilobed from above and prominently beaked in profile, but lacking an acute transverse cutting edge. Midbody scales in 22 rows. Nasal cleft extends from preocular scale to nostril; not visible from above. Pinkish brown above and cream below. ♀ much larger; this may also apply to other spp. ■ **NOTES** Arid Pilbara region, WA, in catchments of Yule R. and de Grey R. Known from areas with shrublands over spinifex.

Fat Blind Snake *Anilios pinguis* TL 445mm

Extremely robust, with snout weakly trilobed from above and slightly angular in profile. Midbody scales in 20 rows. Nasal cleft extends from 2nd upper labial scale to between nostril and rostral scale; not visible from above. Shades of grey, sometimes with pale smudge on each scale aligning to form longitudinal series. Ventral surfaces whitish, sharply to weakly contrasting with upper lateral colour. ■ **NOTES** Humid to subhumid sw. WA, occurring in DSF and woodlands. Feeds largely or solely on the eggs, larvae and pupae of bulldog ants (*Myrmecia* spp.), and recorded in association with their nests.

Anilios nema.
Darwin, NT. B. Maryan

Anilios nigrescens.
Mt Nebo, Qld. S. Wilson

Anilios pilbarensis.
Meentheena Cons. Park, WA. B. Maryan

Anilios pinguis.
Canning Dam, WA.
S. Wilson

Woodland Blind Snake *Anilios proximus* TL 750mm

Robust, with snout bluntly trilobed from above and weakly angular in profile. Midbody scales in 20 rows. Nasal cleft extends from 1st upper labial scale to between nostril and rostral scale; visible from above. Pinkish brown to grey or brown, merging with pale yellowish brown to cream ventral surfaces. Small dark patch may be present on either side of vent. ■ **NOTES** Variety of habitats, from mid-estn Qld through estn interior of NSW to nthn Vic, with a possibly isolated pop. on Atherton Tableland of ne. Qld. Feeds on the eggs, larvae and pupae of stinging bulldog ants (*Myrmecia* spp.) and recorded in the nests of large harmless sugar ants (*Camponotus* spp.). ■ **STATUS** Near threatened (Vic).

Roberts' Blind Snake *Anilios robertsi* TL 290mm

Moderately slender, with snout rounded from above and in profile. Midbody scales in 22 rows. Nasal cleft extends from 2nd upper labial scale nearly to rostral scale; just visible from above. Very dark purplish brown above and cream below, the **dark upper and pale ventral colours very sharply delineated and straight-edged.** ■ **NOTES** Known only from 1 specimen collected in open eucalypt forest at Romeo Creek near Shipton's Flat, ne. Qld. Recorded emerging from hollow fallen timber and feeding on ants' eggs.

Cooloola Blind Snake *Anilios silvia* TL 175mm

Slender, with snout rounded from above and in profile. Midbody scales in 20 rows. Nasal cleft extends from 2nd upper labial scale nearly to rostral; visible from above. Immaculate glossy black above (rarely 11 broad black stripes obscuring a creamy yellow background) and white below, the **dark upper and pale ventral colours jagged and very sharply delineated.** ■ **NOTES** Coastal RF, woodlands and heaths growing on white sand, from Fraser Is. s. to Palmwoods. Shelters in sand and decomposed wood under logs and leaf litter. ■ **STATUS** Near threatened (Qld).

Splendid Blind Snake *Anilios splendidus* TL 511mm

Robust, with snout weakly trilobed from above and angular in profile. Midbody scales in 20 rows. Nasal cleft extends from 2nd upper labial scale to just past nostril; not visible from above. Dull grey above and white below, the **dark upper and pale ventral colours sharply delineated along a jagged boundary.** ■ **NOTES** Known only from a single specimen collected at Milyering Well, an area with shrublands on coral limestone and a thin veneer of sand, on the wstn edge of North West Cape, WA.

Anilios proximus.
Eidsvold, Qld.
S. Wilson

Anilios robertsi.
Romeo Ck, Shipton's Flat area, Qld. L. Roberts

Anilios silvia.
Pile Valley, Fraser Is, Qld. S. Wilson

Anilios splendidus.
Milyering Well, North West Cape, WA.
M. Cowan

North-eastern Blind Snake *Anilios torresianus* TL 400mm

Moderately robust, with snout rounded from above and in profile. Midbody scales in 22 rows. Nasal cleft extends from 2nd upper labial scale, or from suture between 1st and 2nd, nearly to rostral scale; visible from above. Pinkish brown to dark greyish brown, paler on snout and usually on tail-tip, with each scale narrowly pale-edged. Dark upper colours grade evenly with pale ventral surfaces. ■ **NOTES** Occurs in a variety of habitats, including woodlands, monsoon forests and vine thickets, from mid-estn Qld to islands of Torres Strait. Also present in NG and estn Indonesia.

Darwin Blind Snake *Anilios tovelli* TL 122mm

Snout rounded from above and in profile. Midbody scales in 20 rows. Nasal cleft extends from preocular scale to just beyond nostril. Not visible from above. Dark pinkish brown, merging to dark grey or black on tail, with a darker centre on each scale forming obscure narrow lines. Ventral surfaces pale pinkish grey. ■ **NOTES** Ne. NT in vicinity of Darwin and Cobourg Pen. The snake pictured was collected in a vine thicket edging a creek.

Sandamara Blind Snake *Anilios troglodytes* TL 402mm

Very slender, with depressed head, and snout rounded from above and in profile. Midbody scales in 22 rows. Nasal cleft extends from 2nd upper labial scale to rostral scale, completely dividing nasal scale and visible from above. Brown above with pale snout and tail, merging evenly with pale ventral surfaces. ■ **NOTES** Kimberley, WA, from Napier Ra. to Kununurra.

Claw-snouted Blind Snake *Anilios unguirostris* TL 490mm

Moderate to slender, with long snout, weakly trilobed from above, and hooked in profile with prominent transverse cutting edge. Midbody scales in 24 rows. Nasal cleft extends from 1st upper labial scale to or toward rostral scale. Barely or not visible from above. Pink to dark olive brown above, in moderately sharp contrast to cream lower lateral and ventral colour. ■ **NOTES** Tropical woodlands from estn Qld to the Kimberley, WA.

Southern Beaked Blind Snake *Anilios waitii* TL 614mm

Very slender, with snout trilobed from above and strongly hooked in profile. Midbody scales in 20 rows. Nasal cleft extends from 2nd upper labial scale nearly to rostral. Not visible from above. Yellowish brown to dark purplish brown, often paler on snout and merging gradually with cream ventral surfaces. ■ **NOTES** Subhumid to arid sthn and estn WA. Recorded in association with meat ants (*Iridomyrmex* spp.) on pale sand-plains and heavy red loams.

Anilios torresianus
Cardwell, Qld. S. Wilson

Anilios tovelli.
Humpty Doo area, NT. S. Wilson

Anilios troglodytes.
Emma Gorge, El Questro Stn, WA. R. Ellis

Anilios unguirostris.
Kununurra, WA. S. Wilson

Anilios waitii.
Marchagee Reserve, WA. S. Wilson

Brown-snouted Blind Snake *Anilios wiedii* **TL 300mm**

Moderate to slender, with snout rounded from above and in profile. Midbody scales in 20 rows. Nasal cleft extends from 2nd upper labial scale nearly to rostral scale, occasionally reaching it to completely divide nasal scale. Visible from above. Bright pink to pinkish brown, fading to cream on ventral surfaces, and with a dark streak on rostral scale. ■ **NOTES** Various woodland and open habitats, from Mackay, Qld s. to about Koorawatha, NSW.

Yampi Blind Snake *Anilios yampiensis* **TL 128mm**

Slender, with snout rounded from above and in profile. Midbody scales in 18 rows. Nasal cleft extends from preocular to rostral scale, completely dividing nasal scale; not visible from above. Brown, darker on head and tail and paler on snout and ventral surfaces. ■ **NOTES** Known only from a single specimen from Koolan Is. in Yampi Sound, nw. Kimberley, WA. No known live image available.

Yirrkala Blind Snake *Anilios yirrikalae* **TL 200mm**

Moderately slender, with snout rounded from above and in profile. Midbody scales in 24 rows. Nasal cleft extends from 1st upper labial scale to just beyond nostril. Brown above and whitish below. ■ **NOTES** Known only from subhumid ne. tip of Arnhem Land, NT. No known live image available.

West Kimberley Blind Snake *Anilios zonula* **TL 187mm**

Small and moderately slender with snout bluntly rounded from above and in profile, and **no spine on tail-tip**. Midbody scales in 18 rows. Nasal cleft extends from 2nd upper labial scale, and contacts rostral scale to completely divide nasal scale but not visible from above. Purplish pink to pale pink, darkest anteriorly and paler posteriorly. ■ **NOTES** Known only from two specimens, from Augustus Is. and Storr Is. off nw. coast of Kimberley region. Both collected under sandstone slabs, and the Storr Is. specimen is recorded from a stony slope in vine thicket.

Genus *Indotyphlops*

Flowerpot Snake *Indotyphlops braminus* **TL 170mm**

Only one sp. in Aust. Slender, with snout rounded from above and in profile. Midbody scales in 20 rows. Nasal cleft extends from preocular scale to rostral, completely dividing nasal scale and visible from above. Dark purplish brown to almost black, paler on snout and sometimes tail-tip. ■ **NOTES** Aust.'s only introduced snake, presumed to have arrived in the 1960s from South-East Asia. Pops occur in Darwin area, NT, Perth, towns along Pilbara coast and Kimberley region, WA and in Qld between Torres Strait islands and Brisbane. Now widespread in the world's tropical regions, sheltering in moist soil beneath garden debris, in compost and under flowerpots. Parthenogenetic, existing as all-♀ pops.

Anilios wiedii.
Toogoolawah, Qld.
S. Wilson

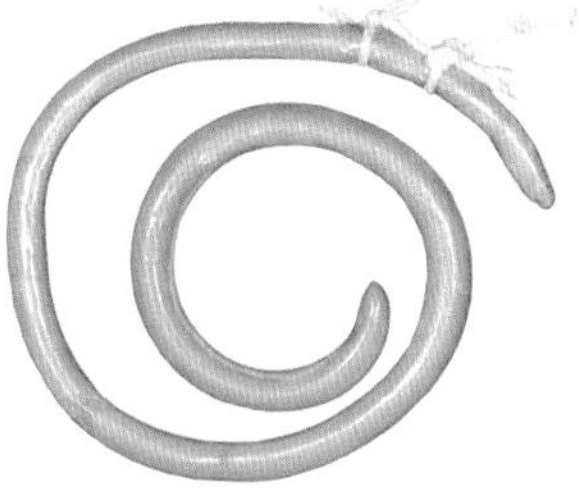

Anilios yampiensis. Preserved holotype.
Koolan Island, WA. R. Ellis

Anilios yirrikalae. Preserved holotype.
Yirrikala, NT. G. Shea

Anilios zonula.
Storr Island, WA. M. Lyons, Dept of Parks and Wildlife

Indotyphlops braminus.
Honiara, Solomon Islands. E. Vanderduys

PYTHONS
Family Pythonidae

Pythons are an essentially tropical group of non-venomous, constricting snakes ranging from Australia through Asia to sub-Saharan Africa. Australia is home to 14 species, roughly half of the world's total of about 34 species.

Australian pythons are most common and diverse in the north, with up to six species occurring at some localities. The Diamond and Carpet Pythons (*Morelia spilota*) reach Victoria and southern Western Australia, while the Woma (*Aspidites ramsayi*) and Stimson's Python (*Antaresia stimsoni*) extend across the arid interior.

Pythons are best known for the massive sizes attained by some species, and for their ability to swallow enormous meals. At about 10 metres, the Reticulated Python (*Malayopython reticulatus*) of South-East Asia is arguably the world's largest snake. Adults normally consume mammals such as deer and pigs, but on rare occasions humans are taken. Australia's largest snake, the Scrub Python (*Simalia kinghorni*) exceeds 5 metres and can easily dispatch large wallabies. The world's smallest python, Western Australia's aptly named Pygmy Python (*Antaresia perthensis*), grows to only 610mm and eats geckos.

Pythons can eat bulky prey thanks to loosely articulated skull bones and numerous very small body scales, which allow greater elasticity of the skin. They locate prey by gathering tell-tale chemical cues with their forked tongues. Most can also detect warm-blooded animals using heat-sensitive pits set along the lips. Sensitive to within about 1/30th of a degree Celsius, the pits are present on all pythons except the Woma and the Black-headed Python (*Aspidites melanocephalus*), which eat mainly reptiles.

Pythons normally hunt by ambush, lying coiled, sometimes for days, beside well-used trails. They also frequent caves or barns containing ready supplies of bats or rats. Pythons may lack venom, but their impressive set of long recurved teeth ensure a secure grip. After a rapid strike they envelop prey in tight coils, killing by suffocation and possibly disruption of blood flow.

Pythons have much in common with a related group, the boas, and have often been classified together in the family Boidae. There is now a growing consensus that pythons should be recognised as a distinct family.

They are regarded as primitive because they retain features believed to have been lost in other snakes. The most significant features are hips and hindlimbs. The hips are minute and the limbs reduced to internal femurs tipped with external spines called cloacal spurs. These remain as visible evidence linking pythons and boas to the limbed ancestors of lizards and snakes. Cloacal spurs are employed by the male to stroke the female's flanks prior to mating.

Pythons exhibit maternal care, extremely rare in snakes. All are egglayers (boas are livebearers), and the females coil around their eggs and guard them until they hatch. By basking they can transfer acquired heat to the clutch, and can even raise their temperatures by shivering. Once the eggs hatch, care ceases and the young disperse.

Unfortunately, many pythons are of conservation concern. They tend to be large and attractively marked, features that have led to their persecution for food and leather in many parts of the world.

Eastern Carpet Python (*Morelia spilota mcdowelli*), swallowing a flying fox. Moggill, Qld. K. Aland

Genus *Antaresia*

Four small to very small spp. (including the world's smallest python), rarely exceeding 1m, with **head scales enlarged to form symmetrical plates, heat-sensory pits present** on some lower labial scales but none in rostral, **3 or more loreal scales** and prominent to weak pattern of **dark blotches or transverse bars on pale ground colour.** ■ **NOTES** Widespread across nthn two-thirds of Aust., normally in dry to well-drained habitats. Though often found in sparsely timbered areas, numbers are highest where rock outcrops, and particularly caves, are present. Excepting the smallest sp., *A. perthensis*, which eats mainly geckos, adults have broad diets, including mammals such as bats or mice, plus birds, lizards, frogs and even other snakes. Pops sharing caves with bat colonies can often be found around cave entrances at dusk, seizing bats as they pour forth into the night. ■ **SEE ALSO** *Liasis*.

Children's Python *Antaresia childreni* TL 1.02m

Pattern weak or sometimes absent on adults but discernible on juv. Tan to reddish brown or purplish brown with numerous slightly darker, **smooth-edged, roughly circular blotches.** ■ **NOTES** Outcrops, escarpments and woodlands from the Kimberley, WA to nw. Qld.
■ **SEE ALSO** *A. maculosa; A. stimsoni.*

Spotted Python *Antaresia maculosa* TL 1.05m

Pattern usually prominent. Cream to yellowish brown with numerous **ragged-edged, dark brown to purplish brown blotches tending to coalesce to form broad wavy longitudinal vertebral streaks anteriorly and posteriorly.** ■ **NOTES** Outcrops, escarpments, woodlands and RF margins from nthn Cape York Pen., Qld to Tamworth, NSW. ■ **SEE ALSO** *A. childreni; A. stimsoni.*

Pygmy Python *Antaresia perthensis* TL 61cm

World's smallest python, with **midbody scales in only 31–35 rows.** Pattern obscure: pale brown to pale reddish brown with slightly darker, irregularly sized blotches and spots. ■ **NOTES** Shrublands and outcrops in semi-arid Pilbara, Gascoyne and upper Murchison regions of WA. Often associated with termite mounds, dwelling in the chambers and preying on geckos that share the mounds. Also common on rock outcrops, sheltering under slabs and in crevices. The scientific name incorrectly implies that it occurs in Perth.

Antaresia childreni.
Kununurra, WA.
S. Wilson

Antaresia maculosa.
Moranbah, Qld.
S. Wilson

Antaresia perthensis.
Waldburg Stn, WA.
S. Wilson

Stimson's Python *Antaresia stimsoni* TL 89cm

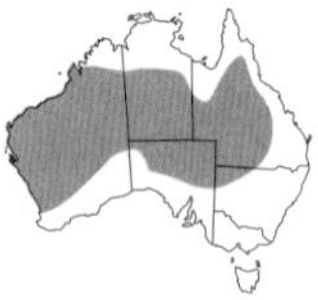

Pattern usually prominent and **including pale ventrolateral line.** ■ **SSP.** *A. s. stimsoni* has 260–302 ventral scales and usually 6th and 7th upper labial scales contacting eye. Pale brown, yellowish brown to cream, irregularly marked with numerous darker brown to reddish brown, **smooth-edged, circular to elongate blotches.** *A. s. orientalis* has 243–284 ventral scales and usually 5th and 6th upper labial scales contacting eye. Pale brown, yellowish brown to cream, with darker brown to reddish brown, **smooth-edged, transversely elongate bars or blotches.** ■ **NOTES** Widespread in outcrops, escarpments and woodlands. *A. s. stimsoni* is restricted to wstn half of WA; *A. s. orientalis* occupies remainder, from central WA eastwards. ■ **SEE ALSO** *A. childreni; A. maculosa.* ■ **STATUS** Vulnerable (NSW).

Genus *Aspidites*

Two large robust spp., **unique in lacking heat-sensory pits.** Head narrow, not markedly distinct from neck, with head shields enlarged to form symmetrical plates. **Eyes with dark irises. Pattern comprises simple bands.** ■ **NOTES** Endemic to Aust., from semi-arid to arid interior to subhumid n. Terrestrial, sheltering in soil cracks, abandoned burrows, hollow logs and rock crevices. Diets consist mainly of reptiles, including venomous snakes, but they also eat mammals and birds. This preference for reptiles is cited as a likely reason for the narrow head and the absence of heat-sensory pits.

Black-headed Python *Aspidites melanocephalus* TL 2.6m

Very distinctively patterned, with **prominent black head, neck and throat.** Body and tail cream, brown to reddish brown with numerous dark brown to blackish bands. Palest with sharpest pattern in far w. of range. ■ **NOTES** Dry tropical nthn areas, in open woodlands, shrublands and outcrops, s. to about North West Cape, WA and Gladstone, Qld. Glossy black head and nape may enable maximum heat absorption while exposing minimum body surface.

Woma *Aspidites ramsayi* TL 2.3m

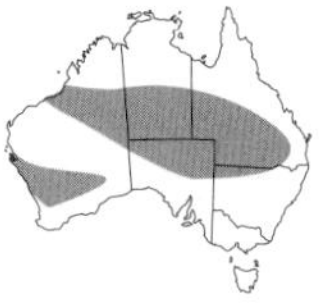

Pale brown, yellowish brown, reddish brown to olive, with numerous irregular darker bands. Juv. have a conspicuous dark patch above each eye, a feature normally lost on adults, but retained to adulthood in pops from se. interior of Qld and sometimes those from central Aust. **Head, neck and throat never black.** ■ **NOTES** Subhumid to arid interior, from nw. coast to about Moonie and Tara districts, sthn Qld. Also present in sw., where land-clearing and possibly predation by feral animals has caused serious declines. Woodlands, heaths and shrublands, often with spinifex. Shelters mainly in abandoned monitor and mammal burrows and in soil cracks. ■ **STATUS** Endangered (IUCN Red List); near threatened (Qld; NT); vulnerable (NSW); rare (SA).

Antaresia stimsoni orientalis.
Sturt NP, NSW.
G. Swan

Antaresia stimsoni stimsoni.
Broome, WA. S. Wilson

Aspidites melanocephalus.
Pardoo, WA. R. Browne-Cooper

Aspidites melanocephalus.
Moranbah area, Qld. S. Wilson

Aspidites ramsayi.
Dove Meadow Stn, Qld. S. Wilson

Genus *Liasis*

Two large to very large spp. with **head scales enlarged to form symmetrical plates, heat-sensory pits present** on some lower labial scales but none in rostral, **1 (rarely 2) loreal scale**, and **pattern absent**; no blotches, stripes or spots. ■ **NOTES** Restricted in Aust. to tropical n., extending to NG and estn Indonesia. Predominantly terrestrial, with one sp. semi-aquatic. They feed mainly on mammals and birds, though reptiles are often taken. Lizards feature prominently in juv. diets. ■ **SEE ALSO** *Antaresia.*

Water Python *Liasis fuscus* TL 2.5m

Glossy dark olive brown, olive grey to almost black, with **distinctive iridescent sheen**. Lower flanks and ventral surfaces yellow. **Midbody scales in 45–48 rows.** ■ **NOTES** Tropical nthn Aust., between Broome, WA and about St Lawrence, Qld. Mainly occurs near freshwater swamps, lagoons, creeks and river edges. In some areas of NT, pops occur in such high densities they are major predators of the floodplains. Predominantly nocturnal. Terrestrial and semi-aquatic. Young freshwater crocodiles (*Crocodylus johnstoni*) are sometimes included in the diet.

Olive Python *Liasis olivaceus* TL 4.5-6.5m

Dark olive, yellowish brown to olive brown with **pearly sheen**. Ventral surfaces white to cream. **Midbody scales in 58 or more rows.** ■ **SSP** *L. o. olivaceus* has **61–72 midbody scale rows** and 321–377 ventral scales. *L. o. barroni* has only **58–63 midbody scale rows**, more ventral scales (374–411) and is larger. ■ **NOTES** Arid to subhumid areas of nthn Aust. Often encountered along watercourses, especially those associated with rocky areas, but generally in drier areas than *L. fuscus*. *L. o. olivaceus* extends from Coulomb Point, WA to wstn half of Qld; *L. o. barroni* is restricted to gorges and escarpments of the Pilbara and Gascoyne regions, WA, isolated by the Gt Sandy Desert. Terrestrial and rock-inhabiting. Adults can consume mammals as large as rock wallabies. ■ **STATUS** *L. o. barroni* is vulnerable (C'wealth; WA).

Genus *Morelia*

Four spp. of moderate to very large pythons with head broad at base and distinct from neck. Head scales **small, irregular and fragmented; heat-sensory pits present on rostral** and some labial scales; pattern consists of bands, blotches and/or stripes. ■ **NOTES** Widespread throughout much of Aust. excluding alps, sthn Vic and Tas, penetrating some arid zones via eucalypt-lined drainage systems. Predominantly nocturnal, though often found basking and foraging by day. Frequently arboreal or rock-inhabiting, though most spp. are regularly encountered on the ground. Diets comprise mainly mammals and birds, including prey such as domestic chickens, possums and fruit bats, but reptiles and amphibians also taken. ■ **SEE ALSO** *Simalia.*

Liasis fuscus.
Iron Range NP, Qld. S. Wilson

Liasis fuscus.
Saibai Is., Qld. S. Wilson

Liasis olivaceus barroni.
Ophthalmia Dam, WA. B. Maryan

Liasis olivaceus olivaceus.
Quamby, Qld. R. Valentic

Centralian Carpet Python *Morelia bredli* TL 2m

Moderately robust. Rich orange red to dark brown with numerous irregular, transversely aligned, dark-edged pale blotches, bands and spots. ■ **NOTES** Central Aust., centred mainly on McDonnell Ra. Occurs on outcrops and creek lines, particularly riverine gorges and along watercourses lined with mature hollow-bearing eucalypts.

Rough-scaled Python *Morelia carinata* TL 2.0m

Slender and large-eyed with **keeled dorsal scales**. Brownish white with many large, angular, dark brown, transversely elongate blotches and coarse variegations. ■ **NOTES** Monsoon forest in sheltered sandstone gorges of nthn Kimberley, WA. Recorded from Mitchell R. Falls on Admiralty Gulf and Hunter R. near Prince Frederick Harbour. ■ **STATUS** Specially protected (WA).

Carpet Python; Diamond Python *Morelia spilota* TL 2.5m

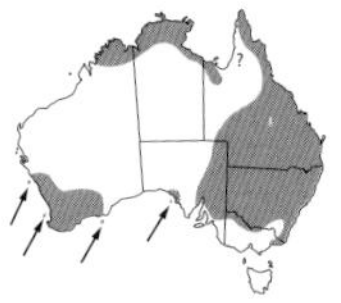

Extremely variable. ■ **SSP.** *M. s. spilota* (Diamond Python) is dark grey to black with a cream spot on most scales, and clusters of all cream or predominantly cream scales arranged to form roughly diamond-shaped blotches over back and flanks. *M. s. variegata* (Top End Carpet Python) is reddish brown to blackish brown with simple ragged, dark-edged pale bands. *M. s. mcdowelli* (Eastern Carpet Python) is extremely variable; typically shades of brown to olive green with many dark-edged pale blotches, tending to be transversely elongated on back and coalescing to form a longitudinal stripe on anterior flanks. Some individuals are wholly striped. *M. s. cheynei* (Jungle Carpet Python) normally has extremely prominent pattern: blackish brown to black with sharply contrasting yellow bands, blotches or stripes. *M. s. metcalfei* (Murray/Darling Carpet Python) is shades of grey with a reddish flush and dark-edged pale grey blotches, nearly circular and arranged roughly in pairs dorsally, and coalescing to form broken stripes laterally. *M. s. imbricata* (Western Carpet Python) is brown to blackish brown with dark-edged pale blotches, tending to be transversely elongated on back and coalescing to form a longitudinal stripe on anterior flanks. ■ **NOTES** It remains to be demonstrated whether these represent valid ssp. or mere colour variants, but collectively they occupy the most diverse habitats of any Aust. python. *M. s. spilota* occurs in estn NSW and ne. Vic; *M. s. variegata* in nthn NT and WA, and may include NG pops; *M. s. mcdowelli* in estn Aust., from Northern Rivers region of NSW to Cape York Pen. and islands of Torres Strait, Qld; *M. s. cheynei* in Wet Tropics of ne. Qld; *M. s. metcalfei* in Murray/Darling drainage basin of estn interior; *M. s. imbricata* occurs in sthn WA., n. to about Houtman's Abrolhos Is and e. to Eyre, with isolated pops on wstn Eyre Pen. and adjacent St Francis Is, SA. Carpet and Diamond Pythons shelter in hollow trunks and limbs, disused burrows, caves, rock crevices and beneath boulders. The various forms occupy most habitats within their broad distributions, though *M. s. cheynei* is restricted to RF. *M. s. metcalfei* is commonly associated with large eucalypts along interior watercourses. *M. s. spilota, M. s. variegata* and *M. s. mcdowelli* thrive in some urban environments, often dwelling in the rafters of houses, yet *M. s. imbricata* appears to be declining markedly as urban areas expand. It is still widespread on the sw. mainland but seems most abundant on offshore islands. These are Aust.'s most familiar pythons, due to their broad distribution and frequent occurrence in large towns and cities. Combat has been observed

Morelia bredli.
Alice Springs, NT. S. Wilson

Morelia spilota imbricata.
Tutanning Nature Reserve, WA. B. Maryan

Morelia spilota cheynei.
Millaa Millaa area, Qld. K. Aland

Morelia carinata.
Prince Frederick Harbour, WA. J. Weigel

Morelia carinata.
Prince Frederick Harbour, WA. J. Weigel

Morelia spilota metcalfei.
Currawinya NP, Qld. S. Wilson

Morelia spilota spilota.
Sydney, NSW. S. Wilson

between ♂ *M. s. mcdowelli* during spring, yet ♂ *M. s. spilota* aggregate near a receptive ♀ and are highly tolerant of each other. Such a behavioural difference between races of 1 sp. is extraordinary. Clutches of 9–52 eggs have been recorded. Individuals differ markedly in temperament. Some readily allow themselves to be handled while others hiss loudly and strike with mouth agape when approached. ■ **STATUS** *M. s. spilota* is endangered (Vic). *M. s. metcalfei* is endangered (Vic); rare (SA).

Green Python *Morelia viridis* TL 1.5m

Slender. **Adults are bright green**, with a vertebral row of white scales. **Juv. are bright yellow** with pale-centred purplish brown streak through eye and lines or blotches on body. Juv. colour and pattern is apparently retained for about 3 years, with transition to green reaching completion over several weeks or months. ■ **NOTES** Restricted in Aust. to RF and vine thickets of Iron and McIlwraith Ranges, ne. Cape York Pen., Qld. Widespread in NG, where additional adult and juv. colour forms occur. Rests in a distinctive looped coil on a branch or vine in dense foliage. It illustrates an excellent example of convergent evolution, mirroring the Emerald Tree Boa (*Corallus caninus*) of South America. Both species are arboreal, with similar adult and juv. colours, feed mainly on birds and rest in the same distinctive coils.
■ **STATUS** Near threatened (Qld).

Genus *Simalia*

Two Aust. spp. Others in NG and estn Indonesia. Very large slender pythons with head long and broad at base, distinct from neck; **enlarged, symmetrically arranged head shields**; and **heat sensory pits present on rostral** and some labial scales. ■ **NOTES** Nthn Aust., in ne. Qld and far nthn NT. These are Aust's largest snakes, often exceeding 4m in length. Adults feed primarily on mammals, taking prey as large as tree kangaroos and rock wallabies. ■ **SEE ALSO** *Morelia*.

Australian Scrub Python *Simalia kinghorni* TL up to 5m, with unconfirmed reports of 8m

Pale yellowish brown to brown, with a milky iridescent sheen and many irregular, angular dark bands, blotches and streaks, tending to become obscure on posterior body and tail. Aust.'s largest snake. ■ **NOTES** RF, vine thickets and occasionally DSF and woodlands, from Townsville n. through Cape York Pen. and islands of Torres Strait to sthn NG. Apparently disjunct pop. in Conway Ra. near Airlie Beach. Distended individuals containing wallabies or tree kangaroos are occasionally encountered basking during the day.

Oenpelli Rock Python *Simalia oenpelliensis* TL 4.3m

Pale brown to pale olive brown with longitudinal rows of dark brown to dark brownish grey blotches, largest dorsally, becoming smaller on lower flanks and fading posteriorly. ■ **NOTES** Arnhem Land escarpment and adjacent outliers. Predominantly rock-inhabiting, sheltering in deep crevices and caves. Adults feed largely on mammals, such as rock wallabies, possums and flying foxes.
■ **STATUS** Vulnerable (NT).

Morelia spilota mcdowelli.
Teviot Falls, Qld. S. Wilson

Morelia spilota variegata.
Darwin district, NT. S. Wilson

Morelia viridis. Juvenile.
Iron Range, Qld. S. Wilson

Morelia viridis. Adult.
Iron Range, Qld. S. Wilson

Simalia kinghorni.
Iron Range area, Qld. S. Wilson

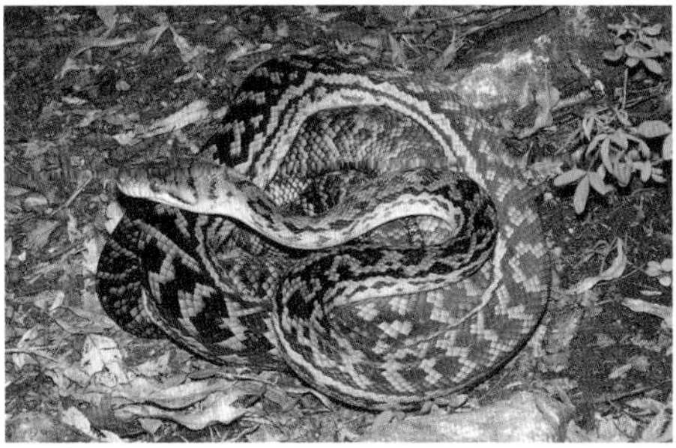

Simalia kinghorni.
Cairns, Qld. S. Wilson

Simalia oenpelliensis.
Kakadu NP, NT. S. Swanson

FILE SNAKES
Family Acrochordidae

Small and unusual family comprising only three species of specialised non-venomous water snakes named for their minute rasp-like scales. They are distributed from South Asia through New Guinea to the Solomon Islands. Two species occur in northern Australia: a freshwater inhabitant of tropical lagoons, rivers and floodplains, and a mainly marine species in coastal mangroves.

File snakes are wholly aquatic. Both Australian species inhabit environments subject to great fluctuation in area on either a daily tidal or seasonal basis. Beneath the water they are graceful swimmers, moving their laterally compressed bodies in easy undulating movements. On land they are ungainly and slow, moving with all the elegance of a wet sock.

Thanks to a very low metabolic rate, file snakes can remain submerged for long periods; they feed infrequently, are generally very sluggish, have lengthy gestation periods and are probably long-lived. They shelter by day in shaded areas among submerged roots, in recesses under banks and beneath sediment, and catch fish by ambush or through active foraging. They can subdue and consume very large prey. Their rasp-like scales are probably suited to maintaining a firm grip on struggling slippery prey, and are tipped with microscopic hair-like structures, suggesting that food detection may, in part, be through tactile response.

Males have been recorded to aggregate in a writhing ball endeavouring to mate with a single female. File snakes are livebearers, with Australian species producing litters of up 25 young.

Genus *Acrochordus*

Moderate to large, very robust, non-venomous snakes with loose baggy skin, blunt snouts, valvular nostrils placed well forward on the snout and small, slightly protrusive eyes with vertically elliptic pupils. Scales are tiny and keeled to pointed, in 80 or more midbody rows with no enlarged ventral scales. Head scales are minute and granular, with no large symmetrical shields.

Arafura File Snake *Acrochordus arafurae* TL 2.1m

Robust. Brown to olive brown **with coarse dark reticulum** enclosing paler blotches over dorsal and ventral surfaces. ■ **NOTES** Freshwater habitats, particularly pandanus-lined lagoons, sheltered riverbanks and floodplains associated with major drainage systems connected to the Arafura Sea, from nw. NT to Cape York Pen., Qld and sthn NG. Disperses widely through temporary waterways and seasonal wetlands during wet season flooding, but during the dry season large numbers contract together as pools shrink.

Little File Snake *Acrochordus granulatus* TL 1.62m

Small, relatively slender and **banded**. Dark grey to dark brown with pale grey to pale brown bands, either continuous or disrupted on midline, usually extending onto ventral surfaces. ■ **NOTES** Mangrove-lined coast from the Kimberley, WA to Cape York, Qld. Also widespread from the Solomon Is. to South Asia. Largely confined to salt or brackish water, but occasionally enters fresh water.

Acrochordus arafurae. Arafura File Snake. Gregory River, Qld. J. Cann

Acrochordus arafurae.
Anniversary Creek, NT. B. Maryan

Acrochordus granulatus.
Gattokae Is., Solomon Is. S. Wilson

COLUBRID SNAKES
Family Colubridae

Colubridae is the largest family of snakes in the world, with more than 1600 species dominating the snake fauna on almost all continents. They exhibit an enormous variety of form and habit, ranging from extremely slender and arboreal to robust and aquatic. Some are large snakes that forage widely across open terrain, while others are minute burrowers. Their diets are broad, from insects and slugs to large vertebrates.

Despite their huge international success, colubrids are represented by only 6 species in Australia. So few on a continent so well endowed with snakes is remarkable, and suggests their relatively recent arrival. Unlike our dominant group, the elapids, with their numerous species and high level of endemism, it seems Australian colubrids evolved elsewhere. None are endemic; all are shared at least with New Guinea. In Australia they are restricted to the north and east, with none in arid or cool temperate habitats. There is a strong bias towards semi-aquatic and arboreal species, niches poorly exploited by other Australian snakes.

Colubridae is so extraordinarily diverse that it is quite possibly a group of convenience, rather than an assemblage of natural allies. They are difficult to clearly define using external characters, and as a group appear outwardly similar to terrestrial elapids. The two groups share large, symmetrically arranged head shields; large, transversely expanded ventral scales; and midbody scales in fewer (usually much fewer) than 30 rows. Australian colubrids differ from elapids in **possessing a loreal scale (fig.)**. Colubridae is divided into several ill-defined subfamilies, two of which occur in Australia.

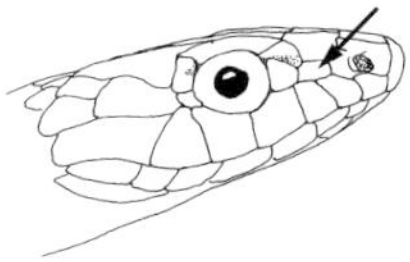

Colubrinae, the largest and most diverse group within the family, is represented here by the tree snakes (*Dendrelaphis* and *Boiga*) and the moisture-loving genus *Stegonotus*. Colubrinae includes completely non-venomous (solid-toothed) and weakly venomous, rear-fanged species.

Natricinae is represented by the Keelback (*Tropidonophis mairii*), a non-venomous, moisture-loving species with strongly keeled scales. Natricines occur worldwide and are common predators of toads. Until the introduction of the Cane Toad (*Rhinella marina*), Australia was toad free. Our only natricine snake is one of the few Australian animals with limited ability to prey on toads. Thanks to its toad-eating ancestry, it may be genetically predisposed to tolerate toad poisons.

Australian colubrids are egglayers and all are predators of vertebrates, occasionally vertebrate eggs. Despite the paucity of species they tend to be abundant in tropical and subtropical areas and can be a conspicuous element in well-vegetated gardens of our northern towns and cities.

No Australian colubrids are considered dangerous to humans.

Brown Tree Snake (*Boiga irregularis*), characterised by enormous, cat-like eyes. Brisbane, Qld. S. Wilson

Genus *Boiga* (Subfamily Colubrinae)

Brown Tree Snake; 'Night Tiger' *Boiga irregularis* TL 2m

Sole Aust. sp.; many others in South-East Asia and South Asia. Long, slender, weakly venomous, rear-fanged snake with **bulbous head distinct from narrow neck** and **large prominent eyes with cat-like vertical pupils**. Scales smooth and weakly glossed, in 19–23 midbody rows; vertebral row enlarged and hexagon-shaped. Anal scale single and subcaudals divided. Loreal scales present. Two regionally distinct colour forms occur. Estn form is pale to rich reddish brown above, with narrow, irregular, dark bands or variegations, and belly orange to salmon pink. Nthn ('Night Tiger') form is cream above and below with prominent rich red bands. ■ **NOTES** Woodlands to RF and rock outcrops, from just s. of Sydney to NG and estn Indonesia (estn form), and in gorges and escarpments from Gulf of Carpentaria, Qld to the Kimberley, WA (nthn form). Arboreal and rock-inhabiting, sheltering in hollow limbs, crevices or caves, and frequently in ceilings of buildings. Adults feed mainly on birds and small mammals, and juv. on lizards. Egglayer. Introduced to Guam, where it appears to have exterminated some bird spp. and seriously threatens others. Aggressive if threatened but not normally regarded as dangerous. Very large specimens could produce uncomfortable symptoms.

Tree Snakes Genus *Dendrelaphis* (Subfamily Colubrinae)

Two Aust. spp., with many others in NG and South-East Asia. Non-venomous, **very slender snakes with long thin tails and an angular ventrolateral keel** along each side of body. Head narrow with large eyes and round pupils. Scales smooth in 13 (rarely 11 or 15) rows, with vertebral series enlarged. Anal and subcaudal scales divided. Loreal scales present. ■ **NOTES** These alert, diurnal snakes are extremely swift and agile among slender branches and foliage. They have acute vision, often raising their heads and swaying to accurately gauge distance. Diets comprise mainly frogs and lizards, swallowed alive. Egglayers, producing 4–16 elongate eggs per clutch. If grasped, they produce an unpleasant odour from anal glands.

Northern Tree Snake *Dendrelaphis calligastra* TL 1m

Extremely slender, with very large eyes. Olive, olive grey to brown with **black streak from snout to forebody** contrasting sharply with white to yellow upper lip. Lower lateral and ventral surfaces white to yellow, usually with darker flecks. ■ **NOTES** RF, monsoon forests and vine thickets, from Townsville, Qld to islands of Torres Strait, NG and Solomon Is. Wary and difficult to approach, but often encountered sleeping coiled in outer foliage at night. Harmless.

Boiga irregularis. 'Night Tiger' form. Bedford Downs Stn, WA. S. Wilson

Boiga irregularis. Eastern form. Winhaven Stn, Qld. S. Wilson

Dendrelaphis calligastra. Iron Range NP, Qld. S. Wilson

Common Tree Snake; Green Tree Snake *Dendrelaphis punctulatus* TL 1.2m

Moderately slender, with **no dark streak from snout to forebody**. Very variable colouration, particularly in e., ranging from black (common in mid-estn Qld), yellow with pale bluish grey head and neck (across nthn Aust.), or olive green, dull green to bluish green or blue (estn Aust.). Ventral surfaces usually yellow, generally most intense on anterior body. ■ **NOTES** Wide variety of habitats, from woodlands to RF and tropical gardens, from just s. of Sydney through Cape York Pen., Qld and islands of Torres Strait to NG and w. to the Kimberley, WA. When cornered, neck and forebody are distended to display contrasting blue skin between scales. Large aggregations recorded over-wintering in hollow trees, disused buildings and caves. Harmless.

Genus *Stegonotus* (Subfamily Colubrinae)

Two non-venomous Aust. spp., with others ranging from NG to South-East Asia. Moderately slender snakes with squarish snouts and moderately small, dark eyes. Scales smooth and very glossy in 17–19 midbody rows. Anal scale single and subcaudal scales divided or single. Loreal scale present. ■ **NOTES** Restricted in Aust. to moist areas in far n. Crepuscular to nocturnal. In addition to vertebrate prey such as mammals, reptiles and frogs, reptile eggs are often eaten. Enlarged broad teeth at the rear of the upper jaw could be designed to slit egg shells. Mainly terrestrial. Egglaying.

Slatey-grey Snake *Stegonotus cucullatus* TL 1.3m

Dark brown to very dark grey, shining iridescent purple when viewed obliquely, becoming paler on flanks. Upper lips cream to pale brown. Ventral surfaces white to cream, sometimes marked with black flecks. Subcaudal scales divided. ■ **NOTES** Largely associated with creeks, swamps and lagoons, extending into various woodland, monsoon forest and RF habitats. Shelters beneath logs, rocks and low vegtn, and in abandoned burrows. Primarily terrestrial, but partially arboreal and semi-aquatic, sometimes encountered climbing in low foliage or on steep rock faces. Feeds largely on frogs, although reptiles and warm-blooded prey are also taken. Pugnacious when provoked, striking repeatedly. Harmless.

Slate-brown Snake *Stegonotus parvus* TL 800mm

Slender, with uniform colouration, dark brown fading to pale brown on lower flanks. Lips white to pale brown, often contrasting sharply with ground colour. Ventral surfaces white to pale yellow. Subcaudal scales of NG specimens mostly single. ■ **NOTES** Poorly known. Restricted in Aust. to Murray Is. in estn Torres Strait, Qld. Widespread in lowland NG. Snake and lizard eggs constitute a significant portion of diet. Lizards are also taken. Harmless.

Dendrelaphis punctulatus.
Humpty Doo, NT. S. Wilson

Dendrelaphis punctulatus.
Lowood, Qld. S. Wilson.

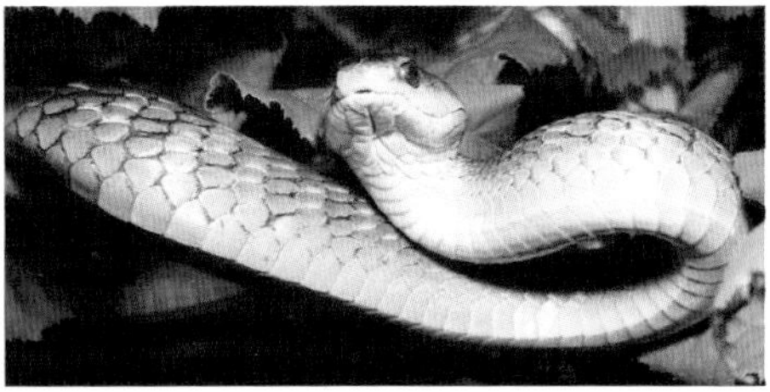

Dendrelaphis punctulatus.
Wynnum, Qld. E. Vanderduys

Stegonotus cucullatus.
Darwin, NT. S. Wilson

Dendrelaphis punctulatus.
Shoalwater Bay, Qld. S. Wilson

Stegonotus parvus.
Baiyer, Papua New Guinea. R. Mackay

Genus ***Tropidonophis*** (Subfamily Natricinae)

Keelback; Freshwater Snake *Tropidonophis mairii* TL 930mm

One Aust. sp., with many others extending from NG to South-East Asia. Non-venomous snake with moderately large eye and round pupil. **Scales strongly keeled** and matt-textured in **15 midbody rows. Anal and subcaudal scales divided. Loreal scale present**. Shades of grey, olive to almost black, or yellow to rich reddish brown, usually with narrow dark bands, spots or variegations mixed with dark and pale flecks. Lips pale with fine dark sutures between scales. ■ **NOTES** Well-watered habitats across nthn Aust., from Northern Rivers region of NSW to the Kimberley, WA. Nocturnal to diurnal. Usually encountered in or near water. Feeds on frogs, tadpoles, lizards and even fish. One of the few native animals able to prey on the introduced poisonous Cane Toad (*Rhinella marina*) without ill effect, though attempts to consume large toads are often fatal. Egglayer, producing clutches of up to 18 eggs. Tail readily broken if handled roughly. Capable of emitting an unpleasant odour from anal glands as a deterrent. Harmless. ■ **SEE ALSO** *Tropidechis carinatus* (terrestrial elapid).

Tropidonophis mairii.
Wynnum, Qld. S. Wilson

Tropidonophis mairii swallowing a toad.
Kurwongbah, Qld. S. Wilson

MANGROVE AND FRESHWATER SNAKES
Family Homalopsidae

Until recently the homalopsid snakes were placed as a subfamily within the unwieldy, diverse and complex family, Colubridae. They are now accorded their own family status, reflecting their unique molecular, physical and behavioural characteristics.

Homalopsids are robust, aquatic to semi-aquatic snakes equipped with valvular nostrils located on the top of the snout, enabling them to breathe from below the surface without exposing too much of the head. All are venomous, with grooved fangs situated at the back of the mouth, but none are regarded as dangerous to humans. They differ from the marine elapids, the true sea snakes, in having a round tail rather than a laterally flattened, paddle-shaped tail. They also retain well-developed, broad ventral scales.

There are about 40 species of homalopsid snakes. Diversity is highest in Indo-China, with species extending west to India and Pakistan and east to New Guinea. Just five species live in tropical northern Australia. Four occupy coastal and estuarine mangrove swamps and mud flats and one inhabits freshwater rivers and streams.

Though not often seen, homalopsids are an extremely successful group of snakes that sometimes comprise a significant proportion of the biomass in the areas they inhabit. This means they can be extremely abundant, so in the right location homalopsids can be seen, not just in ones and twos, but by the dozen.

And it is small wonder that homalopsids are infrequently encountered. The soupy mud and tepid shallow waters of northern Australia's mangrove swamps are physically unpleasant for humans, with stifling humidity, rank smell, a constant whine of biting insects plus a very real risk of being eaten by a crocodile. Naturalists seldom venture into these areas, and no sane person would spend longer there than absolutely necessary.

The marine homalopsids thrive in shallow water and mud. They probably follow rising and falling tides, enabling them to continually occupy their preferred water depth. They shelter in mangrove roots, crustacean burrows, under submerged leaf litter and among debris. Most prey largely on fish such as gobies and mudskippers but one highly specialised species, the White-bellied Mangrove Snake (*Fordonia leucobalia*) is unique among Australian snakes in taking only crustaceans and in frequently dismembering its prey rather than swallowing it whole. The sole freshwater species, Macleay's Water Snake (*Pseudoferania polylepis*), takes fish, frogs and crustaceans.

Homalopsids are primarily nocturnal, though they can be seen active by day, particularly during overcast, drizzly weather. Most Australian species extend at least to southern New Guinea and one reaches South Asia. All are live-bearers.

Macleay's Water Snake (*Pseudoferania polylepis*) is Australia's only freshwater homalopsid snake.
Claudie River, Qld. S. Wilson

Genus *Cerberus*

Australian Bockadam *Cerberus australis* TL 737mm

One Aust. sp. of robust, weakly venomous, rear-fanged water snake with small, **upward-directed, protrusive eyes** with vertically elliptic pupils. Nostrils valvular. Scales moderately strongly keeled in 23–25 midbody rows. Anal and subcaudal scales divided. **Nasal scales in broad contact. Loreal scales present**. Shades of grey to brick red with narrow dark bands above, and cream with broad, prominent, dark bands below. ■ **NOTES** Mangrove-lined tidal creeks, rivers and estuaries in salt to brackish water from wstn Kimberley, WA to tip of Cape York, Qld, and nthn is. of Torres Strait. Mainly nocturnal, although active by day in wet and overcast weather, and occasionally basks on mudflats. Shelters among mangrove roots and beneath submerged detritus, and forages for fish in shallows. Livebearing. Pugnacious if provoked, striking repeatedly and emitting a foul odour from anal glands. Not considered dangerous. ■ **SEE ALSO** *Fordonia; Myron.*

Genus *Fordonia*

White-bellied Mangrove Snake *Fordonia leucobalia* TL 930mm

Sole member of genus. Robust, weakly venomous, rear-fanged water snake with broad head, short rounded snout and small eyes with round pupils. Nostril valvular. Scales smooth and glossy in 23–29 midbody rows. Anal and subcaudal scales divided (occasionally a few subcaudals single). **Loreal scales absent. Nasal scales separated**. Colouration extremely variable, ranging from black through shades of brown and reddish brown to cream. Pattern prominent to absent, typically comprising pale blotches, spots or bands. ■ **NOTES** Mangrove-lined tidal channels and mudflats from Nickol Bay, WA to Cape York and islands of Torres Strait, Qld. Also widespread from NG to South-East Asia. Shelters in crab burrows and among root-tangles, and feeds almost exclusively on crabs, pressing them against substrate with coils, immobilising with venom, and often biting off legs and claws before consuming them. It is the only Aust. snake known to dismember prey in this unique manner. Not considered dangerous. ■ **SEE ALSO** *Cerberus; Myron.*

Cerberus australis.
Grey form.
Wyndham, WA.
S. Wilson

Cerberus australis.
Red form.
Darwin, NT. S. Wilson

Fordonia leucobalia.
Wyndham, WA. S. Wilson

Fordonia leucobalia.
Wyndham, WA. S. Wilson

Genus *Myron*

Two Aust spp. (one other in estn Indonesia) of small, weakly venomous, rear-fanged water snakes each with narrow head distinct from neck and small, slightly protrusive, upward-directed eyes with vertically elliptic pupils. Nostrils valvular, and both Aust. spp. have nasal scales separated. Body scales weakly keeled posteriorly in 19–21 midbody rows. Anal and subcaudal scales divided. Loreal scales present. ■ **NOTES** Amphibious snakes inhabiting mudflats and shallow water associated with tropical coastal and estuarine mangroves. ■ **SEE ALSO** *Fordonia*; *Cerberus*.

Roebuck Bay Mangrove Snake *Myron resetari* **TL 395 mm**

One preocular scale, 19 midbody scale rows. Olive brown with diffuse darker bands, darkest on tail. ■ **NOTES** Very poorly known. Recorded only from Broome area, WA, probably occurring along the mangrove-lined shores of Roebuck Bay. ■ **SEE ALSO** *Myron richardsonii*; *Cerberus*; *Fordonia*.

Richardson's Mangrove Snake *Myron richardsonii* **TL 415mm**

Two preocular scales, 21 midbody scale rows. Brown, olive brown to grey with numerous narrow, irregular dark bands. ■ **NOTES** Mangrove-lined estuaries and tidal creeks on coast and islands of nthn Aust., from nthn WA to Gulf of Carpentaria, Qld. Also extends from NG to estn Indonesia. Shelters among mangrove roots and in crab burrows, foraging for small fish in shallows and on mudflats. Not considered dangerous. ■ **SEE ALSO** *Myron resetari; Cerberus; Fordonia.*

Genus *Pseudoferania*

Macleay's Water Snake *Pseudoferania polylepis* **TL 870mm**

Sole member of genus. Moderately robust, weakly venomous, rear-fanged water snake with long head and small, upward-directed eyes with vertically elliptic pupils. Scales smooth and highly glossy, weakly keeled posteriorly, with an iridescent sheen in 21–23 midbody rows. Anal and subcaudal scales divided. Nasal scales in contact. Loreal scales present. Shades of brown, olive and grey, often with broad darker vertebral stripe and sometimes lateral stripes. Ventral surfaces cream to yellow, usually with dark midventral stripe on body and almost invariably on tail. ■ **NOTES** Freshwater lagoons, swamps and creeks from nthn NT to Cape York Pen. and NG. Shelters among aquatic vegtn, under submerged leaf litter, root-tangles etc. Eats small fish, frogs and tadpoles. In NT, often widely dispersed during wet season sheet-flooding, contracting to permanent pools during dry periods. Not considered dangerous.

Myron resetari. Broome, WA. S. Wilson

Myron richardsonii. Darwin, NT. G. Harold

Pseudoferania polylepis. Anniversary Creek, NT. B. Maryan

VENOMOUS LAND SNAKES
Family Elapidae

The Elapidae are the venomous front-fanged snakes that dominate the Australian snake fauna. They have enlarged syringe-like fangs set at the front of the mouth and connected to a venom gland at the rear of the head via a duct beneath the skin on the upper jaw.

The venomous land snakes and two marine groups, the sea snakes and sea kraits, are so closely related they belong to one subfamily, Hydrophiinae. They appear to have evolved within the Australia and New Guinea region. We adopt that classification here, yet it seems easier to discuss and picture them separately. Their habitats are so starkly different that terrestrial elapids rarely come into contact with the marine groups, and they are so modified for their respective worlds that they appear quite distinctive.

Terrestrial elapids have enlarged, symmetrically arranged scales on top of the head, large, laterally expanded ventral scales and cylindrical pointed tails. At first glance they appear most like some of the non-marine colubrid snakes, but differ in lacking a loreal scale (fig.). See also fig. on page 512

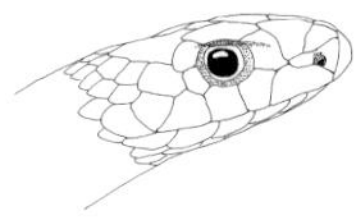

With 106 described species, terrestrial elapids comprise the largest and most diverse group of Australian snakes. They range from large, highly venomous snakes more than 2.5 metres long that forage widely across open terrain to tiny, weakly venomous burrowers less than 30 centimetres long that are seldom seen above ground. Some are short, thick, viper-like snakes lying concealed and sluggish among leaf litter, while others are slender, alert and extremely swift.

Terrestrial elapids occur Australia-wide, with diversity greatest in the tropical to subtropical east. A few thrive in the higher latitudes and altitudes, where cool conditions exclude all other snakes. Hence all snakes in Tasmania and southern Victoria are terrestrial elapids; the occasional sea snake is carried there by ocean currents and washed ashore as a waif.

Terrestrial elapids are predators of vertebrates, which they kill or immobilise with venom and consume whole. Most small species, and juveniles of larger species, are lizard specialists. A few prefer frogs. Large species tend to have more diverse diets, consuming various reptiles, frogs, mammals and birds. The taipans (*Oxyuranus*) eat only mammals and have evolved exceptionally lethal venom to dispatch prey that can retaliate. The shovel-nosed snakes (*Brachyurophis*) are exceptional, with most specialising in reptile eggs.

Terrestrial elapids follow a similar reproductive trend to skinks, with livebearing predominating in cool climates where eggs are difficult to incubate and egglaying predominating in the tropics. Interestingly, all species with undivided anal and subcaudal scales are livebearers.

The rich terrestrial elapid fauna places Australia in a unique situation as the only continent where venomous snakes outnumber non-venomous species. The presence of such a large and diverse assemblage of venomous species may seem alarming, but most are small, inoffensive and secretive, with venom more suited to paralysing skinks than killing humans. That said, some of Australia's terrestrial elapids are among the world's most lethal snakes, and many thrive on the edges of our towns and cities.

Golden-crowned Snake (*Cacophis squamulosus*). Threat posture. Mt Glorious, Qld. S. Wilson

Death Adders Genus *Acanthophis*

Seven **short, very robust** Aust. spp. Head broad, distinct from neck. **Tail slender, terminating in a soft slender spine.** Eye small, with pale iris and vertically elliptic pupil. Head scales smooth to rugose, and body scales smooth to keeled in 19–23 rows at midbody. Anal scale single, and subcaudals single anteriorly and divided posteriorly. **A row of subocular scales between eye and upper labial scales.** ■ **NOTES** Widespread throughout mainland Aust. and some islands, with possible exception of Vic (no recent records), extending n. to NG and estn Indonesia. Slow-moving sedentary snakes, convergent in appearance and behaviour with vipers of other continents. They lie motionless and partly concealed under leaf litter and low vegtn, with the slender segmented tail resting near the snout. At the approach of a small vertebrate the tail is wriggled convulsively in mimicry of a worm or caterpillar, luring the prey within range of the lightning-fast strike. Livebearing, producing up to 33 young. While death adders constitute a distinctive group, differences between them remain unclear. Available names for some additional 'spp.' may yet prove valid. One sp. is among Aust.'s most lethal snakes, but it is prudent to regard all as DANGEROUS.

Common Death Adder *Acanthophis antarcticus* TL 700mm (maximum 1m)

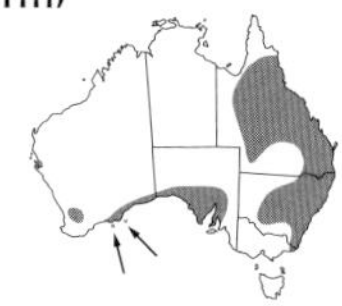

Very stout, with smooth to slightly rugose head shields and **smooth to very weakly keeled dorsal body scales** in **21 midbody rows** (rarely 23). Variable, with most pops including reddish brown and grey individuals, each marked with irregular bands between nape and tail, and dark and pale bars on lips. Segmented tail-tip cream or black. ■ **NOTES** Habitats range from RF to shrublands and heaths. Declining in many areas, probably due to habitat destruction and altered fire regimes. Fangs are long and capable of administering large quantities of powerfully neuro-toxic venom. DANGEROUSLY VENOMOUS. ■ **SEE ALSO** *A. hawkei; A. praelongus.* ■ **STATUS** Vulnerable (Qld); data deficient (Vic).

Plains Death Adder *Acanthophis hawkei* TL 700mm–1.2m

Ill-defined sp. with smooth to moderately rugose head shields and smooth to moderately keeled dorsal body scales in 21–23 midbody rows. Pale brown to grey with numerous irregular bands, and dark and pale bars on lips. ■ **NOTES** Sometimes referred to as the Barkly Tableland Death Adder. Very poorly diagnosed, and not distinguishable on morphological characters but identifiable genetically and said to be the largest death adder in n. Aust. (though reputed maximum of 1.2m requires verification). Associated with cracking clay and Mitchell Grass of Barkly Tablelands, and flood-prone flats in estn. NT and e. of Darwin. Description and map are tentative. DANGEROUSLY VENOMOUS. ■ **SEE ALSO** *A. antarcticus; A. rugosus.* ■ **STATUS** Vulnerable (C'wealth; NT; Qld).

Acanthophis antarcticus. Red form.
Mt Mee SF,. Qld. S. Wilson

Acanthophis antarcticus. Grey form.
Numinbah Valley, Qld. S. Wilson

Acanthophis hawkei.
Fogg Dam, NT.
J. Farquhar

Kimberley Death Adder *Acanthophis lancasteri* TL 645mm

Moderately stout with rugose head shields and dorsal scales prominently keeled anteriorly, in 22–23 rows at midbody. Supraoculars raised to form prominent peaks and **a pair of undivided prefrontal scales**. Dull orange, tan to grey with 44–61 darker bands, black tail-tip and pale lips with dark mottling. **Ventral surfaces cream without pattern; dark pigment restricted to lateral edges.** ■ **NOTES** Kimberley region, WA, incl. some offshore islands, extending from Kununurra area w. to Wotjulum and s. to near Halls Creek. DANGEROUSLY VENOMOUS. ■ **SEE ALSO** *A. pyrrhus; A. rugosus.*

Northern Death Adder *Acanthophis praelongus* TL 600mm

Moderately robust, with moderate to strongly rugose head shields, **strongly keeled anterior dorsal body scales** and 21–23 midbody scale rows. **Supraocular scales have lateral flanges forming prominent raised peaks.** Colour ranges from grey to dark brown or reddish brown, with weak to sharply contrasting bands. Head same colour or darker to almost black, and lips usually barred. Tail-tip cream or black. ■ **NOTES** Grasslands, woodlands, vine thickets, rocky ranges and outcrops of nthn Qld, from Wet Tropics to Cape York Pen. and Torres Strait is. DANGEROUSLY VENOMOUS. ■ **SEE ALSO** *A. antarcticus.*

Desert Death Adder *Acanthophis pyrrhus* TL 708mm

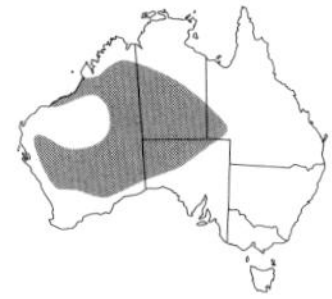

Relatively slender, with **very rugose head shields, divided prefrontal scales, strongly keeled dorsal and lateral scales** and usually **21 midbody scale rows.** Pale reddish brown to rich red, with transversely aligned dark flecks alternating with many narrow cream to yellow bands composed of pale pigment on base of each scale. Lips mottled. Segmented tail-tip usually dark, but often pale or banded. ■ **NOTES** Spinifex deserts, including sand-ridges, sandy or stony flats and rock outcrops. DANGEROUSLY VENOMOUS. ■ **SEE ALSO** *A. lancasteri; A. wellsei.* ■ **STATUS** Vulnerable (SA).

Papuan Death Adder *Acanthophis rugosus* TL 700mm

Moderately robust with moderate to strongly rugose head shields, dorsal scales prominently keeled anteriorly, in 21–23 rows at midbody. Supraoculars raised to form prominent peaks and a pair of undivided prefrontal scales. Grey to reddish brown with numerous darker bands, dark or pale tail-tip and heavily mottled or barred upper lips. **Ventral surfaces cream with distinct dark blotching.** ■ **NOTES** Nthn NT and nw. Qld from near WA border through Mt Isa area to mesas w. of Winton, in a variety of wooded habitats, with a likely preference for stony ridges, outcrops and other rocky sites. Also NG. DANGEROUSLY VENOMOUS. ■ **SEE ALSO** *A. hawkei; A. lancasteri.* ■ **STATUS** Near threatened (NT – as *praelongus*).

Acanthophis lancasteri.
Theda Station, WA.
B. Schembri

Acanthophis praelongus.
Torres Strait, Qld. S. Wilson

Acanthophis pyrrhus.
Port Hedland, WA. S. Wilson

Acanthophis rugosus.
Katherine Gorge, NT. S. Wilson

Pilbara Death Adder *Acanthophis wellsei* TL 520mm

Relatively slender, with **weakly rugose head shields**, usually **undivided prefrontal scales**, and **body scales moderately keeled dorsally and smooth laterally in 19 midbody rows**. Reddish brown and banded, with 2 colour forms occurring: those with pale bands, and strongly patterned individuals with black bands and black heads. Lips not normally barred. ■ **NOTES** Widespread throughout the Pilbara, WA, with an apparently isolated pop. on North West Cape and a possible hybridisation zone with *A. pyrrhus* s. and e. of North West Cape. Occurs among spinifex on stony soils. DANGEROUSLY VENOMOUS. ■ **SEE ALSO** *A. pyrrhus*.

Genus *Antaioserpens*

Two small, moderately robust, short-tailed spp. with weakly shovel-shaped snouts, prefrontal scale contacting upper labials separating nasal from preocular, smooth, glossy scales in 15 midbody rows, and divided anal and subcaudal scales. ■ **NOTES** Secretive burrowing snakes, infrequently encountered foraging at night. They probably feed exclusively on lizards, primarily or solely skinks. Egg-layers. ■ **SEE ALSO** *Brachyurophis*.

North-eastern Plain-nosed Burrowing Snake *Antaioserpens albiceps* TL 420mm

Brown to rich orange, with darker hind edges to body scales forming a reticulum, and sometimes a dark midline caudal stripe. Top of head dark grey with pale mottling, separated from broad black blotch on neck by broad to narrow cream to white band. On juv., reduced pigmentation on head can result in nearly completely white head with dark mottling on snout. ■ **NOTES** Open tropical forests and woodlands of ne. Qld from Mapoon Mission near tip of Cape York Pen. s. nearly to Clermont.

Warrego Burrowing Snake *Antaioserpens warro* TL 438mm

Pale reddish brown to olive with each body scale irregularly dark-edged to create a speckled pattern, and sometimes a dark midline caudal stripe. Top of head with blackish hood extending back and becoming diffuse at about rear edge of parietal scales, separated from broad black band on neck, 6–8 scales long by 3–4 rows of much paler scales. ■ **NOTES** Original faded holotype is from Warro Stn, Port Curtis. All recent specimens are from about 1000km inland at Mitchell, Orkadilla SF near Morven, and from Charleville, along the wstn edge of the Brigalow Belt South and adj. Mulga Lands bioregions. Recorded from Poplar Box/Callitris Pine woodlands, and probably extending into mulga woodlands.

Acanthophis wellsei.
Karratha area, WA.
R. Browne-Cooper

Antaioserpens albiceps.
Harvey Range, Qld.
S. Wilson

Antaioserpens warro.
Orkadilla State Forest, Qld. S. Wilson

Copperheads Genus *Austrelaps*

Three moderate to very large spp. with **barred lips**. Eye moderately large with pale iris and round pupil. Scales smooth and weakly glossed in usually **15 midbody rows; the lowest lateral row enlarged. Anal and subcaudal scales single.** ■ **NOTES** Restricted to se. Aust., including alpine areas and Tas, often occupying habitats too cool for most other snakes. Terrestrial and diurnal, frequently encountered basking tightly coiled in sheltered sunny sites. Copperheads shelter under rocks and logs or in abandoned burrows, and feed on a variety of vertebrates, but mainly frogs and skinks. Livebearers. When cornered, they hiss loudly with necks flattened and raised in a low curve. The two largest spp. have caused fatalities and all should be regarded as DANGEROUSLY VENOMOUS.

Pygmy Copperhead *Austrelaps labialis* TL 870mm

Pale brown or pale to dark grey, with or without a narrow dark vertebral stripe. Dark bar often present across neck, 4 or 5 scales behind head. **Lips very prominently barred.** Ventral surfaces cream, yellow, dark grey to almost black. ■ **NOTES** Restricted to Kangaroo Is., Mt Lofty Ra. and base of Fleurieu Pen., SA. Inhabits broad range of habitats on Kangaroo Is., including coastal dunes, samphire flats, woodlands and agricultural areas. Mainland snakes appear largely confined to high-altitude stringybark forests with dense understorey. Presumed to be DANGEROUSLY VENOMOUS. ■ **STATUS** Vulnerable (IUCN Red List).

Highlands Copperhead *Austrelaps ramsayi* TL 1.1m

Prominently barred lips, with **pale anterior edges to upper labial scales occupying more than one-third of each scale** and meeting dark posterior portion along sharp diagonal junction. Shades of dark reddish brown to dark grey, often paler and redder on lower flanks. ■ **NOTES** Moist habitats in montane heaths, woodlands, WSF and DSF, creek edges and marshes, in cool upland areas between estn Vic and New England Tableland, NSW. DANGEROUSLY VENOMOUS.

Lowlands Copperhead *Austrelaps superbus* TL 1.2–1.8m

Weakly barred lips, with **pale anterior edge to each upper labial scale narrow and often ill-defined.** Colour ranges through shades of brown, reddish brown, grey to almost black, sometimes with dark or pale band across nape and narrow dark vertebral stripe. Lower flanks usually pale; cream to yellow on pale snakes, and pink to orange on dark snakes. Largest specimens occur on King Is., Bass Strait. ■ **NOTES** Closely associated with fresh water or moist low-lying areas in DSF, woodlands or heaths. Especially common where tussock grasses occur. DANGEROUSLY VENOMOUS.

Austrelaps labialis.
Adelaide Hills, SA.
R. Valentic

Austrelaps ramsayi.
Kosciuszko NP, NSW.
S. Wilson

Austrelaps superbus.
Campbell Town area, Tas. E. Vanderduys

Shovel-nosed Snakes Genus *Brachyurophis*

Eight moderately robust spp. with a **wedge-shaped rostral scale tipped with a broad, transverse, weak to acute cutting edge**. Eye small with dark iris. Scales smooth and glossy in **15–17 rows at midbody. Anal and subcaudal scales divided**. Pattern includes **broad dark bands across head and neck**, and usually **narrow prominent bands across body**. ■ **NOTES** Widespread in warm dry areas. Burrowers, dwelling beneath stumps and rocks, in insect holes and loose soil. Egglayers. Some feed only on reptile eggs, cutting the soft shell with uniquely modified blade-like teeth at rear of mouth and consuming both the shell and its contents. Others also take small skinks. Disinclined to bite, even when handled. ■ **SEE ALSO** *Antaioserpens; Simoselaps.*

North-western Shovel-nosed Snake *Brachyurophis approximans* TL 362mm

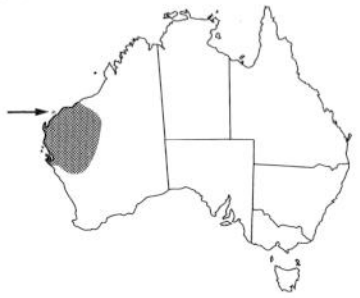

Midbody scales in 17 rows. **Upper labial scales usually 6**. Broad grey to dark greyish brown bands with many very narrow, pale interspaces between nape and tail-tip; the **dark markings are more than 4 times broader than interspaces**, with interspaces less than 1 scale wide, and sometimes reduced to transverse rows of spots. Dark blotch on top of head may be continuous with broad dark nuchal band. ■ **NOTES** Acacia woodlands and shrublands on heavy (often stony) reddish soils in arid nw. interior, coast and some islands of WA, from Broome s. to Shark Bay and Yalgoo. Reptile egg specialist. ■ **SEE ALSO** *B. roperi; B. semifasciatus.*

Australian Coral Snake *Brachyurophis australis* TL 340mm

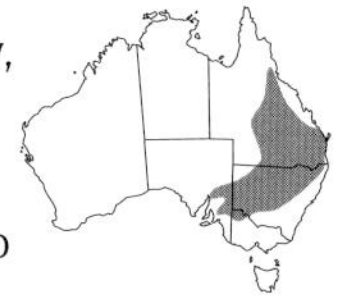

Midbody scales in 17 rows. Pink, pale reddish brown to brick red with many narrow, ragged-edged bands of transverse rows of dark-edged paler scales. Broad dark band extends across head, another across neck. ■ **NOTES** Open habitats, from woodlands and shrublands to spinifex grasslands and rock outcrops in subhumid to semi-arid interior. Feeds on reptile eggs and skinks.

Campbell's Shovel-nosed Snake *Brachyurophis campbelli* TL 353mm

Midbody scales in 15–17 rows, with 15 recorded from Cape York Pen. (Laura, Weipa, Wenlock R. and Archer R.) and Barcaldine, and 17 from Mt Isa and Almaden. Variable, from orange to reddish brown with broad dark blotch on top of head (white blotch in vicinity of Laura) and numerous broad to narrow dark bands across body. ■ **NOTES** Possibly a complex of spp. Relationship with *B. roperi* uncertain, and the name *woodjonesii* (from Lower Archer River) available for pop. with 15 midbody scale rows. Probably a reptile-egg specialist. ■ **SEE ALSO** *B. roperi.*

Brachyurophis approximans.
Tom Price area, WA.
R. Browne-Cooper

Brachyurophis australis.
Greenbank, Qld.
S. Wilson

Brachyurophis campbelli.
Weipa area, Qld.
L. Dibben

Narrow-banded Shovel-nosed Snake *Brachyurophis fasciolatus* TL 390mm

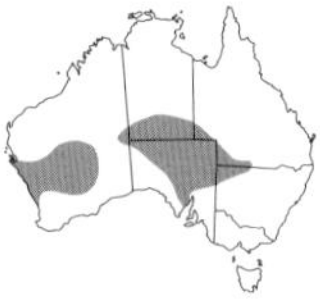

Midbody scales in 17 rows. Cutting edge on rostral scale relatively weak. White, cream to very pale grey or pink, with prominent dark head and nape blotches, many irregular, ragged-edged black bands, and scattered to transversely aligned reddish to blackish spots within pale interspaces. ■ **SSP.** *B. f. fasciolatus* has broad dark nuchal blotch (7–15 scales wide) and narrow dark body bands, 1 scale or less in width. *B. f. fasciatus* has narrower nuchal blotch (3–6 scales wide) and broader body bands, more than 1 scale wide. ■ **NOTES** Variety of habitats, from coastal dunes to spinifex deserts in subhumid to arid sthn Aust. *B. f. fasciolatus* occurs in wstn portion of range, from about Laverton to Shark Bay and s. to coastal areas of Perth, WA; *B. f. fasciatus* extends from estn WA to sw. Qld. Feeds on reptile eggs and skinks. ■ **STATUS** Endangered (NSW).

Unbanded Shovel-nosed Snake *Brachyurophis incinctus* TL 360mm

Midbody scales in 15-17 rows. Pink to brown, **without bands**, and each scale dark-edged, forming reticulum. Black head blotch extends from level of eyes to base of head, widely separated from broad black nuchal bar. ■ **NOTES** Arid interior of Qld to Gulf of Carpentaria and central Aust., mainly on heavy clays, loams, stony soils and rock outcrops supporting woodlands, shrublands or spinifex grasslands. Probably feeds exclusively on reptile eggs.

Arnhem Shovel-nosed Snake *Brachyurophis morrisi* TL 300mm

Midbody scales in 15 rows. Orange-brown **without bands**, each scale dark-edged forming a weak reticulum. **Head very pale yellowish brown with dark head blotch greatly reduced** to heavy dark mottling at about level of eyes. Black nuchal blotch prominent with sharp leading edge. ■ **NOTES** Woodlands of nthn Arnhem Land, NT. Probably feeds exclusively on reptile eggs.

Northern Shovel-nosed Snake *Brachyurophis roperi* TL 368mm

Midbody scales in 15–17 rows, varying geographically (15 in nthn NT, 17 in central NT and sthn Kimberley, WA). **Upper labial scales 6**. Orange, reddish brown to shades of grey with many darker brown to black bands, **less than 3 times as broad as the paler interspaces**, which are occasionally reduced to transverse rows of pale spots. ■ **NOTES** Subhumid to semi-arid areas, from sw. Kimberley, WA to nthn NT s. to about Ti Tree. Heavy soils and rocky ranges. Possibly includes several spp. Reptile egg specialist. ■ **SEE ALSO** *B. approximans; B. campbelli.*

Southern Shovel-nosed Snake *Brachyurophis semifasciatus* TL 353mm

Midbody scales in 17 rows. Upper labial scales 5. Orange to reddish brown with broad dark head and nuchal blotches and many dark brown bands about the same width as pale interspaces. ■ **NOTES** Subhumid to arid sthn Aust. from Eyre Pen., SA to lower w. coast. Common in sandy to stony soils near Perth, WA. Reptile-egg specialist. ■ **SEE ALSO** *B. approximans.*

Brachyurophis fasciolatus fasciolatus.
Perth, WA. S. Wilson

Brachyurophis fasciolatus fasciatus.
Little Sandy Desert, WA. B. Maryan

Brachyurophis incinctus.
Mt Isa, Qld. S. Wilson

Brachyurophis morrisi.
Nabarlek, NT. G. Harold

Brachyurophis roperi.
Darwin district, NT. S. Wilson

Brachyurophis semifasciatus.
Lancelin area, WA. B. Maryan

Crowned Snakes Genus *Cacophis*

Four very small to medium-sized spp. with a **pale band or collar on nape**. Eye small with pale iris and vertical pupil. Scales smooth and glossy in **15 rows at midbody. Anal and subcaudal scales divided**. Spp. are identified by colour and shape of neck markings and by ventral colour. ■ **NOTES** Restricted to moist areas. Secretive nocturnal snakes which shelter under rocks, logs and leaf litter wherever damp conditions prevail. They feed exclusively on skinks, presumably foraging at night for sleeping diurnal prey. When provoked they rear the head and forebody and lunge at aggressor, though the mouth is rarely opened. Egglayers. Regarded as harmless, though bites from large specimens could cause discomfort.

Northern Dwarf Crowned Snake *Cacophis churchilli* TL 450mm

Glossy dark grey with a **narrow pale yellow band across nape**, $\frac{1}{2}$–$2\frac{1}{2}$ scales wide. **Ventral surfaces usually dark grey**, rarely pale yellow with narrow dark bands. ■ **NOTES** RF and eucalypt forests from Atherton Tableland s. to Bluewater Range, Mt Spec and Magnetic Is.

White-crowned Snake *Cacophis harriettae* TL 500mm

Glossy dark grey to almost black with a **broad white band across nape**, 4 or more scales wide, extending forward (and becoming invaded by many dark flecks) onto sides of head and snout. Top of head glossy black. **Ventral surfaces dark grey**. ■ **NOTES** WSF, RF and well-watered urban areas on coast and ranges. Frequently uncovered in suburban compost heaps and abundant in parks and gardens of inner Brisbane, Qld. ■ **STATUS** Vulnerable (NSW).

Southern Dwarf Crowned Snake *Cacophis krefftii* TL 345mm

Dark grey to almost black with **narrow pale yellow band across nape**, $\frac{1}{2}$–2 scales wide, extending forward (becoming broader and invaded by dark flecks) onto sides of head and snout. **Ventral surfaces pale yellow with narrow dark bands**. ■ **NOTES** RF and WSF (occasionally well-watered suburban areas) on coast and ranges, from Gosford, NSW to mid-estn Qld.

Golden-crowned Snake *Cacophis squamulosus* TL 750mm

Dark brown to dark grey with conspicuous **pale brown to yellow streak along each side of neck** forming an incomplete band and extending forward through sides of head to snout. **Ventral surfaces orange, with a mid-ventral line of brown blotches**. ■ **NOTES** RF, moist eucalypt forests or well-watered rock outcrops, on coast and ranges from Wollongong, NSW to mid-estn Qld with isolated inland record in Carnarvon Ras.

Cacophis churchilli.
Tinnaroo Dam, Qld.
S. Wilson

Cacophis harriettae.
Kurwongbah, Qld.
S. Wilson

Cacophis krefftii.
Brisbane, Qld. E. Vanderduys

Cacophis squamulosus.
Mt Glorious, Qld. S. Wilson

Genus *Cryptophis*

Five moderate-sized spp. with relatively depressed heads, squarish snouts and very small to moderate-sized eyes with dark irises. Scales smooth and glossy in 15 midbody rows. Anal and subcaudal scales single. Pattern normally absent (although 1 sp. has a dark head and vertebral stripe) and colouration usually sombre (apart from 1 sp. which is bright pink). ■ **NOTES** Widespread in estn and nthn Aust. and extending to sthn NG. Secretive, terrestrial and nocturnal snakes which tend to seek slightly damp shelter sites beneath rocks and logs and in soil cracks. Livebearers, producing litters of up to 11 young. They feed mainly on lizards, sometimes frogs and occasionally other snakes. Most are not regarded as medically significant but 1 sp. has been implicated in a fatality and should be regarded as POTENTIALLY DANGEROUS.

Carpentaria Snake *Cryptophis boschmai* TL 560mm

Brown to dark orange-brown with dark flush on scale-bases, sometimes a dark vertebral suffusion, and vague pale flush on sides of head, neck and forebody. Ventral surfaces pearly cream. **Nasal scale separated from preocular scale.** ■ **NOTES** DSF and woodlands of estn Qld, n. to wstn Cape York Pen. ■ **SEE ALSO** *C. nigrescens.*

Pink Snake *Cryptophis incredibilis* TL 400mm

Very slender and long-tailed, with relatively large eyes and uniform colour of bright pink. Ventral surfaces pearly white. ■ **NOTES** Known only from Prince of Wales Is. in sthn Torres Strait. Recorded from open eucalypt and paperbark woodlands on sandy soils. The presence of similar habitats on adjacent islands, and ample evidence that these islands have been connected in the recent past, suggest a potentially wider distribution. ■ **STATUS** Vulnerable (Qld).

Eastern Small-eyed Snake *Cryptophis nigrescens* TL 500mm (rarely 1m)

Glossy black, without pattern. Ventral surfaces cream to pale pink, sometimes flecked and blotched with black. **Ventral pigment is wholly confined to ventral scales** (not extending up onto lower flanks). **Nasal scale contacts preocular scale.** ■ **NOTES** E. coast and ranges, from just w. of Melbourne, Vic to Cairns, Qld. Habitats include RF and WSF, woodlands, heaths and rock outcrops. Frequently encountered beneath bark on fallen logs. In addition to skinks and frogs, other snakes (including own kind) are recorded as prey items. Venom toxicity appears to vary geographically, and some pops may be considered DANGEROUSLY VENOMOUS. One recorded fatality. ■ **SEE ALSO** *C. boschmai; Pseudechis porphyriacus.*

Black-striped Snake *Cryptophis nigrostriatus* TL 500mm

Very slender and long-tailed, with relatively large eyes and **dark vertebral stripe**. Dark brown, dull reddish brown to bright pinkish red with glossy black to dark brown head continuous with broad dark vertebral stripe to tail-tip. Ventral surfaces pearly white. ■ **NOTES** DSF and woodlands from Rockhampton to islands of Torres Strait and sthn NG.

Cryptophis boschmai.
Oakey, Qld. S. Wilson

Cryptophis incredibilis.
Prince of Wales Is, Qld. S. Wilson

Cryptophis nigrescens.
Mt Mee, Qld.
S. Wilson

Cryptophis nigrostriatus.
Mareeba, Qld.
S. Swanson

Northern Small-eyed Snake *Cryptophis pallidiceps* TL 550mm

Glossy black, dark grey to brown, paler on head with orange tinge on lower flanks. Ventral surfaces pearly white to pink, often with dark flecks on posterior ventral scales and along middle of tail. ■ **NOTES** Woodlands of nthn NT and nthn Kimberley, WA.

Whipsnakes Genus ***Demansia***

Fourteen **very slender**, long-tailed spp. with **large prominent eyes, pale irises and round pupils**. Scales smooth and matt-textured in **15 midbody rows. Anal and subcaudal scales divided**. Pattern, when present, normally includes **pale rim around eye and dark comma shape below eye**. ■ **NOTES** Dry open habitats over most of Aust. Whipsnakes are diurnal, extremely swift and alert. They feed mainly on lizards, located primarily by sight and pursued with a burst of speed. Egglayers. Most are not medically significant but large specimens should be regarded as POTENTIALLY DANGEROUS.

Narrow-headed Whipsnake *Demansia angusticeps* TL 880mm

Weakly patterned, with no dark band across neck. Narrow, **pale-edged dark line across front of snout,** not meeting eye but curving sharply down at junction of 2nd and 3rd upper labial scales, **prominent pale bar on front and rear edges of eye,** dark brown comma-shape sweeping back to corner of mouth. Olive brown to greyish brown, more yellow-brown on tail and orange-brown on snout, usually with a dark spot on each internasal and prefrontal scale and lower edges of neck. Ventral surfaces cream with grey clouding along inner edges of lower labial scales and **no dark spots along midline.** ■ **NOTES** Tropical woodlands of sthn Kimberley, e. to Victoria River valley, NT. ■ **SEE ALSO** *D. olivacea.*

Black-necked Whipsnake *Demansia calodera* TL 610mm

Pale-edged **dark band across neck**. Olive grey to olive brown, often with dark spots on dorsal scales forming obscure dotted to reticulated pattern. Pattern usually prominent; broad pale-edged dark band across neck; narrow dark brown margin around eye, itself broadly pale-edged, sweeping back as long dark comma-shaped streak to behind corner of mouth; and narrow pale-edged dark line around front of snout. ■ **NOTES** Woodlands, heaths and shrublands along mid-w. coast from North West Cape to Kalbarri, with isolated pop. over 1100km east in Gibson Desert.

Cryptophis pallidiceps.
Kununurra, WA.
S. Wilson

Demansia angusticeps.
Broome, WA.
B. Maryan

Demansia calodera.
Kalbarri area, WA.
S. Wilson

Ornate Whipsnake *Demansia flagellatio* TL 715mm

Small, very slender with long tail (about 40% of SVL) and **prominent yellow and black head markings.** Pale-edged dark line across front of snout not meeting eye but curving sharply down at junction of 2nd and 3rd upper labial scales, prominent pale bar on front and rear edges of eye, and dark brown comma-shape sweeping back to corner of mouth. Top of head dark with yellow band across nape, and two dark bands across neck separated by bright yellow interspace. Body olive-brown, reddish-brown to blue, becoming dull to bright yellow on tail. Ventral surfaces yellow-brown, yellow under throat and tail, occasionally with dark spots forming paired series on anterior ventral scales. ■ **NOTES** Mt Isa and Lawn Hill area, nw. Qld.

Marble-headed Whipsnake; Olive Whipsnake *Demansia olivacea* TL 835mm

Weakly patterned, with **little or no pale-edged dark line across snout, no pale bars beside eye** and no dark band across neck. Brown with weak dark comma-shape extending back to corner of mouth and **dark variegations on lips and snout**. Ventral surfaces shades of yellow to bluish yellow, brighter beneath tail, with prominent **dark variegations on throat, a broken row of dark spots along midline of anterior ventral scales**, and sometimes spots along outer ventral and lower body scales. ■ **NOTES** Woodlands of nthn NT and nthn Kimberley region, WA. ■ **SEE ALSO** *D. angusticeps.*

Greater Black Whipsnake *Demansia papuensis* TL 1.65m

Ventral scales 198–228. Pattern weak, becoming paler and redder posteriorly; dark slate grey on most wstn snakes, dark grey to tan in estn pops. Top of head tan, often with irregular scattered dark spots. Eye usually edged with narrow broken pale margin, and sometimes with a very short dark comma curving back towards corner of mouth. **No dark line around front of snout.** ■ **NOTES** Tropical woodlands of far nthn Aust., from the Kimberley, WA to Cape York and ne. interior of Qld. Despite the name *papuensis*, it is not known from NG. Bites from large individuals should be regarded as POTENTIALLY DANGEROUS. ■ **SEE ALSO** *D. vestigiata.*

Demansia flagellatio. Lawn Hill NP, Qld. G. Stephenson

Demansia olivacea. Darwin, NT. G. Harold

Demansia papuensis. Kakadu NP, NT. B. Maryan

Yellow-faced Whipsnake *Demansia psammophis* TL 1m

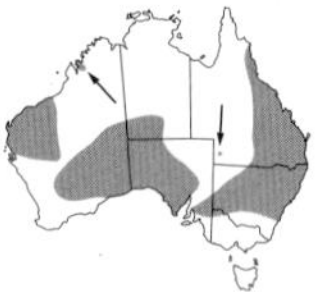

Variable, with prominent dark brown margin around eye, itself pale-edged, sweeping back as a short dark comma-shaped mark curving towards corner of mouth. Narrow, pale-edged dark line extends around front of snout. ■ **SSP.** *D. p. psammophis* is pale grey, bluish grey to olive, often with 2 reddish brown paravertebral stripes from behind neck to anterior third of body in estn pops. *D. p. cupreiceps* has reticulated pattern and head, anterior body and tail flushed with orange to copper. ■ **NOTES** Widely distributed in a variety of habitats, including DSF, woodlands, heaths, WSF and margins of RF, penetrating very arid regions via eucalypt-lined watercourses. *D. p. psammophis* occurs in estn Aust., extending w. to the Goldfields of WA; *D. p. cupreiceps* occupies remaining arid interior from sw. Qld to mid w. coast and nw. of WA. Communal nesting is recorded for *D. p. psammophis*, with one site, containing approximately 500–600 eggs, apparently used repeatedly over consecutive seasons. A bite from a large individual may produce painful local reactions, but not normally considered dangerous. ■ **STATUS** *D. p. psammophis* is near threatened (Vic).

Sombre Whipsnake *Demansia quaesitor* TL 735mm

Weakly patterned with faint **dark band across nape lacking pale edge,** retained by adults in w. but present only laterally on juv. in e. Dark line across front of snout usually present, with or without a faint pale edge, narrowly reaching eye. No pale bars beside eye. Dark comma-shape curves back from below eye to corner of mouth or to lower edge of dark nape band. Greyish brown to almost black, often more brown or yellow on posterior body and tail. **Head paler,** ranging from blue-grey to orange-brown or copper. Ventral surfaces pale and patternless—at most a few dark flecks on throat. ■ **NOTES** Tropical nthn Aust., between Bowthorn Stn, Qld and estn Kimberley region, WA.

Reticulated Whipsnake *Demansia reticulata* TL 1m

Dark brown margin around eye, with prominent pale anterior and posterior margin, sweeping back as short, dark comma-shaped mark to corner of mouth. Narrow pale-edged dark line extends across front of snout from nostril to nostril. Olive green to olive with each scale broadly dark-edged forming prominent reticulum. ■ **NOTES** Variety of open woodlands and shrublands in sw. WA from Dirk Hartog Is. s. to Harvey and inland to Wheatbelt.

Blacksoil Whipsnake *Demansia rimicola* TL 975mm

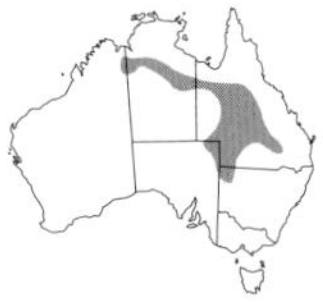

Pale-edged dark band across head, fading on adult, with pale edges persisting longest. Weak dark line across front of snout, often absent centrally, not reaching eye but curving sharply down at junction of 2nd and 3rd upper labial scales. Prominent pale bar on front and rear edges of eye, the **rear bar constricted to form an isolated blotch.** Dark comma-shape curves back from below eye to corner of mouth. Brown with dark spots on top of head. On body, pigment aligns to form broad dark and narrow pale lateral stripes. Ventral surfaces yellow to bright red with a pair of dark brown streaks and marbling on throat, continuous with **two prominent rows of**

Demansia psammophis cupreiceps.
Beyonde, WA. D. Robinson

Demansia psammophis psammophis.
Redbank, Qld. E. Vanderduys

Demansia quaesitor.
Burrell Creek, NT. G. Harold

Demansia quaesitor.
Mt Isa district, Qld. E. Vanderduys

Demansia reticulata.
Kalbarri area, WA. B. Maryan

Demansia rimicola.
Sturt NP, NSW. G. Swan

ventral spots that diverge as they extend back. ■ **NOTES** Semi-arid grasslands and shrublands on plains of cracking clay soils. ■ **STATUS** Vulnerable (NSW); rare (SA).

Rufous Whipsnake *Demansia rufescens* TL 670mm

Weakly patterned with no dark band across nape, prominent pale-edged dark line across snout reaching eye, prominent pale bar on front and rear edges of eye, and dark brown comma-shape sweeping back to corner of mouth. Reddish brown to coppery brown on back and tail, olive grey to dark grey on head and neck. ■ **NOTES** Stony hills and plains with spinifex, often in association with low open woodlands and shrublands, in arid Pilbara, WA. including Dolphin Is., Barrow Is. and an outlying pop. on North West Cape.

Shine's Whipsnake *Demansia shinei* TL 808mm

Brown band across nape edged with lemon yellow. Narrow, pale yellow-edged dark line extends across front of snout not reaching eye, and dark brown comma-shape curves back from below eye to corner of mouth. Prominent pale bars on front and rear edges of eye, the **rear bar very broad** and continuous with pale edge to dark nape band. Pale greyish brown with brown head and yellowish flush on tail. **Ventral surfaces pale yellow and without pattern.** ■ **NOTES** Arid to semi-arid interior to nw. Aust, from Halls Creek, WA, e. to Borooloola and s. to Uluru, NT. Also Little Sandy Desert, WA.

Grey Whipsnake *Demansia simplex* TL 530mm

Robust, with short tail, uniform brownish grey colouration and **fewer than 160 ventral scales**. Eye usually edged with dark brown, and broadly margined with yellow, with short dark brown streak curving back towards corner of mouth. Little or no dark line around front of snout. ■ **NOTES** Grassy woodlands in subhumid areas, from nthn Kimberley, WA to Jabiru, NT.

Collared Whipsnake *Demansia torquata* TL 825mm

Dark band across nape (obscure on adults). Pale brown, olive brown to greyish brown with top of head darker to black. Broad pale-edged dark bar extends across neck. Dark margin around eye, itself pale-edged, sweeps back as a long dark comma-shaped mark to behind corner of mouth. Narrow pale-edged dark line extends across front of snout, through nostril to contact eye. Ventral surfaces blue-grey, yellow beneath throat and tail. ■ **NOTES** Coastal Qld, from Cape York s. to Gladstone and inland to Moranbah area. Abundant on islands off mid-e. coast.

Demansia rufescens.
Newman, WA.
B. Maryan

Demansia shinei.
Three Ways area, NT. R. Valentic

Demansia simplex.
Keep River, NT. P. Horner

Demansia torquata.
Gladstone, Qld.
S. Wilson

Lesser Black Whipsnake *Demansia vestigiata* TL 1.2m

Ventral scales 165–197. Dark brown, reddish brown to dark grey, often flushed with reddish brown on posterior body and tail. Individual scales often with dark markings, forming reticulated or spotted pattern. Small dark blotches usually present on top and sides of head, particularly on estn pops and sometimes absent on wstn pops. Eye usually edged with narrow broken pale margin, and sometimes with a very short dark comma curving back towards corner of mouth. **No dark line around front of snout.** ■ **NOTES** Subhumid woodlands and heaths of far nthn Aust., extending s. on e. coast to Ipswich, Qld, and ne. to Ord R. drainage in the Kimberley, WA. Also present in sthn NG. Bites from large individuals should be regarded as POTENTIALLY DANGEROUS. ■ **SEE ALSO** *D. papuensis*.

Genus *Denisonia*

Two medium-sized, robust spp. with relatively flat heads and moderately large eyes with pale irises and vertically elliptic pupils. Scales smooth and weakly glossy, in 17 midbody rows. Anal and subcaudal scales single. Pattern includes dark patch on head and barred lips. ■ **NOTES** Secretive nocturnal snakes restricted to mid-estn coast and interior. They occur in woodlands and shrublands, mainly in low-lying areas subject to seasonal flooding. Livebearing, producing litters of up to 11 young. Diets are distinctive among small elapids: almost entirely frogs and rarely lizards. Pugnacious when disturbed, flattening body, thrashing and striking wildly if provoked. A bite from 1 sp. has produced severe effects so both should be considered POTENTIALLY DANGEROUS.

De Vis' Banded Snake; 'Mud Adder' *Denisonia devisi* TL 568mm

Yellowish brown to olive with pattern usually prominent, consisting of **many irregular dark brown bands**, often broken along midline, especially on neck and forebody. Large dark blotch present on top of head, and lips prominently barred with cream and dark brown. ■ **NOTES** Favours cracking clay-based soils on moist alluvial flats vegetated with woodlands or shrublands, particularly lignum and brigalow. In addition to frogs, geckos are infrequently recorded prey. POTENTIALLY DANGEROUS. ■ **STATUS** Critically endangered (Vic)

Ornamental Snake *Denisonia maculata* TL 465mm

Extremely robust, with little pattern; dark grey to greyish brown with darker patch on top of head, and black and white barred lips. Outer edges of throat and ventral scales marked with black flecks or spots. ■ **NOTES** Dawson R. drainage and Bowen Basin region of mid-estn Qld. Favours low-lying areas with cracking clay soils. High population densities occur in suitable habitats. Apparently feeds exclusively on frogs. A bite has produced severe local symptoms and should be regarded as POTENTIALLY DANGEROUS. ■ **STATUS** Vulnerable (C'wealth; Qld; IUCN Red List).

Demansia vestigiata.
Beerwah, Qld.
S. Wilson

Denisonia devisi.
Glenmorgan, Qld.
S. Wilson

Denisonia maculata.
Croyden Stn, Lotus Creek area, Qld.
S. Wilson

Genus *Drysdalia*

Three small, moderately robust spp. with large eyes and round pupils. Iris dark brown to grey below, but with a distinct golden upper portion. Scales smooth and matt-textured, in 15 rows at midbody. Anal and subcaudal scales single. Spp. are identified by pattern; the presence or absence of a white stripe along upper lip and pale band across neck. ■ **NOTES** Diurnal snakes, occurring in sthn open forests, shrublands and heaths. In mild to warm sunny weather they bask along the edges of tracks and atop thick low vegtn, wriggling swiftly to cover when disturbed. Livebearing. They feed almost entirely on skinks, rarely frogs. Not regarded as dangerous. ■ **SEE ALSO** *Elapognathus.*

White-lipped Snake *Drysdalia coronoides* TL 450mm

Variable. Olive, reddish brown, pale or dark grey to almost black with prominent **white stripe through upper lip** from nostril to side of neck and **no pale band across neck**. Ventral surfaces usually pink to orange, occasionally cream to olive. ■ **NOTES** Extends from Tas to highlands of ne. NSW. Most cool-adapted Aust. snake, reaching to sthn latitudes and high altitudes where most other snakes cannot survive. Often locally abundant, particularly where ground cover is dominated by tussock grasses. While skinks constitute over 80% of diet, skink eggs, frogs, and even a small mammal have been recorded. ■ **STATUS** Rare (SA).

Masters' Snake *Drysdalia mastersii* TL 330mm

Pale yellowish brown to grey with darker head, **white stripe through upper lip** and **yellow to whitish band across neck**, normally narrowly broken on midline. Ventral surfaces orange centrally (red on juv.); grey speckled with black along outer edges. ■ **NOTES** Semi-arid sthn Aust., extending disjunctly from near Esperance, WA to Big Desert area, Vic. Occurs on coastal dunes and limestones, and on sand-plains supporting heaths or mallee/spinifex associations. ■ **STATUS** Endangered (Vic).

Mustard-bellied Snake *Drysdalia rhodogaster* TL 400mm

Brown to olive grey, darker on top of head, with prominent **orange to yellow band across neck**, usually a narrow dark line running from nostril to eye, but **no white stripe on upper lip**. ■ **NOTES** Coast and ranges of sthn NSW, n. to Newnes Plateau and s. to Merimbula. Favours woodlands, heaths or DSF, usually with tussock-dominated ground cover.

Drysdalia coronoides.
Falls Creek, Vic.
S. Wilson

Drysdalia mastersii.
Madura, WA.
R. Browne-Cooper

Drysdalia rhodogaster.
Wentworth Falls, NSW. S. Wilson

Genus *Echiopsis*

Bardick *Echiopsis curta* **TL 710mm**

Sole member of genus. Short, very stout snake with broad head distinct from neck and moderately large eyes. Iris brown with pale yellow upper portion and round pupil. Scales smooth and matt-textured, in 17–21 (usually 19) midbody rows. Anal and subcaudal scales single. Olive grey, brown to rich reddish brown with little or no pattern; white flecks on sides of head and neck in e., often a diffuse pale streak on rear of head in w., and distinctly dark grey head on mid-w. coast. ■ **NOTES** Three isolated pops occur in sthn Aust.: sw. WA between Kalbarri and Gt Aust. Bight; Eyre Pen., SA; and from se. SA to adjacent Vic and NSW. Favours heaths and mallee/spinifex associations, sheltering among leaf litter and beneath low vegtn. Nocturnal and diurnal. Sedentary and usually encountered motionless, close to shelter. Livebearing, producing litters of 3–14 large young. Feeds on lizards, frogs, and occasionally mammals and birds, probably captured by ambush. Pugnacious when harassed. A bite may cause severe symptoms and should be regarded as POTENTIALLY DANGEROUS. ■ **STATUS** Endangered (NSW); vulnerable (Vic); rare (SA); near threatened (IUCN Red List).

Genus *Elapognathus*

Two small, moderately robust to slender spp. with large eyes and round pupils. Iris dark with pale ring around pupil. Scales smooth and matt-textured, in 15 rows at midbody. Anal and subcaudal scales single. Pattern includes dark band across neck or oblique pale bands on side of neck, pale upper lip and yellow to orange ventral pigments. ■ **NOTES** Restricted to heaths and swamp edges in sthn WA. Diurnal. Livebearing. Feed mainly on frogs, and also eat skinks. Not regarded as dangerous. ■ **SEE ALSO** *Drysdalia.*

Western Crowned Snake *Elapognathus coronatus* **TL 690mm**

Olive grey, olive brown to blackish grey. Top of head bluish grey, margined by **broad black band across nape**, extending forward as black streak through lower portion of eye to snout, and edged below by a prominent white streak along upper lip. Ventral surfaces orange to orange-red, suffused with grey and peppered with black. ■ **NOTES** Coastal woodlands, heaths and swamps of sthn and sw. WA, extending n. to Muchea and e. to Gt Aust. Bight. Shelters beneath rocks and logs, and in abandoned nests of stick-nest ants. Usually encountered foraging or basking in mild sunlight close to cover. Snakes on islands of Archipelago of the Recherche are largest and feed largely or wholly on skinks. Smaller mainland snakes also eat frogs.

Echiopsis curta.
Little Desert, Vic.
R. Valentic

Echiopsis curta.
Guilderton, WA,
R. Browne-Cooper

Elapognathus coronatus.
Albany district, WA.
S. Wilson

Short-nosed Snake *Elapognathus minor* **TL 500mm**

Short snout, large eye and **oblique pale bar on side of neck.** Grey, flushed with reddish brown to bright red on tail. Side of head white to pale grey. Prominent orange-yellow bar sweeps obliquely upward on side of neck, often edged behind by dark streak. Ventral surfaces bright yellow, darkening to orange laterally and posteriorly, with black base to each ventral scale forming distinct bands. ■ **NOTES** Cool, moist sw. corner, from Two Peoples Bay nw. to Busselton. Inhabits heaths edging swamps, though also known from WSF. Shelters in low dense vegtn such as tussocks and sedges. Secretive, poorly known and probably genuinely uncommon, perhaps due to competition from the more abundant *E. coronatus.* ■ **STATUS** Lower risk – near threatened (IUCN Red List).

Genus *Furina*

Five small and slender to medium-sized and moderately robust spp. with weakly depressed heads and small black eyes. Scales smooth and glossy in 15–21 midbody rows. Anal and subcaudal scales divided. ■ **NOTES** Widespread over most of Aust. except the cool moist se. and Tas. Terrestrial nocturnal snakes which shelter under rocks and logs, in soil cracks, insect holes and old termite mounds. Egglayers. All spp. feed almost exclusively on skinks, with diurnal prey probably captured while sleeping. Bites from the larger spp. may cause severe symptoms.

Yellow-naped Snake *Furina barnardi* **TL 500mm**

Midbody scales in 15 rows and nasal scale undivided. Dark brown, dark grey to black, with obscure **pale edges to each scale** forming a reticulum. Head darker brown to black with broad, diffuse, pale brown to yellow band across nape and base of head, darkening to virtual absence with age. ■ **NOTES** Woodlands and rock outcrops. Poorly known. ■ **SEE ALSO** *F. ornata.*

Red-naped Snake *Furina diadema* **TL 400mm**

Slender, with 15 midbody scale rows and nasal scale undivided. Dark brown, orange-brown to reddish brown, with each scale dark-edged, forming a fine reticulum. **Head and neck glossy black, with bright orange-red blotch on neck largely enclosed within dark pigment.** ■ **NOTES** Humid to arid areas of estn Aust., from Port Augusta, SA to Cairns, Qld. Occupies a wide range of habitats, though tends to shun very moist areas such as RF. ■ **SEE ALSO** *F. ornata.* ■ **STATUS** Vulnerable (Vic).

Elapognathus minor.
Ledge Point, WA.
S. Wilson

Furina barnardi.
Townsville area, Qld.
S. Wilson

Furina diadema.
Bendidee SF, Qld.
S. Wilson

Dunmall's Snake *Furina dunmalli* TL 700mm

Robust, with **midbody scales in 21 rows** and nasal scale divided. Pale or dark olive grey to blackish brown with pattern absent, except for a few diffuse pale blotches on upper lips. ■ **NOTES** Woodlands and DSF, particularly areas featuring brigalow, in SE. interior of Qld and adj. NSW. Rarely encountered, and possibly genuinely uncommon throughout its range. Appears to have suffered severe loss of habitat due to its association with brigalow scrub, little of which remains intact. The Tree Skink (*Egernia striolata*) is a recorded prey item. A single known bite produced a severe reaction, so it should be regarded as POTENTIALLY DANGEROUS. ■ **STATUS** Vulnerable (C'wealth; Qld; IUCN Red List).

Orange-naped Snake; Moon Snake *Furina ornata* TL 650mm

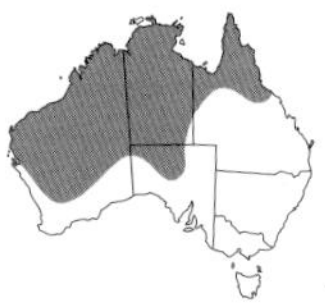

Medium-sized, with 15–17 midbody scale rows and nasal scale undivided. Reddish brown, orange-brown to yellowish brown with **dark edges to each scale** forming a reticulum. **Head and neck glossy dark brown to black, bisected by red to orange band across neck**, tending to darken to virtual absence with age. ■ **NOTES** Widespread over subhumid to arid northern Aust. in a variety of habitats, including woodlands, shrublands and spinifex deserts. ■ **SEE ALSO** *F. barnardi; F. diadema.*

Brown-headed Snake *Furina tristis* TL 1m

Robust, with midbody scales in 17 rows and nasal scale divided. Dark purplish brown to almost black, with narrow pale edge to each scale forming a reticulum, boldest on lower flanks. Broad, diffuse, pale brown to cream band extends across nape, darkening to brown or black on head. ■ **NOTES** Woodlands, monsoon forests and vine thickets, from ne. Cape York Pen. and Torres Strait islands, Qld to sthn NG. Extremely nervous, thrashing wildly when provoked. Care should be taken with large individuals.

Genus *Hemiaspis*

Two medium-sized spp. with large eyes and round pupils. Iris dark brown with pale upper edge. Scales smooth and weakly glossed in 17 midbody rows. **Anal scale divided and subcaudals single.** ■ **NOTES** Restricted to e. coast and estn interior, occurring in moist habitats or in moist retreats within drier regions. Terrestrial and livebearing, producing litters of up to 16 young. The spp. differ markedly in behaviour: one is a diurnal predator of frogs and skinks, the other a nocturnal frog specialist. Bites from large individuals could cause severe symptoms.

Furina dunmalli.
Yuleba State Forest, Qld.
S. Wilson

Furina ornata.
Kununurra, WA.
S. Wilson

Furina tristis.
Weipa, Qld.
S. Wilson

Grey Snake *Hemiaspis damelii* TL 600mm

Pale or dark grey to olive grey with top of head and first few scale rows on nape black on juveniles, contracting to form black band on base of head and neck on adults. ■ **NOTES** Floodplains, usually on cracking soils, in estn interior, reaching coastal districts near Rockhampton, Qld. Shelters under fallen timber and in soil cracks or disused burrows, usually near inland water-courses. Crepuscular to nocturnal frog specialist. ■ **STATUS** Endangered (Qld).

Black-bellied Swamp Snake; Marsh Snake *Hemiaspis signata* TL 700mm

Dark-bellied. Body colour variable but head markings distinctive: **2 narrow pale stripes on each side of face.** Brown to olive brown, or dark olive grey to black, with head often flushed with pale yellow on darker specimens. Cream to yellow stripe extends from snout or eye to side of neck, and another from snout through upper lip to corner of mouth. **Ventral surfaces dark grey to black.** ■ **NOTES** Separate pops occur along humid e. coast and ranges: from se. NSW to se. Qld; in mid-estn Qld; and in ne. Qld. Most abundant on edges of creeks or swamps and in RF or WSF. Predominantly diurnal; crepuscular to nocturnal in hot weather. Feeds on skinks and frogs.

Broad-headed Snakes Genus *Hoplocephalus*

Three moderately large spp. with **broad flattened head** distinct from neck. Eye moderately large with pale iris and round pupil. Scales smooth and weakly glossed in 19–21 midbody rows. Anal and subcaudal scales single. **Ventral scales laterally keeled or notched.** ■ **NOTES** Woodlands, rock outcrops and moist forests, between Nowra, NSW and ne. interior of Qld. Nocturnal. Unusual among Aust. elapids in being arboreal and rock-climbing, sheltering under loose bark, in tree hollows and in narrow rock crevices. Livebearing. Pugnacious if provoked, flattening head, rearing forebody into S-shape and striking repeatedly. Bites from all spp. should be regarded as POTENTIALLY DANGEROUS.

Pale-headed Snake *Hoplocephalus bitorquatus* TL 800mm

Brown, shades of grey to almost black, with very distinctive head and nape pattern; a broad **white to pale grey band across neck** is edged behind by a continuous to broken black bar and in front by a row of angular dark blotches. Top of head pale grey, usually blotched with dark grey. **Lips usually prominently barred** with cream and dark grey. ■ **NOTES** Coast and estn interior. DSF and woodlands, usually on floodplains or near watercourses, mainly in dry areas w. of coastal ranges. Shelters behind loose bark or in hollow trunks and limbs of standing timber. Feeds largely on frogs, but also takes lizards and mammals. POTENTIALLY DANGEROUS. ■ **STATUS** Vulnerable (NSW).

Hemiaspis damelii.
Glenmorgan, Qld.
S. Wilson

Hemiaspis signata.
Mt Nebo, Qld.
S. Wilson

Hoplocephalus bitorquatus.
Lake Broadwater,
Qld. S. Wilson

Broad-headed Snake *Hoplocephalus bungaroides* **TL 900mm**

Strongly and distinctively patterned: **black with many narrow irregular bands of bright yellow scales**. These bands are boldest anteriorly, darkening and breaking posteriorly and tending to form a wavy broken stripe along lower flanks. ■ **NOTES** Restricted to sandstone outcrops and escarpments from about Sydney inland to Blue Mountains and s. to Nowra. Shelters in windblown sandstone caves or beneath slabs resting on bare rock along cliff edges. In summer, ascends into hollows of adjacent eucalypts. Feeds on lizards, particularly skinks and geckos. Though once common in sthn Sydney, indiscriminate collecting of snakes and the removal of sandstone slabs for gardens has caused numbers to severely decline. POTENTIALLY DANGEROUS. ■ **STATUS** Vulnerable (C'wealth; IUCN Red List); endangered (NSW).

Stephens' Banded Snake *Hoplocephalus stephensii* **TL 1.2m**

Colour and pattern variable, but usually dark grey with many narrow brown, orange-brown to cream bands, tending to darken and become obscure posteriorly. Some pops (and occasional individuals throughout range) lack all trace of banded pattern. Sides of head blotched or barred with black and white, even on unbanded snakes. ■ **NOTES** Coastal ranges from Gosford, NSW n. to Kroombit Tops, Qld. Occurs in a variety of habitats, from RF and WSF or DSF to rock outcrops. Shelters beneath loose bark, among epiphytes, in hollow trunks, limbs and rock crevices, or under slabs. Feeds on lizards, frogs, mammals and birds. POTENTIALLY DANGEROUS. ■ **STATUS** Vulnerable (NSW); near threatened (IUCN Red List).

Genus *Neelaps*

Two very small, slender spp. with narrow flat heads and rounded protrusive snouts. Eye very small with black iris. Scales smooth and shiny in 15 midbody rows. Anal and subcaudal scales divided. Pattern includes reddish reticulum on body, black blotch on head, broad black band across neck and sometimes a bold black vertebral stripe. ■ **NOTES** Restricted to dry sandy areas. Secretive sand-swimming, burrowing snakes that dwell in soft upper layers under leaf litter or overhanging foliage of shrubs or tussocks, and beneath embedded logs or stumps. They eat only small skinks, particularly the genus *Lerista*. Egglayers. Harmless.

Black-naped Burrowing Snake *Neelaps bimaculatus* **TL 450mm**

Brown to bright orange-brown, with cream base to each scale forming reticulum. Broad black bands extend across nape and across head forward to level of eyes. ■ **NOTES** Restricted to sandy areas supporting heaths, shrublands and woodlands, from lower w. coast through arid sthn interior to Kingoonya, SA. An isolated pop. occurs on red dunes with spinifex at North West Cape, WA. ■ **STATUS** Rare (SA).

Hoplocephalus bungaroides.
Nowra district, NSW. S. Wilson

Hoplocephalus stephensii.
Samford district, Qld. S. Wilson

Hoplocephalus stephensii.
Mt Glorious, Qld.
S. Wilson

Neelaps bimaculatus.
Burn's Beach, WA.
D. Robinson

Black-striped Burrowing Snake *Neelaps calonotos* TL 280mm

Bright orange-red with cream centre to each scale; broad black crescent-shaped band extending across neck; black bar across top of head; black tip on snout; and black vertebral stripe enclosing cream to white spots, extending from nape to tail-tip. If stripe is broken to absent, indications almost always remain on tail. ■ **NOTES** Restricted to sandy coastal strip near Perth, WA between Mandurah and Cataby, with isolated pops further n. near Eneabba and Dongara. Dunes and sand-plains vegetated with heaths and eucalypt/banksia woodlands. Feeds largely on *Lerista praepedita*, the smallest burrowing skink in its range. Seriously threatened by increasing development within its restricted distribution. ■ **STATUS** Lower risk – near threatened (IUCN Red List).

Genus *Notechis*

Tiger Snake *Notechis scutatus* TL 900mm–2m

Tentatively treated here as 1 highly variable sp., though opinions differ widely, and often regarded as 2 spp. with many ssp. **Frontal shield about as wide as long**, reflecting its broad, relatively flat head. Eye moderately large with dark iris and round, narrowly pale-edged pupil. Scales smooth and weakly glossed in 17–21 midbody rows. Anal and subcaudal scales single. Colouration extremely variable. In much of SA and islands of Bass Strait, snakes are often black and patternless, though pale bands are frequently evident on juv. and some adults. Those from Tas range from black to grey or even yellow, with or without bands. On se. mainland, snakes tend to be paler (shades of brown to olive) with bands of varying width and intensity. Those from WA range from olive to black and bands are often yellow. Size is similarly variable, with the length of some island pops dictated by type of available prey. On Chappell Is. in Bass Strait, dependence on a brief glut of fat muttonbird chicks favours large sizes, commonly exceeding 1.5m. Conversely, on Roxby Is. off Eyre Pen., SA, dwarf pops less than 1m long subsist on small skinks. On the mainland, with a diverse diet of frogs, lizards, birds and mammals, average maximum sizes lie between these extremes. It is surprising, given its abundance near cities and its involvement in many human fatalities, that Tiger Snake taxonomy remains unresolved.
■ **SSP.** The names *N. ater* and *N. scutatus* have generally been used in reference to 2 spp., though there are no unambiguous characters to separate them. Similarly, the following ill-defined ssp. are often cited: *N. s. scutatus* (most of Vic except nw., through estn NSW to sthn Qld, n. to Carnarvon Ra. Nthn pops are usually isolated in upland regions, though lowland pops occur in parts of coastal Qld); *N. s. occidentalis* (sw. WA, from Jurien se. to Pt Malcolm near Esperance); *N. a. ater* (Flinders Ra., SA); *N. a. niger* (sthn Eyre and Yorke Pen. and offshore islands including Kangaroo Is., SA); *N. a. humphreysi* (Tas to King Is. and adjacent islands of wstn Bass Strait); and *N. a. serventyi* (Chappell Is. and other islands of Furneaux group, Bass Strait).
■ **NOTES** Widespread in sthn Aust., favouring cool moist areas such as swamp edges and creek banks. Island pops often occur among tussock grasses. Produces large live litters (up to 64 recorded in Tas). Diurnal, though sometimes nocturnal in very hot weather. When provoked, it flattens its head and neck and raises itself with broadest aspect to aggressor. All forms, whether they prove to be spp., ssp. or local variants, are regarded as DANGEROUSLY VENOMOUS.
■ **STATUS** *N. s. ater* is vulnerable (C'wealth).

Neelaps calonotos.
City Beach, WA. S. Wilson

Notechis scutatus.
Southern Flinders Ranges, SA. S. Eipper

Notechis scutatus.
Ben Lomond NP, Tas. E. Vanderduys

Notechis scutatus.
Hobart, Tas. E. Vanderduys

Notechis scutatus.
Cranbourne, Vic. S. Wilson

Notechis scutatus.
Chappell Is., Tas. S. Wilson

Notechis scutatus.
Kangaroo Is., SA. R. Valentic

Notechis scutatus.
Lake Joondalup, WA. D. Robinson

Taipans Genus *Oxyuranus*

Three spp. with **long narrow heads** and large eyes with dark to pale irises and round pupils. Scales weakly keeled (at least on neck) to smooth and shiny in **21–23 midbody rows. Anal scale single and subcaudals divided.** ■ **NOTES** Restricted to tropical woodlands of nthn and ne. Aust, dry open plains of estn interior and in remote desert near the borders of NT, WA and SA. Also present in sthn NG. The genus includes some of the world's most lethal and feared snakes. They feed exclusively on mammals, mainly rats, and have evolved a unique 'strike-and-release' method of dealing with prey that can retaliate. A massive dose of highly toxic venom is injected and the prey then released and followed until it succumbs. Egglayers. Diurnal, terrestrial snakes, often active during hot weather. DANGEROUSLY VENOMOUS. ■ **SEE ALSO** *Pseudonaja.*

Western Taipan; Inland Taipan; Small-scaled Snake; 'Fierce Snake'

Oxyuranus microlepidotus TL 2m

Variably coloured, with dark iris and smooth scales. Pale yellowish brown to rich dark brown, with seasonal colour change (paler during summer and darker in winter). Most scales dark-edged, forming herringbone pattern. Head and neck uniform glossy black in winter, fading in summer. Ventral surfaces cream to yellow with orange blotches. **Midbody scales in 23 rows.** ■ **NOTES** Bleak, sparsely vegetated cracking plains, associated with Diamantina R. and Cooper Ck drainage systems in arid sw. Qld and ne. SA, s. to Coober Pedy. Old records exist from far nthn NSW and junction of Murray R. and Darling R. Shelters in deep soil cracks and in burrow systems of the Long-haired Rat (*Rattus villosissimus*), foraging and basking on surface for brief periods. Feeds almost exclusively on rats, and together their fortunes rise and fall in the lush seasons followed by lengthy droughts. Venom is the most toxic known for any terrestrial snake, yet it is shy and rarely attempts to bite, even when provoked. DANGEROUSLY VENOMOUS. ■ **STATUS** Presumed extinct (NSW); regionally extinct (Vic).

Taipan *Oxyuranus scutellatus* TL 2m (individuals over 3m recorded)

Orange-brown iris and **long pale head with angular brow**. Scales weakly keeled, at least on neck. **Midbody scales in 21–23 rows.** ■ **SSP.**
O. s. scutellatus is yellowish brown, reddish brown to almost black, with head paler than body; often darkening with age but always discernible at least on snout. Ventral surfaces cream, with scattered orange spots or blotches.
O. s. canni normally has a broad orange vertebral stripe, at least on posterior body. ■ **NOTES** *O. s. scutellatus* extends from nthn Kimberley, WA, through nthn NT to nthn Qld, then down e. coast to Grafton, ne. NSW. *O. s. canni* is recorded from Saibai Is., nthn Torres Strait. Also widespread in NG. Both ssp. occur in a wide variety of habitats from canefields to woodlands, DSF and monsoon forests. Most abundant on well-timbered grassy slopes. Shelters in abandoned burrows, hollow logs or stumps. Swift and extremely alert with keen vision. Quick to flee when approached, but will readily defend itself when cornered and harassed, and may deliver multiple bites in rapid succession. DANGEROUSLY VENOMOUS.

Oxyuranus microlepidotus. Pale summer colour. Goyder's Lagoon, SA. S. Wilson

Oxyuranus microlepidotus. Dark winter colour. Morney Plain, Qld. S. Wilson

Oxyuranus scutellatus scutellatus. Cairns, Qld. S. Wilson

Oxyuranus scutellatus scutellatus. Juvenile feeding. Mt Morgan, Qld. S. Wilson

Oxyuranus scutellatus canni. Moreguina. Central Province, Papua New Guinea. D. Williams

Western Desert Taipan *Oxyuranus temporalis* TL 1.7m

Pale-headed with smooth scales, dark iris and **only 1 primary temporal scale** (other taipans have 2). Midbody scales in 21 rows. Mouth-lining mauve-pink. Subject to seasonal colour change. Uniform brown, or with darker and lighter scale edges on rear body, creating broken 'herring-bone' pattern. Head pale yellowish brown, palest on snout. Belly pale yellowish grey with small weak orange spots anteriorly. ■ **NOTES** Collected at estn margin of Walter James Ra., WA, on a sandy flat with open mallee eucalypts and grevillea over diverse shrubs and spinifex; from vicinity of Ilkurlka Roadhouse in Great Victoria Desert, featuring sand plains, dunes and gravely rises; and an old record from George Gill Ra., NT.

Hooded Snakes Genus *Parasuta*

Six small, moderately robust spp. with slightly depressed heads and moderate to small eyes with dark irises. Scales smooth and glossy in 15–17 midbody rows. **Anal and subcaudal scales single.** Pattern includes **brown to reddish brown body and prominent black blotch on head.** ■ **NOTES** Widespread across sthn Aust., favouring relatively dry or well-drained open habitats. Secretive nocturnal snakes which shelter under rocks and logs, and in soil cracks and insect holes. Livebearers, producing up to 7 relatively large young. They prey almost exclusively on lizards, occasionally on small snakes. If provoked, they flatten their bodies to form tight coils, thrashing abruptly when touched. Large individuals could produce uncomfortable symptoms.

Dwyer's Snake *Parasuta dwyeri* TL 600mm

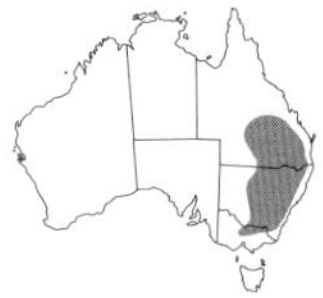

Midbody scales in 15 rows. Brown to reddish brown with dark base to each scale and **black head blotch unbroken from snout to nape**. Lips, tip of snout and area in front of eye cream to pale yellowish brown. ■ **NOTES** DSF, woodlands and rock outcrops, from se. interior of Qld, through wstn slopes and ranges of NSW (approaching coast through Hunter Valley) to about Wedderburn, central Vic. ■ **SEE ALSO** *P. flagellum.*

Little Whip Snake *Parasuta flagellum* TL 450mm

Midbody scales in 17 rows. Dull greyish brown to reddish brown with dark base to each scale and **black head blotch broken by pale bar across snout** between nostril and eye. Side of head yellowish brown to cream. ■ **NOTES** Woodlands, DSF, granite outcrops and basalt plains, from se. NSW s. to Melbourne and w. to se. SA. Adults are often uncovered in pairs or small groups. ■ **SEE ALSO** *P. dwyeri; P. spectabilis.* ■ **STATUS** Vulnerable (NSW).

Oxyuranus temporalis.
Ilkurlka Roadhouse area, WA. J. Vos.

Parasuta dwyeri.
Westmar district, Qld.
S. Wilson

Parasuta flagellum.
Deer Park, Vic.
S. Wilson

Gould's Hooded Snake *Parasuta gouldii* TL 530mm

Midbody scales in 15 rows. Orange-brown to rich reddish brown with **each scale narrowly edged with black**, forming fine reticulum. **Black head blotch indented** by variably sized, pale orange-brown mark in front of each eye. Lips and ventral surfaces white. ■ **NOTES** Heaths, woodlands, shrublands, DSF and rock outcrops of sw. WA, with an apparently isolated pop. further n. in Murchison district. Absent from humid deep sw. ■ **SEE ALSO** *P. monachus; P. spectabilis.*

Monk Snake *Parasuta monachus* TL 460mm

Relatively slender, with midbody scales in 15 rows. Orange-brown to bright brick red, with **black head blotch unbroken from snout to nape** in wstn parts of range, and indented by pale spot in front of each eye in estn pops. Lips and ventral surfaces white. ■ **NOTES** Semi-arid to arid regions, mainly on hard red soils supporting acacia-dominated woodlands and shrublands. Often associated with rock outcrops. ■ **SEE ALSO** *P. gouldii.*

Mitchell's Short-tailed Snake *Parasuta nigriceps* TL 590mm

Robust, with 15 midbody scale rows and **black head blotch unbroken from snout to nape, continuous with prominent dark vertebral stripe or zone** extending to tail-tip. Lateral scales reddish brown to purplish brown with paler posterior margins. Lips pale orange to white. ■ **NOTES** Across sthn Aust.; largely associated with granites of Darling Ra. in far w., extending through various semi-arid habitats (particularly mallee woodlands). In addition to skinks, other small elapids (including own kind) and blind snakes are recorded as prey.

Mallee Black-headed Snake; Port Lincoln Snake *Parasuta spectabilis* TL 400mm

Midbody scales in 15 rows. Greyish brown to reddish brown with **dark base to each scale forming reticulum**. Upper lips and ventral surfaces white. ■ **SSP.** *P. s. spectabilis* is variable. Black head blotch broken by pale bar across snout and deeply indented by pale marking in front of eye; or greatly reduced and mottled, with little or no black pigment forward from level of eye; or broken across nape to include a separate nuchal blotch. *P. s. nullarbor* has unbroken black hood with small pale indentations in front of each eye and longer tail. TL 380mm. *P. s. bushi* has a pale spot behind each eye. Otherwise similar to *P. s. nullarbor*, but larger, with more ventral scales (159–165 vs 135–158). TL 392mm. ■ **NOTES** Sthn Aust., from Big Desert in wstn Vic to n. of Esperance, WA. *P. s. spectabilis* occurs in a variety of sandy and stony woodland and shrubland habitats in estn part of range, to wstn Eyre Pen., SA; *P. s. nullarbor* inhabits limestone-based heavy soils vegetated with chenopod shrublands on Nullarbor Plain of sw. SA and se. WA; *P. s. bushi* is known only from Scaddan, 50km n. of Esperance, WA. ■ **SEE ALSO** *P. flagellum; P. gouldii.* ■ **STATUS** *P. s. spectabilis* is vulnerable (Vic).

Parasuta gouldii.
Ellenbrook, WA. R. Browne-Cooper

Parasuta monachus.
Wialki district, WA. S. Wilson

Parasuta nigriceps.
Samson Brook, WA. R. Browne-Cooper

Parasuta spectabilis bushi.
Scaddan, WA. B. Bush

Parasuta spectabilis nullarbor.
Cocklebiddy, WA. B. Maryan

Parasuta spectabilis spectabilis.
Burra area, SA. S. Swanson

Genus *Paroplocephalus*

Lake Cronin Snake *Paroplocephalus atriceps* TL 569mm

Sole member of genus. Moderately large, slender snake with **broad black head** very distinct from neck, and moderately large eye with pale golden iris and round pupil. Scales smooth and matt-textured in 19 midbody rows. Anal and subcaudal scales single. Uniform brown above with black head and nape and pale spots on lips. ■ **NOTES** Semiarid woodlands and outcrops in sw interior of WA, from vicinity of Lake Cronin, a small ephemeral freshwater lake, and Peak Elenora, a large granite outcrop e. to Fraser Ra., w. of Norseman. Nocturnal. Presumed to be livebearing. A bite has produced severe symptoms, hence it is potentially DANGEROUSLY VENOMOUS. ■ **STATUS** Vulnerable (IUCN Red List).

'Black' Snakes Genus *Pseudechis*

Eight moderate to very large spp. with **relatively broad, depressed heads** (narrow on one sp.) and moderately small eyes with pale to dark irises and round pupils. Scales smooth and weakly to strongly glossed in 17–19 midbody rows. **Anal scale usually divided**, and **subcaudals divided posteriorly and usually at least anterior 20% single** (all single in some small nthn spp.) Despite the name, few spp. are black and the most widespread sp. is brown. ■ **NOTES** Widely distributed throughout Aust., excluding Tas. Also present in sthn NG. Terrestrial. Nocturnal to diurnal according to temperature. Most are egglayers producing clutches of up to 19 eggs; 1 sp. bears live young, born in membranous sacs. Diets are broad, comprising mammals, birds, reptiles, frogs and fish. When threatened they flatten their necks, presenting broadest aspect to aggressor. Relationships are uncertain, and it cannot be assumed that all are closely allied. All should be regarded as DANGEROUSLY VENOMOUS. ■ **SEE ALSO** *Pseudonaja.*

King Brown Snake; Mulga Snake *Pseudechis australis* TL 2-2.5m

Midbody scales in 17 rows. Iris reddish brown. Colour highly variable; pale brown, olive to rich reddish brown, usually with paler bases and darker hind edges to individual scales, forming a reticulated pattern. Ventral surfaces cream to white. ■ **NOTES** Widespread throughout Aust., excepting humid estn and sthn areas. May be encountered in virtually all subhumid to arid habitats throughout its range, from tropical woodlands and monsoon forests to deserts. Shelters in any terrestrial sites available: abandoned burrows, soil cracks or hollow logs. Nocturnal to diurnal according to temperature. Egglaying. DANGEROUSLY VENOMOUS. ■ **STATUS** Near threatened (NT).

Paroplocephalus atriceps.
Peak Elenora, WA. R. Browne-Cooper

Pseudechis australis.
Kununurra, WA. S. Wilson

Spotted Mulga Snake *Pseudechis butleri* TL 1.6m

Yellow-spotted, with midbody scales in 17 rows and dark reddish brown iris. Dark grey to black with prominent cream to yellow blotch on each scale and scattered irregular clusters of wholly black scales. Juv. dark bluish grey and obscurely patterned. **Ventral surfaces cream to bright yellow with each ventral scale dark-based** and occasionally flecked with black. ■ **NOTES** Arid sw. interior of WA, on heavy soils dominated by mulga woodlands and shrublands. Nocturnal to diurnal. Egglaying. DANGEROUSLY VENOMOUS.

Collett's Snake *Pseudechis colletti* TL 1.5m

Pink-blotched, with midbody scales in 19 rows and dark iris. Shades of grey, brown to dark reddish brown with many irregular cream, pink to red bands or transversely aligned blotches, merging to a pink flush on mid- to lower flanks. Ventral surfaces cream to pink. ■ **NOTES** Grasslands on deeply cracking clay plains in dry interior of Qld, south to Tambo area. Secretive and seldom seen, sheltering in soil cracks. Nocturnal to diurnal. Egglaying. DANGEROUSLY VENOMOUS..

Spotted Black Snake; Blue-bellied Black Snake *Pseudechis guttatus* TL 1.5m

Dark-bellied, with midbody scales in 19 rows and dark iris. Black, shades of grey to pale brown or reddish brown, with or without many scattered pale grey, cream or rarely pink spots. Some individuals are cream with black-tipped scales. Ventral surfaces grey to bluish grey. ■ **NOTES** Favours river floodplains, DSF and woodlands, often associated with temporary wetlands. Shelters beneath fallen timber and in abandoned burrows or soil cracks. Nocturnal to diurnal according to temperature. Egglaying. DANGEROUSLY VENOMOUS.

Eastern Pygmy Mulga Snake *Pseudechis pailsei* TL 1.2m

Small, slender and narrow-headed with subcaudal scales often all single. Midbody scales in 17 rows. Iris dark reddish brown. Brown to reddish brown above and cream below, usually with dark sutures on head and dark streaks on neck, and body scales with dark rear edges creating a weak reticulum. ■ **NOTES** Areas of rock and spinifex from Mt Isa area in nw. Qld, s. to about John Hills and Bladensberg NP near Winton. Very poorly known, and status of this sp., a nthn NT pop. and *P. weigeli* remain uncertain. Nocturnal to diurnal. Assumed to be DANGEROUSLY VENOMOUS. ■ **SEE ALSO** *P. weigeli.*

Papuan Black Snake *Pseudechis papuanus* TL 2.14m

Drably marked, with midbody scales in 19 rows and pale brown iris. Glossy to matt black or dark brown above and dark grey below, sometimes with reddish ventral flush on chin, posterior body and tail. ■ **NOTES** Known in Aust. only from Saibai and Boigu Is. in far nthn Torres Strait. The areas are low-lying with an extensive mosaic of freshwater and saline wetlands. Widespread in low-lying habitats in sthn NG. Egglaying. DANGEROUSLY VENOMOUS.

Pseudechis butleri.
Sandstone area, WA. S. Wilson

Pseudechis colletti.
Richmond area, Qld. S. Wilson

Pseudechis guttatus.
Glenmorgan, Qld. S. Wilson

Pseudechis pailsei.
John Hills, Qld. S. Wilson

Pseudechis papuanus.
Saibai Island, Qld.
P. Mirtschin,
Venom Supplies

Red-bellied Black Snake *Pseudechis porphyriacus* TL 1.5–2m

Very distinctive, with midbody scales in 17 rows and dark iris. Uniform **glossy black with red to cream belly, the red ventral pigment extending well up onto lower flanks**. Tip of snout brown. ■ **NOTES** E. coast and adjacent inland, from se. Cape York Pen., Qld to se. SA. Associated with moist areas such as swamps, river banks or WSF and RF. One of Aust.'s most familiar and attractive snakes, often seen basking beside water. Diurnal. Feeds mainly on frogs, but other vertebrates are also taken. Mating occurs in spring, when combat between rival ♂ is often observed. Livebearing, with 5–18 young born enclosed in membranous sacs from which they normally emerge within minutes. Though once common throughout most of range, some Qld and NSW pops appear to have declined dramatically, possibly due to attempted predation on the poisonous introduced Cane Toad (*Rhinella marina*). In se. Qld there are indications that pops may be increasing again. DANGEROUSLY VENOMOUS. ■ **SEE ALSO** *Cryptophis nigrescens.*

Western Pygmy Mulga Snake *Pseudechis weigeli* TL 1.2m

Small, **slender and narrow-headed with all subcaudal scales single.** Midbody scales in 17 rows. Dark reddish brown iris. Greyish brown to reddish brown with little or no pattern; a reticulum formed by paler scale-bases, some narrow dark longitudinal streaks on neck and dark sutures between some head scales. Ventral surfaces cream. ■ **NOTES** Kimberley region, WA, and tentatively incl. a nthn NT pop., though genetic evidence suggests these may be different spp. Very poorly known, and status of this and *P. pailsei* of Qld remain uncertain. Nocturnal to diurnal. Egglaying. DANGEROUSLY VENOMOUS. ■ **SEE ALSO** *P. pailsei.*

Brown Snakes Genus *Pseudonaja*

Nine moderate to very large spp. with **narrow heads and moderately large eyes**, round pupils and normally pale irises (very dark and indistinct in 1 sp.). Scales smooth and weakly glossed in 17–21 midbody rows. **Anal and subcaudal scales divided** (at most a few anterior subcaudals single). Colour variable on all spp., but ventral surfaces usually blotched with orange and **most juv. have black blotch on head and broad black band across neck**. Spp. are identified by mouth colour, number of midbody scale rows and threat posture. ■ **NOTES** Widespread over Aust., excluding far se. Vic and Tas. Most abundant in dry, well-drained areas, tending to avoid closed moist forests and wetlands. Clearing of land and introduction of the house mouse has benefited some spp., which now thrive in disturbed rural and peripheral suburban areas. Brown Snakes feed on a variety of vertebrates, particularly reptiles and mammals. Prey is subdued by a combination of envenomation and constriction, holding the animal in tight coils until venom takes effect. Diurnal to nocturnal according to temperature, tending to forage mainly at night in n. and by day in s. Egglayers, producing clutches of up to 38 eggs. Brown snakes, though generally shy, are nervous and aggressive if cornered and provoked, rearing the head and forebody with mouth agape and striking repeatedly and savagely. The genus includes some of our most lethal snakes, and all except 1 small sp. are regarded as DANGEROUSLY VENOMOUS. ■ **SEE ALSO** *Oxyuranus; Pseudechis.*

Pseudechis porphyriacus.
Sydney, NSW.
G. Swan

Pseudechis weigeli.
Groote Eylandt, NT.
R. Valentic

Pseudechis weigeli.
El Questro Stn, WA.
S. Wilson

Dugite *Pseudonaja affinis* TL 1–2m

Extremely variable, usually with **midbody scales in 19 (WA) or 17 (SA) rows**. Mainland snakes are largest, with variable colouration. ■ **SSP.** *P. a. affinis* is shades of brown to olive brown, with or without light to dense black speckling comprising scattered wholly dark scales. Speckling may be so dense it overrides other colouration and snakes may be completely dark. Juv. have black head and nape, and dark flecks on body forming a herring-bone pattern. Ventral surfaces (incl. **dark grey or brown throat, usually contrasting with paler belly**) brown to greyish white, blotched with orange to brown. *P. a. exilis* and *P. a. tanneri* are much smaller (TL 1.1m) and uniformly dark, including ventral surfaces. ■ **NOTES** *P. a. affinis* is widespread in virtually all habitats, from coastal dunes and semi-arid woodlands to edges of WSF from mainland sw. WA to Eyre Pen., SA. *P. a. tanneri* occupies some islands of Archipelago of the Recherche, off s. coast of WA; *P. a. exilis* occurs on Rottnest Is., off Fremantle, WA. Dwarfism on offshore islands parallels that of the Tiger Snake (*Notechis scutatus*) on some islands off SA, and seems linked to available prey size. While mainland snakes can access various small mammals, adults on several islands subsist for the most part on skinks. When harassed, rears forebody in S-shape. DANGEROUSLY VENOMOUS. ■ **SEE ALSO** *P. inframacula; P. aspidorhyncha.* ■ **STATUS** *P. a. exilis* and *P a. tanneri* are vulnerable (WA).

Strap-snouted Brown Snake *Pseudonaja aspidorhyncha* TL 1.3m

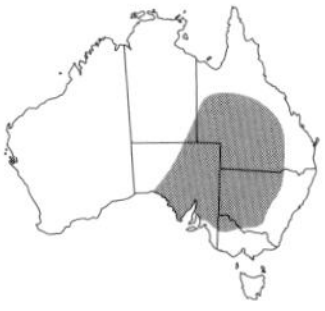

Extremely variable, with **large strap-like rostral scale (fig) creating a chisel-shape to snout in dorsal view, pale mouth-lining** and **midbody scales in 17 rows**. Iris dark with pale orange ring around pupil. Shades of brown to greyish brown, exhibiting numerous colour forms incl: scattered darker scales; a broad darker band on neck; black scales arranged to form a V- or W-shape on neck; darker head; indistinct narrow, oblique darker bands usually most prominent laterally and posteriorly; and broad, prominent to obscure dark bands sometimes alternating with narrower dark bands within pale interspaces. ■ **NOTES** Distributional limits ill-defined pending an Aust. wide examination of museum specimens currently assigned to '*P. nuchalis*'. Sthn central Aust. from Penong, SA. to Hermidale, NSW and most of interior of Qld. In zones of overlap, may inhabit heavier soils than superficially similar *P. mengdeni*. Cornered individuals rear their bodies in an S-shape. DANGEROUSLY VENOMOUS. ■ **SEE ALSO** *P. affinis; P. inframacula; P. ingrami; P. mengdeni; P. nuchalis; P. textilis.* ■ **STATUS** Near threatened (Vic).

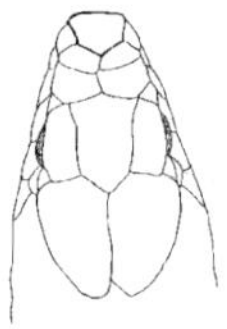

Pseudonaja affinis affinis.
Scarborough, WA. R. Browne-Cooper

Pseudonaja affinis exilis.
Rottnest Is., WA. S. Wilson

Pseudonaja affinis tanneri.
Figure of Eight Is., Recherche Archipelago, WA.
B. Maryan

Pseudonaja aspidorhyncha
Hermidale, NSW. G. Swan.

Pseudonaja aspidorhyncha.
Hermidale, NSW. G. Swan.

Pseudonaja aspidorhyncha.
Bollon, Qld. S. Wilson

Speckled Brown Snake *Pseudonaja guttata* TL 1.4m

Midbody scales in 19 (NT) or 21 (Qld) rows. Mouth-lining bluish black. Iris reddish yellow; inner margin narrowly edged with contrasting white. Orange-yellow to pale greyish brown, occurring as unbanded and banded forms. Unbanded form has lateral edges of most scales black, forming speckled pattern. Banded form has evenly spaced, broad, dark bands, sometimes with 3 narrow transverse lines between each pair of dark bands. Juv. appear to lack the black head and nape markings typifying young of all other *Pseudonaja*. Ventral surfaces white to yellow, often with orange median flush and intense orange peppering, becoming obscure posteriorly. ■ **NOTES** Grasslands on arid, deeply cracking clay plains. Shelters in deep soil cracks. When harassed, raises forebody and flattens neck to form conspicuous hood. DANGEROUSLY VENOMOUS. ■ **SEE ALSO** *P. ingrami; P. nuchalis; P. textilis.* ■ **STATUS** Rare (SA).

Peninsula Brown Snake *Pseudonaja inframacula* TL 1.6m

Variable, with **midbody scales in 17 rows**. Yellowish brown, reddish brown to blackish brown, often with scattered speckling comprising dark individual scales and/or dark edges to scales. **Ventral surfaces grey to dark grey**, usually with **cream chin**, and often a contrasting pale blotch on lateral edge of each ventral scale. ■ **NOTES** Sthn Yorke and Eyre Pen., SA with isolated pop. on Nullarbor Plain. Favours sandy areas vegetated with heaths, chenopod shrublands and mallee woodlands. When harassed, raises forebody in S-shape. DANGEROUSLY VENOMOUS. ■ **SEE ALSO** *P. affinis; P. aspidorhyncha; P. textilis.*

Ingram's Brown Snake *Pseudonaja ingrami* TL 1.8m

Variable, with **midbody scales in 17 rows, 7 lower labial scales** and **dark iris** (dull orange-brown, superficially appearing black). **Mouth-lining bluish black or bluish grey**. Shades of brown, with each scale dark-tipped. Head, neck and forebody sometimes much darker on pale specimens. Ventral surfaces variable; orange spots often fusing to form narrow edge to posterior ventral scales. ■ **NOTES** Grasslands on deeply cracking clay plains, from interior of Qld to mid-estn NT. Disjunct pop. occurs in Kununurra area, WA. Favours low-lying, seasonally flooded habitats and shelters in deep soil cracks. When harassed, raises forebody and flattens neck to form a conspicuous hood. DANGEROUSLY VENOMOUS. ■ **SEE ALSO** *P. aspidorhyncha; P. guttata; P. mengdeni; P. nuchalis; P. textilis.*

Pseudonaja guttata.
Barkly Tableland, NT. G. Swan

Pseudonaja guttata.
Morney Plain, Qld. S. Wilson

Pseudonaja inframacula.
Coffin Bay area, SA. S. Wilson

Pseudonaja inframacula.
Nullarbor Plain, SA. B. Bush

Pseudonaja ingrami.
NT. S. Wilson

Western Brown Snake; Gwardar *Pseudonaja mengdeni* TL 1.2m

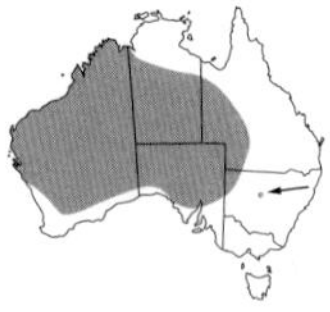

Extremely variable, with **rounded snout (fig), blackish mouth-lining, scales in 17 rows at midbody** and **19-24 rows level with 1st ventral scale**. Iris dark with broken reddish orange ring around pupil. Numerous colour forms occur; 'orange with black head' form is yellow to bright orange with glossy black head, usually a dark reticulated pattern, and occasionally prominent broad dark bands sometimes alternating with 3 narrower dark bands within pale interspaces; 'pale head, grey napè form' is brown to yellowish brown, usually with a fine reticulated pattern, and with paler head and broad dark band across neck, sometimes with several black scales on leading edge, which may form a W- or V-shape. Other forms are shades of brown to reddish brown, ranging from plain to reticulated or banded. ■ **NOTES** Distributional limits ill-defined pending an Aust. wide examination of museum specimens currently assigned to '*P. nuchalis*'. Western and central Aust., occupying a variety of dry to arid habitats, but in areas of overlap with *P. aspidorhyncha*, it may favour more sandy areas. Cornered individuals rear their bodies in an S-shape. DANGEROUSLY VENOMOUS. ■ **SEE ALSO** *P. aspidorhyncha; P. ingrami; P. nuchalis; P. textilis.*

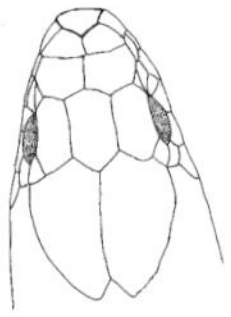

Ringed Brown Snake *Pseudonaja modesta* TL 600mm

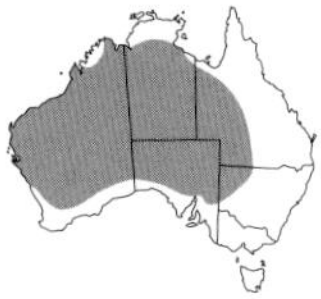

Midbody scales in 17 rows and **widely spaced narrow dark bands**. Iris orange-brown. Pale grey to rich reddish brown with **black patch on top of head, broad black band across neck** and 4–12 evenly spaced narrow dark bands between nape and tail-tip. Pattern may be obscure to virtually absent on large individuals. Ventral surfaces cream to white, flecked with orange. ■ **NOTES** Semi-arid to arid central and wstn interior. Virtually all habitats (with the possible exception of black soil plains) throughout its broad distribution. Feeds largely on diurnal skinks. When threatened, rears forebody in S-shape. Not considered dangerous, but large individuals should be treated with caution. ■ **STATUS** Endangered (NSW).

Northern Brown Snake *Pseudonaja nuchalis* TL 1.3m

Extremely variable, with **large strap-like rostral scale (fig) creating a chisel shape to snout in dorsal view, blackish mouth-lining, scales in 17 rows at midbody and 23-27 rows level with 1st ventral scale**. Iris dark with orange ring around pupil. Shades of brown, occasionally with prominent to obscure broad dark bands, or scattered dark scales on neck. Head and neck may be uniformly dark, or snout may be pale in contrast to darker base of head. ■ **NOTES** Distributional limits ill-defined pending an Aust. wide examination of museum specimens currently assigned to '*P. nuchalis*'. Tropical nthn Aust. incl. nthn NT, Qld s. to Mt Isa, Charters Towers and Innot Hot Springs. DANGEROUSLY VENOMOUS. ■ **SEE ALSO** *P. aspidorhyncha; P. ingrami; P. mengdeni; P. textilis.*

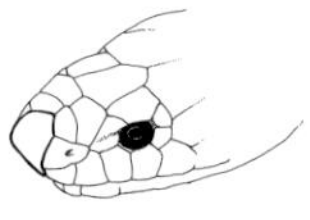

Pseudonaja mengdeni.
Dongara area, WA. B. Maryan

Pseudonaja mengdeni.
Ballidu, WA. B. Maryan

Pseudonaja mengdeni.
Yoting, WA. B. Maryan

Pseudonaja modesta. Strongly patterned.
Durham Downs Stn, Qld. S. Wilson

Pseudonaja modesta.
Weakly patterned.
Eromanga area, Qld. S. Wilson

Pseudonaja nuchalis.
Kununurra, WA. S. Wilson

Pseudonaja nuchalis.
Between Hayes Creek and Adelaide River, NT. P. Horner

Common Brown Snake; Eastern Brown Snake *Pseudonaja textilis* TL 2.2m

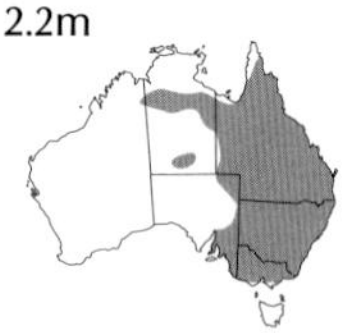

Midbody scales in 17 rows and mouth-lining pink. Iris pale brown. Colour variable: shades of brown to almost black, with dark individuals often having paler heads. Pattern often absent on adults, though some have dark and/ or pale flecking or mottling, or rarely prominent dark bands. Juv. has a black blotch on head, a black band across neck, and sometimes prominent narrow black bands on body. Ventral surfaces marked with scattered orange to brown blotches. ■ **NOTES** Widespread through dry parts of estn Aust. Also se. NG. Virtually all habitats except moist closed forests and alps. Probably estn Aust.'s most frequently encountered large venomous snake. Land clearing has apparently proven beneficial, as it thrives in agricultural regions and on the periphery of nearly all estn Aust. cities and towns. Extremely swift, alert, nervous and quick to retaliate if provoked, rearing head and forebody into an S-shape. DANGEROUSLY VENOMOUS. ■ **SEE ALSO** *P. aspidorhyncha; P. guttata; P. inframacula; P. ingrami; P. mengdeni; P. nuchalis.*

Genus *Rhinoplocephalus*

Square-nosed Snake; Müller's Snake *Rhinoplocephalus bicolor* TL 450mm

Sole member of genus. Relatively robust, with depressed head, squarish snout and **no internasal** scales. Eye small with dark iris. Scales smooth and glossy in 15 midbody rows. Anal and subcaudal scales single. Dark brown to dark grey above and orange on mid- to lower flanks. Juv. pale bluish grey with darker patch on head, occasionally an obscure narrow yellow vertebral line, and pale yellow flanks. Ventral surfaces white. ■ **NOTES** Humid lower sw. WA, favouring sandy, seasonally saturated areas with dense ground cover of low shrubs. Usually encountered in disused stick-ant nests or under rocks and fallen grass trees. Eats only skinks, rarely frogs. Litters of up to 5 young recorded. Rarely attempts to bite, even when handled. Not regarded as dangerous.

Genus *Simoselaps*

Four small, relatively robust spp. with depressed heads and **protruding flattened snouts.** Eye small with dark or pale iris and vertically elliptic pupil. Scales smooth and glossy in 15 midbody rows. Anal and subcaudal scales divided (1st 3–5 single on 1 sp.). Colour pattern is distinctive; **yellow to orange with sharply contrasting black rings**, or a **simple reticulum with black head and nape blotches.** ■ **NOTES** Sandy areas in dry to arid wstn and central Aust. Skilled burrowing sand-swimmers which shelter in loose sand under shrubs, tussocks and leaf litter or beneath partly embedded stumps. Diet consists exclusively of lizards, particularly *Lerista* spp. Harmless and disinclined to bite, even when handled. ■ **SEE ALSO** *Brachyurophis.*

Desert Banded Snake *Simoselaps anomalus* TL 210mm

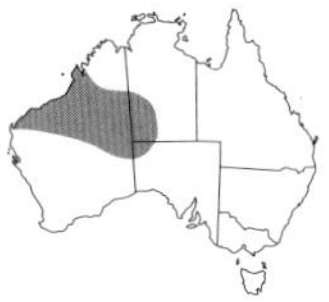

Prominently ringed. Iris dark. Yellowish orange to reddish orange with 24–40 black rings (equal to or narrower than pale interspaces) between nape and tail-tip, commencing with a broad black band across neck. **Head glossy black,** with complete to broken narrow white bar across level of nostrils, continuous with white patch on side of snout. ■ **NOTES** Sandy spinifex deserts.

Pseudonaja textilis.
Rosevale, Qld. S. Wilson

Pseudonaja textilis.
Moggill, Qld S. Wilson

Pseudonaja textilis. Plain juvenile.
Gympie, Qld. S. Wilson

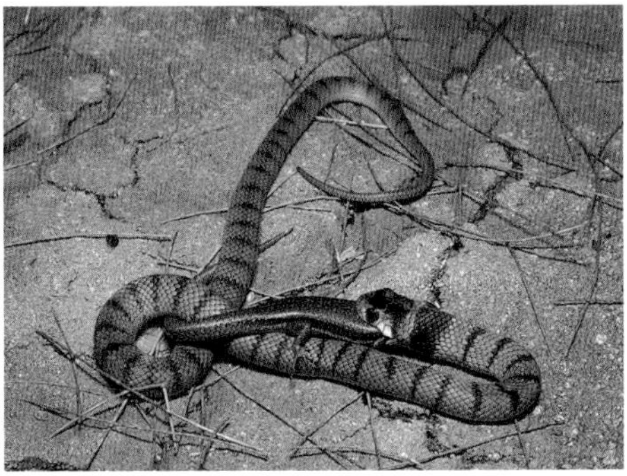

Pseudonaja textilis. Banded juvenile.
Brisbane, Qld. S. Wilson

Rhinoplocephalus bicolor.
Denmark, WA. S. Wilson

Simoselaps anomalus.
Sandfire, WA. D. Robinson

Jan's Banded Snake *Simoselaps bertholdi* TL 300mm

Prominently ringed. Iris pale. Yellow to reddish orange, **each scale usually dark-edged laterally**, with 18–31 black rings, approximately equal to pale interspaces, between nape and tail-tip, commencing with broad band more than 4 scales wide across neck. **Head white to very pale grey** with dark flecks coalescing on base of head to form diffuse dark blotch. ■ **NOTES** Subhumid to arid sandy areas, in coastal dunes, woodlands and heaths. Abundant on the coastal plain around Perth, WA. ■ **SEE ALSO** *S. littoralis.*

West Coast Banded Snake *Simoselaps littoralis* TL 390mm

Prominently ringed. Iris pale. Yellow to yellowish white, with **no dark edges to scales**, marked with 20–42 narrow black rings, usually much narrower than pale interspaces, commencing with a black band 4 or less scales wide across neck. **Head white to very pale grey**, flecked anteriorly and blotched posteriorly with black. ■ **NOTES** Pale coastal dunes and limestones, along subhumid to arid mid- to lower w. coast, from North West Cape s. to Cervantes and including many offshore islands. ■ **SEE ALSO** *S. bertholdi.*

Dampierland Burrowing Snake *Simoselaps minimus* TL 217mm

Reticulated, lacking bands and with 1st 3–5 subcaudal scales single. Cream with dark reddish brown edge to each scale, forming prominent reticulum. Broad black band extends across head, widely separated from a narrower black band across neck. ■ **NOTES** Known only from Dampier Land, sw. Kimberley, WA. Coastal dunes and sandy junction between dunes and adjacent acacia shrublands. Poorly known but presumed to be similar to other *Simoselaps*; a sand-swimmer feeding largely or wholly on skinks of the genus *Lerista.*

Genus *Suta*

Four medium-sized spp. with relatively depressed heads and moderately small eyes with pale irises (dark on 1 sp.) and round or vertically elliptic pupils. Scales smooth and glossy in 15–19 (rarely 21) midbody rows. Anal and subcaudal scales single. ■ **NOTES** Widespread in dry open habitats throughout Aust. and absent from moist areas of s. and e. Livebearing, producing litters of up to 7 young. Terrestrial, nocturnal snakes which shelter beneath rocks or logs, in soil cracks, abandoned burrows or disused termite nests. Some appear to specialise on lizards while others eat a variety of vertebrates. Bites from large individuals can cause severe discomfort.

Rosen's Snake *Suta fasciata* TL 620mm

Prominently banded and blotched, with pale iris and 17 (rarely 19) midbody scale rows. Orange-brown, yellowish brown to pale olive grey with many irregular dark bands or transversely aligned blotches. Head blotched and spotted, with dark streak extending from nostril through eye to temple or side of neck. ■ **NOTES** Semi-arid interior and nw. coast, on sandy to loamy (often stony) soils supporting shrublands or woodlands. Appears to prey largely on sleeping diurnal lizards, particularly dragons. Not regarded as dangerous although a bite has caused severe local swelling.

Simoselaps bertholdi.
City Beach, WA. S. Wilson

Simoselaps littoralis.
Steep Point, WA. S. Wilson

Simoselaps minimus.
Cape Leveque, WA.
G. Harold

Suta fasciata.
Kambalda, WA.
S. Wilson

Ord Snake *Suta ordensis* TL 760mm

Pale iris, **dark ventral bands**, little or no dorsal pattern and 19 midbody scale rows. Brown to greyish brown with obscure dark hood on head (rarely black and conspicuous), fine dark edges to scales and indistinct cream stripe or blotches on upper lip. Ventral surfaces whitish, flushed with grey on leading half of each ventral and subcaudal scale. ■ **NOTES** Far estn Kimberley, WA and adjacent NT. Cracking clay soils associated with drainage systems of Ord R., Victoria R. and Stuart Ck. Presumably shelters in soil cracks. Probably feeds largely on skinks, but may also take snakes, frogs and small mammals. Not listed as dangerous, though a bite may require medical attention. ■ **SEE ALSO** *S. suta.*

Little Spotted Snake *Suta punctata* TL 523mm

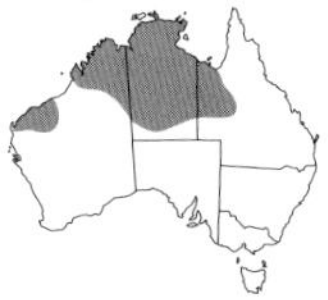

Pale brown to dark iris, **prominent dark spots on head and neck** and 15 midbody scale rows. Yellowish brown to rich reddish brown, with base of each scale usually smudged with darker brown, generally concentrating on anterior lower flanks to form a narrow broken stripe. Head ground colour to yellow with variable dark markings, typically including spots on snout, a streak from nostril through or under eye to base of head, spots on top of head, large blotches on side of neck and a pair of nuchal blotches. ■ **NOTES** Woodlands and spinifex grasslands across subhumid to arid nthn Aust., from interior of Qld through NT to the Kimberley, and on nw. coast and adjacent interior of WA. Feeds largely on sleeping diurnal lizards, particularly skinks and dragons, as well as blind snakes. Not regarded as dangerous.

Myall Snake; Curl Snake *Suta suta* TL 600mm

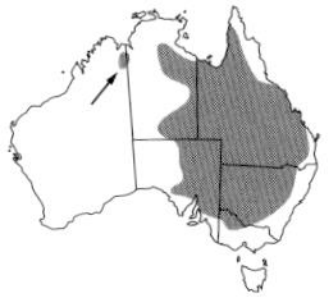

Pale iris, **dark hood, dark-edged pale stripe on side of head**, and 19 (rarely 17 or 21) midbody scale rows. Olive, brown to reddish brown with dark-edged scales. Top of head and nape dark greyish brown to black (sometimes barely discernible on dark individuals). Broad pale streak with dark lower edge extends from snout through eye to temple. Lips and ventral surfaces cream. ■ **NOTES** Widespread through estn interior on a variety of soil types, favouring heavy loams and deeply cracking clays supporting shrublands, woodlands and grasslands. Common name Curl Snake derives from defensive posture, curling body into a tight coil from which it thrashes wildly. Feeds largely on lizards, but also takes frogs and mice. Large individuals could be considered potentially DANGEROUSLY VENOMOUS. ■ **SEE ALSO** *S. ordensis.*

Suta ordensis.
Gordon Downs, NT.
P. Horner

Suta punctata.
Round Knob, WA.
B. Maryan

Suta suta.
Currawinya NP, Qld.
S. Wilson

Genus *Tropidechis*

Rough-scaled Snake; Clarence River Snake *Tropidechis carinatus* TL 900mm

Sole member of genus. **Keeled scales.** Eye moderately large with pale iris and round pupil. Scales matt-textured and strongly keeled in **23 midbody rows. Anal and subcaudal scales single.** Yellowish brown, dark brown to olive with irregular darker bands or transverse series of blotches along body, fading posteriorly and usually most prominent on juv. Ventral surfaces cream, olive to grey. ■ **NOTES** WSF, RF and creek margins on e. coast and ranges. Subtropical pop. extends from the central coast and Barrington Tops, NSW to Fraser Is. area, Qld. A disjunct tropical pop. occurs from Mt Spec to Thornton Peak, ne. Qld. Predominantly terrestrial but frequently climbs low foliage. Feeds largely on frogs and small mammals, but also takes birds and lizards. Nocturnal to diurnal according to temperature. Produces live litters of up to18 young. DANGEROUSLY VENOMOUS. ■ **SEE ALSO** *Tropidonophis mairii* (non-venomous colubrid).

Bandy Bandys Genus *Vermicella*

Five long-bodied **black and white ringed** spp. with rounded snouts, short blunt tails and small dark eyes. Scales smooth and glossy in 15 midbody rows. Anal and subcaudal scales divided. Sharply contrasting dorsal pattern is largely consistent, but spp. differ in number and width of bands, whether they form complete rings, number of ventral scales and presence or absence of internasal scales. Size variable; ♀ largest. ■ **NOTES** Widespread throughout estn, central and nthn Aust., from RF to deserts. Secretive burrowers, seldom seen foraging above ground except at night, often after rain. Most (probably all) are dietary specialists, eating only blind snakes (Typhlopidae). When threatened, some (probably all) spp. contort their bodies into vertically oriented hoops, thrashing and re-positioning when disturbed. In this stance the black and white rings are extremely conspicuous, but in motion the colours merge ('flicker-fusion') and the snakes become obscure.

Common Bandy Bandy *Vermicella annulata* TL 760mm

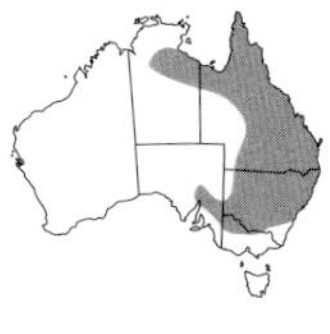

Relatively robust, with **internasal scales present, 195–257 ventral scales** and **48–147 black and white rings** encircling body and tail. ■ **NOTES** Widespread in estn Aust., from Shepparton, Vic to Port Augusta area, SA and n. to Cape York, Qld and ne. NT. Occupies virtually all habitat types within this broad range. The only widespread bandy-bandy and the only sp. encountered with any frequency. ■ **STATUS** Vulnerable (Vic); rare (SA).

Intermediate Bandy Bandy *Vermicella intermedia* TL 605mm

Internasal scales absent, 234–258 ventral scales, and **76–127 black and white rings** on body and tail. The bands either completely encircle the body, or the ventral surface is marked with black and white mottling. ■ **NOTES** Restricted to nthn Aust., with a pop. in nthn NT (Darwin, Humpty Doo and Katherine areas). Specimens also recorded from Liveringa and Mitchell Plateau, WA.

Tropidechis carinatus.
Mt Glorious, Qld. E. Vanderduys

Vermicella annulata.
Mt Glorious, Qld. S. Wilson

Vermicella intermedla.
Kakadu NP, NT. B. Maryan

Narrow-banded Bandy Bandy *Vermicella multifasciata* TL 362mm

Very slender, with **internasal scales absent, 257–269 ventral scales**, and **many (156–188) black and very narrow white rings** on body and tail. The bands either completely encircle the body, or the ventral surface is marked with black and white mottling. ■ **NOTES** Restricted to nthn Aust., with only a small number of specimens known from between Melville Island and Darwin areas, NT, and Victoria R. and Lake Argyle areas of NT and WA.

Pilbara Bandy Bandy *Vermicella snelli* TL 504mm

Slender, with **internasal scales present, 288–295 ventral scales**, and **92–125 broad black and white rings** on body and tail. The bands sometimes completely encircle the body, or the ventral surface is marked with black and white mottling. ■ **NOTES** Pilbara region of WA, from nw. coast e. to Marble Bar and s. to Hamersley Ra., Mundiwindi and Paraburdoo.

Centralian Bandy Bandy *Vermicella vermiformis* TL 525mm

Moderately slender, with **internasal scales present, 260–280 ventral scales**, and **81–90 broad black and white rings** encircling body. ■ **NOTES** Two apparently disjunct pops occur: in Alice Springs region of sthn NT and Roper River Mission in nthn NT.

Vermicella multifasciata. Victoria River Downs Stn, NT. S. Swanson

Vermicella snelli. Port Hedland area, WA. R. Browne-Cooper

Vermicella vermiformis. Alice Springs area, NT. R. Valentic

SEA SNAKES
Family Elapidae

True sea snakes have been variously placed in their own family or (as here) within Elapidae. Biochemical evidence links them so closely to the Australian terrestrial elapids that they are now placed in the same subfamily, the Hydrophiinae.

About 30 spp. have been recorded from Australia. Several are endemic but most extend at least to New Guinea, and many to the Coral Sea and Asia. A few are strays that rarely visit our region and are of doubtful status here, while the Yellow-bellied Sea Snake (*Pelamis platura*) is found virtually worldwide. Sea snakes are essentially tropical. Southern Australian encounters are generally waifs carried by currents into lethally cool waters.

Sea snakes feed and reproduce entirely in the sea, and most never voluntarily venture onto land. Embarking on a wholly marine lifestyle from terrestrial origins has required substantial modifications, both physically and behaviourally. The most obvious is the vertically flattened, paddle-shaped tail. The bodies of most sea snakes are laterally compressed and, as a consequence, the expanded ventral scales found on all terrestrial elapids have become reduced or lost. They also have dorsally placed valvular nostrils and livebearing reproduction.

The degree to which ventral scales have contracted reflects differing lifestyles. *Ephalophis greyae*, *Hydrelaps darwiniensis* and *Parahydrophis mertoni* forage in intertidal shallow water and mudflats, and retain expanded ventral scales for semi-terrestrial locomotion. *Aipysurus*, occurring mainly on shallow coral reefs, are more fully aquatic. Their large ventral scales generally have a median keel and a posterior notch, allowing them to fold along the midline to create a long mid-ventral keel when swimming. Most other sea snakes have ventrals barely distinguishable from remaining scales.

Most sea snakes eat fish. Some are generalists, with fish from 19 families recorded as prey for the Yellow-bellied Sea Snake (*Pelamis platura*). But the group also includes specialists. Several *Hydrophis* spp. are adapted to probe narrow holes for burrowing eels. They have minute heads and thin forebodies, in stark contrast to their robust, deeply compressed hindbodies. The Turtle-headed Sea Snake (*Emydocephalus annulatus*) takes only fish eggs. It has lost some upper labial scales to create broad plates designed to scrape eggs off hard surfaces.

Although sea snakes are fully aquatic, most forage in similar ways to terrestrial snakes. They probe burrows, investigate cavities in corals, and generally remain close to substrates at varying depths. The Yellow-bellied Sea Snake is an exception. It is truly pelagic, often occurring far from land and tending to remain on the surface along slick-lines where currents meet.

Some sea snakes possess a sense unique in reptiles: light-sensitive skin. The tail of the Olive Sea Snake (*Aipysurus laevis*) can detect light, warning it if this part of its body is exposed when the snake shelters in coral cavities. Presumably if the tail is concealed, the rest of the animal is too.

Livebearing reproduction frees sea snakes from any terrestrial obligations. As such the group includes the only living reptiles that dwell completely in water for their entire lives. Other aquatic reptiles, such as crocodiles, turtles and sea kraits, lay eggs on land. The sea snakes occasionally found ashore have been cast up by waves, and are generally relatively helpless and immobile.

Short-nosed Sea Snake (*Aipysurus apraefrontalis*). Ashmore Reef, WA. R. Grace

Genus *Acalyptophis*

Horned Sea Snake *Acalyptophis peronii* TL 1.23m

Sole member of genus, though genetic evidence places it close to, and possibly within, *Hydrophis*. Slender forebody and robust hindbody, small head with head shields fragmented, and supraocular and adjacent scales with free edges raised into **spinose horn-like processes**. Scales each with a central (often dark) keel, overlapping on thin forebody but non-overlapping on robust hindbody, in 21–31 rows at midbody. Ventral scales about as small as adjacent scales. Cream to pale brown, with or without dark cross-bands, broad across back and tapering on flanks. ■ **NOTES** Sandy areas on coral reefs from nw. coast of WA to New Caledonia. Mainly nocturnal. Probes burrows for gobies. Possesses one of the most toxic sea-snake venoms known (based on tests with mice), but no recorded fatalities. DANGEROUSLY VENOMOUS.

Genus *Aipysurus*

Eight moderate to large Aust. spp. with **laterally expanded ventral scales** at least 3 times as broad as adjacent body scales, usually with a distinct median keel and posterior notch (fig.), and **6 or more upper labial scales**. Head scales enlarged to form symmetrical plates, or fragmented. Body scales weakly to strongly overlapping, smooth in ♀ and often tuberculate in ♂, with vertebral row usually enlarged. ■ **NOTES** South-East Asia to New Caledonia; most spp. confined to waters of Aust. region, including NG and Coral Sea. Generally inhabit seas no more than 50m deep, foraging on the bottom for fish and occasionally fish eggs; 1 sp. consumes only fish eggs.

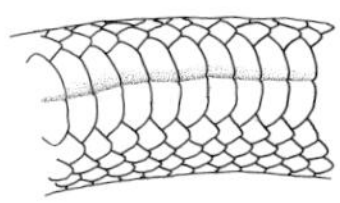

Short-nosed Sea Snake *Aipysurus apraefrontalis* TL 1m

Small-headed, with deeply notched ventral scales, each with a median keel, extremely overlapping body scales with loose, free, pointed hind-edges, and head shields mostly large and symmetrical but with a little fragmention on parietal region and no prefrontals. Midbody scales in 17 rows. Dark olive brown to purplish brown with faint brownish white bands, broadest across back, or with conspicuous bands and white scales scattered mainly on lower flanks. ■ **NOTES** Largely restricted to nw. shelf, from Exmouth to Ashmore Reef, extending nw. to Timor Sea. Forages on reef-flats and reef edges, sometimes sheltering under broken coral and other debris at low tide. Feeds on gobies, eels and possibly other fish. ■ **STATUS** Critically endangered (C'wealth; WA).

Acalyptophis peronii.
Ashmore Reef, WA.
R. Grace

Acalyptophis peronii.
Ashmore Reef, WA. H. Cogger

Aipysurus apraefrontalis.
Ashmore Reef, WA.
H. Cogger

Dubois' Sea Snake *Aipysurus duboisii* TL 1.14m

All **head shields fragmented** except rostral and nasal scales, ventral scales each with a shallow posterior notch and weak median keel, and body scales smooth, weakly keeled to tuberculate, overlapping and in 19 midbody rows. Variable; typically purplish brown with pale edges to scales forming reticulum, and often with cream bands tending to form triangular lateral blotches. ■ **NOTES** Nthn Aust. Also NG to New Caledonia. Reef-flats and coral reefs to depths of about 50m, but often in water so shallow it must crawl rather than swim. Forages in early evening for fish. Possesses one of the most toxic sea-snake venoms known (based on tests with mice), but no recorded fatalities. DANGEROUSLY VENOMOUS.

Leaf-scaled Sea Snake *Aipysurus foliosquama* TL 550mm

Moderately slender and small-headed, with **extensive free hind-edges to greatly overlapping body scales**. Head shields mostly large and symmetrical but with some fragmentation on parietal region. Prefrontal scales present. Ventral scales keeled, and deeply notched posteriorly. Body scales smooth to tuberculate, extensively overlapping, with 1–2 points on hind edges, in 19–21 midbody rows. Dark brown to purplish brown, with or without obscure pale bands and scattered pale spots. ■ **NOTES** Reef-flats, reef edges and shallows on Ashmore and Hibernia Reefs. Eats only fish. ■ **STATUS** Critically endangered (C'wealth; WA).

Dusky Sea Snake *Aipysurus fuscus* TL 940mm

Moderately short, robust and weakly patterned, with some head shields fragmented, mainly on parietal region, loreal scale present, keeled ventral scales each with very shallow posterior notch, and smooth overlapping body scales in 17–19 (rarely 21) rows at midbody. Uniform dark purplish brown, with or without obscure paler bands on lower flanks. ■ **NOTES** Reef-flats, reef edges and shallows from Ashmore and Scott Reefs in nw. WA to Sulawesi, Indonesia. Feeds on fish, particularly gobies and wrasses, and occasionally fish eggs. ■ **STATUS** Endangered (IUCN Red List).

Olive Sea Snake *Aipysurus laevis* TL 1.7m

Extremely large and robust, with head shields mostly large and symmetrical but some partial fragmentation on parietal region, loreal scale present, ventral scales keeled, each with a slight posterior notch, and **smooth overlapping scales** in 21–25 midbody rows. Colouration extremely variable: purplish brown gradually fading to pale ventral surfaces; or with numerous sharply contrasting cream-spotted scales scattered over body; or pale with all ventral and lateral scales creamy white; or golden brown with scattered dark scales. ■ **NOTES** Widespread on coral reefs of nthn Aust., between about Exmouth, WA and central coast of NSW, extending n. to NG and Coral Sea. Active day and night, feeding on a wide variety of fish, occasionally fish eggs or even fresh fish heads and offal. Some reefs support very high densities. Often reported as aggressive, though attacks are rare, with courting snakes normally responsible. DANGEROUSLY VENOMOUS. ■ **SEE ALSO** *A. pooleorum.*

Aipysurus duboisii.
North-eastern Qld.
S. Swanson

Aipysurus foliosquama.
Ashmore Reef, WA. H. Cogger

Aipysurus fuscus.
Ashmore Reef, WA. H. Cogger

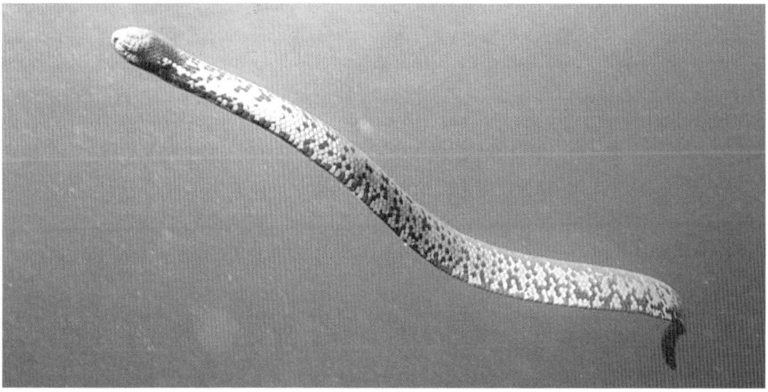

Aipysurus laevis.
Ashmore Reef,
WA. R. Grace

Mosaic Sea Snake *Aipysurus mosaicus* TL 1.1m

Large, symmetrically arranged head shields, weakly keeled ventral scales with no posterior notch, and body scales overlapping and smooth in 17 midbody rows. Cream, salmon or yellowish brown to golden brown with many scales usually dark-edged, marked with numerous irregular, often broken dark bands tending to form staggered half bands on either side. ■ **NOTES** Off-shore waters, estuaries and tidal rivers, 2–22m deep, over soft sand or mud substrates from nthn Aust. to sthn NG. Eats only fish eggs. Weakly venomous and reluctant to bite.

Shark Bay Sea Snake *Aipysurus pooleorum* TL 1.14m

Robust, with head shields mostly large and symmetrical but some partial fragmentation on parietal region, loreal scale present, ventral scales keeled, each with a posterior notch, and **smooth (♀) to tuberculate (♂) overlapping scales** in 20–23 midbody rows. Dark purplish brown with oblique pale lateral bars (♀), or brown becoming gradually paler on flanks (♂). ■ **NOTES** Shark Bay on mid-w. coast, with strays venturing s. to Perth. DANGEROUSLY VENOMOUS. ■ **SEE ALSO** *A. laevis*.

Mjoberg's Sea Snake *Aipysurus tenuis* TL 1.3m

Fragmented head shields, loreal scale present, ventral scales keeled, each with a posterior notch, and body scales smooth (lower rows tuberculate on ♂) and overlapping in 19 midbody rows. Pale brown, darker on head; dark brown spots on tips of scales form longitudinal lines on back and indistinct bars on flanks. ■ **NOTES** Broome s. nearly to Dampier Archipelago. DANGEROUSLY VENOMOUS.

Genus *Astrotia*

Stokes' Sea Snake *Astrotia stokesii* TL 2m

Sole member of genus, though genetic evidence places it close to, and possibly within, *Hydrophis*. Massive, with **extremely robust body**, very large head and thick neck. Body scales overlapping in 46–63 midbody rows. **Ventral scales very small and divided into 2 strongly overlapping rows**, forming a distinct ventral keel. Yellowish brown to dark brown, with or without large dark dorsal blotches alternating with narrow bands. Pattern most pronounced on juv. and often absent on adults. ■ **NOTES** Widespread in turbid coastal water and coral reefs of nthn Aust., s. to Exmouth, WA and central coast of NSW. Extends through South-East Asia to China, Pakistan and Arabian Gulf. Litters of 12–14 young recorded. Feeds on fish. DANGEROUSLY VENOMOUS.

Aipysurus mosaicus.
North-eastern Qld.
S. Swanson

Aipysurus pooleorum.
Shark Bay, WA.
C. Bryce

Aipysurus tenuis.
Dampier Archipelago, WA. C. Bryce.

Astrotia stokesii.
Darwin Harbour, NT P. Horner

Genus *Emydocephalus*

Turtle-headed Sea Snake *Emydocephalus annulatus* TL 900mm

One small Aust. sp. (another in South China Sea) with short blunt head, **only 3 upper labial scales creating a uniquely turtle-like profile**, a conical projection on rostral scale of adult ♂, and wide ventral scales. Colour and pattern variable, from uniform black, dark brown or grey to prominently banded with cream. ■ **NOTES** Apparently patchily distributed in shallow water on coral reefs, from Timor Sea to New Caledonia, including nthn Aust. Primarily diurnal, foraging in shallows for its specialised diet of fish eggs. Venom apparatus greatly reduced. Harmless.

Genus *Enhydrina*

Beaked Sea Snake *Enhydrina zweifeli* TL 1.2m

One Aust sp., though genetic evidence places it close to, and possibly within, *Hydrophis*. Strongly laterally compressed hindbody, enlarged symmetrical head shields, **extremely long, dagger-shaped mental scale (fig.)**, ventral scales scarcely wider than adjacent scales, and body scales overlapping and bluntly keeled. Grey above and paler below, sometimes with diffuse-edged dark bars across back and a dark grey head. ■ **NOTES** Shallow bays and estuaries, from Arabian Gulf to nthn Aust., but recorded here only from scattered localities. Feeds on fish, particularly catfish and pufferfish. Extremely elastic skin on throat may help accommodate large or spinose prey. Responsible for almost 90% of sea-snake fatalities worldwide. DANGEROUSLY VENOMOUS.

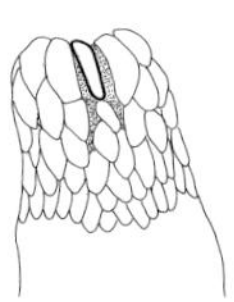

Genus *Ephalophis*

Mangrove Sea Snake *Ephalophis greyae* TL 660mm

Sole member of genus. Slender, with **very broad ventral scales** about 4 times as wide as adjacent scales, preocular scales, enlarged symmetrical head shields, and scales weakly keeled and overlapping on back, but smooth and arranged side by side on lower flanks, in 19–21 midbody rows. Grey with 25–40 darker bands, narrowest on flanks and often joined on back. ■ **NOTES** Mangrove creeks and mudflats between King Sound and Shark Bay. One of the most terrestrial of sea snakes, foraging on mudflats by day for mudskippers and other gobies in their burrows.

Emydocephalus annulatus.
Ashmore Reef, WA. H. Cogger

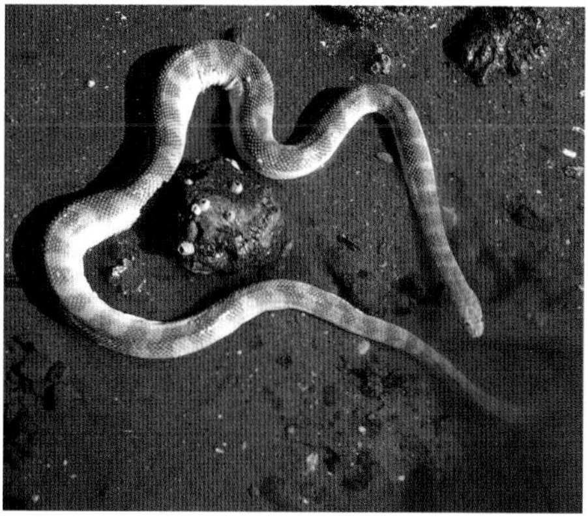

Enhydrina zweifeli.
Weipa, Qld. H. Cogger

Ephalophis greyae. Feeding on a goby.
Port Smith, WA. D. Knowles

Genus *Hydrelaps*

Black-ringed Mangrove Snake *Hydrelaps darwiniensis* TL 530mm

Sole member of genus. Slender, with large symmetrical head shields, **no preocular scales, broad ventral scales** about 2–3 times as wide as adjacent scales, smooth overlapping body scales in 25–30 midbody rows, and **prominent ringed pattern**. Cream to yellowish brown with 30–45 black rings, broadest on back, and sometimes broadening on belly. ■ **NOTES** Intertidal zones associated with mangrove-lined mudflats, from Gulf of Carpentaria to nw. coast of WA and southern NG. Restricted to shallow waters, foraging for fish along rising and falling tidelines.

Genus *Hydrophis*

Fourteen medium to large Aust. spp. (largest sea-snake genus, with nearly 30 spp. worldwide) with small ventral scales scarcely larger than adjacent body scales, head shields arranged as large, non-fragmented symmetrical plates, large anterior chin shields and a broad triangular mental shield. ■ **NOTES** Extremely variable sea snakes, including inhabitants of clear or turbid, and deep or shallow waters. Some have extremely thin forebodies and small heads, enabling them to specialise in removing eels from narrow burrows deep in the sand. Others are more conventionally shaped, with broader diets. Some spp. can be difficult to identify without dissecting the head to examine skull and tooth structure, features not provided here.

Black-headed Sea Snake *Hydrophis atriceps* TL 1m

Very small-headed, with slender forebody, robust, laterally compressed hindbody, and body scales overlapping in 35–49 midbody rows. Yellowish brown with black head and 50–70 dark bands or dorsal blotches (prominent bands or rings on juv.). ■ **NOTES** Poorly known from a few specimens between Darwin and sthn NG, but widespread in South-East Asian waters. Feeds on fish. Litters of 1–7 young recorded. DANGEROUSLY VENOMOUS.

Belcher's Sea Snake *Hydrophis belcheri* TL 1m

Moderate build with head not extremely small. Body scales overlapping in 32–36 rows at mid body. Ventral scales 278 – 320, mostly undivided. Greyish with 48–69 bands on body and tail, broadest dorsally, narrow on flanks and fading on belly. ■ **NOTES** Very poorly known, and primarily occurring from nw. of NG to Gulf of Thailand and South China Sea. One confirmed Aust. record from Arafura Sea. No live image available.

Hydrelaps darwiniensis.
Bing Bong, NT.
P. Horner

Hydrophis atriceps.
Arafura Sea, NT.
G. Gow

Hydrophis belcheri.
Preserved holotype.
New Guinea.
H. Cogger

Dwarf Sea Snake *Hydrophis caerulescens* TL 800mm

Small head, slender forebody and relatively robust, laterally compressed hindbody. Body scales keeled and overlapping in 37–39 midbody rows. Bluish grey with dark head and 41–43 blackish bands which may be disrupted and alternating on midline. Tail banded, or black with 4 pale blotches on dorsal edge. ■ **NOTES** Known in Aust. only from se. Gulf of Carpentaria and estn Qld, but widespread from estn Indonesia to India and China. Litters of up to 13 young recorded. Feeds on bottom-dwelling fish such as eels and gobies. DANGEROUSLY VENOMOUS.

Cogger's Sea Snake *Hydrophis coggeri* TL 1.2m

Small black head, slender forebody and relatively robust, laterally compressed hindbody. Body scales overlapping anteriorly, arranged side by side posteriorly, in 29–34 midbody rows. Juv. prominently marked: pale yellow with 28–40 broad black rings widest dorsally and ventrally, and black head with conspicuous yellow marks on snout and behind eyes. Adults are rather more drab: olive grey with dark rings paler and diffuse-edged. ■ **NOTES** Ashmore and Scott Reefs off nw. coast, where it occurs in deep water off reef edges. Also wstn Pacific, on coral reefs and seagrass beds in shallower waters. Feeds on eels. DANGEROUSLY VENOMOUS.

Geometrical Sea Snake *Hydrophis czeblukovi* TL 1.24m

Small-headed, with slender neck, very thick, strongly laterally compressed hindbody and tail, and **prominent geometrical dorsal and lateral markings**. Body scales each with a short keel, arranged side by side in 51–58 midbody rows. Greyish black with narrow white bars joining and forking to enclose 34–38 dorsal hexagons and lateral pentagons. ■ **NOTES** Poorly known. Recorded from depths of 93–103m on continental shelf off nw. Aust., and from Arafura Sea off nthn Aust. and sthn NG. DANGEROUSLY VENOMOUS.

Rough-scaled Sea Snake *Hydrophis donaldi* TL 878 mm

Moderately robust with **strongly spinose scales** in 33–35 rows at midbody. Yellowish brown with 47-56 darker brown bands on body and tail. Juv. brighter with dark head and turquoise interspaces between bands. ■ **NOTES** Known only from estuarine habitats (< 10 m deep) over shale, mud and sea-grass where mouths of Mission River and Hey Ck enter Albatross Bay in Weipa area, Qld.

Hydrophis caerulescens.
Fitzroy River mouth, Qld. R. Ireland

Hydrophis coggeri.
Ashmore Reef, WA. H. Cogger

Hydrophis czeblukovi.
Eighty Mile Beach, WA. B. Maryan

Hydrophis donaldi.
Weipa area, Qld. K. Ukuwela

Elegant Sea Snake *Hydrophis elegans* TL 2m

Elongate, with slender neck and forebody and robust, laterally compressed hindbody. Body scales smooth or with short keels, and overlapping in 37–49 midbody rows. Juv. prominently marked: pale brown with black head and 35–55 blackish bands, widest dorsally and ventrally and narrowest (often broken) on flanks. Narrower bands often present in pale interspaces, at least on anterior and posterior body. Adults are paler with diffuse pattern. ■ **NOTES** Deep turbid water, and deep water between reefs n. to sthn NG and s. to NSW and sw. coast of WA. Feeds on eels. Litters of up to 30 young recorded. DANGEROUSLY VENOMOUS.

Spectacled Sea Snake *Hydrophis kingii* TL 1.9m

Slender forebody and small **black head with white ring around eye. Anterior chin shields large and easily contacting mental groove (fig.).** Body scales keeled and easily overlapping on back, to smooth and just overlapping on flanks, in 36–40 midbody rows. Ventral scales about twice as wide as adjacent scales. Grey above and cream to pale brown from mid-flanks to ventral surfaces, with numerous dark grey blotches, commencing as black bands on neck and forebody and separated from black head by narrow white bar. Ventral scales black. ■ **NOTES** Deep waters from nthn Aust. to NG. Feeds on fish. DANGEROUSLY VENOMOUS.

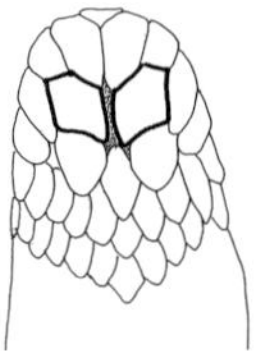

Small-headed Sea Snake *Hydrophis macdowelli* TL 800mm

Extremely small-headed, with very thin forebody and very robust, deeply laterally compressed hindbody. Body scales just overlapping in 35–42 midbody rows. Cream with dark olive to black head, dark grey to black triangular dorsal blotches extending about one-third down flanks, about 3 lateral series of grey, sometimes black-edged marks, and 4–5 pale grey bands on tail. ■ **NOTES** Turbid estuaries and inshore waters of nthn Aust., straying s. to Pilbara, WA and se. Qld, and extending e. to New Caledonia. Reported to take eels and other long-bodied fish. Litters of 2–3 young recorded. DANGEROUSLY VENOMOUS.

Olive-headed Sea Snake *Hydrophis major* TL 1.6m

Robust, with short thick head and **anterior chin shields just contacting or excluded from mental groove by elongate 1st lower labial scales (fig.).** Body scales bluntly keeled and just overlapping in 37–45 midbody rows. Ventral scales each with 2 keels and slightly wider than adjacent scales. Pale grey to olive with 24–30 broad dark bars across back, alternating with narrow dark bar within each pale interspace, each of these aligned with dark spot on flanks. Head olive with dark flecks. ■ **NOTES** Turbid deep water on coasts of nthn Aust. and sthn NG. Feeds on fish. DANGEROUSLY VENOMOUS.

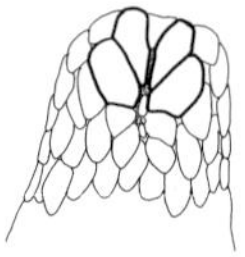

Hydrophis elegans.
Surfers Paradise, Qld. S. Wilson

Hydrophis elegans. Juvenile.
Darwin Harbour, NT. P. Horner

Hydrophis kingii.
Ashmore Reef, WA. H. Cogger

Hydrophis macdowelli.
Arafura Sea, NT. G. Gow

Hydrophis major.
Melville Is., NT.
G. Gow

Ornate Sea Snake *Hydrophis ocellatus* TL 1.5m

Robust, with body of roughly uniform thickness, body scales overlapping in 39–59 midbody rows, and ventral scales about twice as wide as adjacent scales. Grey to bluish grey, with 30–60 broad dark bands or dorsal blotches and a series of large ocellate markings on flanks. Large adults sombre and patternless. ■ **NOTES** Widespread on coral reefs, turbid inshore waters and estuaries across nthn Aust., straying s. to lower w. coast, and even occasionally Tas. Also extends e. to Kiribati and w. to Persian Gulf. Feeds on a variety of fish. Litter of 3 young recorded. DANGEROUSLY VENOMOUS.

Large-headed Sea Snake *Hydrophis pacificus* TL 1.4m

Large-headed, with slender forebody and robust, laterally compressed hindbody. Body scales overlapping in 39–49 midbody rows. Dark grey above, sharply delineated at mid-flanks from whitish ventral colour, with 49–72 dark bands. On juv., bands are black and head is black with yellow spots on snout and behind eyes. ■ **NOTES** Estn Arafura Sea, including Gulf of Carpentaria and sthn NG. Litter of 17 young recorded. DANGEROUSLY VENOMOUS.
■ **STATUS** Near threatened (IUCN Red List).

Genus ***Lapemis***

Spine-bellied Sea Snake *Lapemis curtus* TL 1m

One Aust sp., though genetic evidence places it close to, and possibly within, *Hydrophis*. Robust and large-headed, with head shields enlarged to form symmetrically arranged plates, ventral scales small and virtually unrecognisable and **body scales hexagonal to squarish and arranged side by side** in 23–45 midbody rows. Those on lower flanks are much larger, with prominent tubercles or spines on adult ♂. Olive brown above and cream below, the colours abutting as a deeply indented zigzag along flanks or breaking to form bands, often joined dorsally. ■ **NOTES** Widespread, from Arabian Gulf to nthn Aust., in conditions ranging from clear reefs to turbid estuaries. Feeds on a variety of fish. Litters of up to 15 young recorded. Has caused fatalities. DANGEROUSLY VENOMOUS.

Hydrophis ocellatus.
Cottesloe Beach, WA. B. Maryan

Hydrophis pacificus.
Near Tully Inlet, Gulf of Carpentaria, Qld.
S. Carton

Lapemis curtus. Juvenile.
Darwin Harbour, NT. P. Horner

Lapemis curtus.
Middle Beach, NT. P. Horner

Genus *Parahydrophis*

Northern Mangrove Sea Snake *Parahydrophis mertoni* TL 500mm

Sole member of genus. Slender, becoming more laterally compressed with age, with enlarged symmetrical head shields and **relatively broad ventral scales** about 3 times as wide as adjacent body scales. Body scales smooth and overlapping in 36–39 midbody rows. Bluish grey to greyish brown, with about 40–50 dark bands or rings, broadest and often enclosing a pale patch dorsally. ■ **NOTES** Coastal and estuarine mangrove-lined mudflats of Arafura Sea. Known only from Gulf of Carpentaria, Arnhem Land, and Aru Islands of wstn NG. Probably forages in intertidal shallows. Litter of 3 recorded.

Genus *Pelamis*

Yellow-bellied Sea Snake *Pelamis platura* TL 1m

One Aust sp., though genetic evidence places it close to, and possibly within, *Hydrophis*. Ventral scales very small and divided to indiscernible, enlarged symmetrical head shields, and smooth body scales arranged side by side in 49–69 midbody rows. **Black above and yellow below**, the colours sharply delineated, and tail yellow with black spots or bars. ■ **NOTES** World's most widespread and truly oceanic snake, occupying all tropical and subtropical seas except Atlantic. Occasionally strays n. to Siberia and s. to Tas. and NZ. Primarily inhabits open seas rather than continental shelves, aggregating among floating debris along slicks where surface currents merge. Surface feeder, eating wide variety of fish attracted to shelter of these slicks. Litters of up to 6 recorded. DANGEROUSLY VENOMOUS.

Parahydrophis mertoni.
Darwin, NT. H. Cogger

Pelamis platura. Noumea,
New Caledonia. H. Cogger

SEA KRAITS
Family Elapidae

Like the true sea snakes, sea kraits have often been placed in a family of their own, or have been variously considered a subfamily of sea snakes or of terrestrial elapids. They are now aligned with both, in the subfamily Hydrophiinae.

Sea kraits are truly amphibious. Thanks to their wide ventral scales, they move easily on land, while their paddle-shaped tails propel them effortlessly through water. They forage for fish on coral reefs, with Australian species specialising in crevice-inhabiting eels. After feeding, they return to shore to digest their food, sheltering in hollow logs and rock cavities. They are egglayers, depositing their clutches in soil, debris, rock crevices and caves.

There are no known Australian breeding populations. All records represent waifs, cast from their normal haunts by ocean currents. Their absence is noteworthy, given their extreme abundance to our immediate north, east and west. Explanations include a dearth of coastal limestone, and competition from true sea snakes, particularly *Aipysurus*.

There are 8 species, ranging from Japan and the Bay of Bengal to the western Pacific. They are most common on small offshore islands, sometimes occurring in enormous numbers.

Genus *Laticauda*

Amphibious snakes, represented in Aust. by 2 spp. Head shields enlarged and arranged symmetrically, nasal scales separated by internasals, body scales smooth and overlapping, and lower labial scales moderately fragmented. Sea kraits are intermediate between sea snakes and terrestrial elapids, having a **vertically flattened and paddle-shaped tail** like the sea snakes, and **laterally positioned nostrils** and **broad, laterally expanded ventral scales** like terrestrial elapids. Sea kraits are rarely recorded as strays in Aust. waters. Though normally docile and reluctant to bite, even when handled, they should be regarded as DANGEROUSLY VENOMOUS.

Yellow-lipped Sea Krait *Laticauda colubrina* TL 1.4m

Midbody scales in 21–25 rows. Blue to blue-grey, prominently patterned with 20–65 black rings. Top of head black. Snout and **upper lip yellow.** ■ **NOTES** India and Sri Lanka to islands of sw. Pacific. Rarely recorded as a stray in Aust. waters.

Brown-lipped Sea Krait *Laticauda laticaudata* TL 1m

Midbody scales in 19 rows. Blue to blue-grey, prominently patterned with 25–70 black bands or rings. Top of head black. Snout blue to yellow and **upper lip brown.** ■ **NOTES** Widespread from Bay of Bengal, n. to Japan and e. to islands of wstn Pacific. An old record exists from Tasmania.

Laticauda colubrina.
Darwin, NT. G. Vas

Laticauda colubrina.
Morovo Lagoon, Solomon Is.
S. Wilson

Laticauda laticaudata.
Iriomote Island, Ryukyu Islands, Japan.
H. Cogger

APPENDIX

Late in the publication of this Fifth Edition, the following species of gecko in the family Gekkonidae, was described. It brings the number of described species of Gehyra to 27.

Einasleigh Rock Dtella *Gehyra einasleighensis* SVL 40 mm

Very small. Subdigital lamellae divided, with 5 under expanded portion of 4th toe, 2 pairs of enlarged chin shields, with inner (postmental) contacting 1st and part of 2nd lower labial scales, 2nd lower labial scale notched by subinfralabial scale (**fig**), supranasal scales in broad contact and usually no internasal scale. Golden to dark tan with scattered dark and pale markings: prominent small circular pale spots and slightly larger, irregularly shaped dark blotches, sometimes with yellowish-orange edges. ■ **NOTES** Rock-inhabiting. Associated with small boulders and rock rubble in Einasleigh Uplands Bioregion, Qld, extending across base of Cape York Pen. between Croydon area and Petford, s. to Mingela.

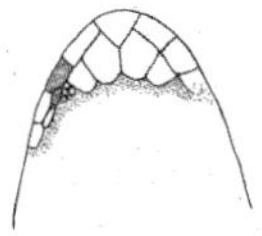

Gehyra einasleighensis
Mt Garnet area, Qld.
E. Vanderduys

SELECTED READING

In writing this book the authors have relied heavily on a wealth of published information. There are many reptile guides devoted to regional, state and national coverage, and numerous scientific papers appearing in a variety of journals. Most of these publications contain comprehensive bibliographies and it has been decided not to repeat them all here. The following list is restricted to recommended books, and the more recent scientific papers that are yet to appear widely in other bibliographies.

Aplin, K. P. & Smith, L. A., 2001. 'Checklist of the frogs and reptiles of Western Australia.' *Records of the Western Australian Museum*, Supplement No. 63: 51–74.

Bennett, R., 1997. *Reptiles and Frogs of the Australian Capital Territory.* National Parks Association of the ACT Inc, Canberra.

Bush, B., Maryan, B., Browne-Cooper, R. & Robinson, D. 2010. *Field Guide to the Reptiles and Frogs of the Perth Region.* Western Australian Museum, Welshpool, W.A.

Bush, B. & Maryan, B. 2011. *Field Guide to Snakes of the Pilbara Western Australia.* Western Australian Museum, Welshpool, WA.

Bush, B., Maryan, B., Browne-Cooper, R. & Robinson, D. 2007. *Reptiles and Frogs in the Bush: Southwestern Australia.* University of Western Australia Press.

Cann, J., 1998. *Australian Freshwater Turtles.* Beaumont Publishing, Singapore.

Cogger, H. G., 2000. *Reptiles and Amphibians of Australia.* Reed New Holland, Sydney.

Couper, P. J. and Hoskin, C. J., 2013. 'Two new subspecies of the leaf-tailed gecko *Phyllurus ossa* (Lacertilia: Carphodactylidae) from mid-eastern Queensland, Australia.' *Zootaxa*, 3664 (4): 537-553.

Couper, P., Melville, J., Emmott, A. and Chapple, S. N. J., 2012. 'A new species of *Diporiphora* from the Goneaway Tablelands of Western Queensland.' *Zootaxa*, 3556: 39-54.

Coventry, A. J. & Robertson, P., 1991. *The Snakes of Victoria. A Guide to their Identification.* Department of Conservation and Environment, East Melbourne.

Dolman, G. & Hugall, A. F., 2008. 'Combined mitrochondrial and nuclear data enhance resolution of a rapid radiation of Australian rainbow skinks (Scincidae: *Carlia*).' *Mol. Phylogenet. Evol.*,

Donnellan, S. C., Couper, P. J., Saint, K. M. & Wheaton, L., 2009. 'Systematics of the *Carlia 'fusca'* complex (Reptilia: *Scincidae*) from northern Australia.' *Zootaxa*, 2227: 1-31.

Doughty, P., Ellis, R. J. and Oliver, P. M., 2016. Many things come in small packages: Revision of the clawless geckos (*Crenadactylus*: Diplodactylidae) of Australia. *Zootaxa*, 4168 (2): 239-278.

Doughty, P., Kealley, L & Melville, J. 2012. 'Taxonomic assessment of *Diporiphora* (Reptilia: Agamidae) dragon lizards from the western arid zone of Australia.' *Zootaxa*, 3518: 1-24.

Doughty, P., Kealley, L., Shoo, P. L. and Melville, J., 2015. Revision of the Western Australian pebble-mimic dragon species-group (*Tympanocryptis cephalus*: Reptilia: Agamidae). *Zootaxa* 4039 (1): 085–117

Doughty, P. and Oliver, P. M. 2013. Systematics of *Diplodactylus* (Squamata: Diplodactylidae) from the south-western Australian biodiversity hotspot: redefinition of *D. ployophthalmus* and the description of two new species. *Rec. West. Aust. Mus.* 28 44-65.

Ehmann, H., 1992. *Encyclopedia of Australian Animals: Reptiles.* Collins Angus & Robertson, Sydney.

Emmott, A. & Wilson, S. G., 2009. *Snakes of Western Queensland. A Field Guide.* Desert Channels Qld, Longreach, Qld.

Gardner, M. G., Hugall, A. F., Donnellan, C., Hutchinson, M. N. & Foster, R., 2008. 'Molecular systematics of social skinks: phylogeny and taxonomy of the *Egernia* group (Reptilia: Scinciadae)' *Zoological Journal of the Linnean Society of London,* 154: 781-794.

Georges, A. & Thomson, S. 2010. 'Diversity of Australasian freshwater turtles, with an annotated synonymy and keys to species' *Zootaxa* 2496: 1-37.

Green, K. & Osborne, W., 1994. *Wildlife of the Australian Snow Country.* Reed Books, Chatswood, New South Wales.

Greer, A. E., 1989. *The Biology and Evolution of Australian Lizards.* Surrey Beatty & Sons, Chipping Norton, New South Wales.

——1997. *The Biology and Evolution of Australian Snakes.* Surrey Beatty & Sons, Chipping Norton, New South Wales.

Griffiths, K., 2006. *Frogs and Reptiles of the Sydney Region.* Reed New Holland, Sydney.

Heatwole, H., 1999. *Sea Snakes.* Australian Natural History Series. University of New South Wales Press, Sydney.

Hedges, S. B., Marion, A. B., Lipp, K. M., Marin, J. and Vidal, N., 2014. 'A taxonomic framework for typhlopid snakes from the Caribbean and other regions (Reptilia, Squamata).' *Caribbean Herpetology,* 49: 1-61.

Horner, P., 2007. '*Ctenotus quirinus* sp. nov. (Reptilia: Sauria: Scincidae) – a new species of skink from the Northern Territory, with the recognition of *C. brevipes* (Storr, 1981) and *C. essingtonii* (Gray, 1842) as distinct species.' *The Beagle, Records of the Museums and Art Galleries of the Northern Territory,* 23: 119-130.

Horner, P., 1992. *Skinks of the Northern Territory.* Northern Territory Museum of Arts and Sciences, Darwin.

Horner, P., 2007. 'Systematics of the snake-eyed skinks, *Cryptoblepharus* Wiegmann (Reptilia: Squamata: Scincidae) –an Australian-based review.' *The Beagle, Records of the Museams and Art Galleries of the Northern Territory,* Supplement 3.

Horner, P., 2009. 'Three new species of *Ctenotus* (Reptilia: Sauria: Scincidae) from the Kimberley region of Western Australia, with comments on the status of *Ctenotus decaneurus yampiensis.*' *Records of the WA Museum,* 25: 181-199.

Hoskin, C. J., 2013. 'A new skink (Scincidae: *Saproscincus*) from rocky forest habitat on Cape Melville, north-east Australia.' *Zootaxa,* 3722: 385-395.

Hoskin, C. J., 2014. 'A new skink (Scincidae: *Carlia*) from the rainforest uplands of Cape Melville, north-east Australia.' *Zootaxa,* 3869 (3): 224-236.

Hoskin, C. J. and Couper, P. J., 2013. 'A spectacular new leaf-tailed gecko (Carphodactylidae: *Saltuarius*) from the Melville Range, north-east Australia.' *Zootaxa,* 3717 (4): 543-558.

Hoskin, C. J. and Couper, P. J., 2014. 'Two new skinks (Scincidae: *Glaphyromorphus*) from rainforest habitats in north-eastern Australia.' *Zootaxa,* 3869 (1): 001-016.

Houston, T. & Hutchinson, M., 1998. *Dragon Lizards and Goannas of South Australia.* South Australian Museum, Adelaide.

Hutchinson, M. N., Doughty, P. & Oliver, P. M., 2009. 'Taxonomic revision of the stone geckos (Squamata: Diplodactylidae: *Diplodactylus*) of southern Australia.' *Zootaxa,* 2167: 25-66.

Hutchinson, M., Swain, R. & Driessen, M., 2001. *Snakes and Lizards of Tasmania.* University of Tasmania, Hobart.

Jenkins, R. & Bartell, R., 1980. *A Field Guide to Reptiles of the Australian High Country.* Inkata

Press, Melbourne.
Johansen, T. 2012. *A Field Guide to the Geckos of Northern Territory.* AuthorHouse, Bloomington, IN USA.
Mecke, S., Doughty, P. & Donnellan, S. C., 2009. 'A new species of *Eremiascincus* (Reptilia: Squamata: Scincidae) from the Great Sandy Desert and Pilbara Coast, Western Australia and reassignment of eight species from *Glaphyromorphus* to *Eremiascincus.*' *Zootaxa,* 2246: 1-20.
Mecke, S., Doughty, P. and Donnellan, S. C., 2013. 'Redescription of *Eremiascincus fasciolatus* (Gunther, 1867) (Reptilia: Squamata: Scincidae) with clarification of its synomyms and the description of a new species.' *Zootaxa,* 3701 (5): 473-517.
Melville, J., Smith, K., Hobson, R. and Shoo, L., 2014. 'The role of integrative taxonomy in the conservation management of cryptic species: The taxonomic status of endangered earless dragons (Agamidae: *Tympanocryptis*) in the grasslands of Queensland, Australia.' P*los One,* 9 (7) e101847:1-13.
Michael, D. & Lindenmayer, D. 2010. *Reptiles of the NSW Murray Catchment.* CSIRO Publishing, Collingwood, Vic.
Murphy, J.C., 2007. *Homalopsid Snakes: evolution in the mud.* Krieger Publishing, Florida, USA.
Oliver, P., Bauer, A. M., Greenbaum, E., Jackman, T. & Hobbie, T. 2012. 'Molecular phylogenetics of the arboreal Australian gecko genus *Oedura* Gray 1842 (Gekkota: Diplodactylidae): Another plesiomorphic grade?' *Molecular Phylogenetics and Evolution,* 63 (2): 255-264.
Oliver, P.M., Couper, P. J and Pepper, M., 2014. Independent transitions between monsoonal and arid biomes revealed by systematic revision of a complex of Australian geckos (*Diplodactylus*; Diplodactylidae) . *Plos One* 9(12): e111895. doi:10.1371/journal.pone.01111895
Oliver, P. M. and McDonald, P. J. 2016. Young relicts and old relicts: a novel paleoendemic vertebrate from the Australian Central Uplands. *R. Soc. Open Sci.* 3 160018. http://dx.doi.org/10.1098/rsos.160018
Pepper, M., Doughty, P. Hutchinson, M. N. & Keogh, J. S. 2011. 'Ancient drainages divide cryptic species in Australia's arid zone: Morphological and multi-gene evidence for four new species of Beaked Geckos (*Rhynchoedura*).' *Molecular Phylogenetics and Evolution,* 61: 810-822.
Pianka, E., King., D. R. and King, R. A., 2004. *Varanoid Lizards of the World.* Indiana University Press, USA.
Rabowski, D. L., Hutchinson, M. N., Donnellan, S. C., Talaba, A. L. and Lovette, I. J., 2014. 'Phylogenetic disassembly of species boundaries in a widespread group of Australian skinks (Scincidae: *Ctenotus*).' *Molecular Phylogenetics and Evolution* 77 (2014): 71-82.
Rasmussen, A. R., Sanders, K. L., Guinea, M. L. and Amey, A. P., 2014. 'Sea snakes in Australian waters (Serpentes: Subfamilies Hydrophiinae and Laticaudinae) – a review with an updated identification key.' *Zootaxa,* 3869 (4): 351-371.
Ross, C. A. (ed.), 1989. *Crocodiles and Alligators.* Golden Press, Silverwater, New South Wales.
Sanders, K. L., Lee, M. S. Y, Mumpuni, Bertozzi, T.& Rasmussen, A. R., 2013. Multilocus phylogeny and recent rapid radiation of the viviparous sea snakes (Elapidae: Hydrophiinae). *Molecular Genetics and Evolution,* 66 (2013): 575–591.
Shea, G., Couper, P., Worthington Wilmer, J. & Amey, A. 2011. 'Revision of the genus *Cyrtodactylus* Gray, 1827 (Squamata: Gekkonidae) in Australia.' *Zootaxa,* 3146: 1-63.
Shea, G.M. and Scanlon, J. D., 2007. 'Revision of the small tropical whipsnakes previously referred to *Demansia olivacea* (Gray, 1842) and *Demansia torquata* (Gunther,

1862) (Squamata: Elapidae).' *Records of the Australian Museum* (2007) 59 (2): 117-142.

Shine, R., 1991. *Australian Snakes: A Natural History.* Reed New Holland, Sydney.

Sistrom, M. J., Hutchinson, M. N., Hutchinson, R. G. & Donnellan, S. C., 2009. ' Molecular phylogeny of Australian *Gehyra* (Squamata: Gekkonidae) and taxonomic revision of *Gehyra variegata* in south-eastern Australia.' *Zootaxa,* 2277: 14-32.

Skinner, A., 2009. 'A multivariate morphometric analysis and systematic review of *Pseudonaja* (Serpentes, Elapidae, Hydrophiinae).' *Zoological Journal of the Linnean Society of London,* 155: 171-197.

Smith, L. A. & Adams, M., 2007. 'Revision of the *Lerista muelleri* species-group (Lacertilia: Scincidae) in Western Australia, with a redescription of *L. muelleri* (Fischer, 1881) and the description of nine new species.' *Records of the WA Museum,* 23: 309-357.

Storr, G. M., Smith, L. A. & Johnstone, R. E., 1983. *Lizards of Western Australia II: Dragons & Monitors.* Western Australian Museum, Perth.

——1990. *Lizards of Western Australia III: Geckos & Pygopods.* Western Australian Museum, Perth.

——1999. *Lizards of Western Australia I: Skinks.* Western Australian Museum, Perth.

—— 2002. *Snakes of Western Australia.* Western Australian Museum, Perth.

Swan, G., Shea, G. & Sadlier, R., 2004. *A Field Guide to Reptiles of New South Wales.* Reed New Holland, Sydney

Swan, M. & Watherow, S., 2005. *Snakes, Lizards and Frogs of the Victorian Mallee.* CSIRO Publishing.

Swanson, S., 2007. *Field Guide to Australian Reptiles.* Steve Parish Publishing, Archerfield, Qld.

Torr, G., 2000. *Pythons of Australia.* Australian Natural History Series. University of New South Wales Press, Sydney.

Weigel, J., 1990. *Australian Reptile Park's Guide to Snakes of South-east Australia.* Australian Reptile Park, Gosford, New South Wales.

Wilson, S. K., 2015. *A Field Guide to Reptiles of Queensland.* Second edition. Reed New Holland. Sydney.

Wilson, S. K. & Knowles, D. G., 1988. *Australia's Reptiles: A Photographic Reference to the Terrestrial Reptiles of Australia.* Collins, Sydney.

Wilson, S. 2012. *Australian Lizards – A Natural History.* CSIRO Publishing, Collingwood, Vic.

INDEX TO SCIENTIFIC NAMES

INDEX TO COMMON NAMES